W9-CEF-168

FROMMER'S

COMPREHENSIVE TRAVEL GUIDE

ARIZONA '93-'94

by Karl Samson

PRENTICE HALL TRAVEL

NEW YORK • LONDON • TORONTO • SYDNEY • TOKYO • SINGAPORE

FROMMER BOOKS

Published by Prentice Hall General Reference
A division of Simon & Schuster Inc.
15 Columbus Circle
New York, NY 10023

ISBN 0-13-333642-5
ISSN 1053-2471

Design by Robert Bull Design
Maps by Ortelius Design

Manufactured in the United States of America

FROMMER'S ARIZONA '93-'94

Editor-in-Chief: Marilyn Wood
Senior Editors: Judith de Rubini, Alice Fellows
Editors: Tom Hirsch, Paige Hughes, Sara Hinsey Raveret, Lisa Renaud, Theodore Stavrou
Assistant Editors: Margaret Bowen, Peter Katucki, Ian Wilker
Managing Editor: Leanne Coupe

CONTENTS

LIST OF MAPS

INVITATION TO THE READERS

In researching this book, I have come across many wonderful establishments, the best of which I have included here. I am sure that many of you will also come across appealing hotels, inns, restaurants, guesthouses, shops, and attractions. Please don't keep them to yourself. Share your experiences, especially if you want to comment on places that have been included in this edition that have changed for the worse. You can address your letters to:

Karl Samson
Frommer's Arizona
c/o Prentice Hall Travel
15 Columbus Circle
New York, NY 10023

A DISCLAIMER

Readers are advised that prices fluctuate in the course of time and travel information changes under the impact of the varied and volatile factors that affect the travel industry. Neither the author nor the publisher can be held responsible for the experiences of readers while traveling. Readers are invited to write to the publisher with ideas, comments, and suggestions for future editions.

SAFETY ADVISORY

Whenever you're traveling in an unfamiliar city or country, stay alert. Be aware of your immediate surroundings. Wear a moneybelt and keep a close eye on your possessions. Be particularly careful with cameras, purses, and wallets, all favorite targets of thieves and pickpockets.

CHAPTER 1
GETTING TO KNOW ARIZONA

Despite the searing summer temperatures of its deserts, which cover much of the state, people have been lured to Arizona for centuries. The Spanish came looking for gold—but settled for saving souls. Cattle ranchers came for Arizona's miles of excellent rangeland. In the mid-19th century, miners scoured the hills for gold (and found more than the Spanish did), but their boom towns soon went bust—the mother lode was copper, which Arizona has in such abundance that it's called the Copper State.

In the 1920s and 1930s Arizona struck a new vein of gold. The railroads made travel to Arizona easy, and wintering here became fashionable with wealthy northerners.

Today it is still the golden sun that lures people to Arizona. Scottsdale, Phoenix, Tucson, and Sedona together are home to some of the most luxurious and expensive resorts in the world. The state has also seen a massive influx of retirees, many of whom have found the few pockets of Arizona where the climate is absolutely perfect—not too hot, not too cold, and plenty of sunshine.

But it is a hole in the ground that attracts most people to Arizona. Though not the deepest or the widest canyon on earth, the Grand Canyon is without a doubt the most spectacular. But it is only one of the natural wonders of Arizona—the largest natural bridge in the world, the largest meteorite crater, the spectacular red-rock country of Sedona, and Monument Valley are just a few of the natural spectacles.

The human hand has also left its mark on Arizona. More than 1,000 years ago Anasazi, Sinagua, and Hohokam Native American tribes built villages on mesas, in valleys, and in the steep cliff walls of deep canyons. In more recent years, it has been the huge dams built along the Colorado River such as the Hoover and Glen Canyon dams that have created the largest man-made reservoirs in the country, attracting millions of visitors each year.

In addition to its sunshine, resorts, and reservoirs, Arizona's fascinating history makes a visit unique. This is the Wild West, the land of cowboys and Indians, of prospectors and ghost towns, coyotes and rattlesnakes. Scratch the glossy surface of modern, urbanized Arizona and you'll strike real gold—the history of the American West.

? DID YOU KNOW . . . ?

- Arizona has more mountainous regions (19,280 square miles) than Switzerland and more forest land (19,902,000 acres) than Minnesota.
- Arizona sided with the South during the American Civil War.
- Arizona was the last territory in the continental U.S. to become a state.
- The Four Corners, in the northeast corner of Arizona, adjoins Utah, Colorado, and New Mexico, the only spot where four states come together.
- The Grand Canyon is one of the seven natural wonders of the world.
- Some rocks in the Grand Canyon are more than two *billion* years old.
- The Hopi village of Oraibi (along with Acoma, New Mexico) is the oldest continuously inhabited settlement in the U.S.
- Wyatt Earp, Ike Clanton, and the McLaury brothers really did have a shootout at the O.K. Corral in Tombstone.
- Arizona has the highest per capita boat ownership of any state.
- The Spanish were in Arizona a quarter century before St. Augustine, Florida, was founded and 70 years before the British founded Jamestown, Virginia.
- The bola tie is the official state neckwear of Arizona.
- Arizona produces more cotton per acre than any other state.
- Arizonan Lorna Lockwood was the first woman chief justice of a state supreme court.
- Arizonan Sandra Day O'Connor was the first woman appointed to the United States Supreme Court.

1. GEOGRAPHY, HISTORY & POLITICS

GEOGRAPHY

Located in the southwestern United States, Arizona is bordered on the east by New Mexico, on the north by Utah, on the west by Nevada and California, and on the south by Mexico. With an area of 114,000 square miles, most of it owned by the federal government, it is sixth-largest state in the nation.

Though most people who have not been to Arizona think of it as one vast desert, in actuality it's one of the most geographically diverse states in the U.S. Mountainous regions throughout the state are clad in forests of pine, aspen, and fir. In the southeast there are rolling grassy plains that support huge cattle ranches. Canyons are filled with deciduous trees that produce colorful autumn leaf changes reminiscent of those in the east. Most surprisingly, there are hundreds of square miles of lakes in Arizona, albeit artificial lakes, that provide the state's population with countless recreational opportunities. And, of course, there are deserts. From north to south and east to west, no region of Arizona lacks for cactus.

Despite the state's large size, it has fewer than 4,000,000 residents and only two major metropolitan areas—Phoenix and Tucson. This relatively small population is due to the lack of areas with drinking water. Before dams were constructed on the Colorado, Salt, and Gila rivers, population growth was at a standstill. Thereafter, however, Arizona became one of the fastest-growing states in the country.

THE REGIONS IN BRIEF

The Valley of the Sun   This name refers to the sprawling metropolitan Phoenix area, which includes more than 20 cities and communities surrounded by several different mountain ranges. It is the economic and population center of modern Arizona.

The Sonoran Desert   Extending from Sonora, Mexico, in the south to central Arizona in the north, the Sonoran Desert is surprisingly green and characterized by the massive saguaro cactus, which can stand 40 feet tall and weigh several tons. It is in the Sonoran Desert that most of Arizona's cities are found.

The Four Corners   The point where Arizona, Utah, Colorado, and New Mexico come together, it's the only place in the U.S. where four states share a common boundary. The Four Corners region of Arizona is almost entirely Hopi and

Navajo reservation land. This high-plateau region of spectacular canyons and towering mesas and buttes features the Painted Desert and the Petrified Forest.

The White Mountains   Located in eastern Arizona, the White Mountains are laced with trout streams, covered by a huge pine forest, and home to far more wildlife than people. Arizona's largest and most popular ski area is located on the Apache Reservation near the town of McNary. Cooler temperatures make this region a very popular summer vacation destination.

✪ **Mission San Xavier del Bac, a beautiful Spanish mission church, is still in active use today.**

Arizona's West Coast   Though Arizona is a land-locked state, its western region is referred to as the West Coast because of the hundreds of miles of lakeshore that were created by the damming of the Colorado River. The low-lying stretches of the Colorado River are the hottest places in Arizona.

Canyon Country   From the Grand Canyon in the north to Oak Creek Canyon in the south, the rugged north-central part of Arizona alternates with high forested mountains and deep canyons. Through this region cuts the Mogollon Rim, a 2,000-foot-high escarpment that stretches for hundreds of miles from central Arizona into New Mexico.

The Arizona Strip   Located north of the Grand Canyon and bordering on southern Utah, this is one of the most remote and untraveled sections of Arizona. The Grand Canyon acts as a natural boundary between this region and the rest of the state.

Southeastern Arizona   Mile-high elevations make this one of the finest temperate climates in the world. Tucson is at the northern edge of this region, but otherwise there are few towns of any size. Mountain "islands" that rise out of the desert are home to more than 200 species of birds, and the wide grassy valleys make this a ranching region.

HISTORY

Arizona is the site of North America's oldest cultures and the longest continuously inhabited settlement (Oraibi). Over the past five centuries it has been Native American territory and part of New Spain, Mexico, and the United States. Early explorers and settlers saw little to profit from in the desert wasteland, but time proved them wrong: Mineral resources, cattle grazing, and particularly cotton (after dams began providing irrigation water)—all became important income sources. In this century the economy has moved from the three Cs (copper, cattle, and cotton) to a service-industries–based economy with tourism one of its major resources.

EARLY HISTORY   More than 11,000 years ago Paleo-Indians known as the Clovis people lived in southeastern Arizona, where stone tools and arrowheads have been found as evidence of their presence, as well as a mammoth-kill site, which has become an important source of information about these people, who were some of the earliest inhabitants of North America.

Few records exist of the next 9,000 years of Arizona's history, but by about A.D. 200, wandering bands of hunters and gatherers began living in Canyon de Chelly in the north. These people would come to be known as the Anasazi, a Navajo word that means "the ancient ones." The earliest Anasazi period, from A.D. 200 to 700, is called the Basketmaker period because of the numbers of baskets that have been found in Anasazi ruins from this time. During

DATELINE

- **9729 B.C.**   Paleo-Indians (the Clovis people) in south-eastern Arizona are the earliest-recorded inhabitants in North America.
- **A.D. 200**   The Anasazi people move into Canyon de Chelly.
- **450**   Hohokam peoples farm the Salt and Gila river valleys, eventually building 600 miles of irrigation canals.
- **650**   The Sinagua cultivate land northeast of present-day Flagstaff.
- **1100s**   Hopi tribes build Oraibi village, the oldest continuously occu-

(continues)

this period the Anasazi gave up hunting and gathering and took up agriculture, growing corn, beans, squash, and cotton on the canyon floors in northern and northeastern Arizona.

During the Pueblo period, between 700 and 1300, the Anasazi began building multistory pueblos (villages) and cliff dwellings. It is unknown why the Anasazi began living in niches and caves high on the cliff walls of the canyons. It may have been to conserve farmland as their population grew and required larger harvests, or for protection from flash floods or attacks by hostile neighbors. Whatever the reason, the Anasazi cliff dwellings were all abandoned by 1300. It is also unknown why the villages were abandoned, but a study of tree rings indicates that the region experienced a severe drought between 1276 and 1299, which suggests that the Anasazi left in search of more fertile farmland. Keet Seel and Betatakin at Navajo National Monument and the many ruins in Canyon de Chelly are Arizona's best-preserved Anasazi ruins.

During the Anasazi Basketmaker period, another culture was beginning to develop in the fertile plateau northeast of present-day Flagstaff and southward into the Verde River valley. The Sinagua, a Spanish name that means "without water," built their stone pueblos primarily on hills and mesas such as those at Tuzigoot near Clarkdale and Wupatki near Flagstaff. They also built some cliff dwellings at such places as Walnut Canyon and Montezuma Castle. By the mid-13th century Wupatki had been abandoned by the Sinaguas, and by the early 15th century they had also abandoned Walnut Canyon and the lower Verde Valley region.

By A.D. 450 the Hohokam culture, from whom the Sinaguas learned irrigation, had begun to farm the Gila and Salt River valleys between Phoenix and Casa Grande. Over a period of 1,000 years they constructed a 600-mile network of irrigation canals, some of which can still be seen today. Because the Hohokam built their homes of earth, few Hohokam ruins remain. However, one building, the Casa Grande, has been well preserved. Throughout this desert region the Hohokam carved many petroglyphs, and recent studies have determined that many of these stone carvings were used for marking the equinoxes and solstices. By the 1450s the tribe had abandoned their villages and disappeared without a sign, hence the name Hohokam: a Tohono O'odham Native American word meaning "all used up" or "the people who have gone." Archeologists believe that the irrigation of desert soil for hundreds of years had left a thick crust of alkali on the surface, and this made farming no longer possible.

HISPANIC HERITAGE The first Europeans to visit the region may have been a motley crew of shipwrecked Spaniards (and one Moor named Estévan) who spent 8 years wandering from a beach in Florida to a Spanish village in Mexico. These wanderers arrived back in Spanish territory with a fantastic story of seven cities filled with goldsmiths, where doorways were encrusted with jewels. No one is sure whether they actually passed through Arizona, but their story convinced the viceroy of New

Spain (Mexico) to send a small expedition, led by Fr. Marcos de Niza and Estévan. Father de Niza's report of finding the fabled Seven Cities of Cíbola also inspired Don Francisco Vásquez de Coronado to set off in search of wealth. However, instead of fabulously wealthy cities, Coronado found only pueblos of stone and mud. A subordinate expedition led by García Lopez de Cárdenas stumbled upon the Grand Canyon, while another group of Coronado's men, led by Don Pedro de Tovar, visited the Hopi mesas.

In the 150 years that followed, only a handful of Spaniards visited Arizona. In the 1580s and 1600s Antonio de Espejo and Juan de Oñate explored northern and central Arizona and found indications that there were mineral riches in the region. In the 1670s the Franciscans founded several missions among the Hopi pueblos, but the Pueblo Revolt of 1680 obliterated this small Spanish presence.

In 1687 Fr. Eusebio Francisco Kino, a German-educated Italian Jesuit, began establishing missions in the Sonora Desert region of northern New Spain. In 1691 he visited the Pima village of Tumacacori. Father Kino taught the inhabitants European farming techniques, planted fruit trees, and gave the natives cattle, sheep, and goats to raise. However, it was not until 1751, in response to a Pima rebellion, that the permanent mission of Tumacacori and the presidio (military post) of Tubac were built, which became the first European settlement in Arizona.

In 1775 a group of settlers led by Juan Bautista de Anza set out from Tubac to find an overland route to California, and in 1776 founded the city of San Francisco. The same year the Tubac presidio was moved to Tucson. Father Kino had visited the Tucson area in 1692 and in 1700 had laid out the foundations for the first church at the mission of San Xavier del Bac. However, construction of the present church, known as the White Dove of the Desert, probably began in 1783.

In 1821 Mexico won its independence from Spain, and Tucson, with only 65 inhabitants, became part of Mexico. Mexico at that time extended all the way to northern California, but in 1848 most of this land, except for a small section of southern Arizona that included Tucson, became U.S. territory in the wake of the Mexican-American War. Five years later, in 1853, Mexico sold the remainder of southern Arizona to the United States in a transaction known as the Gadsden Purchase.

INDIAN CONFLICTS At the time that the Spanish arrived in Arizona, the tribes living in the southern lowland deserts were peaceful farmers, while in the mountains of the east lived the Apaches, a hunting-and-gathering tribe that frequently raided neighboring tribes. In the north, the Navajo, relatively recent immigrants to the region, fought with neighboring Hopis and Utes over land, and the Hopis even fought among themselves.

Coronado's expedition through Arizona and into New Mexico and Kansas was to seek gold. To that end he attacked one pueblo, killed the inhabitants of another, and forced still others to abandon their villages. Spanish-Indian

DATELINE

Tucson to protect the mission of San Xavier del Bac.
- **1821** Mexico gains independence from Spain and takes control of Arizona.
- **1848** Most of present-day Arizona ceded to the U.S. following the Mexican War.
- **1853** The Gadsden Purchase adds the remainder of Mexican land that later becomes Arizona.
- **1862** Arizona becomes the Confederate Territory of Arizona, but is reclaimed by the Union later that same year.
- **1863** Arizona becomes a U.S. territory.
- **1886** Geronimo surrenders to the U.S. Army.
- **1911** Theodore Roosevelt Dam, on the Salt River, enables irrigation and development of the desert.
- **1912** Arizona becomes the 48th state.
- **1919** Grand Canyon National Park established.
- **1936** Hoover Dam completed.
- **1948** Arizona Native Americans receive the right to vote.
- **1963** U.S. Supreme Court upholds Arizona's claim to Colorado River water.

(continues)

DATELINE

- **1974** Construction begins on the Central Arizona Project aqueducts.
- **1975** Raul Castro becomes the first Mexican-American governor of Arizona.
- **1981** Arizona judge Sandra Day O'Connor becomes the first woman appointed to the U.S. Supreme Court.
- **1988** Governor Evan Mecham removed from office.

relations were never to improve, and the Spanish were forced to occupy their new lands with a strong military presence. Around 1600, 300 Spanish settlers moved into the Four Corners region, which at the time supported a large population of Navajos. The Spanish raided Navajo villages to take slaves, and angry Navajos responded by stealing Spanish horses and cattle.

For several decades in the mid-1600s missionaries were tolerated in the Hopi pueblos, but the Pueblo tribes revolted in 1680, killing the missionaries and destroying the missions. Encroachment by farmers and miners moving into the Santa Cruz Valley in the south caused the Pima people to stage a similar uprising in 1751, attacking and burning the mission at Tubac. This revolt led to the establishment of the presidio at Tubac that same year. When the military garrison moved to Tucson, Tubac was quickly abandoned due to frequent raids by Apaches. The Yuman tribe, whose land at the confluence of the Colorado and Gila rivers had become a Spanish settlement, staged a similar uprising that wiped out the Spanish settlement at Yuma in 1781.

By the time Arizona became part of the United States, it was the Navajos and Apaches who were proving the most resistant to white settlers. In 1864 the U.S. Army, under the leadership of Col. Kit Carson, forced the Navajos to surrender by destroying their winter food supplies, then shipped them to an internment camp in New Mexico. Within 5 years they were returned to their land, though they were now forced to live on a reservation.

The Apaches resisted white settlement 20 years longer than the Navajos. Skillful guerrilla fighters, the Apaches were able to attack settlers, forts, and towns despite the presence of U.S. Army troops sent to protect the white settlers. Geronimo and Cochise were the leaders of the last resistant bands of rebellious Apaches. Cochise eventually died in his Chiracahua Mountains homeland and Geronimo was finally forced to surrender in 1886. Geronimo and many of his followers were subsequently relocated to Florida by the U.S. government. Open conflicts between whites and Native Americans finally came to an end.

> ✪ **Many of Arizona's old mining towns are now home to artists and craftspeople as well as ghosts.**

TERRITORIAL DAYS In 1846 the United States went to war with Mexico, which at the time extended all the way to northern California and included parts of Colorado, Wyoming, and New Mexico. When the war ended, the United States claimed almost all the land extending from Texas to northern California; called the New Mexico Territory, it had its capital at Santa Fe. The land south of the Gila River, which included Tucson, was still part of Mexico, but when surveys determined that this land was the best route for a railroad from southern Mississippi to southern California, the U.S. government negotiated the Gadsden Purchase. In 1853 this land purchase established the current Arizona-Mexico border.

IMPRESSIONS

If the world were searched over, I suppose there could not be found so degraded a set of villains as then formed the principal society of Tucson.
—J. ROSS BROWNE, A VISITOR TO TUCSON IN 1863

When the California gold rush began in 1849, many hopeful miners crossed Arizona en route to the gold fields, and some stayed to seek mineral riches in Arizona. However, despite the ever-increasing numbers of settlers, the U.S. Congress refused to create a separate Arizona Territory. When the Civil War broke out, Arizonans, angered by Congress's inaction on their request to become a separate territory, sided with the Confederacy; in 1862 Arizona was proclaimed the Confederate Territory of Arizona. Although Union troops easily defeated the Confederate troops who had occupied Tucson, this dissension convinced Congress, in 1863, to create the Arizona Territory.

The capital of the new territory was temporarily established at Fort Whipple near Prescott, but later the same year the capital was moved to Prescott, and in 1867 to Tucson. Ten years later Prescott again became the capital which it remained for another 12 years before the seat of government moved finally to Phoenix, which is today the Arizona state capital.

During this period mining flourished, and though small amounts of gold and silver were discovered, copper became the source of Arizona's economic wealth.

> ✪ **Tubac is today one of Arizona's most active artists' communities and is filled with galleries and studios.**

With each new mineral strike a new mining town would boom, and when the ore ran out the town would be abandoned. These towns were infamous for their gambling halls, bordellos, saloons, and shootouts in the street. Tombstone and Bisbee became the largest towns in the state, and became known as the wildest towns between New Orleans and San Francisco.

In 1867 farmers in the newly founded town of Phoenix began irrigating their fields using canals that had been dug centuries earlier by the Hohokam peoples. In the 1870s ranching became another important source of revenue in the territory, particularly in the southeastern and northwestern parts of the state. In the 1880s the railroads finally arrived and life in Arizona began to change drastically. Suddenly the mineral resources and cattle of the region were accessible to the East.

STATEHOOD & THE 20TH CENTURY By the turn of the 20th century, Arizonans were trying to convince Congress to make the territory a state. Congress balked at the requests, but finally, in 1910, allowed the territorial government to draw up a state constitution. Territorial legislators were liberal-minded progressive thinkers and the draft of Arizona's state constitution included clauses for the recall of elected officials. President William Howard Taft vetoed the bill that would have made Arizona a state because he opposed the recall of judges. Arizona politicians removed the controversial clause, and, on February 14, 1912, Arizona became the 48th state. One of the new state legislature's first acts was the reinstate the clause providing for the recall of judges.

Much of Washington's opposition to Arizona's statehood had been based on the belief that Arizona could never support economic development. This belief was changed in 1911 by one of the most important events in Arizona history—the completion of the Roosevelt Dam (later to be renamed the Theodore Roosevelt Dam) on the Salt River. The dam provided irrigation water to the Valley of the Sun and tamed the violent floods of the river. The introduction of water to the heart of Arizona's vast desert enabled large-scale agri-

> ✪ **The best preserved Anasazi ruins in Arizona are Betatakin and Keet Seel in Navajo National Monument.**

culture and industry. Over the next decades more dams were built throughout Arizona. Completed in 1936, the Hoover Dam on the Colorado River became the largest concrete dam in the western hemisphere and formed the largest man-made reservoir in North America. Arizona's dams would eventually provide not only water and electricity but recreational areas.

Despite labor problems, copper mining increased throughout the 1920s and 1930s, and with the onset of World War II the mines boomed as military munitions manufacturing increased demand for copper. However, within a few years after the war, many mines were shut down. Arizona is still littered with old mining ghost towns that boomed and then went bust. A few towns, such as Jerome, Bisbee, and Chloride, managed to hang on after the mines shut down and were eventually rediscovered by artists, writers, and retirees. Bisbee and Jerome have now become artists' colonies and major tourist attractions.

○ **The Arizona State Museum in Tucson has a display of Paleo-Indian artifacts.**

World War II also created demand for cotton (which became the state's most important crop), beef, and leather. Clear desert skies were ideal for training pilots and several military bases were established in the state. Phoenix's population doubled during the war years, and after the war many veterans returned with their families. However, it would take the invention of air conditioning to truly open up the desert to major population growth.

During the postwar years Arizona attracted a number of large manufacturing industries and slowly moved away from its agricultural economic base. Today electronics manufacturing, aerospace engineering, and other high-tech industries provide employment for thousands of Arizonans. However, the largest segment of the economy is now in the service industries, with tourism playing a crucial role.

Even by the 1920s Arizona had become a winter destination for the wealthy, and the Grand Canyon, declared a national park in 1919, attracted more and more visitors every year. The clear dry air attracted people suffering from allergies and lung ailments, and Arizona became known as a healthful place. Guest ranches of the 1930s gave way to the resorts of the 1980s. Today Scottsdale and Phoenix together have the greatest concentration of resorts in the United States. In addition, tens of thousands of retirees from as far north as Canada make Arizona their winter home. Called snowbirds, they now play a crucial role in Arizona's economy.

○ **When visiting Cochise Stronghold, it is easy to imagine Cochise and his men eluding capture.**

Continued population growth throughout the 20th century created greater demand for water. However, despite the damming of virtually all of Arizona's rivers, the state still suffered from insufficient water supplies in the south-central population centers of Phoenix and Tucson. It would take the construction of the controversial and expensive Central Arizona Project (CAP) aqueduct to carry water from the Colorado River, over mountains and deserts, and deliver it where it was wanted. Construction on the CAP began in 1974 and is only now reaching completion. However, years of drought in California have once again raised the question of who has legal rights to the waters of the Colorado River.

By the 1960s Arizona had become an urban state with all the problems confronting cities around the nation. The once-healthful air of Phoenix now rivals that of Los Angeles for the thickness of its smog. Allergy sufferers are plagued by pollen from the nondesert plants that have been planted to make the desert look more lush and inviting. Resistance to construction of interstate freeways in the Phoenix area caused that city to become one of the most congested in the nation, and today major highway construction projects are only just beginning to relieve the congestion. In the early 1980s, as industry fled from the north to the Sunbelt states, Arizona experienced an economic boom that by the end of the decade had turned to a bust. Unemployment in the state was high, and yet people continued to move there. The 1990s don't hold much promise of economic

○ **A visit to one of Arizona's major dams will give you an appreciation for what keeps the state alive.**

recovery, and cutbacks in military spending in particular are likely to have profound effects on the Arizona economy.

2. FAMOUS ARIZONANS

Erma Bombeck (1927–) Newspaper columnist who has focused her humorous essays on the life of the American family and particularly the mother's role. Many of her columns have been collected into books.

Lynda Carter (1951–) Star of the television series *Wonder Woman*, which was popular in the late 1970s.

Cesar Chavez (1927–) Founder of the National Farm Workers Association. Throughout the 1960s Chavez organized migrant farm laborers and helped raise wages and living conditions.

Cochise (1829–1909) Led the Chiracahua Apaches against white settlers and the U.S. Army in the 1860s and 1870s. He and his band of warriors were able to elude the military for 10 years by taking refuge in the Chiracahua Mountains in an area now known as Cochise Stronghold.

Andy Devine (1905–77) Squeaky-voiced actor who appeared in hundreds of movies. During the 1950s he played the sidekick Jingles on the television western *Wild Bill Hickok* and in the 1960s appeared as Captain Hap on *Flipper*.

Wyatt Earp (1848–1929) Arizona lawman who was made famous by Hollywood. Earp's famous shootout at the O.K. Corral lasted only a few seconds, but has been reenacted thousands of times over the years.

Geronimo (1812–74) The last great leader of the Apache tribes. Geronimo (his Apache name was Gayathlay) finally surrendered to U.S. Army troops in 1886, and he and all the other Apaches of southeastern Arizona were shipped off to internment camps as far away as Florida.

Barry Goldwater (1909–) Republican elder statesman and former senator from Arizona. Goldwater served in the U.S. Senate for 30 years and unsuccessfully ran for president against Lyndon Johnson in 1964.

Zane Grey (1875–1939) Author of many popular western novels. Grey was not born in Arizona, but spent much of his life here. Many of his novels were set in the Mogollon Rim region of central Arizona. Among his novels are *Riders of the Purple Sage, The Vanishing American, The Arizona Clan,* and *To the Last Man.*

Doc Holiday (1851–87) A frontier dentist who was known for his gunslinging as well. Doc Holiday helped Wyatt Earp shoot down the McLaury brothers at the O.K. Corral in Tombstone.

Stevie Nicks (1948–) Lead singer with the popular rock 'n' roll band Fleetwood Mac.

Sandra Day O'Connor (1930–) The first woman appointed to the United States Supreme Court. O'Connor served in the Arizona senate and as a judge for the Arizona Court of Appeals prior to becoming a Supreme Court Justice.

Linda Ronstadt (1946–) Popular singer who has recorded numerous bestselling albums (primarily in the 1970s). The Ronstadt family has for years been active in Tucson city politics.

3. ART & ARCHITECTURE

ART Though Santa Fe has taken the arts spotlight in recent years, Arizona, too, is a mecca for artists. The Cowboy Artists of America, an organization of artists dedicated to capturing in their art the lives and landscapes of the Old West, was formed in a tavern in Sedona in 1965 by Joe Beeler, George Phippen, Bob McLeod, Charlie Dye, John Hampton, and a few other local artists. Working primarily in oils and bronze, members of this organization depicted the lives of cowboys and Native Americans in minute detail, especially when working in bronze. Today their work is sought after by collectors throughout the country.

As more and more artists and craftspeople headed for Arizona, the towns in which they congregated came to be known as artists' colonies, and galleries sprang up to serve the growing numbers of visitors coming to see their art. Although Sedona is probably the best known of these so-called artists' colonies, others include Jerome and Bisbee, both mining towns that came close to becoming ghost towns before being discovered by artists, and Tubac, the first Spanish settlement in Arizona. All three of these towns have numerous art galleries and crafts shops, with Tubac being the busiest and Bisbee the newest and least developed.

✪ Keep your eyes out for hogans when traveling through Navajo country.

Red-rock canyons, pensive Indians, hard-working cowboys, desert wildflowers, majestic mesas, and stately saguaros have been the themes of this century's representational artists of Arizona. Although contemporary abstract art can be found in museums and galleries, the style pioneered by Frederic Remington and Charles M. Russell in the early 20th century still dominates the Arizona art scene. Remington, Russell, and those who followed in their footsteps romanticized the West, imbuing their depictions of cowboys, Indians, settlers, and soldiers with mythic proportions that would be taken up by Hollywood.

Further back, even before the first Spanish explorers arrived in Arizona, the ancient Anasazis were creating an artistic legacy in their intricately woven baskets, painted pottery, and cryptic petroglyphs and pictographs. In recent years both contemporary Native American artists and non–Native American artists have been drawing on Anasazi designs for their works. Today's Hopi, Navajo, and Zuñi artisans have become well known for their jewelry, which is made of silver and semiprecious stones, primarily turquoise. The Hopi have raised their traditional carved kachina dolls to an art form, and the Navajos continue to weave traditional patterns in their rugs. The Zuñi, noted for their skill in carving stone, have focused on their traditional animal fetishes. However, since the founding of the Santa Fe Indian School in 1932, and later the Institute of American Indian Art, Native American artists have also ventured into the realm of painting. Hopi artist Fred Kabotie and his son, Michael Kabotie, are among the best known Native American artists.

ARCHITECTURE Centuries before the first Europeans arrived in Arizona, the Anasazi people were building elaborate villages, which have come to be known by their Spanish name—pueblos. Many, but not all, of the Anasazi pueblos were built high on cliff walls in the rugged canyon lands of northern Arizona. Built of cut stones

---

IMPRESSIONS

O yes, I have heard of that country—it is just like hell. All it lacks is water and good society.
—A 19TH-CENTURY SENATOR FROM OHIO

mortared together and roofed with logs and earth, the pueblo dwellings had thick walls that provided insulation from heat and cold, and the flat roofs provided a place to do chores. Pueblo architecture was characterized by small rooms with no windows. Some rooms were used for living while others served as grain-storage rooms.

Earlier, the Anasazi developed a type of shelter known as a pit house, which was partially dug into the ground. Eventually these flat-roofed stone houses were adapted to apartment-style construction techniques when they moved up into the canyon walls. The pit-house style of architecture was retained in the form of the kiva, a round ceremonial room that is still used by the Hopis, Arizona's contemporary pueblo dwellers.

○ **Wupatki ruins are a fascinating relic of the ancient Sinagua Indian culture.**

The Sinagua, a culture that developed at the same time as the Anasazi built similar stone pueblos, but most Sinagua pueblos were on hills rather than in the canyons. At the Wupatki ruins, near Flagstaff, there are two unusual stone structures that were built by the Sinagua. One is a ball court similar in many ways to the ball courts of central Mexico and Central America. The other unusual building is a low-walled round structure that may have been an amphitheater or large kiva.

Many Hopis still live in pueblos similar to those built by the Sinagua and Anasazi, with stone-walled rooms and round kivas, with ladders sticking through the roof (entrance to a kiva is prohibited to non-Hopis). The hogan, the traditional home of the Navajo people, displays a very different type of architecture. Usually built with six sides, hogans are constructed of logs and earth and resemble ancient dwellings of central Asia.

When the Spanish arrived in Arizona, they turned to sun-baked adobe bricks as their primary construction material. Because adobe walls must be made very thick, they provide excellent insulation. Very few adobe homes have survived from territorial days because, when not maintained, adobe quickly decays. The best place to see adobe homes is in Tucson, where several have been preserved in that city's downtown historic districts. However, when the railroads arrived in Arizona, many owners of adobe homes hid this fact by putting on

○ **Canyon de Chelly is filled with dozens of Anasazi ruins that can be seen from the canyon rim or floor.**

slanted roofs, Victorian porches, and even siding. In the Barrio Historico district of Tucson, town-house architecture characteristic of Sonora, Mexico, has been preserved. These buildings have no front yards but instead have walls right at the sidewalk. This style of architecture was common during the Mexican and early territorial periods of Arizona history.

With only the two mission churches of San Xavier del Bac and Tumacacori, the Spanish did not leave as great an ecclesiastical architectural legacy as they did elsewhere in the New World. However, mission-revival architecture has been popular for much of this century. A somewhat idealized concept of the style—stucco walls, arches, and courtyards—has come to epitomize the ideal of Arizona living.

In the mid-20th century, architect Frank Lloyd Wright established his winter home and school, called Taliesin West, in Scottsdale and eventually designed several buildings around the Phoenix area. The architect of the Biltmore Hotel, one of the state's oldest resorts, relied on Wright for assistance in designing the hotel, and the hand of Wright is evident throughout. One of Wright's students, an Italian architect named Paolo Soleri, decided to settle in Arizona and has for many years pursued his dream of building an environmentally

○ **Taliesen West, Frank Lloyd Wright's Arizona school, is a must for students of 20th-century architecture.**

sensitive ideal city in the desert north of Phoenix. He calls this city Arcosanti and has partially financed its construction by selling windbells at his Cosanti foundary in Paradise Valley. Arcosanti, the Cosanti foundry, and Taliesin West are open to the public.

4. RELIGION, MYTH & FOLKLORE

Arizona's Native American heritage is rich in myth. Each tribe has its own myths, ceremonies, and dances, and despite the challenges of living in a world dominated by whites, the Native Americans of Arizona have managed to preserve their unique cultural heritage and religious beliefs. Many ceremonies and dances are open to the public, including museum performances, annual festivals, and pow wows.

Arizona's Spanish heritage also left its mark on the religious landscape of Arizona. The missions of San Xavier del Bac and Tumacacori, founded by Fr. Eusebio Francisco Kino in the latter part of the 17th century, are two of the state's greatest architectural treasures, but it is the ruins of a tiny shrine in Tucson that truly captures the imagination. El Tiradito is said to be the only shrine in the United States dedicated to a sinner buried in unconsecrated soil. There are several stories surrounding the shrine, but the most popularly accepted is that of a young man who fell in love with his mother-in-law. When his father-in-law caught his wife with the young man, he shot his son-in-law, who stumbled into the street and fell dead on the spot where El Tiradito now stands. The people of the neighborhood began burning candles on the spot to try to save the soul of the young man, and eventually people began burning candles in hopes that their own wishes would come true. To this day, devout Catholics still burn candles at the shrine in hopes that God will intercede on their behalf.

5. CULTURAL & SOCIAL LIFE

Arizona is one of the most culturally diverse states in the U.S. Its heritage combines Native American, Hispanic, and European influences. The oldest and most distinctive of these is the Native American culture. Arizona is home to nearly two dozen different Native American tribes. Many of these tribes number only a few hundred people on a tiny reservation, but the Navajos, Hopis, Apaches, and Tohono O'odham (formerly known as the Papago) have large populations on reservations that cover large portions of the state. Each tribe pursues its own separate culture, which is reflected in language, religious beliefs and ceremonies, livelihoods, and architecture. Visitors are welcome on reservations and most tribes have some sort of craft specialty that they offer for sale.

Arizona has also preserved its western heritage. Although Arizonans are today more likely to ride Hondas and Toyotas than pintos and appaloosas, western wear is still the preferred fashion of rich and poor alike. Cowboy boots, cowboy hats, blue jeans, and bola ties are acceptable attire at almost any function in Arizona. Horses are still used on ranches around the state, but most are kept simply for recreational or investment purposes. Scottsdale is one of the nation's centers of Arabian horse breeding. Arabian horse auctions attract a very well-heeled (read lizard-skin boots) crowd with horses selling for tens of thousands of dollars. Cowboy bands, western theme villages serving steaks and staged gunfights, and guest ranches all help to preserve the ethos of the Wild, Wild West.

In recent years entire cities such as Sun City and Green Valley have been created exclusively for senior citizens. There are also retirement communities and RV parks where retirees come to stay for the winter months. These latter Arizona visitors have played a major role in the development and character of towns such as Yuma.

6. PERFORMING ARTS & EVENING ENTERTAINMENT

Although it hasn't been too many years since evening entertainment in Arizona meant dance-hall girls or a harmonica by the campfire, Phoenix and Tucson have become centers for the performing arts and share an opera company and a ballet company, both of which split their performance season between the two cities. The Valley of the Sun (Phoenix area) is home to a number of symphony orchestras and theater companies. Smaller cities and towns, too, such as Sedona, with its affluent cosmopolitan atmosphere, stages jazz and classical music festivals, and has a busy performing arts center. Flagstaff's Coconino Center for the Arts also offers a full season of performances by musicians and dance companies from around the country. Even little Grand Canyon Village, on the South Rim of the Grand Canyon, hosts an annual chamber music festival.

Open-air amphitheaters in Phoenix and Tucson stay busy from early spring through late fall. Another Arizona favorite with both adults and children are old-fashioned melodramas, which are staged regularly in Tucson and old mining towns such as Bisbee and Chloride. Audience participation—hiss the villain, cheer the hero—is required.

Dinner itself has been raised to an entertainment form at Arizona's many Wild West steakhouses, where families are entertained by cowboy bands, staged gunfights, hayrides, and sing-alongs, all in the name of reliving the glory days of "cowboys and Indians."

Phoenix and Tucson also support a very active and diverse nightclub scene. From country-western to rock to jazz, there is everything you'd expect of a major metropolitan area. Arizona's resorts are also a good place to look for evening entertainment, and nearly every lounge has some sort of live entertainment at least a couple of nights a week.

7. SPORTS & RECREATION

SPORTS   As elsewhere in the U.S., **sports bars** are everywhere in Arizona, even on the rim of the Grand Canyon. The athletic teams of the **University of Arizona and Arizona State University** have devoted followings, as does the **Phoenix Cardinals** professional football team.

And the state serves as the spring training headquarters for more than half a dozen **baseball** teams, including the Chicago Cubs, Oakland As, San Francisco Giants, and Seattle Mariners. These teams play exhibition games that are very popular with winter visitors and Arizona residents alike.

Greyhound racing is another popular sport in Arizona. There are several dog-racing tracks around the state and off-track betting is permitted.

Professional rodeo had its start in Prescott, Arizona, in 1888 and is still going strong. Throughout the year there are rodeos all over the state.

RECREATION   With more than 300 days of sunshine in most of the state, Arizona

IMPRESSIONS

Do nothing to mar its grandeur . . . keep it for your children, your children's children, all who come after you, as the one great sight which every American should see.
—PRESIDENT THEODORE ROOSEVELT, AFTER VISITING THE GRAND CANYON IN 1903

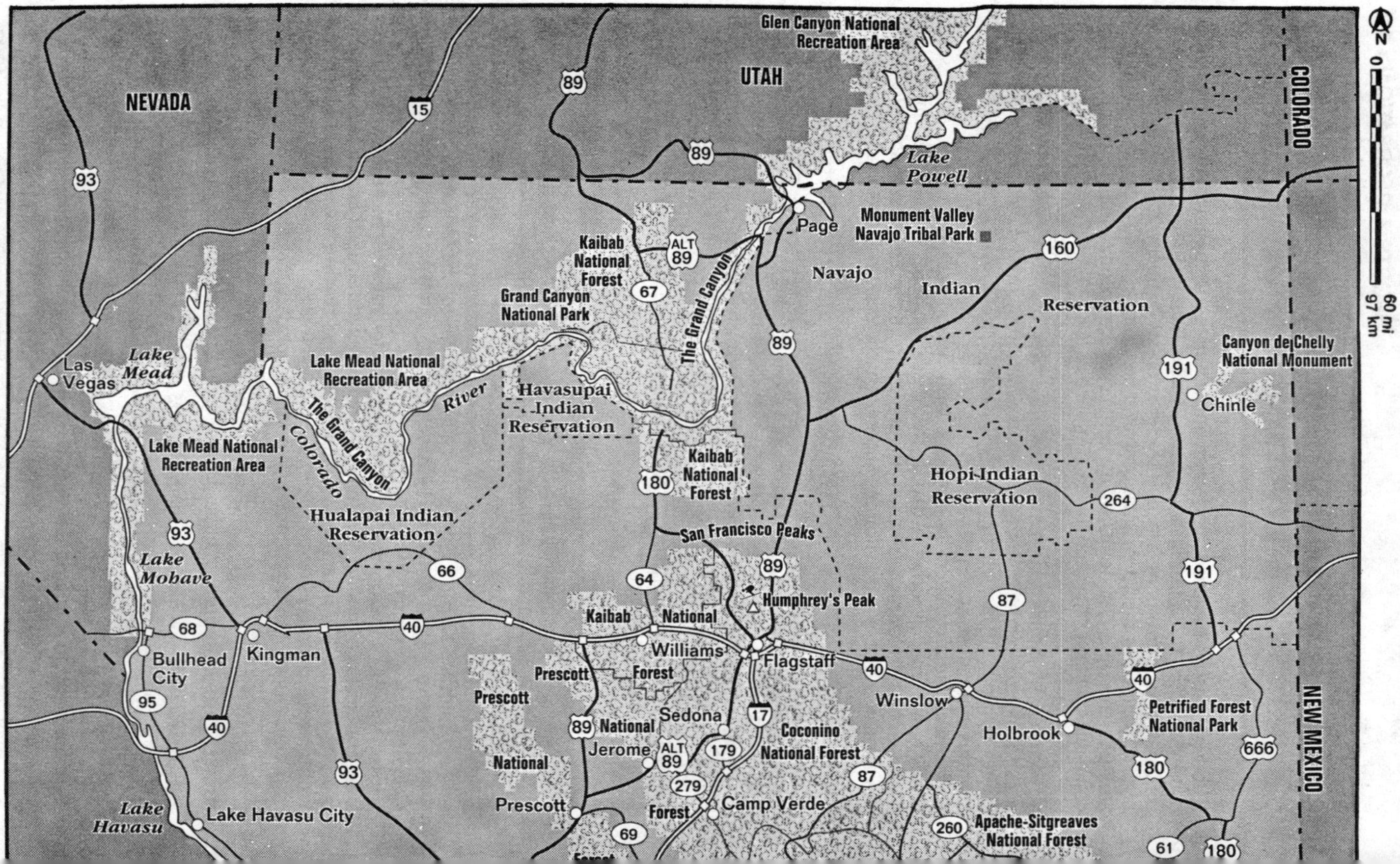

N
0
60 mi
97 km
NEVADA
UTAH
COLORADO
NEW MEXICO
Glen Canyon National Recreation Area
Lake Powell
Page
Monument Valley Navajo Tribal Park
Navajo Indian Reservation
Canyon de Chelly National Monument
Chinle
Hopi Indian Reservation
Kaibab National Forest
Grand Canyon National Park
The Grand Canyon
Lake Mead National Recreation Area
Havasupai Indian Reservation
Colorado River
Hualapai Indian Reservation
Las Vegas
Lake Mead
Lake Mohave
Bullhead City
Kingman
Lake Havasu
Lake Havasu City
San Francisco Peaks
Humphrey's Peak
Williams
Flagstaff
Winslow
Holbrook
Petrified Forest National Park
Prescott National Forest
Prescott
Sedona
Jerome
Camp Verde
Coconino National Forest
Apache-Sitgreaves National Forest
15
93
89
ALT 89
67
160
191
264
87
180
64
66
68
40
95
17
179
279
69
260
61
666

offers year-round opportunities for outdoor recreation, the most popular being **golf** and **tennis.** There are hundreds of golf courses and thousands of tennis courts.

As for **water sports,** fishing, waterskiing, sailboarding, and jet skiing are also popular pursuits on Arizona's many human-made lakes. **Rafting** through the Grand Canyon is ranked as one of the most exciting white-water adventures in the world. Dozens of companies offer trips lasting from 1 day to 2 weeks. Hiking and riding mules are two alternative ways to see the Grand Canyon. Most of the state is publicly owned land, and **camping and hiking** are permitted.

8. FOOD

In the past few years regional cuisines have become all the rage with chefs and diners across the U.S. Southwestern cuisine—which combines the spices of Mexico (especially chile peppers), the unusual fruit-and-meat pairings of nouvelle cuisine, and flame broiling over mesquite—is rapidly becoming one of the most popular new cuisines in the country. Pacific salmon might be served with smoked yellow-pepper sauce and roasted black-bean and corn relish, while roast squab might be served with twice-cooked bacon and chipotle-pepper and cider sauce. Other dishes might include marinated ahi with avocado-papaya salsa and cilantro-scallion aïoli, or southwestern bouillabaisse with grilled nopal cactus. Don't expect to find this sort of cooking at just any corner restaurant. It is still the realm of expensive gourmet restaurants where you can expect to pay at least $30 per person for dinner. In the Phoenix and Tucson chapters of this book, you'll find several restaurants specializing in southwestern cuisine.

Arizona also offers some of the best Mexican food in the country. A few years back the mayor of Tucson even declared that the city was the Mexican restaurant capital of the universe. One specialty that you are likely to encounter at Arizonan Mexican restaurants is carne seca, which is air-dried beef that's shredded and added to various sauces. It has a very distinctive texture and shouldn't be missed.

9. RECOMMENDED BOOKS & FILMS

BOOKS

GENERAL   Few places on earth have inspired as much writing as Arizona's Grand Canyon. John Wesley Powell's *Down the Colorado: Diary of the First Trip down the Grand Canyon* (E. P. Dutton, 1969), which was first published in 1869, and David Lavendar's *River Runners of the Grand Canyon* (University of Arizona, 1985), an illustrated history of river exploration, provide the explorers' and adventurers' view of the canyon. *The Grand Canyon: Early Impressions* (Pruett, 1989), edited by Paul Schullery, is a collection of first impressions by famous writers including John Muir and Zane Grey. *The Man Who Walked Through Time* (Random House, 1972), by Colin Fletcher, is a narrative of one man's hike through the rugged inner canyon. Even Barry Goldwater, a rather accomplished writer, had his say on the Grand Canyon in his book *Delightful Journey: Down the Green and Colorado Rivers* (Arizona Historical Foundation, 1970). In *Grand Canyon* (Morrow, 1968), Joseph W. Krutch, a brilliant observer of nature, distills his observations of the canyon into expressive prose.

Water rights and man's impact on the deserts of the Southwest have raised many controversies this century, none more heated than those centering around the Colorado River. *Cadillac Desert: The American West and Its Disappearing Water* (Penguin, 1987), by Marc Reisner, focuses on the West's insatiable need for water, while *A River No More: The Colorado River and the West* (Borzoi, 1981), by Philip L. Fradkin, addresses the fate of just the one river.

The famous Lost Dutchman mine has inspired at least two books: *Fool's Gold* (Golden West, 1983) by Robert Si; orsky, and *The Treasure of the Superstitions* (Norton, 1973) by Gary Jennings.

Arizona, A Bicentennial History (Norton, 1976), by Lawrence Clark Powell, provides a thorough history of the state. *Arizona Memories* (University of Arizona, 1984), edited by Anne H. Morgan and Rennard Strickland, is an engaging collection of historical recollections by cowboys, miners, an Apache scout, a frontier doctor, a soldier's wife, and many other Arizonans. In *Home Is the Desert* (University of Arizona, 1984), Ann Woodin addresses the mental and spiritual development that her family experienced when they moved to the desert outside Tucson. In his book *The Desert Year* (Viking, 1963), naturalist Joseph W. Krutch combines his observations of Arizona's deserts with his own personal philosophical observations.

Southwestern Indian Arts & Crafts (current edition by Tom Bahti's son, Mark Bahti), *Southwestern Indian Ceremonials*, and *Southwestern Indian Tribes* (all KC Publications) is a trio of softcover books illustrated with color photos by Southwest Native American authority Tom Bahti and provides an accessible source of information on several aspects of Southwest tribal life. Other books on Arizona's Native American tribes include *The Navajo* (Harvard University Press, 1974), by Clyde Kluckhohn and Dorothea Leighton; *The People Called Apache* (Prentice-Hall, 1974), by Thomas E. Mails; and *Anasazi: Ancient People of the Rock* (Crown, 1974), with text by Donald G. Pike and photos by David Muench.

FICTION Arizona's rugged landscape, colorful history, and rich Native American culture have long served as backdrops for fiction writers. Zane Grey spent many years living in north-central Arizona and based many of his western novels on life in this region of the state. Among his books are *Riders of the Purple Sage, West of the Pecos, The Vanishing American, The Arizona Clan*, and *To the Last Man*.

Tony Hillerman is another author whose books rely on Arizona settings. Hillerman's contemporary murder mysteries are almost all set in the Navajo Reservation in the Four Corners area and include many references to actual locations that can be seen by visitors to the area. Among Hillerman's Navajo mysteries are *Thief of Time, The Blessing Way, Listening Woman*, and *The Ghostway*.

Edward Abbey's *The Monkey Wrench Gang* and *Hayduke Lives!* are tales of an unlikely gang of "eco-terrorists" determined to preserve the wildernesses of the Southwest. The former book helped inspire the founding of the radical Earth First! movement. Abbey is also well known as a brilliant, though cynical, observer of the desert and captures the desert's many moods in such works as *Desert Solitaire* (McGraw-Hill, 1968), a nonfiction work based on his time spent in southern Utah's Arches National Monument.

Laughing Boy (Buccaneer Books, 1981) by Oliver LaFarge is a somewhat idealized narrative of Navajo life that won the Pulitzer Prize in 1929. Many novels of pioneer life in Arizona have been made into popular films. These include *Foxfire* (Houghton, 1950) by Anya Seton, the story of a young woman from the East moving to Arizona to marry a part-Apache mining engineer and Henry Will's *Mackenna's Gold* (Random House, 1963), a story of the search for a lost mine in the Arizona mountains.

TRAVEL *Arizona Highways* is a monthly magazine with brilliant color photography and stories on history and attractions.

FILMS

Since before the movies could speak, Arizona has been popular with filmmakers. Its spectacular landscapes, rugged deserts, ghost towns, and cowboy ethos have made it the location for hundreds of films. Old Tucson Studios is a western town that was built for the movie *Arizona* in 1939 and is still in use today as both a movie location and a tourist attraction. Movies and television shows that have been filmed here include John Wayne's *Rio Lobo, Rio Bravo*, and *El Dorado;* Clint Eastwood's *The Outlaw Josey Wales;* Kirk Douglas's *Gunfight at the O.K. Corral;* and Paul Newman's *The Life and Times of Judge Roy Bean*. Old Tucson doubled as Mankato on the television series *Little House on the Prairie*.

Patagonia, in southeastern Arizona, is another town that has served as backdrop for quite a few films, including *Oklahoma, Red River, McClintock, Broken Lance, David and Bathsheba,* and *A Star Is Born,* and television programs including *Little House on the Prairie, The Young Riders,* and *Red Badge of Courage.*

Monument Valley has also been a very popular setting for western movies such as *Stagecoach, How the West Was Won, My Darling Clementine, The Searchers, The Trial of Billy Jack,* and *The Legend of the Lone Ranger.*

Broken Arrow, 3:10 to Yuma, The Cowboy and the Redhead, The Riders of the Purple Sage, and *The Call of the Canyon* were all filmed in the Sedona and Oak Creek area.

CHAPTER 2

PLANNING A TRIP TO ARIZONA

Before heading off to the wide-open spaces of Arizona, you probably have a few questions you'd like answered. When should I go? Where should I stay? What shouldn't I miss? What's the best way to get there? How much is it going to cost? These are the kinds of questions that this chapter addresses.

1. INFORMATION & MONEY

SOURCES OF INFORMATION

If you have more questions than I can answer in this book, there are a number of places that may have the answers for you. For statewide travel information, contact the **Arizona Office of Tourism,** 1100 West Washington Avenue, Phoenix, AZ 85007 (tel. 602/542-TOUR; fax 602/542-4068). Also keep in mind that every city and town in Arizona has either a tourism office or chamber of commerce that can provide you with information. See the individual chapters for addresses of these sources. Also, keep in mind that if you are a member of the **American Automobile Association (AAA),** you can get a map and guidebook covering Arizona and New Mexico.

MONEY

What will a vacation in Arizona cost? That depends on your comfort needs. If you drive an RV or carry a tent, you can get by very inexpensively and find a place to stay almost anywhere in the state. If you don't mind staying in motels that date back to the Great Depression and can sleep on a sagging mattress, you can stay for less money in Arizona than almost anyplace else in the U.S. (under $25 a night for a double). On the other hand, you can easily spend several hundred dollars a day on a room at one of the state's world-class resorts. However, if you're looking to stay in clean, modern motels at Interstate highway off-ramps, expect to pay $40 to $65 a night for a double room in most places. When it comes time to eat, you can get a great meal almost anywhere in the state for under $25, but if you want to spend more, or less, that's also possible. Below are charts of what you can expect to pay in Phoenix and Flagstaff.

Traveler's checks are accepted at hotels, motels, restaurants, and most stores, as are credit cards. Cities and towns throughout the state have banks with automatic teller machines, so you can get cash as you travel. If you plan to rent a car, you'll need a credit card for the deposit.

WHAT THINGS COST IN PHOENIX	**U.S. $**
Taxi from the airport to Scottsdale	15.00
Local telephone call	.25
Double room at The Phoenician (deluxe)	270.00
Double room at the Fiesta Inn (moderate)	78.00
Double room at the Tempe Vagabond Inn (budget)	49.00
Lunch for one at Monti's (moderate)	10.00
Lunch for one at Guedo's (budget)	6.00
Dinner for one, without wine, at Christopher's (deluxe)	60.00
Dinner for one, without wine, at the Paniolo Grill (moderate)	24.00
Dinner for one, without wine, at Ed Debevic's (budget)	10.00
Bottle of beer in a restaurant	1.50
Coca-Cola in a restaurant	1.00
Cup of coffee	.50
Roll of ASA 100 Kodacolor film, 36 exposures	5.50
Admission to the Heard Museum	4.00
Movie ticket	6.50
Theater ticket to Gammage Auditorium	10.00–40.00

WHAT THINGS COST IN FLAGSTAFF	**U.S. $**
Taxi from the airport to the city center	9.50
Local telephone call	.25
Double room at the Woodlands Plaza (moderate)	89.00
Double room at the Monte Vista Hotel (budget)	55.00
Lunch for one at the Woodlands Café (moderate)	12.00
Lunch for one at Café Espress (budget)	8.00
Dinner for one, without wine, at Cottage Place (deluxe)	28.00
Dinner for one, without wine, at Sakura (moderate)	23.00
Dinner for one, without wine, at El Charro Café (budget)	13.00
Bottle of beer in a restaurant	1.50
Coca-Cola in a restaurant	1.00
Cup of coffee	.50
Roll of ASA 100 Kodacolor film, 36 exposures	5.50

Admission to the Museum of Northern Arizona	3.00
Movie ticket	6.00
Theater ticket to the Flagstaff Symphony	10.00–17.50

2. WHEN TO GO—CLIMATE, HOLIDAYS & EVENTS

CLIMATE

The first thing you should know is that the desert can be cold as well as hot. Although winter is the prime tourist season in Phoenix and Tucson, night temperatures can be below freezing and days can even be too cold for sunning or swimming. However, on the whole, winters in Arizona are positively delightful. The all-around best times to visit are in spring and autumn, when temperatures are cool in the mountains and warm in the desert but without extremes (although you shouldn't be surprised to get a bit of snow as late as Memorial Day in the mountains and thunderstorms in the desert in September).

In the winter, sunseekers flock to the deserts where temperatures average in the high 60°s by day. In the summer when desert temperatures are topping 110°, the mountains of eastern and northern Arizona are pleasantly warm with daytime averages in the low 80°s. Yuma is one of the desert communities where winter temperatures are the highest in the state. Prescott and Sierra Vista, in the 4,000- to 6,000-foot elevation range, are two cities that claim to have among the best climates in the world—not too cold, not too hot.

Here are a couple of climate charts to give you an idea of the state's climatic diversity:

Phoenix's Average Temperatures & Days of Rain

	Jan	Feb	Mar	Apr	May	June	July	Aug	Sept	Oct	Nov	Dec
Average Highs	65	69	75	84	93	102	105	102	98	88	75	66
Average Lows	38	41	45	52	60	68	78	76	69	57	45	39
Days of Rain	4	4	3	2	1	1	4	5	3	3	2	4

Flagstaff's Average Temperatures & Days of Rain

	Jan	Feb	Mar	Apr	May	June	July	Aug	Sept	Oct	Nov	Dec
Average Highs	41	44	48	57	67	76	81	78	74	63	51	43
Average Lows	14	17	20	27	34	40	50	49	41	31	22	16
Days of Rain	7	6	8	6	3	3	12	11	6	5	5	6

HOLIDAYS

Arizona celebrates holidays on the following days: January 1 (New Year's Day), February 12 (Lincoln's Birthday), third Monday in February (Washington's Birthday), last Monday in May (Memorial Day), July 4 (Independence Day), first Monday in September (Labor Day), second Monday in October (Columbus Day), November 11 (Veterans' Day/Armistice Day), last Thursday in November (Thanksgiving), and December 25 (Christmas Day). The Tuesday following the first Monday in November is Election Day and is a legal holiday in presidential election years.

ARIZONA
CALENDAR OF EVENTS

JANUARY

☐ **Northern Telecom Open,** Tucson. First PGA golf tournament of the year. 2nd weekend.

FEBRUARY

☐ **Flagstaff Winter Festival,** Flagstaff. Arts and crafts festival, games, sports events. Early to mid-February.

☐ **Tubac Festival of the Arts,** Tubac. Exhibits by North American artists and craftspeople. Early February.

☐ **O'odham Tash,** Casa Grande. Tohono O'odham tribal festival featuring rodeos, crafts shows, dance performances. Mid-February.

☐ **Festival in the Sun,** Tucson. Art exhibitions and performances by world-class musicians and dancers. Mid-February to mid-March.

☐ **Fiesta de los Vaqueros,** Tucson. Largest midwinter outdoor rodeo in the U.S. Late February.

MARCH

☐ **Territorial Days,** Tombstone. Tombstone's birthday celebration. 1st weekend.

APRIL

☐ **San Xavier Pageant & Fiesta,** Tucson. Celebration of the founding of Mission San Xavier del Bac. Early April.

☐ **Yaqui Easter Lenten Ceremony,** Tucson. Holy Week ceremonies combining Christian and Yaqui tribal beliefs. Holy Week.

☐ **Wyatt Earp Days,** Tombstone. Gunfight reenactments in memory of the shootout at the O.K. Corral. Late April.

MAY

☐ **Cinco de Mayo,** Tucson and other cities. Celebration of Mexican victory over the French in the famous battle. May 5.

☐ **Annual Zuñi Artists Exhibition,** Flagstaff. Exhibition and sale at the Museum of Northern Arizona. Late May.

☐ **Phippen Western Art Show & Sale,** Prescott. Premier western art sale. Memorial Day weekend.

☐ **White Mountain All-Indian Pow-Wow,** Whiteriver. Rodeo and Native American fair. Memorial Day weekend.

JUNE

☐ **Annual Festival of Native American Arts,** Flagstaff. Native American market, dances, art exhibition. Late June to early August.

JULY

- ☐ **Prescott Frontier Days,** Prescott. Oldest rodeo in the U.S. 1st week.
- ☐ **Annual Navajo Artists Exhibition,** Flagstaff. Exhibition and sale at the Museum of Northern Arizona. Late July to early August.

AUGUST

- ☐ **Vigilante Days,** Tombstone. Hangings, fist and gunfights, stagecoach rides. Early August.

SEPTEMBER

- ☐ **Navajo Tribal Fair,** Window Rock. Rodeo, dances, parade, food. Early September.
- ☐ **Jazz on the Rocks,** Sedona. Open-air jazz festival. Late September.

OCTOBER

- ☐ **Helldorado Days,** Tombstone. 1880s fashion show, tribal dancers, street entertainment. Late October.

NOVEMBER

- ☐ **Tucson Art Expo,** Tucson. Citywide celebration of the arts. Early to mid-November.

DECEMBER

- ☐ **Festival of Lights,** Sedona. The city is illuminated by *luminarias*. Mid-December.
- ☐ **Las Posadas,** Tucson. Children reenact Mary and Joseph's search for an inn. Mid-December.

PHOENIX CALENDAR OF EVENTS

JANUARY

- ☐ **Fiesta Bowl Football Classic,** Tempe. College football classic. New Year's Day.
- ☐ **Phoenix Open Golf Tournament,** Tournament Players Club. Prestigious PGA golf tournament. Late January.

FEBRUARY

- ☐ **Parada del Sol Parade and Rodeo,** Scottsdale. Longest horse-drawn parade, street dance, rodeo. Early February.
- ☐ **Arizona Renaissance Festival,** Apache Junction. 16th-century English country fair with costumed participants. Early February to mid-March.
- ☐ **All-Arabian Horse Show,** Scottsdale's Horseworld. A celebration of the Arabian horse. Mid-February.

MARCH

- **Phoenix Formula One Grand Prix,** downtown Phoenix. Grand Prix race through the streets of Phoenix. Early March.
- **Heard Museum Guild Indian Fair,** Heard Museum. Showcase of Native American arts and heritage, with more than 150 artists displaying work. 1st weekend.
- **Scottsdale Arts Festival,** Scottsdale Mall. Visual- and performing-arts festival with free concerts, art show, children's events. 2nd weekend.
- **Phoenix Jaycee's Rodeo of Rodeos,** Arizona Veterans Memorial Coliseum. One of the biggest and most popular indoor rodeos in the world. Early March.
- **Maricopa County Fair,** Arizona State Fairgrounds. Midway, agricultural and livestock exhibits, entertainment. Mid-March.
- **Spring Festival of the Arts,** old town Tempe. The largest arts and entertainment festival in the Southwest features more than 450 artists and artisans. Late March to early April.

APRIL

- **Desert Botanical Garden Cactus Show,** Desert Botanical Garden. Display and sale of cactus during blooming season. Early April.
- **Scottsdale All-Indian Days Annual Pow-Wow,** Scottsdale. More than 50 tribes from all over North America perform music and dances and exhibit arts and crafts. 2nd weekend.

MAY

- **Cinco de Mayo,** all over the city. Celebration to commemorate victory of the Mexicans over the French. May 5.

SEPTEMBER

- **Fiesta Patrias,** Phoenix Civic Plaza and Heritage Square. Celebration of Mexican Independence Day. Mid-September.
- **Scottsdale Center for the Arts Annual Gala,** Scottsdale Center for the Arts. Jazz, ballet, music, a sculpture exhibit, and special events. Late September.

OCTOBER

- **Wrangler Jeans Rodeo Showdown & Arizona Festival,** Rawhide. Top rodeo stars from the U.S. and Canada compete. Early October.
- **Arizona State Fair,** Arizona State Fairgrounds. Rodeos, top-name entertainment, ethnic food. Mid- to late October.
- **Annual Cowboy Artists of America Exhibition,** Phoenix Art Museum. Most prestigious and best-known western art show. Late October to late November.

NOVEMBER

- **Hot Air Balloon Race & Thunderbird Balloon Classic,** Glendale. Dozens of hot-air balloons fill the Arizona sky. Early November.

DECEMBER

- **Winter Festival of the Arts,** Mill Avenue, Tempe. Hundreds of artists and artisans, free entertainment, plenty of food. Early December.
- **Fiesta Bowl Festival,** Tempe. All manner of sports competitions and a big block party on December 31. 1st to last week.

3. HEALTH & INSURANCE

HEALTH PRECAUTIONS If you have never been to the desert before, you should be sure to prepare yourself for this harsh environment. No matter what time of year it is, the desert sun is strong and bright. You should be sure to use sunscreen when you are outdoors—and this holds true even if you are up in the mountains, where altitude makes sunburns more likely. The bright sun also makes sunglasses a necessity.

Even if you don't feel hot in the desert, the dry air still steals moisture from your body, so drink plenty of fluids. You may want to use a body lotion as well. The desert air quickly dries out skin.

It's not only the sun that makes the desert a harsh environment. There are poisonous creatures out there, too, but with a little common sense and some precautions you can avoid them. Rattlesnakes are very common in the desert, but your chances of meeting one are slight (except during the mating season in April and May) because they tend not to come out in the heat of the day. However, never stick your hand into holes among the rocks in the desert, and look to see where you are going to step before putting your foot down.

Arizona also has a large poisonous lizard called the Gila monster. These black-and-orange lizards are far less common than rattlesnakes and your chances of meeting one are slight.

Although the tarantula has developed a nasty reputation, the tiny black widow is more likely to cause illness. Scorpions are another insect danger of the desert. Be extra-careful whenever turning over rocks or logs that might harbor either black widows or scorpions.

INSURANCE Before going out and spending money on various sorts of travel insurance, check your existing policies to see if they'll cover you while you're traveling. Make sure your health insurance will cover you when you are away from home. Most credit cards offer automatic flight insurance when you purchase an airline ticket with that credit card. These policies insure against death or dismemberment in the case of an airplane crash. Also, check your credit cards to see if any of them pick up the collision damage waiver (CDW) when you rent a car. The CDW can run as much as $10 a day and can add 50% or more to the cost of renting a car. Check your automobile insurance policy, too; it might cover the CDW as well. If you own a home or have renter's insurance, see if that policy covers off-premises theft and loss wherever it occurs. If you are traveling on a tour or have prepaid a large chunk of your travel expenses, you might want to ask your travel agent about trip-cancellation insurance.

If, after checking all your existing insurance policies, you decide that you need additional insurance, a good travel agent can give you information on a variety of different options. **Teletrip (Mutual of Omaha),** 3201 Farnam Street, Omaha, NE 68131 (tel. 402/345-2400), offers four different types of travel insurance policy for 1 day to 6 months. These policies include medical, baggage, trip cancellation or interruption insurance, and flight insurance against death or dismemberment.

4. WHAT TO PACK

Whenever and wherever you travel, it's always a good idea to travel light. Limit your luggage to what you can easily carry yourself and you will probably enjoy your trip more than if you have to lug around half a dozen bags.

CLOTHING Although typical Arizona attire is casual—blue jeans and cowboy boots are acceptable almost anywhere (as long as you wear a bola tie)—its diverse geography can make packing a real puzzler. How do you pack your bags for snow skiing in Flagstaff and sunning by the pool in Phoenix? The best solution is to take

IMPRESSIONS

From the hygienic point of view, whiskey and cold lead are mentioned as the leading diseases at Tombstone.
—A TOMBSTONE VISITOR IN THE 1880s

---

along a little of everything, but not so much that it won't all fit into your one checked bag and your carry-on bag. If you choose carefully so that all your tops can be worn with all your bottoms and if you bring a bathing suit, shorts, wool sweater or jacket, and a down jacket, you should be prepared for any Arizona weather. Don't forget your blue jeans, cowboy boots, cowboy hat, and bola tie, but if you don't have any of these items, you can shop for them while you're here. A very few restaurants (only the most expensive) require men to wear a jacket and tie (bola ties count) at dinner, so play it safe and bring a jacket and tie.

OTHER ITEMS   Most hotels and motels will give you a wake-up call or have alarm clocks in the room, but you may want to carry a little travel alarm clock just in case. A small flashlight can prove invaluable in the event of an emergency after dark, especially if your car breaks down. A Swiss army knife is another item that everyone should carry. They are handy for picnics, removing splinters, opening wine bottles, and countless other unexpected little tasks.

---

5. TIPS FOR THE DISABLED, SENIORS, SINGLES, FAMILIES & STUDENTS

FOR THE DISABLED   When making airline reservations, always mention your disability. Airline policies differ regarding wheelchairs and Seeing Eye dogs. If you are in a wheelchair, be sure to request a wheelchair-accessible room when making hotel reservations.

FOR SENIORS   When making airline reservations, always mention that you are a senior citizen. Many airlines offer discounts. You should also carry some sort of photo ID card (drivers license, passport, etc.) to avail yourself of senior-citizen discounts on attractions, hotels, motels, and public transportation, as well as one of the best deals in Arizona for senior citizens—the **Golden Age Passport,** which is available for free to U.S. citizens and permanent residents age 62 and older. This federal government pass allows free admission and half-price camping at national parks, monuments, and recreation areas. Passes are issued at all parks, monuments, and recreation areas where they are accepted, or you can obtain one by writing to the National Park Service, Public Inquiry, Dept. of the Interior, 18th Street and C Street NW, Washington, DC 20013.

If you are not a member of the **American Association of Retired Persons (AARP),** 1909 K Street NW, Washington, DC 20049 (tel. 202/872-4700), you should consider joining. This association provides discounts at many lodgings throughout Arizona.

If you'd like to do a bit of studying on vacation, consider **Elderhostel** (see "Alternative/Adventure Travel," below).

FOR SINGLE TRAVELERS   There's no doubt about it, single travelers are discriminated against by hotels and motels. A lone traveler often has to pay the same room rate as two people, and if you want to spend time at a fancy resort, this can make a vacation in Arizona a very costly experience. Unless you are dead set on staying at a particular hotel or resort, you might be able to save some money by finding a comparable hostelry that offers separate rates for single and double rooms.

FOR FAMILIES   Arizona offers something for everyone and is a popular family vacation destination. Kids love the "cowboy and Indian" lore of Arizona, and there are plenty of opportunities for them to explore this aspect of American history. Dude ranches (now known as guest ranches) are popular with families. The kids can go off for a day of horseback riding while the parents relax by the pool, or vice versa. Cookouts and wagon rides are geared as much toward kids as toward adults. Old Tucson and Tombstone are two attractions that kids find fascinating (though parents may be less than enchanted with all the souvenir shops).

Keep in mind that most hotels and motels allow kids to sleep free in their parents room as long as a crib or extra bed is not necessary. Also, when dining, watch for children's dinners on the menu. These will save you quite a bit of money and are likely to be more appealing to the young ones.

Last, remember that Arizona is a very large state. Driving times are long, so bring plenty to keep the kids entertained. Looking out the window at the desert for hours and hours is even boring for adults.

FOR STUDENTS   Because Arizona is a popular destination with young European travelers, it has quite a few youth hostels. You can also get special student discounts on admission to many attractions if you show a current student ID card. Arizona's three major universities—Arizona State University in Tempe, the University of Arizona in Tucson, and Northern Arizona University in Flagstaff—all have an active nightlife in the surrounding neighborhoods. If you'd like to meet other students your age, head for the cafés and bars near the universities.

6. ALTERNATIVE/ADVENTURE TRAVEL

EDUCATIONAL/STUDY TRAVEL   Older travelers who want to learn something from their trip to Arizona or who simply prefer the company of like-minded older travelers should look into programs by **Elderhostel,** 80 Boylston Street, Suite 400, Boston, MA 02116 (tel. 617/426-7788). To participate in an Elderhostel program, either you or your spouse must be 60 years old. In addition to 1-week educational programs, Elderhostel also offers short getaways with interesting themes.

The **Nature Conservancy,** 300 East University Boulevard, Suite 230, Tucson, AZ 85705, is a nonprofit organization dedicated to the global preservation of natural diversity. It does this by identifying and purchasing land that is home to endangered plants, animals, and natural communities. The organization has several preserves in Arizona to which they operate educational field trips of 1 to 4 days. These trips are open to Nature Conservancy members only.

WORK CAMPS   If you enjoy the wilderness and want to get more involved in preserving it, consider a Sierra Club Service Trip. These trips are for the purpose of building, restoring, and maintaining hiking trails in wilderness areas. It's a lot of work, but it's also a lot of fun. For more information on Service Trips, contact the **Sierra Club Outing Department,** 730 Polk Street, San Francisco, CA 94109.

Another sort of service trip is being offered by the National Park Service. They're accepting volunteers to pick up garbage left by thoughtless visitors to Lake Powell National Recreation Area. In exchange for picking up trash, you'll get to spend 5 days on a houseboat called the *Trash Tracker* cruising the gorgeous canyonlands scenery of Lake Powell. Volunteers must be at least 18 years old, and must provide their own food and sleeping bag. For more information, contact **Lake Powell National Recreation Area,** P.O. Box 1507, Page, AZ 86040.

ADVENTURE/WILDERNESS TRAVEL   In the world of adventure travel, Arizona ranks very high on most people's list for the sole reason that this state is home to the Grand Canyon—the most widely known white-water-rafting spot in the world. There are quite a few companies offering rafting trips of various lengths in the Grand Canyon. (see Chapter 6 for companies licensed to operate in the canyon.)

Despite its reputation as a desert state, a large percentage of Arizona is forest land, and within these forests are wilderness areas and countless miles of hiking trails. One of the most popular backpacking spots in the state is Havasu Canyon, which connects to the Grand Canyon. Havasu Canyon is the home of the Havasupai tribe, whose name means "people of the blue-green waters." This tribe takes its name from the beautiful waterfalls that cascade through their canyon. See Chapter 6 for details.

With its cowboy heritage, it comes as no surprise that horseback trips are very popular in Arizona. Whether you want to explore the desert, the forest, or canyons, there are outfits that will lead you down the trail. **Adventure Trails of the West,** P.O. Box 1494, Wickenburg, AZ 85358 (tel. 602/684-3106 or 602/346-4403), offers trips to different areas of the state including Canyon de Chelly, Monument Valley, the Superstition Mountains, and the Bradshaw Mountains.

7. GETTING THERE

BY PLANE With all its resorts, Arizona is a major destination and consequently there are plenty of different airlines flying to both Phoenix and Tucson from around the United States.

The Major Airlines Phoenix and Tucson are both served by quite a few airlines, including the following: **Aero México** (tel. toll free 800/237-6639), **Alaska Airlines** (tel. toll free 800/426-0333), **America West** (tel. toll free 800/247-5692), **American** (tel. toll free 800/433-7300), **Continental** (tel. toll free 800/525-0280), **Delta** (tel. toll free 800/221-1212), **Northwest** (tel. toll free 800/225-2525), **Southwest** (tel. toll free 800/531-5601), **TWA** (tel. toll free 800/221-2000), **United** (tel. toll free 800/241-6522), and **USAir** (tel. toll free 800/428-4322).

Regular Fares At press time fares from New York to Phoenix on Continental ranged from a low of $346 for a nonrefundable, minimum-14-day advance-purchase round-trip ticket, to $970 for a full-fare round-trip coach ticket to $1,710 for a first-class round-trip ticket.

BY TRAIN Phoenix and Tucson both have **Amtrak** service from Los Angeles in the west and Dallas, St. Louis, and Chicago in the east aboard the *Texas Eagle*. The

---

 FROMMER'S SMART TRAVELER: AIRFARES

1. Make reservations as far in advance as possible for best availability and prices. The lowest fares usually require making reservations at least 2 weeks before the scheduled flight.
2. Shop all the airlines flying to your destination, and be sure to watch the newspaper for special fares.
3. Always ask for the lowest-priced fare, not just for a discount fare.
4. Keep calling the airline—availability of cheap seats changes daily. Airline managers would rather sell a seat than have it fly empty. As the departure date nears, additional low-cost seats sometimes become available.
5. Remember that Tucson's airport has almost as many flights as Phoenix's Sky Harbor Airport. If your final destination is Tucson or somewhere in southern Arizona, there is no reason to fly into Phoenix.
6. Look into combination air/land packages if you're planning on spending your time at a resort. Several of the airlines flying to Arizona offer these packages, and often you'll get a lower room rate by booking this way.
7. Always ask what car-rental agencies offer frequent-flyer miles if you participate in a frequent-flyer plan.

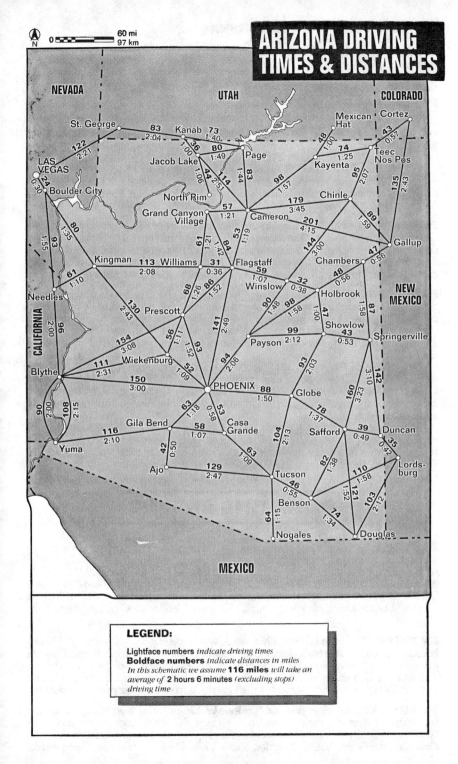

Sunset Limited connects New Orleans, Houston, San Antonio, El Paso, and Los Angeles with Phoenix and Tucson. The *Southwest Chief* connects Flagstaff with Chicago, Kansas City, Albuquerque, and Los Angeles. For information and reservations, call toll free 800/872-7245 in the United States or 800/426-8725 in Canada. At press time, the round-trip fare from Los Angeles to Phoenix was $82 one way and ranged from $89 to $164 for a round-trip ticket. This trip takes about 8½ hours.

BY BUS **Greyhound/Trailways Lines** offers service to several Arizona cities from Los Angeles, San Diego, Las Vegas, and Albuquerque. Travel by bus is economical, especially if you are planning on doing a lot of traveling and purchase a special unlimited travel pass. The trip from Los Angeles to Phoenix takes about 8 hours. The one-way fare is $30.60 Friday through Sunday and $28.60 Monday through Thursday; round-trip fare is $48.90 Friday through Sunday and $44.75 Monday through Thursday.

BY CAR Major highways through Arizona are **I-8** from San Diego to I-10 at Casa Grande, which is about midway between Phoenix and Tucson. **I-10** from Los Angeles passes through Phoenix and Tucson and continues east to Florida. **I-40** connects northern Arizona (including Kingman and Flagstaff) with California, and continues east all the way to North Carolina. **I-19** runs from the Mexican border up to Tucson.

PACKAGE TOURS If you prefer to let someone else do all your travel preparations, then a package tour might be for you—whether you just want to lie by the pool at a resort for a week or see the whole state in 2 weeks. The best way to find out about package tours to Arizona is to visit a travel agent, who will likely have several booklets about different tours and airfare/hotel-room packages being offered by different airlines.

   Gray Line of Phoenix, 3415 South 36th Street, Phoenix, AZ 85040-1607 (tel. toll free 800/628-2449), offers excursions of 1 to 5 days. Tours include the Grand Canyon by way of Sedona and Oak Creek Canyon; the Grand Canyon by train; and a canyon lands tour that includes the Grand Canyon, Lake Powell, and stops in Utah, and at Las Vegas.

   Maupintour, 1515 St. Andrews Drive, Lawrence, KS 66047 (tel. 913/843-1211, or toll free 800/255-4266), one of the largest tour operators in the world, offers several Arizona itineraries that cover the Grand Canyon, the Four Corners region, Phoenix, and Tucson.

8. GETTING AROUND

BY PLANE Arizona is a big state (the sixth largest), so if your time is short, you might want to consider flying between cities. Several small commuter airlines offer service within the state. These include **Air Sedona** (tel. toll free 800/535-4448), **Mesa** (tel. toll free 800/637-2247), **Skywest** (tel. toll free 800/453-9417), and **USAir Express** (tel. toll free 800/428-4322). Cities served by these airlines include Flagstaff, Sedona, Sierra Vista, Yuma, Kingman, Bullhead City/Laughlin, Lake Havasu City, and Page.

BY TRAIN The train is not really a viable way of getting around much of Arizona because there is no **Amtrak** train service between Flagstaff in the north and Phoenix in the south. However, you can travel between Phoenix and Tucson by train. There is also an excursion train that runs from Williams (30 miles west of Flagstaff) to Grand Canyon Village at the South Rim of the Grand Canyon. (See Chapter 6 for details.)

BY BUS Although **Greyhound/Trailways Lines** offers bus service to quite a few cities in Arizona, their routes do not cover the entire state. Cities served by Greyhound/Trailways include Phoenix, Tucson, Tempe, Mesa, Chandler, Sacaton, Casa Grande, Green Valley, Nogales, Sierra Vista, Douglas, Prescott, Camp Verde,

IMPRESSIONS

If this was my lake, I'd mow it.
—WILL ROGERS TO FORMER PRESIDENT CALVIN COOLIDGE ABOUT SAN CARLOS LAKE,
WHICH WAS FORMED BY THE COOLIDGE DAM

Flagstaff, Williams, Ash Fork, Seligman, Kingman, Bullhead City/Laughlin, Houck, Holbrook, and Winslow.

Nava-Hopi Tours (tel. 602/774-5003) offers bus service between Flagstaff and the Grand Canyon, and the **Navajo Transit System** (tel. 602/729-5457) provides service on the Navajo Reservation, which includes such major destinations as Canyon de Chelly National Monument and Monument Valley Navajo Tribal Park.

BY CAR   A car is by far the best way to see Arizona. There just isn't any other way to get to the more remote natural spectacles and historic sites.

Rentals   Because Phoenix and Tucson are major resort destinations, they both have dozens of car-rental agencies. Prices at rental agencies elsewhere in the state tend to be higher, so if at all possible, try to rent your car in either Phoenix or Tucson. Major rental-car companies with offices in Arizona include **Alamo** (tel. toll free 800/327-9633), **Avis** (tel. toll free 800/331-1212), **Budget** (tel. toll free 800/527-0700), **Hertz** (tel. toll free 800/654-3131), and **Thrifty** (tel. toll free 800/367-2277).

Rates for rental cars vary considerably between companies and with the model you wish to rent. Also, keep in mind that the rate for any given date will fluctuate depending on availability and demand. If you call the same company three times and ask about renting the same model car, you may get three different quotes. It pays to start shopping early. At press time, **Budget** was charging $128 per week or $31.70 per day for a compact car with unlimited mileage.

If you are a member of a frequent-flyer program, check to see which rental-car companies participate in the program. Also, when making a reservation be sure to mention any discount you might be eligible for, such as corporate, military, or AAA, and any specials offered. Beware of coupons offering discounts on rental-car rates—often these discount the highest rates only. It's always cheaper to rent by the week, so if you don't really need a car for 7 days, you might find that it's still cheaper than renting for 4 days only.

One last tip: Check with your credit-card and auto-insurance companies to see if you can decline the collision-damage waiver (CDW). Many credit cards now cover the charges if you decline the CDW, and your insurance may already be sufficient to pay for any damage you do to the rental car. CDW insurance can add $10 or more per day to the price of renting a car, so you'll save quite a bit if you're renting for a week or more.

Gasoline   Always be sure to keep your gas tank topped off. It's not unusual for it to be 60 miles between gas stations in many parts of Arizona.

Driving Rules   A right turn on a red light is permitted after first coming to a complete stop. Seatbelts are required for the driver and any front-seat passenger, and children four years and younger or who weigh 40 pounds or less must be in a children's car seat. General speed limits are 25 to 35 m.p.h. in towns and cities, 15 m.p.h. in school zones, and 55 m.p.h. on highways, except rural interstates where the speed limit is 65 m.p.h.

Breakdowns/Assistance   It's a long way between towns in Arizona and a breakdown in the desert can be more than just an inconvenience—it can be dangerous. Always carry drinking water with you while driving through the desert, and if you plan to head off on back roads, it's a good idea to carry extra water for the car as well.

If you are a member of the **American Automobile Association** and your car breaks down, call toll free 800/AAA-HELP for 24-hour emergency road service.

HITCHHIKING   Hitchhiking is illegal on the Interstate system, but you can stick out your thumb at the beginning of on-ramps and on any other roads. Because of the great distances between towns, the harshness of the desert environment, and the general reluctance of drivers to pick up hitchhikers, it's a good idea to take only rides that are going all the way to another town.

SUGGESTED ITINERARIES

HIGHLIGHTS

Cities and Towns	Parks, Monuments, and Natural Areas
Phoenix	Grand Canyon National Park
Tucson	Oak Creek Canyon
Sedona	Havasu Canyon
Prescott	Petrified Forest National Park
Jerome	Painted Desert
Bisbee	Monument Valley Navajo Tribal Park
Tubac	Chiracahua National Monument
The Hopi Mesas	Canyon de Chelly National Monument
	Navajo Indian Reservation
	Glen Canyon National Recreation Area
	Lake Mead National Recreation Area
	Organ Pipe Cactus National Monument

PLANNING YOUR ITINERARY

Because Arizona is such a diverse state, it's difficult to suggest an itinerary that will fit everyone's needs. However, if your goal is to get to know Arizona rather than just lie by the pool or play golf, here are some suggestions.

IF YOU HAVE 1 WEEK

Days 1 and 2: Spend your first 2 days in Tucson.
Days 3 and 4: Drive to Phoenix, stopping at the Casa Grande Ruins on the way.
Day 5: Drive north to Sedona, stopping at Arcosanti and Montezuma Castle on the way.
Day 6: Drive to the Grand Canyon.
Day 7: Wake up for sunrise on the canyon, and then drive back to Phoenix or Tucson.

IF YOU HAVE 2 WEEKS

Days 1–3: Explore Tucson, with trips to Saguaro National Monument, San Xavier del Bac, Tubac/Tumacacori, Tombstone, and Bisbee.
Days 4 and 5: Drive to Phoenix, stopping at the Casa Grande Ruins on the way.
Days 6 and 7: Drive to Sedona by way of Prescott and Jerome.
Days 8 and 9: Explore the Flagstaff area and the Grand Canyon.
Days 10–13: Explore the Four Corners region including Navajo National Monument, Monument Valley, Canyon de Chelly, the Painted Desert, and the Petrified Forest.
Day 14: Return to Phoenix or Tucson, stopping at Montezuma Castle and Arcosanti on the way back.

IF YOU HAVE 3 WEEKS

With this much time you can indulge in whatever your personal interest happens to be. Spend several days or even the whole week at a resort or guest ranch. Rent a houseboat on Lake Powell, Lake Mead, Lake Mohave, or Lake Havasu. Raft the Grand Canyon. Hike or ride a mule down into the Grand Canyon and spend several days exploring the inner canyon.

9. WHERE TO STAY

From rustic cabins in the woods to ultra-luxurious resorts in cosmopolitan Phoenix, Arizona has every possible accommodation option. Whatever your budget, you should have no problem finding an affordable place to stay.

If money is no object, the resorts in Phoenix, Scottsdale, Tucson, and Sedona will pamper you and provide you with all manner of activity or inactivity, whichever you prefer. The Valley of the Sun claims to have the greatest concentration of **world-class resorts** in the United States, and it's hard to argue with this statement. The majority of these resorts are in Scottsdale, particularly along Scottsdale Road, which is known as resort row. If you prefer to get away from all the hustle and bustle of downtown Scottsdale, try the Scottsdale Princess, which is a ways north of town. The Boulders, north of Scottsdale in Carefree, has one of the most spectacular settings of any resort in the state. Tucson's foothills resorts are also well known for their stunning locations at the foot of the Santa Catalina Mountains, while Sedona's resorts have the legendary red-rock country for a backdrop, with the Enchantment Resort claiming the best location, right at the mouth of Boynton canyon.

Back in the old days there were dude ranches, but as the definition of "dude" changed, so, too, did the name. No matter what you call them, Arizona's **guest ranches** are loads of fun no matter what your age. Located in rugged areas surrounded by acres of wilderness, guest ranches cater to folks who want to live out their cowboy dreams—riding the range, sitting around the campfire, singing old cowboy songs, pitching horseshoes. You might also be able to go for a swim in the pool, learn a bit about the local wildlife, go birdwatching, play tennis, play golf, or soak in the hot tub. Arizona's greatest concentrations of guest ranches are in Wickenburg (northwest of Phoenix) and Tucson. Guest ranches aren't cheap, but all your meals are included, and often plenty of horseback riding, too.

Arizona's best lodging bargains are the many motels at Interstate off-ramps. These **chain motels** are reliably clean and fairly economical, with rooms going for $30 to $50. However, you can spend even less on a room if you're willing to stay in a motel that was built back in the 1940s or 1950s. These old motels are found primarily in Phoenix, Tucson, and towns along old Route 66 (U.S. 66) in northern Arizona. Rates are often $30 or less, but you have to be willing to put up with someplace that isn't all that clean or is a bit small. If this is your budget range, when you pull into town, take a look at a few motels before making a decision.

Young or young-at-heart travelers will also find quite a few private **hostels** around the state. These are often old motels in which rooms are set up as four-bed dormitories. The price for a bed in a hostel is usually around $10 to $12 a night.

Cheaper still are the state's many **campgrounds and RV parks,** located throughout the state in national parks, national forests, national recreation areas, state parks, and on private land. Campsite fees range from free at some national-forest campgrounds to $12 or more for a campsite in Grand Canyon National Park. RV spaces are a bit higher.

10. WHERE TO DINE

Arizona is only just north of the border, and in fact was part of Mexico at one time, so wherever you go in Arizona, you can count on finding a Mexican restaurant in town, and though not all of them are great, most are far better than what you can find outside the Southwest.

In recent years, southwestern, or New Mexican cuisine, has become the quintessential Arizonan cooking style. Southwestern cuisine takes the spices of Mexico, the mesquite-broiling of the Southwest, and the fruit-and-meat combinations of nouvelle cuisine and mixes them all together to produce such unusual offerings as filet mignon served with four types of grilled peppers, breast of chicken with ancho-chile sauce and tequila beurre blanc, and duckling with prickly-pear cactus glaze. Southwestern cuisine tends to be expensive, and consequently is mostly served where the wealthy congregate—Phoenix, Tucson, and Sedona.

11. WHAT TO BUY

The best buys in Arizona are those that reflect the state's heritage. Artworks by southwestern artists are popular and there are galleries all over the state. The best places to look for southwestern and the so-called cowboy or western art are in Scottsdale, Tucson, Sedona, Tubac, and Jerome. If the desert has gotten into your blood, nothing says Arizona quite like cowboy boots, a cowboy hat, and a pair of blue jeans. Top it all off with a bola tie and you could be an Arizona rancher.

Native American arts and crafts are perhaps the most sought-after of Arizona purchases, and though they're not cheap, they are the state's most distinctive creations. Tribal arts and crafts are available in shops all over the state, but there's nothing quite like buying at a trading post on a reservation. The best known of these is the Hubbell Trading Post in Ganado on the Navajo reservation, but there are trading posts all over the state and almost all offer excellent selection and quality. It's a good idea to make your jewelry purchases from reputable stores rather than from roadside stalls, of which there are many in the Four Corners region of the state. Many of these stalls sell cheap imitation jewelry.

The Native American tribes of Arizona tend to have one or two specialty crafts that they produce with consummate skill. Many of these crafts were disappearing when the first traders came to the reservations a century ago. Today most of the crafts are alive and well, but primarily as sale items. Prices are high because of the many hours that go into producing these crafts. However, keep in mind that what you're buying is handmade using a skill that has been handed down for generations.

NAVAJO RUGS Rugs have been made only since traders came to the Navajo reservation. Prior to that the Navajo had woven only blankets. Women are the weavers in the Navajo tribe, with the skill passed down from mother to daughter. A single rug only a few feet square takes hundreds of hours to make, much of the time spent in preparing the wool, dyeing it, and setting up the primitive loom. The best rugs are those made from hand-spun wool from local Navajo sheep and goats. Vegetal dyes, which generally produce very muted colors, are considered superior to chemical dyes, but are of course more time-consuming to prepare. When shopping for a rug, check the fineness of the weave and the amount of detail in the design. Finer weave and detail mean higher prices because of the additional time required to produce such a rug. Be prepared to spend $1,000 or more for even a small Navajo rug, and even at this price the women who make the rugs are making less than minimum wage for their labor. At the Hubbell Trading Post in Ganado you can see Navajo women weaving rugs.

HOPI KACHINAS Kachina, the colorful and often grotesque dolls of the Hopi people, are representations of the spirits of animals, ancestors, places, and many other things. Styles of kachinas vary from village to village. Carved from cottonwood root or other wood, kachinas are then colorfully painted and decorated with feathers, leather capes, and bits of yarn. The finished doll is meant to closely resemble the costume and mask worn by kachina dancers during the annual religious ceremonies held in Hopi villages. Traditionally, kachina dolls have been given to young Hopi girls to help them learn about the different kachina spirits. However, today many carvers are creating kachinas to sell. Among the more popular kachinas are the humorous *tsuku* or clown kachinas, which are often painted with bold black and white stripes. A detailed kachina will cost several hundred dollars.

ZUÑI FETISHES A fetish is an object in which a spirit dwells, and such objects have always been important to the Zuñi people. The Zuñi have long been known for their stone-carving skills, which are best demonstrated in their small carved animal fetishes. Carved from various types of stone, including turquoise and jet, Zuñi fetishes traditionally depict eagles, bears, wolves, mountain lions, horses, and goats, each of which is associated with a particular compass direction. Often fetishes are decorated with turquoise and coral beads, feathers, and miniature arrowheads, all of which are tied to the body of the fetish with gut. Bear fetishes often feature inlaid heartlines, arrow-shaped lines running from the mouth down the side to the center of the body.

Before buying a fetish, it's a good idea to look at enough of them so that you can see the difference between one that's crudely carved and one that exhibits fine detail. Fetish prices start as low as $30 but most are at least $100.

TOHONO O'ODHAM BASKETS Although virtually all the Arizona tribes produce some sort of basketry, the Tohono O'odham tribe, which has its reservation near Tucson, has come to be known for their baskets. Most Tohono O'odham baskets are made using the coil method. Bear grass is used as the center of the coil, which is then stitched together with bleached yucca and the dark outer covering of the devil's-claw seed pod. The Tohono O'odham also make miniature baskets from horse hair. These baskets require all the skill of full-size baskets but are often no more than 2 inches across. One of the most common Tohono O'odham designs shows a human figure in the middle of a maze. This figure is I'itoi (Elder Brother) and the maze represents the route to his home in the Baboquivari Mountains. Simple small baskets can be purchased for less than $50, but a basket that is finely woven and has a complex design may cost several hundred dollars.

JEWELRY The Navajo, Hopi, and Zuñi all make jewelry, and each tribe has its own distinctive style. The Navajo are well known for heavy silver jewelry that is made primarily by sandcasting. The squash-blossom necklace, which is based on an old Spanish symbol, actually features pomegranate blossoms rather than squash blossoms, but was adapted to Navajo tastes. The Navajo tend to place the emphasis on fine silver work accented by turquoise stones.

The Zuñi, on the other hand, use silver primarily as a setting for their stone carvings. Using turquoise, jet, coral, and cut seashells, the Zuñi create colorful inlaid images. Another style of Zuñi jewelry features tiny pieces of cut and polished turquoise individually set in delicate grid and starburst patterns.

The Hopi are known for their overlay silverwork, which uses two sheets of silver fused together. The upper sheet of silver has a design cut into it with a tiny saw, while the lower sheet is treated to produce a contrasting black background to the upper layer. In recent years Hopi jewelry has featured ancient Anasazi designs taken from baskets and pottery.

Prices for jewelry vary widely depending on the amount of detail, amount of silver, and number of stones.

POTTERY Although the tribes of New Mexico are much better known for their pottery, Arizona tribes such as the Hopi, Navajo, and Tohono O'odham also make pottery. For years Navajo pottery was crudely made and not very attractive, but in recent years Navajo potters have begun experimenting with new and ancient designs and have begun to produce appealing pottery for sale.

Hopi pottery is almost all made in the village of Hotevilla on First Mesa. It's an orange color and is sometimes incised or decorated with geometric designs in black.

Tohono O'odham pottery is very simple and not as well known as their basketry.

Pottery prices vary considerably, but generally are not nearly as high as that produced in the New Mexico pueblos.

 ARIZONA

American Express There are offices in Phoenix, Tucson, Cottonwood, Green Valley, Flagstaff, Scottsdale, and Tempe.

Area Code   The telephone area code for all of Arizona is 602.

Business Hours   The following are general open hours; specific establishments may vary. Banks: Monday through Thursday from 10am to 3pm, Friday 10am to 5pm (some are also open on Saturday from 9am to noon). Offices: Monday through Friday 9am to 6pm. Stores: Monday through Saturday 10am to 6pm, Sunday noon to 5pm (malls usually stay open until 9pm Monday through Saturday). Bars: Sunday through Thursday 11am to midnight, Friday and Saturday 11am to 1am.

Camera/Film   Because the sun is almost always shining in Arizona, you can use a slower film, that is, one with a lower ASA number. This will give you sharper pictures. If your camera accepts different filters and especially if you plan to travel in the higher altitudes of the northern part of the state, you'd do well to invest in a polarizer, which reduces contrast, deepens colors, and eliminates glare. Also, be sure to protect your camera and film from heat. Never leave your camera or film in a car parked in the sun—temperatures inside the car can climb to more than 130°, which is plenty hot enough to damage sensitive film.

Climate   See "When to Go," in this chapter.

Crime   See "Safety," below.

Currency   See Chapter 3.

Customs   See Chapter 3.

Documents Required   See Chapter 3.

Driving Rules   See "Getting Around," in this chapter.

Emergencies   Throughout Arizona, **911** is the number to call in case of a fire, police, or medical emergency.

Fruits, Vegetables, and Live Plants   Because Arizona is one of the main citrus-growing states in the U.S., there are restrictions on what fruits, vegetables, and live plants can be brought into the state. These restrictions are designed to protect local crops from imported insects and plant diseases and apply primarily to citrus fruits, but other plant matter may also be confiscated. If you'd like to find out more about restrictions, telephone 602/255-4373.

Hitchhiking   See "Getting Around," in this chapter.

Holidays   See "When to Go," in this chapter.

Information   See "Information & Money," in this chapter, and individual city chapters and sections for local information offices.

Legal Aid   If you are in need of legal aid, first look in the White Pages of the local telephone book under "Legal Aid." You may also want to contact the **Travelers Aid Society,** which can also be found in the White Pages of local phone books. In Phoenix, the phone number for **Community Legal Services** is 258-3434. In Tucson, the number for **Southern Arizona Legal Aid** is 623-9461 and for Travelers Aid of Tucson is 622-8900.

Liquor Laws   The legal age for buying or consuming alcoholic beverages is 21. It is illegal to bring liquor in from another state and only 1 quart per month can be brought in from a foreign country. You cannot purchase any alcoholic drinks before 10am on Sunday.

Mail   For the address of the nearest post office, look in the Blue Pages of the local telephone directory.

Maps   The best road maps of Arizona are produced by the American Automobile Association (you have to be a member to get these) and by *Arizona Highways,* a local magazine. This latter map is available from tourist information offices in Phoenix and Tucson. You can also pick up state road maps at almost any gas station.

Newspapers/Magazines   Arizona supports dozens of daily and weekly newspapers. Among these are the morning and evening dailies of Phoenix and Tucson, and those two cities' weekly arts and entertainment newspapers. *Arizona Highways* is nationally known for its stunning color photography that shows Arizona at its very best.

Passports   See Chapter 3.

Pets   Many hotels and motels in Arizona accept pets, though there is sometimes a small fee charged to allow the pet to stay in your room. Others don't allow pets at all, especially bed-and-breakfast inns. If you plan to travel with a pet, it's always best to check when making hotel reservations. At Grand Canyon Village, there is a kennel where you can board your pet while you hike down into the canyon.

Police In most places in Arizona, phone **911**. A few small towns have not adopted this emergency phone number, so if 911 doesn't work, dial 0 (zero) for the operator and state the type of emergency.

Radio/TV All the major television networks have affiliates throughout Arizona. There are also many independent television stations in both Phoenix and Tucson. Most hotels get cable or satellite television.

There are plenty of radio stations around the state, but don't be surprised if you find yourself out of range of every single one of them. It's a big state and towns are often farther apart than a small station can broadcast.

Rest Rooms You will find public rest rooms at highway rest areas, gas stations, in shopping centers, department stores, and public buildings such as museums.

Safety When driving long distances, always carry plenty of drinking water, and if you're heading off onto dirt roads, extra water for your car's radiator is also a good idea. When hiking or walking in the desert, keep an eye out for rattlesnakes; these poisonous snakes are not normally aggressive unless provoked, so give them a wide berth and they'll leave you alone. Black widow spiders and scorpions are also desert denizens that can be dangerous, though the better known tarantula is actually much less of a threat. If you go turning over rocks or logs, you're likely to encounter one of Arizona's poisonous residents.

Taxes There is a state sales tax of 5%, a restaurant food tax of 6.7%, a car-rental tax of 8.7%, and a hotel room tax of 8.5%.

Time Arizona is in the mountain time zone. However, the state does not observe daylight saving time, and so time differences between Arizona and the rest of the country vary with the time of year. From the last Sunday in October until the first Sunday in April, Arizona is 1 hour later than the West Coast and 2 hours earlier than the East Coast. The rest of the year Arizona is on the same time as the West Coast and is 3 hours earlier than the East Coast. There is an exception, however—the Navajo reservation observes daylight saving time. However, the Hopi Reservation, which is completely surrounded by the Navajo Reservation, does not.

Tipping The accepted tip in restaurants is 15% if service has been good. Taxi drivers get 15% also. Bellhops are usually tipped $1 or $2 per bag, while airport Skycaps are generally tipped half this amount. Chambermaids are tipped $1 per night.

Tourist Offices See "Information & Money," in this chapter; and also specific cities.

Visas See Chapter 3.

FOR FOREIGN VISITORS

The American West is well known and well loved in many countries. Images of "cowboys and Indians" are familiar from western novels, movies, television shows, and advertisements. And of course, the Grand Canyon is one of the wonders of the world. However, despite Arizona being the Wild West, there will likely be typically American situations that you will encounter in Arizona, and this chapter should help you prepare for your trip.

1. PREPARING FOR YOUR TRIP

INFORMATION

For information on Arizona, contact the **Arizona Office of Tourism,** 1100 West Washington Street, Phoenix, AZ 85007 (tel. 602/542-TOUR; fax 602/542-4068). For information on Phoenix, contact the **Phoenix & Valley of the Sun Convention & Visitors Bureau,** 505 North Second Street, Suite 300, Phoenix, AZ 85004 (tel. 602/254-6500). For information on Tucson, contact the **Metropolitan Tucson Convention & Visitor's Bureau,** 130 South Scott Avenue, Tucson, AZ 85701 (tel. 602/624-1817).

ENTRY REQUIREMENTS

DOCUMENTS Canadian nationals need only proof of Canadian residence to visit the United States. Citizens of Great Britain and Japan need only a current passport. Citizens of other countries, including Australia and New Zealand, usually need two documents: a valid passport with an expiration date at least 6 months later than the scheduled end of their visit to the United States, and a tourist or business visa, available at no charge from a U.S. embassy or consulate in your country.

To obtain a tourist or business visa, present your passport, a passport-size photo of yourself, and a completed application, which is available through the embassy or consulate. You may be asked to provide information about how you plan to finance your trip or show a letter of invitation from a friend with whom you plan to stay. Those applying for a business visa may be asked to show evidence that they will not receive a salary in the United States.

Be sure to check the length of stay on your visa; usually it's 6 months. If you want to stay longer, you may file for an extension with the Immigration and Naturalization

Service once you're in the country. If permission to stay is granted, a new visa is not required unless you leave the United States and want to reenter.

The visitor arriving by air, no matter what the port of entry—Los Angeles, New York, Anchorage, Honolulu, or any other—should expect Immigration control procedures to take as long as 2 hours on some days, especially summer weekends. Add the time it takes to clear Customs and you'll see that you should make very generous allowance for delay in planning connections between international and domestic flights—an average of 2 to 3 hours at least.

In contrast, for the traveler arriving by car or by rail from Canada, the border-crossing formalities have been streamlined to the vanishing point. And for the traveler by air from Canada, you can sometimes go through Customs and Immigration at the point of departure, which is much quicker.

MEDICAL REQUIREMENTS No inoculations are needed to enter the U.S. unless you are coming from, or have stopped in, areas known to be suffering from epidemics, especially of cholera or yellow fever. Applicants for immigrants' visas (and only they) must undergo a screening for AIDS under a law passed in 1987.

If you have a disease or condition requiring treatment with medications containing narcotics or requiring use of a syringe, carry a valid signed prescription from your physician to allay any suspicions that you are smuggling drugs.

CUSTOMS REQUIREMENTS Every adult visitor may bring in, free of duty: 1 liter of wine or hard liquor; 200 cigarettes or 100 cigars (but no cigars from Cuba) or 3 pounds of smoking tobacco; and $400 worth of gifts. These exemptions are offered to travelers who spend at least 72 hours in the U.S. It is altogether forbidden to bring into the country foodstuffs (particularly cheese, fruit, cooked meats, and canned goods) and plants (vegetables, seeds, tropical plants, etc.). Foreign tourists may bring in or take out up to $10,000 in U.S. or foreign currency with no formalities; larger sums must be declared to Customs on entering or leaving.

INSURANCE

Unlike most other countries, there is no national health system in the United States. Because the cost of medical care is extremely high, I strongly advise every traveler to secure health coverage before setting out. In addition, you may want to take out a travel policy (for a relatively low premium) that covers loss or theft of your baggage; trip-cancellation costs; guarantee of bail in case you are involved in a lawsuit; sickness or injury costs (medical, surgical, and hospital); costs of accident, repatriation, or death. Such packages (for example, "Europe Assistance" in Europe) are sold by automobile clubs at attractive rates, as well as by insurance companies and travel agencies.

MONEY

CURRENCY The U.S. monetary system has a decimal base: one American **dollar ($1)** = 100 **cents** (100¢).

Dollar bills commonly come in $1 ("a buck"), $5, $10, $20, $50, and $100 denominations (the last two are not welcome when paying for small purchases and are not accepted in taxis). There are also $2 bills (seldom encountered).

There are six denominations of coins: 1¢ (one cent, or "penny"); 5¢ (five cents, or "nickel"); 10¢ (ten cents, or "dime"); 25¢ (twenty-five cents, or "quarter"); 50¢ (fifty cents, or "half dollar"); and the rare (outside of Las Vegas, Nevada, and Atlantic City, New Jersey) $1 piece (both the older, larger Eisenhower dollars and the newer, small Susan B. Anthony coin).

TRAVELER'S CHECKS Traveler's checks *denominated in U.S. dollars* are readily accepted at most hotels, motels, restaurants, and large stores. Traveler's checks in other than U.S. dollars will almost always have to be changed at a bank or currency-exchange office, with the possible exception of those in Canadian dollars. Because of the proximity of the Canadian border, many hotels, restaurants, and shops will accept Canadian currency.

CREDIT CARDS The method of payment most widely used for hotel and restaurant bills and for major purchases is the credit card: VISA (BarclayCard in Britain), MasterCard (EuroCard in Europe, Access in Britain, Diamond in Japan), American Express, Diners Club, Discover, and Carte Blanche, in descending order of acceptance. You can save yourself trouble by using "plastic money," rather than cash or traveler's checks, in 95% of all hotels, motels, restaurants, and retail stores (except for those selling food or liquor). A credit card can serve as a deposit for renting a car, as proof of identity (often carrying more weight than a passport), or as a "cash card," enabling you to draw money from banks that accept them.

CURRENCY EXCHANGE The foreign-exchange bureaus so common in Europe are rare even at airports in the U.S., and nonexistent outside major cities. Try to avoid having to change foreign money, or traveler's checks denominated other than in U.S. dollars, at a small-town bank, or even a branch in a big city; in fact, leave any currency other than U.S. dollars at home—it may prove more nuisance to you than it's worth.

---

2. GETTING TO & AROUND THE U.S.

Travelers from overseas can take advantage of the APEX (Advance Purchase Excursion) fares offered by all the major U.S. and European carriers. Aside from these, attractive values are offered by Icelandair on flights from Luxembourg to New York and by Virgin Atlantic from London to New York/Newark.

Some large airlines (for example, TWA, American, Northwest, United, and Delta) offer travelers on their transatlantic and transpacific flights special discount tickets under the name **"Visit USA,"** allowing travel between any U.S. destinations at minimum rates. They are not on sale in the U.S., and must therefore be purchased before you leave your foreign point of departure. This system is the best, easiest, and fastest way of seeing the U.S. at low cost. You should obtain information well in advance from your travel agent or the office of the airline concerned, because the conditions attached to these discount tickets can be changed without advance notice.

Travel by train in the U.S. is not nearly as common nor as easy as it is in Europe or many other countries. **Amtrak** is the only passenger rail service in most of the country and connects Phoenix, Tucson, Flagstaff, and a few other Arizona towns with other cities and towns throughout the U.S. Fares on Amtrak can be higher than airfares, so it always pays to compare costs. For reservations and information call toll free 800/872-7245.

The cheapest way of getting around the U.S. is by bus. The only nationwide bus line is **Greyhound/Trailways Lines,** which offers service to major cities and small towns all across the U.S. Greyhound/Trailways Lines does not have a toll-free telephone number, so check a U.S. telephone book or call directory information for the telephone number of a bus station near you when you reach the U.S.

The U.S. is a nation of car drivers and the most cost effective, convenient, and comfortable way to travel through the U.S. is by car. The interstate highway system connects cities and towns all over the country, and in addition to these high-speed, limited-access roadways, there is an extensive network of federal, state, and local highways and roads. Another convenience of traveling by car is the easy access to inexpensive motels at interstate-highway off-ramps. Such motels are almost always less expensive than hotels and motels in downtown areas. Though driver's license requirements vary from state to state, if you are 18 and hold a valid international driver's license and a valid driver's license from your home country, you should have sufficient proof of ability to operate an automobile. Keep in mind, however, that a separate motorcycle-driver's license is required in most states.

For further information about travel to and around Arizona, see "Getting There" and "Getting Around" in Chapter 2.

FAST FACTS FOR THE FOREIGN TRAVELER

Accommodations It's always a good idea to make hotel reservations as soon as you know the dates of your travel. To make a reservation, you will need to leave a deposit of 1 night's payment. Phoenix, Scottsdale, and Tucson are particularly busy during the winter months and hotels book up in advance. The Grand Canyon is busy all year. If you want to stay at one of the lodges in Grand Canyon National Park, you should make a reservation at least a year in advance. Also, because distances in Arizona are so great (it might be 60 miles or more to the next town) it's crucial to have a room reservation before heading off to remote, yet very popular sections of the state such as the Four Corners region. If you don't have a room reservation, it's best to look for a room in the midafternoon. If you wait until later in the evening you run the risk of hotels being full. In the U.S., major downtown hotels, which cater primarily to business travelers, commonly offer weekend discounts of as much as 50% to entice vacationers to fill up the empty hotel rooms. However, resorts and hotels near tourist attractions tend to have higher rates on weekends.

Hotel room rates in most of Arizona tend to go up in the winter months when there is a greater demand. If you wish to save money and don't mind hot weather, you should consider visiting sometime other than winter. The really unbearable temperatures usually don't hit until mid-May and are over by the end of September.

Auto Organizations If you're planning to drive a car while in the U.S. and you're a member of an automobile organization in your home country, check before leaving home to see if they have a reciprocal agreement with one of the large U.S. automobile associations such as the AAA. However, if you will only be driving a rented car, the rental company should provide free breakdown service.

Business Hours Most **banks** are open Monday through Friday from 9am to 3pm, sometimes with later hours on Friday. Many banks are now also open on Saturday. There is 24-hour access to banks through automatic teller machines. **Bars** in Arizona generally stay open until 1am. Most **offices** are open Monday through Friday from 9am to 5pm, and most **post offices** from 8am to 5pm. Larger **stores,** and many smaller ones as well, are open daily from 9am to 5pm; on Thursday and Friday department stores usually stay open until 9pm.

Climate See Chapter 2.

Currency & Exchange See above.

Customs & Immigration See above.

Drinking Laws The legal drinking age in Arizona is 21. The penalties for driving under the influence of alcohol are stiff.

Electricity In the U.S. it's 110–120 volts, 60 cycles, compared to 220–240 volts, 50 cycles, in most of Europe. Besides a 110-volt transformer, small appliances of non-American manufacture, such as hairdryers or shavers, will require a plug adapter with two flat, parallel pins.

Embassies & Consulates All embassies are located in the national capital, Washington, D.C.; some consulates are located in major cities, and most nations have a mission to the United Nations in New York City.

Listed here are the embassies and consulates of the major English-speaking countries—Australia, Canada, Ireland, New Zealand, and the United Kingdom. If you're from another country, you can get the telephone number of your embassy by calling "information" in Washington, D.C. (tel. 202/555-1212).

The **Embassy** of **Australia** is at 1601 Massachusetts Avenue NW, Washington, DC 20036 (tel. 202/797-3000). There is no consulate in Arizona; the nearest is at 611 North Larchmont Boulevard, Los Angeles, CA 90004 (tel. 213/469-4300).

The **Embassy** of **Canada** is at 501 Pennsylvania Avenue NW, Washington, DC

20001 (tel. 202/682-1740). There is no consulate in Arizona; the nearest is at 300 South Grand Avenue, 10th Floor, Los Angeles, CA 90071 (tel. 213/687-7432).

The **Embassy** of the Republic of **Ireland** is at 2234 Massachusetts Avenue NW, Washington, DC 20008 (tel. 202/462-3939). There is no consulate in Arizona; the nearest is at 655 Montgomery Street, Suite 930, San Francisco, CA 94111 (tel. 415/392-4214).

The **Embassy** of **New Zealand** is at 37 Observatory Circle NW, Washington, DC 20008 (tel. 202/328-4800). The only consulate is in Los Angeles, in the Tishman Building, 10960 Wilshire Boulevard, Suite 1530, Westwood, CA 90024 (tel. 213/477-8241).

The **Embassy** of the **United Kingdom** is at 3100 Massachusetts Avenue NW, Washington, DC 20008 (tel. 202/462-1340). There is no consulate in Arizona; the nearest is at 3701 Wilshire Boulevard, Suite 312, Los Angeles, CA 90010 (tel. 213/385-7381).

Emergencies   Call **911** for fire, police, or an ambulance. If you encounter such travelers' problems as sickness, accident, or lost or stolen baggage, it will pay you to call **Travelers Aid,** an organization that specializes in helping distressed travelers, whether American or foreign. Check the local telephone book for the nearest office, or dial 0 (zero) and ask the telephone operator.

Gasoline [Petrol]   Most cars in the U.S. now use unleaded gasoline (gas) only, and leaded gasoline is not available in most parts of the country, except Washington and Oregon.

Holidays   On the following legal national holidays, banks, government offices, post offices, and many stores, restaurants, and museums are closed: January 1 (New Year's Day), third Monday in January (Martin Luther King, Jr. Day), third Monday in February (President's Day, Washington's Birthday), last Monday in May (Memorial Day), July 4 (Independence Day), first Monday in September (Labor Day), second Monday in October (Columbus Day), November 11 (Veterans' Day/Armistice Day), last Thursday in November (Thanksgiving Day), and December 25 (Christmas Day). The Tuesday following the first Monday in November is Election Day, and is a legal holiday in presidential-election years. However, Arizona does not observe Martin Luther King, Jr. Day, but does observe Lincoln's Birthday (February 12).

Information   See above.

Legal Aid   The foreign tourist, unless positively identified as a member of the Mafia or of a drug ring, will probably never become involved with the American legal system. If you are pulled up for a minor infraction (for example, of the highway code, such as speeding), never attempt to pay the fine directly to the police officer; you may wind up arrested on the much more serious charge of attempted bribery. Pay fines by mail, or directly into the hands of the clerk of the court. If accused of a more serious offense, it is wise to say and do nothing before consulting a lawyer. Under U.S. law, an arrested person is allowed one telephone call to a party of his choice. Call your embassy or consulate.

Liquor Laws   See "Drinking Laws," above.

Mail   The post office will hold your mail for up to 1 month. If you aren't sure of your address, your mail can be sent to you, in your name, **"c/o General Delivery"** at the main post office of the city or region where you expect to be. The addressee must pick it up in person, and produce proof of identity (driver's license, credit card, passport, etc.).

Mailboxes are blue with a red-and-white logo, and carry the inscription "U.S. MAIL." The international postage rates at the time of publication are 40¢ for a half-ounce letter and 30¢ for a postcard mailed to Canada. For all other countries, the cost is 50¢ for a half-ounce letter and 40¢ for a postcard.

Medical Emergencies   Dial **911** for an ambulance.

Post   See "Mail," above.

Post Office   In Phoenix the main post office is at 4949 East Van Buren Street (tel. 225-3434). In Tucson, the main post office is at 141 South Sixth Avenue (tel. 622-8454).

Radio & Television   Audiovisual media, with three coast-to-coast networks—ABC, CBS, and NBC—joined in recent years by the Public Broadcasting

System (PBS), the Fox network, and a growing network of cable channels, play a major part in American life. In addition there are the pay-TV channels showing recent movies or sports events. Throughout Arizona there are dozens of radio stations, each broadcasting a particular type of music—classical, country, jazz, Top-40, oldies—punctuated by news broadcasts and frequent commercials. You will usually find the affiliates of the National Public Radio system at the bottom of the radio dial. These stations broadcast in-depth news programs, classical and jazz music, as well as talk shows and other eclectic programming.

Safety Whenever you're traveling in an unfamiliar city or country, stay alert. Be aware of your immediate surroundings. Wear a moneybelt and don't flash expensive jewelry and cameras in public. This will minimize the possibility of your becoming a crime victim. Be alert even in heavily touristed areas.

Taxes In the U.S. there is no VAT (Value-Added Tax), or other indirect tax at a national level. Every state, and each city in it, is allowed to levy its own local tax on all purchases, including hotel and restaurant checks and airline tickets. In Arizona, the state **sales tax** is 5% but communities can add local sales tax on top of this. For additional taxes, see "Fast Facts: Arizona" in Chapter 2.

Telephone, Telex & Fax Pay phones can be found on street corners, in bars, restaurants, hotels, public buildings, stores, and service stations. **Local calls** cost 25¢. Almost all shops that make photocopies offer fax service as well.

For **long-distance or international calls,** stock up on a supply of quarters; the pay phones will instruct you when, and in what quantity, you should put them into the slot. For direct overseas calls, first dial 011, followed by the country code (Australia, 61; Republic of Ireland, 353; New Zealand, 64; United Kingdom, 44; and so on), and then by the city code (for example, 71 or 81 for London, 21 for Birmingham) and the number of the person you wish to call. For long-distance calls in Canada and the U.S., dial 1 followed by the area code and number you want.

Before calling from a hotel room, always ask the hotel phone operator if there are any telephone surcharges. These are best avoided by using a public phone, calling collect, or using a telephone charge card.

For **reverse-charge, or collect calls,** and for **person-to-person calls,** dial 0 (zero, not the letter "O") followed by the area code and number you want; an operator will then come on the line and you should specify that you are calling collect, or person-to-person, or both. If your operator-assisted call is international, ask for the overseas operator.

For local **directory assistance** ("information"), dial 555-1212; for long-distance information, dial 1, then the appropriate area code and 555-1212.

Like the telephone system, **telegraph** and **telex** services are provided by private corporations like ITT, MCI, and above all, Western Union. You can bring your telegram in to the nearest Western Union office (there are hundreds across the country), or dictate it over the phone (a toll-free call: 800/325-6000). You can also telegraph money, or have it telegraphed to you, very quickly over the Western Union system.

Time The U.S. is divided into six time zones. From east to west these are eastern standard time (EST), central standard time (CST), mountain standard time (MST), Pacific standard time (PST), Alaska standard time (AST), and Hawaii standard time (HST). Always keep changing time zones in your mind if you are traveling (or even telephoning) long distances in the U.S. For example, noon in Phoenix (MST) is 1pm in Chicago (CST), 2pm in New York City (EST), 11am in Los Angeles (PST), 10am in Anchorage (AST), and 9am in Honolulu (HST).

Arizona is in the mountain time zone, but it does not observe **daylight saving time (summer time).** Consequently, from the first Sunday in April until the last Sunday in October, there is no time difference between Arizona and Los Angeles and elsewhere on the West Coast. However, there is a 2-hour difference to Chicago, and 3 hours to New York.

Tipping See "Fast Facts: Arizona" in Chapter 2.

Toilets Often euphemistically referred to as rest rooms, public toilets can be found in bars, restaurants, hotel lobbies, museums, department stores, and service stations—and will probably be clean (although the last-mentioned sometimes leave much to be desired). Note, however, that some restaurants and bars display a notice that toilets are for the use of patrons only. You can ignore this sign or, better yet, avoid arguments by paying for a cup of coffee or soft drink, which will qualify you as a patron. The cleanliness of toilets at railroad stations and bus depots may be questionable; some public places are equipped with pay toilets which require you to insert one or two 10¢ coins (dimes) into a slot on the door before it will open.

Yellow Pages   The local phone company provides two kinds of telephone directory. The general directory called the "White Pages," lists subscribers (business and personal residences) in alphabetical order. The inside front cover lists emergency numbers for police, fire, and ambulance, and othe vital numbers (such as the Coast Guard, poison control center, and crime-victims hotline). The first few pages are devoted to community-service numbers, including a guide to long-distance and international calling, complete with country codes and area codes.

The second directory, the *Yellow Pages,* lists all local services, businesses, and industries by type, with an index at the back. The listings cover not only such obvious items as automobile repairs by make of car, or drugstores (pharmacies), often by geographical location, but also restaurants by type of cuisine and geographical location, bookstores by special subject, places of worship by religious denomination, and other information that the tourist might otherwise not readily find. The *Yellow Pages* also include city plans or detailed area maps, often showing postal ZIP Codes and public transportation.

THE AMERICAN SYSTEM OF MEASUREMENTS

LENGTH

1 inch (in.)	=	2.54cm				
1 foot (ft.)	=	12 in.	=	30.48cm	=	.305m
1 yard	=	3 ft.	=	.915m		
1 mile (mi.)	=	5,280 ft.	=	1.609km		

To convert miles to kilometers, multiply the number of miles by 1.61 (for example, 50 miles × 1.61 = 80.5 km). Note that this conversion can be used to convert speeds from miles per hour (m.p.h.) to kilometers per hour (km/h).

To convert kilometers to miles, multiply the number of kilometers by .62 (example, 25km × .62 = 15.5 mi.). Note that this same conversion can be used to convert speeds from kilometers per hour to miles per hour.

CAPACITY

1 fluid ounce (fl. oz.)	=	.03 liter				
1 pint	=	16 fl. oz.	=	.47 liter		
1 quart	=	2 pints	=	.94 liter		
1 gallon (gal.)	=	4 quarts	=	3.79 liter	=	.83 imperial gal.

To convert U.S. gallons to liters, multiply the number of gallons by 3.79 (example, 12 gal. × 3.79 = 45.48 liters).

To convert U.S. gallons to imperial gallons, multiply the number of U.S. gallons by .83 (example, 12 U.S. gal. × .83 = 9.95 imperial gal.).

To convert liters to U.S. gallons, multiply the number of liters by .26 (example, 50 liters × .26 = 13 U.S. gal.).

To convert imperial gallons to U.S. gallons, multiply the number of imperial gallons by 1.2 (example, 8 imperial gal. × 1.2 = 9.6 U.S. gal.).

WEIGHT

1 ounce (oz.)	=	28.35 grams		
1 pound (lb.)	=	16 oz.	= 453.6 grams	= .45 kilograms
1 ton	=	2,000 lb.	= 907 kilograms	= .91 metric ton

To convert pounds to kilograms, multiply the number of pounds by .45 (example, 90 lb × .45 = 40.5kg).
To convert kilograms to pounds, multiply the number of kilos by 2.2 (example, 75kg × 2.2 = 165 lb.).

AREA

1 acre	=	.41 hectare		
1 square mile (sq. mi.)	=	640 acres	= 2.59 hectares	= 2.6km

To convert acres to hectares, multiply the number of acres by .41 (example, 40 acres × .41 = 16.4ha).
To convert square miles to square kilometers, multiply the number of square miles by 2.6 (example, 80 sq. mi. × 2.6 = 208km).
To convert hectares to acres, multiply the number of hectares by 2.47 (example, 20ha × 2.47 = 49.4 acres).
To convert square kilometers to square miles, multiply the number of square kilometers by .39 (example, 150km × .39 = 58.5 sq. mi.).

TEMPERATURE

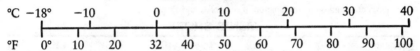

To convert degrees Fahrenheit to degrees Celsius, subtract 32 from °F, multiply by 5, and then divide by 9 (for example, 85°F − 32 × 5/9 = 29.4°C).
To convert degrees Celsius to degrees Fahrenheit, multiply °C by 9, divide by 5, and add 32 (example, 20°C × 9/5 + 32 = 68°F).

CLOTHING SIZES

WOMEN'S DRESSES, COATS, AND SKIRTS

American	3	5	7	9	11	12	13	14	15	16	18
Continental	36	38	38	40	40	42	42	44	44	46	48
British	8	10	11	12	13	14	15	16	17	18	20

WOMEN'S BLOUSES AND SWEATERS

American	10	12	14	16	18	20
Continental	38	40	42	44	46	48
British	32	34	36	38	40	42

WOMEN'S STOCKINGS

American	8	8½	9	9½	10	10½
Continental	1	2	3	4	5	6
British	8	8½	9	9½	10	10½

WOMEN'S SHOES

American	5	6	7	8	9	10
Continental	36	37	38	39	40	41
British	3½	4½	5½	6½	7½	8½

CHILDREN'S CLOTHING

American	3	4	5	6	6X
Continental	98	104	110	116	122
British	18	20	22	24	26

CHILDREN'S SHOES

American	8	9	10	11	12	13	1	2	3
Continental	24	25	27	28	29	30	32	33	34
British	7	8	9	10	11	12	13	1	2

MEN'S SUITS

American	34	36	38	40	42	44	46	48
Continental	44	46	48	50	52	54	56	58
British	34	36	38	40	42	44	46	48

MEN'S SHIRTS

American	14½	15	15½	16	16½	17	17½	18
Continental	37	38	39	41	42	43	44	45
British	14½	15	15½	16	16½	17	17½	18

Note: Shirts are sized on a combination of the collar and sleeve length.

MEN'S SHOES

American	7	8	9	10	11	12	13
Continental	39½	41	42	43	44½	46	47
British	6	7	8	9	10	11	12

Note: Foot width should also be taken into account.

MEN'S HATS

American	6⅞	7⅛	7¼	7⅜	7½	7⅝
Continental	55	56	58	59	60	61
British	6¼	6⅞	7⅛	7¼	7⅜	7½

CHAPTER 4

PHOENIX

Like the phoenix of ancient mythology, Arizona's capital city of Phoenix has risen from its own ashes, in this case the ruins of an ancient Native American village. The name Phoenix, given to the city by an early settler from Britain, has proven to be very appropriate. Rising from the dust of the desert, Phoenix has become one of the largest metropolitan areas in the country.

Why the phenomenal growth in Phoenix? In large part it's due to the climate. More than 300 days of sunshine a year is a powerful attraction. Sure, summers are hot, but the mountains, and cooler air, are only 2 hours away. However, it's in the winter that Phoenix truly shines. When most of the country is frozen solid, Phoenix is basking in warm sunshine. This great winter climate has helped make Phoenix and Scottsdale the resort capitals of the world.

After 50 years of entertaining visitors, Phoenix knows how to show its guests a good time. Golf, tennis, and lounging by the pool are only the tip of the iceberg (so to speak). With the cooler weather comes the cultural season, and between Phoenix and the neighboring city of Scottsdale, there's an astounding array of music, dance, and theater to be enjoyed. Scottsdale is also well known as a center of the visual arts, with dozens of art galleries concentrated in the old town shopping area. You'll also find many excellent, and expensive, restaurants in Phoenix and Scottsdale.

Phoenix has enjoyed the benefits and suffered the problems of rapid urban growth. It has gone from tiny agricultural village to sprawling cosmopolitan metropolis in little more than a century. Along the way it has lost its past amid urban sprawl and unchecked development while at the same time it has forged a city that is quintessentially 20th-century American. Shopping malls, the gathering places of America, are raised to an art form in Phoenix. Luxurious resorts create fantasy worlds of waterfalls and swimming pools. Wide boulevards stretch for miles across land that was once desert but has been made green through irrigation. Perhaps it is this willingness to create a new world on top of an old that attracts people to Phoenix. Then again, maybe it's all that sunshine.

1. ORIENTATION

Phoenix, the capital of Arizona, is centrally located in the middle of the state and makes an ideal starting point for exploring the rest of the state. As the eighth-largest city in the U.S., Phoenix is a sprawling metropolis. Together with Scottsdale and the 20 or so other smaller cities, the area of Phoenix and its environs is now referred to as the Valley of the Sun. Phoenix has lagged far behind other cities in building Interstate highways and beltways to facilitate travel around the city. Consequently, there is no freeway to Scottsdale, the valley's most prestigious city and home to dozens of major resorts. This lack of freeways tends to make getting from one side of town to the other a very time-consuming affair. Add to that the fact that most tourist maps show only major avenues at 1-mile intervals, and you'll find yourself spending far longer than you thought to cover that small distance on the map. Leave yourself plenty of time, or better yet, call your destination beforehand and ask how long it should take.

ARRIVING

BY PLANE Centrally located only 3 miles from downtown Phoenix, **Sky Harbor Airport** has recently undergone major renovation and expansion. Let's hope by the time you arrive all the construction will have been completed. Currently there are three terminals—2, 3, and 4—in use at Sky Harbor. Within these three terminals, you'll find car-rental desks, information desks, hotel reservation centers with direct lines to various valley hotels, and a food court. There is a free 24-hour shuttle bus operating every 6 minutes between the three terminals. For general airport information, call 273-3300; for airport paging, call 273-3455; for airport parking, call 273-0955; for lost and found, call 273-3307.

Getting to and from the Airport There are two entrances to the airport. The west entrance can be accessed from either the Squaw Peak Parkway (Ariz. 51) or 24th Street, and the east entrance can be accessed from the Hohokam Expressway, which is an extension of 44th Street. If you're headed downtown, leave by way of the 24th Street exit and turn right (north) as you leave the airport. If you're headed to Scottsdale, Tempe, or Mesa, take the 44th Street exit. Scottsdale is north, so turn left as you exit the airport. Tempe and Mesa are southeast and are reached by turning right as you leave the airport and getting onto I-10 headed east.

The **SuperShuttle** (tel. 602/253-6300, or toll free 800/331-3565) and **Courier Transportation** (tel. 602/232-2222) offer 24-hour door-to-door van service between Sky Harbor Airport and resorts, hotels, and homes throughout the valley. When heading back to the airport for a departure, call 602/244-9000.

Taxis can also be found waiting outside all three airport terminals, or you can call **Yellow Cab** (tel. 602/275-8501).

The **City of Phoenix Transit System** provides public bus service throughout the valley with bus lines 2 and 13 operating between the airport and downtown Phoenix, Tempe, and Mesa. The tourist information desks at the airport have copies of *The Bus Book,* a guide to using the local bus system that includes detailed information on all routes. Note that bus no. 2 operates Monday through Friday between 5am and 9pm only, with no service on weekends. Bus no. 13 operates similar hours, with Saturday service as well.

BY TRAIN The **Amtrak** (tel. toll free 800/872-7245) train *Texas Eagle* connects Phoenix with Los Angeles in the west and Dallas, St. Louis, and Chicago in the east. The *Sunset Limited* connects New Orleans, Houston, San Antonio, El Paso, and Los Angeles with Phoenix.

The Phoenix Amtrak terminal is at 401 West Harrison Street (tel. 602/253-0121).

BY BUS **Greyhound/Trailways** connects Phoenix to the rest of the U.S. with its

WHAT'S SPECIAL ABOUT PHOENIX

Buildings

☐ Arcosanti, Paolo Soleri's fascinating city of the future in the desert north of Phoenix.

☐ Cosanti Foundation, a smaller-scale complex by Soleri in Paradise Valley.

☐ Taliesin West, Frank Lloyd Wright's school of architecture and former winter residence.

Museums

☐ The Heard Museum, one of the country's finest collections of Native American artifacts, arts, and crafts.

☐ Pueblo Grande Museum and Cultural Park, excavated Hohokam ruins dating as far back as A.D. 1.

Parks/Gardens

☐ Desert Botanical Garden, devoted to the plants of the desert with a special section on historical uses of Sonoran Desert plants.

☐ Phoenix South Mountain Park, a desert wilderness said to be the largest city park in the country.

Events/Festivals

☐ Phoenix Formula One Grand Prix through the streets of downtown Phoenix.

☐ Fiesta Bowl, New Year's Day's college football classic.

For the Kids

☐ Waterworld USA, a water amusement park in a town with no beaches.

Natural Spectacles

☐ Camelback Mountain, said to look like a camel lying down.

☐ Mummy Mountain, from the north vaguely resembles the sarcophagus of an Egyptian mummy.

☐ Papago Buttes, a park northeast of downtown Phoenix with a natural window through the sandstone rock of the buttes.

Shopping

☐ Old Scottsdale and the Fifth Avenue Shops, an area of old western-style buildings filled with boutiques, Native American arts and crafts stores, and art galleries; considered the Rodeo Drive of Phoenix.

☐ The Borgata, also in Scottsdale, a shopping mall built to resemble a medieval European village that's filled with expensive boutiques.

Great Neighborhoods

☐ Mill Avenue in Tempe, a hangout for Arizona State University students and site of unusual little shops, numerous bars, and frequent live-music performances.

Offbeat Oddities

☐ Mystery Castle, a bizarre and sprawling home in south Phoenix built by one man for his daughter.

☐ The world's tallest water fountain, in the town of Fountain Hills, 30 miles northeast of Phoenix.

---

extensive bus system. Their terminal is at 525 East Washington Street (tel. 602/248-4040).

BY CAR Phoenix is connected to Los Angeles and Tucson by I-10 and to Flagstaff via I-17. If you are headed to Scottsdale, the easiest route is to take the Hohokam Expressway north; after it becomes 44th Street it will curve to the right and become McDonald Drive, which leads straight to Scottsdale Road and resort row. The Superstition Freeway (Ariz. 360) leads to Tempe, Mesa, and Chandler.

TOURIST INFORMATION

You'll find a tourist information desk in the baggage claim area of all three terminals at Sky Harbor Airport. The **Phoenix & Valley of the Sun Convention & Visitors Bureau,** 505 North Second Street, Phoenix, AZ 85004-3998 (tel. 602/254-6500), operates its main visitors bureau at the northwest corner of Adams Street and Second Street in the same block as the Hyatt Regency and directly across the street from Civic Plaza.

The **Information Hotline** (tel. 602/252-5588) has recorded information about Phoenix.

CITY LAYOUT

MAIN ARTERIES & STREETS Phoenix and the surrounding cities of Mesa, Tempe, Scottsdale, Chandler, and even those cities farther out in the valley are laid out in a grid pattern with major avenues and roads about every mile. I-17, called the **Black Canyon Freeway,** comes in from the north. Just south of downtown, I-17 curves to the east and merges with I-10, which heads east and south from downtown Phoenix connecting the city with Los Angeles and Tucson. In the west, I-10 is called the **Papago Freeway** and in the south it's called the **Maricopa Freeway.** At the west end of the Sky Harbor Airport, Ariz. 51, called the **Squaw Peak Parkway,** heads north to Squaw Peak. On the east side of the airport, Ariz. 143, called the **Hohokam Expressway,** heads north to become 44th Street. Just south of a section of I-10 called the **Broadway Curve,** Ariz. 360, called the **Superstition Freeway,** heads east to Tempe, Chandler, Mesa, and Gilbert.

Secondary highways in the valley include the **Beeline Highway** (Ariz. 87), which starts out as Country Club Drive in Mesa and leads to Payson, and **Grand Avenue** (U.S. 60 and U.S. 89), which starts downtown and leads to Sun City and Wickenburg.

For traveling east to west across Phoenix, your best choice is **Camelback Road.** For traveling north and south, 44th Street, 24th Street, and **Central Avenue** are good choices.

FINDING AN ADDRESS **Central Avenue,** which runs north to south through downtown Phoenix, is the starting point for all east and west street numbering. **Washington Street** is the starting point for north and south numbering. North and south numbered streets are to be found on the east side of the city, while north and south numbered avenues will be found on the west. For the most part, street numbers change by 100 with each block. Odd-numbered addresses are on the south and east sides of streets, while even-numbered addresses are on north and west sides of streets.

For example, if you're looking for 4454 East Camelback Road, you'll find it 44 blocks east of Central Avenue between 44th Street and 45th Street on the north side of the street. If you're looking for 2905 North 35th Avenue, you'll find it 35 blocks west of Central Avenue and 29 blocks north of Washington Street on the east side of the street.

STREET MAPS The street maps handed out by rental-car companies are almost useless for finding anything in Phoenix. However, the Phoenix Chamber of Commerce publishes a compact but detailed map that's very useful. You can get one of these maps from the tourist information desks at the airport or downtown, or by contacting the Phoenix Chamber of Commerce directly at 34 West Monroe Street, Phoenix, AZ 85003 (tel. 602/254-5521).

NEIGHBORHOODS IN BRIEF

Because of urban sprawl, Phoenix has yielded its importance to the Valley of the Sun, an area encompassing Phoenix and its metropolitan area of more than 20 cities. Consequently, neighborhoods, per se, have lost significance as outlying cities take on regional importance.

Downtown Phoenix Roughly bordered by Thomas Road on the north, Buckeye Road on the south, 19th Avenue on the east, and Seventh Street on the west, downtown Phoenix is primarily a business, financial, and government district, with both the city hall and state capitol buildings. However, there are also a number of tourist attractions including several art museums, Heritage Square, the Civic Plaza, and Symphony Hall.

Biltmore District   The Biltmore District centers along Camelback Road between 24th Street and 44th Street and is Phoenix's upscale shopping, residential, and business district. The area is characterized by modern office buildings and is anchored by the Biltmore Hotel and Biltmore Fashion Park shopping mall.

Scottsdale   A separate city of more than 130,000 people, Scottsdale extends from Tempe in the south to Carefree in the north, a distance of more than 20 miles, much of which is still desert. "Resort Row" is the name given to Scottsdale Road between Indian School Road and Shea Boulevard. Along this section of road are more than a dozen major resorts. Old Scottsdale capitalizes on its cowboy heritage and has become the valley's main shopping district, with boutiques, jewelers, Native American crafts stores, and numerous restaurants.

Old Town Tempe   Tempe is the home of Arizona State University and has all the trappings of a university town. The presence of so many young people keeps a very active nightlife going year round. The center of activity, both day and night, is Mill Avenue, which has dozens of unusual shops along a stretch of about four blocks. Tempe is in the process of building a historic park a block west of Mill Avenue.

Paradise Valley   If Scottsdale is Phoenix's Beverly Hills, then Paradise Valley is its Bel-Air. The most exclusive neighborhood in the valley is almost exclusively residential, but you won't see too many of the more expensive homes because they're set on large tracts of land.

2. GETTING AROUND

BY PUBLIC TRANSPORTATION

Unfortunately the **Phoenix public bus system** is not very useful to tourists. It's primarily meant for use by commuters and stops running before 9pm at night. There is no bus service on Sunday, and in Tempe and Mesa, none on Saturday either. However, if you decide that you want to take the bus, you should pick up a copy of *The Bus Book,* either at one of the tourist information desks in the airport or downtown or at the Downtown Bus Terminal at Washington Street and First Street. There are both local and express buses. Local bus fare is 85¢ and express bus fare is $1.15. Monthly passes are also available.

Of more value to visitors is the **Downtown Area Shuttle (DASH),** which provides free bus service within the downtown area. These purple buses with orange racing stripes operate Monday through Friday between 6:30am and 6pm. The buses stop at regular bus stops and run every 5 to 10 minutes. Attractions along the bus's route include the state capitol, the tourist information center, the Arizona Museum of Science and Technology, Heritage Square, and the Arizona Center shopping mall.

BY TAXI

Because distances in Phoenix are so large, the price of an average taxi ride can be quite high. However, if you haven't got your own wheels and the bus isn't running because it's late at night or the weekend, you don't have any choice but to call a cab. **Yellow Cab** (tel. 275-8501) provides service throughout the valley. Fares start at $2.05 for the first mile and then increase by $1 for each additional mile.

IMPRESSIONS

As the mythical phoenix rose reborn from its ashes, so shall a great civilization rise here on the ashes of a past civilization. I name thee Phoenix.
—"LORD" BRYAN PHILIP DARREL DUPPA, THE BRITISH SETTLER WHO NAMED PHOENIX

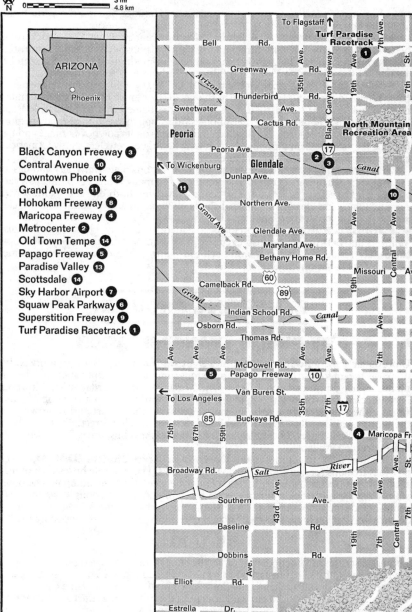

Black Canyon Freeway **3**
Central Avenue **10**
Downtown Phoenix **12**
Grand Avenue **11**
Hohokam Freeway **8**
Maricopa Freeway **4**
Metrocenter **2**
Old Town Tempe **14**
Papago Freeway **5**
Paradise Valley **13**
Scottsdale **14**
Sky Harbor Airport **7**
Squaw Peak Parkway **6**
Superstition Freeway **9**
Turf Paradise Racetrack **1**

PHOENIX ORIENTATION

Cave Creek Rd.

Bell Rd.

Frank Lloyd Wright Blvd.

Greenway Rd.

Thunderbird Rd.

Paradise Valley Mall

32nd St.

Sweetwater Ave.

Cactus

Shea Blvd.

56th St.

Invergordon

Scottsdale

Hayden Rd.

Pima Rd.

96th St.

104th St.

Shea Blvd.

Dreamy Draw Recreation Area

Tatum

Doubletree Ranch Rd.

Paradise Valley

13

Squaw Peak Recreation Area

Lincoln Dr.

Indian Bend Rd.

McDonald Dr.

64th St.

Pima Rd.

Campbell Ave.

To Payson

87

Camelback Rd.

6

Osborn Rd.

56th St.

Indian School Rd.

14

Beeline Hwy.

51

40th St.

44th St.

Thomas Rd.

Scottsdale

48th St.

52nd St.

Papago Park

68th St.

Scottsdale

Miller

Hayden

McDowell Rd.

Dobson Rd.

Sky Harbor International Airport

Van Buren St.

Salt River

McKellips Rd.

Mesa

7

7

10

143

Hohokam Expy.

Dr.

14

Tempe

Mill Ave.

Apache Blvd.

University

60

89

Club Dr.

Country Club Rd.

Dr.

Mesa Dr.

Main St.

Stapley Dr.

Broadway

8

Priest

24th St.

32nd St.

Southern Ave.

360

9

Superstition Freeway

Baseline Rd.

Guadalupe Rd.

Elliot Rd.

10

Rural Rd.

Dr.

McClintock

Price Rd.

Dobson Rd.

School Rd.

Alma

Arizona Ave.

87

McQueen Rd.

Cooper Rd.

Gilbert Rd.

Warner Rd.

Ray Rd.

Chandler Blvd.

↓ To Tucson

Williams Field Rd.

Pecos Rd.

Airport ✈

BY CAR

RENTALS   All the major rental-car companies have offices in Phoenix, with desks inside the airline terminals at Sky Harbor Airport; because this is a major tourist destination, there are often excellent rates because of all the competition. Start calling as far in advance of your visit as possible. The best rates are those made at least a week in advance, but car-rental companies change what they charge for their cars as the demand goes up and down. I recently paid $119 per week for a Geo Metro through Budget Rent-a-Car. To save money on your rental, check to see if your credit-card company picks up the tab for the collision-damage waiver; if not, you'll have to pay an extra $10 or so for this insurance coverage. The state tax on car rentals is high, so if you want to know what your total rental cost will be before making a reservation, be sure to ask about the tax and the collision-damage waiver. Frequent flyers may get bonus miles for renting a car from a particular company—check with your airline plan to find out. If you happen to be making a last-minute reservation, ask if there are any weekend or other specials in effect.

All the major rental-car companies have offices in Phoenix. Among them are the following: **Alamo,** 2246 East Washington Street (tel. 602/244-0897); **Avis,** Sky Harbor Airport (tel. 602/273-3222); **Hertz,** Sky Harbor Airport (tel. 602/267-8822), which has nine other locations around the area; **Budget,** Sky Harbor Airport (tel. 602/267-4000) and five other locations; **Dollar,** Sky Harbor Airport (tel. 602/275-7588); and **Thrifty,** 4114 East Washington Street (tel. 602/244-0311). For toll-free numbers of the major rental-car companies, see the "Getting Around" section of Chapter 2.

PARKING   Phoenix is a new city and, like Los Angeles, has grown up around the automobile. Outside downtown Phoenix, there is almost always plenty of free parking around wherever you go.

DRIVING RULES   A right turn is permitted on red unless otherwise posted. See also "Driving Rules" in Chapter 2.

ON FOOT

Unless you happen to be in downtown Phoenix on business or out in Scottsdale shopping, there really isn't anywhere in the valley that's suitable for exploring on foot. Distances are large and the heat and bright sun make walking a chore rather than a pleasure.

FAST FACTS   PHOENIX

American Express   There are American Express offices at 2508 East Camelback Road (tel. 468-1199) and 6900 East Camelback Road (tel. 949-7000).

Area Code   The telephone area code is 602.

Baby-sitters   First check with your hotel, and if they can't recommend or provide a baby-sitter, contact **Golden Grandmas** (tel. 371-8486) or the **Granny Company** (tel. 264-5454).

Business Hours   See "Fast Facts: Arizona" in Chapter 2.

Car Rentals   See "Getting Around," in this chapter.

Climate   See "When to Go" in Chapter 2.

Currency   See "Preparing for Your Trip," in Chapter 3.

Currency Exchange   You can exchange money at the following banks, or by calling the phone numbers listed and asking for the nearest bank branch that can change your money for you: **Citibank,** 3300 North Central Avenue (tel. 263-7226); **First Interstate Bank,** 100 West Washington Street (tel. 528-6000); **Security Pacific Bank,** 101 North First Avenue (tel. 262-2891); or **Valley National Bank,** 241 North Central Avenue (tel. 261-1387).

Drugstores   Check the *Yellow Pages* of the local telephone directory for the location of a drugstore near you. **Specialty Pharmacy,** 7300 East Fourth Street, Scottsdale (tel. 481-4444), is open 24 hours a day.

Embassies/Consulates None of the English-speaking nations maintains a consulate in Phoenix. The nearest are in Los Angeles. See "Fast Facts" in Chapter 3 for addresses and phone numbers.

Emergencies For police, fire, or medical emergency, phone **911.**

Eyeglasses The **Nationwide Vision Center** has 10 locations around the valley, including 933 East University Drive, Tempe (tel. 966-4991), 5130 North 19th Avenue (tel. 242-5292), and 4615 East Thomas Road (tel. 952-8284).

Hairdressers/Barbers Check with your hotel to see if they have a salon on the premises or can recommend one nearby. Otherwise, **Cutters Hair,** 352 East Camelback Road (tel. 263-1138), and **Mane Attraction,** 3156 East Camelback Road (tel. 956-2996), are both reliable.

Holidays See "When to Go," in Chapter 2.

Hospitals The **Good Samaritan Regional Medical Center,** 1111 East McDowell Road (tel. 239-2000), and the **Desert Samaritan Medical Center,** at 1400 South Dobson Road, Mesa (tel. 835-3000), are two of the largest hospitals in the valley.

Hotlines There is a **visitor hotline** (tel. 252-5588) that provides recorded tourist information on Phoenix and the Valley of the Sun.

Information See "Tourist Information," in "Orientation" in this chapter and "Information & Money" in Chapter 2.

Laundry/Dry Cleaning Ask first at your hotel for a laundry or dry-cleaning service, or try one of the following: **40th Street East,** 4041 East Thomas Road (tel. 955-5337), does both laundry and dry cleaning. **Supermat V,** 1860 North Country Club Road, Mesa (tel. 833-9884), and **Supermat,** 3 West Baseline, Tempe (tel. 839-9177), offer laundry service. **Maroney's,** 4902 North Central Avenue (tel. 264-5964) and 3192 East Indian School Road (tel. 956-2560), is a good dry cleaner.

Libraries The **Phoenix Central Library** is at Central Avenue and McDowell Road (tel. 262-4766).

Lost Property If you lost something in the airport, call 273-3307; on a bus, call 261-8549.

Luggage Storage/Lockers You'll find luggage-storage lockers at the **Greyhound/Trailways bus station** at 525 East Washington Street.

Newspapers/Magazines *The Arizona Republic* is Phoenix's morning daily newspaper, and the *Phoenix Gazette* is the afternoon daily. You'll find both in newspaper boxes, convenience stores, grocery stores, and other places. The Friday papers have special sections with schedules of the upcoming week's movie, music, and cultural performances. *New Times* is a free weekly news and arts journal with comprehensive listings of cultural events, film, and rock-music club and concert schedules. The best place to find *New Times* is at Circle K convenience stores all over the valley.

Photographic Needs Should you need some additional camera equipment or have any other photo needs, try **Photomark,** 1916 West Baseline Road, Mesa (tel. 897-2522); 2202 East McDowell Road (tel. 244-1133); or 204 East University Drive, Tempe (tel. 894-8337).

Police For police emergencies, phone **911.**

Post Office The **Phoenix General Mail Facility** (main post office) is at 4949 East Van Buren Street (tel. 225-3434).

Radio Phoenix has dozens of AM and FM radio stations broadcasting every type of music.

Religious Services The local *Yellow Pages* telephone directory has churches listed by denomination.

Safety Don't leave valuables in view in your car, especially when parking in downtown Phoenix. Put anything of value in the trunk or under the seat if you're driving a hatchback. Many hotels now provide in-room safes, for which there is a daily charge. Others will be glad to store your valuables in a safety-deposit box at the front office.

Shoe Repairs   Try **Tony's Shoe Repair,** Christown Mall, 19th Avenue and Bethany Home Road (tel. 433-0915), Central Avenue and Osborne Road (tel. 266-8081), or 20 West Adams Street (tel. 253-8067).

Television   Valley of the Sun stations are ABC (3), Independent (5), PBS (8), CBS (10), and NBC (12).

Taxes   In addition to the 5% state sales tax, Phoenix imposes hotel room taxes of 8.5% and a car-rental tax of 8.7%.

Taxis   See "Getting Around," in this chapter.

Telegrams/Telex   You can send a telegram by calling **Western Union** (tel. toll free 800/325-6000).

Transit Information   For Phoenix Transit System public bus information, call 253-5000. For Greyhound/Trailways intercity bus information, call 248-4040. For Amtrak intercity train information, call 253-0121 or toll free 800/872-7245. For general airport information at Sky Harbor Airport, call 273-3300. (For specific airline information, contact the individual airline; phone numbers are listed under "Getting There" in Chapter 2.)

Weather   The phone number for weather information is 256-7706.

3. ACCOMMODATIONS

Because Phoenix has long been popular as a winter refuge from cold and snow, it supports an amazingly large and diverse selection of resorts, hotels, motels, and bed-and-breakfast inns. Whatever your budget, you can find something here—from the luxury of Scottsdale to the old motels of Van Buren Street. No matter where you stay, even in a budget motel, you're likely to find a swimming pool and whirlpool spa on the premises.

If you're the kind of person who likes to stay in bed-and-breakfast inns, you may be surprised that, rather than being housed in historic buildings, the B&Bs of Phoenix are in modern homes. **Mi Casa—Su Casa,** P.O. Box 950, Tempe, AZ 85281 (tel. 602/990-0682), is a reservation service that offers accommodations in homes in Phoenix and across the state. Rates range from $30 to $100 for a double room, depending on the location and luxury of the home. The **Arizona Association of Bed & Breakfast Inns,** 3661 North Campbell Avenue (P.O. Box 237), Tucson, AZ 85719 (tel. 602/231-6777), is another organization representing B&Bs across the state, including Phoenix. Contact them for a list of their members.

PHOENIX

VERY EXPENSIVE

ARIZONA BILTMORE, 24th St. and Missouri Ave., Phoenix, AZ 85016.
   Tel. 602/955-6600, or toll free 800/528-3696. Fax 602/954-0469. Telex 165-709. 500 rms and suites. A/C TV TEL
$ **Rates:** Jan to late May, $195–$280 single; $220–$305 double; from $580 suite. Late Sept to Dec, $185–$265 single; $210–$290 double; from $550 suite. Summer rates are lower. Children under 18 stay free in parents' room. Special packages available. AE, CB, DC, DISC, MC, V.

The architecturally aware will immediately recognize the hand of Frank Lloyd Wright in the design of this premier resort at the foot of Squaw Peak. Wright, who worked with the building's main architect, is credited with the design of the precast concrete blocks that are used throughout the interior and exterior of the resort's buildings. Wright also designed a stained-glass window and several sculptures that decorate the facilities.

The Biltmore, opened in 1929, completed an extensive renovation of its public areas in 1991, and in 1992 began upgrading and modernizing its guest rooms. When you visit, you may get one of the new rooms or one of the older rooms that were decorated in the 1970s by Frank Lloyd Wright's widow. There are three styles and sizes of rooms, with the resort rooms being the largest and most comfortable. Both the resort rooms and the terrace court rooms have patios or balconies, and some offer views of Squaw Peak. The traditional rooms in the main building are the smallest and do not have balconies or patios.

Dining/Entertainment: The Orangerie serves new American and continental cuisine in a garden setting inspired by Frank Lloyd Wright. All the furnishings are original Wright designs (see "Dining," below, for details). The Gold Room Grille, with its classic art deco decor and gold-leaf-covered ceiling, serves breakfast, a tempting lunch buffet, dinner, and a superb Sunday brunch. Men must wear a jacket in both of these restaurants after 6pm. Café Sonora serves American favorites and spicy southwestern fare amid a casual atmosphere. The Lobby Lounge is a quiet spot to meet for a drink and some conversation. In the Gold Room, there is a live jazz pianist during happy hour, dinner, and Sunday brunch. The Cabaña Club and Pool Bar serve drinks and light meals beside the pool.

Services: 24-hour room service, concierge, limousine, airport shuttle, shopping shuttle, massages, shoeshine service, valet/laundry service, car-rental service, baby-sitting, physician.

Facilities: Two 18-hole golf courses, three swimming pools, two whirlpool baths, 12 lighted tennis courts, complete fitness center, sauna, steam room, jogging paths, rental bicycles, lawn games, board games, beauty salon, several shops.

THE PHOENICIAN RESORT, 6000 E. Camelback Rd., Scottsdale, AZ 85251. Tel. 602/941-8200, or toll free 800/888-8234. Fax 602/947-4311. 442 rms, 107 casitas, 31 suites. A/C MINIBAR TV TEL

$ Rates: Sept–June, $270–$405 single or double; $270–$405 casita; $750–$1,275 suite. June–Sept, $145–$275 single or double; $185–$275 casita;

Ⓕ FROMMER'S SMART TRAVELER: HOTELS

1. Consider traveling during the shoulder seasons of late spring and late summer. Temperatures are not at their midsummer peak nor are room rates at their midwinter heights. If you can stand the heat of summer you'll save more than 50% on room rates.

2. Be flexible when making reservations. Unless you ask, you may not find out that rates are scheduled to go down a week before or after you have planned your vacation. Changing your dates by a few days or a few weeks may save you hundreds of dollars.

3. Always ask about possible discounts or packages that you might be able to take advantage of. Phoenix resorts often offer weekend rates and golf packages that can save you money.

4. Be sure to find out if the hotel you'll be staying at offers free airport transfers. This can save you an expensive taxi or shuttle-bus ride.

5. Request a room with a view of the mountains whenever possible. You can overlook a swimming pool anywhere, but one of the main selling points of Phoenix hotels are the views of Mummy Mountain, Camelback Mountain, and Squaw Peak.

6. If you'll be traveling with children, always ask what the age cutoff is if children get to stay for free and whether there is a limit to the number of children who can stay for free.

$425–$950 suite. Children 12 and under stay free in parents' room. AE, CB, DC, DISC, MC, V.

This is by far Arizona's most impressive resort. Situated on 130 acres at the foot of Camelback Mountain, the Phoenician makes the most of its location. At night the mountain is dramatically lit, and day or night there are views across the valley. Marble floors, a bubbling fountain, walls of glass, and pieces of the resort's $2-million art collection create a grand lobby.

Guest rooms here are as impressive as the public areas and include sunken bathtubs large enough for two people, Berber carpets, muted color schemes, three phone lines, large patios, a huge TV, two closets, terry robes, bathroom scales, hairdryers, and wall safes. And this is just the standard room.

Dining/Entertainment: Mary Elaine's offers elegant dining with the best views at the resort. French and northern Italian cuisines are featured. In the Terrace Dining Room, the atmosphere is slightly less formal and Italian and American dishes are served, as well as Sunday brunch. Windows on the Green features southwestern cuisine and a view of the golf course. For quick snacks, there are the Oasis at poolside and the Café & Ice Cream Parlor in the shopping arcade. The Lobby Tea Court serves afternoon tea. After a round of golf, there's the 19th Hole. Charlie Charlie's is the resort's disco.

Services: 24-hour room service, valet/laundry service, concierge, tour desk, car-rental desk, children's program.

Facilities: Seven pools, including an oval pool lined with mother-of-pearl tiles, pools for children, a water slide, a lap pool, a pool for playing water volleyball and water polo, and a large tiled whirlpool bath. Connecting these pools are waterfalls and bridges. Other facilities include an 18-hole golf course, a putting green, 11 lighted tennis courts, croquet lawn, lawn bowling, volleyball court, badminton, oversize chess board, backgammon, table tennis, and billiards. Spa including a fitness center, saunas, steam rooms, whirlpool baths, aerobics room, beauty salon, barber; shopping arcade.

THE POINTE ON SOUTH MOUNTAIN, 7777 S. Pointe Pkwy., Phoenix, AZ 85044. Tel. 602/438-9000, or toll free 800/876-4683. Fax 602/438-0577. 638 suites. A/C MINIBAR TV TEL

$ Rates: Jan–Apr, $195–$225 single; $205–$235 double. Apr–May, $120–$140 single; $130–$150 double. May–Sept, $90–$110 single; $100–$120 double. Sept–Jan, $160–$190 single; $170–$200 double. Weekend and special packages available. AE, CB, DC, DISC, MC, V.

Located on the flanks of South Mountain, this Pointe resort is surrounded by a 16,000-acre nature preserve. You'll immediately have a sense of being in an exclusive residential neighborhood when you turn onto the resort's private road. A large fountain stands in the middle of a traffic circle on the way up to the grand entrance. The lobby, with its high ceiling, sweeping stairs, marble railings, and crystal chandeliers, is calculated to impress.

All the guest rooms are suites, and even the smallest is quite roomy. French doors lead from the bedrooms out onto private balconies, while in the living rooms there are marble-top wet bars. The mountainside suites offer the best views of the golf course and South Mountain. Arched alcoves for the bureaus and dark hardwood trim against white walls give the rooms a very Spanish feel.

Dining/Entertainment: Another Pointe in Tyme features a clubby mahogany-paneled interior and continental cuisine, and there's live jazz here in the evenings. Rustler's Rooste is a western-theme restaurant complete with live cowboy bands, rattlesnake appetizers, and a slide from the lounge to the main dining room. Aunt Chilada's serves Mexican food. Sports Club Dining provides light and healthy meals.

Services: Room service, concierge, valet/laundry service, massages, rental-car desk, no-smoking rooms, complimentary afternoon cocktails, baby-sitting.

Facilities: 18-hole golf course, 10 tennis courts, five racquetball courts, six swimming pools, two volleyball courts, riding stables, hiking trails, fitness center with aerobics classes, fitness equipment, free weights, and a lap pool; beauty salon; gift shop.

THE POINTE AT SQUAW PEAK, 7677 N. 16th St., Phoenix, AZ 85020. Tel. 602/997-2626, or toll free 800/876-4683. Fax 602/943-4633. 580 suites. A/C MINIBAR TV TEL

$ Rates: Jan–Apr, $195–$235 single; $205–$245 double. Apr–May, $120–$150 single; $130–$160 double. May–Sept, $90–$120 single; $100–$130 double. Sept–Jan, $160–$200 single; $170–$210 double. Weekend and special packages available. AE, CB, DC, DISC, MC, V.

Though it's at the foot of Squaw Peak, you won't catch more than a glimpse of the mountain through the tall trees of this lushly landscaped resort in northern Phoenix. Spanish-villa styling surrounds you when you stay at this or any of the other Pointe properties. Large courtyards with Mexican fountains offer quiet garden and pool areas. Those seeking peace and quiet will be glad to know that certain pools are off-limits to children.

All the guest rooms here are suites or studios with stucco walls and a mixture of Spanish colonial-style and contemporary furnishings. There are wet bars with marble counters and marble vanities in all the rooms, as well as coffee makers.

Dining/Entertainment: Avanti Trattoria serves expertly prepared Italian meals at reasonable prices. Aunt Chilada's Mexican restaurant is housed in an old adobe building that was built in 1880. Hole-in-the-Wall, the resort's western-theme restaurant is housed in a building that dates to the 1930s. Beside the Pointe restaurant is in a busy corner of the property near the entrance. All the restaurants but Beside the Pointe feature live music several nights a week, from a strolling guitarist at Hole-in-the-Wall to bands playing popular dance music at Aunt Chilada's to a DJ and live band at Avanti. Beside the Pointe also has a sports lounge. There are also poolside cabañas and a swim-up bar for snacks and libations.

Services: Room service, concierge, valet/laundry service, massages, rental-car desk, no-smoking rooms, complimentary afternoon cocktails, baby-sitting.

Facilities: 18-hole golf course, six swimming pools, whirlpool tub, eight tennis courts, riding stables, jogging trails, table tennis, putting green, racquetball courts, games room, bike rentals, gift shop, fitness center with aerobics classes, free weights, exercise machines, a lap pool, sauna, steam room, whirlpool tub, and exercise instructors.

THE POINTE AT TAPATIO CLIFFS, 11111 N. Seventh St., Phoenix, AZ 85020. Tel. 602/866-7500, or toll free 800/876-4683. Fax 602/863-2510. 600 suites. A/C MINIBAR TV TEL

$ Rates: Jan–Apr, $195–$235 single; $205–$245 double. Apr–May, $120–$150 single; $130–$160 double. May–Sept, $90–$120 single; $100–$130 double. Sept–Jan, $160–$200 single; $170–$210 double. Weekend and special packages available. AE, CB, DC, DISC, MC, V.

If you travel north to the aptly named North Mountain, you'll find another Pointe resort. The Spanish-villa architecture is the same as at other Pointe properties, but the location is the most dramatic. The grounds here are so steep that many people just park their cars in the main parking lot and allow bellmen to shuttle them around in golf carts. The resort backs up to a nature preserve where guests can hike in the desert.

As at other Pointe resorts, all the rooms here are spacious suites. Furnishings are all new in shades of pale gray. Wet bars have marble counters, coffee makers, and minibars. Some rooms have high ceilings; corner rooms, with their extra windows, are particularly bright. Bedroom bureaus are set back into arched alcoves that give the rooms a very Spanish feel.

Dining/Entertainment: At the top of the hill on which the resort is built stands Etienne's Different Pointe of View, with stupendous views from the circular lounge and dining room. The menu is international, and the wine cellar is one of the largest in the Southwest. For Wild West dining, there's the Waterin' Hole, which serves steaks, barbecued ribs, and seafood in an old house with sawdust on the floor. For elegant dining without a view, try Pointe in Tyme. Marble floors and mahogany paneling give this restaurant a classic clublike atmosphere. For light poolside meals there's La Cabaña.

Services: Room service, concierge, complimentary afternoon cocktails, massages, rental-car desk, free shuttle between Pointe properties, horseback riding, baby-sitting.

Facilities: 18-hole golf course, 16 tennis courts, four racquetball courts, six swimming pools, whirlpool tubs, fitness room, steam room, sauna, gift shop, tennis shop, golf shop, beauty salon.

EXPENSIVE

SHERATON PHOENIX HOTEL, 111 N. Central Ave. (at Civic Plaza), Phoenix, AZ 95004. Tel. 602/257-1525, or toll free 800/325-3535. Fax 602/253-9755. 534 rms and suites. A/C MINIBAR TV TEL

$ Rates: Late Mar to late Aug, $64–$124 single; $74–$134 double; $119–$480 suite. Late Aug to late Mar, $99–$167 single; $109–$172 double; $159–$500 suite. AE, CB, DC, DISC, MC, V. **Parking:** $5.

Formerly the Phoenix Hilton, this high-rise hotel one block from the Civic Plaza in downtown Phoenix is popular with business travelers who are attending conventions at the nearby Phoenix Convention Center. Guest rooms are fairly standard.

Dining/Entertainment: The Sand Painter Restaurant is open for lunch and dinner and is the more elegant of the hotel's two restaurants. The Cactus Café serves lighter fare amid casual surroundings. The Adams Lounge serves a lunch buffet and offers rock music and dancing in the evenings, often to live bands.

Services: Room service, massages, airport shuttle, in-room movies, valet/laundry service, car-rental desk.

Facilities: Fitness room, swimming pool, whirlpool tub, jogging track, beauty salon and barber, gift shop, women's clothing store.

MODERATE

HOTEL WESTCOURT, 10220 N. Metro Pkwy. E., Phoenix, AZ 85021. Tel. 602/997-5900, or toll free 800/858-1033. Fax 602/997-1034. Telex 706629. 284 rms, 22 suites (all with bath). A/C TV TEL

$ Rates: Mon–Fri $75–$109 single; $85–$119 double. Sat–Sun $49–$69 single or double. AE, CB, DC, DISC, MC, V.

The Westcourt is located in the heart of Phoenix's growing high-tech district adjacent to Metrocenter, the largest shopping mall in Arizona. The contemporary styling of the soaring atrium lobby, with its potted trees and southwestern art, is continued in the guest rooms, where you'll find live plants, ceiling fans, and contemporary furnishings, including platform beds. There are also hairdryers, coffee makers, and refrigerators in all the rooms.

Trumps Restaurant offers both indoor and patio dining with mesquite-broiled steaks and continental cuisine the specialties. Trumps Bar is a dark and sparkling place with lots of polished brass and varnished oak. There's live Top-40 music in the evenings, and a happy-hour seafood bar.

The hotel offers room service, airport shuttle, concierge floor, valet/laundry service, car-rental desk, an Olympic-size swimming pool, whirlpool tub, putting green, croquet lawn, tennis courts, exercise room, and sauna.

SAN CARLOS HOTEL, 202 N. Central Ave., Phoenix, AZ 85004. Tel. 602/253-4121, or toll free 800/528-5446. 120 rms and suites (all with bath). A/C TV TEL

$ Rates (including full breakfast): $59–$69 single; $59–$79 double; $99–$159 suite. AE, CB, DC, DISC, MC, V.

Built in 1927 and reopened in early 1991 after an extensive renovation, the San Carlos is on the National Register of Historic Places. This small European-style hotel provides that touch of elegance and charm missing from the other standardized high-rise hotels of downtown Phoenix. You're close to shopping, the Phoenix Convention Center, sightseeing, and theaters, which makes this a good choice both for vacationers and conventioneers. Crystal chandeliers, a travertine check-in desk, deep-blue carpets, and comfortable couches give the small lobby a touch of class. Rooms, though smaller than today's standard hotel room, feature wingback chairs, ceiling fans, and coffee makers.

The Bistro San Carlos, with its sunken dining room just off the lobby, hints at the art deco aesthetic that was in vogue at the time the hotel first opened. Continental cuisine is served. There are also two casual sandwich shops, the Purple Cow and Philly's.

There is access to a nearby health club, tennis courts, and golf course; and the hotel features valet/laundry service, no-smoking rooms, complimentary coffee, free local phone calls, a beauty salon, shops, and a swimming pool.

BUDGET

HAMPTON INN AIRPORT, 4234 S. 48th St. (at Broadway), Phoenix, AZ 85040. Tel. 602/438-8688, or toll free 800/426-7866. Fax 602/431-8339. 132 rms (all with bath). A/C TV TEL

$ Rates (including continental breakfast): $56–$64 single; $61–$69 double. AE, DC, DISC, MC, V.

You'll find this modern motel just south of the airport at Exit 152A of Interstate 10. At these room rates, it's hard to beat the amenities and service of this Hampton Inn. You'll find contemporary furnishings, comfortable beds, plenty of space, and a soothing pastel decor. Best of all is the Hampton Inn's satisfaction guarantee: If you aren't entirely satisfied with your stay, they won't charge you for the room!

The adjacent Country Kitchen Restaurant is open 24 hours a day. The hotel also offers free airport shuttle, free local phone calls, in-room movies, no-smoking rooms, and a swimming pool.

TRAVELODGE METROCENTER I-17, 8617 N. Black Canyon Hwy., Phoenix, AZ 85021. Tel. 602/995-9500, or toll free 800/255-3050. Fax 602/995-0150. 180 rms (all with bath). A/C TV TEL

$ Rates (including continental breakfast): Jan–Apr, $40–$55 single; $45–$60 double. May–Sept, $31–$50 single; $35–$55 double. Sept–Dec, $35–$50 single; $40–$55 double. AE, CB, DC, DISC, MC, V.

Located just off the Black Canyon Freeway (I-17) at the Northern Boulevard exit, this economical motel is across the freeway from the huge Metrocenter shopping mall and only a short drive from downtown or the airport. Rooms are standard motel rooms but the grounds are grassy and the pool is isolated a bit from the noise of the freeway. There is also a coin-operated laundry, in-room movies, free shuttle to shops and restaurants, and a whirlpool tub.

IN SCOTTSDALE

VERY EXPENSIVE

HYATT REGENCY SCOTTSDALE RESORT AT GAINEY RANCH, 7500 E. Doubletree Ranch Rd., Scottsdale, AZ 85258. Tel. 602/991-3388, or toll free 800/233-1234. Fax 602/483-5550. 493 rms and suites. A/C MINIBAR TV TEL

$ Rates: Jan–May, $275–$335 single or double; $400–$2,200 suite. June–Sept, $115–$175 single or double; $225–$1,700 suite. Sept–Dec, $225–$285 single or double; $325–$1,900 suite. Special packages available. AE, DC, MC, V.

Located just north of Scottsdale Road's resort row, the Resort at Gainey Ranch is a visually stunning $80-million complex. The focal point of the resort is its half-acre water playground surrounded by 7 acres of waterways, fountains, fish ponds, a lake, and manicured gardens. This extravagant complex of 10 swimming pools includes a water slide inside a clock tower, a sand beach, areas for playing water volleyball, waterfalls, fountains, and a whirlpool spa. The grounds are abundantly planted with tall palm trees.

Glass blocks are used extensively in fountains throughout the grounds. You may also notice original works of art throughout the resort. This collection, which can be viewed on a weekly tour, includes a complete restrike set of Remington's western bronzes. For those who prefer nature, there are gorgeous views of the McDowell Mountains and guided plant walks around the gardens. The lobby features a huge wall of glass that is rolled away to create an open outdoor feeling.

The guest rooms are everything you'd expect in this price range, with terry robes, hairdryers, scales, marble-top tables, and attractive pastel color schemes.

Dining/Entertainment: The Golden Swan, serving southwestern cuisine, extends out to a fish pond and garden. The Squash Blossom provides a more casual atmosphere, and also serves southwestern cuisine. Ristorante Sandolo is a casual Italian café with indoor or patio seating. The Lobby Bar features nightly piano music. There are also two bars and a grill near the pool.

Services: 24-hour room service, valet parking, concierge, valet/laundry service, children's programs.

Facilities: 27-hole golf course, 10 swimming pools, eight tennis courts, croquet court, a health spa with exercise equipment, aerobics classes, sauna, jogging and bicycling trails.

MARRIOTT'S CAMELBACK INN, 5402 E. Lincoln Dr., Scottsdale, AZ 85253. Tel. 602/948-1700, or toll free 800/228-9290. Fax 602/951-8469. 423 rms, 23 suites. A/C MINIBAR TV TEL

$ Rates: Jan–May, $225–$275 single or double; $350–$1,450 suite. May–Sept, $95–$135 single or double; $150–$710 suite. Sept–Dec, $185–$230 single or double; $285–$1,190 suite. AE, CB, DC, DISC, MC, V.

The Camelback Inn opened its doors in 1936 and later became the first Marriott resort. Today it is one of the oldest and most traditionally southwestern of Phoenix's dozens of resorts. A few years ago the resort added the most complete resort spa in the valley, which makes this the ideal place to come if you feel like being pampered while you get fit. Set at the foot of Mummy Mountain and overlooking Camelback Mountain, the resort offers a tranquil setting only 5 minutes from Scottsdale's busy shopping areas.

You'll know as soon as you approach the main building that your pace of life is about to slow down. A sign over the door states WHERE TIME STANDS STILL. Inside, the lobby has the feel of a southwestern ranch house with open beamed ceilings, sandstone floor, adobe walls, wagon-wheel chandeliers, cowhide throw pillows on the window seats, and a large rounded fireplace.

Guest rooms have all been recently renovated and are decorated with contemporary southwestern furnishings and art. All have balconies or patios, and some even have their own sun decks. Bathrooms are well lit and come with hairdryers, a large basket of toiletries, and a shaving mirror.

Dining/Entertainment: The Chaparral Dining Room features a great view of Camelback Mountain and is one of the best restaurants in the valley. The cuisine is continental, with tableside cooking a specialty of the house. The Navajo Room is the resort's casual restaurant and is decorated with Native American arts and crafts. Sunday brunch is served in the North Garden, and light snacks are available at Dromedary's or the Oasis Lounge. You'll find healthy but flavorful meals at Sprouts in the health spa. Golfers can dine at the 19th Hole. For a quiet drink in the evening, there's the Chaparral Lounge.

Services: Room service, concierge, baby-sitting, valet/laundry service, car-rental desk; spa services include six types of massage, facials, herbal body wraps, loofah salt glow treatments, and aloe or seaweed mud body masks.

Facilities: Two 18-hole golf courses (nearby), 10 tennis courts, three swimming pools, three whirlpool spas, shuffleboard court, full-service European health spa with beauty salon, lap pool, large aerobics room, saunas, steam rooms, whirlpool tub, and well-equipped fitness room.

RED LION'S LA POSADA RESORT HOTEL, 4949 E. Lincoln Dr., Scottsdale, AZ 85253. Tel. 602/952-0420, or toll free 800/547-8010. 264 rms, 10 suites. A/C TV TEL

$ Rates: Jan–May, $185–$210 single or double; $750–$1,050 suite. May–Sept,

$85–$110 single or double; $390–$800 suite. Sept–Jan, $146–$171 single or double; $690–$950 suite. AE, CB, DC, DISC, MC, V.

If you prefer to spend your time by the pool rather than on the courts or the fairways, you'll love the pool at La Posada. It covers half an acre and features its own two-story waterfall that cascades over human-made pink boulders. There is a swim-through grotto connecting the two halves of the pool, and inside the grotto, a cool (and wet) bar. There's also a fabulous view of Camelback Mountain from the pool.

The resort features Mediterranean styling with red-tile roofs and many fountains and arches. The lobby is a grand high-ceilinged affair that incorporates a bit of French country decor into its villa atmosphere. Guest rooms are larger than average and have all been recently renovated. The new rooms feature pale southwestern-style furnishings, including a glass-top table with verdigris-finish copper legs. Bathrooms have two sinks with elegant fixtures, plenty of counter space, and tile floors.

Dining/Entertainment: The Garden Terrace restaurant features continental cuisine with many southwestern touches, and an excellent view of Camelback Mountain. A pianist plays during dinner. Mangia Bene is an upscale Italian restaurant located in the La Posada Plaza building across the parking lot from the lobby. The Terrace Lounge features live Top-40 and Latin-influenced music Wednesday through Saturday, and a weekday-evening happy hour with a complimentary appetizer bar.

Services: Room service, concierge, laundry/valet service, complimentary airport shuttle, tee-time reservations at local golf courses.

Facilities: Two swimming pools, three whirlpool tubs, sauna, six tennis courts, racquetball courts, volleyball court, horseshoe pits, pitch-and-putt green, pro shop, beauty salon.

REGAL McCORMICK RANCH, 7401 N. Scottsdale Rd., Scottsdale, AZ 85253. Tel. 602/948-5050, or toll free 800/528-3130. 125 rms, 3 suites, 50 condominium villas. A/C MINIBAR TV TEL

$ Rates: Jan–Apr, $145–$190 single; $155–$200 double; $265–$600 suite; $185–$340 villa. May, $80–$105 single; $85–$110 double; $195–$450 suite; $95–$210 villa. June–Sept, $49–$90 single or double; $110–$210 suite; $65–$150 villa. Sept–Jan, $90–$140 single; $100–$150 double; $205–$450 suite; $95–$210 villa. AE, CB, DC, DISC, MC, V.

The Inn at McCormick Ranch is a low-rise lakeside resort surrounded by green lawns and a golf course. The architecture hints at adobe styling with very simple lines, while the lobby is a jewel of southwestern decor. The color scheme incorporates turquoise and purple trim on a pink stucco background. There are huge old amphoras, tables of cast stone, wire-frame lamps, rustic mission-style furniture, a high ceiling, and a huge window. Guest rooms are done in pastel hues and all have their own private balcony or patio, and more than half the rooms overlook the lake, while others overlook the pool or the mountains.

Dining/Entertainment: The Pinyon Grill leaves no doubt that you're in the Southwest. Tree-trunk pillars flank the entry and Native American handcrafts and southwestern art decorate the walls. The menu features all manner of creative southwestern offerings. The terrace offers a view over Camelback Lake. Diamondbacks Lounge continues the southwestern decor with colorfully painted wood carvings of desert animals. There's live jazz and pop music on the weekends and happy-hour specials during the week.

Services: Room service, concierge, valet/laundry service, tennis lessons and clinics, complimentary coffee in the lobby, golf course shuttle.

Facilities: Two 18-hole golf courses, four lighted tennis courts, swimming pool, whirlpool spa, boat rentals, walking and jogging paths, tennis shop, rental bikes.

SCOTTSDALE PRINCESS, 7575 E. Princess Dr., Scottsdale, AZ 85255. Tel. 602/585-4848, or toll free 800/344-4758. Fax 602/585-0086. 400 rms, 125 casitas suites, 75 villa suites. A/C MINIBAR TV TEL

$ Rates: Jan–May, $225–$295 single or double; $410–$2,000 suite. May–Sept, $90–$120 single or double; $165–$1,000 suite. Sept–Dec, $190–$240 single or double; $340–$1,500 suite. Special packages available. AE, CB, DC, DISC, MC, V.

★ Way up at the north end of Scottsdale, a 15-minute drive from all the other resorts and the downtown shopping areas, stands the Scottsdale Princess, a Moorish fantasy in the Arizona desert. It's easy to imagine oneself in a Moorish or Spanish palace here at the Princess, what with royal palms, tiled fountains, and an abundance of classical art and antiques. In the courtyard to the right of the main entrance is a beautiful waterfall that cascades down into a pool underneath the building.

Guest rooms all have distinct living and work areas, wet bars, small refrigerators, and private balconies. The decor is elegant southwestern, with earth-tone colors and furniture with a regional flare. The bathrooms are roomy enough for even the most fastidious guest, and include two sinks, separate shower and tub, a vanity, and a telephone. You'll find two more telephones in the main room, one of which is a speaker phone.

Dining/Entertainment: The Marquesa is Arizona's first restaurant serving the cuisine of the Catalán region of Spain, melding both Spanish and French flavors. Dine by the fire or out on the terrace overlooking the mountains. Las Ventanas is a casual coffee shop with a tropical feel. The menu features heart-healthy dishes and Caribbean cuisine. Only open for dinner, La Hacienda features regional Mexican cuisine and strolling mariachis. Over in the golf clubhouse you'll find the Grill at TPC, where there is both indoor and outdoor seating and a lounge. For a bite to eat in between swimming laps and power tanning, there's the Cabaña Café. Cazadores lounge, overlooking the pool area, is known for its late-night desserts. For dancing and drinking, there's Caballo Bayo, where you'll hear a mixture of today's and yesterday's popular dance music.

Services: Room service, concierge, valet/laundry service, baby-sitting, safety-deposit boxes, health and beauty treatments including massages, facials, and herbal wraps.

Facilities: Two 18-hole golf courses, nine tennis courts, three swimming pools, racquetball court, squash court, exercise room, aerobics classes, steam room, sauna, whirlpool tubs, gift shop, boutiques, beauty parlor, tennis and golf pro shops.

EXPENSIVE

CLARION HOTEL AT SCOTTSDALE MALL, 7353 E. Indian School Rd., Scottsdale, AZ 85251. Tel. 602/994-9203, or toll free 800/695-6995. Fax 602/941-2567. 206 rms and suites. A/C MINIBAR TV TEL
$ **Rates:** Jan–Apr, $99–$139 single; $99–$149 double; $175–$300 suite. Apr–Sept, $59–$89 single; $69–$99 double; $125–$200 suite. Sept–Jan, $70–$99 single; $89–$109 double; $150–$225 suite. Weekend packages available. AE, CB, DC, DISC, MC, V.

If you're a shopoholic or a culture vulture, you can't do any better than the Clarion in this price range. This low-rise hotel is located on the beautifully landscaped Scottsdale Civic Center Mall and is adjacent to the Scottsdale Center for the Arts and the popular Fifth Avenue Shops, the heart of Scottsdale's shopping district. Guest rooms are of medium size and come with bedspreads that look like quilts, patios, TV armoires, and comfortable chairs. The color scheme is pastel with interesting splashed-color patterns on both the chairs and the headboards. The tile bathrooms feature contemporary fixtures.

Dining/Entertainment: The Rôtisserie Bar & Grill features an exhibition kitchen and grilled steaks and seafoods. There is patio dining overlooking the park, and in the evening there's dancing to live and recorded popular music.

Services: Room service, in-room movies, no-smoking rooms.

Facilities: Swimming pool, tennis court, whirlpool tub.

MARRIOTT'S MOUNTAIN SHADOWS, 5641 E. Lincoln Dr., Scottsdale, AZ 85253. Tel. 602/948-7111, or toll free 800/228-9290. 338 rms, 39 suites. A/C MINIBAR TV TEL
$ **Rates:** Jan–May, $215 single; $225 double; $225–$410 suite. May–Sept, $90

single; $100 double; $90–$165 suite. Sept–Dec, $185 single; $195 double; $185–$335 suite. AE, CB, DC, DISC, MC, V.

Located almost directly across the street from the Camelback Inn (another Marriott resort), Mountain Shadows is a little bit closer to Camelback Mountain and offers just a little bit better view. However, the ambience is entirely different. Mountain Shadows was built in the late 1950s and maintains an Eisenhower-years timelessness. The lobby features a stone wall and flagstone floor, travertine-top tables, and comfortable pink and green leather chairs. Beyond the lobby is a large terrace dining area.

There are three sections to the resort, each section with a different type of room. Arranged around the main pool area are a circle of suites that were once cabañas and look as if they had been modeled after a cruise-ship design. These suites all have king-size beds and a wall of glass overlooking the pool. This area sees a lot of activity and should be avoided by those seeking peace and quiet. Standard rooms are large and have high ceilings, wet bars, king-size beds, and balconies. Those in the Palm section offer the best view of the mountain, golf course, and a smaller pool. Other suites above the poolside suites include whirlpool tubs, brass beds, and large private patios.

Dining/Entertainment: Shell's Oyster Bar & Seafood Restaurant features Mexican-influenced decor with colorful fish images all around. There is both indoor and terrace dining. Family dining can be had at the Cactus Flower, which sports southwestern decor, moderate prices, and terrace dining. Maxfield's Lounge, at the country club, is a casual restaurant and features dancing to both live and recorded popular music. From 5 to 8pm on weekdays, there is a hungry hour with great hors d'oeuvres.

Services: Room service, concierge, valet/laundry service, baby-sitting, guided mountain hikes, golf and tennis lessons, massages.

Facilities: Three 18-hole golf courses (one on the grounds, two nearby), eight tennis courts, three swimming pools, two whirlpool spas, saunas, water volleyball, fitness center (and access to the spa at the Camelback Inn), sand volleyball, table tennis, shuffleboard, beauty shop, gift shop, pro shop.

REGISTRY RESORT, 7171 N. Scottsdale Rd., Scottsdale, AZ 85253.
Tel. 602/991-3800, or toll free 800/528-3154. Fax 602/948-9843. Telex 165826. 318 rms, 42 suites. A/C TV TEL
$ Rates: $185–$215 single or double; $250–$1,500 suite. Packages available. AE, CB, DC, DISC, MC, V.

Located in the heart of Scottsdale's resort row, the Registry commands a view of both Camelback and Mummy mountains from its entryway, and the spacious grounds are planted with many flowering shrubs and citrus trees.

There is a variety of guest rooms. The studio rooms come with Murphy beds and a day bed that's perfect for afternoon naps. For relaxing in the evening there are sunken bathtubs. Regular rooms feature marble bathrooms with two sinks, marble-top tables with comfortable chairs, and private patios. The bilevel suites feature traditional European furniture, kitchenettes, sleeping lofts, second-floor decks, and two bathrooms. The golf-course rooms are my favorite simply because of the views of the McDowell Mountains.

Dining/Entertainment: La Champagne serves continental and American regional cuisines amid sparkling crystal, fine china, and pink linens. Sunday champagne brunch is as elegant a meal as you will have anywhere. Café Brioche is a more casual French restaurant serving all three meals both inside and on the patio. There's more patio dining at the Garden Patio. The Kachina Lounge is a quiet place for a drink early in the evening, but picks up the pace with live dance music later on. During the day the Pool Lounge caters to swimmers and sunbathers.

Services: 24-hour room service, valet/laundry service and coin laundry, concierge, tour desk, car-rental desk, massages, reflexology, body polishes, tennis lessons.

Facilities: Two 18-hole golf courses, 21 lighted tennis courts, pro shop, gift shop, three swimming pools, whirlpool tub, health club with fitness room, steam room, and sauna.

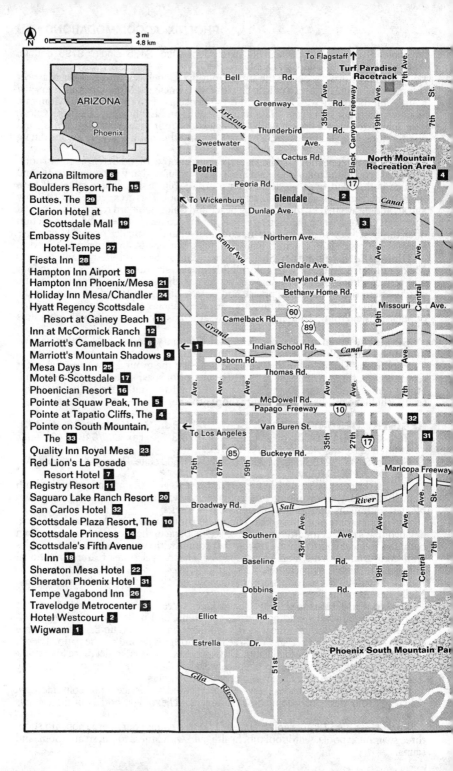

ARIZONA
Phoenix

Arizona Biltmore **6**
Boulders Resort, The **15**
Buttes, The **29**
Clarion Hotel at
    Scottsdale Mall **19**
Embassy Suites
    Hotel-Tempe **27**
Fiesta Inn **28**
Hampton Inn Airport **30**
Hampton Inn Phoenix/Mesa **21**
Holiday Inn Mesa/Chandler **24**
Hyatt Regency Scottsdale
    Resort at Gainey Beach **13**
Inn at McCormick Ranch **12**
Marriott's Camelback Inn **8**
Marriott's Mountain Shadows **9**
Mesa Days Inn **25**
Motel 6-Scottsdale **17**
Phoenician Resort **16**
Pointe at Squaw Peak, The **5**
Pointe at Tapatio Cliffs, The **4**
Pointe on South Mountain,
    The **33**
Quality Inn Royal Mesa **23**
Red Lion's La Posada
    Resort Hotel **7**
Registry Resort **11**
Saguaro Lake Ranch Resort **20**
San Carlos Hotel **32**
Scottsdale Plaza Resort, The **10**
Scottsdale Princess **14**
Scottsdale's Fifth Avenue
    Inn **18**
Sheraton Mesa Hotel **22**
Sheraton Phoenix Hotel **31**
Tempe Vagabond Inn **26**
Travelodge Metrocenter **3**
Hotel Westcourt **2**
Wigwam **1**

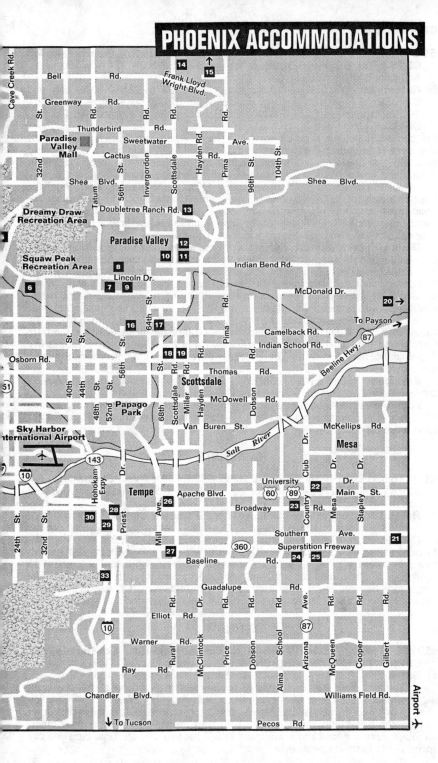

PHOENIX ACCOMMODATIONS

SCOTTSDALE PLAZA RESORT, 7200 N. Scottsdale Rd., Scottsdale, AZ 85253. Tel. 602/948-5000, or toll free 800/832-2025. 224 rms, 180 suites. A/C MINIBAR TV TEL

$ Rates: Jan–Apr, $195–$215 single or double; $275–$2,500 suite. May and Sept–Dec, $145–$165 single or double; $200–$2,000 suite. June–Sept, $85–$95 single or double; $125–$1,800 suite. Special packages available. AE, CB, DC, DISC, MC, V.

Located on Scottsdale Road's resort row, the 40-acre Scottsdale Plaza consists of dozens of red-tile-roofed Mediterranean villas. The main building is a classic grand villa with red-tile floors and a colonnade along one side of the lobby. Tucked in behind this colonnade is a quiet lounge with a fireplace. Rooms here are all very spacious and come with plenty of amenities. There are terry robes, safes, minibars, large changing rooms, a TV armoire, and comfortable chairs. The furnishings are done in whitewashed oak that has an antique southwestern feel. More expensive rooms have wet bars, and many of the suites feature beehive fireplaces and private patios. There are also bilevel suites with two bathrooms.

Dining/Entertainment: Remington's Restaurant and Lounge is located in its own building in the southeastern corner of the property and takes its name from the two Remington bronze statuettes that are displayed in the restaurant entry. The restaurant features Mediterranean decor and feels a bit like a men's club. In the evening there is live jazz performed on the baby grand piano. In the dining room, you'll think you're dining outside when you look up through the ramada over your table and see clouds painted on the sky-blue domed ceiling. The Garden Court is a casual café with a garden atmosphere. For poolside light meals there are the Café Cabaña and the Courtyard Cabaña. JD's Lounge in the main building features live Top-40 dance music, while the Lobby Lounge offers a quiet little niche for a romantic drink by the fireplace.

Services: Room service, concierge, valet/laundry service, in-room movies, tennis lessons, car-rental desk, bike rentals.

Facilities: Five swimming pools, five tennis courts, three racquetball courts, three whirlpool tubs, croquet court, pro shop, fitness room, beauty salon, jogging trails, gift shop, business center.

MODERATE

SCOTTSDALE'S FIFTH AVENUE INN, 6935 Fifth Ave., Scottsdale, AZ 85251. Tel. 602/994-9461, or toll free 800/528-7396. Fax 602/994-0493. 92 rms (all with bath). A/C TV TEL

$ Rates (including full breakfast): Jan–Apr, $71 single; $82–$87 double. May–Sept, $35 single; $40–$45 double. Oct–Dec, $44 single; $52–$57 double. Children under 16 stay free in parents' room. AE, DC, DISC, ER, MC, V.

Located at the west end of Scottsdale's Fifth Avenue Shops shopping district, this motel is within walking distance of some of the best shops and restaurants in Scottsdale. Guest rooms are large and were redecorated just a few years ago. The three-story building is arranged around a central courtyard where you'll find the swimming pool. There is also a whirlpool tub and facilities for the disabled.

BUDGET

MOTEL 6–SCOTTSDALE, 6848 E. Camelback Rd., Scottsdale, AZ 85251. Tel. 602/946-2280. 122 rms (all with bath). A/C TV TEL

$ Rates: $25–$32 single; $31–$38 double. AE, DISC, MC, V.

S You just can't stay in Scottsdale for any less than this, and even this is an anomaly. Scottsdale likes to think of itself as a very exclusive town, so you won't find any new budget motels opening anytime soon. Located at the corner of Camelback and 69th, this Motel 6 is your basic motel—clean, but nothing fancy, although there is a pool and a whirlpool tub. What you save on room rates you can spend in the fancy shops all over town.

CAREFREE

BOULDERS RESORT, 34631 N. Tom Darlington (P.O. Box 2090), Carefree, AZ 85377. Tel. 602/488-9009, or toll free 800/553-1717. Fax 602/488-4118. 136 casitas. A/C MINIBAR TV TEL

$ Rates (including breakfast and dinner): Jan and Oct–Dec, $320 single; $395 double. Jan–Apr and late Dec, $420 single; $495 double. Apr–May, $360 single; $435 double. May–Oct, $210 single; $285 double. AE, CB, DC, DISC, MC, V.

 Located 45 minutes north of Scottsdale in the retirement community of Carefree, the Boulders is a very exclusive resort and residential community. Only the Enchantment Resort in Sedona comes anywhere close to offering the spectacular setting, unusual accommodations, and outstanding service that the Boulders offers. This is the way a desert resort should be. Set amid giant weatherbeaten boulders, cactus, and palo verde trees, the Boulders epitomizes the Southwest aesthetic. Adobe buildings blend with the pastel desert hues and the native rocks.

The lobby is a grand adobe structure with tree-trunk pillars, flagstone floor, and a large fireplace. Navajo rugs and a collection of Native American arts and crafts is displayed around the room. Guest rooms continue the adobe styling with rounded interior stucco walls, beehive fireplaces, and high beamed ceilings. Refrigerators, ceiling fans, and coffee makers are included. The bathrooms are so large and luxuriously appointed that you might spend all of your time in this room. There are tubs for two, separate showers, double sinks, vanities, plenty of high-quality toiletries, and even loofahs for a good scrub. The second-floor rooms offer the best views, but there really isn't a bad view anywhere at the Boulders.

Dining/Entertainment: The resort's premier restaurant is the Latilla Room. The name means ceiling in Spanish, so be sure to glance over your head while you're eating. Stucco walls and log beams contrast with the fine china and pink napery. Gourmet American cuisine is served and jackets are required for men at dinner. The Palo Verde Room features a beautiful tile-front exhibition kitchen brimming with polished copper, dried herbs, and chile peppers hanging from the ceiling. This is where to dine if you enjoy imaginative creations with a southwestern flare. Over at the country club is another dining room open only to club members and hotel guests. The menu emphasizes grilled meats and seafoods. Yet another restaurant, the Cantina del Pedregal, is located in the El Pedregal Shopping Center a short distance by foot or car from the main resort area. This last is the most casual of the resort's dining rooms and serves Mexican food.

Services: Room service, concierge, valet/laundry service, airport shuttle, Jeep tours, balloon rides, bike rentals.

Ⓕ FROMMER'S COOL FOR KIDS:
HOTELS

Hyatt Regency Scottsdale at Gainey Ranch *(see p. 61)* Not only is there a totally awesome water playground complete with sand beach and water slide, but the Kamp Hyatt Kachina program provides supervised structured activities. Like, rad, dude.

The Phoenician Resort *(see p. 57)* The Funicians Club is a supervised activities program for children ages 5 to 12. Kids get to play games, make crafts, and burn up lots of excess energy.

Marriott's Mountain Shadows *(see p. 64)* Kids age 5 to 15 can participate in the Kactus Kids Klub, a recreation program that includes field trips, hay rides, games, pool activities, and arts and crafts activities.

Facilities: 27-hole golf course, six tennis courts, swimming pool, jogging trails, hiking trails, pro shop, gift shop, fitness center with lap pool, men's sauna, exercise machines, whirlpool tub.

MESA

EXPENSIVE

SAGUARO LAKE RANCH RESORT, 13020 Bush Hwy., Mesa, AZ 85205. Tel. 602/984-2194. 25 rms (all with bath).
$ Rates (including three meals daily): $85 per person. AE, MC, V.

Though the address is in Mesa, the Saguaro Lake Ranch Resort is actually 20 miles outside town at the foot of the Superstition Mountains. This rustic guest ranch has been owned by the same family since the 1940s and recently reopened its doors after being closed for several years because of construction on the nearby Saguaro Lake dam. The ranch is in a spectacular setting on the banks of the Salt River with rugged and convoluted cliffs towering above the far side of the river. Cactus-covered hills surround the ranch, and it's in these hills that guests horseback ride, hike, and birdwatch.

This ranch has not been fancied up to attract folks away from the resorts in Scottsdale; it's still as simple and rugged as the day it opened. If you have longed to play cowboy all your life, this is your chance. Furniture throughout the ranch is original and well-worn, but this authenticity is what the guests enjoy most about this place. Guest rooms are small, but the dining room and main lounge, with its four-sided fireplace and stuffed bison heads is where most guests spend their time when they aren't out riding the range.

Dining/Entertainment: Meals are served family style at long tables in the paneled and wood-floored dining room. A stone fireplace warms the room in the winter.

Services: Raft rentals, complimentary inner tubes for floating on the river, horseback riding, sunset cookouts, summer barbecues.

Facilities: Swimming pool, riding stables, basketball court.

SHERATON MESA HOTEL, 200 N. Centennial Way, Mesa, AZ 85201. Tel. 602/898-8300, or toll free 800/456-6372. Fax 602/964-9279. 274 rms, 5 suites. A/C MINIBAR TV TEL
$ Rates: Jan–Apr, $120 single; $130 double. May–Sept, $80 single; $90 double. Sept–Dec, $110 single; $120 double. Children 18 and under stay free in parents' room. AE, CB, DC, DISC, MC, V.

Mesa has become one of the valley's centers for high-tech industries and as such is now filled with modern office and business complexes. In the heart of downtown Mesa and convenient to the convention center, amphitheater, and area businesses, the high-rise Sheraton Mesa Hotel offers great views of the entire valley from its upper floors. Between the main building and the restaurant and lounge building is a noisy waterfall that cascades over four tiers to a small pond. Guest rooms are very attractively decorated with cherrywood furnishings, rattan chairs, and rose carpeting.

Dining/Entertainment: Encore, the hotel's dining room, sports a high ceiling with warehouselike exposed beams. Meals, primarily American standards, are moderately priced. Memories is a large lounge that features karaoke singing on Wednesday night, fashion shows on Thursday, and a DJ playing hits from the '60s to the '90s on Friday and Saturday nights.

Services: Room service, concierge, valet/laundry service, free airport shuttle, free golf course transportation, no-smoking rooms.

Facilities: Swimming pool, whirlpool tub, two tennis courts, fitness room, business center.

MODERATE

HAMPTON INN PHOENIX/MESA, 1563 S. Gilbert Rd., Mesa, AZ 85204. Tel. 602/926-3600, or toll free 800/426-7866. 118 rms (all with bath). A/C MINIBAR TV TEL

$ Rates (including continental breakfast): $50–$60 single; $56–$66 double. Children 18 and under stay free in parents' room. AE, DC, DISC, MC, V.

Located just off the Superstition Freeway (Ariz. 360) in a small shopping center, the Hampton Inn, though a bit far removed from most of the attractions and shopping around the Valley of the Sun, is still a good choice, especially for families. Both children and third and fourth additional adults stay free in the same room. Rooms are new and attractively furnished in shades of seafoam green and other pastels. The large tiled bathrooms come with hairdryers. There's a medium-sized swimming pool on the highway side of the building. The hotel also offers a whirlpool tub, no-smoking rooms, free in-room movies, and free local phone calls.

HOLIDAY INN MESA/CHANDLER, 1600 S. Country Club Dr., Mesa, AZ 85202. Tel. 602/964-7000, or toll free 800/465-4329. Fax 602/964-7000, ext. 118. 245 rms, 83 suites. A/C TV TEL

$ Rates: $49–$119 single or double. AE, CB, DC, DISC, MC, V.

Located just off the Superstition Freeway, this Holiday Inn features a large atrium with a swimming pool that extends outside. Within the lobby itself, there are numerous potted palms, which give the hotel a gardenlike feel. Many rooms in this high-rise hotel have excellent views of the Superstition Mountains to the east, so be sure to request a room as high up as possible. Regardless of what room you stay in, you'll have a small private balcony. Furnishings are of wicker to match the Casablanca decor downstairs.

Dining/Entertainment: Michelle's, which overlooks the pool atrium, serves continental and American food amid a garden of greenery and 1920s decor. In the Lobby Bar beside the indoor swimming pool is live piano music 6 nights a week. Jubilations is a large two-level disco with a live DJ and large dance floor.

Services: Rental-car desk, safety-deposit boxes, complimentary airport shuttle.

Facilities: Indoor/outdoor pool, whirlpool tub, sauna, gift shop.

QUALITY INN ROYAL MESA, 951 W. Main St., Mesa, AZ 85201. Tel. 602/833-1231, or toll free 800/228-5151. 100 rms and suites (all with bath). A/C TV TEL

$ Rates (including continental breakfast): Jan–Apr, $69–$99 single; $72–$109 double. May–Sept, $38–$48 single; $40–$52 double. Oct–Dec, $48–$65 single; $55–$69 double. AE, CB, DC, DISC, MC, V.

Take the Alma School Road exit north off the Superstition Freeway, drive north 2 miles, and then turn right on Main Street. This Quality Inn offers standard motel rooms close to downtown Mesa's business district. Rooms are large and clean, and some come with a kitchenette or a small refrigerator. You'll find a restaurant and a lounge on the premises, and receive a complimentary daily cocktail. Facilities include an outdoor swimming pool, indoor whirlpool tub, sauna, and a fitness center.

BUDGET

MESA DAYS INN, 333 W. Juanita Ave., Mesa, AZ 85210. Tel. 602/844-8900, or toll free 800/325-2525. 125 rms (all with bath). A/C TV TEL

$ Rates (including continental breakfast): $29–$55 single; $29–$60 double. AE, CB, DC, DISC, MC, V.

Located just south of the Superstition Freeway off the Country Club Drive exit, this Days Inn offers huge guest rooms that feature refrigerators and large windows that let in plenty of light. The decor reflects a bit of the Southwest with its pink stucco walls and southwestern motif in the lobby. The motel offers valet service, a swimming pool, whirlpool tub, sauna, exercise room, no-smoking rooms, and wheelchair accommodations.

TEMPE

VERY EXPENSIVE

THE BUTTES, 2000 Westcourt Way, Tempe, AZ 85282. Tel. 602/225-9000, or toll free 800/843-1986. Fax 602/438-8622. Telex 5106015124. 350 rms, 12 suites. A/C TV TEL

$ Rates: Jan–May, $165–$195 single; $175–$205 double. May–Sept, $65–$95 single; $75–$105 double. Sept–Dec, $125–$155 single; $135–$165 double. Year round, suites $375–$1,500. Children under 18 stay free in parents' room. Weekend and special packages available. AE, CB, DC, DISC, MC, V.

The rugged beauty of the desert's rocky buttes lend this modern resort an otherworldly air. Located only 3 miles from Sky Harbor Airport, The Buttes is a truly spectacular resort that makes the most of its location. From its hilltop restaurant and lounge to its free-form swimming pool and desert landscaping, every inch of this resort is calculated to take the breath away. At the front door an old saguaro cactus grows through an opening in the roof, and just inside there are huge amethyst crystal geodes on display. The lobby, which is built right into the side of the hill, is a stunning minimalist room with flagstone floors. Behind the simple check-in desk is a cactus garden beneath skylights. A stream flows across the rocks of the cactus garden and cascades down to a fish pond in the dining room on the floor below the lobby. On the north side of the lobby is a wall of glass with a view across the Valley of the Sun.

You'll find the guest rooms to be as visually striking as the lobby. Each room features louvered shutters on the windows and almost all have stunning views. In keeping with the craggy location of the Buttes, coffee tables are built with artificial stone bases. Dressers, TV cabinet, and a minibar are all built into the wall beneath the picture windows, which gives the room a very streamlined and uncluttered appearance. There is a cassette/clock radio by the bed and phones all have two lines. Live potted cacti will remind you that you're in the desert. In the bathroom, you'll find a very romantic wide oval bathtub, a hairdryer, and drawers beneath the marble counter.

Dining/Entertainment: Set at the end of a cantilevered bridge, the Top of the Rock is the resort's premier restaurant. Featuring an exhibition kitchen and panoramic views of the valley, this dining room actually does sit on top of the rock, which is visible in the center of the dining room. Don't miss sunset dinner here. The Market Café is an informal dining room and is located just below the lobby. You can sit beside the indoor fish pond and waterfall or out on the covered patio. For lively evening entertainment, Chuckawalla's features the latest dance music, a huge video screen, and karaoke sing-along nights.

Services: 24-hour room service, concierge, valet/laundry service, complimentary airport shuttle, rental-car desk.

Facilities: Two free-form swimming pools with waterfalls and a connecting swim-through canal, four secluded whirlpool tubs, four tennis courts, fitness center, jogging trails, gift shop.

EXPENSIVE

EMBASSY SUITES HOTEL–TEMPE, 4400 S. Rural Rd., Tempe, AZ 85282. Tel. 602/897-7444, or toll free 800/362-2779. Fax 602/897-6112. 224 suites. A/C TV TEL

$ Rates (including full breakfast): Jan–May, $115 single; $125 double. May–Sept, $64 single; $74 double. Sept–Dec, $89 single; $99 double. Children 12 and under stay free in parents' room. AE, CB, DC, DISC, MC, V.

Located just off the Superstition Freeway at the Rural Road exit, the Embassy Suites Hotel provides good value and a convenient location in the booming East Valley business district. All the rooms here are suites and all come with extra amenities that make this a great choice for families or business travelers. The two-room suites are all attractively decorated in pastel colors with a mixture of contemporary and rattan furnishings. There are wet bars, coffee makers, microwaves, and small refrigerators in all the suites, so you can fix your own simple meals.

Dining/Entertainment: The Brown Derby restaurant serves American meals and has nightly specials. There is also patio dining in the palm-shaded courtyard garden.

Services: Free airport shuttle, car-rental desk, free evening cocktails, valet service.

Facilities: Swimming pool, whirlpool tub, sauna, steam room, exercise room, games room, gift shop, no-smoking suites, coin laundry.

MODERATE

FIESTA INN, 2100 S. Priest Dr., Tempe, AZ 85282. Tel. 602/967-1441, or toll free 800/528-6481. 269 rms, 10 suites (all with bath). A/C TV TEL
$ Rates: Mon–Fri $61–$98 single; $68–$108 double. Sat–Sun $45–$79 single or double. AE, CB, DC, DISC, MC, V.

When you see the luxurious grounds of this conveniently located hotel, you'll be as surprised at I was at their affordable rates. The portico features a copper-clad roof and there are big chunks of copper ore on display in the front gardens. Inside the tile-floored lobby you'll notice numerous antique bureaus on display, and the stained-glass windows show a touch of Frank Lloyd Wright styling. In winter a pianist plays in the lobby and guests can sit by the fireplace while enjoying the music. Rooms are large and all have small refrigerators and hairdryers. Minisuites are slightly larger than the standard rooms and also have cassette/clock radios and windows overlooking the pool.

Ole Anderson's Other Place serves reliable American fare. There is seating both inside by the fireplace or outside on the patio. The hotel's lounge features a copper bar and a big-screen TV. The hotel also offers free airport shuttle, room service, valet/laundry service, swimming pool, three tennis courts, a health club, sauna, whirlpool tub, jogging trails, and a golf practice facility.

BUDGET

TEMPE VAGABOND INN, 1221 E. Apache Blvd., Tempe, AZ 85281. Tel. 602/968-7793, or toll free 800/522-1555. Fax 602/966-4450. 100 rms (all with bath). A/C TV TEL
$ Rates (including continental breakfast): $34–$46 single; $39–$60 double. AE, CB, DC, DISC, MC, V.
Just a short drive from the Arizona State University campus and the Old Town Tempe, this motel is clean, economical, and well situated. To reach the motel from the airport, take the Broadway Road exit off I-10 and go east to Rural Road, turn left on Rural Road, and then right on Apache Boulevard. Rooms are average size for motels and are nothing fancy, but the list of freebies makes the rooms good values: airport shuttle; free coffee, tea, fresh fruit, local phone calls, and weekday newspaper. The hotel also features a swimming pool, whirlpool tub, and no-smoking rooms.

LITCHFIELD PARK

THE WIGWAM, Indian School Rd. at Litchfield Rd., Litchfield Park, AZ 85340. Tel. 602/935-3811, or toll free 800/SAY-PUTT. Fax 602/935-3737. 241 rms, 68 suites. A/C MINIBAR TV TEL
$ Rates: Jan–Apr, $210–$250 single or double; $355 suite. Apr–May, $160–$195 single or double; $255 suite. May–Sept, $80–$95 single or double; $130 suite. Sept–Jan, $165–$205 single or double; $265 suite. Children 18 and under stay free in parents' room. Special packages available. AE, DC, MC, V.
If you're looking for a classic Arizona resort with southwestern flare, you may want to consider heading out to the Wigwam, which was originally built as executive housing for the Goodyear corporation. The resort opened its doors to the public in 1929 and ever since has been one of the finest resorts in the Southwest. Located 40 minutes west of downtown Phoenix, the resort is a secluded getaway surrounded by the small town of Litchfield Park. Three challenging golf courses make the resort very popular with golfers.

Most of the guest rooms are in small casita buildings and are surrounded by green lawns and colorful gardens. All the rooms have contemporary southwestern furniture, bathrobes, hairdryers, magnifying mirrors, Caswell-Massey toiletries, and walk-in closets. Some room have fireplaces and others have VCRs. There are also large patios with chaise lounges.

Dining/Entertainment: The Terrace Dining Room is the resort's traditional gourmet restaurant, serving continental cuisine on the terrace beside the pool, or inside at an elegantly set table beneath a rustic log-beam ceiling. There is live jazz piano to accompany dinner. Equally elegant, the Arizona Kitchen serves southwestern cuisine and features an exhibition grill. Golfers have their own conveniently located restaurant with Grille at the Greens, which specializes in grilled prime meats and seafoods. The breakfast buffet is particularly popular with golfers off to an early start. The Lobby Lounge, just off the main lobby, serves afternoon tea and evening cocktails. Sports fans can retreat to the Arizona Bar and catch the games on the big-screen TVs.

Services: Room service, concierge, valet/laundry service, massages, golf lessons, tennis lessons, horseback riding.

Facilities: Three golf courses, putting green, nine tennis courts, swimming pool, horse stables, bicycles, volleyball, croquet, shuffleboard courts, trap and skeet fields, exercise room, sauna, pro shop, gift shop.

4. DINING

Just as the Valley of the Sun is full of excellent resorts, so, too, is it full of excellent restaurants. Scottsdale and the Biltmore District are home to most, but not all. If you can afford only one expensive meal while you're here, be sure to make it at one of the resort restaurants that offers a view of the city lights. Other meals not to be missed are the cowboy dinners served amid Wild West decor at such places as Pinnacle Peak and Rustler's Rooste. Mexican food and southwestern cuisine are two other Phoenix specialties.

Pricing categories are as follows: "Budget," under $15; "Moderate," $15 to $25; "Expensive," $25 to $35; and "Very Expensive," more than $35.

PHOENIX
VERY EXPENSIVE

CHRISTOPHER'S, in the Biltmore Financial Center, 2398 E. Camelback Rd. Tel. 957-3214.
   Cuisine: FRENCH. **Reservations:** Required.

 FROMMER'S SMART TRAVELER:
RESTAURANTS

1. While in Phoenix, don't miss the opportunity to try the nouvelle southwestern cuisine created by the city's top chefs.
2. If a restaurant is out of your budget at night, try having lunch there instead. Lunch prices are often half those at dinner.
3. Eat as much Mexican food as you can while you're here.
4. For some reason, Scottsdale's French restaurants have very reasonable prices, which makes this a great place to try French cuisine if it's usually above your budget.
5. Before ordering the delicious-sounding daily special, be sure to ask the price. Specials are usually a bit more expensive than other menu items.
6. Don't leave town without dining at one of the restaurants with a view of the city. The twinkling lights at night are magical.

$ Prices: Appetizers $7.75–$42; main courses $28; menu gourmand $60 ($85 with U.S. wines); menu prestige $75 ($110 with French wines). AE, CB, DC, DISC, MC, V.

Open: Dinner only, daily 6–10pm.

Plush burgundy carpeting, floral draperies, and brocade-upholstered chairs set a tone of traditional elegance at Christopher's, which is located in a modern office building at the corner of Camelback Road and 24th Street. The dining room is small with only a handful of tables. Conversation tends to be in hushed tones, and the clientele sport top-of-the-line suits and multicarat diamonds.

Chef Christopher Gross calls his creations contemporary French cuisine, and his versions of traditional dishes are truly memorable. For an appetizer, try the smoked salmon that Christopher smokes himself as well as one of the appetizers that include Christopher's own foie gras. The menu changes regularly, but on a recent visit the sautéed venison with huckleberries and a red wine sauce was enough to transport you to a hunt club deep in the French countryside. For those who crave the full treatment whatever the cost, there are two *menus dégustation,* with a choice of five or seven courses, and California or French wines. If the prices here are beyond your means, don't despair. Christopher's also operates the Bistro (see below), where the prices are more down to earth.

ORANGERIE, in the Arizona Biltmore, 24th St. and Missouri Ave. Tel. 954-2507.

Cuisine: CONTINENTAL. **Reservations:** Required.

$ Prices: Appetizers $7–$11.50; main courses $16.50–$26. AE, DC, MC, V.

Open: Lunch daily 11:30am–2:30pm; dinner daily 6–11pm.

Though not the most expensive restaurant in the valley, the Orangerie is still considered one of the best. The dining room, which was recently redecorated as part of the Biltmore's major renovation, features original Frank Lloyd Wright–designed furniture. During the restoration, paneling along one wall of the restaurant was removed to reveal a hidden wall of the original concrete blocks that were also designed by Wright. Service is charming and knowledgeable. The menu, which changes seasonally, is imaginatively international. On a recent summer visit, I found the duck sausage with sweet fennel and warm apple slaw to be a succulent starter. Gourmands can expect the unexpected—roast rack of sika deer with herb gnocchi and plum port-wine sauce and seared beef tenderloin with bone marrow and Roquefort showed up on a recent menu. Game and seafood are mainstays of the menu in any season, and are often served with redolent sauces such as rhubarb-and-tamarind chutney and tarragon pan juice. Desserts are equally as imaginative with such combinations as green-tea infused orange-and-raspberry terrine and pistachio parfait. The wine collection is worth half a million dollars, so you should be able to find something to your liking.

VINCENT GUERITHAULT ON CAMELBACK, 3930 E. Camelback Rd. Tel. 224-0225.

Cuisine: SOUTHWESTERN. **Reservations:** Highly recommended.

$ Prices: Appetizers $4–$9 at lunch, $8–$10 at dinner; main courses $7–$10 at lunch, $19–$23 at dinner. AE, DC, MC, V.

Open: Lunch Mon–Fri 11:30am–2:30pm; dinner Mon–Fri 6–10:30pm, Sat 5:30–10:30pm, Sun (winter only) 6–10:30pm.

You'll find Vincent's just west of 40th Street on the north side of the road. Let the valet park your car, and step inside the French country-style dining room. Though most of the diners here will be sporting evening dresses and suits, you can still be served in casual attire (this is Phoenix). The restaurant's several small dining rooms create an intimate atmosphere. Despite the continental decor, the cuisine is solidly southwestern, with chipotle chiles appearing in numerous guises. For a starter, it's hard to beat the aggressive flavors of a lobster chimichanga with leeks, goat cheese, and basil beurre blanc. Moving on to the main course, I suggest duck confit with garlic and Anasazi beans. Health-conscious diners will be glad to see the heart-smart menu that includes such appetizing offerings as a salad of jicama and watercress in an olive oil and grapefruit dressing, and scallops and shrimp steamed with flour tortillas, ginger, lime, cilantro, and chile flakes. The long dessert menu includes such southwestern sweets as a pine nut–and-raisin caramel tart and crème brûlée served in a sweet taco shell with fresh berries. The extensive wine list is equally divided between Californian and French wines.

EXPENSIVE

THE BISTRO, in the Biltmore Financial Center, 2398 E. Camelback Rd., Suite 220. Tel. 957-3214.
   Cuisine: FRENCH/INTERNATIONAL. **Reservations:** Recommended.
$ **Prices:** Appetizers $4.50–$42; main courses $6–$15 at lunch, $14–$22 at dinner. AE, CB, DC, DISC, MC, V.
   Open: Mon–Fri 6:45am–midnight, Sat 11am–midnight, Sun 5–11pm.

The meals here are created in the same kitchen that prepares the pricey dishes for Christopher's, the adjacent restaurant. In fact some of the same dishes, such as Christopher's tender alder-smoked salmon, are also available at the Bistro. So what's the difference other than price? Well, noise level for one. This is a bistro, with marble floors and cherrywood paneling, and the customers tend to be young, upwardly mobile types who enjoy lively conversation. This should not be your first choice for a quiet romantic dinner. The menu reflects influences from around the world while still including traditional bistro fare. Most of the dishes are grilled on the exhibition grill. The panache of fish, a saffron-laced fish soup, makes a flavorful starter, though the smoked salmon is nearly a requirement of dining here. Main courses tend to be straightforward, with grilled rack of lamb, grilled duck, and a mixed grill of fish. Desserts run the gamut from soufflés in the flavor of your choice to a banana split made with homemade ice cream and fresh seasonal fruits.

ROXSAND, 2594 E. Camelback Rd. Tel. 381-0444.
   Cuisine: CONTINENTAL. **Reservations:** Recommended.
$ **Prices:** Appetizers $4–$10; main courses $9.50–$24. AE, DC, MC, V.
   Open: Lunch Mon–Fri 11am–5pm; dinner Mon–Thurs 5–10pm, Fri–Sat 5–10:30pm (11pm for dessert), Sun 4–9:30pm.

Located on the second floor of the exclusive Biltmore Fashion Park shopping mall, Roxsand serves what it calls transcontinental cuisine. The cuisine combines international influences and daring creativity, culminating in a lengthy menu certain to chagrin the indecisive. Where else must you choose between Morrocan b'stilla, Japanese sea-scallop salad, or petite snails served on toasted brioche rounds with grilled chèvre and veal-port sauce? And those are just appetizers. Spin the globe when you reach the main dishes: offerings include stir-fried Asian vegetables with a Thai curry sauce, confit of African pheasant with Evil Jungle Prince sauce on a spun potato nest and deep-fried spinach, or Grandma Rose's braised veal and polenta with parmesan. If the choices on the menu haven't left you quivering with indecision, take another glance at the dessert counter, which nearly blocks the front door. Many a night customers never make it past the counter as the hostess begins reciting her mantra of delicacies: raspberry tarts, cheesecake, crème brûlée, and on and on.

MODERATE

BOBBY MCGEE'S CONGLOMERATION, 8501 N. 27th Ave. Tel. 995-5982.
   Cuisine: AMERICAN. **Reservations:** Suggested.
$ **Prices:** Appetizers $3.25–$5; main courses $6–$15. AE, CB, DC, MC, V.
   Open: Dinner only, Mon–Thurs 5–10pm, Fri–Sat 5–11pm, Sun 5–10pm (lounge stays open until 1am).
Bobby McGee's is not just a restaurant, it's an event. This is where local families head for special occasions, where Phoenicians take their out-of-town guests, and where the younger set cruises for the opposite sex on weekends. The restaurant is always full so be sure to make a reservation or you may be in for a long wait. From the outside

Bobby McGee's looks a bit like an old, dilapidated warehouse, but on the inside it's crammed full of antiques and old photos that give it the feel of a Wild West saloon. Waiters and waitresses are all dressed in costumes that range from antebellum gowns to Boy Scout uniforms. Steaks and prime rib are the specialties here, but there is also a menu of lighter fare such as grilled mahi mahi and mesquite-smoked chicken.

Other branches are at 1320 West Southern Avenue, Mesa (tel. 969-4600), and 7000 East Shea Boulevard, Scottsdale (tel. 998-5591).

THE FISH MARKET, 1720 E. Camelback Rd. Tel. 277-3474.

Cuisine: SEAFOOD. **Reservations:** Recommended.
$ Prices: Downstairs, appetizers $3.25–$12.50; main courses $6–$25. Upstairs, appetizers $6–$13; main courses $7.50–$30. AE, CB, DC, DISC, MC, V.
Open: Mon–Thurs 11am–9:30pm, Fri–Sat 11am–10:30pm, Sun noon–9:30pm.

The Fish Market is divided into two restaurants: the large and casual downstairs dining room and the smaller, tonier, and slightly more expensive Top of the Market upstairs. If you feel more comfortable in jeans than in a suit and tie, stay downstairs. The Fish Market offers seafood from around the world, including fish caught by the restaurant's own two-boat fishing fleet. The first thing you'll see when you enter is the fish-market counter where locals buy the freshest fish in Phoenix. Across from this is a tin-ceilinged and tile-floored oyster bar where you might want to start your evening with some Puget Sound oysters. Mesquite char-broiling is the specialty downstairs, though there are a few blackened or fried dishes. Upstairs you'll find delicious seafood pastas and a greater variety of preparation styles, including tempura calamari; prawns in garlic, butter, white wine, and basil pesto; and salmon with lemon-dill butter.

GARCIA'S MEXICAN RESTAURANT, 4420 E. Camelback Rd. Tel. 952-8031.

Cuisine: MEXICAN. **Reservations:** Suggested.
$ Prices: Appetizers $3–$6.25; main courses $4–$10. AE, CB, DC, DISC, MC, V.
Open: Sun–Thurs 11am–10pm, Fri–Sat 11am–11pm.

For more than 30 years Garcia's has been serving some of the best Mexican food in Phoenix. The lively atmosphere, large portions, and low prices guarantee an enjoyable evening. Located next to a tennis complex on busy Camelback Road, this Garcia's looks like a fortress from the outside, though the huge fan-shaped stained-glass windows soften the appearance a bit. Inside, however, you are transported to an elegant Mexican colonial home with a sunken courtyard. The menu is long, so I'll give you a couple of tips. Try the espinaca con queso, which is a concoction of spinach, jalapeño cheese, onions, and tomatoes all served with tortillas. After that fresh start, skip to the house specialties, and, if you're hungry and have a dining companion, order the Lollapalooza Platter, which consists of seven dishes plus beans and rice. If you aren't that hungry, try the pollo fundido.

Other branches of this popular restaurant are at 3301 West Peoria Avenue (tel. 866-1850); 5509 North 7th Street, at Missouri Avenue (tel. 274-1176); Thunderbird Avenue at 40th Street (tel. 992-2650); 1604 East Southern Avenue, Tempe (tel. 820-0400); 7633 East Indian School Road, Scottsdale (tel. 945-1647); 1940 East University Avenue, Mesa (tel. 844-0023); and 2394 North Alma School Road, Chandler (tel. 963-0067).

PANIOLO GRILL, 2566 E. Camelback Rd. Tel. 381-8772.

Cuisine: INTERNATIONAL. **Reservations:** Recommended.
$ Prices: Appetizers $3–$9; main courses $6.50–$23. AE, DC, MC, V.
Open: Sun–Thurs 11am–10pm, Fri 11am–10:30pm, Sat 9am–10:30pm, Sun 9am–10pm (dinner starts at 5pm and weekend brunch is served until 5pm).

Located on the second floor of the stylish Biltmore Fashion Park shopping mall, Paniolo Grill serves an international menu that focuses on southwestern and south-of-the-border dishes. The decor is meant to create the ambience of a Mexican cantina, but if you're wondering why there is a giant sculpture of a pineapple hanging from the wall, it's a reference to the restaurant's name: A *paniolo* is a Hawaiian cowboy, and pineapples grow in Hawaii. But, whoa!—you won't find poi on the menu; the Kalúa pig sandwich is the token Hawaiian dish. More typical dishes include

Guatemalan tamales, Philippine spring rolls, and El Salvadoran stuffed corn cakes. The priciest dishes are those from the grill, such as grilled tuna pico de gallo served with fresh tomatoes, cilantro, chiles, and onions for a little under $20. The Paniolo Grill is under the same ownership as Roxsand, across the terrace, and I strongly urge you to head over to Roxsand for a choice of 20 or more irresistible desserts.

RICHARDSON'S, 1582 E. Bethany Home Rd. Tel. 265-5886 or 230-8718.
Cuisine: NEW MEXICAN. **Reservations:** Recommended.
$ Prices: Appetizers $3–$10; main courses $5–$16. MC, V.
Open: Mon–Sat 11am–11pm, Sun 11am–10pm.

Tucked into an older corner shopping center with far too few parking spaces, Richardson's is almost invisible amid the glaring lights and flashing neon of this otherwise unmemorable neighborhood. However, once you finally find the restaurant, you'll be glad you did. Downstairs is a crowded bar and a dozen or so booths and tables. It's always crowded and noisy down here, so you might want to ask for a table upstairs where it's quieter. If you enjoy creative, spicy cookery, you'll find yourself making repeat visits to Richardson's just so you can try as much of the menu as possible. If you aren't very hungry, try the Taos club sandwich made with turkey, bacon, and avocado wrapped in a flour tortilla with melted cheese and salsa. A more substantial hunger may be assuaged by a chorizo-stuffed pork chop topped with cilantro chutney and accompanied by green-chile potatoes.

RUSTLER'S ROOSTE, at the Pointe on South Mountain, 7777 S. Pointe Hwy. Tel. 231-9111.
Cuisine: STEAKS. **Reservations:** Not necessary.
$ Prices: Appetizers $4.25–$7.95; main courses $7.95–$19.95. AE, CB, DC, DISC, MC, V.
Open: Mon–Thurs 5–11pm, Fri–Sat 5pm–midnight, Sun 4–11pm.

This doesn't exactly seem like cowboy country. However, up at the top of the hill you'll find one of my favorite Phoenix restaurants. How many other restaurants do you know of where you can slide from the bar down to the main dining room? The view north across Phoenix is entertainment enough for most people, but there are also western bands playing for those who like to kick up their heels. Out on the patio are regular barbecues. If you've ever been bitten by a snake, you can exact your revenge here by ordering the rattlesnake appetizer. Follow that with the enormous cowboy platter if you've got the appetite of a hard-working cowpoke.

BUDGET

ED DEBEVIC'S SHORT ORDERS DELUXE, 2102 E. Highland Ave. Tel. 956-2760.
Cuisine: AMERICAN. **Reservations:** Not accepted.
$ Prices: Burgers $4.25–$5.25; blue plate specials $5–$6. MC, V.
Open: Sun–Thurs 11am–10pm, Fri–Sat 11am–11pm.

Hidden away behind the Smitty's supermarket in the Town & Country Shopping Center, Ed's is a classic 1950s diner right down to the little jukeboxes in the booths. Not only do they make their own burgers, chili, and bread, but they serve the best malteds in Phoenix. The sign in the front window that reads WAITRESSES WANTED—NO PEOPLE SKILLS NECESSARY should give you a clue that service here isn't going to be like service in other restaurants. This place stays busy and the waitresses are overworked (though they do break into song now and again), so don't be surprised if your waitress sits down in the booth with you to wait for your order. Wait a little too long and she may give up and never come back. That's just the kind of place Ed runs, and as Ed says, "If you don't like the way I do things—buy me out."

MATADOR RESTAURANT, 125 E. Adams St. Tel. 254-7563.
Cuisine: MEXICAN/GREEK. **Reservations:** Accepted.
$ Prices: Appetizers $2.75–$7.75; main courses $5–$10. AE, CB, DC, MC, V.
Open: Daily 7am–11pm.

There's none of the usual Mexican kitsch decor here at the Matador, just a plain old-fashioned American coffee shop/diner atmosphere. Located across the street from the Tourist Information Center and the Civic Plaza, this inexpensive restaurant is a great place for lunch if you happen to be visiting the downtown museums. Breakfast and lunch are always packed with folks from the nearby office buildings and convention center, but waits usually aren't very long. The menu is primarily Mexican with a handful of Greek specialties thrown in.

SING HIGH CHOP SUEY HOUSE, 27 W. Madison St. Tel. 253-7848.
Cuisine: CHINESE. **Reservations:** Not necessary.
$ Prices: Appetizers $1.25–$5; main courses $4–$8. AE, CB, DC, MC, V.
Open: Mon–Thurs 11am–9pm, Fri 11am–11pm, Sat noon–11pm, Sun noon–9pm.

It isn't easy to find an inexpensive meal in downtown Phoenix, so you just might have to sing for your supper—Sing High, that is. This large chop-suey house has been around for years serving decent Cantonese meals. Be forewarned, though, that the waitresses can be a bit brusque. Located just one block south of Patriot's Park and two blocks from the Civic Plaza, Sing High is short on atmosphere, but prices are low and portions are big.

SCOTTSDALE

EXPENSIVE

8700 RESTAURANT, 8700 E. Pinnacle Peak Rd. Tel. 994-8700.
Cuisine: SOUTHWESTERN. **Reservations:** Highly recommended.
$ Prices: Appetizers $4.50–$11; main courses $14–$20. AE, DC, MC, V.
Open: Dinner only, daily 6–10pm.

You'll find 8700 in an office complex at the corner of East Pinnacle Peak Road and Pima Road, 20 minutes north of downtown Scottsdale. The restaurant has a large lounge and balcony seating area on the second floor, where the views are worth coming early to enjoy. However, it's the creative cuisine and artistic surroundings that keep people coming back. When you first arrive you can pick up a brochure that tells you about all the original artwork that's on display in the restaurant. Of particular interest are the paintings by Elmry de Hory, who specialized in duplicating the style of famous artists. Meals are presented with the same artistic flair in this genteel atmosphere, and the desserts in particular are veritable works of art. Though much of the menu is southwestern in slant, there is also a very definite leaning toward Italian flavorings and combinations. For a starter I'm partial to the tapas of applewood-

FROMMER'S COOL FOR KIDS:
RESTAURANTS

Ed Debevic's *(see p. 78)* This classic 1950s diner is full of cool stuff, including little jukeboxes in the booths. You can tell your kids about hanging out in places like this when you were a teenager.

Pinnacle Peak Patio *(see p. 81)* Way out in north Scottsdale, this restaurant is a Wild West steakhouse complete with cowboys, shootouts, hayrides, and live western music nightly.

Rustler's Rooste *(see p. 78)* Similar to Pinnacle Peak, but closer in, Rustler's Rooste has a slide from the lounge to the main dining room, a big patio for cookouts and play, and live cowboy bands nightly. See if you can get your kids to try the rattlesnake appetizer—it tastes like chicken.

smoked salmon, cilantro pesto and goat cheese on toasted croutons, roast garlic, and roasted peppers. If you don't mind fruit and fish in combination, you may enjoy the grilled salmon with pineapple, melon, and date salsa. Less adventurous diners may want to stick to the likes of charred and braised baby back ribs or the quesadilla Maricopa, which consists of a flour tortilla stuffed with pork, chicken, fontina cheese, scallions, roasted tomato, and fresh herbs.

EL CHORRO LODGE, 5550 E. Lincoln Dr. Tel. 948-5170.
Cuisine: CONTINENTAL. **Reservations:** Highly recommended.
$ Prices: Full dinners $12–$24. AE, CB, DC, DISC, MC, V.
Open: Lunch Mon–Fri 11am–3pm; breakfast/lunch Sat 9am–3pm; dinner daily 6–11pm; brunch Sun 9am–3pm.

Built in 1934 as a school for girls and converted to a lodge and restaurant 3 years later, El Chorro Lodge is a valley landmark set on its own 22 acres of desert. At night spotlights shine on the palo verdes and cacti and the restaurant takes on a timeless tranquility. The adobe building houses several dining rooms, but the patio, with its crackling fireplace, is the place to sit. On the way in from the parking lot you'll pass a quarter-size bronze statue of a cowboy stopping stampeding longhorns. Both decor and menu offerings are traditional, with such classic dishes as chateaubriand and rack of lamb. In addition to the old favorites there are several dishes that are low in salt and fat. Regardless of what you order for a main course, be sure to save room for one of El Chorro's legendary sticky buns.

LA CHAUMIERE, 6910 Main St. Tel. 946-5115.
Cuisine: FRENCH. **Reservations:** Recommended.
$ Prices: Appetizers $4–$8; main courses $12–$15. AE, DC, MC, V.
Open: Daily 11am–11pm.

S Set amid a shady garden of palms and ficuses, La Chaumière is a French country inn in downtown Scottsdale. A white rail fence surrounds the property and inside the main dining rooms there are antique farm and kitchen implements on the paneled walls. If all this sounds too un-Arizona to you, rest assured that there is also a glass-enclosed garden room and an open-air patio for enjoying the warm desert nights. A jazz pianist provides a touch of sophistication to the evening. This is hearty country French cooking at its best, with a few unexpected dishes tucked into the menu. Warm goat cheese on ratatouille is my favorite starter here; the pungent goat cheese is complemented by the fresh flavor of the vegetables. If they have Dover sole on the night of your visit, count yourself lucky and indulge. Otherwise the New York steak sautéed with peppercorns, cognac, and cream is a knockout. Dinners come with a crispy fresh salad and perfectly cooked vegetables, but no French meal of this type would be complete without ordering a side of french fries. Though the fresh-fruit tarts are colorful and not too sweet, I'm partial to the crème brûlée for dessert.

MANCUSO'S, at the Borgata, 6166 N. Scottsdale Rd. Tel. 948-9988.
Cuisine: ITALIAN/CONTINENTAL. **Reservations:** Recommended.
$ Prices: Appetizers $4.50–$59; pastas $13–$17; main courses $15–$23. AE, CB, DC, DISC, MC, V.
Open: Dinner only, daily 5–10pm.

★ The Borgata is built in the style of a medieval European village with ramparts, towers, stone walls, and narrow, uneven alleyways leading through the complex. When you reach your castle banquet hall for a repast of gourmet Italian cuisine, a pianist will be playing soft jazz (alas, no Gregorian chants) amid a soaring ceiling, stone walls, arched windows, and huge roof beams (which make the restaurant seem far larger than it really is). If you lack the means to start your meal with the beluga caviar, perhaps carpaccio di manzo, sliced raw beef with mustard sauce and capers, will do. Although there is an extensive selection of main courses, including an entire page of veal dishes, I find it difficult to get past the pasta offerings. Mancuso's serves no fewer than 10 different types in 16 different sauces. If you want something other than pasta, there are dozens of meat and seafood dishes all perfectly prepared. Flawless service will have you feeling like royalty by the time you finish your dessert and coffee.

MODERATE

JEAN-CLAUDE'S PETIT CAFE, 7340 E. Shoeman Lane. Tel. 947-5288.
Cuisine: FRENCH. **Reservations:** Highly recommended.
$ Prices: Appetizers $5–$7; main courses $7–$11 at lunch, $13–$18 at dinner. AE, CB, DC, MC, V.
Open: Lunch Mon–Sat 11:30am–2:30pm; dinner Mon–Sat 6–10pm.

⑤ It's small and quiet, and those who know about it prefer to keep it a secret. Shoeman Lane runs parallel to Camelback Road east of Scottsdale Road, and you'll find the restaurant a few blocks east of the latter road. There are several small dining rooms, the nicest of which overlook the lighted fountain in the courtyard. Other than this little fountain, there's nothing in the simple decor to distract you from the well-prepared French food. All the favorites of the French kitchen are here—escargots bourguignons, pâté, Brie with apples and pears—but for an hors d'ouevre you can't miss with the steamed mussels in a cream sauce liberally sprinkled with fennel seeds. For a main dish, try the fragrant grilled loin of lamb with rosemary-and-ginger sauce or poached trout stuffed with seafood mousse in a lobster sauce. Desserts are as tempting as the rest of the menu with crème caramel à l'orange my favorite choice.

LOS OLIVOS, 7328 E. Second St. Tel. 946-2256.
Cuisine: MEXICAN. **Reservations:** Suggested.
$ Prices: Appetizers $4–$7.50; main courses $6–$13.50. AE, CB, DC, DISC, MC, V.
Open: Sun–Thurs 11am–10pm, Fri–Sat 11am–11:30pm.

Mi casa es su casa (My house is your house) is an old Mexican saying that is wholeheartedly embraced by the Corral family who run this Mexican eatery only steps away from the Scottsdale Civic Plaza. At one point there were plans to tear the restaurant down because it didn't fit in with Scottsdale's new image, but such an uproar was raised that the building was preserved. It isn't that the building is of historic interest, but the cast-concrete entryway with its colored-glass panels is an example of Mexican-American folk art. Inside, monster heads hang from the ceiling alongside a chandelier that was made by an uncle. One of the dishes on the menu you might want to try is the colorful Mexican flag, a combination of three enchiladas each covered with a different color sauce.

PINNACLE PEAK PATIO, 10426 E. Jomax Rd. Tel. 967-8082 or 563-5133.
Cuisine: STEAK. **Reservations:** Not necessary.
$ Prices: Main courses $4.50–$21. AE, DISC, MC, V.
Open: Mon–Thurs 4–10pm, Fri–Sat 4–11pm, Sun noon–10pm.

Businessmen beware! Wear a tie into this restaurant and you'll have it cut off and hung from the rafters. The casual dress code is strictly enforced at this Wild West restaurant. A meal at the Pinnacle Peak Patio is more an event than an opportunity to satisfy your hunger. Though you can indulge in mesquite-broiled steaks (they even have a 2-pound porterhouse monster) with all the traditional trimmings, the real draw here is all the free Wild West entertainment—gunfights, cowboy bands, two-stepping, cookouts.

You'll find Pinnacle Peak Patio about 20 minutes north of downtown Scottsdale up in the hills overlooking the valley. To get there, take Scottsdale Road north to Pinnacle Peak Road, turn right and continue to Pima Road where you turn left. At this point just follow the signs.

TEMPE

HOUSE OF TRICKS, 114 E. Seventh St. Tel. 968-1114.
Cuisine: SOUTHWESTERN/INTERNATIONAL. **Reservations:** Suggested.
$ Prices: Appetizers $6.50–$7; main courses $11.75–$12.50. AE, CB, DC, DISC, MC, V.
Open: Mon 11am–4pm, Tues–Fri 11am–9pm, Sat 5–9pm.

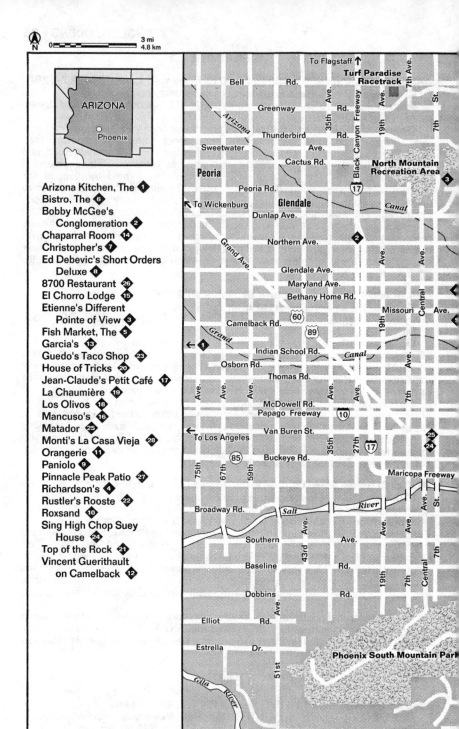

Arizona Kitchen, The ●1
Bistro, The ◆6
Bobby McGee's
  Conglomeration ◆2
Chaparral Room ◆14
Christopher's ◆7
Ed Debevic's Short Orders
  Deluxe ◆8
8700 Restaurant ◆26
El Chorro Lodge ◆15
Etienne's Different
  Pointe of View ◆3
Fish Market, The ◆5
Garcia's ◆13
Guedo's Taco Shop ◆23
House of Tricks ◆20
Jean-Claude's Petit Café ◆17
La Chaumière ◆19
Los Olivos ◆18
Mancuso's ◆16
Matador ◆25
Monti's La Casa Vieja ◆28
Orangerie ◆11
Paniolo ◆9
Pinnacle Peak Patio ◆27
Richardson's ◆4
Rustler's Rooste ◆22
Roxsand ◆10
Sing High Chop Suey
  House ◆24
Top of the Rock ◆21
Vincent Guerithault
  on Camelback ◆12

S Arizona State University is surrounded by neighborhoods of old Craftsmen bungalows and in one of them is the area's trendiest restaurant. There are only a few tables inside the tiny dining room, which has a cozy fireplace, and slightly more outside on the patio. The clientele tends to be students and professors who know a good value when they taste it. The menu changes regularly and consists of a single page of salads, appetizers, and main dishes, all of which are tempting. On my last visit, the roast poblano chile stuffed with corn, cheese, and herbs came with two creamy sauces that were so good I had to order extra bread to sop them up. Mint marinated flank steak with black beans and curry-and-tomato salsa was an unusual combination of flavors that worked well. Grilled pork tenderloin with sautéed figs and red onions was another surprising, but delicious, pairing.

MONTI'S LA CASA VIEJA, 3 W. First St. Tel. 967-7594.
   Cuisine: AMERICAN. **Reservations:** Suggested.
$ **Prices:** Appetizers $3–$6.25; main courses $6–$23. AE, CB, DC, DISC, MC, V.
   Open: Sun–Thurs 11am–11pm, Fri–Sat 11am–midnight.
If you're tired of the glitz and glamor of the Valley of the Sun and are looking for Old Arizona, head down to the corner of Mill Avenue and First Street in Tempe to Monti's La Casa Vieja. The name means "the old house" in Spanish and that's exactly what this building is. The adobe building was constructed in 1871 on the site of the Salt River ferry, in the days when the Salt River flowed year round and Tempe was nothing more than a ferry crossing. Today local families who have been in Phoenix for generations know Monti's well and rely on the restaurant for solid meals and low prices. You can get a filet mignon for under $10, even less when it's the Monday-night special. Dining rooms are dark and filled with memorabilia of the Old west.

CHANDLER

GUEDO'S TACO SHOP, 71 E. Chandler Blvd. Tel. 899-7841.
   Cuisine: MEXICAN. **Reservations:** Not accepted.
$ **Prices:** Main dishes $1.35–$1.80. No credit cards.
   Open: Tues–Sat 11am–9pm.
✪ I have friends who will drive 40 miles to eat at Guedo's. The freshness of the ingredients and the authenticity of the recipes here have made this place the best little taco house in Phoenix. There are no piles of tasteless rice or beans, **S** just whatever you order, so be sure to order at least two dishes—three if you're hungry. Wash it all down with fresh *horchata,* a creamy drink made from rice and almonds.

SPECIALTY DINING
HOTEL DINING

THE ARIZONA KITCHEN, at the Wigwam Resort, W. Indian School Rd., Litchfield Park. Tel. 935-3811, ext. 1424.
   Cuisine: SOUTHWESTERN. **Reservations:** Highly recommended.
$ **Prices:** Appetizers $6–$11.50; main courses $11–$27. AE, CB, DC, DISC, MC, V.
   Open: Dinner only, daily 5–10pm.
It's a long way out to Litchfield Park and the Wigwam Resort, but if you have succumbed to the spicy flavors of southwestern cuisine and want to taste some of the best, you won't mind the drive. In the Arizona Kitchen the Wigwam's southwestern ambience takes the guise of a blue-and-white tiled exhibition kitchen in a dining room paved with bricks and filled with Spanish colonial-style furnishings. Here you'll find true regional offerings. Don't miss the opportunity to sample the traditional mainstay of the Hopi diet, piki bread. This paper-thin cornmeal bread is served with chicken molé vanilla-bean sauce. Rattlesnake fritters are another specialty. Be sure to start your meal with the silky butternut squash and black-bean soup, which is not only visually striking but rich and creamy. Though the main dishes are almost all in the over-$20 range, you can order an innovative pizza for half as much. These pizzas are made with a jalapeño-and-corn fried bread crust. Venison makes an appearance on

the menu accompanied by braised nopale cactus and black muscat and pink peppercorn sauce.

CHAPARRAL ROOM, in the Camelback Inn, 5402 E. Lincoln Dr. Tel. 948-1700 or 948-6644.
  Cuisine: CONTINENTAL. **Reservations:** Required.
$ Prices: Appetizers $8–$11; main courses $23–$30. AE, CB, DC, DISC, MC, V.
  Open: Dinner only, Sun–Thurs 6–10pm, Fri–Sat 6–11pm.

The Camelback Inn has been around since 1936, and ever since opening its doors, it has been known as the home of some of the valley's finest restaurants. The Chaparral Room is possibly the most consistently reliable continental restaurant in the valley. The decor is southwestern, with a view of Camelback Mountain through the curving glass wall and a carved silhouette of the mountain on the back of each chair. Tableside cooking is one of the specialties of the house, so be sure to ask your waiter what you can have cooked at your table. The menu features a balanced mixture of exquisitely prepared old standards and nouvelle offerings displaying the chef's creative flair. Cherrywood-smoked shrimp hors d'oeuvres are served with a mild papaya chutney that doesn't overpower the flavor of the shrimp. For a bit of culinary showmanship, try the wilted-spinach salad, which is prepared and flamed at your table. The chateaubri-and is tender and juicy with a creamy béarnaise sauce, while the Muscovy duck with a passionfruit sauce offers adventurous diners an unusual combination of flavors.

DINING WITH A VIEW

ETIENNE'S DIFFERENT POINTE OF VIEW, at the Pointe at Tapatio Cliffs, 11111 N. Seventh St. Tel. 866-7500, ext. 7200.
  Cuisine: FRENCH. **Reservations:** Highly recommended.
$ Prices: Appetizers $6.50–$12.50; main courses $22–$30. AE, CB, DC, DISC, MC, V.
  Open: Dinner only, Tues–Thurs 6:30–10pm, Fri–Sat 6–10pm.

For a view of the valley from the north, Étienne's is the place. In fact, you can enjoy two different views if you arrive early enough to have a drink in the lounge. The lounge faces north and the restaurant faces south, but both have curving walls of glass that let in sweeping vistas of the city, mountains, and the desert. The building is built right into the top of the mountain, with the entry walk passing between walls of rock. (the road to the restaurant is incredibly steep, so I advise leaving your car at the bottom of the hill and taking the free shuttle up to the front door). The restaurant has all the glimmer and glitz of Las Vegas, and there's even dancing and a Vegas-style floor show each night. However, despite the excellent food, award-winning wine list, and live entertainment, it's still the view that's the star of the show here. If you can't afford dinner, you can still stop by for a drink in the lounge.

TOP OF THE ROCK, at the Buttes, 2000 Westcourt Way, Tempe. Tel. 225-9000.
  Cuisine: SOUTHWESTERN. **Reservations:** Recommended.
$ Prices: Appetizers $7–$9; main courses $8.50–$11 at lunch, $15–$25 at dinner. AE, CB, DC, DISC, MC, V.
  Open: Lunch Mon–Fri 11am–3pm; dinner Mon–Thurs 5–11pm, Fri–Sat 5pm–midnight, Sun 5:30–11pm; brunch Sun 10am–2pm.

All the best views in Phoenix are from the resorts and their restaurants, so if you want to dine with a view of the valley, you're going to have to pay the price. Luckily, quality accompanies the high prices, and here at the Top of the Rock in the stunning setting of the Buttes resort, you can enjoy creative southwestern cuisine. There is no question as to which appetizer to order on your first visit: Get the appetizer assortment so you can sample such delicacies as scallops sautéed in passionfruit, orange, and tarragon; spicy shrimp; marinated duck glazed with red chili sauce; and peperred tenderloin. The breast of chicken soaked in prickly-pear-cactus marinade, topped with melted herbed-havarti cheese, and accompanied by a roasted-pepper and sweet-corn beurre blanc was both an unusual and a delicious dish. Even if you aren't familiar with southwestern cuisine, you'll find the margarita duck breast extremely

❷ DID YOU KNOW . . . ?

- The Phoenix metropolitan area has more than 100 major golf courses and more than 1,000 tennis courts.
- Phoenix is home to more Mobile five-star resorts than any other city in the country.
- Phoenix is the eighth-largest metropolitan area in the U.S.
- The Valley of the Sun hosts the spring training camps of eight major-league baseball teams: the Oakland As, San Francisco Giants, Chicago Cubs, Milwaukee Brewers, Seattle Mariners, Cleveland Indians, California Angels, and San Diego Padres.
- Phoenix is home to the world's largest indoor sand sculpture display; it's in the Chris-town Shopping Center.
- Each year Phoenix enjoys sunshine during 86% of all daylight hours, for a total of 300 to 315 sunny days.
- Phoenix was founded on the site of an ancient Hohokam village and received its name from an early British settler who predicted that a great city would rise from the ruins of the prehistoric village just as the phoenix of ancient mythology rises from its own ashes every 500 years.

flavorful and succulent; it's served with a tequila-lime glaze. In addition to the regular menu there are also nightly specials, and don't overlook the fact that lunch is half the price of dinner and you get a daytime view of the valley.

BREAKFAST/BRUNCH

Most of Phoenix's best Sunday brunches are to be had at the major hotels, including the Arizona Biltmore, Camelback Inn, Hyatt Regency Scottsdale, Sheraton Phoenix, Hotel Westcourt, the Wigwam, and the Wyndham Paradise Valley Resort.

5. ATTRACTIONS

SUGGESTED ITINERARIES

IF YOU HAVE 1 DAY Head downtown to the Heard Museum and Pueblo Grande Museum and Ruins. After lunch, visit the Desert Botanical Gardens, then cross town to Scottsdale for some shopping in old Scottsdale. Have dinner at a restaurant with a view of the valley.

IF YOU HAVE 2 DAYS Spend your first day as suggested above. On the second day, early in the morning hike up one of the Phoenix mountains (Squaw Peak, Mummy Mountain, Camelback Mountain), and afterward visit the Phoenix Art Museum. In the afternoon, head out to north Scottsdale to the Desert Foothills Drive to see a bit more of the desert. Have dinner at Pinnacle Peak Patio for a bit of western kitsch along with your steak.

IF YOU HAVE 3 DAYS Spend your first 2 days as suggested above. On Day 3, drive north from Phoenix to the Pioneer Arizona Living History Museum to see what life was like in Arizona 100 years ago, and then continue north to Arcosanti to see what life would be like in Paolo Soleri's future. In the late afternoon, go for a horseback ride in the desert. Eat dinner at a restaurant serving southwestern cuisine.

IF YOU HAVE 5 DAYS OR MORE For the first 3 days, follow the suggestions above. On Days 4 and 5, take an overnight trip out from Phoenix. Two days is enough time to visit the Grand Canyon, or Sedona and Oak Creek Canyon, or some of the mountain scenery in eastern Arizona, or one of the lakes on the Colorado River.

THE TOP ATTRACTIONS

ARIZONA STATE UNIVERSITY ART MUSEUM, Nelson Fine Arts Center, 10th St. and Mill Ave., Tempe. Tel. 965-ARTS.

Though it isn't very large, the Arizona State University Art Museum is memorable for its innovative architecture. The building, stark and angular, captures the colors of sunset on desert mountains with its purplish-gray stucco facade and pyramidal shape. The museum entrance is down a flight of stairs that lead to a cool underground garden area. Inside are galleries for crafts, prints, contemporary art, American artists, a temporary exhibition gallery, and two outdoor sculpture courts. The museum's collection of works by American artists includes works by Georgia O'Keeffe, Edward Hopper, and Frederic Remington. On Sunday there is a free public tour at 1:15pm. The Mathews Center, at the corner of Cady and Taylor malls, is also part of the museum and contains Latin American art, American ceramics, South Pacific and African art, folk art, and a whimsical collection of animal figures known as the ASU zoo.

Admission: Free.

Open: Mon–Fri 8:30am–4:30pm, Sat 10am–4pm, Sun 1–5pm. **Closed:** Major hols. **Bus:** 2.

DESERT BOTANICAL GARDEN, 1201 N. Galvin Pkwy. Tel. 941-1225.

✪ Devoted exclusively to cacti and other desert plants, the Desert Botanical Garden is adjacent to the Phoenix Zoo and Papago Park. There are more than 10,000 desert plants from all over the world on display throughout the different sections of the garden. The most fascinating section of the garden is the "Plants and People of the Sonoran Desert" trail. This trail explains the science of ethnobotany through interactive displays that demonstrate how the inhabitants of the Sonoran Desert once utilized wild and cultivated plants. You can practice grinding corn and pounding mesquite beans, make a yucca-fiber brush, and examine the type of dwelling once built by the local Hohokam tribe.

Admission: $4 adults, $3.50 senior citizens, $1 children 5–12, free for children under 5.

Open: Sept–May, daily 9am–sunset; June–Aug, daily 8am–sunset. **Closed:** Dec 25. **Bus:** 3.

HEARD MUSEUM, 22 E. Monte Vista Rd. Tel. 252-8848.

✪ Considered one of the finest museums in the country that deals exclusively with Native American cultures, the Heard Museum should be among your first stops in Arizona. "Native Peoples of the Southwest" is an extensive exhibit that explores the culture of each of the major tribes of the region. Included in the exhibit are a Navajo hogan, an Apache wickiup, and a Hopi corn-grinding room. A large kachina gallery will give you an idea of the number of different kachina spirits that populate the Hopi and Zuñi religions. "Our Voices, Our Land" is an audiovisual presentation in which contemporary Native Americans express their thoughts on their heritage. "Old Ways, New Ways" is an unusual interactive exhibit that is aimed at children, but is interesting to adults as well. You can join a drumming group on a video, duplicate a Northwest tribal design, or design a Navajo rug. On weekends there are performances by Native American singers and dancers, and during the week, artists demonstrate their art forms.

The biggest event of the year is the annual Annual Guild Indian Fair & Market, which is held on the first weekend in March and includes numerous performances of traditional dances as well as arts and crafts demonstrations and sales.

There are guided tours of the museum daily. September through May they are held Monday through Saturday at noon, 1:30pm, and 3pm, and on Sunday at 1:30 and 3pm. June through August, they are held Monday through Friday at 1:30pm, on Saturday at 11am, 1:30, and 3pm, and on Sunday at 1:30 and 3pm.

Admission: $4 adults, $3 senior citizens, $2 college students, $1 children age 7–17, free for Native Americans and children 6 and under.

Open: Mon–Sat 10am–5pm, Sun noon–5pm. **Closed:** First Mon in Mar and some hols. **Bus:** 0.

PHOENIX ART MUSEUM, 1625 N. Central Ave. Tel. 257-1222.

The Phoenix Art Museum is the largest art museum in the Southwest and has a very respectable collection that spans the major artistic movements from the Renaissance to the present. The collection of modern and contemporary art is particularly good, with works by Diego Rivera, Frida Kahlo, Pablo Picasso, Karel Appel, Willem de Kooning, Alexander Calder, Henry Moore, Georgia O'Keeffe, Henri Rousseau, and Auguste Rodin. The large first-floor gallery is used for special exhibits including major touring retrospectives. The Thorne Miniature Collection is one of the museum's most popular exhibits and consists of tiny rooms on a scale of 1 inch to 1 foot. The rooms are exquisitely detailed right down to the leaded-glass windows of an English lodge kitchen. Other exhibits include historic fashions in a gallery used by the Arizona Costume Institute, a large collection of Asian art, Spanish colonial furnishings and religious art, and of course, a western American exhibit featuring works by members of the Cowboy Artists of America. Tours of the museum are offered Tuesday through Sunday at 1:30pm and on Wednesday also at 7pm.

Admission: $3 adults, $2.50 senior citizens, $1.50 students and children 6–12, free for children under 6.

Open: Tues and Thurs–Sat 10am–5pm, Wed 10am–9pm, Sun noon–5pm. **Bus:** 0.

PUEBLO GRANDE MUSEUM AND CULTURAL PARK, 4619 E. Washington St. Tel. 495-0900.

Located not far from the Sky Harbor Airport and downtown Phoenix, the Pueblo Grande Museum and Cultural Park houses the ruins of an ancient Hohokam tribal village. This was one of several villages located along the Salt River between A.D. 300 and 1400. Sometime around 1450, this and other villages were mysteriously abandoned. One speculation is that drought and a buildup of salts from irrigation water reduced the fertility of the soil and forced the people to leave their homes and seek more fertile lands. Before touring the grounds to view the partially excavated ruins, you can walk through the small museum, which exhibits many of the artifacts that have been dug up on the site. There are also changing exhibits focusing on different aspects of ancient and contemporary Native American cultures. On a recent visit there was a fascinating photographic exhibit on the use of petroglyphs and pictographs as astronomical observations.

Admission: 50¢.

Open: Mon–Sat 9am–4:45pm, Sun 1–4:45pm. **Closed:** Major hols. **Bus:** 1.

MORE ATTRACTIONS

HISTORIC BUILDINGS/MONUMENTS

HERITAGE SQUARE, 115 N. Sixth St., at Monroe. Tel. 262-5029.

Though the city of Phoenix was founded as recently as 1870, much of its history has been obliterated. Heritage Square is a collection of some of the few remaining houses in Phoenix that date to the last century and the original Phoenix townsite. All the buildings here are listed on the National Register of Historic Places and most display Victorian architectural styles popular just before the turn of the century. Among the buildings on Heritage Square are the ornate **Rosson House,** which is open for tours; the **Silva House,** a neoclassical-revival-style home that now houses historical exhibits on water and electricity use in the Valley of the Sun; the **Burgess Carriage House,** which houses the Arizona Historical Society gift shop; the **Bouvier-Teter House,** an 1899 bungalow that houses the Heritage Café; and the **Arizona Doll and Toy Museum,** housed in a 1912 schoolhouse.

Admission: Rosson House tours, $3 adults, $2 senior citizens and children 6–13, free for children under 6.

Open: Wed–Sat 10am–4pm, Sun noon–4pm (shorter hours in summer). **Closed:** Arizona Doll and Toy Museum, Aug. **Bus:** 1 or 2.

ARIZONA STATE CAPITOL MUSEUM, 1700 W. Washington St. Tel. 542-4675.

In the years before Arizona became a state, the territorial capital moved from Prescott to Tucson, then back to Prescott, and finally to Phoenix. In 1898 a stately territorial capitol building was erected with a copper roof to remind the local citizenry of the importance of that metal in the Arizona economy. A statue of *Winged Victory* stands atop the polished copper dome of the capitol building, while inside there are portraits of the state's governors. This museum no longer serves as the actual state capitol, but has recently been restored to its original appearance in 1912, the year Arizona became a state. Among the rooms on view are the senate and house chambers, as well as the governor's office and historical exhibits.

Admission: Free.
Open: Mon–Fri 8am–5pm. **Bus:** 1.

 FROMMER'S FAVORITE
PHOENIX EXPERIENCES

Hiking on Camelback Mountain Hiking up to the top of Camelback Mountain very early on Sunday morning is a tradition among the city's more active residents, including the mayor.

Dinner with a View There is something quite bewitching about gazing down at the twinkling lights of the city while enjoying a delicious meal at one of Phoenix's many restaurants, priced for all pocketbooks.

Lounging by the Pool Nothing is more relaxing than lounging by the pool and gazing up at the desert mountains from one of Phoenix's or Scottsdale's world-class resorts.

Tubing down the Salt River The best way to see the desert is from an inner tube . . . floating down a river. A few companies provide inner tubes and shuttles.

Scottsdale Art Walk Thursday evenings from October to May is the chance for dilettantes and connoisseurs to visit nearly 60 art galleries in downtown Scottsdale, often with complimentary refreshments and artists on hand.

Spring Training Baseball Games Get a headstart on all your fellow baseball fans by going to a spring-training game while you're in Phoenix.

MUSEUMS/GALLERIES

ARIZONA MUSEUM OF SCIENCE AND TECHNOLOGY, 80 N. Second St. Tel. 256-9388.

Aimed primarily at children, the Arizona Museum of Science and Technology is a hands-on museum with more than 100 interactive exhibits. You can walk inside a giant camera obscura, conduct electricity with your own body, or build an arch. There are frequent physics and chemistry demonstrations, and a small collection of reptiles. Throughout the year there are different traveling exhibits on display. For several years the museum has been in the process of constructing and moving to a new building on Washington Street between Fifth Street and Seventh Street. Be sure to call first to find out if they have made the final move and reopened at the new location.

Admission: $4.50 adults, $3.50 senior citizens and children 4–12, free for children under 4.
Open: Mon–Sat 9am–5pm, Sun noon–5pm. **Bus:** 1, 2, or 8.

CHAMPLIN FIGHTER MUSEUM, 4636 Fighter Aces Dr., Mesa. Tel. 830-4540.

This aeronautical museum is dedicated exclusively to fighter planes and the men who flew them. Aircraft from World Wars I and II, the Korean War, and the Vietnam War are on display, with a strong emphasis on the wood-and-fabric biplanes and triplanes of World War I. There are several Sopwiths and Fokkers. From World War II, there are a Grumman Hellcat, a Grumman Wildcat, a Spitfire, a Messerschmitt, and a Goodyear Corsair. Jet fighters from more recent battles include a MiG-15, a MiG-17, and an F4 Phantom. In addition to the restored fighter planes, there is memorabilia of famous flying fighter aces.

Admission: $5 adults, $2.50 children 14 and under.
Open: Daily 10am–5pm.

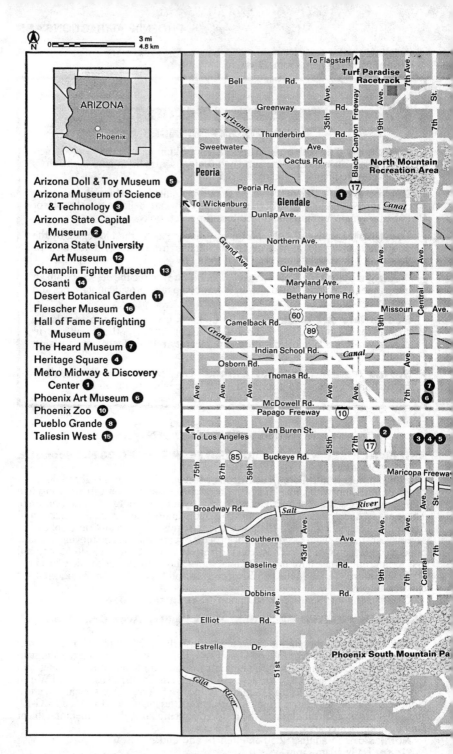

0 ____ 3 mi
         4.8 km

ARIZONA

Phoenix

Arizona Doll & Toy Museum ⑤
Arizona Museum of Science
  & Technology ③
Arizona State Capital
  Museum ②
Arizona State University
  Art Museum ⑫
Champlin Fighter Museum ⑬
Cosanti ⑭
Desert Botanical Garden ⑪
Fleischer Museum ⑯
Hall of Fame Firefighting
  Museum ⑨
The Heard Museum ⑦
Heritage Square ④
Metro Midway & Discovery
  Center ①
Phoenix Art Museum ⑥
Phoenix Zoo ⑩
Pueblo Grande ⑧
Taliesin West ⑮

To Flagstaff ↑
Turf Paradise Racetrack

Bell   Rd.
Greenway   Rd.
Arizona
Thunderbird   Rd.
Sweetwater   Ave.
Cactus Rd.   North Mountain Recreation Area
Peoria
Peoria Rd.   ①
Glendale   Canal
To Wickenburg
Dunlap Ave.
Grand Ave.
Northern Ave.
Glendale Ave.
Maryland Ave.
Bethany Home Rd.
Missouri   Ave.
Central
Camelback Rd.   (60)
Grand   (89)
Indian School Rd.   Canal
Osborn Rd.
Thomas Rd.
Ave.   7th   ⑦ ⑥
McDowell Rd.
Papago Freeway   (10)
Van Buren St.   ②   ③④⑤
To Los Angeles   35th   27th   (17)
(85)   Buckeye Rd.
75th   67th   59th   Maricopa Freeway
Broadway Rd.   Salt   River   Ave.   St.
Southern   Ave.   Ave.
43rd
Baseline   Rd.   19th   7th   Central
Dobbins   Rd.
Elliot   Rd.
Estrella   Dr.   Phoenix South Mountain Pa
51st
Gila River

PHOENIX ATTRACTIONS

Cave Creek Rd.
Bell Rd.
Greenway Rd.
Frank Lloyd Wright Blvd.
Thunderbird
Paradise Valley Mall
Sweetwater
Cactus
Shea Blvd.
32nd St.
56th St.
Invergordon
Scottsdale
Hayden Rd.
Pima Rd.
96th St.
104th St.
Shea Blvd.
Ave.
Tatum Blvd.
Doubletree Ranch Rd.
Dreamy Draw Recreation Area
Paradise Valley
Squaw Peak Recreation Area
Lincoln Dr.
Indian Bend Rd.
McDonald Dr.
64th St.
Pima Rd.
To Payson
Camelback Rd.
Indian School Rd.
Beeline Hwy.
Osborn Rd.
51
40th St.
44th St.
56th St.
Thomas Rd.
Scottsdale
Miller
Hayden
McDowell Rd.
Dobson Rd.
48th St.
52nd St.
Papago Park
68th St.
Scottsdale
Van Buren St.
McKellips Rd.
Mesa
Sky Harbor International Airport
Salt River
Club Dr.
143
Hohokam Expy.
Priest Dr.
Tempe
Mill Ave.
Apache Blvd.
University
60
89
Country Club Rd.
Mesa Dr.
Main St.
Stapley Dr.
Broadway
10
24th St.
32nd St.
Southern Ave.
360
Superstition Freeway
Baseline Rd.
Guadalupe Rd.
Elliot Rd.
Rural Dr.
McClintock Dr.
Price Rd.
Dobson Rd.
School Rd.
Alma
Arizona Ave.
McQueen Rd.
Cooper Rd.
Gilbert Rd.
10
Warner Rd.
Ray Rd.
87
Chandler Blvd.
To Tucson
Williams Field Rd.
Pecos Rd.
Airport

FLEISCHER MUSEUM, in the Perimeter Center, 17207 N. Perimeter Dr., Scottsdale. Tel. 585-3108.

This is the only museum in the U.S. devoted exclusively to the California school of American impressionism, which drew extensively on French impressionist styles, and holds a quiet place in American art history.

Admission: Free.

Open: Daily 10am–4pm. **Closed:** Major hols.

HALL OF FLAME FIREFIGHTING MUSEUM, 6101 E. Van Buren St. Tel. ASK-FIRE.

The world's largest firefighting museum houses a fascinating collection of vintage fire trucks. The displays date back to an 1855 hand-pumper from Philadelphia, but also includes several class fire engines from the early part of this century. All are beautifully restored and, of course, fire-engine red. In all there are more than 100 vehicles on display.

Admission: $3 adults, $2 senior citizens, $1 children 6–17, free for children under 6.

Open: Mon–Sat 9am–5pm. **Closed:** Jan 1, Thanksgiving, and Dec 25. **Bus:** 3.

PARKS & GARDENS

PHOENIX ZOO, 5810 E. Van Buren St. Tel. 273-7771.

Home to more than 1,200 animals, the Phoenix Zoo, which is adjacent to Papago Park in central Arizona, is known for its 4-acre African veldt exhibit and its baboon colony. The southwestern animal exhibits are also of particular interest. All the animals in the zoo are kept in naturalistic enclosures and can be viewed from a train that makes a 30-minute circuit of the grounds. Narrators aboard the train explain each exhibit. Kids will love the 11-acre children's zoo, where they can see baby animals and pet some of the more friendly residents.

Admission: $6 adults, $3 children 4–12, free for children 3 and under.

Open: May–Labor Day, daily 7am–4pm; Labor Day–Apr, daily 9am–5pm. **Bus:** 3.

COOL FOR KIDS

ARIZONA DOLL & TOY MUSEUM, 602 E. Adams St. Tel. 253-9337.

Located in the Stevens house on Heritage Square in downtown Phoenix, the Arizona Doll & Toy Museum is as interesting to adults as it is to kids. There is a 1912 schoolroom display in which the children are all antique dolls.

Admission: Free.

Open: May 29–July, Tues–Sat 10am–3pm, Sun 11am–3pm; Sept–May 28, Tues–Sat 10am–4pm, Sun noon–4pm. **Closed:** Aug. **Bus:** 1, 2, 7, or 16.

METRO MIDWAY & DISCOVERY CENTER, Metrocenter, 9615 Metro Pkwy. W. Tel. 997-6900.

Inside the largest regional shopping mall in the Southwest, your kids will discover 300 arcade and video games that give this amusement center the feel of a county fair. There's even a carousel for the youngest. The Discovery Center is an interactive science learning center with 40 displays that kids can manipulate to help them understand scientific principles. Other fun facilities include a kid-size bank and grocery store.

Admission: Free.

Open: Metro Midway, Sun–Thurs 9am–10pm, Fri–Sat 9am–1am; Discovery Center, daily 10am–6pm. **Bus:** 3.

SPECIAL-INTEREST SIGHTSEEING

FOR THE ARCHITECTURE BUFF

COSANTI, 6433 Doubletree Ranch Rd., Scottsdale. Tel. 948-6145.

This complex of cast-concrete structures served as a prototype and learning

project for architect Paolo Soleri's much grander Arcosanti project, which is under construction north of Phoenix (see "Easy Excursions from Phoenix," below, for details). It is here at Cosanti that Soleri's famous bells are cast.
Admission: $1 donation.
Open: Daily 9am–5pm. **Closed:** Major hols.

TALIESIN WEST, 180th St., Scottsdale. Tel. 860-2700.
Architect Frank Lloyd Wright fell in love with the Arizona desert and in 1937 opened a winter camp here that served as his office and school. Today Taliesin West is the headquarters of the Frank Lloyd Wright Foundation and School of Architecture. Tours offer a general-background introduction to Wright and his theories of architecture and the buildings of this campus. Wright believed in using local materials in his designs and this shows up at Taliesin West in the use of local stone for building foundations. Wright developed a number of innovative methods for dealing with the extremes of the desert climate such as sliding wall panels to let in varying amounts of air and light. Architectural students, and anyone interested in the work of Wright, will find the gift shop full of excellent books.
Admission: Oct–May, $10 adults, $8 senior citizens and students, $3 children 4–12, free for children under 4; June–Sept, $6 adults and senior citizens, $3 children 4–12, free for children under 4.
Open: Oct–May, Mon–Thurs 1–4pm, Fri–Sun 9am–4pm; June–Sept, daily 8–11am. **Closed:** Major hols and occasional special events.

ORGANIZED TOURS

There are numerous companies offering guided tours of both the Valley of the Sun and the rest of Arizona. Tours of the valley tend to include only brief stops at highlights. **Gray Line of Phoenix,** 3415 South 36th Street (tel. 602/437-3701, or toll free 800/426-7532), is one of the largest tour companies in the valley. They offer a 5-hour tour of Phoenix and the Valley of the Sun for $20 per adult. The tour points out such local landmarks as the state capitol, downtown Phoenix, the Arizona Biltmore, Barry Goldwater's home, the Wrigley Mansion, and Camelback Mountain. There's also a stop in Scottsdale for lunch and shopping.
Far more popular and more fun are the desert Jeep tours. Though the Pink Jeep tours in Sedona are perhaps the best-known Jeep tours, there are also plenty of options in the Valley of the Sun. **Arizona Desert Jeep Tours,** 10110 East Jenan Drive, Scottsdale (tel. 860-1777), has been leading Jeep tours through the desert for longer than any other company in the valley. Their trips include a bit of six-gun shooting practice, nature walks, and Native American folklore as told by cowboy guides. They'll pick you up at your resort or hotel.

6. SPORTS & RECREATION

SPECTATOR SPORTS

AUTO RACING   At the **Firebird International Raceway Park,** at Maricopa Road and Exit 162A of I-10 (tel. 268-0200), you can see NHRA races and amateur drag racing. At the **Phoenix International Raceway,** 1313 North Second Street (tel. 252-3833), there is NASCAR racing in November and Indy car racing in April on the world's fastest 1-mile oval. Each spring the streets of downtown Phoenix are taken over for the **Phoenix Formula One Grand Prix;** contact the Visitors Bureau for further information.

BASEBALL   The **Phoenix Firebirds** play AAA Pacific Coast League professional ball at Phoenix Municipal Stadium, 5999 East Van Buren Street (tel. 275-0500). This is the farm club of the San Francisco Giants.
In addition, eight major-league baseball teams have their **spring-training camps**

in the Valley of the Sun during March and April. You can catch exhibition games several nights a week.

BASKETBALL   The NBA's **Phoenix Suns,** play at Veteran's Memorial Coliseum, 1826 West McDowell Road (tel. 263-SUNS).

FOOTBALL   The **Phoenix Cardinals,** 8701 South Hardy Road, Tempe (tel. 379-0101), became Phoenix's NFL football team in 1988. Games are played at the Arizona State University's Sun Devil Stadium, which is also home to the **Fiesta Bowl Football Classic.**

GOLF   Among the many PGA tournaments held in the Valley of the Sun, the **Phoenix Open Golf Tournament** in January is the largest. It is held at the Tournament Players Club in Scottsdale.

HORSE/GREYHOUND RACING   The **Phoenix Greyhound Park,** East Washington Street at 40th Street (tel. 273-7181), is one of the nation's premier greyhound tracks. The large fully enclosed and air-conditioned facility offers seating in various grandstands, lounges, and restaurants. There is racing throughout the year.

   Turf Paradise, 1501 West Bell Road (tel. 942-1101), is Phoenix's horse-racing track. The season runs from October to May with post time at 1pm. Admission ranges from $2 for a grandstand seat to $10 for a reserved seat in the Turf Club dining room.

RECREATION

BALLOONING   The still morning air of the Valley of the Sun is perfect for hot-air ballooning, and not surprisingly, there are quite a few companies offering balloon rides around Phoenix. **Aeronautical Adventure,** 10001 North 28th Place (tel. 992-2627), offers daily sunrise flights, and between November and March they also have sunset flights.

BICYCLING   Though the Valley of the Sun is a sprawling place, it's mostly flat, which makes bicycling a breeze as long as it isn't in the heat of summer. **Eagle Bike & Sport,** 8435 East McDonald Road (tel. 951-3675), in Scottsdale, rents bikes and leads escorted tours of the desert and nearby mountains.

FISHING   There are six large lakes in the mountains northeast of Phoenix and all offer good fishing. You'll need to get a fishing license from the Arizona Game & Fish Commission. These licenses are generally available wherever fishing gear is sold. If you prefer to have a professional lead you to where the fish are biting, contact **Neal's Fishing Guide Service,** 8715 East Amelia Avenue (tel. 945-6122), in Scottsdale.

GOLF   With more than 100 courses in the Valley of the Sun, golf is the most popular sport in Phoenix. Many of the golf resorts around the valley are open to the public. You can get more information on Valley of the Sun golf courses from the **Phoenix & Valley of the Sun Convention & Visitors Bureau,** 505 North Second Street, Suite 300, Phoenix, AZ 85004 (tel. 602/254-6500). You can also pick up a copy of the *Arizona Golf Course Directory* for $2.95 at the Visitors Bureau, golf courses, and many hotels and resorts.

HIKING   Mummy Mountain, Camelback Mountain, and Squaw Peak all have a portion of land that is a public park, the largest of which is **Phoenix South Mountain Park,** claimed to be the largest city park in the country. There are many nature, hiking, and horseback-riding trails in South Mountain Park, and the views of Phoenix are spectacular, especially at sunset. To reach the park, simply drive south on Central Avenue.

   Another popular spot for hiking is **Camelback Mountain,** near the boundary between Phoenix and Scottsdale. This is the highest mountain in Phoenix, and the 1.2-mile trail to the summit is very steep. Don't attempt this one in the heat of day, and take at least a quart of water with you. The reward for your effort is the city's finest view. To reach the trailhead for Camelback Mountain, drive up 44th Street until it becomes McDonald Drive, then turn right on 54th Street and continue up the hill until the road ends.

Squaw Peak in the Phoenix Mountains Preserve offers a slightly less strenuous hike and views that are almost as spectacular as those from Camelback Mountain. Squaw Peak is reached from Squaw Peak Drive off Lincoln Drive between 22nd Street and 23rd Street.

Farther afield there are numerous hiking opportunities in the **Superstition Mountains** to the east and the **McDowell Mountains** to the north.

HORSEBACK RIDING There are plenty of places around Phoenix to rent a horse. **South Mountain Stables,** 10005 South Central Avenue (tel. 276-8131), rents horses on an hourly or daily basis and also leads different rides through South Mountain Park. **Ponderosa Stables,** 10215 South Central Avenue (tel. 268-1261), offers similar rates and rides in the same area.

SOARING The thermals that form above the mountains in the Phoenix area are ideal for soaring in a sailplane (glider). **Estrella Sailport,** on Cottonwood Lane in Maricopa (tel. 568-2318), offers sailplane rides as well as instruction.

TENNIS Tennis is second only to golf in popularity in the Valley of the Sun. Most major hotels have a few tennis courts and there are several tennis resorts around the Valley. Some racquet clubs that open their doors to the public include the **City Center Tennis Courts,** 121 East Adams Street (top of the Hyatt Regency Parking Garage), Phoenix (tel. 256-4120); the **Gold Key Racquet & Swim Club,** 12826 North Third Street, Phoenix (tel. 993-1900); the **Jordan Tennis & Racquetball Center,** 9540 North 75th Drive, Peoria (tel. 878-1588); the **Scottsdale Racquet Club,** 8201 East Indian Bend Road, Scottsdale (tel. 948-5990); and the **Waterin' Hole Racquet Club,** Waterin' Hole Complex, 11111 North Seventh Street, Phoenix (tel. 997-7237).

WATER SPORTS A human-made lake at **Arizona Ski Springs,** 537 North McQueen Road, Gilbert (tel. 892-7868), is the site of what promises to be America's next big water-sports craze. Skiers are pulled by an overhead cable system on double or slalom skis, kneeboards, skurfers, shoeskis, or trick skis. Skiing costs $16 for 2 hours, $21 for 4 hours, and $26 for the whole day. They are open daily from 10am to 10pm.

At **Waterworld USA,** 4243 West Pinnacle Peak Road (tel. 266-5299), you can free-fall 6½ stories down the Avalanche speed water slide or catch a gnarly wave in the wave pool. Other water slides offer tamer times. Admission is $10.95 for adults, $8.95 for children 4 to 11. Waterworld is open from Memorial Day to Labor Day, daily from 10:30am to 10pm.

WHITE-WATER RAFTING The desert may not seem like the place for white-water rafting, but when the Salt River isn't completely dry, it offers some exciting rafting. **Desert Voyagers** (tel. 998-RAFT) offers half-day to 4-day trips on the Salt River and the Rio Verde. Prices range from $50 for a half-day float to $375 for the 4-day expedition.

Tamer river trips can be had from **Salt River Recreation** (tel. 984-3305), which has its headquarters 20 miles northeast of Phoenix on the Bush Highway at the intersection with Usery Pass Road in the Tonto National Forest. For $8 they'll rent you a large inner tube and shuttle you by bus upriver.

7. SAVVY SHOPPING

THE SHOPPING SCENE

Phoenix and Scottsdale have long been winter meccas for the moneyed classes, so it's no surprise that the same fashionable shopping establishments you're likely to find in

Beverly Hills, New York, London, and Paris are also here. In addition to these are the many boutiques and shops of local designers who have gained a dedicated following in the Southwest, where a very distinctive style has emerged in recent years.

For the most part, shopping in the valley means malls. They're everywhere and they're air-conditioned, which, I'm sure you'll agree, makes shopping in the desert far more enjoyable than in the 100° heat. Scottsdale and the Biltmore District of Phoenix are the valley's main upscale shopping areas. Old Scottsdale (one of the few outdoor shopping areas) plays host to hundreds of boutiques, galleries, jewelry stores, and Native American crafts stores. The western atmosphere of Old Scottsdale is partly real and partly a figment of the local merchants' imaginations, but nevertheless it's the single most popular tourist shopping area in the valley. It also happens to be the heart of the valley's art market, with dozens of art galleries along Main Street.

SHOPPING A TO Z

ANTIQUES

ARIZONA ANTIQUE GALLERY, 1126 N. Scottsdale Rd., Scottsdale. Tel. 921-3343.

Arizona's largest antiques mall houses 126 dealers selling all manner of antiques and collectibles in a half-acre covered building.

YE OLDE CURIOSITY SHOPPE, 7245 E. First Ave., Scottsdale, Tel. 947-3062.

Since 1959 Ye Olde Curiosity Shoppe has been providing local residents with antiques, dolls, laces, vintage clothing, and more.

ART

LISA SETTE GALLERY, 4142 N. Marshall Way, Scottsdale. Tel. 990-7342.

If you aren't a fan of cowboy or Native American art, you may think that Phoenix has little serious art to offer. Think again, then stop by Lisa Sette. International, national, and local artists all share wall space here, with a wide mix of media represented.

ORTEGA FINE INDIAN ARTS, 7150 E. Fifth Ave., Scottsdale. Tel. 947-8914.

Housed in a two-story adobe-style building on Fifth Avenue, this gallery features only the finest Native American arts, including paintings, baskets, kachinas, pottery, alabaster carvings, and Navajo rugs. You'll also find both contemporary and southwestern paintings, bronzes, ceramics, and art glass.

OVERLAND TRAIL GALLERY, 7155 Main St., Scottsdale. Tel. 947-1934.

Traditional western paintings and sculptures are the specialty of this gallery, where you'll find amazingly detailed bronzes of bucking broncos, wagon trains, longhorn steers, and many other scenes of cowboy life.

TRAILSIDE GALLERIES, 7330 Scottsdale Mall, Scottsdale. Tel. 945-7751.

Western realism, American impressionism, and wildlife art are the specialties of this gallery, which features the work of more than 80 artists.

CRAFTS

MIND'S EYE CRAFT GALLERY, 4200 N. Marshall Way, Scottsdale. Tel. 941-2494.

You'll find the finest contemporary crafts from around the nation at this Scottsdale gallery. There is a distinct emphasis on southwestern craftspeople in the collection of jewelry, ceramics, wood, clothing, paper, and glass.

FASHIONS
Western Wear

BOOT BARN, 2949 N. Scottsdale Rd., Scottsdale. Tel. 946-1381.
These boots are made for walking . . . and riding. Arizona's largest selection of cowboy boots.

SABA'S WESTERN STORES, 7254 Main St., Scottsdale. Tel. 949-7404.
Since 1927 this store has been outfitting Scottsdale's cowboys and cowgirls, visiting dude ranchers, and anyone else who wants to adopt the look of the Wild West.

Women's

CITADEL, 8700 E. Pinnacle Peak Rd., Suite 109. Tel. 585-4527.
Southwestern designs by Arizona Woman provide the look of the Southwest.

GALERIA DOS CABEZAS, in the Borgata, 6166 N. Scottsdale Rd., Scottsdale. Tel. 991-7004.
The address alone should give you some idea that this is not the sort of place for people who are watching their spending. The designs are fun, colorful, and thoroughly southwestern. There's another Dos Cabezas in the Arizona Biltmore Hotel, 24th Street and Missouri Avenue (tel. 955-3205).

GIFTS/SOUVENIRS

ABSOLUTELY ARIZONA UNIQUE GIFTS, 7655 E. Evans, Suite 2, Scottsdale. Tel. 483-3223.
Every item in this shop is grown, manufactured, or packaged in Arizona, which makes this a great one-stop shop for gifts to take back to family and friends.

HEARD MUSEUM GIFT SHOP, Heard Museum, 22 E. Monte Vista Rd. Tel. 252-8848.
As museum stores go, this place is pretty big, and there's no better place to buy Native American arts and crafts. The museum sells only the best, with the prices to prove it.

JEWELRY

CHIEF DODGE INDIAN JEWELRY STORE, 601 S. Mill Ave., Tempe. Tel. 967-9365.
You can watch Native American craftspeople create beautiful silver jewelry right in the store, and then peruse the cases searching for just the right accessory.

GILBERT ORTEGA'S INDIAN ARTS, 1803 E. Camelback Rd. Tel. 265-4311.
You'll find only the finest Native American jewelry at Gilbert Ortega shops. Other branches are located at the Hyatt Regency Hotel, 122 North Second Street (tel. 265-9923); 6208 North Scottsdale Road, Scottsdale (tel. 991-4072); 7227 East Main Street, Scottsdale (tel. 947-2805); 7252 East First Avenue, Scottsdale (tel. 945-1819); 7155 East Fifth Avenue (tel. 941-9281); and at Koshari in the Borgata, 6166 North Scottsdale Road (tel. 998-9699).

MALLS/SHOPPING CENTERS

BILTMORE FASHION PARK, E. Camelback Rd. and 24th St. Tel. 955-8400.
Since this is a "fashion park" and not just a shopping mall, it comes as no surprise that the shops bear the names of international designers and exclusive boutiques. Saks Fifth Avenue anchors the mall, with the likes of Gucci and Elizabeth Arden filling the

smaller stores. Limousine service from certain hotels and valet parking are both available.

THE BORGATA OF SCOTTSDALE, 6166 N. Scottsdale Rd. Tel. 998-1822.

✪ Designed to resemble a medieval Italian village with turrets, stone walls, and ramparts, the Borgata is far and away the most architecturally interesting shopping mall in the valley. There are 50 upscale boutiques, art galleries, and restaurants.

EL PEDREGAL FESTIVAL MARKETPLACE, Scottsdale Rd. and Carefree Hwy. Tel. 258-3609.

✪ Located adjacent to the spectacular Boulders Resort, El Pedregal is the most self-consciously southwestern shopping center in the valley. It's worth the long drive out here just to see the new pueblo architecture and colorful accents. The shops offer high-end merchandise, fashions, and art.

METROCENTER, 9617 Metro Pkwy. W. Tel. 997-2641.

This is the largest shopping center in the Southwest, with more than 200 specialty shops, four major department stores (Dillard's, Broadway Southwest, Robinson's, and Sears), and 50 eating establishments. Personal-shopper service and shuttle from selected hotels are available.

PAPAGO PLAZA, E. McDowell Rd. and N. Scottsdale Rd. Tel. 947-0800.

✪ This new shopping center made a bold move when it chose not to enclose. What with all the air-conditioned malls around the valley, Papago Plaza had to offer something very special to attract customers, and it does. New pueblo architecture with bright colors and rounded stucco walls make this a southwestern shopping fantasy.

SCOTTSDALE FASHION SQUARE, 7000 E. Camelback Rd., Scottsdale. Tel. 990-7800.

Scottsdale has long been the valley's shopping mecca, and for years this huge mall was the reason why. In addition to two major department stores, it houses the Nature Company and the Museum Store.

SCOTTSDALE GALLERIA, Scottsdale Rd. and Fifth Ave., Scottsdale. Tel. 949-3222.

As if Old Scottsdale and the Scottsdale Fashion Square weren't enough shopping for one small area, the Scottsdale Galleria opened and put everyone in the neighborhood to shame. Four floors contain more than 200 shops, restaurants, nightclubs, a seven-screen multiplex movie theater, and an IMAX theater. The centerpiece of this marble-lined mall is the 80-foot-high atrium that features a computerized musical fountain, which is only outdone by the million-gallon aquarium that is viewed from a 450-foot-long acrylic tunnel.

THE SHOPS AT ARIZONA CENTER, Third St. and Van Buren St. Tel. 271-4000.

Revitalizing downtown Phoenix, this mall houses several nightclubs as well as shops and a food court. The gardens and fountains are a peaceful oasis amid downtown's asphalt.

TOWER PLAZA MALL, 38th St. and E. Thomas Rd. Tel. 275-2991.

This enclosed, air-conditioned mall houses 70 shops, Phoenix's only ice rink, 10 movie theaters, several nightclubs, and restaurants.

NATIVE AMERICAN ARTS & CRAFTS

ATKINSON'S TRADING POST, 3957 N. Brown Ave., Scottsdale. Tel. 949-9750.

Handcrafted and hand-painted pottery, statues, and other accent pieces feature southwestern motifs.

GREY WOLF, 7101 Stetson Dr., Scottsdale. Tel. 423-0004.

You'll find the valley's largest selection of Native American artifacts, quality handcrafted kachinas, rugs, pottery, baskets, and souvenirs.

8. EVENING ENTERTAINMENT

THE PERFORMING ARTS

THE MAJOR PERFORMING ARTS COMPANIES

Opera & Classical Music

ARIZONA OPERA COMPANY, Symphony Hall, 225 E. Adams St. Tel. 266-7464.
The Arizona Opera Company splits its performances between Phoenix and Tucson, so if you miss a performance here, you might be able to catch one in Tucson. The 1991–92 season included *Tosca, Aïda, La Sonnambula,* and *Cinderella.*
Admission: Tickets, $9–$40.

PHOENIX SYMPHONY ORCHESTRA, 3707 N. Seventh St., Suite 107. Tel. 264-6363.
The Southwest's leading symphony orchestra performs classical, chamber, pops, morning Coffee Classics, and Sunday-afternoon family concerts during their November-to-April season.
Admission: Tickets, $10–$35.

SCOTTSDALE SYMPHONY ORCHESTRA, 3817 N. Brown Ave., Scottsdale. Tel. 945-8071.
For 17 years the Scottsdale Symphony Orchestra has been providing Scottsdale with excellent classical music performed in the Scottsdale Center for the Arts. The season runs from November to June and includes five concerts.
Admission: Tickets, $8–$10.

Theater Companies

ACTOR'S THEATER OF PHOENIX [ATOP], Herberger Theater, 222 E. Monroe St. Tel. 254-3475.
In less than 10 years, ATOP has become one of Phoenix's premier acting companies. Plays tend to be smaller, lesser-known works with musicals, dramas, and

---

THE MAJOR CONCERT & PERFORMANCE HALLS

Chandler Center for the Arts, 250 North Arizona Avenue, Chandler (tel. 786-3954).
Desert Sky Pavilion, North 83rd Avenue (tel. 254-7200).
Grady Gammage Memorial Auditorium, Mill Avenue and Apache Boulevard, Tempe (tel. 965-3434).
Herberger Theater Complex, 222 East Monroe Street (tel. 252-TIXS).
Kerr Cultural Center, 6110 North Scottsdale Road, Scottsdale (tel. 965-KERR).
Phoenix Civic Plaza and Symphony Hall, 225 East Adams Street (tel. 262-6225).
Scottsdale Center for the Arts, 7383 Scottsdale Mall, Scottsdale (tel. 994-2301).
Sundome Center for the Performing Arts, 19403 R.H. Johnson Boulevard, Sun City West (tel. 584-3118).
Tempe Performing Arts Center (tel. 833-5875).

comedies equally represented. The September to May season includes not only five multi-act productions, but also numerous one-act plays. These latter productions are part of the popular Brown Bag Theatre—lunchtime performances that start at 12:15pm Tuesday through Thursday.

Admission: Tickets, $10–$25; Brown Bag Theatre, $3.50.

ARIZONA THEATRE COMPANY [ATC], 1040 E. Osborn Rd. Tel. 279-0534.

For big productions, well-known works, and first-rate acting, the Arizona Theatre Company can't be beat. Founded in 1967, the ATC has since grown into a major force in the Arizona thespian scene with performances split between Phoenix and Tucson. The season runs from October to June with six productions. Among the 1991–92 season offerings were *Who's Afraid of Virginia Woolf?*, *Ain't Misbehavin'*, and *The Heidi Chronicles*.

Admission: Tickets, $19–$25.

VALLEY BROADWAY SERIES, Gammage Auditorium, Arizona State University, Mill Ave. and Apache Blvd. Tel. 965-3434.

This high-ticket-price series brings the best of Broadway past and present to the stage at the Gammage Auditorium. The emphasis is on rousing musicals, but the 1991–92 season also saw Joan Collins appearing in Noël Coward's *Private Lives*. The five-show season almost guarantees you a chance to see a Broadway-style production during your visit.

Admission: Tickets, $25–$40.

Dance Companies

BALLET ARIZONA, 3645 E. Indian School Rd. Tel. 381-0184.

Ballet Arizona brings to Phoenix performances of both familiar and innovative ballet. The 1991–92 season included *A Midsummer Night's Dream* and *The Nutcracker,* as well as a Southwest festival of dance and a tribute to George Balanchine.

Admission: Tickets, $16–$26.

CENTER DANCE ENSEMBLE, Herberger Theatre Center, 222 E. Monroe St. Tel. 252-8497.

The valley's premier modern dance company stages four productions during its October-to-May season at the Herberger Theatre. Many of the productions are adaptations of better-known works such as Stravinsky's *Rite of Spring* and Hans Christian Andersen's *The Snow Queen*. Other performances include original works by local choreographers.

Admission: Tickets, $12.50 adults, $10.50 senior citizens and students.

MAJOR CONCERT HALLS & ALL-PURPOSE AUDITORIUMS

DESERT SKY PAVILION, N. 83rd Ave. Tel. 254-7200 or 254-7299.

Why go to performances indoors when you can sit under the desert stars at this 18,500-seat amphitheater. From Broadway musicals to rock 'n' roll, the Desert Sky Pavilion hosts a wide variety of entertainment.

Admission: Tickets, $10–$40.

GRADY GAMMAGE MEMORIAL AUDITORIUM, Arizona State University, Mill Ave. and Apache Blvd., Tempe. Tel. 965-3434.

Designed by architect Frank Lloyd Wright, the Gammage Auditorium is at once graceful and massive. From September to May the auditorium hosts a wide variety of performances in such series as the Great Orchestras of the World, the Valley Broadway Series, Dance Directions (ballet and modern dance), and World Rhythms, and such performers as Victor Borge, Peter, Paul, and Mary, and George Winston. The box office is open Monday through Friday from 10am to 6pm and on Saturday from 10am to 4pm.

Admission: Tickets, $10–$40.

KERR CULTURAL CENTER, 6110 N. Scottsdale Rd., Scottsdale. Tel. 965-5377.

Located just off North Scottsdale Road behind the Cottonwoods Resort, the Kerr Cultural Center is an adobe building that provides a more intimate setting than the Gammage Auditorium and offers a much more eclectic and diversified season. From outrageous dinner theater to harp soloists, from cowboy bands to classical jazz, from old-time fiddlin' to steel-band orchestras, you never know who or what might be on the stage here. The box office is open Monday through Friday from 10am to 5pm.
Admission: Tickets, $8–$30 (mostly $10).

SCOTTSDALE CENTER FOR THE ARTS, 7383 Scottsdale Mall, Scottsdale. Tel. 994-2787.

Anchoring the Scottsdale Mall sculpture park at the heart of downtown Scottsdale, this cultural center hosts both visual-art exhibitions and performing-arts productions. The packed season of performances always manages to include the very best performers from around the world. The 1991–92 season included the Irish band The Boys of the Lough, Dizzy Gillespie, the Peking Acrobats, Ladysmith Black Mambazo, the Windham Hills Winter Solstice Concert, and the Duke Ellington Orchestra, as well as several plays. The box office is open Monday through Saturday from 10am to 5pm (to 8pm on Thursday) and on Sunday from noon to 5pm.
Admission: Tickets, $10–$35.

THEATERS

ACTOR'S LAB THEATER, 7223 E. Second St., Scottsdale. Tel. 990-1731.

If you're feeling like you need a serious dose of nonsense, give a call to the Actor's Lab and see if they happen to be staging one of their outrageous comedies. The long-running favorite, *Six Women with Brain Death or Expiring Minds Want to Know*, was an all-woman musical revue based on soap operas and supermarket tabloids.
Admission: Tickets, $15–$20.

HERBERGER THEATER CENTER, 222 E. Monroe St. Tel. 252-8497.

Located downtown across the street from the Civic Plaza, the Herberger vaguely resembles a colonial church from the outside. Its two Broadway-style theaters together host more than 600 performances each year, including productions by the Arizona Theatre Company, Actors Theatre of Phoenix, the Arizona Opera, Center Dance Ensemble, and traveling shows.
Admission: Tickets, $7–$25.

PHOENIX LITTLE THEATRE, 25 E. Coronado Rd. Tel. 258-1974 or 254-2151.

For more than 70 years the Phoenix Little Theatre has been entertaining stagestruck Phoenicians with its excellent productions of both the familiar and the obscure. The theater stages two different series each season, with eight plays included in the Mainstage series and another four, slightly more daring productions staged in the Stage II series.
Admission: Tickets, $12–$20.

THE CLUB & MUSIC SCENE

The Valley of the Sun has a very diverse club and music scene that is spread out across the length and breadth of the valley. However, there are a few concentrations of clubs and bars that you might want to know about. **Phoenix Live! at Arizona Center,** 455 North Third Avenue, is playing a big part in the renaissance of downtown Phoenix. With four different bars and clubs side by side in the modern shopping mall, Phoenix Live! offers downtown bar-hoppers a chance to do all their hopping under one roof. Another place to wander around until you hear your favorite type of music is Mill Avenue in Tempe. Because Tempe is a college town, there are plenty of clubs and bars on this short stretch of road. Looking for a more upscale crowd and more sophisticated surroundings? Head for Scottsdale, both the Old Scottsdale neighborhood and resort row along Scottsdale Road have plenty of choices for evening entertainment.

NIGHTCLUBS/CABARET/COMEDY

THE IMPROVISATION, 930 E. University Dr., Tempe. Tel. 921-9877.
With the best of the national comedy circuit harassing the crowds and rattling off one-liners, the Improv is the valley's most popular comedy club. Weekend lines are long, but your reward is a chance to see the same folks that appear on TV stand-up comedy shows. Dinner is served and reservations are advised.
Admission: $4–$8; dinner $10.

TROCADERO'S, 7117 E. Third Ave., at Scottsdale Rd., Scottsdale. Tel. 990-3466.
A Caribbean theme sets the stage at this classic nightclub just off Scottsdale Road. With its walls of glass, you can even check out the action before heading inside. There is live music Tuesday through Sunday and a happy hour free buffet.
Admission: Free–$4.

YESTERDAY'S, 9035 N. Eighth St. Tel. 861-9080.
Singing waiters and waitresses perform Broadway show tunes and other songs from the '20s to the '60s. There's no cover charge but there is a $10 minimum per person. Meals range from $11.85 to $17.95, and reservations are required. In the winter you should book at least a week in advance.
Admission: $10-per-person minimum.

FOLK & COUNTRY

HANDLEBAR-J, 7116 E. Becker Lane, Scottsdale. Tel. 948-0110.
I'm not saying that this is a genuine cowboy bar, but cowpokes do make this one of their stops when they come in from the ranch. You'll hear git-down two-steppin' music and can even get free dance lessons on Wednesday and Thursday.
Admission: Free–$3.

TOOLIE'S COUNTRY SALOON AND DANCE HALL, 4231 W. Thomas Rd. Tel. 272-3100.
Once a Safeway supermarket, Toolie's is now the best country-and-western bar in the valley. A false-front cowtown facade beckons cowboys and cowgirls to come on in and git down. Nationally known acts make this their Phoenix stop, and when they aren't on stage Toolie's books the best of the C&W bands.
Admission: Free–$3.

ROCK

ANDERSON'S FIFTH ESTATE, 6820 Fifth Ave. Tel. 994-4168.
Phoenix has a thriving alternative music scene and even manages to support an alternative music radio station (KUKQ-AM). This club is where you can hear the music that gets played on KUKQ. Most nights there's a DJ spinning the dance music, but there are also occasional live shows.
Admission: $3–$13.

CHUY'S, 410 S. Mill Ave., Tempe. Tel. 967-2489.
Overlooking the Hayden Square Amphitheatre in the heart of Tempe's Mill Avenue college hangout district, Chuy's is a glossy club decked out in bright white. Step through the door and you almost trip onto the dance floor. High above you is the stage and higher still is a huge video screen. Local bands perform on weekends with touring groups filling up the weeknight slots.
Admission: $2–$6.

EDCEL'S ATTIC, 414 S. Mill Ave., Tempe. Tel. 894-0015.
Another Mill Avenue hangout for the college crowd, Edcel's is on the second floor

of a little courtyard shopping area. Rock, reggae, pop, funk, and soul—it all gets played by local bands and the occasional out-of-town group.

Admission: $2–$3.

HAYDEN SQUARE AMPHITHEATRE, 350 S. Mill Ave., Tempe. Tel. 921-7337.

Phoenix loves to brag about its 350 days of sunshine, but its nights aren't too shabby either. Warm temps and balmy breezes make outdoor concerts a year-round entertainment, and this bricked-in square behind the shops of Tempe's Mill Avenue stages some of the best rock, blues, and jazz concerts in town.

Admission: Free.

10 DOWNING STREET, 7135 E. Camelback Rd., Scottsdale. Tel. 481-0970.

This big cylindrical building overlooks the very busy intersection of Scottsdale Road and Camelback Road with walls of glass to make sure that all the passing cars can see what a good time you're having. Wednesday is classic rock 'n' roll night. On Thursday there's a karaoke contest. Weekends it's time for Top-40 and alternative dance music.

Admission: Fri–Sat, $5.

JAZZ & BLUES

Call the **Arizona Jazz Hotline** (tel. 254-4545) for a schedule of jazz performances all over the state.

CHAR'S HAS THE BLUES, 4631 N. Seventh Ave. Tel. 230-0205.

Yes, indeed, Char's does have those mean-and-dirty, lowdown blues, and if you want the blues, too, this is where you head when you're in Phoenix. All the best blues brothers and sisters from around the city and around the country make the scene here to the enjoyment of hard-drinkin' crowds.

Admission: Free.

PUZZLES, Arizona Center, 455 Third St. Tel. 252-2112.

Downtown at the Arizona Center's something-for-everyone entertainment complex, Puzzles features live jazz, blues, and salsa Tuesday through Saturday nights with primarily local acts on stage. Occasionally reggae or rock bands play as well.

Admission: $3–$5.

TIMOTHY'S, 6335 N. 16th St. Tel. 277-7634.

For an elegant evening of dining and listening to lively jazz, Timothy's is hard to beat. The restaurant and lounge both attract a well-off crowd. Sunday is live jam night.

Admission: Free, but there's a food and drink minimums.

DANCE CLUBS/DISCOS

CLUB RIO, 430 N. Scottsdale Rd. Tel. 894-0533.

You may find yourself in a strange town dancing with a stranger, and if the town happens to be Scottsdale, you can blame it on Rio. This cavernous club has a dance floor big enough for football practice. From barely legal ASU students to the Porsche-and-pony set from Scottsdale, everyone agrees that Club Rio's *de rigueur* if you love to dance to the lastest in Euro-pop. Plenty of live shows, too.

Admission: $2–$4.

THE BAR SCENE
PUBS/WINE BARS

ANOTHER POINTE IN TYME, at the Pointe on South Mountain, 7777 S. Pointe Pkwy. Tel. 438-9000.

If you feel most comfortable when surrounded by walls of mahogany and sitting on brocade or velvet, or if a pianist tickling the ivories is your idea of the perfect music to drink by, then you'll be content at Another Pointe in Tyme. There's another Another Pointe in Tyme up north at the Pointe at Tapatio Cliffs.

DURANTS, 2611 N. Central Ave. Tel. 264-5967.

If you prefer martinis to Bud light, and all your friends prefer martinis too, then you probably belong at Durants. For many years this has been *the* place for downtown money merchants to stop on their way back to their rooms with a view.

RICHARDSON'S, 1582 E. Bethany Home Rd. Tel. 265-5886.

It's small, it's crowded, it's noisy, and it's southwestern. It also happens to be a fave hangout with young politicos, and if you can spot it in its nondescript strip-mall disguise, you can pull up a chair at the C-shaped bar and be a part of the Phoenician scene.

OUTSTANDING HAPPY HOURS

AUNT CHILADA'S, at the Pointe at Squaw Peak, 7330 N. Dreamy Draw Dr. Tel. 997-2626.

The Pointe at Squaw Peak took an old adobe building and turned it into a first-rate Mexican restaurant and then did themselves one better with the Friday-evening happy hour in the bar. The young downtown business crowd jams the patio to chow down on free Mexican snacks and cheap drinks.

DON & CHARLIE'S, 7501 E. Camelback Rd., Scottsdale. Tel. 990-0900.

Tucked in behind the sprawling Scottsdale Galleria, Don & Charlie's is well known for its Chicago-style ribs, but working stiffs tend to gravitate here more for the awesome happy hour food buffet. After an hour or so of quaffing cold ones and noshing on free eats, who has room for dinner?

SINGLES BARS

STUDEBAKERS, 705 S. Rural Rd., Tempe. Tel. 829-8495.

A sort of Hard Rock Café rip-off with an old Studebaker coupe parked in the middle of the club, this is Tempe's biggest singles scene. On Tuesday night there's a male dance revue for ladies only between 7 and 9pm. After 9pm the doors are opened to men, and well, you can probably imagine what happens then.

Admission: Thurs $2, Fri–Sat $3.

COCKTAILS WITH A VIEW

The Valley of the Sun has more than its fair share of spectacular views. Unfortunately, most of them are in expensive restaurants. Fortunately, however, all these restaurants also have lounges, where for the price of a drink, and perhaps valet parking, you can sit back and ogle a crimson sunset and the purple mountains' majesty. Your choices include **Etienne's Different Pointe of View** at the Pointe at Tapatio Cliffs, **Rustler's Rooste** at the Pointe on South Mountain, and the **Top of the Rock** at the Buttes. All these restaurants can be found in the restaurant section of this chapter. One other choice is **The Thirsty Camel** at the Phoenician resort. You may never drink in more ostentatious surroundings than here at Charles Keating's Xanadu.

SPECIALTY BARS

A Sports Bar

MAX'S, 6727 N. 47th Ave., Glendale. Tel. 937-1671.

These days it seems that sports bars are as common as knee injuries on the football field. But most of these sports bars are little more than a bar with a big-screen TV. Max's is *not*. It's the real thing! In fact it's a sports museum, restaurant, dinner theater, and off-track betting parlor all wrapped up in one. Yes, after perusing the glass cases full of football helmets and other sports memorabilia, you can sit down to some prime ribs and a cold glass of beer, and wager on the greyhounds.

A Gay Bar

NU TOWNE SALOON, 5002 E. Van Buren St. Tel. 267-9959.

A big red truck parked inside this bar acts as a visual focal point, but the real draws are the food-and-drink specials every Sunday. After 20 years of popularity it's obvious that the friendly, funky atmosphere here works.

9. NETWORKS & RESOURCES

FOR STUDENTS   Arizona State University is located in Tempe, one of the valley's many city's. Mill Avenue is the center of activity for ASU students. You'll find inexpensive restaurants, cafés, unusual shops, and of course, numerous bars and nightclubs featuring nightly live and recorded music. *University Guide* is a student-oriented directory with information on everything from apartments to student aid, concerts to where to go skiing.

FOR GAY MEN & LESBIANS   To help get in touch with the Phoenix gay community, there are a several phone numbers you can try: the **Gay and Lesbian Community Switchboard** (tel. 234-2752), the **Gay Exchange** (tel. 1-976-1100), the **Gay and Lesbian Alternative Service Switchboard** (tel. 266-3733), and the **Gay Help Line** (tel. 265-1100).

FOR SENIORS   Phoenix and the Valley of the Sun have long been popular with retirees. Over the years entire cities have developed for senior citizens. You or at least one member of your household must be at least 55 to live at Del Webb's Sun City in the northwest part of the valley. *Senior World Newspaper* is a weekly newspaper with information relevant to senior citizens. You can find it in supermarkets and convenience stores.

10. EASY EXCURSIONS FROM PHOENIX

NORTH OF THE CITY

PIONEER ARIZONA LIVING HISTORY MUSEUM, I-17 at Pioneer Rd. Tel. 993-0212.
   If a visit to a "cowtown" restaurant with false-front buildings and shootouts in the street just doesn't fulfill your need to learn more about the history of Arizona and the west, a visit to this living-history museum certainly should. With more than 20 original and reconstructed buildings, and costumed interpreters practicing traditional pioneer occupations, the museum is one of the best introductions to life on the western frontier 100 years ago. Among the buildings of this quaint little village are a carpenter shop, blacksmith shop, wagonmaker's shop, miner's cabin, stagecoach station, one-room schoolhouse, opera house, church, two farmhouses, and a Victorian mansion from Phoenix. Each year in November there are Civil War battle reenactments and a gathering of modern mountain men. The museum is located 12 miles north of Phoenix (measured from Bell Road) at the Pioneer Road exit from I-17.
   Admission: $4.50 adults, $4 senior citizens and students 13 to college, $3 children 4–12, free for children under 3.
   Open: Nov–May, Wed–Sun 9am–5pm. **Closed:** June–Oct.

ARCOSANTI, I-17 at Cordes Junction, Mayer. Tel. 632-7135.
   Paolo Soleri, an Italian architect who came to Arizona to study with Frank Lloyd Wright at Taliesin West, has a dream of merging architecture and ecology. He calls this merger *arcology,* and Arcosanti is the realization of his

ideas. Located 50 miles north of Phoenix down a rough dirt road, Arcosanti is an experiment in urban living, an energy-efficient town that merges with the desert and preserves as much of the surrounding landscape as possible. Using cast concrete, arches, and domes, Soleri and his many students have over the years been slowly expanding Arcosanti in an ongoing project that attracts both the mildly curious visitor and the zealously enthusiastic architectural student. The latter work and live at Arcosanti for various periods of time, performing either building construction or the casting of bronze bells. These wind bells are all individually designed by Soleri and their sale has helped finance the building of Arcosanti. You'll see Soleri's wind bells in shops all over Arizona, but the best selection is here in the gift shop at Arcosanti. You can also watch the bells being cast both here and at Cosanti, Soleri's gallery and studio in Scottsdale. Visitors are not allowed to wander around Arcosanti unescorted, so you must take one of the hourly tours. There is also a café here.

Admission: $4.

Open: Daily 9am–5pm (tours on the hour 10am–4pm). **Closed:** Thanksgiving and Christmas.

SOUTHEAST OF PHOENIX

CASA GRANDE RUINS NATIONAL MONUMENT, 1100 Ruins Dr., Coolidge. Tel. 723-3172.

In Spanish, Casa Grande means "large house," and that's exactly what you'll find at this national monument. However, the large house is an earth-walled ruin that was built 650 years ago by the Hohokam peoples. The Casa Grande ruins have perplexed visitors to this region ever since the first Spanish explorers saw them in the 17th century. Was the main building an astronomical observatory? A ceremonial building? The answer is still unknown, but one thing is certain—this ruin is an amazing example of ancient architecture in the Southwest. Built of shaped earth rather than adobe bricks, the Casa Grande ruin had a 4-foot-deep foundation and was three stories high. The large ruin is surrounded by many smaller buildings, which were probably homes and indicate that the Casa Grande was not used as living quarters. Among the other ruins here is a ball court similar to those built by the ancient cultures of Mexico, which indicates that there was contact between central Mexico and the Southwest.

The Hohokam people began farming in the Gila and Salt river valleys about 1,500 years ago and eventually built an amazing network of canals for irrigating their crops. Throughout these two valleys there are more than 600 miles of canals, some of which are 6 feet wide and 3 feet deep. Crops grown on irrigated land included corn, beans, squash, and cotton. By the middle of the 15th century, the Hohokam had abandoned their villages and disappeared without a trace.

Admission: $1.

Open: Daily 7am–6pm.

GILA RIVER ARTS & CRAFTS CENTER, Colo. 587 and I-10. Tel. 963-3981.

Located on the Gila River Indian Reservation, this center is well worth a stop if you're in the area and wish to learn more about the history and culture of the tribes that inhabit this region of the Arizona desert. In Heritage Park, you will see replicas of villages of five different tribes, including the Tohono O'odham, Pima, Maricopa, Apache, and the ancient Hohokam, who disappeared in the 15th century. Inside the museum there are historical photos, artifacts, and an excellent collection of Pima baskets. Other exhibits tell the story of the Gila River Basin, of which this area is a part. In the winter months there are frequent tribal dance performances and craft demonstrations. Of particular interest are the **Pima-Maricopa Arts Festival** the first weekend of November and the **Native American Dance Festival** the weekend after Thanksgiving. The arts and crafts shop has a good selection of kachinas, baskets, pottery, rugs, sculptures, and paintings by members of many southwestern tribes.

Admission: Free.

Open: Daily 9am–5pm.

EAST OF PHOENIX

APACHE TRAIL (Ariz. 88).

Heading east from Phoenix on U.S. 60 will take you to the town of Apache Junction, which is the start of the historic Apache Trail (Ariz. 88). This trail is now one of the most scenic roads in Arizona and winds its way up through narrow canyons past Canyon, Apache, and Theodore Roosevelt lakes, all of which have been formed by dams on the Salt River. These lakes provide the water that has made it possible for Phoenix to develop into the metropolis it is today. The oldest of the dams is the Theodore Roosevelt Dam, which was built in 1911 and is the largest masonry dam in the world. All three lakes offer camping, picnicking, fishing, boating, and swimming. A fourth lake, Saguaro Lake, is below Canyon Lake, but is only accessible from Ariz. 87. From just beyond Tortilla Flat to Roosevelt, a distance of about 25 miles, the road is not paved, though it is well graded. The road is slow but the views are gorgeous.

TONTO NATIONAL MONUMENT, Ariz. 88, 5 miles south of Roosevelt Dam. Tel. 602/467-2241.

Tonto National Monument preserves the southernmost cliff dwellings in Arizona. Built between 1100 and 1400 by the Salado peoples, the three cliff dwellings here are some of the only remaining pueblos of the Salado culture, which, like that of the Anasazi, Sinagua, and Hohokam, disappeared around 1400. Most of the remains of the Salado culture now lie beneath the waters of Theodore Roosevelt Lake, which was formed by the Theodore Roosevelt Dam in 1911. The three ruins here—Upper Ruin, Lower Ruin, and the Lower Ruin Annex—are built into the caves above the Salt River where they were protected from the elements and thus were well preserved. All three ruins are built of stone, and the largest ruin, Upper Ruin, has 40 rooms and is three stories high in some places. The only time the public may visit Upper Ruin is on Saturday at 9:30am. It's a 3-mile round-trip hike and reservations are required. A shorter trail leads to the Lower Ruin, which is open daily until 4pm. There's also a museum and visitor center that displays relics of the Salado culture.

Besh Ba Gowah Ruins, the only other Salado pueblo ruins, are 30 miles away near the town of Globe. This 200-room pueblo was built atop a mesa. The ruins are open daily and are administrated by the city of Globe, which displays some Salado artifacts in its city hall. To reach Besh Ba Gowah from Globe, take South Broad Street to Ice House Canyon Road.

Admission: $3 per car.
Open: Daily 8am–5pm.

BOYCE THOMPSON SOUTHWESTERN ARBORETUM, U.S. 60, Superior. Tel. 602/689-2811.

Located 45 miles east of Mesa in the small mining town of Superior, the Boyce Thompson Arboretum is jointly operated by the Arizona State Parks, the University of Arizona, and the nonprofit Arboretum corporation. Because of its wealth of information on gardening in the desert and its large selection of potted plants for sale, this arboretum is of most interest to residents of the Southwest who have or wish to have a desert garden. However, visitors from rainier climates will certainly enjoy the varied landscape and plantings of this arboretum. Built in the 1920s as an educational facility to promote the gardening of drought-tolerant plants, the arboretum's visitor center building is on the National Register of Historic Places. Because of the presence of both a creek and a small lake, the arboretum has displays on the more water-demanding plants of the desert. Though the cactus gardens are impressive, it's the two boojum trees from Baja California that visitors find most fascinating. These spiny trees have thick, tapering trunks and few leaves. With a bit of imagination it's possible to see them as giant turnips stood on end. Spring, when the desert wildflowers are in bloom, is the best time to visit.

Admission: $3 adults, $1.50 children 5–12, free for children under 5.
Open: Daily 8am–5pm. **Closed:** Christmas Day.

CHAPTER 5

TUCSON

Founded by the Spanish in 1775, Tucson is built on the site of a much older Native American village. The city's name comes from the Pima Native American word *chukeson,* which means "at the base of black mountain," a reference to the peak now known simply as "A Mountain." From 1867 to 1877 Tucson was the territorial capital of Arizona, but eventually the capital was moved to Phoenix. As pacification, it was given Arizona's first university— University of Arizona. Tucson did not develop as quickly as Phoenix and holds fast to its Hispanic and Western heritage, with three downtown historic districts and a number of excellent museums.

Tucson also supports a very active cultural life, with symphony, ballet, opera, and theater companies and many festivals celebrating aspects of Tucson life. The natural surroundings make Tucson really unique, however. Four mountain ranges ring the city, and within those mountains and their foothills are giant saguaro cactus, an oasis, one of the finest zoos in the world, a ski area, and miles of hiking and horseback-riding trails. Understandably, the Tucson life-style is oriented toward the great outdoors.

History, culture, and nature are the major attractions, but another aspect of the city is currently being developed—that of a resort destination. With its mild, sunny climate and mountain vistas, Tucson is a natural for resorts, and although it doesn't have as many world-class resorts as Scottsdale, it certainly has finer views.

1. ORIENTATION

Not nearly as large and spread out as Phoenix and the Valley of the Sun, Tucson is small enough to be convenient, yet large enough to be sophisticated. The mountains ringing the city are bigger and closer than those of Phoenix, and the desert is equally close.

ARRIVING

BY PLANE Located 6 miles south of downtown, **Tucson International Airport** is served by 12 airlines including Alaska Airlines (tel. 602/622-0455, or toll free 800/426-0333), America West (tel. 602/894-0800, or toll free 800/548-8969), American (tel. 602/888-1818, or toll free 800/433-7300), Continental (tel. 602/273-1096, or toll free 800/

WHAT'S SPECIAL ABOUT TUCSON

Buildings
☐ Mission San Xavier del Bac, called the White Dove of the Desert, a Spanish mission church.

Cowboy Adventures
☐ Guest ranches (formerly dude ranches) for riding the range.
☐ Cowboy steakhouses featuring hayrides, staged gunfights, barbecues, and sing-alongs.

Natural Spectacles
☐ Sabino Canyon Park, an oasis of waterfalls.
☐ Saguaro National Monument, with the massive saguaro cactus, symbol of the American desert.

Activities
☐ Mount Lemmon, a forested mountain with hiking and skiing.
☐ Excellent golf courses.

Zoos
☐ The Arizona–Sonora Desert Museum, one of the leading zoos in the country.

Religious Shrines
☐ El Tiradito, the only shrine in the U.S. dedicated to a sinner buried in unconsecrated soil.

TV and Film Locations
☐ Old Tucson, where dozens of western movies and television shows have been filmed.

Great Neighborhoods
☐ El Presidio Historic District (1880s).
☐ Barrio Historico, the largest concentration of Sonoran-style adobe homes in the U.S.

Offbeat Oddities
☐ The Titan Missile Museum, the world's only ICBM that has become a museum.
☐ Biosphere II, with eight "biospherians" living in a self-contained air-tight greenhouse for 2 years.

525-0280), Delta (tel. 602/886-7178, or toll free 800/221-1212), Northwest (tel. toll free 800/225-2525), TWA (tel. 602/747-1011, or toll free 800/221-2000), United (tel. 602/622-1214, or toll free 800/241-6522), and USAir (tel. 602/623-3428, or toll free 800/428-4322). At the airport you'll find car-rental desks, regularly scheduled shuttle vans to downtown, taxis, and, in the baggage claim area, two visitor information centers where you can pick up brochures about Tucson and reserve a hotel room if you haven't done so already.

Transportation to Town   Many resorts and hotels in Tucson provide airport shuttle service and will pick you up and return you to the airport either for free or for a competitive fare. **Arizona Stagecoach** (tel. 602/889-1000) operates a daily 24-hour van service to downtown Tucson and the foothills resorts. You'll find their vans outside the center of the baggage-claim area. Just follow the signs that say SCHEDULED VAN SERVICE. Fares range from $10.50 to downtown up to $16.50 to the foothills resorts. To return to the airport, be sure to call at least 4 hours before your scheduled departure.

You'll also find taxis waiting in the same area or you can call **Airline Transport Taxi Cab & Tour** (tel. 602/292-0126 or 575-5186) or **Yellow Cab** (tel. 602/624-6611). A taxi to downtown costs around $11 to $12.

Sun Tran (tel. 602/792-9222), the local public transit, operates a bus service to and from the airport, though you'll have to make a transfer to reach downtown. The bus at the airport is no. 25 (ask for a transfer when you board); at the Roy Laos Transit Center you should transfer to no. 16 for downtown. The fare is 60¢. Route 25 from the airport operates daily: on weekdays between 7am and 8pm, on Saturday between 8am and 7pm, and on Sunday between 9am and 7pm. Departures are every 30 minutes in the early morning and late afternoon on weekdays and every hour on weekends and during the middle of the day on weekdays.

BY TRAIN   Tucson is served by **Amtrak** passenger rail service (tel. toll free 800/872-7245 in the U.S., 800/426-8725 in Canada). Both the *Sunset Limited,* which runs between New Orleans and Los Angeles, and the *Texas Eagle,* which connects Chicago and Los Angeles, stop in Tucson. The train station is at 400 East Toole Avenue (tel. 602/623-4442) in the heart of downtown Tucson and is within walking distance of the Tucson Convention Center, the El Presidio Historic District, and a few hotels. You'll find taxis waiting to meet the train.

BY BUS   Greyhound-Trailways Lines (tel. 602/792-0972 or 882-4386) connects Tucson to the rest of the United States through its extensive system. The bus station is at 2 South Fourth Avenue, across the street from the Hotel Congress in the Downtown Arts District. For service to Phoenix, call 622-1777; for service to Nogales, call 622-1555.

BY CAR   I-10, the main east-west interstate across the southern United States, passes through Tucson as it swings north to Phoenix. I-19 connects Tucson with the Mexican border at Nogales. Ariz. 86 heads southwest into the Papago Indian Reservation and U.S. 89 leads north toward Florence and eventually connects with U.S. 60 into Phoenix. If you're headed downtown, take the Congress Street exit off I-10. If you're headed for one of the foothills resorts north of downtown, you'll probably want to take the Ina Road exit.

TOURIST INFORMATION

The **Metropolitan Tucson Convention & Visitors Bureau,** 130 South Scott Avenue, Tucson, AZ 85701 (tel. 602/624-1889), is an excellent source of information on Tucson and environs. You can contact them before leaving home or stop at their Visitor Center, which is well stocked with brochures and has helpful people at the desk to answer your questions. The Visitor Center is open Monday through Friday from 8:30am to 5pm, and also on Saturday and Sunday from 9am to 4pm during the cooler months.

CITY LAYOUT

MAIN ARTERIES & STREETS   Tucson is laid out on a grid that is fairly regular in the downtown areas, but which becomes less orderly the farther you go from the city center. In the foothills, where Tucson's most recent growth has occurred, the grid system breaks down completely because of the hilly terrain. Major thoroughfares are spaced at 1-mile intervals, with smaller streets filling in the squares created by the major roads.

The **main east-west roads** are (from south to north) 22nd Street, Broadway Boulevard, Speedway Boulevard, Grant Road (with Tanque Verde Road as an extension), and Ina Road/Skyline Drive. The **main north-south roads** are (from west to east) Miracle Mile/Oracle Road, Park Avenue, Campbell Avenue, Country Club Road, and Alvernon Road. I-10 cuts diagonally across the Tucson metropolitan area from northwest to southeast.

In **downtown Tucson,** Congress Street and Broadway Boulevard are the main east-west streets and Stone Avenue, Fourth Avenue, and Sixth Avenue are the main north-south streets.

FINDING AN ADDRESS   Because Tucson is laid out on a grid, finding an address is relatively easy. The zero (or starting) point for all Tucson addresses is the corner of Stone Avenue, which runs north and south, and Congress Street, which runs east and west. From this point, streets are designated either north, south, east, or west. Addresses usually, but not always, increase by 100 with each block so that an address of 4321 East Broadway Boulevard should be 43 blocks east of Stone Avenue. In the downtown area, many of the streets and avenues are numbered, with numbered streets running east and west and numbered avenues running north and south.

STREET MAPS   The best way to find your way around Tucson is to pick up a *Valley National Bank of Arizona Tucson, Arizona, Street Map.* This free folding map is available from the Metropolitan Tucson Convention & Visitors Bureau (see "Tourist Information," above). The map includes numbers indicating addresses on major roads, thereby taking the guesswork out of finding an address. The maps handed out by car-rental agencies are not very detailed, but will do for most purposes.

NEIGHBORHOODS IN BRIEF

El Presidio Historic District Named for the Spanish military garrison that once stood on this site, the neighborhood is bounded by Alameda Street on the south, Main Avenue on the west, Franklin Street on the north, and Church Avenue on the east. El Presidio District was the city's most affluent neighborhood in the 1880s, and many large homes from that period have been restored and now house restaurants, arts and crafts galleries, and bed-and-breakfast inns. The Tucson Museum of Art anchors the neighborhood.

Barrio Historico District Another 19th-century neighborhood, the Barrio Historico is bounded on the north by Cushing Street, on the west by the railroad tracks, on the south by 18th Street, and on the east by Stone Avenue. Barrio Historico is characterized by Sonoran-style adobe rowhouses that directly abut the street with no yards, a style typical in Mexican towns. Although a few restaurants and art galleries dot the neighborhood, most restored buildings serve as offices.

Armory Park Historic District Bounded by 12th Street on the north, Stone Avenue on the west, 19th Street on the south, and Second Avenue and Third Avenue on the east, the Armory Park neighborhood was Tucson's first historic district. Today this area is undergoing a renaissance driven by the renovation of the Temple of Music and Art and the reopening of the Carnegie Library building as the Tucson Children's Museum.

Downtown Arts District This neighborhood encompasses a bit of the Armory District, a bit of the El Presidio District, and the stretch of Congress Street and Broadway Boulevard west of Toole Avenue. Home to galleries, boutiques, nightclubs, and hip cafés, it is Tucson's liveliest neighborhood.

Fourth Avenue Running from University Drive in the north to Ninth Street in the south, Fourth Avenue is Tucson's hippest shopping district, with boutiques selling ethnic clothing and shops offering handcrafted items from around the world. In April and December the street is closed to traffic for a colorful street fair.

The Foothills Encompassing a huge area of northern Tucson, the foothills contain the city's most affluent neighborhood. Elegant shopping centers, modern malls, world-class resorts, golf courses, and expensive residential neighborhoods are surrounded by hilly desert at the foot of the Santa Catalina Mountains.

2. GETTING AROUND

BY PUBLIC TRANSPORTATION

DISCOUNT PASSES Most discount buses passes for the **Sun Tran** public bus system are designed for Tucson residents. These include the Daily Rider pass ($20), the Class Pass for students through 12th grade ($14), and the Reduced Fare pass for senior citizens, low-income riders, and the disabled ($8.50). Contact Sun Tran (tel. 792-9222) for the nearest place to purchase a pass. Visitors will be more interested in the Weekend Pass ($1.20), good for unlimited rides from 6:30pm on Friday until the last bus on Sunday.

BY BUS Operating over much of the Tucson Metropolitan area, **Sun Tran** (tel. 792-9222) public buses cost only 60¢ for adults, 40¢ for students, 25¢ for senior citizens, free for children under 6. The bus system does not extend to such tourist attractions as the Arizona–Sonora Desert Museum, Old Tucson, Saguaro National Monument, or the foothills resorts, and consequently is of limited use to visitors.

Bus stops are marked by red-and-yellow signs that provide information on which

N

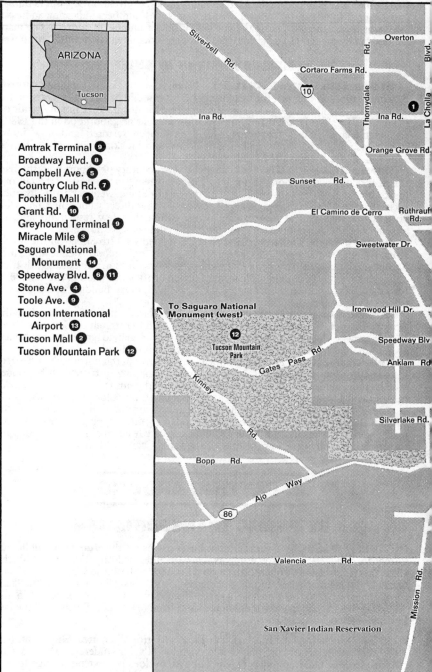

ARIZONA

Tucson

Silverbell Rd.

Overton

Rd.

Blvd.

Cortaro Farms Rd.

Thornydale

10

Ina Rd.

La Cholla

Ina Rd.

1

Orange Grove Rd.

Sunset   Rd.

El Camino de Cerro

Ruthrauf
Rd.

Sweetwater Dr.

Ironwood Hill Dr.

**To Saguaro National
Monument (west)**

Speedway Blv

12
Tucson Mountain
Park

Anklam   Rd

Gates   Pass   Rd.

Kinney

Silverlake Rd.

Rd.

Bopp   Rd.

Ajo   Way

86

Valencia   Rd.

Mission   Rd.

San Xavier Indian Reservation

TUCSON ORIENTATION

Magee Rd.

La Canada Dr.

Ina Rd.

Orange Grove Rd.

Skyline Dr.

To Sabino Canyon Park ↗

Canyon Rd.

Kolb Rd.

Sunrise Dr.

Craycroft Rd.

Swan Rd.

Sabino Canyon Rd.

River Rd.

2

Wetmore Rd.

Flowing Wells Rd.

Roger Rd.

Prince Rd.

Ave.

Ft. Rd.

Lowell

Snyder Rd.

Bear Canyon

To Mount Lemmon ↗

Catalina Hwy.

3

Miracle Mile

4

Grant Rd.

Oracle Rd.

Stone Ave.

1st

Campbell Ave.

Tucson Blvd.

Country Club Rd.

Alvernon Way

Rd.

10

Tanque Verde Rd.

Grant Rd.

10

Speedway Blvd.

11

Grande Ave.

9

6

5

6th St.

5th St.

Congress

8

Broadway Blvd.

Reid Park

Randolph Park

To Saguaro National Monument (east)

14 ↘

Sentinel Peak Park

22nd St.

Tucson Greyhound Park

7

29th St.

36th St.

Swan Rd.

Craycroft Rd.

Wilmot Rd.

Kolb Rd.

22nd St.

Golf Links Rd.

Ajo Way

Kino Blvd.

10

Escalante

Pantano Rd.

Camino Seco Rd.

Irvington Rd.

Irvington Rd.

Drexel Rd.

Palo Verde Rd.

Davis Monthan AFB

Kolb Rd.

12th Ave.

6th Ave.

Valencia Rd.

13

Los Reales Rd.

19

✈ Tucson International Airport

10

Airport ✈

buses stop there, major streets they serve, and their final destinations. The Downtown–Ronstadt Transit Center at the corner of Congress Street and Sixth Avenue is served by nearly 30 regular and express bus routes to all parts of Tucson. The Roy Laos Transit Center serves the southern part of the city.

Another option, and one likely to be more useful to tourists, is the **Sun Tran Trolley,** a trolley–style bus that operates Monday through Saturday in downtown Tucson. It stops at the University of Arizona, along Fourth Avenue, in the Downtown Arts District, and at the Tucson Visitor's Bureau, the Tucson Convention Center, and the Tucson Museum of Art, among other places. Best of all, it costs only 25¢.

BY TAXI

If you need a taxi, you'll have to phone for one. **Yellow Cab** (tel. 624-6611), **Allstate Cab** (tel. 798-1111), and **ABC Cab** (tel. 623-7979) all provide service throughout the city. Fares start at $1.10 and increase by $1.40 per mile. Although distances in Tucson are not as great as those in Phoenix, it's still a good 10 or more miles from the foothills resorts to downtown Tucson, so expect to pay at least $10 for any taxi ride. Most resorts offer or can arrange taxi service to the major tourist attractions around Tucson.

Shoppers should keep in mind that several Tucson shopping malls offer free shuttle service from hotels and resorts. Be sure to ask at your hotel before paying for a ride to a mall.

BY CAR

RENTALS Unless you plan to stay by the pool or on the golf course at one of Tucson's world-class resorts, you'll probably want to rent a car to get around town. See "Getting Around" in Chapter 2 for details on renting a car in Arizona. Luckily, rates are fairly economical, especially if you can skip the collision-damage waiver. You can usually rent a subcompact for $120 to $150 per week or $30 to $40 per day.

Among the rental-car agencies with offices in Tucson are **Alamo,** 2340 East Elvira Road (tel. 602/746-0196, or toll free 800/327-9633); **Avis,** Tucson International Airport (tel. 602/294-1494, or toll free 800/331-1212); **Budget,** Tucson International Airport (tel. 602/889-8800, or toll free 800/527-0700); **Hertz,** Tucson International Airport (tel. 602/294-7616, or toll free 800/654-3131); **National,** Tucson International Airport (tel. 602/573-8050, or toll free 800/227-7368); and **Thrifty,** 7051 South Tucson Boulevard (tel. 602/889-5761, or toll free 800/367-2277). These are the main offices of the rental-car agencies. Several also have branch offices in other parts of the city, so be sure to ask if they have a more convenient location for pick up or drop off of your car.

PARKING Downtown Tucson is still a relatively easy place to find a parking space, and parking fees are low. There are two huge parking lots at the south side of the Tucson Convention Center, a couple of small lots on either side of the Tucson Museum of Art, and parking garages beneath the main library and El Presidio Park. You'll also find plenty of metered parking on the smaller downtown streets. Almost all Tucson hotels and resorts provide free parking.

DRIVING RULES Lanes on several major avenues in Tucson change direction at rush hour to facilitate traffic flow, so pay attention to signs hung over the street. These tell you the time and direction of traffic in the lanes.

ON FOOT

Downtown Tucson is compact and easily explored on foot. Many old streets in the downtown historic neighborhoods are narrow and much easier to appreciate if you leave your car in a parking lot. On the other hand, several major attractions, including Arizona–Sonora Desert Museum, Old Tucson, Saguaro National Monument, and Sabino Canyon, require quite a bit of walking, often on uneven footing, so be sure to bring a good pair of walking shoes.

TUCSON

American Express　The local American Express representative in the Tucson area is **Bon Voyage Travel.** They have 10 offices, the most convenient located at 990 East University Boulevard (tel. 622-5842).

Area Code　The telephone area code is 602.

Baby-sitters　Most hotels can arrange a baby-sitter for you, and many resorts feature special programs for children on weekends and throughout the summer. If your hotel can't help, call **A-1 Messner Sitter Service** (tel. 881-1578).

Business Hours　See "Fast Facts: Arizona" in Chapter 2 for details.

Car Rentals　See "Getting Around" in this chapter.

Climate　See "When to Go" in Chapter 2.

Currency Exchange　Contact the **Valley National Bank,** 2 East Congress Street (tel. 792-7200), to exchange major currencies.

Drugstores　**Walgreen's** has stores all over Tucson. Some of the more convenient locations are 44 North Stone Avenue (tel. 622-3310), 3330 East Speedway Boulevard (tel. 327-3445), 1900 East Grant Road (tel. 323-9304), and 4080 North Oracle Road (tel. 887-5632).

Embassies/Consulates　The **Mexican Consulate** is at 553 South Stone Avenue (tel. 882-5595). For information on the consulates and embassies of the U.K., Canada, Ireland, Australia, and New Zealand, see "Embassies and Consulates" in "Fast Facts: For the Foreign Traveler" in Chapter 3.

Emergencies　For fire, police, or medical emergency, phone **911.**

Eyeglasses　**Alvernon Optical** has several stores around town where you can have your glasses repaired or replaced. Convenient locations include 440 North Alvernon Way (tel. 327-6211), 7043 North Oracle Road (tel. 297-2501), and 7123 East Tanque Verde Road (tel. 296-4157).

Hairdressers/Barbers　Most Tucson resorts have beauty salons, as do some larger hotels. **Hair in Motion,** 6272 East Grant Road (tel. 721-7920), offers computerized imaging of what you would look like with various changes to your hair. The Tucson *Yellow Pages* telephone book also lists dozens of beauty salons and barbers.

Holidays　See "When to Go" in Chapter 2.

Hospitals　The **Tucson General Hospital** is at 3838 North Campbell Avenue (tel. 327-5431), the **Tucson Medical Center** is at 5301 East Grant Road (tel. 327-5461), and the **University Medical Center** is at 1501 North Campbell Avenue (tel. 694-0111).

Hotlines　Call **Ask-a-Nurse** (tel. 544-2000), **crisis counseling/suicide prevention** (tel. 323-9373), or the **Rape Crisis Hotline** (tel. 623-7273).

Information　See "Tourist Information" in "Orientation" in this chapter.

Laundry/Dry Cleaning　The **Wildcat Wash Well,** 902 East Speedway Boulevard (tel. 792-3656), has a laundry and dry-cleaning drop-off service, and will wash, dry, fold, and package your laundry for you. It's open Monday through Saturday from 8am to 9pm and on Sunday from 10am to 9pm.

Libraries　Tucson's main library is a large modern building in the center of downtown at 101 North Stone Avenue (tel. 791-4010).

Lost Property　If you've lost something and you don't know where, try the **Tucson Police Department Found-Recovered Property office** (tel. 791-4458). If you lost something at the **airport,** call 573-8156; if you lost something on a **Sun Tran bus,** call 792-9222.

Luggage Storage/Lockers　You'll find baggage-storage lockers at the **Greyhound-Trailways bus station,** 2 South Fourth Street (tel. 882-4386).

Newspapers/Magazines　The *Arizona Daily Star* is Tucson's morning daily and the *Tucson Citizen* is the afternoon daily. *Tucson Weekly* is the city's weekly news-and-arts journal; it is published on Wednesday.

Photographic Needs　Tucson's largest camera store is **NuArt Photo,** with three locations: 3954 East Speedway Boulevard (tel. 326-9606), 7000 East

Tanque Verde Road (tel. 290-1266), and El Con Mall, 3601 East Broadway Boulevard (tel. 327-7062).

Police In case of an emergency, phone 911.

Post Office The main Tucson post office is at 141 South Sixth Avenue (tel. 622-8454), open Monday through Friday from 8am to 5pm.

Radio Tucson has dozens of radio stations playing all types of music. Just tune the dial till you hear something that catches your fancy.

Religious Services The Tucson *Yellow Pages* has a complete list of churches listed by denomination.

Safety Tucson is surprisingly safe for a city of its size. However, take the same precautions you would in any other city. Lock your car and put valuables in the trunk or out of sight. Don't carry large amounts of cash when you're walking the streets; it's much better to carry traveler's checks, which can be replaced if stolen. Many streets in the Tucson area are subject to flooding when it rains. Heed warnings about possible flooded areas and don't try to cross a low area that has become flooded. Find an alternate route instead.

Shoe Repairs In the El Con Shopping Center, 3601 East Broadway Boulevard, **El Con Custom Cobblers** (tel. 795-2436) is centrally located and will repair your shoes while you wait or while you shop.

Taxes In addition to the 5% state sales tax, Tucson levies a 2% city sales tax. The hotel room tax is 8.5%.

Taxis See "Getting Around" in this chapter.

Telegrams/Telex The **Western Union** telegraph office is at 4550 South 12th Avenue (tel. 294-4505).

Television Channel Numbers 9 (ABC), 4 (NBC), 6 (PBS), 11 (Fox), 13 (CBS), 18 (Independent), 52 (Independent).

Transit Information **Sun Tran** public buses (tel. 792-9222), the **Amtrak** station (tel. 623-4442), the **Greyhound-Trailways** bus station (tel. 792-0972). See "Arriving" in "Orientation," above, for phone numbers of airlines serving Tucson.

Useful Telephone Numbers **AAA emergency road service** (tel. 298-3358), **Alcoholics Anonymous** (tel. 624-2229), **Alanon** (tel. 323-2229).

Weather Phone 623-4000 for the local weather forecast.

3. ACCOMMODATIONS

Though Phoenix still holds the title of resort capital of Arizona, Tucson is also rapidly becoming known as a resort destination. With the opening in recent years of such world-class full-service resorts as the Sheraton El Conquistador, Westin La Paloma, and Loew's Ventana Canyon Resort, Tucson has taken on a more upscale feel. I personally think that the settings of these Tucson resorts are much more spectacular than comparable resorts in Phoenix and Scottsdale.

For travelers who can't afford the high prices of the major resorts, Tucson has a wider variety of accommodations than Phoenix. This is in part due to the fact that several historic neighborhoods around Tucson are becoming home to bed-and-breakfast inns and also to the presence of several guest ranches within 20 minutes' drive of Tucson. Business and budget travelers are also well served with downtown all-suite and conference hotels and Interstate budget motels.

If you're looking to stay in a bed-and-breakfast inn while in Tucson, you can contact several agencies. The **Arizona Association of Bed & Breakfast Inns,** 3661 North Campbell Avenue (P.O. Box 237), Tucson, AZ 85719 (tel. 602/231-6777), has listings of B&Bs in Tucson and the rest of the state. **Old Pueblo Homestays B & B Reservation Service,** P.O. Box 13603, Tucson, AZ 85732

(tel. 602/790-2399), will book you into one of its many homestays in the Tucson area.
Mi Casa–Su Casa, P.O. Box 950, Tempe, AZ 85281 (tel. 602/990-0682), has accommodations in the Tucson area, as well as all over the Southwest.

Something else to consider when planning a trip to Tucson is that room rates are roughly half in summer as in winter at the more expensive hotels and resorts. Rates usually are lowest from May to September or October. If you want to save money and don't mind the higher temperatures of early and late summer, plan to visit in May or September, when the low rates are in effect. Hotels change their rates on different dates, so always ask when rates go up or down.

For the following listings, the "Budget" category is under $60 double per night, "Moderate" is between $60 and $90, "Expensive" is $90 to $120, and "Very Expensive" is $120 and up.

DOWNTOWN & THE UNIVERSITY AREA

VERY EXPENSIVE

ARIZONA INN, 2200 E. Elm St., Tucson, AZ 85719. Tel. 602/325-1541,
or toll free 800/933-1093. Fax 602/881-5830. 63 rms, 15 suites. A/C TV TEL
$ Rates: Jan–May, $108–$135 single; $118–$145 double; from $155 suite.
May–Sept, $52–$85 single; $62–$95 double; from $105 suite. Sept–Dec,
$69–$105 single; $82–$115 double; from $140 suite. AE, MC, V.

The Arizona Inn, which opened in 1930, offers individually decorated rooms, many with furniture made by handicapped World War I veterans. Many guests return again and again, and the familylike old Arizona atmosphere makes this the most unique resort in Tucson. Just off the lobby is a large high-ceilinged library lounge where guests can sit back with a newspaper or good book and relax in the grand style. The ever-peaceful grounds are a welcome oasis from hectic city life. A private courtyard surrounds the year-round outdoor swimming pool.

All guest rooms are situated in pink stucco buildings surrounded by mature gardens. Although bathrooms are small and have older fixtures, the guest rooms themselves are often very spacious. Old Audubon and floral prints decorate the walls. Most suites have private patios or enclosed sun porches, as well as sitting rooms. Some have their own fireplaces and others have sun terraces.

Dining/Entertainment: The restaurant's main dining room is a casually elegant hall with a high, beamed ceiling, wrought-iron chandeliers, and grilles on the

---

Ⓕ FROMMER'S SMART TRAVELER: HOTELS

1. Consider traveling during the shoulder seasons of late spring and late summer, when temperatures and room rates are somewhat lower. If you can stand the heat of summer, you'll save more than 50% on room rates.
2. Be flexible when making reservations. Rates might go down a few days or a week before or after your scheduled travel. By changing your dates, you might save hundreds of dollars.
3. Always ask about possible discounts or packages. Tucson resorts often offer weekend rates and golf packages that can save you money.
4. Be sure to find out if your hotel offers free airport transportation.
5. If you plan to stay at a guest ranch, be sure to clarify whether the rates include horseback rides or if you'll be charged extra.
6. Request a room with a view of the mountains or the city lights whenever possible (you can overlook a swimming pool anywhere).
7. If you'll be traveling with children, always ask the age of children permitted to stay free and the number of children who can stay free.

windows. Three meals a day are served, with continental cuisine at dinner. The Audubon Lounge is filled with greenery and Audubon prints. A pianist performs in the evening.

Services: Room service, concierge.

Facilities: Swimming pool, two Har-Tru tennis courts, croquet court, table tennis.

EXPENSIVE

DOUBLETREE TUCSON, 445 S. Alvernon Way, Tucson, AZ 85711. Tel. 602/881-4200, or toll free 800/528-0444. 300 rms, 8 suites. A/C TV TEL

$ Rates: Jan–May, $110 single; $120 double. May–Sept, $49 single or double; Sept–Dec, $95 single; $105 double. AE, DC, DISC, MC, V.

Located directly across the street from the Randolph Park public golf course, the Doubletree is midway between the airport and downtown Tucson. Although the hotel does much convention business and sometimes feels quite crowded, the gardens, with their citrus trees and roses, are almost always tranquil. Rooms are divided between a nine-story building that offers views of the valley and a two-story building with patio rooms overlooking the quiet garden and pool area. All rooms are comfortably appointed with contemporary furnishings. Live potted plants in most rooms are a homey touch.

Dining/Entertainment: The Cactus Rose Restaurant serves southwestern cuisine. The Javelina Cantina, a more lively place, serves Mexican food in a western atmosphere. For drinks and live piano music there's the Lobby Bar.

Services: Room service, valet service, car-rental desk.

Facilities: Swimming pool, whirlpool spa, exercise room, three tennis courts, no-smoking rooms, gift shop, beauty salon.

RAMADA DOWNTOWN, 475 N. Granada Rd., Tucson, AZ 85701. Tel. 602/622-3000, or toll free 800/228-2828. 297 rms, 10 suites. A/C TV TEL

$ Rates: Jan–May, $65–$90 single; $75–$100 double. May–Sept, $55 single; $65 double. Sept–Dec, $60 single; $70 double. AE, CB, DC, DISC, MC, V.

Pink stucco walls, red-tile roofs, and arched windows give this hotel a classic Spanish colonial flavor. Located just off I-10 and only a few blocks from the El Presidio Historic District and Tucson Museum of Art, the Ramada Downtown is an excellent choice for anyone who wants to be close to Tucson's past and its lively cultural present. The lobby, with its bubbling fountain and sweeping stairway with a wrought-iron railing, is reminiscent of a colonial hacienda. Guest rooms are attractively furnished in contemporary style and pastel colors. There are alarm clocks and coffee makers to get you going in the morning and balconies overlooking the pool for relaxing.

Dining/Entertainment: El Centro Grill serves American and continental meals at reasonable prices and has a large salad bar. There is also a brightly lit lounge.

Services: Free airport shuttle, valet service.

Facilities: Olympic-size swimming pool, no-smoking rooms.

MODERATE

BEST WESTERN GHOST RANCH LODGE, 801 W. Miracle Mile, Tucson, AZ 85705. Tel. 602/791-7565, or toll free 800/456-7565. Fax 602/791-3898. 81 rms (all with bath). A/C TV TEL

$ Rates (including continental breakfast): Jan–May, $54–$74 single; $60–$80 double. June–Dec, $31–$64 single; $37–$70 double. AE, CB, DC, DISC, MC, V.

Although Miracle Mile was once Tucson's main drag and home to dozens of motor hotels, today it's looking a bit shabby. One exception is the Ghost Ranch, which opened back in 1941 and was for many years one of Tucson's desert resorts catering to northern visitors who stayed for the winter. Situated on 8 acres, the lodge has a justly famous cactus garden, orange grove, and extensive lawns that together create an oasis atmosphere. Guest rooms have all been recently refurbished but still have a bit of western flavor to them such as high beamed ceilings, painted brick walls, and patios covered by red-tile roofs. If you're looking for Old Tucson, this is it. The lodge's dining room serves southwestern-style meals and offers dining on a poolside patio or inside with a view of the Santa Catalina Mountains. Facilities of the Ghost Ranch include a swimming pool, a whirlpool spa, a games room, and no-smoking rooms. Laundry service is available.

A Bed & Breakfast

EL PRESIDIO BED & BREAKFAST INN, 297 N. Main Ave., Tucson, AZ 85701. Tel. 602/623-6151. 1 rm, 3 suites (all with bath). TEL
$ Rates (including full breakfast): $85–$95 single or double. No credit cards.

⭐ In Tucson's early years the only building material was adobe, but when the railroad arrived, homeowners quickly took advantage of newly available building materials. El Presidio is a merger of the Victorian and adobe architectural styles and is a truly unique lodging in Tucson. You're only steps away from the Tucson Museum of Art, Old Town Artisans, and Janos, one of Tucson's best restaurants. Owners Patti and Jerry Toci spent many years restoring the old house and today it is a little oasis with lush gardens, fountains, and a courtyard filled with birds. Guest rooms are arranged around the courtyard, and three of the four are suites with little kitchens. All are decorated with antiques and original art (some by Jerry Toci) and come with bathrobes. In addition to the filling breakfast in the sun room, there are complimentary drinks, fruit, and treats in the afternoon and evening.

BUDGET

DAYS INN SANTA RITA, 88 E. Broadway Blvd., Tucson, AZ 85701. Tel. 602/622-4000, or toll free 800/325-2525. Fax 602/620-0376. 162 rms, 6 suites (all with bath). A/C TV TEL
$ Rates: $39–$61 single; $45–$67 double; $55–$130 suite. Children 18 and under stay free in parents' room. AE, DC, DISC, MC, V.

Almost across the street from the convention center and around the corner from Tucson's downtown arts district and the El Presidio Historic District, this high-rise hotel is surprisingly inexpensive for such an excellent location. You wouldn't think so to look at it, but this hotel is nearly 90 years old. Today there is a sunken lobby with a fountain and original art on the walls. The guest rooms are done in Spanish colonial decor with southwestern-motif bedspreads and framed prints. The hotel's Cafe Poca Cosa is a wildly painted café that's popular with the downtown art crowd. The hotel offers free local phone calls and complimentary coffee and pastries. Facilities include a swimming pool, saunas, and no-smoking rooms.

HOTEL CONGRESS, 311 E. Congress St., Tucson, AZ 85701. Tel. 602/622-8848. 40 rms (all with bath). TEL
$ Rates: $26–$35 single; $29–$45 double. Discount to University of Arizona students and faculty. Lower rates for shared hostel rooms. AE, MC, V.

⭐ Located in the heart of Tucson's burgeoning arts district, the Hotel Congress is one of the few historic downtown hotels left in Arizona. Built to serve the needs of railroad passengers, the hotel once played host to John Dillinger. Today it is operated as a youth hostel and budget hotel, and is conveniently located near the Greyhound and Amtrak stations as well as the downtown transit mall. Although the hotel is not luxurious, it has been restored to its original southwestern elegance, with Native American–motif paintings decorating the lobby walls. Some bathrooms have bathtubs only and others have showers only. There is a pleasant little café off the lobby, as well as a properly western saloon bar. At night the Club Congress is a very popular disco.

RODEWAY INN–TUCSON NORTH, 1365 W. Grant Rd., Tucson, AZ 85745. Tel. 602/622-7791, or toll free 800/228-2000. Fax 602/629-0201. 146 rms, 2 suites (all with bath). A/C TV TEL
$ Rates: Jan–Apr, $52 single; $58 double; $80 suite. May–Dec, $43 single; $49 double; $65 suite. AE, CB, DC, DISC, MC, V.

Located only a mile north of downtown and just off I-10 at the Grant Road exit, the

Rodeway Inn is centrally located for visiting almost all of Tucson's tourist attractions. Guest rooms are large and have modern furnishings and clock radios. Sonora Sam's Restaurant and Cantina is a casual coffee shop serving a wide variety of dishes from southwestern to continental. The hotel provides complimentary coffee and muffins in the morning, plus a complimentary afternoon cocktail. Its facilities include a swimming pool and a volleyball court.

EAST TUCSON

EXPENSIVE

EMBASSY SUITES HOTEL/TUCSON–BROADWAY, 5335 E. Broadway, Tucson, AZ 85711. Tel. 602/745-2700, or toll free 800/EMBASSY. Fax 602/790-9232. 142 suites. A/C TV TEL
$ Rates (including full breakfast): Jan–Apr, $85–$120 single; $95–$130 double. May–Sept, $70–$80 single; $80–$90 double. Sept–Dec, $75–$90 single; $80–$95 double. Weekend rates available. AE, DC, DISC, MC, V.
For the traveler who needs plenty of room, Embassy Suites offers an all-suite hotel close to eastern Tucson businesses and restaurants. Mission revival decor sets the tone for the hotel, with red-tile floors and huge carved ceiling beams in the lobby. Suites are arranged around two courtyards, one containing a small pool and the other a three-story atrium garden. French doors and a wall of glass let plenty of light into each suite. There are kitchenettes, and sofa beds allow up to six people to stay in a suite.
    Dining/Entertainment: There is no restaurant on the premises, but a full cooked-to-order breakfast is served. In the evening there is a 2-hour complimentary happy hour. Gas grills and utensils are available if you want to barbecue.
    Services: Room service, concierge, complimentary health club passes, complimentary afternoon cocktails, valet service.
    Facilities: Swimming pool, sauna, whirlpool bath, billiards room, no-smoking suites, wheelchair accommodations, gift shop.

TUCSON HILTON EAST, 7600 E. Broadway, Tucson, AZ 85710. Tel. 602/721-5600, or toll free 800/445-8677. Fax 602/721-5696. 223 rms, 8 suites. A/C MINIBAR TV TEL
$ Rates: Oct–Apr, $105–$135 single; $118–$148 double; $158–$178 suite. May–Sept, $69 single or double; $125 suite. Special packages and weekend rates available. AE, DC, DISC, MC, V.
Located on the east side of town in Tucson's business corridor, the Tucson Hilton East is a high-rise hotel with unobstructed views across the valley. The lobby is large and spartan, the view through the seven-story wall of glass serving as the focal point.
    Rooms are decorated in sea-green or rose color schemes, with contemporary furnishings. Bathrooms are what you'd expect, but nothing more unless you stay in a suite or VIP room, in which case you might find a tiny TV on the bathroom counter, a telephone, and a plush bathrobe. Suites also have large private sun decks.
    Dining/Entertainment: The Propre Place is the proper place for an elegant meal of nouvelle American cuisine with a hint of southwestern flavoring. For more casual dining, there is the Atrium Café. Both restaurants provide outstanding views of the mountains. The Terrace Café, beside the pool, features 16 wines and champagnes on tap.
    Services: Room service, concierge floor, passes to nearby fitness center, free shopping shuttle, complimentary shuttle to within 3 miles.
    Facilities: Swimming pool, whirlpool bath, no-smoking rooms.

TUCSON VISCOUNT SUITE HOTEL, 4855 E. Broadway, Tucson, AZ 85711. Tel. 602/745-6500, or toll free 800/255-3050. 215 suites. A/C TV TEL
$ Rates (including full breakfast): Summer, $65 single; $75 double. Winter, $122 single; $132 double. AE, CB, DC, DISC, MC, V.

The Viscount is centrally located in the eastern Tucson business district only a few minutes from downtown. All accommodations at this four-story atrium-style hotel are spacious suites. The atrium, with its garden atmosphere, serves as a breakfast room. Suites are done in pinks and pale aqua with a mixture of contemporary and classic European furnishings. Some have a small refrigerator or microwave. In the bathroom you'll find a marble counter and tile floors. Large windows let sunshine flood the bedrooms.

Dining/Entertainment: Breakfast and afternoon cocktails are served in the Atrium Café. For more formal dining there's the Oxford. Wilbur's is a sports bar named after the University of Arizona mascot.

Services: Room service, concierge, complimentary afternoon cocktails, shopping shuttle.

Facilities: Swimming pool, whirlpool bath, sauna, exercise room, no-smoking rooms, wheelchair accommodations.

MODERATE

THE LODGE ON THE DESERT, 306 N. Alvernon Way (P.O. Box 42500), Tucson, AZ 85733. Tel. 602/325-3366, or toll free 800/456-5634. Fax 602/327-5834. 37 rms (all with bath). A/C TV TEL

$ Rates (including continental breakfast): Nov–May, $72–$97 single; $82–$109 double. June–Oct, $48–$66 single; $52–$70 double. AE, CB, DC, MC, V.

A sort of poor-man's Arizona Inn, the Lodge on the Desert offers the same adobe-style buildings in a garden compound. Conveniently located close to downtown and not far from Tucson's restaurant row, this is an old Arizona resort at affordable rates. It is still owned by the same family that founded it in 1936. The lodge's greatest draw is its old-world charm and hacienda styling. Manicured lawns and flower gardens offer a relaxing retreat. The main building was once a private residence, and several guest rooms are housed in buildings made of adobe blocks. There are basically three types of rooms, though all are individually furnished with old Monterey furniture. Some rooms have beamed ceilings and others have fireplaces. Larger rooms have Mexican tile floors rather than carpeting. One room even has its own private swimming pool. Years ago Duncan Hines would stay at the Lodge on the Desert because the meals met his high standards. Those high standards still prevail. One section of the dining room has a fireplace and a bench built into the adobe wall. Among the lodge's other features are a swimming pool with a view of the Santa Catalina Mountains, shuffleboard, table tennis, a croquet court, and a library.

SMUGGLER'S INN, 6350 E. Speedway (at Wilmot), Tucson, AZ 85710. Tel. 602/296-3292, or toll free 800/525-8852. Fax 602/722-3713. 150 rms and suites (all with bath). A/C TV TEL

$ Rates: Jan–Apr, $77–$85 single; $87–$95 double; $115 suite. May–Sept, $44–$49 single; $51–$56 double; $78 suite. Oct–Dec, $53–$59 single; $63–$69 double; $96 suite. AE, CB, DC, DISC, MC, V.

The Smuggler's Inn is a very comfortable and economically priced hotel. The guest rooms are arranged around a beautiful garden that features a small lake with curving rocky banks. Neatly trimmed lawns and tall palm trees give the garden a tropical look. Guest rooms are spacious and all have a balcony or patio. Furnishings are modern, and there are clock radios and bathroom telephones. The inn's restaurant sports a Caribbean nautical theme both in decor and on the menu, which features good fish dishes. There is also a cocktail lounge. The inn offers room service, a complimentary morning newspaper, and golf privileges. Its facilities include a swimming pool, whirlpool bath, fitness room, putting green, tennis court, and no-smoking rooms.

TANQUE VERDE INN, 7007 E. Tanque Verde Rd., Tucson, AZ 85715. Tel. 602/298-2300, or toll free 800/882-8484. 89 rms, 2 suites (all with bath). A/C TV TEL

$ Rates (including continental breakfast): Feb–Mar, $75–$90 single or double; $130 suite. Apr–May and Oct–Jan, $55–$70 single or double; $100 suite. May–Oct, $39–$55 single or double; $85–$90 suite. AE, DC, MC, V.

Though it looks like a fortress or a prison from the outside, the Tanque Verde Inn, located beside a shopping center on Tucson's restaurant row, is surprisingly pleasant inside. The modest motel is built around four courtyards that provide tranquil garden settings. Each courtyard has fountains, tile benches, and lush plantings. Most rooms are quite large; some have kitchenettes and all have coffee makers. Numerous excellent restaurants are along East Tanque Verde Road. The inn provides complimentary evening cocktails, free local phone calls, and free in-room movies. Among its facilities are a swimming pool, whirlpool bath, coin laundry, no-smoking rooms, and wheelchair accommodations.

NORTH TUCSON
VERY EXPENSIVE

LOEW'S VENTANA CANYON RESORT, 7000 N. Resort Dr., Tucson, AZ 85715. Tel. 602/299-2020, or toll free 800/234-5117. Fax 602/299-6832. 398 rms, 26 suites. A/C TV TEL

$ Rates: Jan–May, $225–$285 single; $245–$305 double; $450–$1,400 suite. May–Sept, $95–$125 single; $105–$135 double; $190–$1,400 suite. Sept–Jan, $195–$235 single; $215–$275 double; $350–$1,400 suite. Special packages available. AE, CB, DC, MC, V.

The rugged Santa Catalina Mountains and Ventana Canyon stand in striking contrast to the pampered luxury and comforts of this full-service resort. Majestic saguaro cactuses cover the rocky slopes, yet the manicured greens of the golf course soften the desert picture. Outside the grand entrance to the resort, a low man-made waterfall cascades into a lake, while up the Ventana Canyon nature trail you'll find a breathtaking natural waterfall. Flagstone floors in the lobby and tables with boulders for bases give the resort's public rooms a rugged but luxurious appeal.

Guest rooms are designed to impress. Beds angle out from a corner with drapes hanging from the headboard and a floral arrangement providing an accent. Pale peaches and desert pastels give the rooms a tranquil and bright feel, while contemporary overstuffed chairs add comfort. Some of the rooms have fireplaces made of the same cast stone blocks found in the lobby. Private balconies overlook either the city lights or the mountains. Bathrooms are designed for enjoyment, with a tiny television, hairdryer, scales, a telephone, travertine marble floors, oversize towels, and a bathtub big enough for two people.

Dining/Entertainment: The Ventana Room is one of the finest restaurants in Tucson and serves nouvelle American cuisine amid views of the city lights. The Canyon Café offers a view of the canyon waterfall. For lakeside terrace dining there is the Flying V Bar and Grill. Southwestern meals, steaks, and seafood are served, and at

---

FROMMER'S COOL FOR KIDS:
HOTELS

The Westin La Paloma (see p. 126) Kids get their own lounge and games room, and in summers and holidays there are special programs for the kids so parents can have a little free time.

Guest Ranches (see pp. 129–130) Tucson has several guest ranches, most of which are family oriented. Kids can play cowboy to their heart's content, riding the range, singing songs by the campfire, or whatever.

night a disco takes over. The Cascade Lounge serves afternoon tea and then becomes an evening piano bar. On weekends there is live dance music.

Services: 24-hour room service, concierge, valet/laundry service, free shopping shuttle, massages, mountain bike rentals, fitness classes, car-rental desk, tour desk.

Facilities: 18-hole golf course, two swimming pools with mountain views, whirlpool baths, 10 tennis courts, croquet court, health spa (including a lap pool, a fitness trail, aerobics room, exercise room with machines and free weights, steam rooms, saunas), beauty salon.

SHERATON TUCSON EL CONQUISTADOR, 10,000 N. Oracle Rd., Tucson, AZ 85737. Tel. 602/742-7000, or toll free 800/325-7832. 440 rms, 100 suites. A/C MINIBAR TV TEL

$ Rates: Jan–May, $175–$275 single or double; $200–$1,100 suite. May–Sept, $90–$145 single or double; $115–$650 suite. Sept–Dec, $120–$230 single or double; $150–$1,100 suite. Weekend and special packages available. AE, CB, DC, DISC, MC, V.

No doubt about it, El Conquistador has the most spectacular setting of any resort in Tucson. Each day at sunset, nature provides El Conquistador with a light show unsurpassed anywhere in Arizona. However, you must stay farther away from downtown to see it. The resort is decorated in mission-revival style throughout, with red-tile roofs and stucco walls. The lobby captures a traditional southwestern feel with a blue-tile fountain, red-tile floors, and rustic furniture.

The guest rooms were all redecorated in 1991 and feature southwestern-influenced contemporary furniture in shades of pale green. The pale-wood television armoires have hammered-tin insets that are reminiscent of old Mexican cabinets. All rooms have a balcony or patio and a view of the mountains, the desert, or a courtyard. There are fireplaces in most suites. Bathrooms are spacious and come with a large basket of toiletries.

Dining/Entertainment: The White Dove is a small, elegant dining room that incorporates touches of Arizona's mission history. Meals display an appropriately southwestern flavor. For Mexican food, there is Dos Locos Cantina with its strolling mariachis and lively dance floor at night. At the Last Territory Steakhouse, cowboy vittles and music are the order of the day. The Sundance Café offers a casual and quiet atmosphere and international cuisine at moderate prices. The El Conquistador Country Club's La Vista, which capitalizes on its outstanding view, serves continental and southwestern dishes.

Services: Room service, concierge, valet/laundry service, airport shuttle ($16 per person each way), shopping shuttle, baby-sitting, rental-car desk, tour desk, massages, horseback riding.

Facilities: Three golf courses (45 holes total), 31 lighted tennis courts, 11 indoor racquetball courts, large swimming pool, whirlpool baths, sauna, fitness room, jogging paths, volleyball, basketball, rental bikes, gift shop, art gallery.

TUCSON NATIONAL GOLF & CONFERENCE RESORT, 2727 W. Club Dr., Tucson, AZ 85741. Tel. 602/297-2271, or toll free 800/528-4856. Fax 602/742-2452. 167 rms. A/C MINIBAR TV TEL

$ Rates: Jan–Apr, $175–$195 single or double. Apr–Sept, $80–$100 single or double. Sept–Jan, $135–$155 single or double. Special packages available. AE, CB, DC, MC, V.

Formerly a country club, Tucson National sits on 650 acres in the foothills north of downtown Tucson. The lobby, which should not be mistaken for the golf club entrance, is designed in mission-revival style with a tree-of-life fountain capturing your attention the moment you walk through the door. A further glance around reveals colorful floral wall murals and a carved stone check-in desk reminiscent of old church facades in Mexico. Rustic Mexican furniture is arranged in private seating areas around the lobby. As the resort's name implies, golf is the driving force behind most stays; however, the full-service health spa is one of the best in Arizona and makes for very relaxing visits.

The guest rooms here are in two-story buildings and most overlook the golf

N

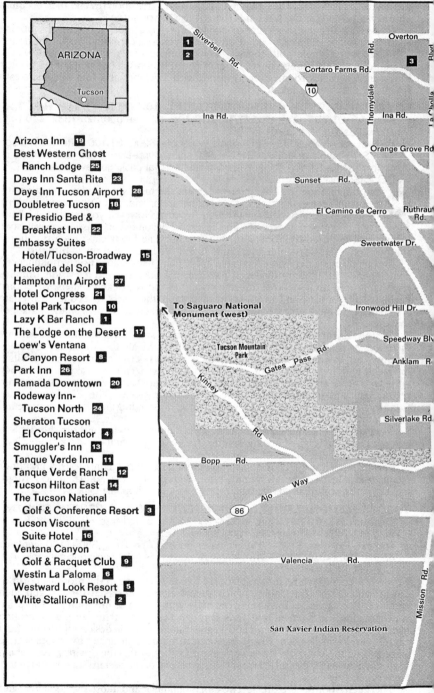

TUCSON ACCOMMODATIONS

To Sabino Canyon Park ↗

Magee Rd.

La Canada Dr.

5 Ina Rd.

Orange Grove Rd.

Skyline Dr.

Kolb Rd. **8**

9

6

7

Sunrise Dr.

River Rd.

Wetmore Rd.

Roger

Prince

Flowing Wells Rd.

Sabino

Snyder Rd.

Canyon Rd.

To Mount Lemmon ↗

Catalina Hwy.

Bear Canyon

Miracle Mile **25**

Ft. Lowell Rd.

Campbell

Stone

Tucson Blvd.

Country Club Rd.

Alvernon Way

Swan Rd.

Craycroft Rd.

Tanque Verde Rd.

Grant Rd. **24**

(10)

Oracle

1st

19

Swan Rd. **10**

Grant Rd.

11

12 →

Speedway Blvd.

13

20

21

6th St.

Broadway Blvd.

5th St. **16** **15**

17

Wilmot Rd.

Kolb Rd.

To Saguaro National Monument (east) ↗

14

Congress

22 **23**

Grande Ave.

Sentinel Peak Park

22nd St.

Tucson Greyhound Park

36th St.

Reid Park

Randolph Park **18**

29th St.

Craycroft Rd.

22nd St.

Golf Links Rd.

Escalante Rd.

Pantano Rd.

Camino Seco Rd.

Ajo Way

Irvington Rd.

Kino Blvd.

(10)

28

Palo Verde Rd.

Davis Monthan AFB

Kolb

Irvington Rd.

Drexel Rd.

12th Ave.

6th Ave.

Valencia Rd. **26**

27

Los Reales Rd.

Tucson International Airport

(19)

(10)

Airport ↗

course, the mountains, or the swimming pool. There are several different styles, but all are very spacious and have their own patio or balcony. Hand-carved doors and Mexican hand-painted tile counters in the bathrooms give the rooms a Spanish colonial feel. For convenience there are two sinks and large dressing areas in all the rooms.

Dining/Entertainment: The Fiesta Room and Bar plays up Arizona's copper-mining history with copper-top tables and copper chandeliers. At the back of the lobby is the Bella Vista Lounge with a shiny copper fireplace and a distant view of the Santa Catalina Mountains. There are free hors d'oeuvres here during happy hour and live contemporary jazz in the evening.

Services: 24-hour room service, business services, valet parking, valet/laundry service, exercise classes, massages, herbal wraps, loofah scrubs, salt scrubs, Scotch water massage, dietary assistance, facials.

Facilities: 27-hole golf course (home of the Tucson Open), two tennis courts, swimming pool, whirlpool bath, volleyball court, gift shop, pro shop, and full-service health spa with exercise machines, free weights, an aerobics room, steam rooms, saunas, whirlpool baths, tanning beds, Russian baths, and a skin-care salon.

VENTANA CANYON GOLF & RACQUET CLUB, 6200 N. Clubhouse Lane, Tucson, AZ 85715. Tel. 602/577-1400, or toll free 800/828-5701, 800/233-4569 in Arizona. Fax 602/299-0256. 48 suites. A/C MINIBAR TV TEL
$ Rates: Jan–Apr, $255 one bedroom, $360 two bedrooms. Apr–May, $220 one bedroom, $315 two bedrooms. May–Oct, $90 one bedroom, $185 two bedrooms. Oct–Jan $210 one bedroom, $295 two bedrooms. AE, MC, V.

Golf is the raison d'être of this small luxury resort. However, even the nongolfer will be impressed by the spectacular setting at the foot of the rugged Santa Catalina Mountains, and the 1,100 acres of tranquil desert. The lobby is a streamlined, low-key room decorated in mauve colors and glass-block walls. Small size with big-resort amenities is what makes this resort so appealing.

Guest quarters are all spacious and attractive suites. Most have walls of windows so you can enjoy the views from the comfort of your room. All include small kitchens. Some have balconies, soaring cathedral ceilings, and spiral stairs that lead up to a loft sleeping area. All feature a large bathroom with oversize tub, two sinks, and a separate changing room.

Dining/Entertainment: The Clubhouse Dining Room, a few steps from the lobby, offers fine dining with a view of the looming Santa Catalina Mountains. Drinks are served at the Terrace Lounge and the Fireside Lounge. There's also a poolside snack bar.

Services: Room service, concierge, golf lessons, tennis lessons, massages, baby-sitting, valet/laundry service, complimentary daily newspaper and shoeshine, free shuttle to Loew's Ventana Canyon Resort.

Facilities: Two 18-hole golf courses, 12 tennis courts, swimming pool, whirlpool baths, exercise room, aerobics room, exercise course, steam rooms, saunas, beauty salon, pro shop.

WESTIN LA PALOMA, 3800 E. Sunrise Dr., Tucson, AZ 85718. Tel. 602/742-6000, or toll free 800/876-3683. Fax 602/577-5886. 487 rms, 43 suites. A/C MINIBAR TV TEL
$ Rates: Jan–May, $260–$290 single; $280–$310 double; from $350 suite. May–Sept, $120–$150 single; $140–$170 double; from $175 suite. Sept–Jan, $190–$220 single; $210–$240 double; $280 suite. Special packages available. AE, CB, DC, DISC, MC, V.

La Paloma (The Dove) roosts in the middle of Tucson's prestigious foothills neighborhoods, with sweeping panoramas from its hilltop perch. Mission-revival architecture in a pale pink that mimics the mountains at sunset gives La Paloma a timeless feel. Even the walkways are made to look old, and the native vegetation has been left intact.

Guest rooms are situated in 27 two-story buildings. Decor is in desert pastels with such colorful accents as textured cotton on the furniture, woven raffia headboards, and verdigris-finished metal-and-glass tables. Bathrooms are extremely spacious, with separate tub and shower, two sinks, a telephone, and kimono-style bathrobes.

Dining/Entertainment: The casual Desert Garden, with views of the mountains, is open all day. Gourmet American cuisine is highlighted in the La Paloma Dining Room at the La Paloma Country Club (jacket required for dinner). La Villa is set in its own hacienda and is well known for its delicious fish dishes and view of the city (dinner only). For snacks there is the Courtside Deli and another snack bar on the golf course. Sabinos is a swim-up bar that also serves light meals. The Desert Garden Lounge in the lobby provides great views and evening piano music. Sports fans can retreat to the Cactus Club sports bar, which becomes a disco in the late evening. Golfers have their own bar at the 19th Hole.

Services: 24-hour room service, concierge floor, valet service, massages, day-care center, fitness classes, bike rentals, shopping shuttle.

Facilities: 27-hole golf course, driving range, putting green, free-form swimming pool with swim-up bar and water slide, 12 tennis courts (3 clay), indoor racquetball courts, three whirlpool baths, golf pro shop, tennis pro shop, table tennis, volleyball, croquet court, jogging trails and health club with exercise machines, aerobics room, beauty salon, children's lounge.

WESTWARD LOOK RESORT, 245 E. Ina Rd., Tucson, AZ 85704. Tel. 602/297-1151, or toll free 800/722-2500. Fax 602/297-9023. 244 rms, 10 suites. A/C MINIBAR TV TEL

$ Rates: Jan–Apr, $145–$190 single or double; from $300 suite. Apr–May and Sept–Jan, $115–$160 single or double; from $240 suite. May–Sept, $70–$100 single or double; from $150 suite. Special packages available. AE, CB, DC, DISC, MC, V.

Opened in 1929 as a dude ranch, the Westward Look has since grown to become one of Tucson's foremost resorts. Offering quiet, traditional luxury in the foothills of the Santa Catalina Mountains, the resort is surrounded by desert that is home to the saguaro cactus and palo verde trees. The low-ceilinged lobby maintains a western ranch atmosphere with hardwood floors, a fireplace, and cushioned wicker furniture.

Guest rooms are all quite large and many have exposed-beam ceilings in keeping with the ranch heritage. All rooms are slightly different, but each has a private balcony or patio and comes with amenities like a coffee maker, clock radio, small refrigerator, and an iron and ironing board.

Dining/Entertainment: The Gold Room features two walls of glass that provide sweeping views of Tucson. The continental cuisine is reliably excellent. The Lobby Café serves breakfast and lunch in a casual atmosphere. The Lookout Lounge, near the main swimming pool, offers live Top-40 music Tuesday through Friday and jazz and blues on Saturday and Sunday.

Services: Room service, massages, tennis lessons.

Facilities: Three swimming pools (including a lap pool), eight tennis courts ($8 per hour court fee), three whirlpool baths, softball, basketball, volleyball, horseshoes, table tennis, jogging trail, pro shop, gift shop, and a fitness center with free weights, an aerobics room, and exercise machines.

EXPENSIVE

HACIENDA DEL SOL, 5601 N. Hacienda del Sol Rd., Tucson, AZ 85718, Tel. 602/299-1501, or toll free 800/444-3999. Fax 602/299-7950. 37 rms and suites. A/C TV TEL

$ Rates: $50–$75 single; $110–$120 double; $180–$295 suite. AE, DC, DISC, MC, V.

Built in 1929 as a girls' school, Hacienda del Sol offers a bit of old southwestern hospitality and atmosphere. Perched on a ridge overlooking the city, the lodge has gorgeous views in all directions. The main building is in the traditional hacienda style with covered tile walkways around the courtyard. The lobby features a huge hearth around the stucco fireplace, and in the adjacent library are hand-carved ceiling beams. The small pool, situated on its own terrace below the main lodge, overlooks the mountains and foothills. Although the rooms are not luxurious, in their early years they were patronized by the Westinghouses, Joseph Cotton, Clark Gable, and Spencer Tracy, among others. Size and comfort levels vary considerably among the rooms, the least expensive being the cement-floored rooms in the old hacienda building. Newer and more modern accommodations are available in several casita buildings. Some suites have tile floors and counters, while others include fireplaces or kitchens.

Dining/Entertainment: The lodge's dining room features great views of the city and the Santa Catalina Mountains. A high beamed ceiling, rustic hand-painted chairs, old Navajo sand paintings, and colorfully painted door frames give the room a very southwestern mood. A classical guitarist plays on Friday and Saturday evenings, and there is a Sunday champagne brunch. The kitchen prepares continental dishes in the $15 to $20 range.

Services: Horseback riding.

Facilities: Swimming pool, whirlpool bath, tennis court, volleyball.

HOTEL PARK TUCSON, 5151 E. Grant Rd., Tucson, AZ 85712. Tel. 602/323-6262, or toll free 800/257-7275, 800/344-0189 in Arizona. Fax 602/325-2989. 215 suites. A/C TV TEL
$ Rates (including full breakfast): Jan–Apr, $105–$115 single; $115–$125 double. May–Sept, $75–$85 single; $85–$95 double. Sept–Jan, $95–$105 single; $105–$115 double. AE, CB, DC, DISC, MC, V.

Located between the prestigious foothills of northern Tucson and the business corridor of eastern Tucson, this all-suite hotel is a very convenient choice both for business travelers and vacationers who want to play the numerous nearby golf courses. Huge wall murals of Mexican village life and an unusual fountain that surrounds a raised seating area give the Hotel Park Tucson's lobby a bit of visual interest. Swimmers should note that the hotel's pool features one of the few swim-up bars in Tucson.

All suites come with small refrigerators and Colonial American-style furnishings. However, there are plans to remodel the hotel's guest rooms in a southwestern style with tile floors and rustic Mexican furnishings. The hotel's best rooms are on the north side, with views of the mountains.

Dining/Entertainment: The Ranchers Club serves the tastiest steaks in Tucson at expectedly high prices. Cowboy decor would make John Wayne feel right at home. (See "Dining," below, for details.) Trophies is one of the most popular sports bars in Tucson and is decked out with University of Arizona and Phoenix Cardinals decorations.

Services: Valet service, shopping shuttle, car-rental desk, secretarial service.

Facilities: Swimming pool, whirlpool bath, sauna, steam room, exercise room, no-smoking rooms, rooms for women only, wheelchair accommodations.

NEAR THE AIRPORT
BUDGET

DAYS INN TUCSON AIRPORT, 3700 E. Irvington Rd., Tucson, AZ 85714. Tel. 602/571-1400, or toll free 800/325-2525. Fax 602/571-1400. 117 rms (all with bath). A/C TV TEL
$ Rates: $39–$49 single; $45–$52 double. AE, CB, DC, DISC, MC, V.

This motel is close to the airport, conveniently located just off I-10 at the Palo Verde exit. It also happens to be next door to a large indoor swap meet (flea market) and three blocks from a factory-outlet shopping mall. Most rooms contain two double beds and all are clean and new. There's also a swimming pool and whirlpool bath.

HAMPTON INN AIRPORT, 6971 S. Tucson Blvd., Tucson, AZ 85706. Tel. 602/889-5789, or toll free 800/HAMPTON. Fax 602/889-4002. 125 rms and suites (all with bath).
$ Rates (including continental breakfast): $39–$54 single; $45–$59 double. AE, CB, DC, DISC, MC, V.

I'm a big fan of Hampton Inns because of their satisfaction guarantee. If you aren't completely satisfied with your stay, you don't have to pay. Obviously, the staff at a Hampton Inn will go out of its way to please you, and this makes for excellent and friendly service. This Hampton Inn is right outside the entrance to the airport. Rooms here are modern and of medium size; the only drawback are their small windows. There are several restaurants nearby. Services include in-room movies, an airport shuttle, and free local phone calls. The inn has a swimming pool and whirlpool bath.

PARK INN, 2803 E. Valencia Rd., Tucson, AZ 85706. Tel. 602/294-2500, or toll free 800/437-PARK. Fax 602/741-0851. 89 rms, 3 suites (all with bath). A/C TV TEL
$ Rates: $39–$70 single; $43–$75 double; $65–$112 suite. AE, CB, DC, DISC, MC, V.

One of the nicest budget-price lodgings in the area, the Park Inn is located just off the road leading to the airport. You can't miss the blue pillars at the entrance portico. Inside, there are pink pillars and a pink-tile floor. Standard rooms are not large but are attractively decorated in dusty rose and blue. Room service and an airport shuttle are available, and there are a swimming pool, whirlpool bath, no-smoking rooms, and wheelchair accommodations.

OUTSIDE THE CITY
GUEST RANCHES

LAZY K BAR RANCH, 8401 N. Scenic Dr., Tucson, AZ 85743. Tel. 602/744-3050. 23 rms and suites. A/C
$ Rates (including all meals): $105–$140 single; $160–$210 double; $210–$240 suite. AE, DC, DISC, MC, V. **Closed:** June 15–Sept 1.

Homesteaded in 1933 and converted to a dude ranch in 1936, the Lazy K Bar Ranch covers 160 acres adjacent to Tucson Mountain Park. There are plenty of nearby hiking and riding trails, and if you have a hankering for city life, it isn't difficult to reach downtown (20 minutes away). Guest rooms vary in size and comfort level. The newest are the most comfortable, with exposed brick walls and sliding glass doors that open onto a patio. I prefer the corner rooms with windows on two sides. Birdwatchers will appreciate the six bird-feeding stations around the property; hummingbirds are frequently seen.

Dining/Entertainment: All meals are included in room rates and are served family style in a dining room that features Mexican tile floors and an open-pit fireplace. Food is hearty American ranch style with a Saturday-night cookout. Each evening there's a happy hour at the ranch's BYOB bar.

Services: Complimentary airport transfer, horseback riding twice daily, Sunday shuttle to Old Tucson and Arizona–Sonora Desert Museum, hayrides, lunch rides, cookouts, square dances.

Facilities: Swimming pool, whirlpool bath, tennis courts, volleyball, basketball, shuffleboard, horseshoes, stables, library, TV lounge, games, cards.

TANQUE VERDE RANCH, 14301 E. Speedway Blvd. (Rte. 8, Box 66), Tucson, AZ 85748. Tel. 602/296-6275, or toll free 700/234-DUDE. Fax 602/721-9426. 65 rms. A/C TEL
$ Rates (including all meals): Dec–Apr, $215–$260 single; $240–$300 double. May–Sept, $155–$195 single; $195–$235 double. Oct–Dec, $160–$210 single; $200–$250 double. AE, CB, DC, DISC, MC, V.

Far and away the most luxurious guest ranch in Tucson, the Tanque Verde Ranch has a worldwide reputation and is very popular with both Americans and Europeans who come to live their cowboy dreams in the Old West. This is a resort that happens to be a ranch rather than a guest ranch and happens to include some resort amenities. Tanque Verde encompasses 640 acres and borders both Saguaro National Monument and the Coronado National Forest. Its 100 plus horses provide unlimited horseback riding opportunities. The ranch was founded in the 1860s and some of the original buildings still stand. The main building and dining room were recently renovated and expanded, so the ranch is looking better than ever these days.

Guest rooms are all very spacious and comfortable, but don't expect a television here—ranch policy encourages guests to participate in various activities. Many rooms have fireplaces and patios. In front of numerous rooms are bird feeders that attract as many deer as birds. Bathrooms are large with tile floors and counters.

Dining/Entertainment: The large new dining room features continental and American dishes. Its wall of glass overlooks the swimming pool and Rincon Mountains. There are also breakfast horseback rides, poolside luncheons, and cookout rides. The Doghouse is an old foreman's cabin now housing a cantina.

Services: Complimentary riding and tennis lessons, children's programs, evening lectures and performances, nature and bird-banding hikes.

Facilities: Indoor and outdoor swimming pools, riding stables, five tennis courts, exercise room, saunas, whirlpool bath, shuffleboard, horseshoes, basketball, volleyball, tennis pro shop, rodeo arena.

WHITE STALLION RANCH, 9251 W. Twin Peaks Rd., Tucson, AZ 85743. Tel. 602/297-0252, or toll free 800/782-5546. Fax 602/744-2786. 20 rms, 9 suites.
$ Rates (including all meals): $119–$125 single; $194–$224 double; $226–$268 suite. Weekly rates available. No credit cards. **Closed:** May–Nov.

Set on 3,000 acres of desert just over the hill from Tucson, the White Stallion Ranch is perfect for those who crave wide-open spaces. Despite the proximity to the city, you won't see any city lights—just mile after mile of desert and the Tucson Mountains. Operated for nearly 30 years by the True family, this spread has a more authentic ranch feel than any other guest ranch in the Tucson area. With more than 60 horses on the ranch, there are plenty of choices for any riding skill level: two fast rides and two slow rides are offered daily. Kids will love the petting zoo. Guest rooms vary considerably in size and comfort from the tiny, spartan single rooms to suites with beamed ceilings, paneled walls, ceiling fans, small refrigerators, modern bathrooms, and patios with lounging furniture. In the busy winter months, there is a 4-night minimum stay.

Dining/Entertainment: All meals are served family style in the main dining room, which is housed in a 90-year-old ranch building with 24-inch-thick adobe walls. There is an honor bar with a longhorn steer head on the wall, cowhide stools, and a stone fireplace.

Services: Airport pickup, four horseback rides a day, hayrides, barbecue, guided nature walk, trip into Tucson, car-rental desk, tours available at additional charge.

Facilities: Swimming pool, indoor hot tub, tennis courts, horseback riding, shuffleboard, basketball, volleyball, billiards, table tennis, library, TV lounge.

4. DINING

A few years back the mayor declared Tucson the Mexican restaurant capital of the universe. Though Mexico City might want to contest the claim, it isn't far off the mark. There is authentic Mexican food down in the barrio district of South Fourth Avenue, heart-healthy Mexican at El Adobe, historic Mexican at El Charro, Mexico City Mexican at La Parilla Suiza, family-style Mexican at Casa Molina, and upscale Mexican at La Placita Cafe. If you like Mexican food, you'll be in heaven. If you don't like Mexican food, there are dozens of other restaurants serving everything from the finest French cuisine to innovative American to Italian to southwestern. Be sure to take one of your first meals here in a southwestern-style restaurant. This cuisine can be brilliantly creative, and after trying it you may want all your meals to be southwestern. There are enough of these imaginative restaurants around town that you could dine at a different excellent southwestern restaurant every day for a week or more. Keep in mind, however, that southwestern cuisine tends to be a bit pricey.

In the following listing, "Budget" restaurants are those where dinner (without wine) for one costs less than $15, "Moderate" are those charging between $15 and

$25, "Expensive" are those ranging from $25 to $35, and "Very Expensive" are those where the bill will exceed $35 per person.

DOWNTOWN & THE UNIVERSITY AREA

VERY EXPENSIVE

THE RANCHERS CLUB, in the Hotel Park Tucson, 5151 E. Grant Rd. Tel. 79-RANCH.
   Cuisine: STEAK. **Reservations:** Recommended.
$ Prices: Appetizers $7.50–$8; main courses $16–$30. AE, CB, DC, MC, V.
   Open: Lunch Mon–Fri 11:30am–2pm; dinner Mon–Sat 5:30–10pm.
There's no question as to where to get the very best steak in Tucson—the Ranchers Club. But before you saddle up the palomino and trot over, be sure you're prepared for the hefty tab. And if you're offended by stuffed animal heads, you might want to pass it by. The Ranchers Club glorifies the Old West with its decor. There are old saddles and chaps, steer horns, cowhide upholstered chairs, and bear, javelina, and deer heads on the walls. Antiques, brass, and brocade chairs lend the dining room a touch of elegance that seems only fitting considering the steep prices. Hefty steaks are grilled over mesquite, hickory, sassafras, and cherrywood fires. Each type of wood adds its own subtle flavor to the meat. The appetizer and salad sections of the menu provide a touch of continental flare, while the list of sauces and condiments offers such choices as curried apple chutney, wild-mushroom sauce, basil butter, and Cajun remoulade. So you don't like steak? How about mesquite-grilled lobster, shrimp, or swordfish? If you can eat a 24-ounce porterhouse steak and still have room for dessert, you're a bigger man than I.

EXPENSIVE

JANOS, 150 N. Main St. Tel. 884-9426.
   Cuisine: SOUTHWESTERN/CONTINENTAL. **Reservations:** Highly recommended.
$ Prices: Appetizers $5.50–$8.50; main courses $16 50–$27; summer sampler $13. AE, DC, MC, V.
   Open: Dinner only, Mon–Sat 5:30–9:30pm.
 Across the courtyard from the Tucson Museum of Art, in one of the El Presidio Historic District's old adobe homes, is one of Tucson's best and most frequently recommended restaurants. Janos owes its popularity as much to its

---

(F)   FROMMER'S SMART TRAVELER: RESTAURANTS

1. Don't miss the nouvelle southwestern cuisine turned out by the city's top chefs.
2. If a restaurant is beyond your dinner budget, try eating lunch there instead, often for half the price of dinner.
3. Eat as much Mexican food as possible. Tucson has been proclaimed the "Mexican restaurant capital of the universe," and features its own specialty, carne seca, an unusual dried-beef dish.
4. Pack picnic lunches at a grocery store before heading to Sabino Canyon, Saguaro National Monument, Mount Lemmon, or other natural areas, most of which have picnic grounds.
5. Before ordering the delicious-sounding daily special, be sure to ask the price. Specials are usually a bit more expensive than other menu items.

setting as to its stellar cuisine. This is a spot for the well-heeled to dine before attending the theater and is at once traditional and contemporary. The menu is limited but changes both daily and seasonally. The last time I visited Janos, the menu included an appetizer of grilled oyster mushrooms with smoked poblano chile flan served with black beans and salsa fresca. Among the main dishes, the pepito roasted rack of lamb, rubbed with mustard and rosemary, coated with pepitos (pumpkin seeds), and served with mint jus caught my fancy. Even those on a limited budget can enjoy Janos in the summer, when an amazingly low-priced sampler menu is available. This is probably the best restaurant value in Tucson.

PENELOPE'S, 3619 E. Speedway Blvd. Tel. 325-5080.

Cuisine: FRENCH. **Reservations:** Recommended.

$ Prices: Fixed-price dinner $27.50 without wine, $39.50 with wine; lunch dishes $7–$10. MC, V.

Open: Lunch Tues–Fri 11:30am–2pm; dinner Tues–Sun 5:30–10pm.

As you drive down Speedway Boulevard past used-car dealers, topless bars, and tattoo parlors, you may become convinced that the above address is wrong. Don't despair: Though it's located in a nondescript little building on an otherwise unremarkable section of road, Penelope's is indeed a memorable restaurant. The owners are dedicated to presenting exquisite meals at reasonable prices and have chosen not to spend money on a pretentious setting. The food is the star attraction at Penelope's. For under $30 (without wine) you can enjoy an outstanding six-course meal. On my last visit, dinner began with a leek tart followed by a choice of cream of cauliflower or onion soup. There was a choice of four dishes including frogs' legs with tomato-garlic sauce and filet mignon with creamy white-pepper-and-dill sauce. This was followed by salad and cheese courses, and then a dessert of either black- and white-chocolate mousse or caramelized apple tart. For those who wish to include wine with their meal, there are appropriately chosen selections for each course and each dish. If you can't afford dinner, you can stop by for lunch and sample dishes that are every bit as good as the evening fare. The crêpes are light and delicious, especially the tangy Roquefort crêpe.

MODERATE

CAFE MAGRITTE, 254 E. Congress St. Tel. 884-8004.

Cuisine: INTERNATIONAL. **Reservations:** Recommended.

$ Prices: Appetizers $3–$6.50; main courses $5–$8.50.

Open: Tues–Thurs 11am–11pm, Fri 11am–midnight, Sat noon–midnight, Sun 6–10pm.

The Café Magritte is a little cubbyhole of the surreal in a downtown neighborhood that in recent years has experienced a cultural renaissance as the young, the hip, and the artistic stake out the area as their own turf. Shoulder to shoulder with galleries, nightclubs, and curious boutiques, this trendy café serves up inexpensive, creative meals amid a thoroughly urban atmosphere, with changing works of cutting-edge art by local artists. I always have a hard time leaving the appetizer section, where Sonoran pesto made with cilantro, pistachios, and olives appears—one of my favorites. If you're feeling blue, you might want to try the fragrant bleu hearts—chopped artichoke hearts and prosciutto simmered in bleu cheese sauce and served with green apple slices and bread.

CARLOS MURPHY'S, 419 W. Congress St. Tel. 628-1958.

Cuisine: MEXICAN. **Reservations:** Recommended.

$ Prices: Appetizers $4–$6; main courses $5–$14; lunch $4.40–$10. AE, DISC, MC, V.

Open: Mon–Thurs 11am–10pm, Fri–Sat 11:30am–11pm, Sun noon–10pm (lounge stays open until 1am).

If you think you made a wrong turn and ended up at the train station instead of Carlos Murphy's, you're right . . . and you're wrong. It is, make that *was,* the train station but now it's a cavernous Mexican restaurant with a sense of humor. On the left as you enter the building is Carlos's sports bar, complete with a punching bag hanging from the ceiling. You might find yourself gazing at the ceilings—you'll see a red, white, and blue canoe and a Mexican air force biplane. The walls throughout the several dining rooms are brick and the floors are tile, so the restaurant still has much of the feel of the old train station. Carlos claims to scour the Southwest and Mexico for recipes, and fills you in on the details of many of the dishes. There are Mexican favorites, shark fajitas, barbecued baby back ribs, even tortas (a Mexican sandwich), but the all-time favorite dish at Carlos Murphy's is the iwanna iguana taco. Unfortunately it's only available during iguana season, which runs from February 30 to 31 each year.

EL CHARRO CAFE, 311 N. Court Ave. Tel. 622-5465.
Cuisine: MEXICAN. **Reservations:** Recommended.
$ Prices: Appetizers $1–$12; main courses $4.50–$15.50. AE, MC, V.
Open: Sun–Thurs 11am–9pm, Fri–Sat 11am–10pm.

El Charro, located in the El Presidio Historic District in an old stone building, claims to be Tucson's oldest Mexican restaurant. A front porch has been glassed in for a greenhouselike dining area overlooking the street, and there is also dining downstairs. Look at the roof of El Charro as you approach, and you might see a large metal cage containing beef drying in the sun. This is the main ingredient in carne seca, El Charro's well-known specialty, which is oft copied but never duplicated at other Mexican restaurants around town. You'll rarely find carne seca on a Mexican menu outside Tucson, so indulge in it while you're here. A warning—the café is packed at lunch, so arrive early or late.

PRESIDIO GRILL, 3352 E. Speedway Blvd. Tel. 327-4667.
Cuisine: SOUTHWESTERN. **Reservations:** Recommended.
$ Prices: Appetizers $2.50–$11; main courses $6.50–$9.50 at lunch, $8–$18 at dinner. MC, V.
Open: Tues–Thurs 11:30am–10pm, Fri 11:30am–midnight, Sat 8am–midnight, Sun 8am–10pm.

One glance at the contemporary decor and well-dressed diners at Presidio Grill and you'd expect to be somewhere in the foothills. Instead, this ever-trendy restaurant is located in one of my least-favorite sections of town, along busy Speedway Boulevard. However, it's obvious from the continuing accolades and lines at the door that a less-than-appealing location has not had ill effects on the Presidio. This is another of Tucson's fine restaurant's serving southwestern cuisine, and if you're like me, you'll be dragging chile peppers home with you so you can attempt to duplicate your favorite dishes. I'm crazy about chorizo, so the appetizer of Anaheim chile stuffed with chorizo, fresh corn, cilantro, and havarti cheese got me off to just the right start. The Sonoran Caesar salad, made with grilled shrimp, roasted peppers, and a spicy dressing, was a novel twist on an old standard. Whether you want pizza, pasta, or something from the grill, all the dishes here are tempting and show a variety of international influences. However, I'd stick with something that's solidly southwestern, such as the Sonoran mixed grill of hand-rolled sausages, grilled chicken breast, and marinated ribeye served with poblano polenta and grilled peppers.

BUDGET

EL ADOBE, 40 W. Broadway Blvd. Tel. 791-7458.
Cuisine: MEXICAN. **Reservations:** Recommended.
$ Prices: Appetizers $4.50–$6; main courses $4–$9. AE, DC, DISC, MC, V.
Open: Oct–May, Mon–Thurs 11am–9pm, Fri–Sat 11am–10pm; June–Sept, Mon–Thurs 11am–9pm, Fri 11am–10pm, Sat 5–10pm.

El Adobe is housed in the historic Charles O. Brown House, an adobe home built sometime in the 1850s. One of the oldest buildings in Tucson, it is surrounded by the skyscrapers that almost succeeded in replacing old Tucson. Fig, pomegranate, orange, and palm trees provide shade for the garden and make El Adobe an oasis protected from the hustle and bustle of Broadway Boulevard. Most of the dishes on the menu have been approved by the American Heart Association, while others can be modified slightly to meet the guidelines of that organization. So a meal here is not only delicious but healthy, too.

EAST TUCSON

EXPENSIVE

JEROME'S, 6958 E. Tanque Verde Rd. Tel. 721-0311.
  Cuisine: SEAFOOD. **Reservations:** Recommended.
  $ Prices: Appetizers $4.50–$7.50; main courses $9–$18; Sun brunch $15. AE, CB, DC, DISC, MC, V.
  Open: Lunch Tues–Sat 11am–2pm; dinner Tues–Sun 5–10pm; brunch Sun 11am–2pm.

Although you may not be thinking of seafood in the middle of the desert, there are those folks who tire of Mexican and southwestern fare and crave a bit of fish. For those people there is Jerome's, preparing contemporary seafood and New Orleans specialties. Located in the middle of Tucson's restaurant row, Jerome's is situated in an adobe-style building with a red-tile roof. The interior decor is dark with wood paneling, making Jerome's a good choice for either romantic dinners or business lunches. A long list of appetizers includes such standout dishes as calamari ceviche, a sort of Mexican sushi in that the calamari is not cooked—but marinated in a spicy lime dressing. Mesquite grilling is a specialty, and the grilled shrimp with tomatillo relish is always delicious. There are also a few meat dishes, such as mesquite-grilled chicken breast with citrus sauce. The Sunday New Orleans buffet is an extravaganza of Créole and Cajun dishes.

PAINTED DESERT RESTAURANT, 3055 N. Campbell Ave., Suite 113. Tel. 795-8440.
  Cuisine: SOUTHWESTERN. **Reservations:** Highly recommended.
  $ Prices: Appetizers $4–$7; main courses $5–$10 at lunch, $11–$20 at dinner. AE, CB, DC, DISC, MC, V.
  Open: Lunch Mon–Fri 11:30am–2pm; dinner Sun–Thurs 5–10pm, Fri–Sat 5–11pm.

Located in a small pueblo-style shopping center, which also houses art galleries, the Painted Desert is a trendy little restaurant. Original work by local artists decorates the walls, and classical and light jazz pulses from the stereo. The menu is short and changes seasonally. The pear and Brie quesadilla is a melding of classic French and Mexican to create a unique southwestern dish. Creative southwestern dishes such as pork saddle with purple mole and fried yams, and grilled scallops in a blue-corn tortilla with chipotle-pepper-cream sauce, are served full dinner size or appetizer size for those who prefer to leave room for dessert. Lunches are quite a bit cheaper than dinner and many of the same dishes are on the menu.

MODERATE

BOBBY MCGEE'S CONGLOMERATION, 6464 E. Tanque Verde Rd. Tel. 886-5551.
  Cuisine: AMERICAN. **Reservations:** Recommended.
  $ Prices: Appetizers $3.50–$5; main courses $6–$15. AE, CB, DC, DISC, MC, V.
  Open: Dinner only, Sun–Thurs 5–10pm, Fri–Sat 5–11pm (lounge until 1am).

Bobby McGee's has a dual personality. On the one hand it's an incredibly popular family restaurant, and on the other hand it's a popular singles bar. Luckily the two are kept separate, though the dance music from the lounge can still be a bit loud in the restaurant. Although the decor is Old West, with stained glass, wood paneling, and antiques, the servers are all dressed in costumes that range from superheros to dowdy school marms. The menu emphasizes steaks and prime rib, but there is also a list of lighter meals such as Santa Fe–style chicken or grilled mahi mahi macadamia. Both kids and adults love the wild atmosphere here, and that's why Bobby McGee's has been packing 'em in for more than 20 years. Don't be surprised to find yourself seated on an old toilet that's been converted into a dining room chair.

LOTUS GARDEN, 5975 E. Speedway Blvd. Tel. 298-3351.
  Cuisine: CHINESE. **Reservations:** Recommended.

$ Prices: Appetizers $3–$9; main courses $7.50–$13; combination and family dinners $8–$20. AE, DC, DISC, MC, V.
Open: Sun–Thurs 11:30am–11pm, Fri–Sat 11:30am–midnight.
Look around the parking lot at the Lotus Garden and you're likely to see Cadillacs and pickups. Inside, you'll find people in blue jeans and people in business suits. Nearly everyone agrees that the Lotus Garden serves some of the best Cantonese and Szechuan cuisine in Tucson. The interior decor is elegant, with a very contemporary rose, gray, and black color scheme. The Wong family has owned and operated the restaurant since it opened in 1968, and the Wongs go to great lengths to make sure patrons enjoy their meals. The menu is extensive, but if you don't see your favorite dish, the chef will be happy to fix it for you.

PINNACLE PEAK STEAKHOUSE, 6541 E. Tanque Verde Rd. Tel. 886-5012.

Cuisine: STEAKS. **Reservations:** Recommended.
$ Prices: Main courses $4–$12. DC, DISC, MC, V.
Open: Dinner only, daily 5–10pm.
Located in the Trail Dust Town, a Wild West–theme shopping and dining center, the Pinnacle Peak Steakhouse specializes in family dining in a fun cowboy atmosphere. Be prepared for crowds—this place is very popular with tour buses. Stroll the wooden sidewalks past the opera house and saloon to the grand old dining rooms of the Pinnacle Peak Steakhouse. You'll be surprised at the authenticity of the restaurant, which really resembles a dining room in old Tombstone or Dodge City.

BUDGET

CASA MOLINA, 6225 E. Speedway Blvd. Tel. 886-5468.

Cuisine: MEXICAN. **Reservations:** Recommended.
$ Prices: A la carte $1.50–$6; main courses $9–$14. AE, DC, MC, V.
Open: Daily 11am–11pm.
For years this has been Tucson's favorite family-run Mexican restaurant. You can't miss it—just watch for the larger-than-life-size bull and bullfighter in front. Casa Molina sports a casual atmosphere, with waiters and members of the Molina family sometimes lounging by the fireplace in the entry hall. I recommend that you dine on the patio beneath the tile-roofed overhangs. Be sure to start dinner with a tangy margarita—one of the best in town. The carne seca (sun-dried beef) shouldn't be missed. Lighter eaters will enjoy the layered topopo salad made with tortillas, refried beans, meat, lettuce, celery, avocado, tomato, and jalapeños.
Other Casa Molina locations include Foothills Mall, 7401 North La Cholla Boulevard, no. 146 (tel. 297-5000); 3001 North Campbell Avenue (tel. 795-7593); and 4240 East Grant Road (tel. 326-6663).

THE GOOD EARTH, in the El Mercado Shopping Center, 6366 E. Broadway Blvd. (at Wilmot). Tel. 745-6600.

Cuisine: AMERICAN. **Reservations:** Recommended.
$ Prices: Appetizers $2–$3.50; main courses $5–$10. No credit cards.
Open: Mon–Thurs 7am–10pm, Fri–Sat 7am–11pm, Sun 9am–10pm.
This large family restaurant and bakery believes that good food can also be healthy food. To that end the menu is dominated by vegetable and chicken dishes. Homemade soups and crisp salads are ideal fare for a hot summer day in Tucson. More substantial offerings include pastas, Mexican favorites, and dishes ranging from Malaysian cashew shrimp to beef Stroganoff. The Good Earth is well known for baked goods, such as freshly baked fruit pies.

LA PARILLA SUIZA, 5602 E. Speedway Blvd. Tel. 747-4348.

Cuisine: MEXICAN. **Reservations:** Recommended.
$ Prices: Main courses $4.50–$9.50. AE, DISC, MC, V.
Open: Mon–Thurs 11am–10pm, Fri–Sat 11am–11pm, Sun 11am–10pm.
Most Mexican food served in the U.S. is limited to Sonoran style, originating just south of the border. However, the cuisine of Mexico is nearly as varied as that of

N

ARIZONA

Tucson

Arizona Inn ⓻
Anthony's in the Catalinas ㉕
Bobby McGee's
  Conglomeration ⓮
Boccata ⓲
Cafe Magritte ⓺
Cafe Terra Cotta ㉒
Carlos Murphy's ⓸
Casa Molina ⓬
El Adobe ⓹
El Charro Cafe ⓶
El Corral Restaurant ㉗
The Gold Room ㉖
The Good Earth ⓭
Janos ⓷
Jerome's ⓯
La Placita Cafe ㉓
Le Rendez-Vous ⓴
Lotus Garden ⓫
Painted Desert Restaurant ㉑
La Parilla Suiza ⓵⓪
Penelope's ⓽
Pinnacle Peak
  Steakhouse ⓰
Presidio Grill ⓼
The Ranchers Club ⓳
Scordato's ⓵
The Tack Room ⓱
Ventana Room ㉔

Silverbell Rd.
Overton
Cortaro Farms Rd.
Thornydale
10
Ina Rd.
Ina Rd.
Orange Grove Rd
Sunset Rd.
El Camino de Cerro
Ruthrau
Rd.
Sweetwater Dr.
To Saguaro National
Monument (west)
Ironwood Hill Dr.
Tucson Mountain
Park
Gates Pass Rd.
Speedway Blv
Anklam R
Kinney
Rd.
Silverlake Rd
Bopp Rd.
Ajo Way
86
Valencia Rd.
Mission Rd.
San Xavier Indian Reservation

TUCSON DINING

China, and the meals served at La Parilla Suiza are based on the style popular in Mexico City, where most of the chain's restaurants are located. Many menu items are sandwiched between two flour tortillas, much like a quesadilla, but the charcoal broiling of meats and cheeses lend the sandwiches special status.

There is another La Parilla Suiza at 2720 North Oracle Road (tel. 624-4300).

NORTH TUCSON

VERY EXPENSIVE

THE TACK ROOM, 2800 N. Sabino Canyon Rd. Tel. 722-2800.
   Cuisine: CONTINENTAL. **Reservations:** Required.
$ **Prices:** Appetizers $9–$16; main courses $25–$35. AE, CB, DC, MC, V.
   Open: June–Dec, Tues–Sun 4:30–11pm; Dec–June, daily 4:30–11pm.

In the years when the wealthy were just discovering Arizona's allure as a winter retreat from the northern cold, the Tack Room was a rustic resort. Today the Italianate villa surrounded by palo verde trees is the only *Mobil Travel Guide* five-star restaurant in Arizona. As you're driving up Sabino Canyon Road, watch for the giant cowboy boot that acts as the restaurant's sign. From the boot it's a quarter-mile drive to the restaurant itself. The large clublike lounge with stone fireplace and stuffed elk head is a very comfortable place for a drink before dinner. Although the rough hewn beams in the high ceiling and rustic lounge indicate a casual atmosphere, waiters in tuxedos immediately dispel this notion. A glance out across the desert to the mountains will confirm that this is the height of southwestern elegance.

The menu changes daily and never fails to impress with both variety and creativity, and though dishes are primarily southwestern in flavor, there are also several well-loved continental offerings. For an appetizer you might try a shrimp-and-crab tamale with roasted garlic and banana sauce or escargots. The tortilla moltacqua soup is a favorite that's almost always on the menu. Popular dishes that also make frequent appearances are the Arizona four-pepper steak (with jalapeño, Anaheim, serrano, and sweet peppers) and the roast duckling with merlot wine sauce, which is sometimes flavored with raspberry and sometimes with orange. If you still have room, there's always a tempting assortment of pastries.

EXPENSIVE

ANTHONY'S IN THE CATALINAS, 6440 N. Campbell Ave. Tel. 299-1771.
   Cuisine: CONTINENTAL. **Reservations:** Highly recommended.
$ **Prices:** Appetizers $7–$10; main courses $12–$25. AE, CB, DC, MC, V.
   Open: Dinner only, daily 5:30–10pm.

If you head north on Campbell Avenue up into the foothills of the Catalinas, you'll reach a modern hacienda-style building overlooking the city. Anthony's exudes southwestern elegance from the moment you drive under the portico and let the valet park your car. Waiters are smartly attired in tuxedos and guests are almost as well dressed. Quiet classical music plays in the background, with the clinking of crystal and fine china punctuating the hushed conversations. Through the window of the main dining room the lights of the city twinkle below. In such rarified atmosphere one would expect only the finest meal, and that's what you get. I suggest starting with the air-dried beef from Switzerland, a dish infrequently encountered in the U.S. Another good choice would be shrimp stuffed with chorizo, a nod to southwestern influences. The crayfish-stuffed chicken in a saffron sauce is a delicately flavored winner. The pastry cart may tempt you, but you'd miss out on the best part of a meal if you didn't order either the day's soufflé (order early) or a flambé dessert.

BOCCATA, in River Center, 5605 E. River Rd. Tel. 577-9309.
   Cuisine: ITALIAN. **Reservations:** Recommended.
$ **Prices:** Appetizers $3.50–$8; main courses $7.50–$13. AE, MC, V.
   Open: Lunch Fri 11am–2:30pm; dinner Sun–Thurs 5:30–9pm, Fri–Sat 5–10pm; brunch Sun 10am–2:30pm.

FROMMER'S COOL FOR KIDS:
RESTAURANTS

Pinnacle Peak Steakhouse *(see p. 135)* Dinner here is a Wild West event with cowboys, shootouts, and an entire western town outside. Kids love it.

Bobby McGee's Conglomeration *(see p. 134)* The waiters and waitresses are dressed in unusual costumes and the dining rooms are filled with antiques.

Carlos Murphy's *(see p. 132)* Situated in Tucson's former train station, this trendy Mexican place features a mock-up of a Mexican air force biplane hanging from the ceiling.

You'll find this casually elegant upscale restaurant at the back of an office and shopping complex in the foothills. The decor is minimal, with pink floral tablecloths and pale-green chairs. Elegant curtains frame the panoramic view of Tucson in the valley below. Marble floors and a few works of contemporary art add finishing touches. The food is Italian as you may have never had it before. Sun-dried tomatoes show up in everything from insalata Boccata, which also includes seasonal greens, radiccio, mozzarella, pesto croutons, and vinaigrette provençal, to melanzane ripiene, thin slices of eggplant rolled with goat cheese, mozzarella, sun-dried tomatoes, and garlic and then baked in a tomato-basil sauce. Pasta dishes are as creative as any on the menu. My favorite is penne ciao bella, made with grilled chicken, roast peppers, artichoke hearts, pine nuts, and a cream sauce with white wine, chives, and Gorgonzola. Save room for dessert. The pear la chaise, poached in red wine and port and served with candied pecans and mascarpone cheese sweetened with cabernet, brown sugar, and poire William, is absolutely heavenly.

CAFE TERRA COTTA, 4310 N. Campbell Ave. Tel. 577-8100.
   Cuisine: SOUTHWESTERN. **Reservations:** Recommended.
$ Prices: Appetizers $5–$7.50; main courses $10–$18. AE, DC, MC, V.
   Open: Sun–Thurs 11am–10pm, Fri–Sat 11am–11pm.

Located in upscale St. Philip's Plaza shopping center, at the corner of River Road, Café Terra Cotta is one of Tucson's most highly acclaimed restaurants. A casual atmosphere and creative southwestern cooking are a combination that appeals to trendy Tucsonans, who stop by both for dinner at the restaurant or to pick up gourmet food to go. Before you even make it through the door, you will be struck by the artistic flare of this fine restaurant. The front door is done in a verdigris finish with the restaurant's name in shiny copper.

Inside you are immediately tempted by counters holding colorful salads and rich desserts. You'll see a large brick oven, used to make imaginative pizzas. How about a pizza with mesquite-smoked bacon, wild mushrooms, roasted poblano chiles, and fontina cheese? With excellent salads, small plates, soups, sandwiches, and main dishes as well, it's often very difficult to make a choice. If you like garlic, you'll love the appetizer of garlic custard with warm salsa vinaigrette and herbed hazelnuts. Large prawns stuffed with herbed goat cheese and southwestern tomato coulis is one of my favorite dishes. As I'm sure you'll notice when you walk in, Café Terra Cotta gives equal importance to dessert. Try the tiramisu with crème anglaise and raspberry sauce.

LE RENDEZ-VOUS, 3844 E. Ft. Lowell Rd. Tel. 323-7373.
   Cuisine: FRENCH. **Reservations:** Highly recommended.
$ Prices: Appetizers $4–$11; main courses $14–$20. AE, CB, DC, MC, V.

Open: Lunch Tues–Fri 11:30am–2pm; dinner Tues–Sun 6–10pm.

Chef Jean-Claude has become legendary among the gustatory cognoscenti of Tucson for his phenomenal duck à l'orange. Consequently, patrons are almost exclusively locals who return again and again for the duck, mussels cooked in white wine, and the ultimate spinach salad. If it's hot out, cool off with a bowl of creamy vichyssoise. If you're inclined to expand your own culinary horizons, you won't go wrong with the frogs' legs provençal or the veal sweetbreads with mushrooms dijonnaises. You might expect such rich and savory fare to be served amid rarified elegance, but instead Le Rendez-vous is housed in an unpretentious little stucco cottage near the busy corner of Fort Lowell Road and Alvernon Way. Waiters are dressed in black tie, but aside from this little concession, the atmosphere is strictly bistro. When the pastry cart comes around, ask for the tarte St-Claude, Jean-Claude's own creation, which sandwiches a layer of hazelnut cream between layers of crispy, light meringue.

MODERATE

LA PLACITA CAFE, in the Plaza Palomino, 3800 E. Sunrise Dr. Tel. 881-1150.

Cuisine: MEXICAN. **Reservations:** Recommended.

$ Prices: Appetizers $2.50–$6; main courses $6–$15. MC, V.

Open: Lunch Mon–Sat 11am–2pm; dinner Mon–Sat 5–9pm.

The Plaza Palomino is an upscale, modern shopping center in northern Tucson, and La Placita is a rather upscale Mexican restaurant. The decor is pastel with a few Mexican crafts on display, not your usual garish Mexican hacienda design. The varied menu includes not only dishes from around Mexico, but also some gringo fare. The menu offers four soups, including menudo, the classic Mexican hangover cure. There are all the usual tacos, enchiladas, burritos, tostadas, and tamales, but you'd do well to try one of the special dinners. Mole oaxaqueño is my favorite. It's served in a spicy chocolate-based sauce.

BUDGET

EL CORRAL RESTAURANT, 2201 E. River Rd. Tel. 299-6092.

Cuisine: STEAKS. **Reservations:** Recommended.

$ Prices: Complete dinner $10–$15. DISC, MC, V.

Open: Dinner only, daily 5–10pm.

⑤ Owned by the same folks who brought you Tucson's Pinnacle Peak Steakhouse, El Corral is another inexpensive steakhouse. The hacienda building has flagstone floors and wood paneling that make it dark and cozy, while outside in the bright sunlight a cactus garden flourishes. In keeping with the name, there is a traditional corral fence of mesquite branches around the restaurant parking lot. Prime rib is the house specialty, but there are also plenty of steaks, pork ribs, and burgers for the kids.

WEST TUCSON

SCORDATO'S, 4405 W. Speedway Blvd. Tel. 792-3055.

Cuisine: ITALIAN. **Reservations:** Highly recommended.

$ Prices: Appetizers $4.50–$8; main courses $12–$22. AE, CB, DC, DISC, MC, V.

Open: Dinner only, Tues–Sun 5–10pm.

It's a long way out to Scordato's but that doesn't bother the loyal clientele who enjoy the setting near Saguaro National Monument. The restaurant looks a bit like a lost Italian villa searching for the Mediterranean coast, with a saguaro standing side by side with a cypress out front. Inside, plush carpets, comfortable brocade chairs, and big windows allow diners to enjoy desert views in comfort. Despite the crystal chandeliers and tapestries on the walls, you don't have to dress up for dinner here.

Families and business types both enjoy the regional Italian cuisine. The menu contains page after page of tempting dishes, although it's difficult to move beyond the variety of veal dishes. Veal stresa is my favorite—it's stuffed with prosciutto and mozzarella and then sautéed in marsala and white wine sauce. For an appetizer, I like the scampi sauté. The extensive wine list will satisfy the wine connoisseur.

SPECIALTY DINING

HOTEL DINING

ARIZONA INN, 2200 E. Elm St. Tel. 325-1541.
 Cuisine: CONTINENTAL. **Reservations:** Recommended.
 $ Prices: Appetizers $5–$7; main courses $10–$15; fixed-price dinner $16; lunch $4.75–$8.50. AE, MC, V.
 Open: Breakfast daily 7–10:30am; lunch daily 11:30am–2pm; early dinner 5–6pm; dinner daily 6–10pm.
Opened in 1930, the Arizona Inn is one of the state's first resorts, and the dining room has established itself as a consistently excellent restaurant with reasonable prices. The rose-pink stucco pueblo-style buildings of the resort are surrounded by neatly manicured gardens that have aged gracefully, and it's a treat to dine on the terrace overlooking the garden and croquet lawn. The menu is not extensive, but every dish is perfectly prepared. Flavors are predominantly continental, with hints of southwestern. The fixed-price dinner, which changes daily, is an excellent value. Wednesday through Saturday in the winter season a classical guitarist plays in the evening. Lunches tend toward salads and sandwiches, including buffalo burgers.

THE GOLD ROOM, in the Westward Look Resort, 245 E. Ina Rd. Tel. 297-1151.
 Cuisine: CONTINENTAL. **Reservations:** Recommended.
 $ Prices: Appetizers $6–$12.50; main courses $16.50–$24. AE, CB, DC, DISC, MC, V.
 Open: Breakfast daily 7–10am; lunch daily 11am–2pm; dinner daily 5:30–10pm.
For more than 20 years the Gold Room has been one of the best hotel dining rooms in Tucson. Located in the Westward Look Resort, which opened in 1929 as a dude ranch, the Gold Room is a casual restaurant featuring southwestern ranch decor that includes pine paneling and viga beams in the ceiling. There are views of the city through two walls of glass and a terrace for al fresco dining. Despite the casual decor, place settings are elegant and service is very professional. The menu is French with an occasional chile to remind diners of the Arizona location. There is a distinct seafood slant to the hors d'oeuvres list, with escargots showing up on their own and stuffed into jumbo mushrooms. My personal favorite is the quail sautéed with cream and walnut liqueur. Although it's possible to order classics like chateaubriand and roast rack of lamb, the chef excels in preparing veal. The medallion of veal loin with ricotta and prosciutto baked in a pastry shell is the brightest star.

VENTANA ROOM, in Loew's Ventana Canyon Resort, 7000 N. Resort Dr. Tel. 299-2020.
 Cuisine: NOUVELLE AMERICAN. **Reservations:** Highly recommended.
 $ Prices: Appetizers $7–$55; main courses $17–$26. AE, CB, DC, MC, V.
 Open: Dinner only, daily 6–10:30pm.
With the spectacular setting and waterfall at the head of Ventana Canyon, it would be worth eating at the Ventana Room even if the food weren't so good. *Ventana* means "window" in Spanish, and the views are emphasized here. The twinkling lights of the city in the valley below and the strains of ethereal harp music set the mood. The menu, which changes daily, is not long, but its memorable quality compensates for lack of variety. Appetizers tend toward continental flare, with a ragoût of escargots and wild forest mushrooms outstanding. If offered, be sure to try the hearts-of-palm salad. Venison and quail make regular appearances, and on my last visit, venison was served with cranberries and smoked pear sauce. Quail might come with

❓ DID YOU KNOW . . . ?

- Mount Lemmon, named for the woman who first climbed it, is the southernmost ski area in the continental United States.
- Tucson is the sunniest city in the U.S.
- The Sonoran Desert is the only place in the world where the saguaro cactus grows, and Saguaro National Monument outside Tucson has the greatest concentration of these plants.
- Singer Linda Ronstadt is part of a Tucson family very active in local politics. A public bus station is named for one of the Ronstadts.
- More astronomical observatories are within a 50-mile radius of Tucson than in any other area of comparable size in the world.
- The world's largest dry cavern is just outside Tucson.
- The University of Arizona was established in Tucson to appease the citizenry after the territorial capital was moved to Phoenix.

cactus pear jelly or roasted garlic sauce and foie gras. Don't let the dessert cart pass you by.

DINING WITH A VIEW

Virtually all the foothills resorts offer dining with a view, including the **Ventana Room** and the **Gold Room,** both listed above. Outside the foothills resorts, there are many additional choices for dining with a view. **Anthony's in the Catalinas, Boccata, Scordato's,** and the **Tack Room** offer superb views of the city's twinkling lights or the jagged mountains surrounding the valley. These restaurants are listed above.

---

5. ATTRACTIONS

SUGGESTED ITINERARIES

IF YOU HAVE 1 DAY Start your day at the Arizona–Sonora Desert Museum, then continue to Saguaro National Monument. After lunch, visit Old Tucson Studios if you're a fan of western movies, then head downtown to the El Presidio Historic District. Have drinks or dinner at one of the foothills resorts and enjoy the view.

IF YOU HAVE 2 DAYS Spend your first day as suggested above. Start your second day at the Arizona Historical Society Tucson Museum, then cross the street to the Arizona State Museum. After lunch, visit the University of Arizona Museum of Art, then head out to Sabino Canyon to experience a desert oasis.

IF YOU HAVE 3 DAYS Spend your first 2 days as suggested above. On Day 3, head south to visit Mission San Xavier del Bac and then continue south to Tubac and Tumacacori.

IF YOU HAVE 5 DAYS OR MORE For Days 1 to 3, see the suggestions above. Start your fourth day with a hike or some horseback riding, then later in the day, head up to Mount Lemmon to see how close the mountains are to downtown Tucson. On Day 5, drive to Tombstone and Bisbee for the day (or start on Day 4 and make it an overnight trip).

THE TOP ATTRACTIONS

ARIZONA–SONORA DESERT MUSEUM, 2021 N. Kinney Rd. Tel. 883-1380.

⭐ Don't be fooled by the name. This is a zoo, and it's one of the best in the country. Don't be surprised to find yourself spending more hours than intended.

The Sonoran Desert is the arid region that encompasses much of central and southern Arizona as well as parts of northern Mexico. In this desert are not only arid lands but also forested mountains, springs, rivers, and streams. The full spectrum of Sonoran Desert life, from plants to insects to fish to reptiles to mammals, is on display in natural settings. There are black bears and mountain lions, beavers and otters, frogs and fish, tarantulas and scorpions, prairie dogs and javelinas. In addition, there is a simulated cave with exhibits on prehistoric desert life and more than 400 species of native plants, including the giant saguaro cactus, which abounds in adjacent Saguaro National Monument. My favorite exhibit is an aviary holding a dozen species of hummingbird. The tiny birds buzz past your ears and stop only inches in front of your face. A separate aviary contains many other bird species. Guides explain everything from the life cycle of the saguaro to the feeding habits of the tarantula.

Admission: $6 adults, $1 children 6–12, free for children under 6.

Open: Labor Day–Memorial Day, daily 8:30am–5pm; Memorial Day–Labor Day, daily 7:30am–6pm. **Directions:** The Arizona–Sonora Desert Museum is located 14 miles west of Tucson between Tucson Mountain Park and Saguaro National Monument (West). To reach the museum/zoo from downtown Tucson, take Speedway Boulevard, which becomes Gates Pass Boulevard.

SAGUARO NATIONAL MONUMENT, 3693 S. Old Spanish Trail. Tel. 883-6366 (Saguaro West) or 296-8576 (Saguaro East).

The saguaro cactus has been called the monarch of the desert and is the quintessential symbol of the American desert. It is the largest cactus native to the United States and can attain a height of 50 feet and a weight of more than 8 tons, which makes it the largest living organism in the Sonoran Desert. With life spans of 200 years, saguaros may not sprout their first branches until they are 75 years old. Many species of bird live in holes in the cactus trunk. Coyotes, foxes, squirrels, and javelinas (a wild pig) all eat the sweet fruit and seeds of the saguaro. Tohono O'odham Native Americans have for centuries started their new year with the saguaro fruit harvest season.

Since 1933 the two sections of Saguaro National Monument have protected the saguaro and all the other inhabitants of this section of the Sonoran Desert. The west section is the more popular because of its proximity to both the Arizona–Sonora Desert Museum and Old Tucson Studios. In the area near the Red Hills Information Center is a waterhole that attracts wild animals, which you are most likely to see at dawn, dusk, or at night. The east section of the park contains an older area of forest at the foot of the Rincon Mountains. This section is popular with hikers because most of it has no roads. There is also a visitor center here. Both sections have loop roads, nature trails, hiking trails, and picnic grounds.

Admission: $3 per car (east section only).

Open: Park, daily 24 hours; visitor centers, daily 8am–5pm. **Directions:** To reach the west section, take Speedway Boulevard west from downtown Tucson (it becomes Gates Pass Boulevard); to reach the east section, take Speedway Boulevard east, then head south on Freeman Road to Old Spanish Trail.

OLD TUCSON STUDIOS, 201 S. Kinney Rd. Tel. 883-6457.

This is not the genuine old Tucson—it's a movie set. After more than 50 years of filming western movies and television shows here, however, Old Tucson Studios has a longer history than much of the real city of Tucson. If you're a fan of the western genre, you'll doubtless recognize Old Tucson, which first appeared in the 1939 epic *Arizona*. Among the memorable films shot here are John Wayne's *Rio Lobo, Rio Bravo,* and *El Dorado;* Clint Eastwood's *The Outlaw Josey Wales;* Kirk Douglas's *Gunfight at the O.K. Corral;* and Paul Newman's *The Life and Times of Judge Roy Bean.* Old Tucson also doubled as Mankato on the long-running television series "Little House on the Prairie." Kids, and some adults, love Old Tucson. There are shootout enactments on Main Street, rodeos, stagecoach rides, an old steam train, and plenty of stores where you can spend your money.

Admission: $9.95 adults, $5.95 children 4–11, free for children 3 and under; after 5pm, $5.95 adults, $5.20 children.

Open: Daily 9am–5pm. **Closed:** Thanksgiving and Christmas. **Directions:** Take Speedway Boulevard west, continuing in the same direction when it becomes Gates Pass Boulevard. Turn left on South Kinney Road.

ARIZONA HISTORICAL SOCIETY TUCSON MUSEUM, 949 E. Second St. Tel. 628-5774.

As Arizona's oldest historical museum, this repository of all things Arizonan is a treasure trove for the history buff. If you've never explored a real mine, you can do the next best thing by looking at the museum's full-scale reproduction of an underground mine tunnel. You'll also see an assayer's office, miner's tent, blacksmith's shop, and a stamp mill in the mining exhibit. Transportation through the years is another interesting exhibit, with silver-studded saddles of Spanish ranchers, steam locomotives that opened Arizona to the world, and "horseless carriages" that revolutionized life in the Southwest. There is even an exhibit on the history of air conditioning and refrigeration.
Admission: Free.
Open: Mon–Sat 10am–4pm, Sun noon–4pm. **Closed:** Major hols. **Bus:** 1.

ARIZONA STATE MUSEUM, University of Arizona, University Blvd. and Park Ave. Tel. 621-6302.

Founded in 1892, Arizona State Museum houses an extensive collection of artifacts from prehistoric and contemporary Native American cultures of the Southwest. The first floor features a mock-up of a cave with displays of artifacts from ancient cave-dwelling cultures of the Southwest. Also on this floor are exhibits on the modern Hopi, Navajo, and Apache. There are exquisite Apache baskets and beadwork, as well as ceremonial clothing and dolls in Native American dress. Don't miss the sand painting in the Navajo section. Sandpaintings are rarely displayed in museums because they are used for religious purposes and are traditionally destroyed on the day they are made. On the second floor, the cultures of other ethnic groups of southern Arizona—the Pima and Tohono O'odham—are explored. A large exhibit covers the Hohokam, an ancient farming culture that lived in the desert and built extensive networks of irrigation canals until it disappeared mysteriously around 1450.
Admission: Free.
Open: Mon–Sat 9am–5pm, Sun 2–5pm. **Closed:** Major hols. **Bus:** 1.

TUCSON MUSEUM OF ART AND HISTORIC BLOCK, 140 N. Main Ave. Tel. 624-2333.

Situated in a large modern building surrounded by historic adobes and a spacious patio, the Tucson Museum of Art boasts a large collection of western art, notably realistic and romantic portrayals of life in the West. Cowboys, horses, cattle, and wide-open spaces are depicted in the paintings and bronzes. An excellent collection of pre-Columbian art representing 3,000 years of life in Mexico and Central and South America rounds out the museum's permanent collection. On the patio outside the museum are large sculptures. In addition, the museum always hosts temporary exhibitions, such as an annual celebration of women in the arts.

The restored homes on the block bordering the museum date from 1850 to 1907 and are all built on the former site of the Tucson presidio. La Casa Cordova, the oldest house on the block, is one of the city's earliest houses. It serves as a Mexican Heritage Museum. The Leonard Romero House is now the museum's art school, while the Stevens House is home to Janos, one of the best restaurants in Tucson. The Fish House contains an art gallery. A map and descriptive brochures on the houses are available at the museum's front desk. Free guided tours of the block from October 1 to May 1 begin on Wednesday at 11am and on Thursday at 2pm.
Admission: $2 adults, $1 students and seniors, free for children 12 and under, free for everyone on Tues.
Open: Tues–Sat 10am–4pm, Sun noon–4pm. **Closed:** All national hols. **Bus:** All downtown-bound buses.

UNIVERSITY OF ARIZONA MUSEUM OF ART, Park Ave. and Speedway Blvd. Tel. 621-7567.

Founded in 1942, this art museum has a more extensive and diverse art collection than the Tucson Museum of Art. The collection includes European works from the

Renaissance to the 17th century, notably works by Tintoretto, Lucas Cranach, and Tiepolo. The star attraction is the *Retable of Ciudad Rodrigo,* which consists of 26 paintings from 15th-century Spain. The retable was originally above a cathedral altar. The museum also has a collection of 20th-century art that includes sculpture by Rodin, Picasso, Isamu Noguchi, and George Segal. Other artists whose work is displayed include Henry Moore, Joan Miró, Mark Rothko, and Karel Appel. A new building is being constructed adjacent to the old building.
   Admission: Free.
   Open: Sept 2–May 14, Mon–Fri 9am–5pm, Sun noon–4pm; May 15–Sept 1, Mon–Fri 10am–3:30pm, Sun noon–4pm. **Bus:** 1.

SABINO CANYON, 5900 N. Sabino Canyon Rd. Tel. 749-2861.
   Located in the Santa Catalina Mountains of Coronado National Forest, Sabino Canyon is a desert oasis that has attracted people and animals for thousands of years. Along the length of the canyon are waterfalls and pools where you can swim. For those who prefer just to gaze at the beauty of crystal-clear water flowing over rock, there's a narrated tram ride through the lower canyon. There are also many trails and picnic tables. If you enjoy horseback riding, a great way to see the canyon is on a moonlight ride, held three times each month between April and December (phone 749-2327 for reservations).
   Admission: $5 adults, $2 children 3–12, free for children under 3.
   Open: Daily 9am–4:30pm. **Directions:** Take Grant Road east to Tanque Verde Road, continuing east; at Sabino Canyon Road, turn north and watch for the sign.

MORE ATTRACTIONS
CHURCHES & SHRINES

EL TIRADITO, S. Granada Ave. at West Cushing St.
   El Tiradito has long played an important role in the life of Roman Catholic Tucsonans. The crumbling shrine, listed on the National Register of Historic Places, is dedicated to a sinner who was buried on unconsecrated ground at this spot. There are several stories regarding the identity of the sinner, the most widely accepted being a tale of a young herder who fell in love with his mother-in-law. The father-in-law shot the youth after catching him in a tryst with his wife. The herder staggered into the street and died on the spot where El Tiradito now stands. Townsfolk soon began burning candles for the herder and a shrine was later erected. Long after the young man's death, people burned candles in hope that their own wishes would come true, believed to happen if the candle burned through the night. Today you can still see candles burning at El Tiradito.
   Directions: One block south of Tucson Convention Center on South Grenada Avenue.

MISSION SAN XAVIER DEL BAC, San Xavier Rd. Tel. 294-2624.
   Called the White Dove of the Desert and considered to be the finest example of mission architecture in the United States, Mission San Xavier del Bac incorporates Moorish, Byzantine, and Mexican Renaissance architectural styles into a single beautiful church. Brilliantly white in the desert sun, the church serves the residents of the surrounding San Xavier Indian Reservation. Although a church had existed near here as early as 1700, the existing structure was only built in 1783–97. Why only one church tower was completed is a mystery, but you'll immediately notice the missing dome of the right-hand tower. The building consists of domes and arches made of adobe brick. Faded murals cover the walls and a statue of St. Francis Xavier, the mission's patron saint, is to the left of the main altar. Outside, a small hill just east not only affords an interesting view of the church but is also the site of a replica of the famous grotto in Lourdes, France. The mission is an active Roman Catholic church. Masses are held Monday through Saturday at 8:30am and on Sunday at 8, 9:30, and 11am, and 12:30pm.
   Admission: Free.
   Open: Daily 8:30am–5:30pm. **Directions:** Take I-19 south about 9 miles to the Valencia Road exit and follow signs.

Map Legend

Arizona Historical Society
Tucson Museum **9**
Arizona-Sonora Desert
Museum **1**
Arizona State Museum **10**
Center for Creative
Photography **7**
El Tiradito **14**
Flandrau Science
Center & Planetarium **11**
Fremont House Museum **13**
Mission San
Xavier del Bac **18**
Old Pueblo Museum **4**
Old Tucson Studios **2**
Pima Air Museum **17**
Reid Park Zoo **16**
Sabino Canyon Park **5**
Saguaro National
Monument **3**
Tucson Botanical
Gardens **6**
Tucson Children's
Museum **15**
Tucson Museum of Art **12**
University of Arizona
Museum of Art **8**

ARIZONA

Tucson

N

Silverbell Rd.

Overton

Cortaro Farms Rd.

10

Thornydale Rd.

Ina Rd.

Ina Rd.

4

Orange Grove R

Sunset Rd.

El Camino de Cerro

Ruthra
Rd.

Sweetwater Dr.

Ironwood Hill Dr.

To Saguaro National
Monument (west)

3

1

Tucson Mountain
Park

2

Gates Pass Rd.

Kinney Rd.

Speedway B

Anklam F

Silverlake Rc

Bopp Rd.

Ajo Way

86

Valencia Rd.

Mission Rd.

San Xavier Indian Reservation

TUCSON ATTRACTIONS

To Sabino Canyon Park ↗

Magee Rd.

Ina Rd.

Orange Grove Rd.   Skyline Dr.

La Canada Dr.

Kolb Rd.

Sabino Canyon Rd.

Sunrise Dr.

5

River Rd.

Snyder Rd.

Wetmore Rd.

Roger Rd.

Prince Rd.

Swan Rd.

Craycroft Rd.

Kolb Rd.

River Rd.

To Mount Lemmon ↗

Bear Canyon

Catalina Hwy.

Miracle Mile

Ft. Lowell Rd.

Way

Tanque Verde Rd.

ant Rd.

Grant Rd.

10

Oracle

Stone

1st Ave.

Campbell Ave.

Tucson Blvd.

Country Club Rd.

Alvernon Way

Flowing Wells Rd.

Speedway Blvd.

To Saguaro National Monument (east) ↘

8 **7**

5th St.

9 **10** **11** 6th St.

6

3

12 Congress

Broadway Blvd.

Wilmot Rd.

Kolb Rd.

22nd St.

Grande Ave.

13

Reid Park

Randolph Park

15

entinel eak ark

14

22nd St.

16

Swan Rd.

Craycroft Rd.

Tucson Greyhound Park

29th St.

36th St.

Golf Links Rd.

Ajo Way

Kino Blvd.

10

Escalante Rd.

Pantano Rd.

Camino Seco Rd.

Irvington Rd.

Davis Monthan AFB

Irvington Rd.

Drexel Rd.

Palo Verde Rd.

Kolb Rd.

12th Ave.

6th Ave.

Valencia Rd.

17

Los Reales Rd.

18

✈ Tucson International Airport

19

10

Airport ✈

FROMMER'S FAVORITE
TUCSON EXPERIENCES

The Arizona—Sonora Desert Museum One of the world's finest zoos, the museum focuses exclusively on the animals and plants of the Sonoran Desert of southern Arizona and northern Mexico.

Full-Moon Desert Hikes There is no better time to explore the desert than at night (when the desert comes alive) under a full moon. Drive to the east or west section of Saguaro National Monument for your hike.

The Drive to Mount Lemmon From the desert, the road twists and turns up into the Santa Catalina Mountains, with cactus and palo verde gradually replaced by pine and juniper and breathtaking views of Tucson along the way.

First and Third Saturday Nights Tucson's Downtown Arts District abounds with open art galleries, boutiques, crafts shops, street performers, and free entertainment in hip cafés.

A Day in Tubac As the first European settlement in what would later become Arizona, Tubac has a long history now complemented by nearly 100 arts and crafts studios, galleries, and shops. A day here is a great outing.

HISTORIC BUILDINGS/MONUMENTS

FREMONT HOUSE MUSEUM, 151 S. Granada Ave. Tel. 622-0956.
    Located on the shady grounds of the modern Tucson Convention Center, between Broadway Boulevard and Cushing Street, Fremont House is a classic example of Sonoran Mexican adobe architecture. Originally built in 1858 as a small adobe house, the structure was enlarged after 1866. In 1878 it was rented to Territorial Governor John Charles Frémont, who had led a distinguished military career as an explorer of the West. It is to this period that the building has been restored, with the living room and bedrooms opening off a large central hall known as a *zaguán,* and all rooms decorated with period antiques. The flat roof is made of pine beams, called *vigas,* covered with saguaro cactus ribs and topped, by a layer of hard-packed mud.
    Admission: Free.
    Open: Wed–Sat 10am–4pm. **Closed:** All major hols. **Bus:** All downtown-bound buses.

MUSEUMS/GALLERIES

CENTER FOR CREATIVE PHOTOGRAPHY, east of the corner of Park Ave. and Speedway Blvd. Tel. 621-7968.
    Have you ever wished you could see an original Ansel Adams print up close, or perhaps an Edward Weston or a Richard Avedon? You can at the Center for Creative Photography. Originally conceived by Ansel Adams, the center now holds more than 500,000 negatives, 200,000 study prints, and 40,000 master prints by the world's greatest photographers, making it one of the best and largest collections in the world. Although the center does mount photography exhibits year-round, it is primarily a research facility, whose main goal is to preserve the complete photographic archives of various photographers, including Adams. Prints may be examined in a special room. It is suggested that you make an appointment and decide beforehand whose works you would like to see. You are usually limited to two photographers per visit.
    Admission: Free.
    Open: Mon–Fri 10am–5pm, Sun noon–5pm. **Bus:** 1.

OLD PUEBLO MUSEUM, in the Foothills Center, 7401 N. La Cholla Blvd. Tel. 742-7191.

Its name sounds as if this museum is in a dusty old adobe building, but in fact it's a very modern museum inside a shopping mall. A large and beautiful mineral collection is sparklingly displayed, and a mock-up of a cave used by paleo-Indians 12,000 years ago contains the bones of a mammoth.
Admission: Free.
Open: Mon–Fri 10am–9pm, Sat 10am–6pm, Sun noon–5pm. **Bus:** 103.

PIMA AIR MUSEUM, 6000 E. Valencia Rd. Tel. 574-9658.

Located just south of Davis Monthan Air Force Base, reachable from I-10, Pima Air Museum displays more than 160 aircraft covering the evolution of American aviation. This is the third-largest collection of historic aircraft in the world. A 20,000-square-foot building houses part of the collection, though most of the aircraft are outside. The collection includes replicas of the Wright Brothers' 1903 Wright Flyer and the X-15, the world's fastest aircraft. World War II bombers and later jet fighters are popular attractions.

The Pima Air Museum also operates the **Titan Missile Museum** in nearby Grass Valley. This is the only intercontinental ballistic missile (ICBM) complex in the world open to the public. Hours and admission fees are the same as for the Pima Air Museum.
Admission: $5 adults, $4 seniors, $3 children 10–17, free for children under 10.
Open: Daily 9am–5pm. **Closed:** Christmas Day. **Bus:** 26 to the Pima Air Museum. **Directions:** Take I-19 south to Exit 69 to the Titan Missile Museum.

PARKS & GARDENS

REID PARK ZOO, Country Club Rd. and 22nd St. Tel. 791-4022.

Although small and overshadowed by its neighbor, Arizona–Sonora Desert Museum, Reid Park Zoo is an important breeding center for several endangered species. Among the animals in the zoo's breeding programs are giant anteaters, white rhinoceroses, tigers, ruffed lemurs, and zebras.
Admission: $2 adults, $1.50 seniors, 50¢ children 5–14, free for children under 5.
Open: Mar 15–Sept 14, Mon–Fri 8:30am–3:30pm, Sat–Sun and hols 8:30am–5:30pm; Sept 15–Mar 14, daily 9:30am–4:30pm. **Bus:** 14.

TUCSON BOTANICAL GARDENS, 2150 N. Alvernon Way. Tel. 326-9255.

These gardens form an oasis of greenery in suburban Tucson. Within the 5-acre grounds are several small gardens that not only have visual appeal but are also historic and educational. If you live in the desert, you'll benefit from a visit when you learn about harvesting rainfall for your garden and designing a water-conserving landscape. The sensory garden stimulates all five senses, while in another garden traditional southwestern crops are grown for research purposes.
Admission: $2 adults, $1.50 seniors, free for children under 12.
Open: Sept–May, daily 8:30am–4pm; May–Sept, daily 8:30am–4:30pm.
Closed: Jan 1, July 4, Thanksgiving, and Dec 24–25. **Bus:** 11.

FLANDRAU SCIENCE CENTER & PLANETARIUM, Cherry and University Aves. Tel. 621-STAR.

Located on the campus of the University of Arizona, the Flandrau Planetarium offers stargazers a chance to learn more about the universe. The dome theater offers programs on the stars as well as very popular laser shows set to music. Other programs explore such natural wonders as Australia's Great Barrier Reef. Exhibit halls contain displays on the sun, moon, and planets; asteroids and meteorites; and the exploration of space. On clear nights, Tuesday through Saturday, you can gaze through the planetarium's 16-inch telescope. (Arizona has become a magnet for stargazers, and several famous telescopes are near Tucson. See "Easy Excursions from Tucson," below, for information on the **Kitt Peak National Observatory.**)
Admission: Exhibits, free. Theater, $3.75 adults, $3 senior citizens, students, and children; $2 for 10:30am shows in summer. Laser shows $5 (Sat–Sun $3.75 for 2:30pm show).

Open: Daytime, Mon–Fri 8am–5pm, Sat–Sun 1–5pm; evenings, Tues 7–9pm, Wed–Thurs 7–10pm, Fri–Sat 7pm–12:30am. **Closed:** Major hols. **Bus:** 1.

COOL FOR KIDS

TUCSON CHILDREN'S MUSEUM, 200 S. Sixth Ave. Tel. 792-9985.

In late 1991 the Tucson Children's Museum moved into these spacious new quarters in the restored Carnegie Library. In recognition of its heritage, the Children's Museum's first exhibition was of giant books that children could walk into and through while trying to solve a puzzle. Hands-on activities continue to be a museum feature. In one activity, children can pedal a bicycle and produce enough electricity to project their image onto a television screen by way of a video camera.

Admission: $3 adults, $1.50 seniors, $1.50 children 3–18, free for children 2 and under.

Open: Labor Day–Memorial Day, Tues–Sat 10am–5pm, Sun 1–5pm; Memorial Day–Labor Day, Tues–Sat 9am–3pm, Sun 1–5pm. **Closed:** Jan 1, Memorial Day, July 4, Labor Day, Thanksgiving, Dec 25. **Bus:** All downtown-bound buses.

WALKING TOUR —— Downtown Historic Districts

Start: The Fish House.
Finish: Congress Hotel.
Time: 3 hours, but with browsing you could take all day.
Best Times: Weekends, when restaurants aren't packed at lunch.
Worst Times: Monday, when the museum is closed.

Tucson has a long and varied cultural history, which is most easily seen on a walking tour of the city's downtown historic districts. Downtown Tucson is also the city's arts and crafts center, so a walk through this area provides interesting shopping opportunities.

Start your tour at the Fish House at the corner of Alameda Street and Main Avenue. With your back to the modern high-rise office buildings of downtown Tucson, you'll be facing the El Presidio Historic District, which is named for the Presidio of San Augustín del Tucson (1775), the Spanish garrison that once stood here to protect the San Xavier del Bac Mission from Apaches. For many years this was the heart of Tucson. No original building still stands, and those you'll see date from the mid-19th century. The building directly in front of you is the:

1. **Fish House,** 120 North Main Avenue, built in 1868 in the Sonoran architectural style and named for Edward Nye Fish, a local merchant. Today it houses El Presidio Gallery. Next along Main Avenue is the:
2. **Stevens Home,** 150 North Main Avenue. Together with the Fish House, this was the cultural heart of Tucson in the latter 19th century. It now houses Janos, one of Tucson's best restaurants. From Janos, take a right on Washington Street and then another right onto Meyer Avenue where you'll see the:
3. **Romero House.** Built in 1868, it now contains the Tucson Museum of Art School. Next door is:
4. **La Casa Cordova,** 175 North Meyer Avenue, which dates to about 1848 and is one of the oldest buildings in Tucson. As a part of the art museum, it's furnished in the style of the period and is dedicated as a Mexican Heritage Museum. Diagonally across Meyer Avenue is Tucson's premier crafts market:
5. **Old Town Artisans,** 186 North Meyer Avenue. Within this adobe building dating from 1862 are several rooms full of handmade southwestern crafts (see "Savvy Shopping," below, for details). You could spend hours browsing through the amazing assortment of crafts.

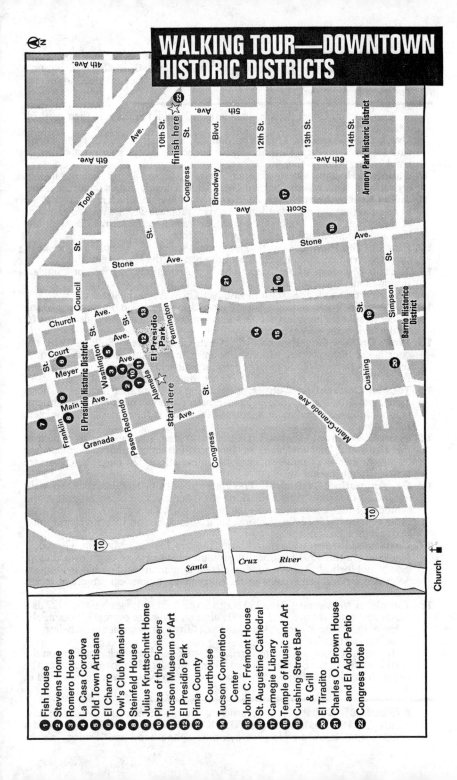

WALKING TOUR—DOWNTOWN HISTORIC DISTRICTS

N

start here

finish here

4th Ave.
5th Ave.
6th Ave.
10th St.
12th St.
13th St.
14th St.
6th Ave.

Congress St.
Broadway Blvd.
Stone Ave.
Scott Ave.
Stone Ave.
Toole Ave.
Council St.
Church Ave.
Court St.
Meyer Ave.
Main Ave.
Washington St.
Franklin St.
Alameda St.
Granada Ave.
Paseo Redondo
Pennington St.
Simpson St.
Cushing St.
Main-Granada Ave.
Congress St.

El Presidio Park
El Presidio Historic District
Armory Park Historic District
Barrio Historico District

Santa Cruz River

Church

1 Fish House
2 Stevens Home
3 Romero House
4 La Casa Cordova
5 Old Town Artisans
6 El Charro
7 Owl's Club Mansion
8 Steinfeld House
9 Julius Kruttschnitt Home
10 Plaza of the Pioneers
11 Tucson Museum of Art
12 El Presidio Park
13 Pima County Courthouse
14 Tucson Convention Center
15 John C. Frémont House
16 St. Augustine Cathedral
17 Carnegie Library
18 Temple of Music and Art
19 Cushing Street Bar & Grill
20 El Tiradito
21 Charles O. Brown House and El Adobe Patio
22 Congress Hotel

REFUELING STOP If you started your tour late in the morning you're probably hungry by now, so head up Court Avenue to: **6. El Charro,** Tucson's oldest Mexican restaurant. Be sure to order carne seca (see "Dining," above, for complete information).

Continue up Court Avenue, turn left on Franklin Street and then right on Main Avenue to reach the:

7. **Owl's Club Mansion,** 378 North Main Avenue, built in 1901 as a gentlemen's club for some of Tucson's most eligible bachelors. At the southwest corner of Franklin and Main is the:

8. **Steinfeld House,** 300 North Main Avenue, built in 1899 in Spanish mission-revival style. This was the original Owl's Club. Directly across the street is the:

9. **Julius Kruttschnitt Home,** 297 North Main Avenue, which now serves as the El Presidio Bed and Breakfast Inn. Victorian trappings disguise the adobe origins of this unique home. Continue down Main Avenue to the archway between the Fish and Stevens homes, turn left, and cross the:

10. **Plaza of the Pioneers,** with fountains and sculptures. The plaza is the site of summer-evening jazz concerts. Across the plaza is the entrance to the:

11. **Tucson Museum of Art** (see "The Top Attractions," above, for complete information). This modern building houses collections of pre-Columbian art and western art, as well as Spanish furnishings. Cross Alameda Street to:

12. **El Presidio Park,** once the parade ground for the presidio and now a shady gathering spot for homeless people and downtown office workers. Just to the east of the park is the very impressive:

13. **Pima County Courthouse,** 155 North Church Street. Built in 1928, the courthouse incorporates Moorish, Spanish, and southwestern architectural features. A portion of the original presidio wall is in a glass case on the second floor. Walking south on Church Street for three blocks will bring you to the:

14. **Tucson Convention Center,** a sprawling complex that includes a sports arena, grand ballroom, concert hall, theater, pavilions, meeting halls, gardens, craft and souvenir vendors, and, near the fountains in the center of the complex, the historic:

15. **John C. Frémont House,** 151 Granada Avenue, an adobe structure built in the 1850s and later the home of Territorial Governor John C. Frémont (see "More Attractions," above, for complete information). The large church you see across Church Avenue is:

16. **St. Augustine Cathedral.** The entrance is from Stone Avenue, so walk around to the front. Above the door you'll see a statue of St. Augustine and symbols of the Arizona desert—the horned toad, the saguaro, and the yucca. From the south side of the cathedral, walk a block east on 13th Street and you'll be facing the back of the:

17. **Carnegie Library,** which now houses Tucson Children's Museum. The recent renovation of this 1901 building has promoted the revival of downtown Tucson. (See "Cool for Kids," above, for complete information.) Walk a block south on Scott Avenue and you'll come to the other major renovation project of recent years, the:

18. **Temple of Music and Art,** 330 South Scott Avenue. It was built in 1927 as a movie and stage theater, and in 1991, after its complete overhaul, became the home of the Arizona Theatre Company (see "Evening Entertainment, below, for complete information).

If you turn right on Cushing Street and walk another block, you'll be on the northern edge of the Barrio Historico District with its 150 adobe rowhouses, the largest collection of 19th-century Sonoran-style adobe architecture preserved in the United States.

REFUELING STOP At the corner of Cushing Street and Meyer Avenue stands the: **19. Cushing Street Bar & Grill,** housed in an old home and a country store. Inside are old photos of the neighborhood (see "Dining," above, for complete information).

Continue another block west to Granada Avenue and turn left. On the far side of the street stands:

20. El Tiradito (see "More Attractions," above, for complete information). This is the only shrine in the United States dedicated to a sinner buried in unconsecrated soil. People still light candles here in hope of having their wishes come true. Wander a while through the Barrio Historico District admiring the Sonoran-style homes that are built right out to the street. Head back up Church Avenue when you're ready and turn right on Broadway.

REFUELING STOP   Though it's surrounded by high-rise buildings now, the:
21. Charles O. Brown House and El Adobe Patio remains a quiet oasis in the city and is now a restaurant and gift shop. The shady patio, planted with fruit trees, is a great place for healthy Mexican food and tasty margaritas. (See "Dining," above, for complete information.)

There is one more place you might want to see before ending your walking tour of the real Old Tucson. Walk a block north to Congress Street, turn right, and walk four blocks until you come to the:

22. Congress Hotel, 311 East Congress Street. The famous gangster John Dillinger stayed here shortly before he was captured. The Congress Hotel was recently renovated as a youth hostel. Be sure to look around the lobby.

ORGANIZED TOURS

Tucson Tours (tel. 297-2911) offers half-day guided city tours with pickups at several downtown hotels. The tours head up to the top of A Mountain for an overview of the city, then visit the three downtown historic districts and the University of Arizona. This company also offers a shuttle service to the Arizona–Sonora Desert Museum and Old Tucson Studios and tours to Mission San Xavier del Bac.

6. SPECIAL & FREE EVENTS

Because of the excellent weather year round, Tucson hosts numerous outdoor festivals, celebrations, and events. Many are free and are held downtown and in the city's parks.

One year-round favorite free event is **Downtown Saturday Night,** a celebration of the Downtown Arts District held on the first and third Saturday of each month. From 7 to 10pm on these nights, the district, which includes East Pennington Street, East Congress Street, and East Broadway Boulevard between Fourth Avenue and Stone Avenue, comes alive with music performances on the street and in cafés, art gallery openings, and late-evening shopping. You'll also hear live music if you wander over to the Old Town Artisans crafts market in the El Presidio Historic District. First Saturdays are primarily for art gallery openings and third Saturdays are mainly for late-shopping, but either night is loads of fun.

January

Northern Telecom Open Golf Tournament, Tucson National Golf Course. Mid-January.

February

Indian Arts Benefit Fair, Old Town Artisans. Native American handcrafts and entertainment. Early February.
Old Pueblo Balloon Classic, Midvale Park. More than 40 hot-air balloons compete. Mid-February.

Festival in the Sun, University of Arizona. Arts and music festival. Late February to early March.
Tucson Rodeo Parade, downtown. World's largest nonmotorized parade. Late February.
La Fiesta de los Vaqueros, Tucson Rodeo Grounds. Cowboy festival and rodeo. Late February.

March

Walk Pow Wow, Mission San Xavier del Bac. Tohono O'odham celebration featuring many southwestern Native American groups. Early March.
Yaqui Easter Lenten Ceremony, Barrio Libre and Pasqua Villages. Religious ceremonies blending Christian and Yaqui Native American beliefs. Holy Week.

April

San Xavier Pageant and Festival, Mission San Xavier del Bac. Celebration of the mission's founding. Early April.
Fiesta del Presidio, Tucson Museum of Art. A celebration of Hispanic heritage. Mid-April.
Tucson International Mariachi Conference, Tucson Convention Center. Mariachi bands from all over come to compete. Mid-April.
Taste of Tucson, Tucson Convention Center. Showcase of the best fare from Tucson's finest restaurants. Late April.

May

Cinco de Mayo, Kennedy Park. Mexican food, music, dancing. May 5.
Summerset Suites, Tucson Museum of Art. Open-air jazz concerts. Saturday May to July.

June

Mount Lemmon Music Festival, Mount Lemmon Ski Area. Open-air concerts. Early June.

September

Mexican Independence Day Celebration, Kennedy Park. Music, arts, and food. September 14–16.

October

Tucson Meet Yourself, El Presidio Park. Celebration of Tucson's ethnic diversity. Mid-October.
Chile Fiesta, Tucson Botanical Gardens. Mid-October.
Tucson Blues Festival, Reid Park. Regional and national blues masters. Mid-October.
Tucson International Film Festival, around the city. Late October.

November

A Southwestern Celebration, Old Town Artisans. Arizonan, southwestern Native American, and Latin American artisans exhibit and demonstrate their crafts. Early November.
Western Music Festival, Old Tucson Studios. Concerts and workshops by country-and-western music performers. Late November.

December

Fourth Avenue Street Fair, Fourth Avenue. Outdoor arts and crafts festival. Early December.
Fiesta de Guadelupe, De Grazia Gallery in the Sun. Celebration of Mexico's patron saint. Early December.
Las Posadas, Barrio Historico District. Children reenact Joseph and Mary's search for an inn. Mid-December.

7. SPORTS & RECREATION

SPECTATOR SPORTS

AUTO RACING   Stock cars race at **Tucson Raceway Park,** 12500 South Houghton Road (tel. 629-0707). Tickets range from $8 to $15.

BASEBALL   The **Cleveland Indians** (tel. 325-2621) pitch spring training camp at Hi Corbett Field in Reid Park, at South Country Club Road and East 22nd Street. This is also where you can watch the **Tucson Toros** (tel. 325-2621), the Houston Astros AAA team in the Pacific Coast League. Game starting times vary. Tickets range from $3.50 to $5.50.

GREYHOUND RACING   Greyhounds race year-round at **Tucson Greyhound Park,** South Fourth Avenue at 36th Street (tel. 884-7576). Admission ranges from $1.25 for general admission to $3 for the clubhouse.

RECREATION

BALLOONING   **Balloon America,** P.O. Box 64600, Tucson, AZ 85740 (tel. 299-7744), offers breakfast flights over the foothills of the Santa Catalina Mountains with free pickups at most resorts. Because of strong thermals in the summer, the ballooning season runs only from October to June. At $195 per person for a 1- to 2-hour flight, ballooning is not cheap. The flights start at the golf course of the Westin La Paloma and end with a champagne toast and breakfast back at the resort.

BICYCLING   You can explore the Arizona backcountry with a rental bicycle from **Desert Pedals,** 2131 East Fifth Avenue (tel. 884-8838). They also offer guided bicycle trips.

GOLF   Golf is one of the most popular sports in Arizona and golf courses abound in Tucson. Tucson Parks & Recreation operates five public golf courses: **Randolph North** and **Randolph South,** 600 South Alvernon Way (tel. 791-4161); **El Rio,** 1400 West Speedway Boulevard (tel. 791-4229); **Silverbell,** 3600 North Silverbell Road (tel. 791-5235; and **Fred Enke,** 8250 East Irvington Road (tel. 791-2539). Greens fees range from a summer weekday low of only $3.50 for 9 holes to a high of $19 for 18 holes at Randolph North. A special $5 rate pertains weekdays from 4pm to dark. The advance reservation fee is $2. Golf carts are available for $9 to $14.
   In addition to the public links, there are two resort courses open to the public. These are the **Sheraton Tucson El Conquistador Golf & Tennis Resort,** 10000 North Oracle Road (tel. 297-0404), and the **Ventana Canyon Golf & Racquet Club Canyon Course,** 6200 North Clubhouse Lane (tel. 577-6258). Greens fees at these clubs vary with the season, and are always considerably higher than at the public courses.

HIKING   Tucson is nearly surrounded by mountains that are protected as city and state parks, a national forest, and a national monument. Within these areas are hundreds of miles of hiking trails.
   Sections of **Saguaro National Monument** are off Old Spanish Trail east of Tucson and past the end of Speedway Boulevard west of the city. In these areas you can observe Sonoran Desert vegetation and wildlife and hike among the huge saguaro cactuses for which the park is named.
   Tucson Mountain Park, also at the end of Speedway Boulevard, is adjacent to Saguaro National Monument and preserves a similar landscape.
   Sabino Canyon, at the end of Sabino Canyon Road, is Tucson's most popular recreation area. A cold mountain stream here cascades over waterfalls and forms pools that make great swimming holes. The most popular trail is the 4½-mile-long Seven Falls Trail, which follows the canyon deep into the mountains.
   Catalina State Park, north of the city on North Oracle Road, is set on the

rugged northwest face of the Santa Catalina Mountains, between 2,500 and 3,000 feet high. Hiking trails beginning in the park lead into the Pusch Ridge Wilderness.

Mount Lemmon Recreation Area, at the end of the Catalina Highway, is set amid high alpine forests on this 8,250-foot mountain. The cool air at this elevation makes this a popular summertime retreat.

HORSEBACK RIDING If you want to play cowboy or just go for a leisurely ride through the desert, there are plenty of stables around Tucson where you can saddle up. In addition to renting horses and providing guided trail rides, all stables below also offer breakfast and sunset rides with cookouts. Though reservations are not always required, they're a good idea.

Pusch Ridge Stables, 11220 North Oracle Road (tel. 297-6908), is adjacent to Catalina State Park and Coronado National Forest. Rates are $12.50 for 1 hour, $20 for 2 hours, and $18 for a 1½-hour sunset ride.

El Conquistador Stables, 10000 North Oracle Road (tel. 742-4200), is part of the Sheraton Tucson El Conquistador Resort, but the public is welcome. Rates are $10 for 1 hour, $18 for 2 hours, and $15 for a 1½-hour sunset ride. Reservations are required.

Desert–High Country Stables, 6501 West Ina Road (tel. 744-3789), is located 2 miles west of I-10 and offers a variety of rides in the Tucson Mountains and Saguaro National Monument West. Rates range from $15 for 1½ hours to $50 for a full day. Reservations are requested.

SKIING One hour (35 miles) from Tucson, **Mount Lemmon Ski Valley,** P.O. Box 612, Mount Lemmon, AZ 85619 (tel. 576-1321), offers 15 slopes for experienced downhill skiers as well as a beginners' ski area. This is the southernmost ski area in the continental United States, and at times there's insufficient snow for good skiing. Be sure to call ahead before driving here. The ski season runs from mid-December to mid-April. Lift tickets are $25.

TENNIS Tucson boasts more than 220 public tennis courts, many lighted for night playing. **Randolph Tennis Center,** 100 South Alvernon Way (tel. 791-4896), convenient to downtown, offers 24 courts, 21 lighted. Many of the city's hotels and resorts provide courts for guest use.

8. SAVVY SHOPPING

Tucsonans have a very strong sense of their place in the Southwest, and this is reflected in the city's shopping scene. Southwestern clothing, food, crafts, furniture, and art abound (and often at reasonable prices), as do shopping centers built in a southwestern architectural style.

THE SHOPPING SCENE

Although Tucson is overshadowed by Scottsdale and Phoenix, the city provides a very respectable diversity of merchants. Its population center has moved steadily northward for some years, and you'll find the most expensive shops selling the best-quality merchandise as well as large enclosed shopping malls in the **northern foothills.**

Aside from the foothills, there are plenty of new, hip, and unusual shops downtown. On **Fourth Avenue,** between Congress Street and Speedway Boulevard, are more than 100 shops, galleries, and restaurants in the North Fourth Avenue historic shopping district. The buildings here were built in the early 1900s, and a drive to keep the neighborhood humming has helped maintain Tucson's downtown vitality. Notable Fourth Avenue places include The Metal Man, selling metal sculptures; Antigone Books, a women's bookstore; La Zia, featuring North American Indian arts; the Zenith Center of Spiritual Arts; SaraSol and Del Sol, offering southwestern women's fashions; and interesting restaurants and bars. Through the underpass at the south end of Fourth Avenue is **Congress Street,** the heart of the downtown Arts

District. Here you'll find numerous galleries specializing in contemporary art, avant-garde boutiques, and a few trendy eating establishments. The **El Presidio Historic District** around the Tucson Museum of Art is the city's center for crafts shops. Here are Old Town Artisans and Ocotillo Artisans Gallery, as well as the El Presidio Art Gallery and the Tucson Museum of Art museum shop.

SHOPPING A TO Z
ANTIQUES

ACCENT ANTIQUES, 505 S. Sixth Ave. Tel. 624-8118.
This complex of antiques shops is in a restored building that is on the National Register of Historic Homes. You'll find antiques, fine art, and other collectibles from all over the world.

ART

AMERICA WEST GALLERY, 363 S. Meyer Ave. Tel. 623-4091.
Although this gallery specializes in works by Native Americans, you'll also find pre-Columbian art and pieces from Africa, Oceania, and Asia.

DE GRAZIA GALLERY IN THE SUN, 6300 N. Swan Rd. Tel. 299-9191.
Southwestern artist Ettore "Ted" De Grazia is a Tucson favorite son, and his gallery, set in an adobe home in the foothills, is a Tucson landmark. De Grazia is said to be the most reproduced artist in the world because many of his impressionistic images are found on greeting cards and numerous other places. Connected to the gallery is a small adobe chapel that De Grazia built in honor of the missionary explorer Father Eusebio Kino. No original works are for sale, but there are many reproductions and other objects with De Grazia images.

EL PRESIDIO GALLERY, 120 N. Main Ave. Tel. 884-7379.
Housed in a historic building in the El Presidio District, this gallery deals primarily in traditional paintings of the Southwest, although some contemporary works are also available.

STUDIO 346, 346 N. Fourth Ave. Tel. 623-6646.
This is one of the best places in town to look for contemporary southwestern art.

CRAFTS

MANY HANDS COURTYARD, 3054 N. First Ave. Tel. 798-3454.
Meet the artists and artisans in their own studios while you shop for handcrafted southwestern items. The studios and shops are built in Mexican village style.

OCOTILLO ARTISANS GALLERIA, 182 N. Court Ave. Tel. 884-8846.
Across the street from Old Town Artisans is a smaller shop selling more crafts with southwestern motifs.

OLD TOWN ARTISANS, 186 N. Meyer Ave. Tel. 623-6024.
★ Housed in a restored 1850s adobe building covering an entire city block of the El Presidio district are 15 rooms brimming with the best of southwestern arts and crafts. You'll find traditional and contemporary designs by more than 400 artisans.

FASHIONS
Western Wear

ARIZONA HATTERS, 3600 N. First Ave. Tel. 292-1320.
If you've decided to outfit yourself in proper Arizona cowboy or cowgirl attire, this is the place to start for the essential cowboy hat by Stetson or any of the other less-well-known makers.

THE BOOTERY, 2511 S. Craycroft Rd. Tel. 790-1212.

After you've shaded your brow with a 10-gallon hat, it's time to slip into some pointy-toed cowboy boots, and this store has the largest selection in the city.

WESTERN WAREHOUSE, 3719 N. Oracle Rd. Tel. 293-1808.
If you'd rather put together your western-wear ensemble under one roof, this is the place. It's the largest western-wear store in Tucson and can deck you out in jeans, hats, boots, and Native American jewelry.

Women's
JASMINE, 423 N. Fourth Ave. Tel. 629-0706.
Fine natural fibers, including washable silks, are the specialty here. The styles range from classic to exotic and fabrics are often hand-loomed. There are southwestern accessories and jewelry to go with the clothes, and the store even provides round-trip transportation from your hotel.

SARASOL, 735 N. Fourth Ave. Tel. 623-6680.
Imported textiles from South and Central America form the basis of uniquely southwestern fashions available here.

SEÑOR COYOTE, Tucson Mall, 4500 N. Oracle Rd. Tel. 888-8884.
The bright colors of contemporary southwestern art have become all the rage in the past few years, and at Señor Coyote you'll find those great colors in T-shirts and sweatshirts. Howling coyotes and cow skulls are very popular designs. Lots of hand-painted cover-ups too.

GIFTS/SOUVENIRS
B&B CACTUS FARM, 11550 E. Speedway Blvd. Tel. 721-4687.
This plant nursery is devoted exclusively to cacti and succulents. The store can pack your purchase for traveling or ship it anywhere in the U.S., including California and Hawaii. Even if you're not in the market for your very own barrel cactus or saguaro, the farm is worth a visit to see the amazing variety of cactus on display.

JEWELRY
BETH FRIEDMAN JEWELRY, 186 N. Meyer Ave. Tel. 622-5013.
Located in the Old Town Artisans complex, this shop sells jewelry from southwestern Native American, and international designers.

THUNDERBIRD SHOP, in the Old Adobe Building, 40 W. Broadway Blvd. Tel 623-1371.
 In business since 1927, this shop specializes in high-quality Native American jewelry. It is housed in a landmark adobe building erected in the 1850s.

MALLS/SHOPPING CENTERS
EL CON MALL, 3601 E. Broadway Blvd. Tel. 327-6787.
With more than 135 establishments, including major department stores, this is Tucson's oldest regional shopping mall. Although convenient to downtown, it lacks the style of the newer malls in northern Tucson.

EL MERCADO DE BOUTIQUES, 6336 E. Broadway Blvd. Tel. 790-8333.
This small Mexican-style mercado (market) contains 19 one-of-a-kind shops and several restaurants, including the popular The Good Earth.

FOOTHILLS MALL, 7401 N. La Cholla Blvd. Tel. 742-7191.
This large mall not only has dozens of specialty shops, boutiques, movie theaters, restaurants, and department stores, but also houses the Old Pueblo Museum, which features exhibits on southwestern history, culture, arts, and natural sciences.

PARK MALL SHOPPING CENTER, 5870 E. Broadway Blvd., at Wilmot Rd. Tel. 748-1222.
Offering everything from department stores to a post office, this mall has 120 shops and provides a courtesy hotel shuttle.

ST. PHILIP'S PLAZA, 4300 N. Campbell Ave., at River Rd. Tel. 299-6676.
This *yup*scale southwestern-style shopping center includes three excellent restaurants, a luxury beauty salon, and numerous shops and galleries, including Bahti Indian Arts and Café Terra Cotta.

TUCSON MALL, 4500 N. Oracle Rd. Tel. 293-7330.
The foothills of northern Tucson have become shopping center central, and this is the largest of the malls. You'll find more than 170 merchants in this two-story skylit complex.

MARKET

TUCSON PUBLIC MARKET, 135 S. Sixth Ave. Tel. 792-2623.
Saturday mornings from early April until the first frost, there's a farmers market here, while on the first and third Saturday nights of each month there's a crafts market. Live entertainment makes shopping at either an event.

NATIVE AMERICAN ARTS & CRAFTS

BAHTI INDIAN ARTS, in St. Philip's Plaza, 4300 N. Campbell Ave. Tel. 577-0290.
For more than 35 years this store has been selling fine Native American arts and crafts. You'll find jewelry, baskets, sculpture, prints, weavings, kachina dolls, and much more.

JAY'S INDIAN ARTS, 6637 S. 12th Ave. Tel. 294-3397.
A wide selection and good prices make this one of the best places in Tucson to shop for authentic Native American arts, crafts, and jewelry. You'll find kachina dolls, rugs, pottery, sand painting, and more.

9. EVENING ENTERTAINMENT

THE PERFORMING ARTS

MAJOR PERFORMING ARTS COMPANIES

ARIZONA OPERA COMPANY, P.O. Box 42828, Tucson, AZ 85733. Tel. 293-4336.
The Arizona Opera Company turns 25 in 1992, and with performances in both Phoenix and Tucson, the company stays busy entertaining the state's opera fans. The season runs from October to March with four scheduled productions each year. In

---

THE MAJOR CONCERT & PERFORMANCE HALLS

A.K.A. Theatre, 125 East Congress Street (tel. 623-7852).
Centennial Hall, University Boulevard and Park Avenue (tel. 621-3341).
Demeester Outdoor Performance Center, Reid Park, Country Club Road and East 22nd Street (tel. 791-4079).
Gaslight Theatre, 7000 East Tanque Verde Road (tel. 886-9428).
Invisible Theatre, 1400 North First Avenue (tel. 882-9721).
Temple of Music and Art, 330 South Scott Avenue (tel. 884-8210).
Tucson Convention Center Music Hall, bounded by Church Avenue, Broadway Boulevard, Cushing Street, and Granada Avenue (tel. 791-4266).

Tucson, performances are held at the Tucson Convention Center Music Hall. The box office is open Monday through Saturday from 10am to 6pm.
Admission: Tickets, $9–$40.

ARIZONA THEATRE COMPANY [ATC], Temple of Music and Art, 330 S. Scott Ave. Tel. 622-2823 or 884-8210.

With six productions a year performed in both Tucson and Phoenix, the Arizona Theatre Company is the state's main professional acting company. Each season sees a mix of comedy, drama, and Broadway-style musical shows. The ATC has also been bringing writers, directors, and actors to Tucson to develop new plays, one of which is performed each year. The box office is open Monday through Friday from 10am to 6pm, on Saturday from 10am to 5pm, and on Sunday from 10am to 2pm.
Admission: Tickets, $14–$21.

BALLET ARIZONA, 3645 E. Indian School Rd., Phoenix. Tel. 882-5022 (in Tucson).

Yet another company that splits its performances between Tucson and Phoenix, Ballet Arizona offers four regular productions during its December-to-May season. Productions usually include well-known ballets as well as new works by regional choreographers. Performances are at different venues around town.
Admission: Tickets, $16–$26.

SOUTHERN ARIZONA LIGHT OPERA COMPANY, Tucson Convention Center Music Hall. Tel. 323-7888 or 884-1212.

This local company does not employ professional actors or singers for its productions, so don't expect international caliber performances. However, the company always does a commendable job. Productions tend to be Broadway musicals rather than true light opera. The box office is open Monday through Friday from 9am to 5pm, and also on Saturday if there's a performance that day.
Admission: Tickets, $11–$22.

TUCSON SYMPHONY ORCHESTRA, 443 S. Stone Ave. Tel. 792-9155 for information or 882-8585 for tickets.

The Tucson Symphony Orchestra is the oldest continuously performing symphony in the Southwest. The season runs from October to May with a wide variety of performances, most of which are given in the Tucson Convention Center Music Hall. The season includes classics, pops, chamber, and family music performances. The box office is open Monday through Friday 9am to 5:30pm.
Admission: Tickets, $9–$35.

MAJOR CONCERT HALLS & ALL-PURPOSE AUDITORIUMS

CENTENNIAL HALL, University of Arizona, University Blvd. and Park Ave. Tel. 621-3341.

This is one of Tucson's main stops for touring national musical acts, international performing companies, and Broadway shows. A large stage and excellent sound system permit large-scale productions. The 1991 season included *Les Misérables*, the Moscow-Studio Theatre, the Bulgarian National Folk Ensemble, and Wynton Marsalis, among many others. The box office is open Monday through Friday from 10am to 6pm and 1½ hours before curtain time.
Admission: Tickets, $12–$40.

DEMEESTER OUTDOOR PERFORMANCE CENTER, Reid Park, Country Club Rd. and E. 22nd St. Tel. 791-4079.

Located in the middle of the sprawling Reid Park, which also contains Tucson's zoo, the DeMeester Outdoor Performance Center is the site of summer performances by the A.K.A. Theatre and other production companies, as well as frequent music performances. Shows are scheduled for the warm months only, from April on into late October.
Admission: Free.

TEMPLE OF MUSIC AND ART, 330 S. Scott Ave. Tel. 884-8210.

✪ This historic theater was completely restored in 1991 and reopened to a very warm welcome from the citizens of Tucson. Tucson's downtown Arts District was well on its way to becoming a major gathering area for the city's arts community, and the renovation of this landmark 1927 theater gave the neighborhood another lift. The 605-seat Holsclaw Theatre is the temple's main venue, but there is also a 90-seat Cabaret Theatre. You'll also find an art gallery and a restaurant here. Free tours of the Temple of Art and Music are available three or four times a month for most of the year. The box office is open Monday through Friday from 10am to 6pm, on Saturday from 10am to 5pm, and on Sunday from 10am to 2pm.

Admission: Tickets, $10–$30.

TUCSON CONVENTION CENTER MUSIC HALL, bounded by Church Ave., Broadway Blvd., Cushing St., and Granada Ave. Tel. 791-4101 or 791-4266.

This large performing arts and convention complex is home to the Tucson Symphony Orchestra, the Arizona Opera Company (when in town), and Ballet Arizona, and also hosts many touring companies. The box office is open Monday through Saturday from 10am to 6pm.

Admission: Tickets, $10–$40.

THEATERS

A.K.A. THEATRE, 125 E. Congress St. Tel. 623-7852.

Small but growing, the A.K.A. Theatre likes to take chances. Well known for its avant-garde productions, this downtown Arts District theater company scored a big success with *Macbeth*. Productions also include lesser-known but equally entertaining plays. Friday and Saturday night late shows. Phone reservations only.

Admission: Tickets, $9.

THE GASLIGHT THEATRE, 7000 E. Tanque Verde Rd. Tel. 886-9428.

✪ The West just wouldn't be the West without good old-fashioned melodramas, and the Gaslight Theatre is Tucson's home of evil villains, stalwart heroes, and defenseless heroines. You can boo and hiss, cheer and sigh as the predictable stories unfold on stage. It's all great fun for kids and adults. The box office is open Monday through Tuesday from 10am to 5:30pm, Wednesday through Friday from 10am to showtime, and on Saturday and Sunday from noon to showtime.

Admission: Tickets, $10 adults, $9 students and senior citizens, $5.50 children.

INVISIBLE THEATRE, 1400 N. First Ave. Tel. 882-9721.

This tiny theater has been home to Tucson's most experimental theater for more than 30 years. The box office is open daily from 10am to 5pm.

Admission: Tickets, $10–$12.

THE CLUB & MUSIC SCENE

A COMEDY CLUB

LAFFS COMEDY CLUB & CAFE, The Village, 2900 E. Broadway Blvd. Tel. 32-FUNNY.

Tucson hasn't yet gone comedy crazy as have other U.S. cities. This is still the only comedy club in town, but comedians from around the country perform. Shows are Sunday through Thursday at 8pm and on Friday and Saturday at 8 and 10:30pm.

Admission: $1–$8.

COUNTRY & MARIACHI

EL MARIACHI RESTAURANTE Y CANTINA, 106 W. Drachman St. Tel. 791-7793.

With their big hats and spangled outfits, mariachi musicians have come to symbolize Mexico to many Americans. Their lively acoustic music and traditional Mexican love songs are essential to any festivity south of the border. Here in Tucson

the band International Mariachi America performs Tuesday through Sunday night at this restaurant and nightclub. The menu features steaks and Mexican food in the $8 to $16 range. Shows are at 7, 8:30, 10, and 11:30pm.
Admission: $2.

LA FUENTE, 1749 N. Miracle Mile. Tel. 623-8659.

⭐ La Fuente is another good spot to catch Mexico's most popular traditional music. The music starts after 6:30pm Tuesday through Sunday night. La Fuente is the largest Mexican restaurant in Tucson and serves up good food as well as music. If you just want to listen to the music, you can sit in the lounge.
Admission: Free.

WILD WILD WEST, 4385 W. Ina Rd. Tel. 744-7744.

This country-western club used to be a bowling alley, and since the conversion, it has the biggest and best dance floor in Tucson. In fact there's an acre of floorboard for all you two-steppers. Rock 'n' rollers aren't forgotten either—there's a rock bar within the huge complex.
Admission: Free Sun–Thurs, $2–$3 Fri–Sat.

ROCK

CHICAGO BAR, 5954 E. Speedway Blvd. Tel. 748-8169.

Transplanted Chicagoans love to watch their home teams on the TVs here, but there's also live music ranging from rockabilly to reggae. Monday night is open-mike night if you want to catch a bit of undiscovered local talent.
Admission: Free–$3.

CLUB CONGRESS, 311 E. Congress St. Tel. 622-8849.

Just off the lobby of the restored Hotel Congress, which is now a youth hostel, Club Congress is one of Tucson's main alternative music venues. There are usually a couple of nights of live music each week.
Admission: $1–$5.

CUSHING STREET BAR & RESTAURANT, 343 S. Meyer Ave. Tel. 622-7984.

The building may be 100 years old, but the music is up-to-the-minute. The Cushing Street Bar is in the Barrio Historico District in a 100-year-old adobe building. Live rock, blues, and folk music by local and national acts can be heard nightly.
Admission: $2–$10.

JAZZ & BLUES

BERKY'S BAR, 5769 E. Speedway Blvd. Tel. 296-1981.

The blues wail 6 nights a week from Tuesday through Sunday at this smokey bar.
Admission: Free Sun and Tues–Thurs, $2 Fri–Sat.

CAFE SWEETWATER, 340 E. Sixth Ave. Tel. 622-6464.

Downtown in the Fourth Avenue District, you can hear live jazz Tuesday through Saturday night. Thursday is jam session night.
Admission: Free.

DANCE CLUBS/DISCOS

BOBBY MCGEE'S CONGLOMERATION, 6464 E. Tanque Verde Rd. Tel. 886-5551.

Though known primarily as a fun family restaurant, Bobby McGee's is also a very popular singles disco that attracts a very young crowd. Music is loud and there are long happy hours with lots of free hors d'oeuvres.
Admission: $2.

THE BAR SCENE

PUBS

BAY HORSE TAVERN, 2802 E. Grant Rd. Tel. 326-8554.

Basically just a neighborhood bar, the Bay Horse has a giant chair chained to a post in the middle of the bar. The owners claim it's identical to the chair used by Lily Tomlin when she played Edith Ann on "Laugh In." The jukebox has been designated one of the best in Tucson.

GENTLE BEN'S BREWING CO., 841 N. Tyndall Ave. Tel. 624-4177.

With daily food and drink specials, live music on Friday and Saturday nights, and a Sunday barbecue, Gentle Ben's is Tucson's newest microbrewery. The crowd is young and active.

SAN FRANCISCO BAR & GRILL, 3922 N. Oracle Rd. Tel. 292-2233.

This was the first microbrewery to open in Tucson, and still turns out a respectable brew. Sports fans can join like-minded folks rooting for the U.A. Wildcats and the Phoenix Cardinals.

COCKTAILS WITH A VIEW

Just about all the best vistas in town are at foothills resorts, but luckily they don't mind sharing with nonguests.

CACTUS CLUB AND DESERT GARDEN LOUNGE, in the Westin La Paloma, 3800 E. Sunrise Dr. Tel. 742-6000.

The Cactus Club is the resort's disco and features DJ dance music of the past 30 years. Open Tuesday through Saturday, the Cactus Club has a big wrap-around patio for viewing the city below. If you'd rather gaze up at the Santa Catalina Mountains, head over to the Desert Garden Lounge where there's live entertainment amid a southwestern decor. Both spots tend to attract an upscale 30-something crowd.

CASCADE LOUNGE, in Loew's Ventana Canyon Resort, 7000 N. Resort Dr. Tel. 299-2020.

If you can't afford the lap of luxury, at least you can pull up a chair in the grand lobby of this *très moderne* resort. The lobby lounge takes its name from the narrow ribbon of waterfall that cascades out of Ventana Canyon a few hundred yards away.

LOOKOUT LOUNGE, in the Westward Look Resort, 245 E. Ina Rd. Tel. 297-1151.

The Westward Look is one of Tucson's oldest resorts and took to the hills long before it became the fashionable place to be. The nighttime view of twinkling city lights and stars is unmatched. Monday is sports night, but the rest of the week there's live jazz.

10. NETWORKS & RESOURCES

FOR STUDENTS The University of Arizona, the state's oldest university, is located between Sixth Street and Speedway Boulevard and Fourth Avenue and Campbell Avenue. Fourth Avenue has many shops, restaurants, and bars catering primarily to the university crowd. Be sure to carry a current student ID so you can get into attractions and purchase show tickets for the student rates.

FOR GAY MEN & LESBIANS The **Tucson Old Pueblo**, 4210 North Saranac Drive, Tucson, AZ 85718 (tel. 602/577-6018; fax 602/577-0340), is a small bed-and-breakfast inn serving the gay and lesbian community. Located on 2½ acres of desert, the inn features a swimming pool, hot tub, and great views of the Santa

Catalinas. Rates range from $55 to $95 for a double. Complimentary airport transfers are provided.

The **Gay and Lesbian Tucson Community Center—Wingspan** is at 240 North Court Avenue (tel. 624-1779). The community center's hotline number is 624-1778.

FOR WOMEN   Though it's large, Tucson is still a fairly safe city. However, women alone should avoid downtown streets late at night. When making a hotel reservation, ask if the hotel has special women's rooms. These rooms are outfitted with amenities that traveling women, especially those on business, find helpful.

The **Women's Bookstore,** 403 East Fifth Avenue (tel. 792-3715), is just what its name implies and is located just off Fourth Avenue.

The **crisis hotline** phone number is 323-9373 and the **rape crisis center** phone number is 623-7273.

FOR SENIORS   Senior citizens should be sure to carry IDs wherever they go so they can take advantage of discounts at attractions and hotels. Many hotels offer discounts to members of the American Association of Retired Persons (AARP), 1909 K Street NW, Washington, DC 20049 (tel. 202/872-4700), but you can usually get the same discount simply by showing your ID.

---

11. EASY EXCURSIONS FROM TUCSON

BIOSPHERE 2, Ariz. 77 mile marker 96.5. Tel. 896-2108.

On September 26, 1991, four men and four women were sealed inside a large and elaborate greenhouse to begin an experiment they hope will lead to a better understanding of the human role in the future of Planet Earth. Actually, Biosphere is far more than a 3-acre greenhouse. It's an airtight, self-sustaining habitat, and if all goes well, the eight biospherians inside will be able to live for 2 years without further inputs of food, water, or air. (One needed outside medical attention early on, however.) More than 4,000 species of plant and animal are part of the experiment, which includes a rain forest, a desert, a savannah, a marsh, and even a tiny "ocean" complete with waves and tides. The biospherians will use intensive agricultural practices to grow vegetables and grains. Chickens, pygmy goats, and tilapia fish provide protein. During the 2 years the eight-member team will conduct experiments to better science's understanding of how the earth, which is basically a gigantic closed system fueled by the sun, manages to support all the planet's life forms.

There are daily tours of Biosphere 2, but reservations are required. Of course you won't be able to enter the Biosphere when you visit, but during your escorted tour you'll see a slide presentation on the history and purpose of Biosphere 2, view both a model of Biosphere and a prototype, walk through the research and development center, and then proceed to a viewing point overlooking the actual Biosphere 2 structure. Unfortunately you won't be able to get any closer than about 50 yards. Biosphere 2 has become a major tourist attraction and has its own hotel, conference center, restaurant, and gift shop.

Admission: $9.95 adults, $7 seniors and students 13–17, $5 children 6–12, free for children under 6.

Open: Daily 9am–4pm. **Directions:** Biosphere 2 is located 35 miles north of Tucson near the town of Oracle. Take Oracle Road north out of Tucson continuing north on U.S. 89 and Ariz. 77 until you see the Biosphere sign.

KITT PEAK NATIONAL OBSERVATORY. Tel. 325-9200.

Southern Arizona likes to brag about how many sunny days it has each year, and the nights are just as clear. The starry skies have lured more astronomical observatories to the Tucson vicinity than to any other region of the world. Southern Arizona has come to be known as the Astronomy Capital of the World, and the largest of the astronomical observatories here is the famous Kitt Peak National Observatory. Located in the Quinlan Mountains, 56 miles southwest of Tucson, the observatory is atop 6,882-foot Kitt Peak. The lack of lights in the surrounding Tohono O'odham Reservation makes the night sky here as brilliant as anywhere else on earth.

There are five major telescopes operating at Kitt Peak. The McMath telescope is the world's largest solar telescope. Its system of mirrors channels an image of the sun deep into the mountain before reflecting it back up to the observatory where scientists study the resulting 30-inch-diameter image of the sun. The 158-inch Mayall telescope features a 30,000-pound quartz mirror and is used for studying distant regions of the universe.

Though the observatory is open daily, there are guided tours only on weekends and holidays; on weekdays you can pick up a brochure for a self-guided walking tour. There is also a visitor center and museum. A film detailing the construction of the observatory and the work done here is shown daily at 10:30am and 2:30pm. A gift shop sells books on astronomy, posters, souvenirs, and crafts made by the Tohono O'odham people. There is no restaurant at the observatory, but there is a picnic area.

Admission: Free.

Open: Daily 10am–4pm. **Closed:** Dec 24–25. **Directions:** Take Ariz. 86 southwest from Tucson; in about 40 miles you'll see the turnoff for Kitt Peak.

TUBAC & TUMACACORI

Before Phoenix and Tucson there was Tubac. First settled by the Spanish in 1691 when Fr. Eusebio Francisco Kino established the nearby Tumacacori mission, Tubac was the first European settlement in what is today Arizona. However, the Tubac area had long been home to Native Americans. Archeologists have found evidence that there have been people living along the nearby Santa Cruz River for nearly 10,000 years. The Hohokam dwelt in the area from about A.D. 300 until their mysterious disappearance around 1500. Between 1691 and the present, seven different flags have flown over Tubac, including those of Spain, Mexico, the New Mexico Territory, the Confederacy, the United States Territory of Arizona, and the State of Arizona.

Sixty miles due south of Tucson on I-19, today, Tubac is one of Arizona's arts communities (others include Sedona, Jerome, and Bisbee). The town's old buildings now house more than 80 shops selling fine arts, crafts, and unusual gifts. This amazing collection of artists' studios and galleries makes Tubac one of southern Arizona's most popular destinations, and a small retirement community is beginning to develop in the area. After visiting Tubac Presidio State Historic Park and Tumacacori National Monument to learn about the area's history, you'll probably want to spend the rest of the day browsing through these interesting shops. Keep in mind, however, that many of the local artists leave town during the summer, so it's best to visit on weekends then. The busy season is from October to May, and during these months shops are open daily.

The **Tubac Festival of the Arts** is held each year in February. Artists from all over the country participate. In October, **De Anza Days** commemorate Capt. Juan Bautista de Anza's 1775 trek to found San Francisco.

WHAT TO SEE AND DO

TUBAC CENTER OF THE ARTS, Plaza Rd. Tel. 602/398-2371.

Tubac is an arts community, and this Spanish colonial building serves as its center for cultural activities. In addition to the permanent collection of artworks by members of the Santa Cruz Valley Art Association, the center acts as a sale gallery. Throughout

---

IMPRESSIONS

It has a melancholy appearance. The walls of the church still stand, no roof, and only the upright piece of the cross. It looks desolate indeed.
—A TRAVELER NAMED HAYS, UPON SEEING THE RUINS OF TUMACACORI IN 1849

the season there are also workshops, traveling exhibitions, juried shows, an annual craft show, and theater and music performances.

Admission: Free.

Open: Oct–May, Tues–Sat 10am–4:30pm, Sun 1–4:30pm. **Closed:** June–Sept.

TUBAC PRESIDIO STATE HISTORIC PARK, Presidio Dr. Tel. 602/398-2252.

Tubac Presidio has a long and fitful history. Though the Tumacacori mission had been founded in 1691, it was not until 1752 that the Tubac Presidio was established in response to a Pima uprising. The Tubac Presidio housed a garrison of 50 Spanish soldiers, and it was from here that Capt. Juan Bautista de Anza set out in 1775 on the overland expedition that led to the founding of San Francisco. That same year the presidio's military garrison was moved to Tucson, and, with no protection from raiding Apaches, most of Tubac's settlers also left the area. A military presence was reestablished in 1787, but after Mexican independence in 1821 insufficient funds led to the closing of the presidio. Villagers once again abandoned Tubac because of Apache attacks. After the Gadsden Purchase, Tubac became part of the United States and was again resettled.

Though little but buried foundation walls remain of the old presidio, Tubac Presidio State Historic Park has exhibits that explain the history of Tubac. There are displays on the Spanish soldiers, Native Americans, religion, and contemporary Hispanic culture in southern Arizona. In 1859 Arizona's first newspaper was published in Tubac and the press is on display here. In fact, Tubac claims quite a number of Arizona firsts, including being the first European town, and having the first Spanish land grant and the first Arizona state park. Also on the museum grounds is an old adobe schoolhouse built in 1885.

Admission: $1.

Open: Daily 8am–5pm. **Closed:** Dec 25.

TUMACACORI NATIONAL MONUMENT, Frontage Rd. Tel. 602/398-2341.

We in the United States often forget our Spanish heritage, but these mission ruins are a silent reminder of the role that Spanish missionaries played in settling the Southwest. Tumacacori mission was founded by Jesuit missionary and explorer Fr. Eusebio Francisco Kino in 1691 to convert the Pima. Much of the old brick-and-stucco mission church still stands, and the Spanish architectural influence can readily be seen. A small museum contains exhibits on mission life, and the Spanish and Native American history of the region. On weekends, Native American and Mexican craftspeople give demonstrations of native arts. The **Tumacacori Fiesta,** a celebration of Native American, Hispanic, and Anglo cultures, is held in early December.

Admission: $3 per car.

Open: Daily 8am–5pm. **Closed:** Major hols. **Directions:** You'll find Tumacacori 3 miles south of Tubac near Exit 29 off I-19.

CHAPTER 6

THE GRAND CANYON & NORTHERN ARIZONA

The Grand Canyon—the name is at once apt and inadequate. How can words sum up the grandeur of two billion years of the earth's history sliced open by the power of a single river? And yet, what else could such a magnificent work of nature be called but grand? Once a barrier to explorers and settlers, today the Grand Canyon attracts visitors from all over the world who gaze wonderstruck into its seemingly infinite depths.

Yet, other parts of northern Arizona also contain worthwhile attractions. Only 60 miles south of the great yawning chasm stand the San Francisco Peaks, the tallest of which is Humphreys Peak which stands 12,643 feet above sea level. These peaks, sacred to the Hopi and Navajo, are ancient volcanoes. Smaller volcanoes in this region once made the land fertile enough to support ancient Sinagua culture that has long since disappeared, leaving only the ruins of its ancient villages.

Amid northern Arizona's miles of windswept plains and ponderosa pine forests is the city of Flagstaff, which at 7,000 feet in elevation is one of the highest cities in the U.S. It's also home to Northern Arizona University, whose students ensure that it's a lively town. Born of the railroads, Flagstaff has preserved its western heritage in its restored downtown historic district.

In the name of progress and developing the desert, the great river canyons of Arizona have been dammed. Their sometimes quiet, sometimes angry waters have been turned into vast lakes. Among these is Lake Powell, created by the construction of the Glen Canyon Dam. The bitter fight to preserve Glen Canyon has been left behind and today the lake is popular with boaters, anglers, and skiers who come to pursue their sports amid the steep canyon walls. This lake, with its miles of water mirroring cliff walls hundreds of feet high, is one of northern Arizona's curious contrasts—a vast human-made reservoir in the middle of barren desert canyons.

1. FLAGSTAFF

150 miles N of Phoenix, 32 miles E of Williams,
80 miles south of Grand Canyon Village.

GETTING THERE   By Plane   Flagstaff's **Pulliam Municipal Airport** is served by Skywest (tel. toll free 800/453-9417), a Delta feeder airline, and America

WHAT'S SPECIAL ABOUT NORTHERN ARIZONA

Indian Ruins
- ☐ The ancient Sinagua pueblos of Wupatki National Monument.
- ☐ The Sinagua cliff dwellings of Walnut Canyon National Monument.

Buildings
- ☐ The Watchtower on the South Rim of the Grand Canyon.
- ☐ El Tovar Hotel in Grand Canyon Village.

Museums
- ☐ The Museum of Northern Arizona in Flagstaff.

Events/Festivals
- ☐ Hopi, Navajo, and Zuñi festivals at the Museum of Northern Arizona.

Natural Spectacles
- ☐ The Grand Canyon, one of the earth's greatest natural wonders.

- ☐ Sunset Crater, a colorful cinder cone near Flagstaff.
- ☐ The waterfalls of Havasu Canyon.
- ☐ The world's largest and best-preserved meteorite crater.

Activities
- ☐ Rafting through the Grand Canyon on the Colorado River.
- ☐ Riding a mule to the bottom of the Grand Canyon.
- ☐ Hiking into Havasu Canyon.
- ☐ Houseboating on Lake Powell, the best way to explore this huge human-made lake.

Beaches
- ☐ Lake Powell, in the middle of the desert.

West (tel. toll free 800/247-5692). The airport is located 2 miles south of town off I-17.

By Train   Flagstaff is served by **Amtrak** (tel. 602/774-8679 for arrival and departure information, or toll free 800/872-7245 for reservations) from Chicago and Los Angeles. The train station is at 1 East Santa Fe Avenue.

By Bus   Flagstaff is served by **Greyhound/Trailways Lines.** The bus station is at 399 South Malpias Lane (tel. 602/774-4573).

By Car   Flagstaff is on I-40, one of the main east-west Interstates in the U.S. I-17 also starts here and heads south to Phoenix. U.S. 89A connects Flagstaff to Sedona by way of Oak Creek Canyon. U.S. 180 connects Flagstaff with Grand Canyon Village, and U.S. 89 with Page.

ESSENTIALS   Orientation   Downtown Flagstaff is located just north of **I-40. Milton Road,** which at its southern end becomes I-17 to Phoenix, leads past Northern Arizona University on its way into downtown. Santa Fe Avenue runs parallel to the railroad tracks. Downtown's main street is **San Francisco Street,** while Humphreys Street leads north out of town toward the San Francisco Peaks and the south rim of the Grand Canyon.

Information   The **Flagstaff Visitors' Center,** at 101 West Santa Fe Avenue (tel. 602/774-9541, or toll free 800/842-7293), is open Monday through Saturday from 8am to 9pm and on Sunday from 8am to 5pm.

Fast Facts   The **area code** is 602. The **bus** system, Pine Country Transit (tel. 779-6624), provides public transit around the city; the fare is 75¢ for adults. **Car rentals** are available from Budget (tel. 602/779-0307 or 774-2763, or toll free 800/527-0700) and Hertz (tel. 602/774-4452, or toll free 800/654-3131). **Foreign**

currency can be exchanged at Valley National bank, which has offices at 100 West Birch Street (tel. 779-7411) and 2520 North Fourth Street (tel. 779-7351. For a **taxi,** call Northland Taxi (tel. 556-0041) or Dream V.I.P. Taxi (tel. 774-2934).

Situated at 7,000 feet above sea level, Flagstaff is one of the highest cities in the country, and is the county seat of Coconino County, the second-largest county in the U.S. it's the best all-around staging point for explorations of the Grand Canyon and the rest of northern Arizona, and its university supports a lively cultural community and is also home to one of the finest museums in Arizona—the Museum of Northern Arizona. The San Francisco Peaks, just outside the city, are one of Arizona's winter playgrounds, with the Fairfield Snowbowl attracting thousands of skiers to the slopes. In summer, sightseers ride the lift to the top of the mountain for the views and hikers come to explore the miles of mountain trails. Hikers and photographers also enjoy exploring Sunset Crater National Monument, a colorful cinder cone created by a volcanic eruption hundreds of years ago. Flagstaff has done much to preserve its pioneer heritage, but its history goes much farther back. Within a short drive of the city are ancient Sinagua cliff dwellings and the ruins of large pueblos that were built more than 700 years ago.

WHAT TO SEE & DO
MUSEUMS & OTHER CULTURAL ACTIVITIES

THE ARBORETUM AT FLAGSTAFF, Woody Mountain Rd. Tel. 774-1441.
Covering 200 acres, this arboretum focuses on plants of the high desert, coniferous forests, and alpine tundra, all of which are environments founded in the vicinity of Flagstaff.
Admission: Free.
Open: Mon–Fri 10am–3pm (guided tours at 11am and 1pm).

COCONINO CENTER FOR THE ARTS, 2300 N. Fort Valley Rd. (U.S. 180). Tel. 779-6921.
Throughout the year various exhibits and performances are held at this small center north of downtown. The gallery regularly exhibits contemporary and traditional arts and crafts from around northern Arizona. You might also catch a performance of Native American dances.
Admission: $2 adults, $1 students, $5 families, free for everyone on Sun.
Open: Winter, Tues–Sat 9am–5pm, Sun 11am–5pm; summer, daily 9am–5pm.
Closed: Thanksgiving, Dec 25–Jan 1, Easter Sun.

LOWELL OBSERVATORY, 1400 W. Mars Hill Rd. Tel. 774-2096.
Located atop aptly named Mars Hill is one of the oldest astronomical observatories in the Southwest. Founded in 1894 by Percival Lowell, the observatory has played important roles in contemporary astronomy. Among the work carried out here was Lowell's study of the planet Mars and his calculations that led him to predict the existence of the planet Pluto. However, it was not until 13 years after Lowell's death that Pluto was finally discovered almost exactly where he had predicted it would be. Today this is still an important research facility, but most astronomical observations are now carried out at Anderson Mesa, which is 10 miles farther away from the lights of Flagstaff.
The facility consists of several observatories and administrative buildings and a visitor center. At times when the visitor center is closed, there are brochures available for a self-guided tour of the site. Keep in mind that the telescope domes are not heated, so if you come up to observe the stars on a wintry night be sure to dress appropriately.
Admission: $1.
Open: Visitors center, June–Aug, Tues–Sat 10am–4:30pm. Lecture and tour, June–Aug, Tues–Sat at 10am and 1:30pm; Sept–May, Tues–Sat at 1:30pm. Evening viewing through telescope (weather permitting), first day of each month 8–10pm; June–Aug, also every Fri 8–10pm.

MUSEUM OF NORTHERN ARIZONA, N. Fort Valley Rd. (U.S. 180). Tel. 774-5211.

★ Located 2 miles north of downtown Flagstaff on U.S. 180, this small but surprisingly thorough museum should be your first stop. Here you will learn in state-of-the-art exhibits about the archeology, ethnology, geology, biology, and fine arts of the region. The most interesting of the museum's exhibits is its "Native Peoples of the Colorado Plateau," an exploration of both the archeology and ethnology of the region. The exhibit traces life on the Colorado Plateau from 15,000 B.C. to the present. Among the more interesting displays are a life-size kiva ceremonial room and an extensive collection of kachinas. In addition to its public educational role, the museum also serves as a research facility containing more than a million archeological artifacts from around the region. A video theater provides continuous showings of documentaries on regional history and Native American culture. The large gift shop is full of contemporary Native American arts and crafts. Throughout the year there are special exhibits focusing on Hopi, Navajo, and Zuñi arts and crafts.

The museum building itself is made of native stone and incorporates into its design a courtyard featuring vegetation from the six life zones of northern Arizona. Outside the museum is a short self-guided nature trail that leads through a narrow canyon strewn with boulders.

Admission: $3 adults, $1.50 children.
Open: Daily 9am–5pm. **Closed:** New Year's Day, Thanksgiving, and Christmas.

ARIZONA HISTORICAL SOCIETY/PIONEER MUSEUM, 2340 N. Fort Valley Rd. (U.S. 180). Tel. 774-6272.

Located next door to the Coconino Center for the Arts, this museum houses a historical collection from northern Arizona's pioneer days. The main museum building is a large stone structure that was built in 1908 as a hospital for the indigent. Among the exhibits are pieces of camera equipment used by Emery Kolb at his studio on the South Rim of the Grand Canyon. Many of Kolb's photos are also on display. Several small exhibit rooms cover various aspects of life in northern Arizona during the pioneer days and later. You'll see a doctor's office filled with frightening instruments; barbed wire and brands; an exhibit on Teddy Roosevelt's Rough Riders; dolls; saddles; and trapping and timber displays. In an old barn behind the main building is a large art gallery featuring works by local artists.

Admission: Free.
Open: Mon–Sat 9am–5pm. **Closed:** New Year's Day, Thanksgiving, and Christmas.

RIORDAN MANSION STATE PARK, Milton Rd. Tel. 779-4395.

Built in 1904 for local lumber merchants Michael and Timothy Riordan, this 13,000-square-foot mansion is unusual in that it's actually two houses connected by a large central hall. Each Riordan brother and his family occupied one half. The two halves of the mansion have different rooflines, so visitors can tell the two apart. The home is built in the Craftsmen style and though it looks like a log cabin, it's actually only faced with log slabs. The Riordans played important roles in the early history of Flagstaff. They built the first Roman Catholic church, the first library, the power company, the phone company, and also donated the land for Northern Arizona University.

Admission: $2 adults, free for children under 17.
Open: Daily 1–5pm (tours at 1, 2, 3, and 4pm).

SPORTS & RECREATION

Flagstaff is northern Arizona's center for outdoor activities. Chief among these is snow skiing at **Fairfield Snowbowl** on the slopes of Mount Agassiz (tel. 602/779-1951 for information or 602/779-4577 for a snow report, or in Phoenix 602/957-0404 for a snow report). There four chair lifts, 32 runs, and 2,300 vertical feet of slopes. There are also ski rentals, a baby-sitting program, and a children's ski program. Lift tickets range from $20 for a half-day midweek pass to $27 for a weekend all-day pass. There is a shuttle bus that operates from the Ft. Valley Lodge at the base of the mountain, as well as parking at the top for 1,000 cars. In the summer the ski lift carries hikers and anyone else who wants to enjoy the views. Summer rates are $7 for adults, $5 for seniors, and $3.50 for children 6 to 12.

There are dozens of trails on the slopes of Mount Agassiz starting either at the top or bottom of the ski lift. There are many other trails throughout the San Francisco peaks and many are open to mountain bikes as well as hikers. Late September, when the aspens have turned to a brilliant golden yellow, is one of the best times of year for a hike in Flagstaff's mountains.

If you feel like saddlin' up and hittin' the trail, contact **Hitchin' Post Stables,** 448 Lake Mary Road (tel. 774-1719 or 774-7131). This horseback-riding stable offers guided trail rides, sunset barbecue rides, and cowboy breakfast rides. The most popular trail ride goes into Walnut Canyon, site of ancient cliff dwellings.

ORGANIZED TOURS

Gray Line/Nava-Hopi Tours (tel. 602/774-5003, or toll free 800/892-8687) operates several day-long tours of northern Arizona. These tours include excursions to the South Rim of the Grand Canyon; Walnut Canyon, Wupatki, and Sunset Crater; Monument Valley and the Navajo Indian Reservation; the Petrified Forest, Painted Desert, and Meteor Crater; and the Hopi Indian Reservation.

WHERE TO STAY
MODERATE

ARIZONA MOUNTAIN INN, 685 Lake Mary Rd., Flagstaff, AZ 86001. Tel. 602/774-8959. 3 rms, 15 cottages and chalets (all with bath). **$ Rates:** $60–$90 single or double. DISC, MC, V.

Located just a few minutes south of downtown Flagstaff, the Arizona Mountain Inn is a quiet mountain retreat set beneath shady pine trees. Though there are three bed-and-breakfast rooms in the main building, all the rest of the accommodations here are cabins that can sleep anywhere from 2 to 20 people. Many of the rustic cabins are A-frames or chalets and all are a little bit different from each other. If you've got a really big group, say, 20 people, you can rent their giant log hogan with a big sleeping loft. The family-oriented inn has 13 acres surrounding it, and beyond this are miles of national forest.

Services: Rental TVs, limited firewood.

Facilities: Volleyball, horseshoes, baseball field, basketball court, playground, coin laundry.

BEST WESTERN WOODLANDS PLAZA HOTEL, 1175 W. Hwy. 66, Flagstaff, AZ 86001. Tel. 602/773-8888, or toll free 800/528-1234. Fax 602/773-0597. 125 rms, 15 suites (all with bath). A/C TV TEL **$ Rates:** $59–$79 single; $69–$89 double; $79–$110 suite. AE, CB, DC, DISC, MC, V.

When the Woodlands Plaza Hotel opened in 1991, it filled Flagstaff's need for a small luxury hotel. With its elegant marble-floored lobby, the Woodlands Plaza would easily fit in on Scottsdale's resort row. A baby grand piano, crystal chandelier, traditional European furnishings, and contemporary sculpture all add to the unexpected luxury. Throughout the hotel's public areas you'll also see intricately carved pieces of furniture and architectural details from different Asian countries. Traditional European styling is used in the guest-room decor with pale pastel colors and southwestern touches. There are large TVs and clock radios in all rooms, and in the tile bathroom you'll find a large basket of toiletries.

The Sakura restaurant serves Teppan-style Japanese meals with tableside cooking and a sushi bar. In the Woodland Café, the menu features traditional American fare with a few international and southwestern touches. The hotel also offers room service, a swimming pool, two whirlpool baths, sauna, steam room, fitness center, wheelchair accommodations, no-smoking rooms, and a coin laundry.

LITTLE AMERICA, I-40 East at Butler Ave., Flagstaff, AZ 86001. Tel.

602/779-2741, or toll free 800/352-4386. Fax 602/774-7553. 248 rms, 9 suites (all with bath). A/C TV TEL
$ Rates: $59–$69 single; $65–$79 double; $69–$85 suite. AE, CB, DC, DISC, MC, V.

At first it might seem as if Little America's, of which there are several around the West, are little more than glorified truck stops, but on closer inspection you'll find that this Little America is an excellent, economical hotel. It's a spread-out complex beneath the pines on the east side of Flagstaff at Exit 198 from I-40. The spacious lobby features a roaring fire most of the year. Rooms vary in size but all have small private balconies. The interior decor is dated but fun, with a French provincial theme throughout the guest rooms. Televisions are absolutely huge.

The restaurant features a lunch buffet and nightly dinner specials. The hotel also offers room service, laundry/dry cleaning, courtesy van, a swimming pool, health club, badminton, volleyball, croquet, jogging/hiking trails, gift shop, and a gas station.

QUALITY SUITES, 706 S. Milton Rd., Flagstaff, AZ 86001. Tel. 602/774-4333, or toll free 800/221-2222. Fax 602/774-0216. 102 suites (all with bath). A/C TV TEL
$ Rates (including full breakfast): $63–$135 single; $79–$135 double. AE, DC, DISC, MC, V.

Conveniently located near Northern Arizona University and downtown Flagstaff, this all-suite hotel is great for families traveling together or business travelers who need some extra space for meeting clients. Modern and attractively furnished, the hotel sports a country-club feel with its stone-walled main building, fireplace with two-story stone chimney, and oak-and-wicker–filled lounge that doubles as a small library. Breakfast is served in the bright, plant-filled Pinyon Pantry. Guest rooms are all divided into sleeping rooms and living rooms, with wet bar, refrigerator, microwave oven, two TVs, two phones, a VCR, and an AM/FM stereo. The hotel also has a swimming pool and whirlpool bath.

Wild Oaks lounge offers a clublike atmosphere for a drink in the evening. There is also a manager's cocktail party in the evening.

BUDGET

EVERGREEN INN, 1008 E. Santa Fe Ave., Flagstaff, AZ 86001. Tel. 602/774-7356. 139 rms (all with bath). A/C TV TEL
$ Rates: $24–$35 single; $37–$55 double; $39–$57 suite. AE, DISC, MC, V.

Located just east of downtown on Flagstaff's old motel row, the Evergreen Inn is a modern, though slightly worn, motel set back from the busy road. The rooms on the upper floor have a bit of view over the forests south of town. The grounds feature a swimming pool, and morning coffee and doughnuts are available in the lobby. There's a good Mexican restaurant right next door.

MONTE VISTA HOTEL, 100 N. San Francisco St., Flagstaff, AZ 86001. Tel. 602/779-6971. 42 rms (39 with bath), 8 suites. TV TEL
$ Rates: $29–$33 single; $35–$55 double; $51–$60 suite. AE, MC, V.

Originally opened in 1927, the Monte Vista Hotel was renovated in the mid-1980s and is today a historic budget hotel with old-fashioned flair. In its heyday the Monte Vista is said to have hosted Clark Gable, John Wayne, Walter Brennan, Alan Ladd, Jane Russell, Spencer Tracy, Lee Marvin, Carole Lombard, and Gary Cooper. Arizona's favorite writer, Zane Grey, was instrumental in having this hotel built. In the small, dark lobby are painted ceiling beams and Victorian furniture. Shops take up most of the space on the ground floor. Rooms vary in size and many are furnished with oak furniture and ceiling fans. You might even find such unusual touches as a rocking chair or oak toilet seat. I like the corner rooms best because they have windows on both sides. You'll find a coffee shop and lounge on the first floor.

SUPER 8 FLAGSTAFF, 3725 Kasper Ave., Flagstaff, AZ 86001. Tel. 602/526-0818, or toll free tel. 800/843-1991. 83 rms, 3 suites (all with bath). A/C TV TEL

$ Rates: $30–$37 single; $33–$45 double. AE, CB, DC, DISC, MC, V.

Located off Exit 201 from I-40, the Super 8 Flagstaff is only a few miles from downtown and is close to several fast-food restaurants. Rooms are clean and modern but with no frills. The hotel offers in-room movies, free local phone calls, a whirlpool spa, sauna, and no-smoking rooms.

A HOSTEL

MOTEL DUBEAU, 19 W. Phoenix Ave., Flagstaff, AZ 86001. Tel. 602/774-6731, or toll free 800/332-1944. 20 rms (all with bath).

$ Rates (including continental breakfast): $25 single or double; $11 per person in dorms.

This old motel right downtown near the train station and the university is now a youth hostel with two to four people sharing the rooms. Popular with students and young people here to see the Grand Canyon, the Motel Dubeau is managed by a friendly young family. They provide free airport, train, and bus station transfers, free bike rentals, free coffee and tea all day, a guest kitchen, and free local phone calls. There's no charge for linens and no curfew. With all these freebies, it's hard to beat this little place.

WHERE TO DINE
EXPENSIVE

COTTAGE PLACE RESTAURANT, 126 W. Cottage Ave. Tel. 774-8431.
   Cuisine: CONTINENTAL. **Reservations:** Required.
$ Prices: Appetizers $4.50–$8.50; main courses $10–$22. AE, MC, V.
   Open: Dinner only, Tues–Sun 5–9:30pm.

There's no question that the best (and priciest) restaurant in Flagstaff is this little cottage. Located in a rather run-down neighborhood between the railroad tracks and the university, Cottage Place is just what its name implies—a little cottage. There are a few tables in each of the dining rooms, so dining here is always an intimate affair. I like the front rooms with their walls of windows, especially at sunset on a summer evening. Though the menu is primarily continental, there are French and southwestern dishes as well, all equally well prepared. The house specialties are chateaubriand and rack of lamb (both served for two), and for vegetarians there's a delicious polenta gratin stuffed with fresh vegetables and chipotle salsa and baked with Cheddar cheese. The southwestern scampi is a spicy rendition of an old standard; the garlic butter has the added bite of jalapeños and the fragrance of cilantro. For starters there are, of course, escargots, but I think the artichoke ratatouille shouldn't be missed. Every evening there's a different selection of tempting desserts.

MODERATE

BLACK BART'S, 2760 E. Butler Ave. Tel. 779-5155.
   Cuisine: STEAK/SEAFOOD. **Reservations:** Suggested.
$ Prices: Appetizers $4; main courses $10–$23. MC, V.
   Open: Dinner only, Sun–Thurs 5–9pm, Fri–Sat 5–10pm.

Arizona is full of odd restaurants and Black Bart's must surely be classified as one of the most unusual. A former RV park and antiques store, this warehouse-size restaurant serves gigantic steaks complete with cowboy beans, "leaves-and-weeds" salads, and sourdough biscuits. But the real draw is the entertainment, provided by a player piano and the waitpersons (local university students), who get up on stage and sing for your supper. Plays are also staged here regularly. A small saloon serves up such libations as snake bite, bronco-buster, and sarsparilla.

KELLY'S CHRISTMAS TREE RESTAURANT, 5200 E. Cortland Blvd. Tel. 779-5888.
   Cuisine: INTERNATIONAL. **Reservations:** Recommended.
$ Prices: Appetizers $4.50–$9; main courses $8–$19. MC, V.
   Open: Lunch daily 11:30am–2pm; dinner daily 5:30–10pm.

This oddly named restaurant has long been a Flagstaff favorite and recently moved to a new location in a shopping center on the east side of town. A festive holiday atmosphere reigns year round in the red, white, and green dining room at Kelly's, while ceiling fans with fluted lights and waiters in black ties give the dining room a casual Victorian feel. The menu runs the gamut from sautéed chicken livers to curried chicken to beef Stroganoff. There are daily seafood specials as well as such menu standards as tender sautéed scallops. The char-broiled prime rib is probably Kelly's most popular dish and is served with apple sauce and horseradish. And what would the holidays be without egg nog or spiced hot cider? For dessert the Mozart parfait is my choice.

SAKURA RESTAURANT, in the Woodlands Plaza Hotel, 1175 W. Hwy. 66. Tel. 773-9118.

Cuisine: JAPANESE. **Reservations:** Recommended.

$ Prices: Appetizers $4–$5; main courses $12–$17. AE, DC, DISC, MC, V.

Open: Lunch Mon–Sat 11:30am–2pm; dinner daily 5–10pm.

Though major cities around the world have had teppanyaki Japanese restaurants in the form of Benihanas for years, this style of tableside cooking is new to Flagstaff, and it has made quite a hit. Sakura is located in the Woodlands Plaza Hotel, which is owned by an Asian-American family. Dinner or lunch here is an event, with the chef's culinary floor show at a grill in front of your table. Steaks, grilled seafood, and chicken are the mainstays of the menu, but there's also sushi made with fresh fish flown in daily, crispy tempura, and warming miso soup for cold winter nights. Shoji screens and potted bamboo give the dining room a Japanese atmosphere.

WOODLANDS CAFE, in the Woodlands Plaza Hotel, 1175 W. Hwy. 66. Tel. 773-9118.

Cuisine: INTERNATIONAL. **Reservations:** Recommended.

$ Prices: Appetizers $4.75–$7; main courses $11–$22. AE, DC, DISC, MC, V.

Open: Daily 6am–midnight.

The Woodlands Plaza Hotel also claims another of Flagstaff's best restaurants: the Woodlands Café, a bright, casual restaurant filled with plants and decorated in a southwestern motif. Though the menu is primarily continental, there are touches of southwestern and Japanese cuisine as well. If you're a daring diner, it's hard to resist the rattlesnake appetizers, but the seafood ceviche, with a touch of tequila in it, is a spicy way to start a meal. Fresh game (such as venison au poivre) is one of the specialties of the Woodlands Café and there are weekly specials as well. The Coconino trout, sautéed with roasted pine nuts, and the Sedona chicken, with roasted peppers and a spicy cream sauce, are two of the menu's southwestern dishes that are well worth trying. Lunches offer a variety of interesting salads and sandwiches, as well as a few dishes that also show up on the dinner menu.

BUDGET

CAFE ESPRESS, 16 N. San Francisco St. Tel. 774-0541.

Cuisine: INTERNATIONAL/VEGETARIAN. **Reservations:** Not necessary.

$ Prices: Sandwiches $3.50–$6; dinners $3.50–$7. MC, V.

Open: Sun–Thurs 7am–10pm, Fri–Sat 7am–11pm.

If you miss your college days of hanging out in the local café eating a tempeh burger and discussing the latest foreign film, you can relive those memories at Café Espress. Grab an alternative newspaper from the table by the front door, sit down at one of the tables in the front window, and ensconce yourself in college life all over again. If you happen to still be in school, this place will certainly be your favorite dining spot in Flagstaff. You can start the day with granola, move on to tempeh or turkey burgers for lunch, and then have spanokopita for dinner.

EL CHARRO CAFE, 409 S. San Francisco St. Tel. 779-0552.

Cuisine: MEXICAN. **Reservations:** Not necessary.

$ Prices: Appetizers $3–$4; main courses $4–$12. MC, V.

Open: Mon–Sat 11am–9pm.

Sunday through Thursday this is a very plain little family Mexican restaurant popular with university students for its low prices and large portions, but on Friday and Saturday the atmosphere is enlivened by mariachis in the evening. Be serenaded while you fill up on all your favorite Mexican dishes. El Charro has been in business since 1950, so you know they're doing something right. It's not a very distinctive building, but you can't miss it—there's a giant boot out front.

SHOPPING

Downtown Flagstaff along Santa Fe Avenue, San Francisco Street, Aspen Avenue, and Birch Avenue is the city's **historic district.** The old brick buildings of this neighborhood are now filled with interesting little shops selling Native American handcrafts, art and crafts by local artists, and various other Arizona souvenirs such as rocks, minerals, and crystals. This historic area is worth a walk through even if you aren't shopping.

EVENING ENTERTAINMENT

Check the local newspaper for events taking place on the campus of Northern Arizona University. The university has many musical and theatrical groups that perform throughout most of the year.

FLAGSTAFF FESTIVAL OF THE ARTS, P.O. Box 1607, Flagstaff, AZ 86002. Tel. 774-7750.
This festival has been enlivening Flagstaff summers for more than a quarter of a century and runs from early July to mid-August. Throughout the city there are music, theater, dance, and film performances, as well as poetry readings and art exhibits.
Admission: Tickets to individual events, $6–$17; dinner theater, $30.

THE MUSEUM CLUB, 3403 E. Santa Fe Ave. Tel. 526-9434.
If you prefer hanging out in saloons to listening to classical music, you should feel right at home in this cavernous log-cabin bar. Built in the early 1900s and often called the Zoo Club, the saloon is filled with deer antlers, stuffed animals, and trophy heads. There's live music, predominantly country-and-western, Tuesday through Thursday with varying admission prices. Willie Nelson, John Lee Hooker, Dr. Hook, Asleep at the Wheel, and Mose Allison are some of the musicians who have appeared here in the past.

EASY EXCURSIONS FROM FLAGSTAFF

METEOR CRATER, I-40, 35 miles east of Flagstaff. Tel. 602/526-5259.
In the middle of the barren desert east of Flagstaff lies a gaping hole in the earth. Standing on a platform on the crater rim it's difficult to imagine the instant devastation that occurred 49,000 years ago when a meteorite estimated to be about 100 feet in diameter slammed into the ground here at 45,000 miles per hour. Today the Meteor Crater is 570 feet deep and nearly a mile across. Billed as "this planet's most penetrating natural attraction," Meteor Crater is the best-preserved crater in the world. The resemblance of the crater landscape to the surface of the moon prompted NASA to use this area as a training site for Apollo program astronauts. There is a small museum, part of which is dedicated to the exploration of space, and an Apollo space capsule on display. The rest of the museum is devoted to astrogeology and includes a meteorite weighing nearly three-quarters of a ton. A short video program and artists' renderings provide an image of how the meteorite's impact must have looked.
Admission: $6 adults, $5 senior citizens, $2 children 13–17, $1 children 6–12, free for children 5 and under.
Open: May 15–Sept 15, daily 6am–6pm; Mar 16–May 14 and Sept 16–Nov 14, daily 7am–5pm; Nov 15–Mar 15, daily 8am–5pm.

WUPATKI NATIONAL MONUMENT, 36 miles north of Flagstaff off U.S. 89. Tel. 602/527-7040.
The landscape northeast of Flagstaff is desolate and windswept, a sparsely populated region carpeted with volcanic ash deposited in the 11th century. It comes as quite a surprise, then, to learn that this area contains hundreds of prehistoric and

historic habitation sites. The most impressive ruins are those left by the Sinagua (the name means "without water" in Spanish) people who inhabited this area from around A.D. 1100 until shortly after A.D. 1200. The land at this time was quite fertile because of the enriching qualities of the volcanic ash that had been deposited in the previous century. Rains were more plentiful than they are today, and the land was able to support a fairly large population of farmers. The Sinagua people built small villages of stone similar to the pueblos on the nearby Hopi reservation and today the ruins of these ancient villages can still be seen.

The largest of the prehistoric pueblos is **Wupatki ruin** in the southeastern part of the monument. Here the Sinagua built a sprawling three-story pueblo containing nearly 100 rooms. It is believed that Wupatki was on the main trade route to Mexico, and the influence of the more developed cultures farther south is evident in the presence of a ball court. Though this ball court is quite different from the courts of the Aztecs and Mayas, there is no doubt that a similar game was played. Another circular stone structure just below the main ruins is believed to have been an amphitheater or dance plaza.

Wupatki ruin is also the site of the **visitor center.** Inside you'll find interesting exhibits on the Sinagua and Anasazi people who once inhabited the region.

The most unusual feature of Wupatki, however, is a natural phenomenon—a **blowhole**—that may have been the reason for building the pueblo on this site. Unlike blowholes that are found along rocky ocean shores, this blowhole blows (and sucks) only air. A network of small underground tunnels and chambers acts as a giant barometer, blowing air when the underground air is under greater pressure than the outside air. On hot days, cool air rushes out of the blowhole with amazing force.

Several other ruins within the national monument are easily accessible by car. These include **Nalakihu, Citadel,** and **Lomaki,** which are the closest to U.S. 89, and **Wukoki,** which is near Wupatki. Wukoki ruin is built atop a huge sandstone boulder and is particularly picturesque.

Admission: $3 per car.

Open: Daily sunrise–sunset; visitor center, daily 8am–6pm.

SUNSET CRATER NATIONAL MONUMENT, 15 miles north of Flagstaff off U.S. 89. Tel. 602/527-7042 or 527-7134.

Dotting the landscape northeast of Flagstaff are more than 400 volcanic craters, of which Sunset Crater is the youngest. Taking its name from the sunset colors of the cinders near its summit, Sunset Crater stands 1,000 feet tall and began forming in A.D. 1064. Over a period of 100 years the volcano erupted repeatedly, creating the red-and-yellow cinder cone we see today and eventually covering an area of 800 square miles with ash, lava, and cinders. Though it's no longer possible to hike to the summit of Sunset Crater, there is a mile-long interpretative trail that passes through a desolate landscape of lava flows, cinders, and ash as it skirts the base. In the visitor center you can learn more about the formation of Sunset Crater and about volcanoes in general.

Near the visitor center at the west entrance to the national monument is a small campground that's open from May to September.

Admission: $3 per car (includes admission to Wupatki National Monument).

Open: Daily sunrise–sunset; visitor center, daily 8am–5pm.

WALNUT CANYON NATIONAL MONUMENT, Walnut Canyon Rd. Tel. 602/526-3367.

The remains of hundreds of 13th-century Sinagua cliff dwellings can be seen in a dry, wooded canyon 7 miles east of Flagstaff. The undercut layers of limestone in this 400-foot-deep canyon proved ideal for building dwellings well protected both from the elements and from enemies. The Sinaguas were the same people who built and then abandoned the stone pueblos found in Wupatki National Monument. It is theorized that when the land to the north lost its fertility, the Sinaguas began migrating southward, settling for 150 years in Walnut Canyon.

A self-guided trail leads from the visitor center on the canyon rim down 185 feet to a section of the canyon wall where 25 cliff dwellings can be viewed and entered. Look

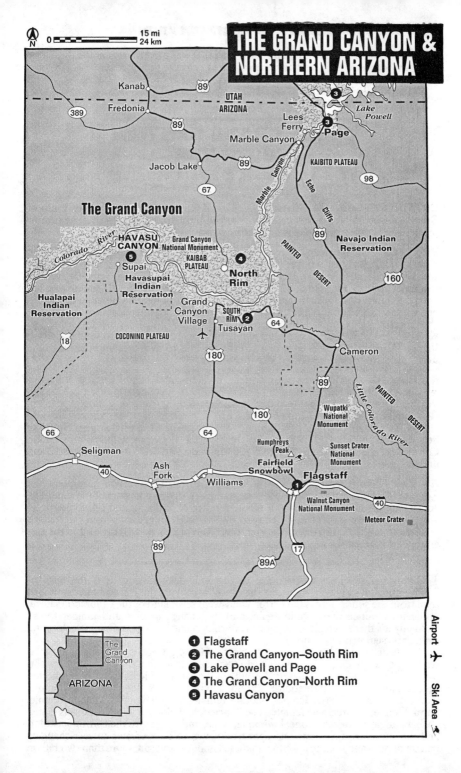

closely and you can see hand prints in the mud that was used to cement the dwellings' stone walls together. There's also a picnic area near the visitor center.

Admission: $3 per car
Open: Daily 8am–5pm. **Closed:** Thanksgiving and Christmas.

2. THE GRAND CANYON: SOUTH RIM

60 miles N of Williams, 80 miles NE of Flagstaff, 230 miles N of Phoenix, 340 miles N of Tucson

GETTING THERE   By Plane   The Grand Canyon Airport is 6 miles south of Grand Canyon Village in Tusayan, but is served by charter airlines only. The nearest regularly scheduled service is in Flagstaff.

By Train   The **Grand Canyon Railway,** Grand Canyon Railway Depot, Grand Canyon Boulevard (tel. toll free 800/843-8724), operates a vintage steam locomotive and 1920s coaches between Williams and Grand Canyon Village. Same-day round-trip fares are $49 for adults, $25 for children age 12 and under (Monday through Friday children ride for half the normal children's fare). It's also possible to ride up one day and return on a different day if you make arrangements ahead of time.

Amtrak (tel. 602/774-8679, or toll free 800/872-7245) provides service to Flagstaff. From Flagstaff it is then possible to take a bus directly to Grand Canyon Village. Another option is to take a Greyhound bus to Williams and then take the steam train from there to Grand Canyon Village.

By Bus   Bus service between Flagstaff, Williams, and Grand Canyon Village is provided by **Nava-Hopi Tours** (tel. 602/774-5003). A round-trip ticket is $25, and the bus leaves the Greyhound station at 8:35am and the Amtrak station at 8:45am. **Greyhound/Trailways Lines** has service to Flagstaff from around the country and also offers service between Flagstaff and Williams. The **Grand Canyon Railway** (tel. toll free 800/843-8724) operates bus service between Williams and Grand Canyon Village. The round-trip fare is $20 for adults and $10 for children age 12 and under.

By Car   Before setting out for the Grand Canyon, be sure you have plenty of gasoline in your car; there are few service stations in this remote part of the state. The South Rim of the Grand Canyon is 60 miles north of Williams and I-40 on Ariz. 64 and U.S. 180. Flagstaff, the nearest city of any size, is 78 miles away. From Flagstaff it's possible to take U.S. 180 directly to the South Rim or U.S. 89 to Ariz. 64 and the east entrance to the park.

A strange hush clings to the edge of this mile-deep canyon. It is the hush of reverential awe. For the first-time visitor to the canyon, there is no better approach than from the south, across the barren windswept scrubland of the Colorado Plateau. You hardly notice the elevation gain, and the change to pine and juniper forest. Suddenly it's there. No preliminaries, no warnings. Stark, quiet, a maze of colors and cathedrals sculpted by nature.

A mile deep and 18 miles wide in places, the Grand Canyon is truly one of the great wonders of the world, and it comes as no surprise to learn that the cartographers who mapped the area sensed the spiritual beauty of the canyon. Their reverence is reflected in the names of its formations: Apollo Temple, Venus Temple, Thor Temple, Zoroaster Temple, Horus Temple, Buddha Temple, Vishnu Temple, Krishna Temple, Shiva Temple, Confucious Temple, The Tabernacle, Solomon Temple, Angels Gate.

Banded layers of sandstone, limestone, shale, and schist give the canyon its color, and the interplay of shadows and light from dawn to dusk creates an ever-changing palette of hues and textures. Written in these bands of stone are more than two billion years of history. Formed by the cutting action of the Colorado River as it flows through the Kaibab Plateau, the Grand Canyon is an open book exposing the secrets of the geologic history of this region. Geologists believe that it has taken between three and six million years for the Colorado River to carve the Grand Canyon, but the canyon's history extends much further back in time. In the distant past of millions of years ago, vast seas covered this region. Sediments carried by sea water were deposited and over millions of years turned into sedimentary limestone and sandstone. When the ancient seabed was thrust upward to form the Kaibab Plateau, the Colorado River began its work of cutting through the plateau. Today 21 sedimentary layers, the oldest of which is more than a billion years old, can be seen in the canyon. However, beneath all these layers, at the very bottom, is a stratum of rock so old that it has been metamorphosed, under great pressure and heat, from soft shale to a much harder stone called schist. Called Vishnu schist, this layer is the oldest rock in the Grand Canyon.

In the more recent past the Grand Canyon has been home to several Native American cultures including the Anasazi, who are best known for their cliff dwellings in the Four Corners region. About 150 years after the Anasazi and Coconino peoples abandoned the canyon in the 13th century, another tribe, the Cerbat, moved into the area. The Hualapai and Havasupai tribes, descendents of the Cerbat people, still live in and near the Grand Canyon on the south side of the Colorado River. On the North Rim lived the Southern Paiutes, and in the west the Navajos.

In 1540 Spanish explorer García Lopez de Cardenas became the first European to set eyes on the Grand Canyon. However, it would be another 329 years before the first expedition would travel through the entire canyon. John Wesley Powell, a one-armed Civil War veteran, was deemed crazy when he set off to navigate the Colorado River in wooden boats. His small band of men spent 98 days traveling 1,000 miles down the Green and Colorado rivers. Their expedition was not without mishap. When some boats were wrecked by the powerful rapids, part of the group abandoned the journey and set out on foot, never to be heard from again.

Today the Grand Canyon is the last major undammed section of the Colorado River, and the river, which once carried more than half a million tons of sand and silt with it every 24 hours, now flows cold and clear from the bottom of the upriver Glen Canyon Dam. By raft, by mule, on foot, in helicopters and small planes, four million people come to the canyon each year seeking one of nature's meccas.

ORIENTATION

ARRIVING   The Grand Canyon Airport is in the village of Tusayan, 6 miles south of Grand Canyon Village and the South Rim. The **Tusayan–Grand Canyon Shuttle bus** operates between Tusayan and Grand Canyon Village hourly from 7am to 7pm and costs $4 one way. It's also possible to take a **taxi** (tel. 638-2822 or 638-2631) from the airport. The fare is $5 per person and does not include the entrance fee.

The **Grand Canyon Railway** operates vintage steam engines and restored 1920s coaches between Williams and Grand Canyon Village. The train arrives at the Grand Canyon Depot, across the street from the El Tovar Hotel and rim of the canyon.

Nava-Hopi Tours (tel. 602/774-5003) operates buses between Flagstaff, Williams, and Grand Canyon Village with a stop at Tusayan (south entrance).

If you're driving to the South Rim of the Grand Canyon, the most direct route is by

---

IMPRESSIONS

We are imprisoned three quarters of a mile in the depths of the earth and the great unknown river shrinks into insignificance as it dashes its angry waves against the walls and cliffs that rise to the world above.
—MAJ. JOHN WESLEY POWELL, ON HIS SUCCESSFUL TRIP THROUGH THE GRAND CANYON

way of I-40 to Ariz. 64 to U.S. 180. A more scenic route is to take U.S. 180 all the way from Flagstaff. If you're coming from the North Rim or the Native American reservations in the northeastern part of the state, take U.S. 89 to Ariz. 64. These routes all lead to Grand Canyon Village from the east. The rim of the canyon will be on your right and there are a couple of view points before you reach the visitor center. If you continue past the visitor center another mile, you'll reach the center of the village, where you'll find five of the South Rim's lodges.

INFORMATION   You can get information on the Grand Canyon before leaving home by contacting the **Grand Canyon National Park,** P.O. Box 129, Grand Canyon, AZ 86023 (tel. 602/638-7888). Once there, you should stop by the Grand Canyon National Park **Visitor Center,** located on Village Loop Drive 6 miles north of the south entrance. Here you'll find an information desk, brochures, exhibits about the canyon, and a bookshop selling maps as well as books about the canyon. The visitor center is open daily from 8am to 7pm. *The Guide,* a small newspaper crammed full of useful information about Grand Canyon National Park, is available at all of the park entrances.

VILLAGE LAYOUT   Grand Canyon Village is built on the South Rim of the canyon and is roughly divided into two sections. At the east end of the village is the visitor center, Yavapai Lodge, Trailer Village, and Mather Campground. At the west end are El Tovar Hotel and Bright Angel, Kachina, Thunderbird, and Maswik lodges, as well as several restaurants and the trailhead for the Bright Angel Trail. Just before the El Tovar Hotel the road becomes one way.

GETTING AROUND

BY BUS   The **Tusayan–Grand Canyon Shuttle** (tel. 602/638-2475) operates between the Grand Canyon Airport in Tusayan at the park's south entrance and Grand Canyon Village with stops at the Canyon Squire Inn, the heliport, the Quality Inn, the IMAX theater, the Village Store, and Moqui Lodge in Tusayan, and at Yavapai Lodge, Bright Angel Lodge, and Maswik Lodge in Grand Canyon Village. The one-way fare is $4.50 and buses leave hourly between 7am and 7pm.

   Trans Canyon (tel. 602/638-2820) offers shuttle-bus service between the South Rim and the North Rim. The vans leave the South Rim at 1:30pm and arrive at the North Rim at 6pm. The return trip leaves the North Rim at 7am, arriving back at the South Rim at 11:30am. The fare is $50 per person one way, $85 per person round-trip.

   During the summer months a **free shuttle** operates between the park's visitor center and village lodges. Also in summer, when the West Rim Drive is closed to private vehicles, another free shuttle covers this route.

BY CAR   Two rental agencies, **Budget** (tel. 602/638-9360) and **Dollar** (tel. 602/638-2625) maintain desks at the Grand Canyon Airport in Tusayan at the south entrance to the park.

   There are **service stations** at Grand Canyon Village, in Tusayan, and at Desert View near the east entrance (this station is seasonal). Because of the long distances within the park and to towns outside the park, be sure that you have plenty of gas before setting out on a drive.

BY TAXI   There is taxi service available to and from the airport, trailheads, and other destinations. Phone 638-2822 or 638-2631.

FAST FACTS: THE GRAND CANYON

   Admission   The Grand Canyon is a national park. Admission to the park is $10 per car or $3 per person if you happen to be coming in on a bus, by taxi, or on foot.

   Area Code   The telephone area code for the Grand Canyon region is 602.

   Climate   The climate at the Grand Canyon is quite different from that of

Phoenix, and between the rim and the canyon floor there is also a considerable difference. Because the South Rim is at 7,000 feet, it gets quite cold in the winter. You can expect snow anytime between November and May and winter temperatures can be below 0° Fahrenheit at night, with daytime highs in the 20°s or 30°s. Summer temperatures at the rim range from highs in the 80°s to lows in the 50°s. The North Rim of the canyon is slightly higher and stays a bit cooler throughout the year, but is only open to visitors from May through October. On the canyon floor temperatures are considerably higher. In summer the mercury can top 100°F with lows in the 70°s, while in the winter temperatures are quite pleasant with highs in the 50°s and lows in the 30°s. July, August, and September are the wettest months because of frequent afternoon thunderstorms. April, May, and June are the driest months, though it might still rain or even snow. Down on the canyon floor there is much less rain year round.

Drugstores   There's a drugstore (tel. 638-2460) in Grand Canyon Village down Center Road, which runs past the National Park Service rangers office. The drugstore is open Monday through Friday from 8:30am to 5:30pm.

Emergencies   Dial 911; from hotel or motel rooms, dial 9-911.

Hospitals/Clinics   The **Grand Canyon Medical Clinic** (tel. 638-2551 or 638-2469) is located down Center Road, which runs past the National Park Service rangers office. The clinic is open Monday through Friday from 8am to 5:30pm and on Saturday from 9am to noon. They also provide 24-hour emergency service.

Laundry   A coin-operated laundry is located near Mather Campground in the Camper Services building.

Lost & Found   Report lost items or turn in found items at the visitor center or Yavapai Museum. Call 638-7798 Monday through Friday between 8am and noon or 1 and 4pm.

Newspapers/Magazines   Current newspapers and magazines are available at souvenir stores and lodges in the village.

Photographic Needs   Film and film processing are available at all village curio shops.

Police   In an emergency, dial 911. Ticketing speeders is one of the main occupations of the park's police force, so obey the posted speed limits.

Post Office   The post office is located in Mather Center near the visitor center. It's open Monday through Friday from 9am to 4:30pm and on Saturday from 11am to 1pm.

Religious Services   There are several churches at Grand Canyon Village including the Shrine of the Ages near the visitor center and the Community Building near Maswik Lodge. The following denominations offer services: **Church of Jesus Christ of Latter-Day Saints,** Shrine of the Ages (tel. 638-2792); **Roman Catholic,** Shrine of the Ages or El Cristo Rey Chapel (tel. 638-2390); **Assembly of God,** Community Building (tel. 638-9415); **Baptist,** Shrine of the Ages (tel. 638-9421); and **interdenominational,** Shrine of the Ages (tel. 638-2340).

Safety   The most important safety tip to remember is to be careful near the edge of the canyon. Footing can be unstable and may give way. Also be sure to keep your distance from wild animals, no matter how friendly they may appear (even chipmunks bite). Don't hike alone, and keep in mind that the canyon rim is more than a mile above sea level (it's harder to breathe up here). Don't leave valuables in your car or tent.

Useful Telephone Numbers   Alcoholics Anonymous (tel. 638-2769).

WHAT TO SEE & DO

MUSEUMS, HISTORIC BUILDINGS & AUDIOVISUAL PROGRAMS

GRAND CANYON IMAX THEATRE, Tusayan. Tel. 638-2203.

⭐ Located in the village of Tusayan at the south entrance to the park, the Grand Canyon IMAX Theatre devotes its seven-story screen to a 34-minute film about the canyon. A reenactment of John Wesley Powell's first navigation of the Colorado River is the central focus of the film, but geology, ancient history, and cultural and natural history are also included. However, the star of the show is, of course, the heart-stopping IMAX cinematography. The huge screen that fills your field of vision and the amazing high definition of the film together create an astoundingly realistic image of the canyon.

Admission: $6.50 adults, $4 children under 12.

Open: Mar–Oct, daily 8:30am–8:30pm; Nov–Feb, 10:30am–6:30pm.

KOLB AND LOOKOUT STUDIOS, on the Rim, Grand Canyon Village. Tel. 638-2631, ext. 6587.

These two buildings cling precariously to the rim of the canyon just west of the Bright Angel Lodge. Though they have very different early histories, both have been listed on the National Register of Historic Places. Kolb Studio is named for Ellsworth and Emory Kolb, two brothers who set up a photographic studio on the rim of the Grand Canyon in 1904. The building became the center of a controversy over whether buildings should be allowed on the canyon rim. Because the Kolbs had friends in high places, their sprawling studio and movie theater remained. Emory Kolb lived here until his death in 1976, by which time the building had been listed as a historic building and could not legally be torn down. Today it serves as a bookstore. Lookout Studio, built in 1914 from a design by Mary Jane Colter, was the Fred Harvey Company's answer to the Kolb brothers' studio. Photographs and books about the canyon were sold at the studio, which incorporates architectural styles of the Hopis and the Anasazis. The use of native limestone and an uneven roofline allows the studio to blend in with the canyon walls and gives it the look of an old ruin. Today the studio houses a souvenir store and two lookout points.

Admission: Free.

Open: Kolb Studio, daily 9am–6pm. Lookout Studio, Mar–Nov, daily 8am–7pm; Nov–Mar, daily 8am–5pm.

OVER THE EDGE THEATRES, Community Building, Village Loop Dr., Grand Canyon Village. Tel. 638-2224.

Not quite as stunning as the IMAX film, this program is, nevertheless, informative and visually exciting. Using slides instead of motion pictures, the audiovisual program introduces the visitor to the geology and history of the canyon. The narration is given from the point of view of Capt. John Hance, one of the canyon's first guides.

Admission: $4 adults, $2 children 8–12, free for children under 8.

Open: Mar–Nov, daily 9am–9pm; Nov–Mar, daily 10am–3pm and 5–8pm.

TUSAYAN MUSEUM, East Rim Dr. Tel. 638-2305.

Located 23 miles east of Grand Canyon Village and 3 miles west of Desert View, the Tusayan Museum is dedicated to the Hopi tribe and ancient Anasazi people who inhabited this region 800 years ago. Inside the small museum are artfully displayed exhibits on various aspects of Anasazi life. Outside is a short self-guided trail through actual Anasazi ruins.

Admission: Free.

Open: Mar–Nov, daily 8am–7pm; Nov–Mar, daily 9am–5pm.

VISITOR CENTER, Village Loop Dr. Tel. 638-7888.

The visitor center, in addition to providing answers to all your questions about the Grand Canyon, also contains exhibits on its natural history, history, and exploration. Throughout the day slide and video programs are shown. There is also an excellent little bookstore here where you can find books on all aspects of the canyon. In the center's courtyard are several boats that have navigated the canyon over the years.

Admission: Free.

Open: Mar–Nov, daily 8am–7pm; Nov–Mar, daily 8am–5pm.

THE WATCHTOWER, Desert View, East Rim Dr. Tel. 638-2736.

Though the watchtower looks as though it were built centuries ago, it's actually only 60 years old. Architect Mary Jane Colter, who is responsible for much of the park's historic architecture, designed the tower to resemble the prehistoric towers that dot the southwestern landscape. Built as an observation tower and rest stop for tourists, the watchtower incorporates Native American designs and art. The curio shop on the ground floor is a replica of a kiva (sacred ceremonial chamber). The tower's second floor features artwork by Hopi artist Fred Kabotie, among which is a sand painting on a snake altar. Covering the walls are pictographs incorporating traditional designs. On the walls and ceiling of the upper two floors are more traditional images, this time reproductions of petroglyphs from throughout the Southwest by Fred Geary. The giftshop offers a pamphlet describing the watchtower in detail.

Admission: Free.

Open: Mar–Nov, daily 8am–8pm; Nov–Mar, daily 9am–5pm.

YAVAPAI MUSEUM, Village Loop Dr. Tel. 638-7890.

Located less than a mile east of the visitor center, the Yavapai Museum features exhibits on the geologic history of the Grand Canyon. There is also a panorama of the canyon through the museum's large windows.

Admission: Free.

Open: Mar–Nov, daily 8am–7pm; Nov–Mar, daily 9am–5pm.

VIEWPOINTS

Sunrise and sunset are the most spectacular times of day in the Grand Canyon. Because so many people want to enjoy the dawn and dusk light shows created by the interplay of shadows and light within the maze of the canyon, the National Park Service includes a table with sunrise and sunset times in *The Guide,* the park's official visitor newspaper.

Tips for Photographing the Canyon   By the time most people leave the Grand Canyon they have shot several roles of film. This is not at all surprising considering the stunning beauty of this rugged landscape. However, it's not always easy to capture the canyon's spirit on film. Here are some tips to help you bring back the best possible photos from your trip.

A polarizing filter is a great investment if you have the kind of camera that will accept lens filters. A polarizing filter will reduce haze, lessen the contrast between shadowy areas and light areas, and deepen the color of the sky.

The best time to photograph the canyon is at sunrise and sunset, when filtered and sharply angled sunlight paints the canyon walls in beautiful shades of lavender and pink. At these times the shadows are also at their most dramatic. To capture these ephemeral moments it's best to use a tripod and a long exposure. The worst time to photograph the canyon is at noon when there are almost no shadows, and thus little texture or contrast.

Something else to keep in mind is that the Grand Canyon is immense. A wide-angle lens may leave the canyon looking like a distant plane of dirt on paper. Try zooming in on narrower sections of the canyon to emphasize a single dramatic landscape element. If you are shooting with a wide-angle lens, try to include something in the foreground (people or a tree branch) to give the photo perspective and scale.

When shooting portraits against a sunrise or sunset, use a flash to illuminate your subjects; otherwise your camera meter may expose for the bright light in the background and leave your subjects in shadow.

THE WEST RIM DRIVE   The West Rim Drive is an 8-mile-long road leading west from Grand Canyon Village to Hermits Rest. Along the length of the road are several scenic overlooks that provide changing views of the canyon. From some of these overlooks it's even possible to see the Colorado River far below. The West Rim Drive is closed to private automobiles during the summer, but a free shuttle operates frequently and stops at all the scenic overlooks. The rest of the year it's possible to drive this scenic road in your own car, stopping whenever and wherever you wish.

The first stops are **Trailview Overlook** and **Paiute Point.** From either of these points you have a view of Grand Canyon Village to the east with the Bright Angel Trail winding down into the canyon from the village. The trail leads 3,000 feet below the rim to the Tonto Plateau, site of Indian Gardens, a grove of cottonwood trees. This is a popular resting spot with both hikers and mule riders. The trail leading north from Indian Gardens goes to Plateau Point, the destination of the 1-day mule rides.

The next stop on the West Rim Drive is **Maricopa Point.** Here you can see the remains of the Orphan Mine, which began operation in 1893. The copper from this mine was raised to the rim of the canyon by a cable system. The mine went out of business because transporting the copper to a city where it could be sold was too expensive. Uranium was discovered here in 1954, but in 1966 the mine was shut down and the land became part of Grand Canyon National Park. If you look carefully at the bottom of the canyon you can see some of the black Vishnu schist, which is among the oldest exposed rock on earth.

The **Powell Memorial,** which is the next stop, is dedicated to John Wesley Powell, who, in 1869 with a party of nine men, became the first person to navigate the Colorado River through the Grand Canyon.

Next along the drive is **Hopi Point,** from which you can see a long section of the Colorado River. Because of the great distance, the river seems to be a tiny, quiet stream, but in actuality the section you see is more than 100 yards wide and races through Granite Rapids.

Mojave Point is the next stop. From here you can see (and sometimes hear) Hermit Rapids, another section of white water. As are almost all rapids in the canyon, these are formed at the mouth of a side canyon where boulders loosened by storms and carried by flooded streams are deposited in the Colorado River.

The next pull-off is at the **Abyss,** the appropriately named 3,000-foot drop-off created by the Great Mojave Wall. This vertiginous view is one of the most awe-inspiring in the park. The walls of the abyss are red sandstone that is more resistant to erosion than the softer shale in the layer below. Other layers of erosion-resistant sandstone have formed the free-standing pillars that are visible from here, the largest of which is called the Monument.

From **Pima Point** it's possible to see the remains of Hermit Camp on the Tonto Plateau. Built by the Santa Fe Railroad, Hermit Camp was a popular tourist destination between 1911 and 1930 and provided cabins and tents. Today only foundations remain.

At the end of the West Rim Drive is **Hermits Rest,** named for Louis Boucher, a prospector who came to the canyon in the 1890s and was known as the Hermit. The log-and-stone Hermits Rest building, designed by Mary Jane Colter and built in 1914, is on the National Register of Historic Places.

THE EAST RIM DRIVE The East Rim Drive extends for 25 miles from Grand Canyon Village to Desert View. Along this scenic drive there are several overlooks with views of the canyon, Colorado River, the Painted Desert, and the San Francisco Peaks to the south. There are also native American ruins, a museum, and the Desert View Watchtower.

The first stop is **Yaki Point,** which is the trailhead for the Kaibab Trail leading to Phantom Ranch. The spectacular view from here encompasses a wide section of the central canyon. The large flat-topped butte to the northeast is Wotan's Throne, one of the canyon's easily recognizable features.

The next stop, **Grandview Point,** affords a view of Horseshoe Mesa, another interesting feature of the canyon landscape. The mesa was the site of the Last Chance Copper Mine in the early 1890s. Later that same decade, the Grandview Hotel was built and served canyon visitors until its close in 1908.

Next along the drive is **Moran Point,** from which can be seen a bright-red layer of shale in the canyon walls. This point is named for a 19th-century landscape painter named Thomas Moran.

The **Tusayan Museum** is the next stop along the East Rim Drive. Inside this small museum are exhibits on the ancient Anasazi people who once inhabited this region. Outside the museum are the ruins of an Anasazi village.

At **Lipan Point** you can see the Grand Canyon supergroup: several strata of rock that are tilted at an angle to the other layers of rock in the canyon. Their angle indicates that there was a period of geological mountain building prior to the layers of sandstone, limestone, and shale. The red, white, and black rocks of the supergroup are composed of sedimentary rock and layers of lava. From **Navajo Point,** the Colorado River and Escalante Butte are both visible.

IMPRESSIONS

Ours has been the first and will doubtless be the last party of whites to visit this profitless locality.
—LT. JOSEPH C. IVES, EXPLORING THE COLORADO RIVER BY STEAMBOAT 1857–58

Desert View, with its trading post, cafeteria, service station, and watchtower, is the end of this scenic drive. However, the road continues east from here. Though the views are breathtaking from anywhere at Desert View, the best lookout is from atop the watchtower. This unusual building was designed by Mary Jane Colter and opened in 1932. From the roof, which is the highest point on the South Rim (7,522 feet above sea level) it's possible to see the Painted Desert to the northeast, the San Francisco Peaks to the south, the Colorado River, and Marble Canyon to the north. Coin-operated binoculars provide close-up views of some of the noteworthy landmarks of this end of the canyon. On the roof are several black-mirror "reflectoscopes" that provide interesting darkened views of some of the most spectacular sections of the canyon.

INTERPRETIVE PROGRAMS

Numerous interpretive programs are held throughout the year at various locations around Grand Canyon Village, at the West Rim Information Booth, and at Desert View. There are ranger-led walks that explore various aspects of the canyon, geology talks, lectures on the cultural and natural resources of the canyon, nature hikes, trips to fossil beds, and star-gazing gatherings. At Tusayan Ruin there are guided tours. Evening programs are held at Mather Amphitheater in the summer and at the Shrine of the Ages the rest of the year. Consult your copy of *The Guide* for information on times and meeting points.

ORGANIZED TOURS

AIR TOURS   Because the Grand Canyon is so immense and remote, the only way to see it all is from an airplane or helicopter. Several companies operating out of the Grand Canyon Airport offer air tours of the canyon. Tours vary from 30 minutes to 2 hours and all are quite expensive.

Companies offering air tours by small plane include the following: **Air Grand Canyon** (tel. 638-2686), $50 to $115 for adults, $35 to $70 for children; **Grand Canyon Airlines** (tel. 638-2407), $50 for adults, $25 for children; and **Windrock Aviation** (tel. 638-9591), $45 to $150 for adults, $30 to $100 for children.

Helicopter tours are available from **Airstar Helicopters** (tel. 638-2622), $75 to $150 per person; **Kenai Helicopters** (tel. 638-2412), $75 to $150 per person; and **Papillon Grand Canyon Helicopters** (tel. 638-2419), $75 to $160 for adults, $60 to $128 for children.

BUS TOURS   If you'd rather leave the driving to someone else and enjoy more of the scenery, you can opt for a bus or van tour of one or more sections of the park. The **Fred Harvey Transportation Co.** (tel. 602/638-2631, ext. 6576) offers several trips ranging in length from 2 to 8 hours. Inside the park, tours visit the East Rim and West Rim, while beyond the park boundaries they visit Monument Valley, Wupatki National Monument, Sunset Crater, and Walnut Canyon National Monument. Tours can be booked by calling the above phone number or by stopping at one of the transportation desks, which are located at Bright Angel, Maswik, and Yavapai lodges. Prices range from $11 to $65 for adults and $5.50 to $32.50 for children.

MULE RIDES

After having a look at the steep drop-offs and narrow path of the Bright Angel Trail, you might decide that this isn't exactly the place to trust your life to a mule. However, the trail guides will be quick to reassure you that they haven't lost a rider yet. Mule rides into the canyon are some of the most popular activities at Grand Canyon Village and have been since the turn of the century when the Bright Angel Trail was a toll road. Trips of various lengths and to different destinations are offered. The 1-day trip descends to Plateau Point, where there's a view of the Colorado River 1,320 feet below. This is a grueling trip requiring riders to spend 6 hours in the saddle. Those who want to spend a night down in the canyon can choose an overnight trip to Phantom Ranch, where there are cabins and dormitories available at the only lodge actually in the canyon. From mid-November to mid-March there's also a 3-day/2-night trip to Phantom Ranch.

There are also 2-hour trail rides along the West Rim from Rowe Well Hitching Post. These rides start at 9am and 1pm, and do not descend into the canyon.

There are a couple of rider qualifications that you should keep in mind before making a reservation. You must weigh less than 200 pounds fully dressed and stand no less than 4 feet, 7 inches tall. Pregnant women are not allowed on mule trips.

Because these trail rides are very popular (especially in summer), make a reservation as soon as you know when you'll be visiting. For more information or to make a reservation, contact the **Grand Canyon National Park Lodges,** Reservations Department, P.O. Box 699, Grand Canyon, AZ 86023 (tel. 602/638-2401). If you arrive without a reservation and decide that you'd like to go on a mule ride, stop by the Bright Angel Transportation Desk to get your name on the day's waiting list.

HORSEBACK RIDING

Horseback riding is available from **Moqui Lodge,** P.O. Box 369, Grand Canyon, AZ 86023 (tel. 602/638-2891 or 638-2424), at the south entrance to the park. There are rides of various lengths; prices range from $16 for a 1-hour ride to $45 for a 4-hour ride.

RAFTING

Rafting down the Colorado River as it roars and tumbles through the mile-deep gorge of the Grand Canyon is an adventure of a lifetime. Ever since John Wesley Powell ignored everyone who knew better and proved that it was possible to travel by boat down the tumultuous Colorado River, running the big river has become a passion and an obsession with adventurers. Today anyone, from grade schoolers to grandmothers, can join the elite group who can claim to have made the run. However, be prepared for some of the most furious white water in the world.

There are 20 companies offering trips through the canyon and there are nearly as many ways to make the trip as there are companies with boats. You can spend as few as 3 days on the river or as many as 16. Many companies also offer half trips. You can go down the river in a huge motorized rubber raft that carries as many as 15 people. Paddled and oar-powered rafts are smaller and more thrilling. For those who seek the utmost in white-water thrills, there are kayak trips and trips by wooden dory rowboat, which is the traditional way to run the Grand Canyon.

Most trips start from Lees Ferry on the Arizona side of the Colorado near Page and Lake Powell. It's also possible to start or finish a trip at Phantom Ranch, hiking in or out from either the North or South Rim. The main rafting season is from April to October, but some companies operate year round. These trips are not cheap; a 6-day trip costs more than $1,000 and a 3-day trip costs about $500. Rates usually include round-trip airfare between Las Vegas and the starting point of the trip, a helicopter trip into or out of the canyon, all meals, and camping equipment.

The following are just a few of the 20 companies currently authorized to operate trips through the Grand Canyon:

ARA-Wilderness River Adventures, P.O. Box 717, Page, AZ 86040 (tel. toll free 800/992-8022, 800/654-7238 in Arizona).

Arizona Raft Adventures, 4050-X East Huntington Drive, Flagstaff, AZ 86004 (tel. toll free 800/786-RAFT).

Arizona River Runners, P.O. Box 47788, Phoenix, AZ 85068-7788 (tel. 602/867-4866, or toll free 800/477-7238).

Colorado River & Trail Expeditions, P.O. Box 57575, Salt Lake City, UT 84157-0575 (tel. 801/261-1789, or toll free 800/253-7328).

Grand Canyon Expeditions, P.O. Box O, Kanab, UT 84741 (tel. 801/644-2691, or toll free 800/544-2691).

Hatch River Expeditions, P.O. Box 1200, Vernal, UT 84078 (tel. 801/789-3813, or toll free 800/433-8966).

Moki Mac River Expeditions, P.O. Box 21242, Salt Lake City, UT 84121 (tel. 801/943-6707, or toll free 800/284-7280).

Outdoors Unlimited, P.O. Box 854-G, Lotus, CA 95651 (tel. 916/626-7668, or toll free 800/637-7238).

Sobek's White Water River Expeditions, P.O. Box 1359, Angels Camp, CA 95222 (tel. 209/736-0427, or toll free 800/888-0229).

Tour West, P.O. Box 333, Orem, UT 84059 (tel. 801/225-0755, or toll free 800/453-9107).

Western River Expeditions, 7258 Racquet Club Drive, Salt Lake City, UT 84121 (tel. 801/942-6669, or toll free 800/453-7450).

TWO WHITE-WATER ALTERNATIVES For those not addicted to adrenalin, there are two Colorado River rafting alternatives. **Wilderness River Adventures,** P.O. Box 717, Page, AZ 86040 (tel. 602/645-3297, or toll free 800/992-8022), operates half-day smooth-water raft trips between Glen Canyon Dam and Lees Ferry. They offer two trips daily (at 7am and 1pm) for $34.75 for adults and $26 for children. It's also possible to arrange this trip through the **Fred Harvey Transportation Company,** P.O. Box 709, Grand Canyon, AZ 86023 (tel. 602/638-2401), which will transport you between Grand Canyon Village and Page. This trip costs $70 for adults and $35 for children.

West of Grand Canyon Village, on the Hualapai Indian Reservation, **Hualapai River Runners,** P.O. Box 246, Peach Springs, AZ 86434 (tel. 602/769-2210 or 769-2219, or toll free 800/622-4409 outside Arizona), operates 1- and 2-day river trips that include a day of white water and a day of smooth water. These trips include accommodations the night before and the night after the trip and cost $225 per person for the 1-day trip and $327 per person for the 2-day trip.

HIKING THE CANYON

There are no roads leading into the Grand Canyon, so if you want to visit the inner canyon you have to fly, float, ride a mule, or hike. The ever-changing views are as spectacular as those from the rim, and up close there are fossils, old mines, petroglyphs, wildflowers, and wildlife to see. Keep in mind, however, that no hike below the rim of the canyon is easy.

The Grand Canyon offers some of the most rugged and strenuous hiking anywhere in the United States, and for this reason anyone attempting even a short walk should be well prepared. Each year several people are injured or killed because they set out to hike the canyon without preparing properly. Most of these injuries and fatalities are day hikers who set out without sturdy footgear and without food or adequate amounts of water. Don't become another Grand Canyon statistic! Take precautions. Unless you have proper footgear and at least 1 quart of water, you won't even be allowed on the daily ranger-led nature walk along the South Kaibab Trail. Even a short 30-minute hike in the summer can dehydrate you, and a long hike into or out of the canyon in the heat can necessitate drinking more than a gallon of water. Remember while hiking that mules have the right of way; always stay to the inside of the trail when being passed by a mule train. Don't attempt to hike from the rim to the Colorado River and back in 1 day. Many people who have tried this have suffered injury or death.

DAY HIKES There are no loop-trail day hikes possible in the Grand Canyon, but the vastly different scenery in every direction makes a return trip on the same trail a totally new experience. The easiest day hikes are those along the rim. There is a 1½-mile paved trail leading from Yavapai Museum to the Powell Memorial. From the Powell Memorial the trail becomes dirt and continues another 8 miles to Hermits

Rest, from which, in summer, you can take a free shuttle back to Grand Canyon Village.

Trails leading down into the canyon include the Bright Angel Trail, the South Kaibab Trail, Grandview Trail, and the Hermit Trail. If you plan to hike for more than 30 minutes, carry 2 quarts of water per person.

The **Bright Angel Trail** starts just west of Bright Angel Lodge in Grand Canyon Village. It's the main route down to Phantom Ranch and is the most popular trail into the canyon. Day hikes on this trail include the trips to Indian Gardens or Plateau Point. Both these trips are long and very strenuous. There are rest houses at 1½ and 3 miles, which make good turn-around points for a 3-mile or 6-mile round-trip hike.

The **South Kaibab Trail** begins near Yaki Point east of Grand Canyon Village and is the alternative route to Phantom Ranch. This trail offers the best views of any of the day hikes in the canyon. From the trailhead it's a 3-mile round-trip to Cedar Ridge. The hike is very strenuous and there's no water available along the trail.

Grandview Trail is a steep, unmaintained trail that should be attempted only by people with experience hiking in the desert. It's a very strenuous 6-mile round-trip hike to Horseshoe Mesa, and there's no water available along the trail. Allow at least 7 hours for this rugged hike.

The **Hermit Trail** begins near Hermits Rest and is also steep and unmaintained. Don't attempt this trail if you don't have some experience hiking in the desert. It's a 5-mile round-trip to Santa Maria Springs and a 6-mile round-trip to Dripping Springs. Water from these springs must be treated before it's safe to drink.

BACKPACKING There are miles of trails deep in the canyon and several established campgrounds for backpackers. The best times of year to backpack in the canyon are spring and autumn. During the summer, temperatures at the bottom of the canyon are regularly over 100° Fahrenheit, while in the winter ice and snow at higher elevations makes footing on trails precarious. Be sure to carry at least 2 quarts, and preferably 1 gallon, of water whenever backpacking in the canyon.

A Backcountry Use Permit is required of all hikers planning to overnight in the canyon unless you'll be staying at Phantom Ranch in one of the cabins or in the dormitory. Because a limited number of hikers are allowed into the canyon on any given day, it's important to make reservations as far in advance as possible. Contact the **Backcountry Reservations Office,** P.O. Box 129, Grand Canyon, AZ 86023 (tel. 602/638-2474 for information). Holiday periods are the most popular and for these times it may be necessary to reserve your permit a year in advance. The office begins accepting reservations on October 1 for the following year and also for the rest of the current year. If you want to hike over the Labor Day weekend, be sure you make your reservation on October 1! If you show up without a reservation, go to the Backcountry Reservations Office (open daily from 8am to noon and 3 to 5pm; from 7am in summer) and put your name on the waiting list. When applying for a permit you will have to specify your exact itinerary and, once in the canyon, you must stick to this itinerary. There are campgrounds at Indian Gardens, Bright Angel Campground (near Phantom Ranch), and at Cottonwood, but hikers are limited to 2 nights per trip at each of these campgrounds. Other nights can be spent camping at undesignated sites along the trail, though you'll have to pick locations where water is available. The Backcountry Reservations Office has information available to help you plan your itinerary.

WHERE TO STAY

GRAND CANYON VILLAGE

Expensive

EL TOVAR HOTEL, P.O. Box 699, Grand Canyon, AZ 86023. Tel. 602/638-2401. Fax 602/638-9247. Telex 297394 FHGCUR. 65 rms, 12 suites (all with bath). A/C TV TEL

$ Rates: $97–$137 single or double; $147–$222 suite. AE, DC, DISC, MC, V.

First opened in 1905 after the Santa Fe Railroad reached the Grand Canyon, the El Tovar is the Grand Canyon's premier lodge. Built of native boulders and Oregon pine by Hopi craftsmen, the El Tovar is a rustic yet luxurious mountain lodge that combines attributes of both a Swiss chalet and a Norwegian villa. The imposing brown log structure perches on the edge of the canyon with awe-inspiring views.

The lobby, entered from an old-fashioned veranda with stone walls and rustic furniture, has a small fireplace, high-beamed ceiling, and dark log walls from which hang moose, deer, and antelope heads. In short, it's a classic mountain lodge.

The rooms, though clean, comfortable, and well appointed with new furnishings, are not done in the same rustic style as the hotel's public rooms. They have been recently renovated with new carpets and colonial-style furniture. The standard rooms are rather small, as are the bathrooms, which were added after the hotel was built. Deluxe rooms provide more legroom, and the suites, with their own private terraces, mini-refrigerator, and stunning views, are extremely spacious.

Dining/Entertainment: The El Tovar Dining Room (see "Where to Dine," below) is the best restaurant in the village and serves exquisite continental and southwestern cuisine. Just off the lobby is a cocktail lounge with a view by day and live music by night.

Services: Concierge, room service, tour desk.

Facilities: Gift shop, necessities shop, clothing shop.

Moderate

THUNDERBIRD & KACHINA LODGES, P.O. Box 699, Grand Canyon, AZ 86023. Tel. 602/638-2401. Fax 602/638-9247. Telex 297394 FHGCUR. 100 rms (all with bath). A/C TV TEL

$ Rates: $82–$88 single or double. AE, DC, DISC, MC, V.

These are the two newest lodges on the canyon rim. They are both two-story motel-style buildings, though the use of native sandstone in their construction helps them blend in a bit with the surrounding historic lodges. Thunderbird Lodge registration is done in Bright Angel Lodge, and Kachina Lodge registration is done in El Tovar Lodge.

Rooms in both lodges have stone walls and large windows, although you'll have to request a canyonside room if you want a view of something more than a parking lot. The canyon-view rooms are only $6 more than those without views and are well worth the extra cost. Neither lodge has its own dining room or lounge, but because they are between the El Tovar and Bright Angel lodges, you don't have to walk far when you get hungry.

YAVAPAI LODGE, P.O. Box 699, Grand Canyon, AZ 86023. Tel. 602/638-2401. Fax 602/638-9247. Telex 297394 FHGCUR. 348 rms (all with bath). TV TEL

$ Rates: $65–$75 single or double. AE, DC, DISC, MC, V.

Located in several buildings in the shadow of towering pine trees at the east end of Grand Canyon Village, the Yavapai is the largest lodge in the park. Rooms are large and comfortable with a southwestern motif used in the decor. Large windows look out into the forest, not the canyon, which is why this lodge is less expensive than the Thunderbird and Kachina lodges. It's also a bit of a hike to the main section of the village.

There is a cafeteria (see "Where to Dine," below) serving burgers, sandwiches, pizza, and salads at relatively economical prices. In one corner of the cafeteria is a combination bar and disco. The lodge also has a tour desk and gift shop.

Budget

BRIGHT ANGEL LODGE & CABINS, P.O. Box 699, Grand Canyon, AZ 86023. Tel. 602/638-2401. Fax 602/638-9247. Telex 297394 FHGCUR. 34

rms (10 with sink, 10 with sink and toilet, 14 with full bath), 54 cabins (all with bath), 1 suite (with bath).

$ Rates: $33 single or double with sink only, $38 single or double with sink and toilet, $45 single or double with full bath; $52–$97 cabin; $182 Buckey Suite. AE, DC, DISC, MC, V.

S Bright Angel Lodge began operation in 1896 as a collection of tents and cabins on the edge of the canyon. The current lodge was opened in 1935 and includes one of the original cabins. With its flagstone floor, huge fireplace, log walls and furniture, and soaring ceiling, the lodge's lobby is the epitome of a rustic retreat. Off this lobby is a museum dedicated to the Fred Harvey Company, which has been running the lodges here since 1905.

This is the most economical lodge in the park and offers the most interesting accommodations. For the budget-minded there are rooms with shared toilet facilities and rooms with private toilets but shared showers. There are also 55 cabins, including four rim cabins that have their own fireplaces. These rim cabins are the most popular and must be booked a year in advance. The other rooms in this lodge are extremely popular, too, because of their low rates and must be booked at least 6 months in advance. Most of the rooms and cabins feature rustic furnishings and painted wood walls. The Buckey Suite, the oldest structure on the canyon rim, is arguably the best room in the park, with a canyon view, fireplace, two rooms, two TVs, king-size bed, and a queen-size sofabed.

The Bright Angel Dining Room (see "Where to Dine," below) is the lodge's main restaurant and serves moderately priced meals. It's open daily for breakfast, lunch, and dinner. The Arizona Steak House (see "Where to Dine," below) is open for dinner only and serves steaks in the $10 to $20 range. For snacks, sandwiches, and ice cream, there is the Bright Angel Fountain. The lodge also has a tour desk, bookstore, museum, and gift shop.

MASWIK LODGE, P.O. Box 699, Grand Canyon, AZ 86023. Tel. 602/ 638-2401. Fax 602/638-9247. Telex 297394 FHGCUR. 288 rms (all with bath). TV TEL

$ Rates: $46–$86 single or double. AE, DC, DISC, MC, V.

Set back a bit from the rim, but still close to the head of the Bright Angel Trail and the historic lodges and restaurants, the Maswik Lodge offers spacious accommodations in several different buildings and cabins at reasonable rates. If you crave modern appointments such as new carpeting, new mattresses, and plum-and-lavender decor, opt for one of the newly remodeled north rooms. More rugged types will prefer the less expensive and more rustic old cabins that have bathtubs but not showers in their bathrooms.

There is a large cafeteria (see "Where to Dine," below) and a sports lounge with a big-screen TV (an odd contrast to the rugged stone walls of the room). A tour desk and gift shop are also on the premises.

An RV Park

TRAILER VILLAGE, P.O. Box 699, Grand Canyon, AZ 86023. Tel. 602/638-2401. Fax 602/638-9247. Telex 297394 FHGCUR. 78 full hookup sites.

$ Rates: $15 for two people, plus 50¢ for each additional person.

Situated amid the trees at the east end of Grand Canyon Village, this RV park is open all year.

Campgrounds

MATHER CAMPGROUND, P.O. Box 129, Grand Canyon, AZ 86023. Tel. toll free 800/452-1111. 310 sites.

This campground is under the pine trees at the east end of Grand Canyon Village. There are pay showers, modern bathrooms, and a coin-operated laundry. No RV hookups are available. All national park campground reservations are handled by Ticketron. You can make reservations in person by going to a Ticketron outlet or you can write to Ticketron, P.O. Box 617516, Chicago, IL 60661-7516, to request a reservation form; be sure to make your reservation at least 3 weeks before your planned departure. You can also make reservations by calling the above toll-free number any day of the week between 8am and midnight, central time. There is a $4 handling charge for each phone reservation.

AT THE PARK'S SOUTH ENTRANCE
Expensive

QUALITY INN GRAND CANYON, P.O. Box 520, Grand Canyon, AZ 86023. Tel. 602/638-2673, or toll free 800/221-2222. 136 rms. A/C TV TEL
$ Rates: $88–$103 single or double. Rates lower Nov–Mar. AE, CB, DC, DISC, MC, V.

Recently changed from the Red Feather to a Quality Inn, this relatively expensive motel provides standard rooms with two double beds. Because of the remodeling, all the rooms have modern appointments, new carpets, and drapes.

Dining/Entertainment: Two restaurants and a lounge provide a choice for dining and drinking.

Services: Free local phone calls, complimentary coffee and tea.

Facilities: Swimming pool, whirlpool bath, no-smoking rooms.

Moderate

GRAND CANYON SQUIRE INN, P.O. Box 130, Grand Canyon, AZ 86023-0130. Tel. 602/638-2681, or toll free 800/528-1234. Fax 602/638-2782. 151 rms (all with bath). A/C TV TEL
$ Rates: $55–$85 single or double; $125–$175 suite (the lower rate available only Dec–Jan, excluding hols). AE, DC, DISC, MC, V.

When you tire of the views up at the canyon rim, or if you prefer playing tennis to riding a mule, you'll be happy staying here. The rooms are large and come with two double beds and comfortable easy chairs. One wall of each guest room is made of local stones and there are large windows that let in light and views.

The Coronado Room is the best restaurant in Tusayan and serves continental cuisine and regional American specialties at reasonable prices. Less expensive fare is available in the Coffee Shop. Before or after dinner you can sit by the fireplace of the Squire Lounge. The inn also offers free airport shuttle service, a swimming pool, tennis courts, whirlpool bath, sauna, bowling alley, pool room, video games, and a gift shop.

MOQUI LODGE, P.O. Box 699, Grand Canyon, AZ 86023. Tel. 602/638-2401. Fax 602/638-9247. Telex 297394 FHGCUR. 127 rms (all with bath) TV TEL
$ Rates: $70 single or double. Rates lower Nov–Mar. AE, DC, DISC, MC, V.
Closed: Jan–Feb.

Operated by the Fred Harvey Company but located at the south entrance to the park, Moqui Lodge captures the feel of a ski lodge with its tall A-frame construction. Just off the main lobby is a lounge with a stone chimney and a beautiful mural. The guest accommodations are standard motel-style rooms with large windows along an open-air hall, floral-print bedspreads on the two double beds, and cinderblock wall construction.

Moderately priced Mexican and American meals are served in the dining room amid Spanish colonial decor. The cocktail lounge has live country music in the evenings. There is also a tour desk and gift shop.

IN THE CANYON

PHANTOM RANCH, P.O. Box 699, Grand Canyon, AZ 86023. Tel. 602/638-2401. Fax 602/638-9247. Telex 297394 FHGCUR. 11 cabins, 40 dorm beds.
$ Rates: Cabins, $53 single or double; $19 dormitory bed. AE, MC, V.

This is the only lodge down in the Grand Canyon and as such is very popular with both hikers and mule riders. Built in 1922, Phantom Ranch has the same western atmosphere as some of the old lodges on the canyon rims. Accommodations are either in rustic stone-walled cabins (mostly reserved for mule riders) or 10-bedded sex-segregated dormitories. Evaporative coolers keep both the cabins and dorms cool in the summer. Make reservations as early as possible (up to a year in advance).

Dining/Entertainment: Family-style meals must be reserved in advance and are served in the dining hall. The menu consists of beef-and-vegetable stew ($16), a vegetarian dinner ($16), or steak ($26). Breakfasts ($10) are hearty and sack lunches ($6.50) can be prepared for you. Between meals there's a canteen in the dining hall. It sells snacks, drinks, gifts, and necessities. After dinner the dining hall becomes a beer hall.

Services: Public phone, mule-back baggage transfer between Grand Canyon Village and Phantom Ranch ($40 down, $30 up).

Facilities: Swimming in Bright Angel Creek, horseshoe pit, fishing.

WILLIAMS

Although it's 60 miles south of the Grand Canyon, Williams is the nearest town. Consequently it has dozens of low-budget motels catering to people who were unable to get a room at the park. The Grand Canyon Railway Depot is located here.

Moderate

COMFORT INN, 911 W. Bill Williams Ave., Williams, AZ 86046. Tel. 602/635-4045, or toll free 800/228-5150. 54 rms (all with bath) A/C TV TEL
$ Rates: $40–$90 single; $50–$95 double. AE, CB, DC, DISC, MC, V.
Clean and modern, the Comfort Inn is located at the west end of Williams. Guest rooms are of average size but are comfortable. The indoor swimming pool and whirlpool bath are the motel's real pluses (even in the summer, nights here in Williams can be quite cool). The motel offers free coffee, a coin laundry, no-smoking rooms, and wheelchair accommodations. There is a small restaurant adjacent to the motel.

MOUNTAINSIDE INN & RESORT, 642 E. Bill Williams Ave., Williams, AZ 86046. Tel. 602/635-4431, or toll free 800/462-9381. Fax 602/635-2292. 96 rms (all with bath). A/C TV TEL
$ Rates: $48–$78 single or double. AE, CB, DC, MC, V.
Located at the east end of town at Exit 167 from I-40, this large motel is popular with tour groups. The live entertainment in the evening also makes it one of Williams's most popular places for dinner and drinks. Rooms are medium size with large windows, some of which have views of the mountains. The large restaurant and lounge off the lobby provides American meals and live entertainment 6 nights a week in summer and on the weekends in winter. In summer there's also a western band on weekends. The hotel also offers room service, a swimming pool, whirlpool bath, picnic area, and a gift shop.

QUALITY INN MOUNTAIN RANCH & RESORT, Rte. 1, at Exit 167 from I-40, Box 35, Williams, AZ 86046. Tel. 602/635-2693, or toll free 800/221-2222. 73 rms (all with bath). A/C TV TEL
$ Rates: $58–$88 single or double (the lower rates only available Nov–Mar). AE, DC, DISC, MC, V.
⑤ Located a few miles east of town, the Mountain Ranch & Resort is close to the Interstate, but is surrounded by 26 acres of forest and meadow that give it a secluded feeling. This seclusion and the activities available here make this the best hotel in Williams. Rooms are large, with two sinks and windows on two sides to let in plenty of light and views of the forest and the San Francisco Peaks. There is a large restaurant with a flagstone fireplace and bubbling fountain. The menu features steaks and American food. The hotel offers horseback riding, a swimming pool, whirlpool bath, sauna, tennis courts, volleyball, basketball, and a putting green.

Budget

CANYON COUNTRY INN, 442 W. Bill Williams Ave., Williams, AZ 86046. Tel. 602/635-2349. 9 rms (all with bath). TV TEL
$ Rates (including continental breakfast): Summer, $45–$75 single or double; winter $35–$65 single or double. AE, CB, DC, DISC, MC, V.

⭐ This quaint country inn is a cross between a motel and a bed-and-breakfast. Though it's not a historic building and is located in the middle of Williams's motel row, all rooms are individually furnished and feature crafts made by local women, ceiling fans, and plenty of teddy bears to keep guests company. The owners, John and Sue Einolander, are a friendly, helpful couple.

NORRIS MOTEL, 1001 W. Bill Williams Ave., Williams, AZ 86046. Tel. 602/635-2202, or toll free 800/341-8000. Fax 602/635-9202. 36 rms. A/C TV TEL

$ Rates: $24–$49 single; $26–$60 double. AE, DISC, MC, V.

Run by a British family, the Norris Motel may not look like anything special from the street, but the friendliness of the welcome will immediately let you know that this is not your ordinary motel. Most of the guest rooms have been recently remodeled and have quilt-patterned bedspreads that give each room a homey feel. Many rooms also have refrigerators. There's even a whirlpool bath to soak away your aches and pains in the evening.

WHERE TO DINE
GRAND CANYON VILLAGE
Expensive

EL TOVAR DINING ROOM, in the El Tovar Hotel. Tel. 638-6292.
   Cuisine: CONTINENTAL/SOUTHWESTERN. **Reservations:** Required at dinner, recommended at lunch.
$ Prices: Appetizers $4.90–$12.50; main courses $12–$24. AE, DC, DISC, MC, V.
   Open: Breakfast daily 6:30–11am; lunch daily 11:30am–2pm; dinner daily 5–10pm.

⭐ Rough-hewn ceiling beams and log walls are a surprising contrast to the fine china, crystal, and linen table settings in the El Tovar Dining Room. World-class continental cuisine with touches of southwestern flavor thrown in for good measure is the hallmark of the restaurant's excellent chef. Most of the ingredients used in the El Tovar's kitchen are flown in daily to assure freshness and quality. On a recent visit the dinner menu featured black-pepper smoked salmon with corn crêpes among the appetizers. For a main course the filet mignon and quail medallions with Gorgonzola polenta was mouth-watering. The view out the picture windows is one of the best in the world.

Moderate

ARIZONA STEAK HOUSE, in Bright Angel Lodge. Tel. 638-6355.
   Cuisine: STEAKS. **Reservations:** Not accepted.
$ Prices: Dinner $10–$20. AE, DC, DISC, MC, V.
   Open: Dinner only, daily 5–10pm.

If you have a craving for a thick juicy steak or a crisp cool salad, a visit to this steakhouse is in order. The decor is contemporary Southwest with a desert palette of pastel colors. A wall of glass along one side of the restaurant assures everyone of a view of the canyon beyond. Since the restaurant is open only for dinner (although group tours dine here at lunch), you should get here as early as possible to enjoy the sunset view.

BRIGHT ANGEL DINING ROOM, in the Bright Angel Lodge. Tel. 638-2631.
   Cuisine: AMERICAN. **Reservations:** Suggested.
$ Prices: Breakfast $3.50–$6; lunch/dinner $10–$14. AE, DC, DISC, MC, V.
   Open: Breakfast daily 6:30–11am; lunch daily 11:15am–4:45pm; dinner daily 5–10pm.

Muted desert tones, lodgepole pine beams and pillars, and wrought-iron chandeliers give this spacious dining room a distinctive southwestern feel. Waiters in black bow ties and vests lend an air of sophistication to an otherwise casual atmosphere.

Budget

BABBITTS DELICATESSEN, Babbitt's General Store. Tel. 638-2262.
   Cuisine: DELI. **Reservations:** Not accepted.
$ **Prices:** $3–$5. No credit cards.
   Open: Daily 8am–7pm.
If you're looking for really fast food and cheap eats, this deli should fill your belly without emptying your wallet. It's across the street from the visitor center. Eat here or take your meal to a scenic overlook.

MASWIK CAFETERIA, in the Maswik Lodge. Tel. 638-2631.
   Cuisine: AMERICAN. **Reservations:** Not accepted.
$ **Prices:** Meals $4–$6. AE, DC, DISC, MC, V.
   Open: Daily 6am–10pm.
Located in the Maswik Lodge, this large cafeteria is a good place for a quick or inexpensive meal. The selection of foods is wide, and in addition to such old standards as barbecued beef ribs, they also offer tostados and a few other popular Mexican dishes.

YAVAPAI CAFETERIA, at the Yavapai Lodge. Tel. 638-2631.
   Cuisine: AMERICAN. **Reservations:** Not accepted.
$ **Prices:** $4–$6. AE, DC, DISC, MC, V.
   Open: Daily 6am–10pm.
If you're staying at the Yavapai Lodge, this is the closest place to get a meal. Early risers and sunrise photographers will be glad to know that they can get that morning cup of coffee as early as 6am. If you happen to be camping or staying in your RV, this convenient eatery is good to keep in mind for that day when you're just too tired to fix dinner.

ELSEWHERE IN THE PARK

DESERT VIEW TRADING POST CAFETERIA. Tel. 638-2360.
   Cuisine: SNACKS. **Reservations:** Not accepted.
$ **Prices:** $2–$4. No credit cards.
   Open: Mar–Nov, daily 8am–6pm; Nov–Mar, daily 9am–5pm.
What the Hermits Rest is for the west end of the South Rim, the Desert View is for the east end. Sandwiches, snacks, and hot and cold drinks are about the extent of dining possibilities here—just enough to tide you over until you get back to the village.

HERMITS REST FOUNTAIN, at the Hermits Rest Curio Shop, end of West Rim Dr. Tel. 638-2351.
   Cuisine: SNACKS. **Reservations:** Not accepted.
$ **Prices:** $2–$4. No credit cards.
   Open: Daily 10am–4pm.
Once you hit the end of this dead-end road, you may be thirsty or hungry. You can fill up with sodas and hot dogs before heading back to places where "real" food is available.

SHOPPING

There are several curio shops along the South Rim of the canyon. The largest and most interesting of these is the **Hopi House** (tel. 638-2631, ext. 6587) in front of the El Tovar Hotel. This shop, the first in the park, was built in 1905 to resemble a Hopi pueblo and to serve as a place for Hopi artisans to work and sell their crafts. Today it's full of Hopi and Navajo arts and crafts, including expensive kachinas, rugs, jewelry, and pottery. The nearby **Verkamps Curios** (tel. 638-2242) originally opened in a tent in 1898, but after John Verkamp went out of business, it was not reopened until 1905. Today it's the main place to look for souvenirs and crafts. The **Desert View**

Watchtower (tel. 638-2736), 23 miles east of Grand Canyon Village, is another fascinating shop housed in a historic building. It's full of souvenirs and southwestern crafts.

EVENING ENTERTAINMENT

Most people visiting the Grand Canyon aren't thinking about anything other than a campfire when they think of evening entertainment, but in fact there's quite a bit of nightlife for those who haven't been exhausted by a day of hiking or mule riding. The **Maswik Cafeteria** has a sports bar with big-screen TV. The **Yavapai Cafeteria** has a disco with dancing to recorded and live music nightly. In the **lounge of the El Tovar Hotel,** there is quiet piano music. Thursday through Saturday night there is live country music at the **Moqui Lodge lounge.**

In addition to these lively pursuits, there are more traditional **national park evening programs** such as star gazing and lecture/slide shows on cultural and natural-history aspects of the Grand Canyon. In September there is the **Grand Canyon Chamber Music Festival.** Most of these programs are held in the Shrine of the Ages near the visitor center.

---

3. LAKE POWELL & PAGE

130 miles N of Flagstaff, 272 miles N of Phoenix,
120 miles W of Monument Valley,
130 miles E of the Grand Canyon North Rim,
130 miles NE of Grand Canyon South Rim

GETTING THERE **By Plane** The **Page Airport,** 1 mile east of town on Ariz. 98 (tel. 602/645-9200), is served by Sky West airlines (tel. toll free 800/453-9417).

By Car Page is connected to Flagstaff by U.S. 89. Ariz 98 leads southeast into the Navajo Indian Reservation and connects with U.S. 160 to Kayenta and Four Corners.

ESSENTIALS For further information on Page and Lake Powell, contact the **Page/Lake Powell Chamber of Commerce,** P.O. Box 727, Page, AZ 86040 (tel. 602/645-2741), or the **John Wesley Powell Memorial Museum,** 6 North Lake Powell Boulevard (P.O. Box 547), Page, AZ 86040 (tel. 602/645-9496). The **telephone area code** is 602.

Had the early Spanish explorers of Arizona suddenly come upon Lake Powell, they would have either taken it for a mirage or fallen to their knees and rejoiced. Surrounded by hundreds of miles of parched desert land, this human-made lake acts like a human magnet, drawing everyone in the region toward its promise of relief from the heat. Though construction began on the Glen Canyon Dam in 1960 and was completed in 1963, Lake Powell did not reach capacity until 1980. Today it's a water playground frequented by boaters, skiers, fishermen, and people who come here to see Rainbow Bridge, one of the natural wonders of the world. Rainbow Bridge is called *nonnozhoshi* or "the rainbow turned to stone," by the Navajo. It's the largest natural bridge on earth and stretches 278 feet across a side canyon in the Glen Canyon National Recreation Area.

The construction of the Glen Canyon Dam came despite the angry outcry of people who felt that this canyon was even more beautiful than Grand Canyon and should be preserved in its natural state. The preservationists lost their battle and today houseboats and skiers cruise where once birds and waterfalls filled the canyons with their songs. Page, a work camp constructed to house the workers who built the Glen Canyon Dam, has now become a town unto itself and, with its many motels and restaurants, is the best place from which to explore Lake Powell.

WHAT TO SEE & DO

GLEN CANYON DAM, U.S. 89 and the Colorado River. Tel. 645-2481.

Built across a section of Glen Canyon that's less than a third of a mile wide, the dam impounds the waters of the Colorado River to form Lake Powell. Standing 710 feet above the bedrock, the dam contains almost five million cubic yards of concrete. Lake Powell extends for more than 180 miles behind the dam and has a shoreline of nearly 2,000 miles. Construction on the dam began in 1960 and was not completed until 1963. It took another 17 years to completely fill Lake Powell. Built to provide water for the desert communities of the Southwest and West, the dam also provides hydroelectric power. Self-guided tours of the dam take 30 to 45 minutes.

Admission: Free.

Open: Nov–Mar daily 8am–5pm; Mar–Nov, daily 7am–7pm.

GLEN CANYON NATIONAL RECREATION AREA AND RAINBOW BRIDGE NATIONAL MONUMENT, P.O. Box 1507, Page AZ 86040. Tel. 602/ 645-2471.

Until the construction of the Glen Canyon Dam and the subsequent formation of Lake Powell, this area was one of the most remote regions in the lower 48 states. Today, however, it's one of the nation's most popular national recreation areas and attracts 2½ million visitors each year. The lake is the main attraction and its stunning setting amid the slick-rock canyons of northern Arizona and southern Utah makes it one of the most beautiful of Arizona's many human-made lakes. More than 500 feet deep in some places, and bounded by more than 2,000 miles of shoreline, Lake Powell is a maze of convoluted canyons. Waterskiing, jet skiing, and fishing are the most popular activities, and five marinas (only Wahweap is in Arizona) help boaters explore the lake. There are, however, few roads penetrating the recreation area, so the only way to appreciate this rugged region is by boat. Bring your own boat or rent one here, and there are even houseboats if you want to spend a few days or a week living in comfort on the water.

The most popular destination on the lake is Rainbow Bridge, the world's largest natural bridge, which is preserved as a national monument. Standing 290 feet high and spanning 275 feet, this sandstone arch is an awesome reminder of the powers of erosion that have sculpted this entire region into the spectacle it is today. Rainbow Bridge is located 50 miles from Glen Canyon Dam and is accessible only by boat or on foot. Traveling there by boat is by far the more popular route. There are daily tours from Wahweap and Bullfrog marinas (see "Organized Tours," below, for details).

There are campgrounds and RV facilities at Wahweap and Lees Ferry in Arizona and at Bullfrog, Hite, and Halls Crossing in Utah. The Carl Hayden Visitor Center (tel. 602/645-2511) in Wahweap is open daily from 8am to 5pm (7am to 7pm in summer). The Bullfrog Visitor Center (tel. 801/684-2243) in Bullfrog, Utah, is open daily from 8am to 4:30pm.

Admission: Free.

Open: Daily 24 hours.

JOHN WESLEY POWELL MEMORIAL MUSEUM, 6 N. Lake Powell Blvd. Tel. 645-9496.

Lake Powell is named after John Wesley Powell, the one-armed Civil War hero who led the first expedition through the Grand Canyon. In 1869 Powell and a small band of men spent more than 3 months fighting the rapids of the Green and Colorado rivers in wooden-hulled boats. This small museum is dedicated to the courageous—some said crazy—Powell and his expedition. Besides documenting the Powell expedition with photographs, etchings, and artifacts, the museum displays Native American artifacts from Anasazi pottery to contemporary Navajo and Hopi crafts. The exhibit of fluorescent minerals is particularly interesting. There are also several informative videos that are regularly screened in the museum's small auditorium. The museum also acts as an information center for Lake Powell and the region, and has a small gift shop.

Admission: Free.

Open: Mon–Sat 8am–6pm, Sun 10am–6pm.

ORGANIZED TOURS

The Glen Canyon National Recreation Area covers an immense area, much of it inaccessible to regular automobiles. If you'd like to see more of the area than is visible from the few roads, you might want to consider a tour by Jeep, boat, or small plane. **Duck Tours** (tel. 602/645-8881 code 81, or 645-2741 or 645-9496), offers the most distinctive overland tours out of Page. The name refers to the open-air 1945 army Duck, a six-wheel-drive vehicle that can be driven into the water and operated as a boat. Unfortunately, the National Park Service will not allow this particular duck on the waters of Lake Powell, so you'll have to be content with a terrestrial tour. Tours cost $24.95 for adults, $14.95 for children 5 to 12, and free for children under 5. **Lake Powell Overland Adventures** (tel. 602/645-5501) offers a similar tour in open Jeeps. A half-day tour that stops at a Navajo village costs $37.10 for adults and $15.90 for children. Tours to Corkscrew Canyon alone cost $21.20 for adults and $10.60 for children and last 1½ hours.

Arizona Air–Lake Powell (tel. 602/645-2494) offers several air tours of northern and northeastern Arizona, including flights to Rainbow Bridge, the Escalante River, the Grand Canyon, Canyonlands, Bryce Canyon, Monument Valley, and the Navajo nation. Rates range from $60 to $225.

Lake Powell Resorts & Marinas (tel. 602/645-2433, or toll free 800/528-6154) offers a variety of boat tours on Lake Powell. Three times daily, the paddlewheeler *Canyon King* embarks on a 1-hour tour out of Wahweap Marina ($8.75 for adults, $6.25 for children). There are also sunset ($18.95 for adults, $12.75 for children) and dinner cruises ($39.95) aboard the *Canyon King*. There are half-day ($46.75 for adults, $23.35 for children) and full-day ($59.95 for adults, $29.95 for children) tours to Rainbow Bridge National Monument, 50 miles up Lake Powell from Wahweap Marina. Colorado River float trips and white-water rafting trips are also available. The float trips depart May through September from just below the Glen Canyon Dam and cost $34.75 for adults and $26 for children. You can also rent your own powerboat and go exploring on your own. The same company that operates the boat tours rents runabouts, skiffs, patio boats, and bass boats. Rental rates range from $60 to $180 a day in the high season and $39 to $116 a day in the low season. Weekly rates are also available.

WHERE TO STAY

EXPENSIVE

LAKE POWELL RESORTS & MARINAS—HOUSEBOATS, 2916 N. 35th Ave., Suite 8, Phoenix, AZ 85017-5261. Tel. 602/278-8888, or toll free 800/528-6154. Fax 602/269-9408.
$ Rates (for 7 nights): Boats that sleep 6, $1,185 May–Oct, $770 Nov–May; boats that sleep 10, $1,465 May–Oct, $952 Nov–May; boats that sleep 12, $1,907 May–Oct, $1,240 Nov–May. Rates also available for 2, 3, or 4 nights.

⭐ Though there are plenty of hotels and motels in and near Page, the most popular accommodations here are not waterfront hotel rooms but houseboats, which function as floating vacation homes. With a houseboat, you can explore Lake Powell's beautiful redrock country, far from any roads. These houseboats are powered by two outboard motors and are as easy to operate as a car. Houseboats, which range in size from 36 to 50 feet, sleep anywhere from 6 to 12 people. They come complete with hot showers, refrigerator/freezer, heating system, stove, oven, and gas grill. Kitchens come equipped with everything you'll need to prepare meals. The only things you'll really need to bring are bedding and towels; however, there are plenty of other items you might want to remember such as a flashlight, camping equipment in case you want to camp on an isolated beach, maps, a compass, fishing gear, binoculars, or whatever. With a houseboat, you can anchor in a quiet cove or tie up on a secluded beach. Swimming, diving, fishing, and just relaxing are houseboating's main pursuits.

WAHWEAP LODGE, Lakeshore Dr., P.O. Box 1597, Page, AZ 86040.

Tel. 602/645-2433, or toll free 800/528-6154. Fax 602/645-2072. 270 rms and suites. A/C TV TEL

$ Rates: Apr–Oct, $80–$88 single; $88–$97 double; $160 suite. Nov–Mar, $52–$58 single; $58–$63 double; $104 suite. AE, DC, DISC, MC, V.

Wahweap Marina is a sprawling complex 4 miles north of the Glen Canyon Dam on the shores of Lake Powell. The resort and nearby marina stay busy with boaters all spring, summer, and fall. Set on a hill a little ways from the lake, this is the biggest and best hotel in Page and features many of the amenities and activities of a resort. Guest rooms are decorated in sky blue or dusty rose and are arranged in two long two-story wings. All the rooms have either a balcony or a patio, TV armoire, and generous bathroom. The west wing has the better view (the east wing overlooks the Navajo coal-fired power plant, which has been under recent attack for allegedly causing smog in the Grand Canyon).

Dining/Entertainment: The Rainbow Room (see "Where to Dine," below) offers fine dining with a sweeping panorama of the lake and desert. The menu is equally divided between American standards and southwestern fare. For light meals, snacks, ice cream, and cookies, there is the Cookie Jar near the boat ramp. The Driftwood Lounge features live Top-40 dance music Monday through Saturday evenings.

Services: Room service (pizza), in-room movies, shuttle to Page.

Facilities: Two swimming pools, whirlpool bath, gift shop, boat rentals, boat ramp.

MODERATE

INN AT LAKE POWELL, 716 Rim Dr., Page, AZ 86040. Tel. 602/645-2466, or toll free 800/826-2718. Fax 602/645-2466. 101 rms, 2 suites (all with bath). A/C TV TEL

$ Rates: Apr–Oct, $39 single; $57 double. Nov–Mar, $56 single; $70–$79 double. AE, DC, DISC, MC, V.

Perched right at the edge of Page and the mesa on which the city is built, the Inn at Lake Powell has a fine view across miles of desert. Half the rooms have views, and of course these are the more expensive rooms. Decor is modern with desert colors and Native American designs used throughout. The hotel's restaurant is in a separate building across the parking lot from the main building. Large windows take in a view of the desert that is slightly marred by the number of powerlines that stretch out from the dam. Steaks and seafood are the menu mainstays. The hotel also offers free coffee in the lobby, airport shuttle, a swimming pool with a hundred-mile view, and a whirlpool bath.

BUDGET

BEST WESTERN WESTON INN, 201 N. Lake Powell Blvd., Page, AZ 86040. Tel. 602/645-2541, or toll free 800/528-1234. 90 rms (all with bath). A/C TV TEL

$ Rates: Apr–Oct, $48–$58 single; $53–$63 double. Nov–Mar, $32–$42 single; $39–$49. AE, CB, DC, DISC, MC, V.

Located right next door to the Holiday Inn, the Weston Inn is a more economical choice that's convenient to restaurants. It doesn't have views, but it's the same distance to Lake Powell as other Page motels. The hotel offers an airport shuttle, swimming pool, no-smoking rooms, and wheelchair accommodations.

LAKE POWELL MOTEL, U.S. 89, P.O. Box 1597, Page, AZ 86040. Tel. 602/645-2477, or toll free 800/528-6154. 24 rms (all with bath). A/C TV TEL

$ Rates: Apr–Oct, $52–$58 single; $58–$63 double. Nov–Mar, $34–$38 single; $38–$41 double. AE, DC, DISC, MC, V.

Located on a barren hill set back from the lake, the Lake Powell Motel offers a budget alternative away from the traffic and lights of downtown Page. If you prefer quiet and a view of the lake and surrounding desert, this should be your first choice in this price range. Accommodations are standard motel rooms with one or two queen-size beds.

You'll find the Lake Powell Motel 3 miles west of Wahweap Marina or 4 miles north of Glen Canyon Dam on U.S. 89.

WHERE TO DINE

MICHAEL'S, 819 N. Navajo Dr. Tel. 645-5458.
   Cuisine: INTERNATIONAL. **Reservations:** Suggested.
   $ Prices: Appetizers $3–$6.50; main courses $7–$14. MC, V.
   Open: Daily 11am–10pm.
This fern-bar restaurant in a Colonial Williamsburg–style building is one of Page's most popular restaurants. Chef Michael Decker, the restaurant's namesake, has nearly 20 years of experience and owned two other restaurants before locating here in Page. The menu has a selection of Mexican dishes that's quite good, but the seafood dishes, in a wide range of preparations, are even better. Cajun shrimp fettuccine and scallops in wine sauce are just two tempting offerings. Steak eaters will enjoy the tender, juicy filet mignon and other char-broiled cuts. Michael's is located just around the corner from the John Wesley Powell Museum.

RAINBOW ROOM, in the Wahweap Lodge, Wahweap Marina, Lakeshore Dr. Tel. 645-2433.
   Cuisine: AMERICAN. **Reservations:** Suggested in summer.
   $ Prices: Appetizers $2.25–$6.50; main courses $8.50–$18. AE, DC, DISC, MC, V.
   Open: Breakfast daily 6–11am; lunch daily 11am–3pm; dinner daily 5–10pm.
With sweeping vistas of Lake Powell through the walls of glass and a menu featuring southwestern and American dishes, the Rainbow Room at the Wahweap Lodge is Page's best restaurant. The southwestern pizza made with a cornmeal crust, jack cheese, roasted chiles, chorizo sausage, and fresh tomatoes is such a great appetizer that it's tempting to have two of them and call it dinner, but you'll want to try one of the southwestern dishes as well. The Mexicali shrimp scampi sautéed in tequila, tomatoes, garlic, oregano, cilantro, cumin, and red pepper is my favorite. If you're heading out on the water for the day, they'll fix you a box lunch, either American or European style.

EN ROUTE TO THE NORTH RIM

Between Page and the North Rim of the Grand Canyon, Alternate U.S. 89 crosses the Colorado River at **Lees Ferry** in Marble Canyon. Lees Ferry is the starting point for raft trips through the Grand Canyon, and for many years was the only place to cross the Colorado River for hundreds of miles in either direction. There is also a campground here. Lees Ferry is well known among anglers for its trophy trout fishing, and when the North Rim closes and the rafting season comes to an end, about the only folks you'll find up here are fishermen and hunters.

Continuing west, the highway passes under the **Vermillion Cliffs,** so named for their deep-red coloring. Along this remote and unpopulated stretch of road there are a couple of very basic lodges. If you don't have a reservation at one of the three lodges at or near the North Rim, you may want to stop at one of the following lodges and continue on to the North Rim the next morning. Lodges near the canyon fill up early if they aren't already fully booked with reservations made months in advance.

West of Marble Canyon 17 miles, you'll see a sign for **House Rock Ranch,** a wildlife area managed by the Arizona Game and Fish Department. House Rock Ranch is best known for its herd of American bison (buffalo). From the turnoff it's a 22-mile drive on a dirt road to reach the ranch.

WHERE TO STAY EN ROUTE

CLIFF DWELLERS LODGE, U.S. 89A, Marble Canyon, AZ 86036. Tel. 602/355-2228. 20 rms (all with bath).
   $ Rates: Apr–Oct, $48–$55 single or double. Nov–Mar, $40 single; $47 double; second night $10. MC, V.
To give you some idea of how remote an area this is, the Cliff Dwellers Lodge is

marked on official Arizona state maps. There just isn't much else out here, so a single lodge can be as important as a town. Newer and more expensive rooms here have combination bathtub/showers, while the older rooms have showers only. It's about 8 miles east to the Navajo Bridge over the Grand Canyon.

LEES FERRY LODGE, U.S. 89A (HC67-Box 1), Marble Canyon, AZ 86036. Tel. 602/355-2231. 9 rms (all with bath). A/C
$ Rates: $30 single; $40 double. MC, V.
Located 3½ miles west of Lees Ferry and the Navajo Bridge over the Colorado River, the Lees Ferry Lodge is a small place with rustic accommodations, built in 1929 of native stone and rough-hewn timber beams. Views of the Vermillion Cliffs are quite spectacular, and there is a very pleasant patio seating area in front of all the rooms. Unfortunately the highway is only a few yards away, so traffic noises occasionally disturb the tranquility. A small dining room provides meals.

MARBLE CANYON LODGE, Marble Canyon, AZ 86036. Tel. 602/355-2225. 50 rms (all with bath). A/C
$ Rates: $40–$45 single; $45–$50 double. MC, V. **Parking:** Free.
Located just 4 miles from Lees Ferry, the Marble Canyon Lodge was built in the 1920s. Its stone walls give it a very rustic feel, and its proximity to Lees Ferry makes it a great place to spend the night before starting a rafting trip. You're right at the base of the Vermillion Cliffs here, and the views are great. There is a cozy restaurant and a trading post.

---

4. THE GRAND CANYON: NORTH RIM

42 miles S of Jacob Lake, 216 miles N of Grand Canyon Village (South Rim), 354 miles N of Phoenix, 125 miles W of Page/Lake Powell

GETTING THERE   By Plane   The nearest airport to the North Rim is in Page, served by Sky West airlines (see "Lake Powell & Page" for details).

By Bus   Trans Canyon (tel. 602/638-2820) operates a shuttle between the North Rim and South Rim of the Grand Canyon. The shuttle leaves the South Rim daily at 1:30pm and arrives at the North Rim at 6pm. The return trip leaves the North Rim at 7am and arrives at the South Rim at 11:30am.

By Car   The North Rim is at the end of Ariz. 67 (the North Rim Parkway), which is reached from Alternate U.S. 89.

ESSENTIALS   The North Rim is only **open** from mid-May to late October. The park **admission fee** is $10 per car and is good for 1 week. There is an **information desk** in the lobby of the Grand Canyon Lodge, open daily from 8am to 5pm. At the entrance gate you will also be given a copy of **The Guide,** a small newspaper with information on park activities. There is a separate edition of *The Guide* for each of the two rims. For information before leaving home, contact **Grand Canyon National Park,** P.O. Box 129, Grand Canyon, AZ 86023 (tel. 602/638-7888). The **telephone area code** is 602.

Though the North Rim is only 10 miles as the raven flies from the South Rim, it's a 200-mile drive. For this reason many people never make it to this rim of the canyon. In addition to the great distance from the more popular South Rim, the North Rim is only open from mid-May to October or early November. At 8,000 feet in elevation, the North Rim is 1,000 feet higher than the South Rim and receives considerably more snow in the winter. Ariz. 67 is not plowed and consequently the Grand Canyon Lodge is closed down for the winter.

Kaibab is a Paiute word meaning "the mountain lying down," so Kaibab is an apt name for the plateau on which the North Rim is located. The Kaibab Plateau averages over 8,000 feet in elevation and is home to a unique white-tailed squirrel called the Kaibab squirrel. Keep your eyes open for this large-eared squirrel whenever you're walking in the forest. The higher elevation of the North Rim's Kaibab Plateau also produces a different vegetation. A dense forest of ponderosa pines interspersed with large meadows gives the North Rim an alpine feel that is lacking at the South Rim. Watch for mule deer grazing in the meadows along Ariz. 67.

WHAT TO SEE & DO

There are far fewer activities on the North Rim than there are on the South Rim, and not surprisingly there are also fewer people. If Grand Canyon Village was too much of a human zoo for you and not the wilderness experience you had expected, then the North Rim will probably be much more to your liking. Though there is an information desk in the lobby of the Grand Canyon Lodge, there is no visitor center or museum here.

The best spots for viewing the canyon are Bright Angel Point, Point Imperial, and Cape Royal. **Bright Angel Point** is the closest to Grand Canyon Lodge, and from here you can see and hear Roaring Springs, which is 3,600 feet below the rim and is the North Rim's only water source. From Bright Angel Point you can also see Grand Canyon Village on the South Rim. At 8,803 feet, **Point Imperial** is the highest point on either rim of the Grand Canyon. A short section of the Colorado River can be seen far below, and off to the east, the Painted Desert is visible. However, **Cape Royal** is the most spectacular setting on the North Rim. Along the 23-mile road to Cape Royal, there are several scenic overlooks. Across the road from the Walhalla Overlook are the ruins of an Anasazi structure. Just before reaching Cape Royal you'll come to the Angel's Window Overlook, which gives you a breathtaking view of the natural bridge that forms Angel's Window. Once at Cape Royal, you can follow a trail across this natural bridge to a towering promontory overlooking the valley.

If you'd like to see the North Rim on a guided tour, contact **TW Recreational Services** in the lobby of the Grand Canyon Lodge. They offer 3-hour van tours that stop at the overlooks mentioned above. The cost is $11.95 for adults and $6.95 for children 4 to 12.

After simply taking in the views, **hiking along the rim** is the most popular activity. There are quite a few day hikes of varying lengths possible on the North Rim. The shortest is the half-mile paved trail to Bright Angel Point and the longest is the North Kaibab Trail to Roaring Springs and back, which takes six to eight hours.

If you want to see the canyon from a saddle, contact **Canyon Trail Rides** (tel. 602/638-2292). This company offers mule rides varying in length from 1 hour to a full day. Prices range from $10 for an hour ride up to $60 for the all-day trip.

WHERE TO STAY & DINE

GRAND CANYON LODGE, TW Recreational Services, P.O. Box 400, Cedar City, UT 84721. Tel. 801/586-7686. 201 rms and cabins (all with bath).

$ Rates: $45–$60 single or double. AE, CB, DC, DISC, MC, V.
Closed: Nov–Apr.

Perched right on the edge of the canyon beneath the ponderosa pines at the end of the North Rim Parkway, the Grand Canyon Lodge is a classic mountain lodge and is listed on the National Register of Historic Places. The stone-and-log main lodge building has a soaring ceiling and a wall of glass overlooking the canyon. Just off the lobby is a viewing room set up with chairs facing the windows. On either side of this room are flagstone terraces set with more rustic chairs, including rocking chairs, all of which face out toward the canyon. When it gets chilly, fires are built in the huge fireplaces on these terraces.

Guest rooms vary from standard motel rooms to rustic mountain cabins to comfortable modern cottages. My favorites are the little cabins, which though cramped and paneled with dark wood, capture the feeling of a mountain retreat better than any of the other rooms. A few rooms have views of the canyon, but most are tucked back away from the rim.

Dining/Entertainment: A large dining hall with two walls of glass serves straightforward American food and is open daily for all three meals. There is also a cafeteria and snack bar outside the lodges's front entrance. Opposite the cafeteria is a saloon.

Services: Tour desk.

Facilities: Gift shop.

JACOB LAKE INN, Jacob Lake, AZ 86022. Tel. 602/643-7232. 12 rms, 22 cabins (all with bath).

$ Rates: May 15–Nov, $45–$58 single or double. Nov–May 15, $37 single; $38 double. AE, DC, DISC, MC, V.

Located 30 miles north of the entrance to the North Rim, the Jacob Lake Inn consists of motel rooms and rustic cabins. The motel rooms are quite a bit nicer than the cabins, which have old shag carpets and cramped bathrooms with showers only. However, if you're looking for a rustic mountain experience, the slab-board cabins may be just what you want. This lodge stays open in winter and is a base for cross-country skiers and snowmobilers.

Dining/Entertainment: Just off the lobby is a coffee shop complete with stools at the counter. Adjacent to this is a more formal dining room. A bakery counter sells fudge and cookies, and the general store sells snacks.

Facilities: Gift shop, gas station, tennis court, playground.

KAIBAB LODGE, P.O. Box 2997, Flagstaff, AZ 86003. Tel. 602/526-0924, or toll free 800/525-0924. 26 rms (all with bath).

$ Rates: $45–$60 single or double. MC, V.

Located 5 miles north of the entrance to the Grand Canyon's North Rim, the Kaibab Lodge was built around 1926 as a cattle ranch and is situated on the edge of a large meadow where deer can be seen grazing. Rooms are in small rustic cabins set back in the pines from the main lodge building. Nights here are cool even in summer and a favorite pastime of guests is to sit by the fireplace in the lobby, where there is also a TV lounge.

Starting in December 1992, the lodge will stay open year round, although the highway from Jacob Lake will not be open. The lodge will operate special vehicles to bring cross-country skiers down over the snow-covered road. This remote setting is ideal for cross-country skiing and makes a very quiet retreat.

Dining/Entertainment: The lodge's small dining room is open daily for three meals, and the kitchen will prepare you a box lunch for day-long outings.

Services: Tour desk, hiking-equipment rentals, mountain-bike rentals.

Facilities: Gift shop, whirlpool bath.

CAMPGROUNDS

Located just north of Grand Canyon Lodge, the **North Rim Campground,** with 82 sites and no hookups for RVs, is the only campground at the North Rim. Reservations can be made by calling Ticketron (tel. toll free 800/452-1111). The fee is $10 per site per night.

There are two campgrounds outside the park in the Kaibab National Forest. These are **DeMotte Park Campground,** which is the closest to the park entrance and has only 25 sites. The fee is $6 per vehicle per night. **Jacob Lake Campground** is 30 miles north of the park entrance. It has 50 sites, half of which are available by reservation by calling Mistix (tel. toll free 800/283-CAMP). The fee is $6 per vehicle per night with a $2 reservation fee.

The **Jacob Lake R.V. Park** is a privately owned campground in the crossroads of Jacob Lake, 30 miles north of the park entrance. This campground has 80 RV sites and 50 tent sites. You can make a reservation by calling 602/643-7804, or 801/628-8851 in winter. You can also camp anywhere in the Kaibab National Forest. So, if you can't find a site in a campground, simply pull off the highway within the national forest and park your RV or pitch your tent.

5. HAVASU CANYON

40 miles NW of Grand Canyon Village, 70 miles N of Ariz. 66,
155 miles NW of Flagstaff, 115 miles NE of Kingman

GETTING THERE **By Car** It isn't possible to reach Supai village or Havasu Canyon by car. The nearest road ends 8 miles from Supai at Hualapai Hilltop. This is the trailhead for the trail into the canyon and is at the end of Indian Route 18, which runs north from Ariz. 66. The turn-off is 6 miles east of Peach Springs and 21 miles west of Seligman. Many Arizona maps show an unpaved road between U.S. 180 and Hualapai Hilltop, but this road is not maintained on a regular basis and is only passable to four-wheel-drive vehicles *when* it is clear of fallen logs.

By Helicopter The easiest and fastest (and by far the most expensive) way to reach Havasu Canyon is by helicopter from the Grand Canyon Airport in Tusayan. Flights are operated by **Grand Canyon Helicopters,** P.O. Box 455, Grand Canyon, AZ 86023 (tel. 602/638-2419, or toll free 800/528-2418 outside Arizona). The round-trip airfare is $300 from May to October, $280 the rest of the year. This company also offers package tours to Havasu Canyon.

By Horse The next easiest way to get to Havasu Canyon is by horse. Both you and your luggage can ride from Hualapai Hilltop, the trailhead for Supai and Havasu Canyon. Pack and saddle horses can be rented from the **Havasupai Tourist Enterprise,** Supai, AZ 86435 (tel. 602/448-2121). Rates are $90 from Hualapai Hilltop to the campground, $70 from Hualapai Hilltop to Supai village, and $35 from Supai village to the campground. One-way rates are also available—many people who hike in decide that it's worth the money to ride out, or at least have their backpack packed out. Be sure to confirm your horse reservation a day before driving to Hualapai Hilltop. Sometimes no horses are available and it's a long drive back to the nearest town.

On Foot The cheapest, slowest, and most difficult way to reach Havasu Canyon is on foot. Start early to avoid the heat of the day. The hike is beautiful; although, it's 10 miles to the campground. The steepest part of the trail is the first mile or so from Hualapai Hilltop. After this section it's relatively flat.

ESSENTIALS There is a $12-per-person **entry fee** to Havasu Canyon from April to October, $8 the rest of the year. Everyone is required to **register** at the Tourist Office across from the sports field as you enter the village of Supai. Because it's a long walk in to the campground, be sure you have a confirmed reservation before setting out from Hualapai Hilltop. It's good to make **reservations** as far in advance as possible, especially for holiday weekends. The **telephone area code** is 602.

Imagine hiking for hours through a dusty brown landscape of rocks and cacti. The sun overhead is blistering and bright. The air is hot and dry. This is desert, canyon country. Rock walls rise up higher and higher as you continue your descent through a mazelike canyon. Eventually the narrow canyon opens up into a wide plain shaded by cottonwood trees—a sure sign of water—and within a few minutes you hear the sound of a babbling stream. The water, when you finally reach it, is cool and crystal clear, a pleasant surprise. Following the stream, you pass through a dusty village of modern homes. Every yard seems to be a corral for horses, not surprising in a village 8 miles beyond the last road. You pass through the village, still following the stream. As the trail descends again, you spot the first waterfall.

The previously crystal-clear water is now brilliant turquoise blue at the foot of the waterfall. The sandstone walls look redder than before. No, you aren't having a heat-induced hallucination—the water really is turquoise, and it fills terraces of travertine to form deep pools of cool water at the base of three large waterfalls. Together these three waterfalls form what many claim is the most beautiful spot in the entire Grand Canyon.

This is Havasu Canyon, the canyon of the Havasupai tribe, whose name means "people of the blue-green waters," and who for centuries have called this idyllic desert oasis home.

WHAT TO SEE & DO

The waterfalls are the main attraction here and most people are content to sun themselves on the sand, go for dips in the cool waters, and gaze for hours at the turquoise waterfalls. When you tire of these pursuits, you can go for a **hike** up the small side canyon to the east of Havasu Falls. Another trail leads along the west rim of Havasu Canyon and can be reached by carefully climbing up a steep rocky area near the village cemetery. If the trail has been restored down to the base of Mooney Falls by the time you visit, there is a trail that leads all the way down to the Colorado River, though this is an overnight hike.

In Supai village is a small **museum** dedicated to the culture of the Havasupai people. Its exhibits and old photos will give you an idea of how little the lives of these people have changed over the years.

WHERE TO STAY & DINE
IN HAVASU CANYON

HAVASUPAI LODGE, General Delivery, Supai, AZ 86435. Tel. 602/448-2111. Telex 165-714. 24 rms (all with bath). A/C
$ Rates: Mar–Nov, $45 single; $50 double. Dec–Feb, $30 single; $35 double. No credit cards.
Located in Supai village just past the school, this modern lodge is, aside from the campground, the only accommodation in the canyon. The two-story building features standard motel-style rooms that are lacking only televisions and telephones, neither of which are in demand at this isolated retreat. People come to Havasu Canyon to get away from it all, and the Havasupai Lodge is happy to oblige. The only drawback of this comfortable lodge is that it's 2 miles from Havasu Falls and 3 miles from Mooney Falls.

Dining/Entertainment: The Havasupai Café, across from the general store, serves breakfast, lunch, and dinner. It's a very casual place, and the prices are high because all ingredients are brought in by horse.

HAVASU CAMPGROUND, Havasupai Tourist Enterprise, Supai, AZ 86435. Tel. 602/448-2161. 400 sites.
$ Rates: Mar–Nov, $9 per person per night; Dec–Feb, $7 per person per night.
The campground is located 2 miles below Supai village between Havasu Falls and Mooney Falls. Campsites are mostly in the shade of cottonwood trees on either side of Havasu Creek. Picnic tables are provided, but no firewood is available at the campground. Cutting of any trees or shrubs is prohibited, so be sure to bring a campstove with you. There is spring water available, and though it's considered safe to drink, I advise treating it first.

NEAR HUALAPAI HILLTOP

GRAND CANYON CAVERNS INN AND CAMPGROUND, P.O. Box 180, Peach Springs, AZ 86434. Tel. 602/422-3223 or 422-3224. 48 rms (all with bath). A/C TV TEL
$ Rates: $16–$32 single; $20–$48 double; campground $10 per site per night. MC, V (no credit cards at campground).
If you're planning to hike or ride into Havasu Canyon, you'll need to be at Hualapai Hilltop as early in the morning as possible, and because it's a 3- to 4-hour drive to Hualapai Hilltop from Flagstaff, you might want to consider staying here—the only place to stay for miles around. As the name implies, this motel is built on the site of the Grand Canyon Caverns, which are open to the public.

Dining/Entertainment: There is a casual restaurant and cocktail lounge.
Facilities: Games room, gift shop, general store with camping supplies and food.

1. SEDONA & OAK CREEK CANYON

• **WHAT'S SPECIAL ABOUT CENTRAL ARIZONA**

2. PRESCOTT

3. WICKENBURG

No other region of Arizona packs so much into so little space. Encompassing the Mogollon Rim, the fertile Verde River valley, Oak Creek Canyon, the red rocks of Sedona, the pine-forested mountains around Prescott, and the desert in the Wickenburg area, central Arizona has played an important role in Arizona history for more than 1,500 years. Ancient Hohokam and Sinagua peoples, as well as early settlers, were drawn to the fertile valley of the Verde River. Though these tribes had disappeared by the time the first white settlers arrived in the area, hostile Apache and Yavapai tribes inhabited the area, so the U.S. Army established Fort Verde to protect the settlers.

When Arizona became a U.S. territory in 1863, Prescott was chosen as its capital because of its central location. Though Prescott would later lose that title to Tucson and eventually to Phoenix, for part of the late 19th century it was the most important city in Arizona, evident in the stately Victorian homes and an imposing county courthouse.

Settlers were lured to this region not only by fertile land, but by the mineral wealth that lay hidden in the ground. Miners founded a number of communities in central Arizona, among them Jerome. When the mines shut down, Jerome was almost completely abandoned, but artists and craftspeople moved in to reclaim and revitalize the old mining town.

Artists also found their way to Sedona, but only after the movie industry had hit upon Sedona's red-rock country as a striking backdrop for exciting westerns. Situated at the mouth of Oak Creek Canyon, one of Arizona's major recreational areas, Sedona now attracts artists, retirees, and New Agers (who come to visit Sedona's mystical vortexes).

Once called the dude ranch capital of the world, Wickenburg clings to its western roots and has restored much of its downtown to its 1880s appearance. There are even a few dude ranches—now called guest ranches—still in business.

---

1. SEDONA & OAK CREEK CANYON

27 miles S of Flagstaff, 106 miles S of the Grand Canyon,
28 miles E of Jerome, 116 miles N of Phoenix, 56 miles NE of Prescott

GETTING THERE By Plane Air Sedona (tel. 602/282-7935, or toll free 800/535-4448) has five flights daily between Phoenix and Sedona Airport (tel. 602/282-4409). The fare is $48 one way, $90 round-trip.

By Train There is **Amtrak** (tel. toll free 800/872-7245) passenger service to Flagstaff (see "Flagstaff") in Chapter 6 for details).

By Bus Sedona Phoenix Shuttle (tel. 602/282-2066) operates three trips daily between the Phoenix Skyharbor Airport and Sedona.

By Car Sedona is on Ariz. 179 at the mouth of scenic Oak Creek Canyon. From

✓ WHAT'S SPECIAL ABOUT CENTRAL ARIZONA

Native American Ruins
- ☐ Sinagua cliff dwellings at Montezuma Castle National Monument.
- ☐ A Sinagua pueblo atop a hill at Tuzigoot National Monument.

Great Towns/Villages
- ☐ Jerome, almost a ghost town until discovered by artists and craftspeople; in a spectacular setting on a steep mountainside
- ☐ Prescott, the former territorial capital of Arizona.

Shopping
- ☐ Jerome, with artists' and craftspeoples' studios and shops.
- ☐ Sedona, one of Arizona's arts communities, with dozens of art galleries.

Natural Spectacles
- ☐ The red rocks surrounding Sedona.
- ☐ Oak Creek Canyon, a small but beautiful canyon with a year-round stream.

Activities
- ☐ The Verde Valley Railroad, a scenic train ride.
- ☐ Searching out vortexes around Sedona.

TV & Film Locations
- ☐ Sedona's red-rock country.

Phoenix, take I-17 to Ariz. 179 north. From Flagstaff, head south on I-17 until you see the turnoff for Ariz. 179 and Sedona. U.S. 89A connects Sedona with Prescott.

ESSENTIALS   For more information in Sedona, contact the **Sedona–Oak Creek Chamber of Commerce,** P.O. Box 478, Sedona, AZ 86336 (tel. 602/282-7722), which also operates a **Tourist Information Center** on the corner of U.S. 89A and Forest Road near uptown Sedona. For a taxi, call **Bob's Taxi of Sedona** (tel. 282-1234). There is also a **free shopping shuttle** that operates Monday through Saturday between 10am and 5pm, making stops at Cedars, L'Auberge, The Orchards, Arroyo Roble, uptown, the Sedona Chamber of Commerce, Los Abrigados, and Hillside. The **telephone area code** is 602.

Though the first settler didn't arrive in the Sedona area until 1877 and the city wasn't incorporated until 1987, it has become one of the most popular destinations in Arizona. The city was named for Sedona Schnebly, one of the first residents of the area, because her name was short enough to fit on a postal cancellation stamp and the postmaster didn't like any of the other names that were suggested for the new town at the mouth of Oak Creek Canyon. Hollywood producers of western movies were among the first people to discover the beauty of Sedona. Next came artists lured by the red-rock landscapes and desert light. More recently the spectacular views and mild climate were discovered by retirees, and when a New Age channeler discovered the Sedona vortexes, a whole new group of people descended on the town. This unusual history has created an ideal destination for lovers of the arts as well as lovers of nature. However, an unfortunate side effect of Sedona's popularity has been unchecked suburban sprawl, which detracts from the beauty of the red rocks.

The waters of Oak Creek Canyon that first lured settlers, and native peoples before them, still lure visitors to Sedona. Two of Arizona's finest swimming holes are located on Oak Creek only a few miles from Sedona. One of these swimming holes has even been made into a state park.

Sedona is also a good base for exploring much of central Arizona. Within easy driving distance are several ancient Native American ruins, including an impressive cliff dwelling. If you don't get your fill of arts and crafts in Sedona, Jerome, another smaller arts community, is an easy day excursion.

WHAT TO SEE & DO
RED ROCKS & VORTEXES

Rugged cliffs, needlelike pinnacles, and isolated buttes rise up from the green forest floor at the mouth of Oak Creek Canyon in Sedona. Layers of different-colored stone deposited during various prehistoric ages, form bands through the cliffs above, the most prominent of these bands being the layer of red sandstone called the Schnebly Hill Formation. Because this rosy sandstone predominates around Sedona, the region has come to be known as the red-rock country. Each evening at sunset the red rocks put on a sunset light show that is reason enough for visiting Sedona.

Page Bryant, a member of the New Age movement, determined through channeling that there were four vortexes around Sedona. A vortex is a site where the earth's unseen lines of power intersect to form a particularly powerful energy field. Scientists may scoff, but Sedona's vortexes have become so well known that the chamber of commerce visitor center has several handouts to explain them and guide you to them. (Many of the most spectacular geological features of the Sedona landscape also happen to be vortexes.)

Days can be spent exploring the red-rock country in any of half a dozen different modes of transport. There are Jeep tours, vortex tours, hot-air balloon flights, horseback rides, mountain-bike trails, hiking trails, and scenic drives suitable for standard cars. (See "Organized Tours" and "Recreation," below.) For a relatively easy and yet spectacular red-rock viewing excursion, head south out of Sedona on Ariz. 179, turn left after you cross the bridge over Oak Creek and head up the unpaved Schnebly Hill Road. The road climbs up into the hills above town and every turn yields a new and breathtaking view. The road eventually climbs to the top of the Mogollon Rim. At the rim is the **Schnebly Hill overlook,** which offers the very best view in the area.

Just south of Sedona, on Ariz. 179, you'll see the aptly named **Bell Rock** on the east side of the road. There is a parking area at the foot of Bell Rock and trails leading up to the top. Bell Rock is one of the vortexes. It is said to contain masculine or electric energy that boosts emotional and spiritual energy. From Bell Rock, you can see **Cathedral Rock** to the west. This rock, besides being the most photographed in Sedona, is also a vortex site that is said to contain feminine or magnetic energy, which is good for facilitating relaxation. Adjacent to Bell Rock is **Courthouse Rock.** Not far from Bell Rock and visible from Chapel Road, are **Eagle Head Rock** (from the front door of the Chapel of the Holy Cross—see "Other Attractions," below—look three-quarters of the way up the mountain to see the eagle's head), the **Twin Nuns** (two pinnacles standing side by side), and **Mother and Child Rock** to the left of the Twin Nuns.

If you head west out of Sedona on U.S. 89A and turn left onto Airport Road, you'll come to the **Airport Mesa** vortex, which consists of three small hills commanding an unobstructed panorama of Sedona and the red rocks. The Airport Mesa vortex is said to be an electric or masculine energy vortex, which means that it will give you a spiritual, emotional, and physical uplift.

One of the most beautiful areas around Sedona is **Boynton Canyon,** which also happens to be the most powerful vortex. Boynton Canyon vortex is considered an electromagnetic energy site, which means it has a balance of masculine and feminine energy. To reach this spectacular canyon, drive west out of Sedona on U.S. 89A, turn right on Dry Creek Road, take a left at the T intersection, and at the next T intersection take a right. On the way to Boynton Canyon, look north from U.S. 89A and you'll see **Coffee Pot Rock,** which is also known as Rooster Rock, rising 1,800 feet above Sedona. Three pinnacles, known as the **Three Golden Chiefs** by the Yavapai tribe, stand beside Coffee Pot Rock. As you drive up Dry Creek Road, you will see on your right **Capitol Butte,** which resembles the U.S. Capitol building. Just outside the gates of the Enchantment Resort is a parking area for the Boynton Canyon trailhead. From the parking area the trail leads 3 miles up into the canyon. The ancient

Sinagua peoples once lived in Boynton Canyon, and the ruins of their homes can still be seen.

On the south of U.S. 89A and just beyond the turnoff for Boynton Canyon is Lower Red Rock Loop Road. Near the end of this road and on the banks of Oak Creek, you will find **Red Rocks State Park** (tel. 282-6907). The views here take in many of the rocks listed above, and you have the additional bonus of being right on the creek. The park admission is $3 per vehicle.

OAK CREEK CANYON

The Mogollon Rim is a 2,000-foot escarpment cutting diagonally across central Arizona and on into New Mexico. At the top of the Mogollon Rim are the ponderosa pine forests of the high mountains, while at the bottom the lowland deserts begin. Among the canyons cutting down from the rim, Oak Creek Canyon is the best known. Ariz. 179 runs down through the canyon from Flagstaff to Sedona, winding its way down from the rim and paralleling Oak Creek. Along the way there are overlooks, parks, picnic areas, campgrounds, cabin resorts, and small inns.

If you have a choice of how to first see Oak Creek Canyon, come at it from the north. In fact if you're coming from Phoenix and have the time, it's worth driving the extra 50 miles up I-17 to come down Ariz. 179 from the north. Your first stop after traveling south from Flagstaff will be the Oak Creek Canyon overlook, which provides a view far down the valley to Sedona and beyond. The overlook is at the edge of the Mogollon Rim with the road suddenly dropping in tight switchbacks after you leave the overlook. You may notice that one rim of the canyon is lower than the other. This is because Oak Creek Canyon is on a geologic fault line with one side of the canyon moving in a different direction from the other.

Though the top of the Mogollon Rim is a ponderosa pine forest and the bottom is a desert, Oak Creek Canyon supports a forest of sycamores and other deciduous trees. In the autumn the canyon is ablaze with red and yellow leaves. Ariz 179 is considered the most beautiful road in Arizona, and there is no better time to drive it than from late September to mid-October, when the leaves are usually changing.

At the foot of the switchbacks that descend from the overlook, you'll see the **Sterling Springs Fish Hatchery,** which supplies the trout for local streams, including Oak Creek, which is well known for its good fishing. A little ways beyond the fish hatchery, you will come to **Cave Spring Campground** where there is a self-guided nature walk that describes the riparian environment of Oak Creek. A riparian area is one along a body of water. Different plants live in this moist environment, and the plants and water often attract a wide variety of animals. Riparian habitats are especially crucial in deserts.

The most popular spot in all of Oak Creek Canyon is **Slide Rock State Park** (tel. 282-3034). Located 7 miles north of Sedona on the site of an old homestead, this park preserves a natural water slide. On hot summer days the park is jammed with people splashing in the water and sliding over the algae-covered sandstone bottom of Oak Creek. Sunbathing and fishing are other popular pastimes here at the park. Admission to the park is $3 per vehicle. There's another popular swimming area at Grasshopper Point, several miles closer to Sedona.

Less than 3 miles south of Slide Rock State Park, you'll pass **Indian Gardens.** This area was once cultivated by local tribes. In 1876 John James Thompson settled here, becoming the first white resident of Oak Creek Canyon.

Within Oak Creek Canyon several hikes of different lengths are possible. By far the most popular is the 6-mile round-trip hike up the West Fork of Oak Creek. This is a classic canyon-country hike with steep canyon walls rising up from the creek. At some points the canyon is no more than 20 feet wide with walls rising up more than 200 feet. You'll see cars parked on both sides of the road at the trailhead, but there are also a couple of parking areas. Stop by the Sedona–Oak Creek Chamber of Commerce to pick up a free map listing hikes in the area. The Coconino National Forest ranger station (tel. 282-4119) on Brewer Road, just west of the intersection of U.S. 89A and Ariz. 179, is also a good source of hiking information.

OTHER ATTRACTIONS

Sedona's most notable architectural landmark is the **Chapel of the Holy Cross,** a small church built right into the red rock on the south side of town. If you're driving up from Phoenix, you can't miss the chapel. It sits high above the road just off Ariz. 179. With its very contemporary styling, the chapel is considered one of the most architecturally important modern churches in the country. Marguerite Brunswig Staude, a devout Catholic painter, sculptor, and designer, had the inspiration for the chapel in 1932, but it wasn't until 1957 that her dream was finally realized here in Sedona. The chapel's design is dominated by a simple cross forming the wall that faces the street. The cross and the chapel seem to grow directly from the rock. The stark beauty of the church leaves the natural beauty of the red rock to speak for itself. The chapel is open daily.

Another Sedona attraction is the **Sedona Museum of Art,** at the corner of Apple Road and Jordan Road (tel. 282-7021). The museum houses a small collection of fine art and contemporary works by local artists and artists who have been inspired by Sedona. The **Sedona Arts Center,** U.S. 89A at Art Barn Road (tel. 282-3809), near the north end of town, serves both as a gallery for artworks by local and regional artists and as a theater for plays and music performances. In April the center holds its annual Fine Arts and Crafts Exhibition.

ORGANIZED TOURS

Traditional tours are offered by **Susie's Trolley** (tel. 602/284-0549), which operates 1-hour tours to introduce visitors to what Sedona has to offer ($8 for adults and $2.50 for children) and **Sedona Tours** (tel. 602/282-2800, or toll free 800/658-5825), which offers a tour of Sedona's main attractions and some lesser-known spots, as well as all-day trips to the Grand Canyon, Navajoland, and the Hopi mesas.

The red-rock country surrounding Sedona is the city's greatest natural attraction, and for more than 30 years **Pink Jeep Tours,** P.O. Box 1447, Sedona, AZ 86336 (tel. 282-5000, or toll free 800/8-SEDONA), has been sharing it with the curious. There is no better way to explore the red-rock country than in a four-wheel-drive vehicle. This company heads deep into the Coconino National Forest on four different tours ranging in length from 1 hour ($15) to 2½ hours ($38). You can take a vortex tour, travel the Sedona backcountry, visit an unexcavated archeological site, or simply visit the best views in the area. **Sedona Red Rock Jeep Tours,** 260 North U.S. 89A (P.O. Box 10305), Sedona, AZ 86336 (tel. 282-6826, or toll free 800/848-7728), offers similar tours at comparable prices.

In recent years Sedona has become one of the world's centers for the New Age movement and attracts ever-growing numbers of people who come to experience the power vortexes of the surrounding red-rock country. Several companies now offer vortex tours. **Sedona Nature Excursions** (tel. 602/282-6735), **Dorian Tours** (tel. 602/282-4562), and **Sacred Earth Tours,** 260 North U.S. 89A (tel. 602/282-6826) and 251 Ariz. 179 (tel. 602/282-2026, or toll free 800/848-7728) all offer vortex tours that combine aspects of Native American and New Age beliefs. Tours last 3 hours and cost $45 per person.

RECREATION

Red Rock Balloon Adventures (tel. 602/284-0040) and **Northern Light Balloon Adventures** (tel. 602/282-2274) offer peaceful hot-air-balloon rides over the canyons and sculpted buttes. **Airstar Helicopters** (tel. 602/638-2622, or toll free 800/962-3869), **Action Helicopter of Arizona** (tel. 602/282-7884), and **Arizona Helicopter Adventures** (tel. 602/282-0904, or toll free 800/282-5141) all offer short flights to different parts of this colorful region.

The **Sedona Golf Resort** (tel. 284-9355) is located south of town on Ariz. 179. The views of the red rocks are magnificent. Sedona's other 18-hole course is the **Oak**

Creek Country Club, 690 Bell Rock Boulevard (tel. 284-1660), which is also south of town and offers equally stunning views from the course.

Kachina Stables, Lower Red Rock Loop Road (tel. 602/282-7252), offers guided horseback trail rides. Prices range from $17.50 for a 1-hour ride to $85 for an all-day ride. There are also breakfast, full moon, lunch, sunset, and Indian sacred pipe ceremony rides. Lower Red Rock Trail is west of Sedona on U.S. 89A. **Blazing Trails,** just before milepost 368 on U.S. 89A (tel. 602/282-1672), charges $20 for a 1-hour ride and $35 for a 2-hour ride.

If your images of Sedona stem from old western movies, you might want to go for a ride in the **Sedona Surrey** (tel. 282-5467), which even has a fringe on top. Rides start at $5 and leave either from Tlaquepaque shopping center or from the Hitching Post Restaurant in uptown Sedona.

You can rent a mountain bike from **Canyon Country Mountain Bikes,** 245 North U.S. 89A (tel. 602/282-6985), or **Sedona Mountain Bike Rental** (tel. 602/282-2164) which offers free pickup and delivery. Rates are $20 for a full day and $15 for a half day.

SPECIAL & FREE EVENTS

With its cosmopolitan population, Sedona is host to a wide variety of annual events. You can find out what will be happening during your visit by contacting the **City of Sedona City Council Arts & Culture Commission,** City Hall Annex, Park Place, 2855 West U.S. 89A, Sedona, AZ 86336 (tel. 602/282-9738). Each year in May, Hopi artists gather for the **Hopi-Tu Tsootsvolla** (tel. 282-1117 or 282-2800), which takes place in uptown Sedona and includes Hopi art, dances, food, and cultural exhibits. One of the year's big events is the **Sedona Chamber Music Festival,** held each June; contact the Sedona Chamber Music Society, P.O. Box 153, Sedona, AZ 86336 (tel. 602/282-7044 or 282-9351), for details. **Jazz on the Rocks,** held each year in September, usually features nationally known jazz musicians who perform at the JOR Amphitheater at the Verde Valley School. For more information contact Sedona Jazz on the Rocks, Inc., P.O. Box 889, Sedona, AZ 86336. In mid-December each year Sedona celebrates the **Festival of Lights** by lighting thousands of luminárias (paper bags partially filled with sand and containing a single candle each) beginning at sunset. Street musicians, Christmas-tree lightings, and late-night shopping are all part of the festival.

WHERE TO STAY

In the past few years Sedona has become one of Arizona's major resort destinations. There are several full-service resorts, as well as hotels, motels, and campgrounds in the area. If you're having trouble finding a place to stay, you can try calling the **Accommodations Bureau of Sedona,** P.O. Box 2435, Sedona, AZ 86336 (tel. 602/282-2773, or toll free 800/845-6773). This free reservation service and general information office will do what it can to find you a place to stay.

VERY EXPENSIVE

ENCHANTMENT RESORT, Boynton Canyon, 525 Boynton Canyon Rd., Sedona, AZ 86336. Tel. 602/282-2900, or toll free 800/826-4180. 160 rms and suites. A/C TV TEL

$ Rates: $155–$210 single or double; $220–$330 one-bedroom suite; $410–$560 two-bedroom suite. AE, DC, MC, V.

Located at the mouth of Boynton Canyon, a rugged red-rock hideaway a few miles west of Sedona, the Enchantment Resort more than lives up to its name. The setting is the most spectacular of all the Sedona resorts and the amenities will keep you busy all day if you're an active type. The pink-stucco, pueblo-style architecture of the hotel blends in perfectly with the remote canyon landscape giving the resort a timeless southwestern feeling. If you're seeking peace and tranquility and an escape from the stresses of a harried and hurried life-style, I can send you to no better place to rejuvenate your body and soul.

The individual *casitas* (little houses) of this resort can all be booked as two-bedroom suites, as one-bedroom suites, or simply as single rooms. If you can afford it, it's worth booking a suite just so you can enjoy the living room, which is the best room in the casita. The living room features high rough-hewn beamed ceilings, a pueblo-style curved corner fireplace, built in shelves that hold sculptures, Native American baskets, and pottery. The large patio includes a built-in barbecue and provides dramatic views of the canyon. A skylight brightens the large bathroom and there's even a shelf along one side of the large bathtub so you have someplace to set your champagne and glasses.

Dining/Entertainment: The resort's restaurant (see "Where to Dine," below) and lounge offer terrace tables as well as indoor dining and drinking. At lunch there's a casual salad bar buffet, while at dinner the dining room is dressed up with pink linens for a more formal atmosphere. The menu features innovative American cuisine and changes daily.

Services: Room service, massages, tennis lessons, fitness programs, aerobics instruction, personal training, guided hikes, stress-management programs, aroma-therapy, complimentary morning juice and newspaper, airport shuttle.

Facilities: Four swimming pools, 12 tennis courts, three croquet courts, whirlpool baths, fitness center, hiking trails, pitch-and-putt golf.

L'AUBERGE DE SEDONA, 301 Little Lane (P.O. Box B), Sedona, AZ 86336. Tel. 602/282-1661, or toll free 800/272-6777, 800/331-2820 in Arizona. 96 rms and suites. A/C TV TEL

$ Rates: Mar–Nov, $105–$155 double in the Orchards or the Lodge, $275–$375 double (including half board) in cottages; Dec–Feb (excluding hols, when rates are higher), $95–$145 double in the Orchards or the Lodge, $250- $350 double (including half board) in cottages. AE, DC, MC, V.

Located in the heart of uptown Sedona, this hotel is the only lodging I know of that has its own private cable car. The car acts as an elevator between the Orchards at the top of the hill and the lodge and cottages on the valley floor. Between these two locations, you have a range of accommodation options. If you want spectacular views and stunning sunsets, opt for the Orchards. If you want romantic seclusion amid shady sycamores, opt for one of the cottages on the banks of Oak Creek. If you want to enjoy a bit of European elegance in Arizona, opt for the lodge. With two restaurants and only a pool and whirlpool bath for activities, this resort definitely aims for the less active guest who prefers fine dining to working up a sweat.

The roomy cottages are decorated in the style of Provence, France, with canopy beds and fireplaces. If you choose to stay in a cottage, a five-course gourmet dinner and full breakfast at L'Auberge Restaurant are both included in the price. Other rooms, though not as spacious, are equally attractive in their decor. Antiqued headboards, custom-designed fabrics, and country French furniture add to the Old World charm of this hotel.

Dining/Entertainment: L'Auberge Restaurant (see "Where to Dine," below) is one of Sedona's finest and certainly its most expensive. Pink linens, bone china, and burgundy decor set the tone for the five-course French dinners that are served. The Orchards Grill, a much more casual restaurant, serves equally fine meals. The menu is strictly nouvelle American.

Services: Room service.

Facilities: Swimming pool, whirlpool bath, French boutique.

LOS ABRIGADOS, 160 Portal Lane, Sedona, AZ 86336. Tel. 602/282-1777, or toll free 800/521-4141, 800/822-2525 in Arizona. 175 suites. A/C MINIBAR TV TEL

$ Rates: $125–$185 standard single or double, $150–$215 deluxe single or double, $150–$215 view single or double; $195–$235 two-bedroom (single or double). AE, CB, DC, DISC, MC, V.

You can't get any closer to Sedona's famous Tlaquepaque shopping center than this resort. The Spanish colonial architecture of Los Abrigados is a natural extension of

Tlaquepaque and together they create a tiny world apart from the rest of Sedona. Antiqued stucco-and-brick walls, red-tile roofs, and arched colonnades re-create a bit of Old Mexico. There's even a little artificial stream running through the grounds.

Los Abrigados tends to attract an active clientele who like to keep in shape. The extensive exercise facilities offer all the latest equipment, and when you've finished your workout, you can relax with a massage or some time in the sauna.

Open the carved-wood door of your guest room and you'll find a spacious suite complete with a stocked minibar, microwave oven, and table with four chairs. In the bathroom you'll find a hairdryer, lighted mirror, and Neutrogena soap. Many of the suites also have fireplaces and whirlpool tubs. Unfortunately, rooms here do not have views of the red rocks.

Dining/Entertainment: The menu at the Canyon Rose (see "Where to Dine," below) focuses on innovative American cuisine. The Sunday brunch is a culinary extravaganza. The lounge, separated from the restaurant by a curving wall of glass, has a separate menu that includes breakfast, lunch, and evening appetizers, and features dancing to live Top-40 music in the evenings.

Services: Concierge, room service, massages, facials, tour desk.

Facilities: Health spa, tennis courts, exercize course, swimming pool, sauna, whirlpool baths, tanning salon, gift shop.

EXPENSIVE

POCO DIABLO, Ariz. 179 (P.O. Box 1709), Sedona, AZ 86336. Tel. 602/282-7333, or toll free 800/528-4275, 800/352-5710 in Arizona. 110 rms. A/C MINIBAR TV TEL

$ Rates: Mar 15–Oct, $105–$155 single or double; $145–$320 suite. Nov–Mar 14, $95–$145 single or double; $135–$330 suite. Lower rates Mon–Fri. AE, MC, V.

This complete golf and tennis resort is located on the south side of Sedona not far from the Tlaquepaque shopping center. Oak Creek runs right through the 25-acre resort, while tiny artificial streams meander through the grounds to quiet ponds. The green fairways of the golf course provide a striking contrast to the red rocks and blue skies.

The small lobby exudes Arizona sophistication with Frank Lloyd Wright–inspired furnishings, fresh flowers on tile-top tables, contemporary southwestern art, and Native American baskets and pottery. About half the guest rooms feature views of the surrounding canyon walls, and all are decorated in pale blue-green, pink, and plum with contemporary southwestern art and furniture. Bathrooms include two sinks set in a tile counter, a basket of toiletries, and a well-lit mirror.

Dining/Entertainment: Willow's Dining Room has a view of the golf course and red rocks. The menu offers southwestern, Cajun, and continental cuisines. Sunset dinners are a bargain. In Brandy's Lounge you can relax over a drink while enjoying the view, or, after the sun goes down, hit the dance floor.

Services: Room service, valet/laundry service.

Facilities: Two swimming pools, three whirlpool baths, four tennis courts, racquetball courts, nine-hole golf course.

A Bed & Breakfast

GRAHAM'S BED & BREAKFAST INN, 150 Canyon Circle Dr. (P.O. Box 912), Sedona, AZ 86336. Tel. 602/284-1425. 5 rms (all with bath).

$ Rates (including full breakfast): $80–$125 single; $95–$140 double. MC, V.

Located just a few miles south of Sedona in the village of Oak Creek, Bill and Marni Graham's B&B offers views of the red rocks from every room. The contemporary southwestern home features a lush garden complete with swimming pool and spa. You can breakfast beside a crackling fire or on the terrace, depending on the time of year. Each of the five rooms is decorated in a different theme. There is the Heritage Room with its red, white, and blue color scheme and memorabilia of Bill's father. The Southern Room is a tribute to Bill's mother, who was raised in the deep South. The Southwest Room reflects the colors of the Sedona countryside and includes a rustic

Taos bed and whirlpool bath. The Garden Room features wicker furniture and has a good view from the balcony. The largest room is the San Francisco Room with a California king-size bed and a double whirlpool bath.

Services: Afternoon refreshments.

Facilities: Swimming pool, whirlpool bath.

MODERATE

BELL ROCK INN, 6246 Ariz. 179, Sedona, AZ 86336. Tel. 602/282-4161. 47 rms, 5 suites (all with bath) A/C TV TEL

$ Rates: $47–$82 single; $69–$91 double; $86–$96 suite. Golf packages available. AE, MC, V.

You'll find this comfortable hotel not far from Bell Rock in the village of Oak Creek, a few miles south of Sedona. A southwestern motif prevails throughout the hotel from the rustic furniture in the small lobby to the pueblo-style architecture. The pink stucco buildings and shaded ramada-style walkways leave no doubt that you're in the Southwest. Most guest rooms feature rough-hewn plank walls, beamed ceilings, and contemporary southwestern art.

The restaurant features southwestern and American meals, with views of the red rocks. There is live Top-40 music in the lounge. The hotel also offers welcoming champagne, weekly cookouts in summer, golf privileges, a swimming pool, whirlpool bath, and two tennis courts.

BEST WESTERN ARROYO ROBLE HOTEL, 400 N. U.S. 89A (P.O. Box NN), Sedona, AZ 86336. Tel. 602/282-4001, or toll free 800/528-1234, 800/252-4483 in Arizona. 53 rms, 9 suites, 7 villas (all with bath). A/C TV TEL

$ Rates: Feb 15–Nov, $85–$90 single or double; $105–$145 suite; $225 villa. Dec–Feb 14, $60–$75 single or double; $95–$145 suite; $225 villa. Senior-citizen discount. AE, CB, DC, DISC, MC, V.

You can't miss this large hotel crowding up against narrow U.S. 89A in uptown Sedona. The five-story hotel perches above Oak Creek with views of the red-rock walls across the canyon and provides all the amenities of a much more expensive resort. In the high-ceilinged lobby an onyx fireplace is the focus of attention. Rooms all come with king- or queen-size beds and a private balcony or patio. Be sure to request a room with a view. Closets are large, though the bathrooms are standard size. Surrounded by Oak Creek Canyon's shady sycamores, the new villas are below the main hotel building. The two-bedroom vacation homes have two fireplaces, 2½ bathrooms, two TVs, a stereo, VCR, and two private patios or balconies. Moderate rates and extensive services and facilities make this an ideal choice for families.

The hotel doesn't have its own restaurant, but there are plenty within walking distance.

QUALITY INN KING'S RANSOM, Ariz. 179 (P.O. Box 180), Sedona, AZ 86336. Tel. 602/282-7151, or toll free 800/228-5151 or 800/221-2222. 65 rms, 1 suite (all with bath). A/C TV TEL

$ Rates: $56–$74 single; $66–$89 double; $135–$150 suite. Lower rates available in winter. AE, CB, DC, DISC, MC, V.

Situated on the outskirts of Sedona on Ariz. 179, the King's Ransom doesn't have the breathtaking views of some of Sedona's other hotels, but it does have a peaceful courtyard garden with a pool and elegant Mediterranean-style covered spa. Some of the guest rooms are a bit cramped but others have plenty of space. Decor is done in tasteful dusty rose and gray. Bathrooms have plenty of counter space and an assortment of toiletries, but have showers only.

A casual dining room and terrace on the second floor offers an American menu at lunch and Middle Eastern cuisine at dinner. There's a tiny bar off to one side of the main dining room.

BUDGET

MATTERHORN MOTOR LODGE, 230 Apple Ave., Sedona, AZ 86336. Tel. 602/282-7176. 21 rms (all with bath). A/C TV TEL

$ Rates: Mar–Nov, $58–$64 single or double; Dec–Feb, $42–$44 single or double. AE, DISC, MC, V.

In the heart of the uptown shopping district, the Matterhorn is convenient to restaurants and shopping and all rooms have excellent views of the red-rock cliffs across the mouth of Oak Creek Canyon. The motel is right on busy U.S. 89A, but if you lie in bed and keep your eyes on the rocks, you won't notice the traffic below you. Guest rooms have older carpets and furnishings and tiny bathrooms. There's also a swimming pool and whirlpool bath.

SEDONA MOTEL, Ariz. 179 (P.O. Box 1450), Sedona, AZ 86336. Tel. 602/282-7187. 13 rms (all with bath). A/C TV TEL
$ Rates: $39–$54 single; $39–$69 double. AE, DISC, MC, V.

Located almost at the intersection of Ariz. 179 and U.S. 89A, the Sedona Motel looks like any other older motel from the outside, but once you check in, you'll find a few surprises. First and foremost is the view across the parking lot. You can pay three times as much in Sedona and not have this good a view. Windows are double-paned so the rooms stay cool and quiet. The next surprise is in the bathrooms, where contemporary fixtures give the rooms a very modern feel. Unfortunately the interior decor is not as attractive as the view out the window.

WHERE TO DINE
VERY EXPENSIVE

L'AUBERGE, in L'Auberge de Sedona, 301 Little Lane. Tel. 282-7131 or 282-1661.
Cuisine: FRENCH. **Reservations:** Required.
$ Prices: Fixed-price five-course dinner $45. AE, CB, DC, MC, V.
Open: Breakfast Mon–Sat 7:30–11am; lunch Mon–Sat noon–2pm; dinner Mon–Sat seatings at 5:45–6:15pm and 8:30–9pm.

L'Auberge—the name conjures up an image of a French country inn, and though this L'Auberge happens to be in the red-rock country of central Arizona, it manages to live up to its name. Oak Creek is just outside the windows and sycamores shade the banks. Inside, all is country elegance with a beamed ceiling, fresh flower arrangements on every table, and morning-glory motifs on the china. The menu is changed daily, but you'll always have a choice of several hors d'oeuvres and main dishes. On a recent evening there were radichio tacos of duckling with papaya nestled in a nectarine cilantro panache for a starter, chilled orange champagne nectar for a soup, baby designer greens with baby corn and eggplant for the salad, and among the main-course choices were broiled mahi mahi accompanied by leeks and flavored with thyme, roast veal ribeye with citrus and a tarragon sauce, and sautéed jumbo scallops with caviar and a boursin-cheese beurre blanc. For dessert there was an array of delicate pastries.

EXPENSIVE

CANYON ROSE, in Los Abrigados, 160 Portal Lane. Tel. 282-7673 or 282-1777.
Cuisine: AMERICAN. **Reservations:** Highly recommended.
$ Prices: Appetizers $7–$8; main courses $15–$24. AE, CB, DC, DISC, MC, V.
Open: Breakfast daily 7–11am; lunch daily 11am–2pm; dinner daily 5–10pm.

Right next door to the Tlaquepaque shopping center, Los Abrigados is a mission-revival-style resort with red-tile roofs, Mexican fountains, arches, and white stucco. Within these elegant environs is one of Sedona's excellent restaurants. To reach your seat at the Canyon Rose you'll have to run a gauntlet of temptation past the pastry case, where hedonistic delights will make you forget about appetizers and entrees. But after you see the wine cabinets and the hostess leads you past the marble-floored salad-bar area, you certainly won't want to miss the opportunity to sample the appetizers or main courses at this casually elegant restaurant. On a recent visit, the dry-aged New York strip steak with sun-dried tomatoes, peppercorns, and burnt brandy sauce captured the attention of my tastebuds. On Wednesday nights there's a wandering troubador, and other nights a pianist plays. For an intimate dinner, you might reserve one of the single-table private dining rooms that have frosted-glass walls.

ENCHANTMENT, in the Enchantment Resort, 525 Boynton Canyon Rd. Tel. 282-2900.

Cuisine: NOUVELLE AMERICAN. **Reservations:** Required.

$ Prices: Appetizers $6–$8.50; main courses $13.50–$22. AE, DISC, MC, V.

Open: Breakfast daily 7–10am; lunch daily 11am–2pm; dinner daily 5:30–9pm.

If you crave a taste of the good life, make a reservation for dinner at the Enchantment Resort's dining room. Put on your best clothes, and ensconce yourself in the realm of the rich and famous. It may be expensive, but where else can you dine inside a genuine power vortex? The best time for dinner is at sunset, when the desert sun paints the red rocks in fiery hues, and the food is as spectacular as the view. For an appetizer, try the grilled jumbo shrimp in a light avocado-wine sauce served with grilled polenta. The salads are made with finest produce of the season, and even simple black-bean soup gets a special touch with applewood-smoked bacon and cumin-scented tortilla strips. The menu changes regularly, but if you're lucky you might get to try the pan-roasted tenderloin of pork marinated in southwestern spices and served with Mexican beer and chile sauce and wild-rice-and-apple griddle cakes. The dessert tray is, of course, enchantingly decadent.

RENE AT TLAQUEPAQUE, Tlaquepaque, Ariz. 179. Tel. 282-9225.

Cuisine: CONTINENTAL/AMERICAN. **Reservations:** Highly recommended.

$ Prices: Appetizers $6–$9; main courses $16–$26. MC, V.

Open: Lunch Wed–Mon 11:30am–2pm (sometimes later); dinner Mon and Wed–Thurs 5:30–8:30pm, Fri–Sat 5:30–9:30pm. **Closed:** Jan.

Located in Tlaquepaque, the city's upscale south-of-the-border–theme shopping center, René's is the quintessential Sedona dining experience. The crowds that come to enjoy chef René's continental creations are always lively and cultured. Original works of art by southwestern artists hang from the walls, reminding you while you dine that Sedona is an art community. Virtually any dish made with lamb is sure to be tender and juicy, but the rack of Colorado lamb, though expensive, is superb. It's served for two people and comes with mint jelly and a sweet-and-sour chutney.

MODERATE

HUMPHREY'S, 1405 W. U.S. 89A. Tel. 282-7745.

Cuisine: SEAFOOD. **Reservations:** Highly recommended.

$ Prices: Appetizers $3–$5; main courses $8–$12. MC, V.

Open: Dinner only, daily 5–9:30pm.

Although the desert doesn't seem to be a likely place for fresh fish, when the urge strikes, you'll be glad that Sedona has Humphrey's. It's nothing fancy, just straightforward fish in pleasant surroundings. For those who don't like fish, there are also a few steaks on the menu.

SHUGRUE'S RESTAURANT, BAKERY & BAR, 2250 W. U.S. 89A. Tel. 282-2943.

Cuisine: INTERNATIONAL. **Reservations:** Recommended.

$ Prices: Appetizers $3.50–$8; main courses $8–$22. AE, MC, V.

Open: Breakfast/lunch Mon 11am–3pm, Tues–Sun 8am–3pm; dinner Sun–Thurs 5–9pm, Fri–Sat 5–10pm.

Sprawling grounds, a maze of dining rooms, and a menu that just goes on and on have given Shugrue's the reputation of being the most popular restaurant in Sedona. A covered entryway leads to a beautiful stained-glass art deco door with a circular window. You may want to come early enough to enjoy the restaurant's sunken fireside lounge. Ceiling fans and old books on shelves in the dining rooms give the restaurant a tropical library feel. The restaurant is located a couple of miles west of uptown Sedona and is surrounded by pleasant shady gardens.

BUDGET

EAT YOUR HEART OUT, 350 Jordan Rd. Tel. 282-1471.
Cuisine: HEALTH ORIENTED. **Reservations:** Not accepted.
$ Prices: Appetizers $3–$5; main courses $8–$12. MC, V.
Open: Lunch daily 11am–2pm; dinner Mon–Thurs 5–9pm.
Located near the corner of Apple Road and Jordan Road, Eat Your Heart Out is where you dine in Sedona if you care about how you treat your heart. Meals here are lighter and healthier than you normally find in restaurants, and many have been approved by the American Heart Association. At lunch, meals are served from a cafeteria-style buffet, while at dinner waitresses take your order from the short menu. Most dishes are baked and imaginative flavor combinations guarantee a satisfying meal.

RINCON DEL TLAQUEPAQUE, Tlaquepaque Village, Ariz. 179. Tel. 282-4648.
Cuisine: MEXICAN. **Reservations:** Recommended.
$ Prices: Combination dinners $6.50–$10. MC, V.
Open: Tues–Thurs 11am–8pm, Fri–Sat 11am–9pm, Sun noon–5pm. **Closed:** Feb.
Located amid the courtyards and fountains of the Mexican-style Tlaquepaque shopping center on the south side of town is Sedona's best and most popular Mexican restaurant. There always seems to be a line at the door, which should give you the idea that the food here is worth waiting for. It mixes traditional Mexican fare with a bit of Navajo cookery. The margaritas are made with real limes and egg whites and are by far the best in town.

SHOPPING

Sedona is well known as an arts community, and it was here that the highly respected Cowboy Artists of American organization was founded in 1965. You'll see many of their works in some of the nearly 50 art galleries in town. Most of these galleries specialize in traditional western, contemporary southwestern, and Native American art. You'll find the greatest concentration of galleries in the **Tlaquepaque** shopping center, where artists are often seen working in their combination gallery-studios. Tlaquepaque, Sedona's premier shopping center, is named after a famous arts-and-crafts neighborhood in the suburbs of Guadalajara, Mexico. It's designed to resemble an old Mexican village with its maze of narrow alleys, connecting courtyards, fountains, even a chapel and a bell tower. Among the galleries not to be missed at Tlaquepaque are **Casa de Artes,** Suite B-105 (tel. 282-4335), and **El Prado,** Suite E-101 (tel. 282-7390).

    Hozho, at 431 Ariz. 179, is a Santa Fe pueblo-style shopping center that houses several art galleries.

    The **Hillside Courtyard,** at 671 Ariz. 179, is yet another shopping center dedicated almost exclusively to art galleries.

    If you are looking for Native American arts and crafts such as Hopi kachinas and jewelry, visit **Kopavi,** at Ariz. 179 and Schnebly Hill Road (tel. 282-4774).

EVENING ENTERTAINMENT

Your best bet for evening entertainment in Sedona will be a resort hotel lounge. **On the Rocks,** at Los Abrigados, beside Tlaquepaque, is one of the nicest lounges in town. The clientele is upscale and there's live popular dance music Tuesday through Saturday. The **Sedona Arts Center,** U.S. 89A at Barn Road (tel. 282-3809), has frequent performances of music and plays.

EASY EXCURSIONS FROM SEDONA
THE VERDE VALLEY

For thousands of years people have been drawn to the Verde (Spanish for "green") Valley. The Verde River, which flows through the valley, has served as a source of irrigation waters for ancient Hohokam and Sinagua peoples, the Yavapai and Apache, and most recently, white settlers. The river got its name from the lush greenery that grows along the banks of the river, for beyond from this flowing oasis the landscape is barren brown desert. With its headwaters in the Juniper Mountains of the Prescott National Forest, the Verde River flows down through a rugged canyon before meandering slowly across the wide Verde Valley plains. These plains are today one of Arizona's richest agricultural and ranching regions, but long before the first white explorers entered the Verde Valley, the Sinagua were living by the river. Sinagua ruins can still be seen along the length of the Verde Valley at such places as Tuzigoot National Monument and Montezuma Castle National Monument. Later when white settlers and Yavapai and Apache tribes clashed, the U.S. Army established Fort Verde to protect settlers. The fort is now a state park.

It was not only water that attracted people to this area. The Spanish passed through searching for gold, but found none. Years later, the town of Jerome became the site of one of Arizona's first copper mines. Following the classic pattern of boom and bust, Jerome nearly became a ghost town when the copper mine shut down, but luckily, it was discovered by artists and has been reborn as one of Arizona's arts communities.

Exploring the Verde Valley is an easy day excursion from Sedona. The route taking in the following sites covers less than 90 miles and is a large loop that can be done in either direction. To follow the order below, head west out of Sedona on U.S. 89A. At Ariz. 279, turn right toward Cottonwood, Clarkdale, and Jerome. Return back southeast on Ariz. 279 to Camp Verde. From Camp Verde, go north on I-17 and take the Ariz. 179 exit to return to Sedona.

Clarkdale

TUZIGOOT NATIONAL MONUMENT, off U.S. 89A near Clarkdale. Tel. 634-5564.

Perched atop a hill overlooking the Verde River, this Sinagua ruin was inhabited between 1125 and 1400. Built of stones and mud, the village had 77 ground-floor rooms and may have housed as many as 200 people: Sometime in the 1200s, the population of Tuzigoot (an Apache word meaning "crooked water") doubled and then doubled again as a drought struck this part of Arizona. (However, in the early 1400s the Sinagua abandoned the Verde Valley, possibly because the land had been overused or perhaps because the Yavapai and Apache had moved into the area and begun raiding the villages of the Sinagua.)

The Sinagua peoples, whose name is Spanish for "without water" were contemporaries of the better-known Anasazi, who lived in the canyonlands of northeastern Arizona. The Sinagua were traditionally dry-land farmers relying entirely on rainfall to water their crops. When the Hohokam, who had been living in the Verde Valley since A.D. 600, moved on to more fertile land around 1100, the Sinagua moved in. Their buildings progressed from individual homes called pit houses to communal pueblos. Here at Tuzigoot they built atop a hill, but in other areas they built into the cliffs, just as the Anasazi were doing at that same time. A Sinagua cliff dwelling can be seen at nearby Montezuma Castle National Monument (see below).

Inside the visitor center at Tuzigoot is a small museum displaying many of the artifacts unearthed at Tuzigoot. An interpretive trail leads through the ruins, explaining different aspects of Sinaguan life. Desert plants, many of which were utilized by the Sinagua, are also identified along the trail.

Admission: $1 adults, free for children 16 and under.
Open: Daily 8am–5pm.

ARIZONA CENTRAL RAILROAD, 300 N. Broadway. Tel. 602/639-0010.

When the town of Jerome was busily mining copper, a railway was built to link the booming town with the territorial capital at nearby Prescott. Because of the rugged mountains between Jerome and Prescott, the railroad was forced to take a longer but less difficult route north along the Verde River before turning back south toward Prescott. Today the Arizona Central Railroad operates excursions from Clarkdale to

Perkinsville. The route through the Verde River Canyon traverses unspoiled desert that is inaccessible by car and is part of the Prescott National Forest. The views of the rocky canyon walls are quite dramatic, and if you look closely, you can even see traces of ancient Sinagua cliff dwellings in the canyon. The railroad operates both sightseeing excursions and western-barbecue dinner excursions.

Admission: Tickets, excursion only, $23.95 adults, $22.95 senior citizens, $13.95 children under 12, $39.95 first class; western-barbecue dinner excursion, $52.95 per person, $74.95 first class.

Open: Dec–Feb, departures Sat–Sun at 1pm; Mar–May and Sept–Nov, departures Wed–Sun at 1pm; June–Aug, departures Mon–Fri at 3pm, Sat–Sun at 9am and 3pm.

Jerome

Clinging to the slopes of Cleopatra Hill high on Mingus Mountain, Jerome beckons to the traveler today just as it once did to miners. The town's fortune was made and lost on copper from several mines that operated between 1882 and 1950. Over the years Jerome experienced an economic roller-coaster ride as the price of copper rose and fell, and when it was finally no longer profitable to mine the ore, the last mining company shut down its operations. Almost everyone left town, and by the early 1960s Jerome looked as if it would soon become just another ghost town. But about that same time, artists discovered the phenomenal views and dirt-cheap rents to be had in Jerome. Before long Jerome was being called an artists' colony and tourists were beginning to visit to see the artwork that was being created.

Today Jerome is far from a ghost town, and on summer weekends the streets are packed with visitors shopping at galleries and crafts shops. The same remote and rugged setting that once made it difficult and expensive to mine copper here has now become one of the town's main attractions. Jerome is divided into two sections by an elevation of 1,500 vertical feet, with the upper part of town 2,000 feet above the Verde Valley. The view from up here is stupendous on a clear day (of which there are quite a few)—it's possible to see for more than 50 miles with the red rocks of Sedona, the Mogollon Rim, and the San Francisco Peaks all visible in the distance.

Because Jerome is built on a 30° slope, the two streets through town are switchbacks from one level of houses to the next. Old brick and wood-frame buildings built into the side of the mountain have windows gazing out into the abyss. Narrow streets, alleys, and stairways connect the different levels of town. Jerome is so steep that in the 1920s a dynamite blast loosened the town jail from its foundations and the building slid 225 feet down the hill to its present location.

In recent years the artists who have moved into town have been restoring and renovating the old houses. Residences, studios, shops, and galleries all stand side by side looking much as they did when Jerome was an active mining town. The entire town has been designated a national historic landmark.

What to See and Do Simply wandering through town soaking up the atmosphere and shopping are the main pastimes in Jerome, but for those interested in learning more about the town's mining history there is the **Jerome State Historic Park** off U.S. 89A in the lower section of town (tel. 634-5381). Located in a mansion that was built in 1916 as a home for mine owner "Rawhide Jimmy" Douglas and as a hotel for visiting mining executives, the Jerome State Historic Park contains both exhibits on mining and many of the mansion's original furnishings. Built on a hill above Douglas's Little Daisy Mine, the mansion overlooks Jerome and, dizzyingly far below, the Verde Valley. Constructed of adobe bricks made on the site, the mansion contained a wine cellar, billiard room, marble shower, steam heat, and a central vacuum system. The mansion's library has been restored as a period room, while other rooms contain exhibits on copper mining and the history of Jerome. Various types of colorful ores are on display, along with the tools that were once used to extract the ore from the mountain. Admission is $1 for adults and free for children under 17. It's open daily from 8am to 5pm, except on Christmas Day.

Jerome's shops offer an eclectic blend of urban art, chic jewelry, one-of-a-kind handmade fashions, and unusual imports and gifts. Fans of bizarre art should be sure to stop by **Wuf Wuf,** 412 Clark Street (tel. 639-0322), which more than lives up to its claim to sell "all manner of strange stuff." **Adornments by Lauren Renée,** at 593 Main Street (tel. 634-2008), features treasure necklaces and treasure capes made with rare beads from around the world. **Sky Fire,** 39 Main Street (tel. 634-8081), has a fascinating collection of southwestern gifts and furnishings, and Mexican and Central American imports. Many of the old storefronts in downtown Jerome have now become artist's studios. You can watch the artists at work and then have a look at some of the completed pieces being offered for sale.

Where to Dine If you're looking for a place to eat, try **The English Kitchen** at 119 Jerome Avenue (tel. 634-2134), which has a long and interesting history as a restaurant. First opened in 1899 and operated until the 1960s as Chinese restaurant, the English Kitchen now serves sandwiches, salads, and burgers in the $4 to $6 range. Good breakfasts are also available. The restaurant is open Tuesday through Sunday from 7:30am to 4pm.

If you know exactly when you'll be in town, and it happens to be a Saturday or Sunday, you might want to make a reservation for dinner at the **House of Joy** on Hull Avenue (tel. 634-5339). This excellent continental restaurant is housed in a building that was once a bordello and the interior decor is reminiscent of its colorful history. Reservations are an absolute necessity and must be made several weeks in advance because there are only seven tables in the restaurant. Dinner will cost between $20 and $25 per person, and credit cards are not accepted.

There are also two parks in town where you can have a picnic lunch while gazing out at the view.

And what would an old mining town be without a saloon? The **Spirit Room** on Main Street (tel. 634-5792) is an old-fashioned high-ceilinged saloon with mannequins in Gay '90s attire in a window above the bar. This big, open saloon becomes a dance hall on weekends, when regional rock and country bands perform.

Camp Verde

FORT VERDE STATE HISTORIC PARK, 3 miles east of I-17. Tel. 567-3275.

Established in 1871, Fort Verde was the third military post in the Verde Valley and was occupied until 1891, by which time tensions with the Native American population had subsided and made the fort unnecessary. The military had first come to the Verde Valley in 1865 at the request of settlers who wanted protection from the local Tonto Apaches and Yavapai. The tribes, traditionally hunters and gatherers, had been forced to raid the settlers' fields for food after their normal economy was disrupted by the sudden influx of whites and Mexicans into the area. Between 1873 and 1875 most of the Native Americans in the area were rounded up and forced to live on various reservations. An uprising in 1882 led to the last clash between Native Americans and Fort Verde's soldiers.

Today the state park, which covers 10 acres, preserves three officers' quarters, an administration building, and some ruins. The buildings that have been fully restored house exhibits on the history of the fort and what life was like on a central Arizona fort in the 19th century. With their white lattices and picket fence, gables, and shake-shingle roofs, the buildings of Fort Verde suggest that life at this remote post was not so bad, at least for officers.

Admission: $2 adults, $1 children 17–12, free for children under 12.
Open: Daily 8am–4:30pm.

MONTEZUMA CASTLE NATIONAL MONUMENT, Exit 289 from I-17. Tel. 567-3322.

Neither a castle nor an Aztec dwelling, as the name implies with its reference to the Aztec ruler Moctezuma (traditionally Montezuma), this Sinagua cliff dwelling is still very impressive. It is perhaps the best preserved of all the cliff dwellings in Arizona and consists of two stone pueblos. The more intriguing of the two is set in a shallow cave 100 feet up in a cliff overlooking Beaver Creek. Construction on this five-story, 20-room village began sometime in the early 12th century. For more than 600 years Montezuma Castle has been protected from the elements by the overhanging roof of the cave in which it is built, the original adobe mud that was used to plaster over the stone walls of the dwelling is still intact. Another structure, containing 45 rooms on a total of six levels, stands at the base of the cliff. This latter dwelling is not nearly as well preserved as the cliff dwelling because it has been subjected to rains and floods over the years. For some as-yet-unknown reason these buildings were abandoned in the early 15th century by the Sinagua people, who disappeared without a trace. In the visitor center there are artifacts that have been unearthed at the ruins.

Deserts are supposed to be dry places where water is scarce, so **Montezuma Well** comes as quite a surprise. Located a few miles north of Montezuma Castle, Montezuma Well is another prehistoric Native American site. Occupied by both the Hohokam and Sinagua at different times in the past, this desert oasis measures 368 feet across and 65 feet deep. The rock of this area is porous limestone, which is often laced with caverns and underground streams, and Montezuma Well resulted when a cavern in the limestone rock collapsed to form a sinkhole. Springs that still flow today soon filled the sinkhole and eventually local tribes discovered this reliable source of year-round water. The water was used for irrigation by both the Hohokam and Sinagua, and their irrigation channels can still be seen. An excavated Hohokam pithouse built around 1100 and Sinagua houses and pueblos stand around the sinkhole.

Admission: $1 adults, free for children 16 and under.
Open: Daily 8am–5pm.

2. PRESCOTT

100 miles N of Phoenix, 60 miles SW of Sedona, 87 miles SW of Flagstaff

GETTING THERE By Plane   There is regularly scheduled service between Prescott's **Ernest A. Love Airport,** U.S. 89 (tel. 602/778-3053), and the **Phoenix Skyharbor Airport** on Mesa airlines (tel. 602/225-5150, or toll free 800/637-2247). The round-trip airfare is $69 or $79, depending on how far in advance you buy your ticket.

By Train   The closest you can get to Prescott on an **Amtrak** (tel. toll free 800/872-7245) passenger train is Phoenix or Flagstaff. You'll have to drive or take a bus from there to Prescott.

By Bus   Prescott is served by **Greyhound/Trailways Lines.** The bus station is at 820 East Sheldon Street (tel. 445-5470).

By Car   Prescott is at the junction of U.S. 89, U.S. 89A, and Ariz. 69. If you're coming from Phoenix, take the Cordes Junction exit (Exit 262) from I-17. If you're coming from Flagstaff, the most direct route is to take I-17 to Ariz. 169 to Ariz. 69. From Sedona, just take U.S. 89A all the way.

ESSENTIALS Orientation   U.S. 89 comes into Prescott on the northeast side of town where it joins with Ariz. 69 coming in from the east. The main street into town is **Gurley Street,** which forms the north side of the Courthouse Plaza. **Montezuma Street,** also known as Whiskey Row, forms the west side of the plaza. If you continue south on Montezuma Street, you'll be on U.S. 89 heading toward Wickenburg.

Information   For more information on Prescott, contact the **Prescott Chamber of Commerce,** 117 West Goodwin Street (P.O. Box 1147), Prescott, AZ 86302-1147 (tel. 602/445-2000). The visitor information center here is open Monday through Saturday from 9am to 5pm.

Fast Facts   The **telephone area code** for Prescott is 602. If you need a taxi, call **Ace-City Cab** (tel. 445-1616). If you need to rent a car, contact **Budget** (tel. 602/778-3806, or toll free 800/527-0700), with three locations around town.

Special Events   The **Prescott Frontier Days Rodeo** is held each year in early July as part of the city's **Prescott Frontier Days** celebration. Also included in

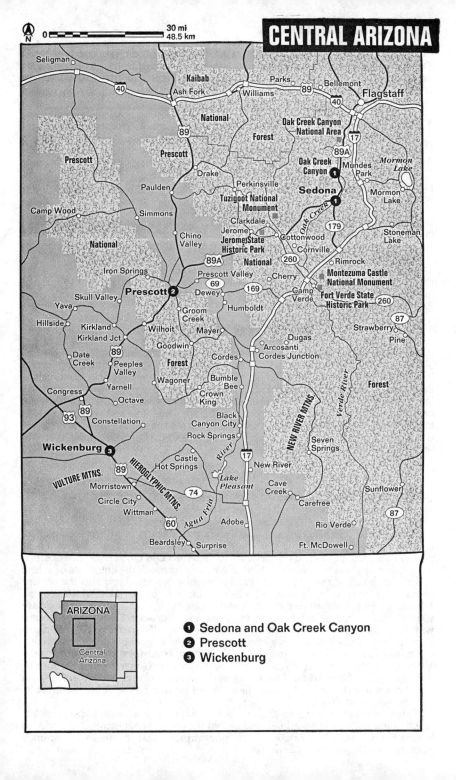

this celebration is a western art show, a golf tournament, dances, and foot races. **Territorial Days,** held in early June, is another big annual festival with special art exhibits, dances, music performances, tournaments, races, and lots of food and free entertainment.

In 1863 the Walker party discovered gold in the mountains of central Arizona, and soon miners were flocking to the area to seek their own fortunes. In 1864 Arizona became a U.S. territory and the new town of Prescott, located right in the center of Arizona, was made the territorial capital. However, Prescott lost its statewide influence when the capital moved to Phoenix, but because of the importance of ranching and mining in central Arizona, Prescott continued to be a very important regional town.

A stately courthouse on a tree-shaded square in the middle of town, a well-preserved historic downtown business district, and quite a few old Victorian homes give Prescott a timeless American hometown atmosphere. Several small museums, a couple of historic hotels, and the nearby Prescott National Forest assure that visitors with a diverse range of interests spend time here.

In summer, when Phoenix is baking, Prescott is generally 20° cooler, which makes this a popular weekend destination with Phoenicians. Prescott is also gaining importance as a retirement community as retirees from California rediscover Arizona's once-bustling territorial capital.

WHAT TO SEE & DO

A walk around the **Courthouse Plaza** should be your first introduction to Prescott. The stately old courthouse in the middle of a tree-shaded plaza captures the former importance of Prescott. The building, far too large for a small regional town such as this, dates from the days when Prescott was the capital of the Arizona territory. Surrounding the courthouse and extending north for a block is Prescott's **historic business district.** Stroll around admiring the brick buildings and you'll get an idea that Prescott was once a very important city. Duck into an old saloon or the lobby of one of the town's two historic hotels. After you've gotten a taste of Prescott, there are several museums you might like to visit.

MUSEUMS

SHARLOT HALL MUSEUM, 415 W. Gurley St. Tel. 445-3122.

At the age of 12, Sharlot Hall traveled to the Arizona territory with her parents in 1882. From an early age she became fascinated by frontier life. As an adult, she became a writer and historian and began collecting artifacts from Arizona's pioneer days. From 1909 to 1911 she was the territorial historian, an official government position. In 1928 she opened this museum in Prescott's **Old Governor's Mansion,** a log home that had been built in 1864. Eventually, through the donations of others and the activities of the local historical society, the museum grew into the present complex of historic buildings and gardens. In addition to the Old Governor's Mansion, which is furnished much as it might have been when it was built, there are several other interesting buildings that can be toured. The **John C. Frémont House** was built in 1875 for the fifth territorial governor. Its traditional wood-frame construction shows how quickly Prescott grew from a remote logging and mining camp into a civilized little town. The 1877 **William Bashford House** reflects the Victorian architecture that was popular throughout the country around the turn of the century. The **Sharlot Hall Building** was built of stone and pine logs in 1934 and now houses museum exhibits on prehistoric and historic Native American artifacts and the history of Prescott.

Other buildings of interest include a blacksmith's shop, a schoolhouse, a gazebo, a ranch house built by Sharlot Hall, and an old windmill. The museum's rose garden honors famous women of Arizona. Each spring artisans, craftspeople, and costumed exhibitors participate in the Folk Arts Fair.

Admission: By donation.
Open: Apr–Oct, Tues–Sat 10am–5pm, Sun 1–5pm; Nov–Mar, Tues–Sat 10am–4pm, Sun 1–5pm.

PRESCOTT'S PHIPPEN MUSEUM OF WESTERN ART, 4701 U.S. 89 N. Tel. 778-1385.

Located on a hill a few miles north of town, the Phippen Museum of Western Art is named after the first president of the prestigious Cowboy Artists of America. The museum exhibits works by both established western artists and newcomers. Throughout the year there are several one-person shows, as well as group exhibitions. Each year on Memorial Day weekend the museum sponsors the Phippen Western Art Show. In the fall there is another show and sale at the museum. In the museum gift shop, more than 100 Arizona artists are represented.

Admission: $2 adults, $1.50 senior citizens, $1 students.
Open: May–Dec, Mon and Wed–Sat 10am–4pm, Sun 1–4pm; Jan–May, Mon and Wed–Sun 1–4pm.

THE SMOKI MUSEUM, 100 N. Arizona St. Tel. 445-1230.

There never was a real Smoki tribe. The Smoki organization was founded in 1921 by a group of non–Native Americans who wanted to inject some new life into Prescott's July Fourth celebrations. Creating their own costumes inspired by Hopi, Navajo, and Plains traditional dress, the Smokis began staging annual ceremonial dances. The tradition continues, and the dances are held each year in August at the Yavapai County Fairgrounds. The Snake Dance is a favorite. Despite its non–Native American origins, the museum contains genuine artifacts from many different tribes. There is also a collection of western art.

Admission: $2.
Open: June–Sept, Tues–Sat 10am–4pm, Sun 1–4pm. **Closed:** Oct–May.

PARKS, NATURAL AREAS & RECREATION

Prescott's most readily recognizable feature is **Thumb Butte,** a rocky outcropping that towers over the forest just outside town. If you'd like to go hiking on Thumb Butte, head west out of town on Gurley Street, which becomes Thumb Butte Road. A few miles north of town is an unusual and very scenic area known at the **Granite Dells.** Jumbled hills of rounded granite suddenly jut up from the landscape, creating a maze of huge boulders and smooth rock. Amid this strange geological feature is a human-made lake that makes the scene even more picturesque. This is a great place to go for a walk or shoot some photos.

Prescott is situated on the edge of a wide expanse of high plains with the pine forests of **Prescott National Forest** at its back. There are hiking trails, several lakes, and campgrounds within the national forest. For maps and information, stop by the Forest Service Office, 344 South Cortez Street.

Reasonably priced golfing is available at the **Antelope Hills Golf Course,** 19 Clubhouse Drive (tel. 445-0583). Prescott bills itself as the "Softball Capital of the World," and on summer weekends it's hard to argue with this claim. At parks all over town, teams from around the world play championship softball.

WHERE TO STAY

EXPENSIVE

SHERATON RESORT & CONFERENCE CENTER, 1500 Ariz. 69, Prescott, AZ 86301. Tel. 602/776-1666, or toll free 800/325-3535, 800/445-4848 in Arizona. 162 rms, 80 suites. A/C TV TEL

$ Rates: $55–$105 single; $65–$125 double; $105–$155 suites. AE, CB, DC, MC, V.

Prescott's only full-service deluxe resort hotel is built high on a hill overlooking the city and the surrounding valley and mountains. The lobby, with its soaring ceiling and wall of glass, is a mixture of urban sophistication and western chic. Red recessed lights, modern furnishings, and a baby grand piano are offset by bronze statues of a mother and child and an eagle. Western art is on display throughout the resort. Guest rooms are spacious and comfortable, and are done in desert pastel tones. Each room also has its own balcony overlooking the valley.

Dining/Entertainment: The Thumb Butte Room, serving innovative American cuisine, is Prescott's best restaurant and offers a stunning panorama to accompany the fine meals. For a drink and conversation, there's the Eagle's Nest bar in the hotel lobby. The Buckey O'Neill Lounge is the resort's disco.

Services: Room service, valet/laundry service.

Facilities: Swimming pool, tennis courts, racquetball courts, exercise room, gift shop, art gallery, beauty salon.

MODERATE

HASSAYAMPA INN, 122 E. Gurley St., Prescott, AZ 86301. Tel. 602/ 778-9434, or toll free 800/322-1927 in Arizona. 67 rms, 10 suites (all with bath). A/C TV TEL

$ Rates (including full breakfast): May–Oct, $70–$80 single; $85–$95 double; $100–$125 suite. Nov–Apr, $65–$80 single; $80–$95 double; $95–$125 suite. AE, CB, DC, DISC, MC, V.

★ Though the recently restored Hassayampa Inn calls itself a bed-and-breakfast inn, it's not your standard family-run inn. The building is on the National Register of Historic Places and was built as a luxury hotel in 1927. Located a block uphill from Courthouse Plaza, it evokes the time when Prescott was the bustling capital of the Arizona territory. The European styling of the brick exterior belies the Spanish colonial design of the tiled lobby. Stenciled exposed ceiling beams, wrought-iron chandeliers, and arched doorways all reflect a southwestern heritage. There are even two pianos that guests may play.

All the guest rooms are a bit different and feature either original furnishings or antiques. There are quilted comforters on the beds, and in the bathroom you may find an old-fashioned porcelain sink with matching porcelain faucets. Most rooms have thick new carpeting, but there are still some with the original hardwood floor. One room here is even said to be haunted and any hotel employee will be happy to tell you the story of the ill-fated honeymooners.

Dining/Entertainment: With its high ceiling, booths of floral tapestry cloth, plenty of shining brass, and frosted-glass windows, the Peacock Room (see "Where to Dine," below) exudes the same classic elegance as the rest of the hotel. A small lounge adjacent to the restaurant provides a quiet place to have a drink in the evening.

Services: Welcoming cocktail, complimentary coffee and cookies.

Bed & Breakfast Inns

THE PRESCOTT COUNTRY INN, 503 S. Montezuma St. (U.S. 89S), Prescott, AZ 86303. Tel. 602/445-7991. 11 rms (all with bath). A/C TV TEL

$ Rates (including continental breakfast): $49–$109 single or double. Children 6 and under stay free in parents' room. Special rates available for 3- to 5-night stays. MC, V.

If you have traveled any sections of old highway in Arizona, you have seen the aging motel courts that sprang up in the 1930s and 1940s to cater to travelers heading to California. Before being totally renovated, the Prescott Country Inn was just such a motel. Today it's a surprisingly comfortable place to stay and should serve as an example to other prospective innkeepers who are overlooking the many old motel courts throughout the Southwest. Despite the name, this bed-and-breakfast inn is located only a few blocks from Courthouse Plaza. All the rooms here feature country decor and have their own kitchenettes. Some also have small gas fireplaces.

The inn also offers courtesy airport shuttle, free access to a nearby health club with swimming pool, tennis courts, racquetball courts, a sauna, and whirlpool bath.

VICTORIAN INN OF PRESCOTT, 246 S. Cortez St., Prescott, AZ 86303. Tel. 602/778-2642. 4 rms (3 with bath).

$ Rates: Apr–Oct, $85–$110; Oct–Apr, $75–$95. MC, V.

As the territorial capital at the turn of the century, Prescott attracted quite a few wealthy families. Ornate Victorian homes were all the rage throughout the United States at that time, and Prescott was no exception. In the blocks surrounding Courthouse Plaza are dozens of beautifully restored Victorian homes, including this bed-and-breakfast inn. There are only four guest rooms here, and each features a different decor. There is the Garden of Eve with its wicker furnishings and mosquito net over the bed, the Teddy Bear Room, the Rose Room, and the Victorian Suite, which has a fireplace, sitting area, private bathroom, and two large bay windows. Breakfasts are large and include such dishes as cheese soufflés and Swedish pancakes.

BUDGET

HOTEL ST. MICHAEL, 205 W. Gurley St., Prescott, AZ 86301. Tel. 602/776-1999, or toll free 800/678-3757. 72 rms, 3 suites (all with bath). A/C TV TEL

$ Rates: $28 single; $32.50–$36.50 double; $46–$65 suite or family unit. AE, MC, V.

Located on Whiskey Row, the most recent addition to the Prescott hotel scene is another restoration that's likely to give the more expensive Hassayampa Inn a bit of competition. The Hotel St. Michael even has its own resident ghost and features the oldest elevator in Prescott. All rooms are different: Some have large closets; others have only bathtubs (no showers) in their bathrooms. If you're a light sleeper, be sure to get a room away from Matt's Wall, the wall separating the hotel from the adjacent cowboy bar. Among the St. Michael's past guests have been Teddy Roosevelt and Barry Goldwater. The casual Café St. Michael is a small restaurant and lounge with brick walls and a pressed-tin ceiling.

SUPER 8 MOTEL, 1105 E. Sheldon St., Prescott, AZ 86303. Tel. 602/776-1282, or toll free 800/800-8000. 70 rms (all with bath). A/C TV TEL

$ Rates: $36–$38 single; $41–$45 double. AE, CB, DC, DISC, MC, V.

U.S. 89 (Gurley Street) on the northeast side of downtown Prescott is the city's motel row, with dozens of old motels offering comparable low rates and quality. If you prefer the expected to the unexpected, though, you can turn off Gurley onto Sheldon Street and stay at Prescott's Super 8 Motel. This national chain provides reliably clean and comfortable lodgings at low rates. The hotel also offers free coffee and doughnuts, free local calls, a swimming pool, no-smoking rooms, and a picnic area with barbecue grills.

A Bed & Breakfast Inn

PRESCOTT PINES INN, 901 White Spar Rd. (U.S. 89S), Prescott, AZ 86303. Tel. 602/445-7270. 13 rms (all with bath). A/C TV TEL

$ Rates: $46–$73 single or double. MC, V.

Just as the name implies, this B&B is located amid the pines in the mountains to the south of downtown Prescott. The main house is a 1902 country Victorian cottage, and the Victorian theme is continued throughout the several cottages that comprise this inn. There are modern furnishings in the guest rooms, all of which have private bathrooms. Numerous porches, verandas, and a garden patio invite guests to sit back and relax in the cool shade of the pines. An A-frame chalet sleeping up to eight people is available for large families and groups. It comes with its own deck, a woodstove, and a kitchen. The B&B also offers free airport pickup, complimentary morning coffee, and no-smoking rooms.

WHERE TO DINE

MODERATE

MURPHY'S, 201 N. Cortez St. Tel. 445-4044.
 Cuisine: AMERICAN. **Reservations:** Recommended.
$ Prices: Appetizers $3.25–$8; main courses $10.50–$18; lunch $5–$10; Sun brunch $6–$7. DISC, MC, V.
 Open: Daily 11am–11pm.

★ "All goods guaranteed to be first class." That was the motto of the store that once occupied this location and it's now the motto of Prescott's most popular restaurant. Located a block from Courthouse Plaza, Murphy's is housed in the oldest mercantile building in the Southwest. The building, which is on the National Register of Historic Places, was built in 1890, and many of the shop's original shelves can be seen in the restaurant's lounge area. Leaded diamond-pane glass doors usher diners into a high-ceilinged room with fans turning slowly overhead. In keeping with the historical nature of the building, antiques are on display throughout the restaurant. The appetizer list features such varied dishes as escargots and buffalo wings. Mesquite-broiled prime rib is the specialty of the house, but the steaks and seafood cooked over the same fire are equally tasty.

OLD PRESCOTT FIREHOUSE, 220 W. Goodwin St. Tel. 776-0911.
Cuisine: AMERICAN. **Reservations:** Suggested.
$ **Prices:** Appetizers $2.50–$5; main courses $6–$14; lunch $4–$9. DISC, MC, V.
Open: Lunch daily 11am–3:30pm; dinner daily 3:30–10pm.
Kids, and anyone else who has ever had a fascination with firefighting, will love this noisy, open restaurant. Just as the name says, this is the old firehouse and even today it's filled with old firefighting equipment. On the walls are photos and information about the famous July 14, 1900, fire that destroyed 25 saloons and bawdy houses along Whiskey Row. To keep firefighting fans up-to-the-minute, the restaurant monitors and broadcasts calls on the emergency radio scanner. If you happen to be a firefighter yourself, you can get a discount on your meal here. The menu includes family favorites with an emphasis on steaks.

THE PEACOCK ROOM, in the Hassayampa Inn, 122 E. Gurley St. Tel. 778-9434.
Cuisine: CONTINENTAL. **Reservations:** Recommended.
$ **Prices:** Appetizers $2.50–$6.25; main courses $9–$16. AE, DC, DISC, MC, V.
Open: Breakfast Mon–Fri 7–11am, Sat–Sun 7–11:30am; lunch Mon–Fri 11am–2pm, Sat–Sun noon–2pm; dinner daily 5–9pm.

⑤ Located in the elegant Hassayampa Inn just off Courthouse Plaza, the Peacock Room evokes a period of history when Prescott played an important role as the capital of the Arizona territory. High ceilings, frosted-glass windows, café curtains, polished brass railings, and floral tapestry-cloth booths give the restaurant a grand old style. Meals are as traditional as the decor, with such continental standards as escargots, schnitzle, and steak au poivre making appearances. The prices are surprisingly low—even a swordfish steak costs less than $14. The dessert tray always has a few irresistible treats on it.

PRESCOTT MINING COMPANY, 155 Plaza Dr. Tel. 445-1991.
Cuisine: STEAK/SEAFOOD. **Reservations:** Recommended.
$ **Prices:** Appetizers $3–$5; main courses $12–$18. DISC, MC, V.
Open: Dinner only daily 4–10pm.
Prescott made its first fortune in mining, so it comes as no surprise that one of the city's favorite restaurants has adopted a mining theme. An old mining-ore car is used as a wine cart, mining lamps shine from the wall, and outside in the garden is a reproduction of a mine entrance. Set on the banks of a small stream west of downtown, the Prescott Mining Company serves simply prepared steaks and seafood, as well as chicken, lamb, and pasta. Meals are large, but be sure to leave room for one of the delicacies on the dessert tray. You can dine in the high-ceilinged, open-beamed main dining room and lounge or out on the patio beside the stream. Mellow jazz music plays on the stereo, and on weekends a pianist plays in the lounge.

BUDGET

KENDALL'S FAMOUS BURGERS AND ICE CREAM, 113 S. Cortez St. Tel. 778-3658.

Cuisine: BURGERS. **Reservations:** Not accepted.
$ Prices: $2.80–$5.50. No credit cards.
Open: Mon–Sat 11am–9pm, Sun 11am–6pm.

"Do I have to eat all this?" asked a customer the last time I was here. "Either that or use it for art," answered the server at the counter. Ask anyone in town where to get the best burger in Prescott and they'll send you to Kendall's on Courthouse Plaza. This bright and noisy luncheonette serves juicy burgers with a choice of toppings and breads. A basket of fries is mandatory accompaniment.

SHOPPING

Downtown Prescott, especially along the historic **Whiskey Row** section of Montezuma Street, has numerous interesting shops selling Native American arts and crafts, antiques, and gifts. There are also a few art galleries to be seen.

One of the most interesting shopping areas in downtown is the brick-paved alley beneath the recently restored Hotel St. Michael. You'll find stores selling imports and exclusive fashions, as well as the **Elizabeth Prince Gallery,** 110 South Montezuma Street, Suite F (tel. 776-8223), which specializes in contemporary art by Arizona and regional artists. The **Four Winds Gallery,** 502 South Montezuma Street (tel. 778-5474), sells Navajo and Hopi pottery, as well as western and traditional art.

McNey's, 160 South Montezuma Street (tel. 445-3563), is where you can outfit yourself in cowboy gear so you'll look like an Arizona native. They also sell Native American jewelry and crafts.

Prescott makes a lot of superlative claims, including being the "Antiques Capital of Arizona." Whether or not this is true, there are plenty of antiques stores downtown. Most of the shops are concentrated along Cortez Street in the block north of Gurley Street and the courthouse. The **Merchandise Mart Mall,** 205 North Cortez Street (tel. 776-1728), houses several dealers under one roof and is the largest antiques store in town.

EVENING ENTERTAINMENT

Back in the days when Prescott was the territorial capital and a booming mining town, it supported dozens of rowdy saloons, most of which were concentrated along Montezuma Street on the west side of Courthouse Plaza. This section of town was known as **Whiskey Row,** and legend has it that there was a tunnel from the courthouse to one of the saloons so lawmakers wouldn't have to be seen ducking into the saloons during regular business hours. On July 14, 1900, a fire consumed most of Whiskey Row, including 25 saloons and bawdy houses. However, concerned cowboys and miners managed to drag the tremendously heavy bar of the Palace Saloon across the street before it was damaged by the fire. The saloon continued to do business in its new open-air location. Today Whiskey Row is no longer the sort of place where respectable women shouldn't be seen, although it does still have a few noisy saloons with genuine Wild West flavor.

THE PERFORMING ARTS

The **Prescott Fine Arts Association,** at the northwest corner of Marina Street and Willis Street (tel. 445-3286), sponsors plays, classical music performances, dinner theater, children's theater, and art exhibits. The association's main building is a former church that was built in 1899 and is on the National Register of Historic Places. The **Hendrix Auditorium,** 300 South Granite Street (tel. 445-5400), is another of the city's venues for classical music concerts. The Phoenix Symphony Orchestra does four performances here a year. The **Yavapai College Community Theater,** 113 East Gurley Street (tel. 445-3557), also schedules quite a few performances throughout the year. Check with the performance halls or the chamber of commerce for a schedule of upcoming events.

Prescott claims to be the home of the world's oldest rodeo.

3. WICKENBURG

53 miles NW of Phoenix, 61 miles south of Prescott,
128 miles SE of Kingman

GETTING THERE   By Plane   The nearest regularly scheduled service is to Phoenix Skyharbor Airport. Drive or take a bus from Phoenix.

By Train   The nearest **Amtrak** (tel. toll free 800/872-7245) passenger service is in Phoenix; drive or take a bus from there.

By Bus   Greyhound/Trailways Lines, 444 East Center Street (tel. 602/684-2601), provides service to Wickenburg from Phoenix and Las Vegas.

By Car   From Phoenix, take U.S. 60, which heads northwest and becomes Ariz. 93 and then U.S. 89. U.S. 89 also comes down from Prescott in the north, while U.S. 60 comes in from I-10 in western Arizona. Arizona 93 comes down from I-40 in northwestern Arizona.

ESSENTIALS   For more information about Wickenburg, contact the **Wickenburg Chamber of Commerce,** 215 Frontier Street (P.O. Drawer CC), Wickenburg, AZ 85358 (tel. 602/684-5479). The **telephone area code** is 602.

Wickenburg was once the "Dude Ranch Capital of the World" and attracted celebrities and families from all over the country. Today there are still several dude ranches, now known as guest ranches, in the Wickenburg area. These guest ranches range from rustic adobe buildings to luxurious country-club resorts.

Located on the northern edge of the Sonoran Desert in central Arizona, Wickenburg stands on the banks of the Hassayampa River, one of the last clear, free-flowing rivers in the Arizona desert. The town was founded in 1863 by Prussian gold prospector Henry Wickenburg, who discovered what would eventually become the most profitable gold and silver mine in Arizona. Today the abandoned mine can be toured.

When the dude ranches flourished back in the 1920s and 1930s, Wickenburg realized that visitors wanted a taste of the Wild West, so the town gave the tenderfoots what they wanted—trail rides, hayrides, cookouts, the works. Wickenburg still likes to play up its western heritage and has preserved one of its downtown streets much as it may have looked in 1900. If you've come to Arizona searching for the West the way it used to be, Wickenburg is a good place to look.

WHAT TO SEE & DO

A stroll around the old section of downtown Wickenburg provides a glimpse of the Old West. Most of the buildings here were built between 1890 and the 1920s, although a few are older. **Frontier Street** is preserved as it looked in the early 1900s. The covered sidewalks and false fronts are characteristic of old western architecture, which often disguised older adobe buildings. The old Santa Fe train station is now the Wickenburg Chamber of Commerce, which should be your first stop in town. They'll give you a map that tells a bit about the history of the town's older buildings. The brick post office building almost across the street from the train station once had a ride-up window providing service to people on horseback. The oldest building in town is the **Etter General Store** adjacent to the Gold Nugget Restaurant. The old adobe-walled store was built in 1864 and has long since been disguised with a false wooden front.

Two of the town's most unusual attractions aren't buildings at all. The **Jail Tree,** behind the Circle K store at the corner of Wickenburg Way and Tegner Street, is an old mesquite tree that served as the local hoosegow. Outlaws were simply chained to the tree. Their families would often come to visit and have a picnic in the shade of the tree. The second, equally curious, town attraction is the **Wishing Well,** which stands beside the bridge over the Hassayampa. Legend has it that anyone who drinks from the Hassayampa River will never tell the truth again, and so drinking water was always drawn from this well. How it became a wishing well is unclear.

DESERT CABALLEROS WESTERN MUSEUM, 21 N. Frontier St. Tel. 684-2272.

Thanks for the Rain, Joe Beeler's life-size bronze statue of a kneeling cowboy and his horse, stands outside Wickenburg's western museum, and inside you'll find more western art depicting life on the range in the days of "cowboys and Indians." Though it's not too large, the museum manages to convey a great deal about the history of this part of Arizona. There's an excellent display of colorful minerals, and a small collection of Native American artifacts. Branding and barbed-wire exhibits cover the ranching history of the area. On the main floor, dioramas depict important scenes from the history of the Wickenburg region. Downstairs a 1900 street scene from a western town is re-created, complete with general store. Rooms from a Victorian home are also on display.

Admission: $2.50 adults, $2 senior citizens, 50¢ children.
Open: Mon–Sat 10am–4pm, Sun 1–4pm.

VULTURE MINE, 12 miles south on Vulture Mine Rd. Tel. 377-0803.

Wickenburg was founded as a mining town in 1863 when Henry Wickenburg discovered gold nearby. The old Vulture Mine, on the site where Wickenburg made his strike, is now a tourist attraction that includes the old mine and the ghost town of Vulture City. Most of the buildings here were built in 1884, including the assay office, which is constructed of ore from the mine. The walls of the assay office contain more than $600,000 worth of gold and silver ore. From 1863 until 1942 (when the government closed down the Vulture Mine), more than $200 million worth of gold and silver was extracted from the mine. You can even pan for gold here.

Admission: $5.
Open: Sept–Apr, Thurs–Mon 9am–5pm; May–July, Mon and Thurs–Fri 9am–5pm, Sat–Sun 8am–4pm. **Closed:** Aug.

HASSAYAMPA RIVER PRESERVE, 3 miles south on U.S. 60. Tel. 684-2772.

At one time the Arizona desert was laced with rivers that flowed for most, if not all, of the year. In the past 100 years these rivers have disappeared at an alarming rate because of damming of rivers and lowering water tables. The riparian (waterside) habitat supports trees and plants that require more water than is usually available in the desert, and this lush growth provides food and shelter for hundreds of species of birds, mammals, and reptiles. The Nature Conservancy, a nonprofit organization dedicated to purchasing and preserving endangered habitats, owns and manages the Hassayampa River Preserve. Nature trails lead along the river beneath cottonwoods and willows and past the spring-fed Palm Lake. More than 230 species of birds have been spotted within the preserve. Naturalist-guided walks are offered on Saturday at 10:30am in the winter and 7am in the summer. Though the guided walks are free, reservations are required.

Admission: $3.
Open: Sept–May, Wed–Sun 8am–5pm; May–Sept, Wed–Sun 6am–noon.

WHERE TO STAY
GUEST RANCHES

FLYING E RANCH, 4 miles west on U.S. 60 (P.O. Box EEE), Wickenburg, AZ 85358. Tel. 602/684-2690. Fax 602/684-5304. 16 rms (all with bath). A/C

$ Rates (including all meals): $100–$140 single; $165–$210 double. No credit cards.

Of the guest ranches still operating in Wickenburg, this is the only one still operating a cattle ranch. There are 21,000 acres for you and the cattle to roam, and if you want, you can help the ranch hands round up cattle or check for newborn calves during calving season. The main lodge features a spacious lounge where guests like to gather by the fireplace. Guest rooms vary in size, but all have rustic western furnishings and small refrigerators. There are either twin or king-size beds in the rooms.

Dining/Entertainment: Three family-style meals are served in the wood-paneled dining room. There's no bar, so you'll need to bring your own liquor. There are also breakfast cookouts, lunch rides, and evening chuckwagon dinners.

Services: Horseback riding (not included in room rates), hayrides, guest rodeos, square dances in the barn.

Facilities: Swimming pool, whirlpool bath, sauna, tennis court, shuffleboard, table tennis, horseshoes.

KAY EL BAR GUEST RANCH, Rincon Rd., off U.S. 93 (P.O. Box 2480) Wickenburg, AZ 85358. Tel. 602/684-7593. 8 rms, 1 cottage (all with bath).

$ Rates (including all meals): $95 single; $175 double; $195 cottage double. MC, V. **Closed:** May–Oct.

S This is the smallest and oldest of the Wickenburg guest ranches, and its old adobe buildings, built between 1914 and 1925, are listed in the National Register of Historic Places. From the moment you're greeted by the resident golden retrievers, you'll feel at home on the range. In the lodge is a rustic lounge with round ceiling beams that were once telegraph poles. The chandelier hanging from the ceiling was made from a telegraph pole crosspiece. An upright piano provides music for guest sing-alongs and a stone fireplace warms the room in winter. A "humane" bearskin rug covers the floor, and a jackalope head puzzles the tenderfoots. Though the ranch has only 60 acres of its own, it abuts thousands of acres of public lands where guests can ride or hike. One horseback ride a day is included in room rates. The two-bedroom/two-bath cottage is ideal for families or two couples vacationing together and gives you plenty of room and your own fireplace. Guest rooms in the main lodge are much smaller and darker since adobes were built with small windows.

Dining/Entertainment: A tile floor and curved corner fireplace in the dining room provide an authentic southwestern feel. Meals vary from Chinese to prime rib to chicken and dumplings, and are served in heaping portions. There is also a fully stocked bar.

Services: Pickup at Wickenburg airport.

Facilities: Swimming pool, stables.

RANCHO DE LOS CABALLEROS, Vulture Mine Rd., off U.S. 60 (P.O. Box 1148) Wickenburg, AZ 85358. Tel. 602/684-5484. Fax 602/684-2267. 74 rms (all with bath). A/C TEL

$ Rates (including all meals): $120–$170 single; $192–$270 double. A 15% gratuity is added to all bills. No credit cards. **Closed:** May–Oct.

Located on 20,000 acres 2 miles west of Wickenburg, Rancho de los Caballeros is a very exclusive resort community, country club, and resort. Peace and quiet are the keynotes of a stay at this ranch, with golfing and horseback riding the most popular activities. Keep in mind, however, that these two activities will cost you extra. The lobby is a classic southwestern lodge, with sandstone floors, brick walls, open ceiling beams, a large copper fireplace, and a painting by Frederic Remington. A cowboy piano with wrought-iron hinges is available to guests, and there is a quiet library for the less athletic to while away the hours. Guest rooms have either tile floors or carpeting and rustic Spanish colonial furnishings. Exposed beam ceilings and Native American rugs complete the southwestern motif. Some rooms have their own fireplaces. Bathrooms are large and done in red tiles.

Dining/Entertainment: The dining room features traditional southwestern furnishings, and the dinner menu includes a choice of four main dishes. At lunch there's a poolside buffet. In the lounge is an old painted bar with large mirrors on the back of the bar. You'll also find complimentary lemonade, iced tea, and cookies in the lounge.

Services: Children's programs, baby-sitting.

Facilities: Swimming pool, four tennis courts, horseback riding ($16–$30 per ride), trap and skeet shooting, 18-hole golf course ($30 greens fee), pro shop.

WICKENBURG INN, U.S. 89 (P.O. Box P), Wickenburg, AZ 85358. Tel. 602/684-7811, or toll free 800/528-4227. Fax 602/684-2981. 46 casitas, 12 studios, 15 suites, 14 deluxe suites (all with bath). A/C MINIBAR TV TEL
$ Rates (including all meals): $90–$160 single; $150–$250 double; $110–$170 single suite; $180–$280 double suite. Higher rates in effect most winter months. MC, V.

⭐ Located 8 miles north of Wickenburg and calling itself a tennis and guest ranch, the Wickenburg Inn caters both to those who want to perfect their backhand and those who want to become trailhands. To that end there are 11 tennis courts and 4,700 acres of desert. Resident cowboys provide instruction and roping and riding exhibitions. Tennis pros give private lessons, and there are also 3- and 5-day clinics.

Most rooms are in adobe casitas (little houses) scattered over the hills near the main lodge. These cottages have the look of old colonial adobes with red-tile roofs and porches made from rough-hewn logs. Inside there are kitchenettes with tile counters, fireplaces, high beamed ceilings, bookshelves with old books, rustic-but-comfortable furniture, walk-in closets, bathrooms with two sinks, and twin beds. Studios are similar but have king-size beds. The deluxe suites have sundecks reached by spiral staircases. The lodge rooms have rough-hewn wood walls and furniture and a deck or balcony.

Dining/Entertainment: Meals, included in the daily rate, a combination of western and continental. On Saturday night there is a campfire cookout in the desert with a sing-along afterward.

Services: Free Wickenburg airport shuttle, fee shuttle to and from the Phoenix airport, horseback riding and lessons, moonlight rides, cookout rides, breakfast rides, sunset rides, tennis lessons, holiday children's programs, baby-sitting.

Facilities: Swimming pool, whirlpool bath, 11 tennis courts, self-service laundry, gift shop, arts-and-crafts center, nature center, stables, archery field, jogging trail.

A MOTEL

BEST WESTERN RANCHO GRANDE, 293 E. Center St. (P.O. Box 1328), Wickenburg, AZ 85358. Tel. 602/684-5445, or toll free 800/528-1234. Fax 602/684-7380. 80 rms, 10 suites (all with bath). A/C TV TEL
$ Rates: $45–$59 single; $48–$69 double. AE, CB, DC, DISC, MC, V.
Right in the heart of downtown Wickenburg, this Best Western motel is built in Spanish colonial style, with tile roof, stucco walls, arched colonnades, and tile murals on the wall. There is a wide range of room types and prices. At the higher end you get a larger room, larger bathroom (with a phone), large towels, and a coffee maker. Suites are housed in 120- and 150-year-old buildings, one of which is an old adobe. However, remodeling has updated these buildings completely.

The motel's restaurant and lounge, the Gold Nugget, is across the street. Meals are filling, and you can dine in one of the main dining rooms or in the coffee shop. The hotel also offers in-room movies, a swimming pool, a whirlpool bath, and a tennis court.

WHERE TO DINE

CHARLEY'S STEAKHOUSE, 1187 W. Wickenburg Way. Tel. 684-2413.
 Cuisine: STEAKS. **Reservations:** Suggested.
$ Prices: $9–$16. DISC, MC, V.
 Open: Dinner only, Tues–Sun 5–10pm.
Out on the west side of town is Wickenburg's favorite steakhouse. Though the building looks quite modern from the outside, the interior is done in rustic pine paneling, and collectors' whiskey bottles are lined up all over the dining room. Dinners come with salad, baked potato, cowboy beans, rolls and butter, tea, and dessert, so bring a hearty appetite.

RANCHO DE LOS CABALLEROS, Vulture Mine Rd. Tel. 684-5484.
 Cuisine: AMERICAN/CONTINENTAL. **Reservations:** Required.

$ Prices: Complete dinner $20.50. No credit cards.
Open: Dinner only, daily 6:30–8:30pm. **Closed:** May–Oct.

Wickenburg's most exclusive guest ranch also opens its excellent restaurant to the public. The menu focuses on continental and southwestern cuisine and changes daily. However, you always have a choice of two soups, two salads, four main courses, and two desserts. If none of the regular entrees appeal to you, there are slightly more expensive alternatives as well. Men are required to wear a jacket and tie, and women must also dress appropriately.

WICKENBURG INN GUEST RANCH, U.S. 89 (Prescott Hwy.). Tel. 684-7811.

Cuisine: AMERICAN/CONTINENTAL. **Reservations:** Required.

$ Prices: Complete dinner $18.75. MC, V.
Open: Dinner only, Sun–Fri 6–8:30pm, Sat 6–10pm (cookout).

The Wickenburg Inn is north of town in a picturesque setting of rolling desert hills. The dining room, which is open to the public with advance reservations, has the feeling of an old-fashioned southwestern lodge. Stone and raw wood give it a rugged feeling, but creature comforts are not overlooked. For the fixed price of $18.75 you get soup, salad, a choice of main dish, beverages, and dessert. Entree choices include steaks, seafood, chicken, pasta, and such southwestern specialties as brochette of flank steak served with cilantro pesto.

CHAPTER 8

THE FOUR CORNERS REGION & EASTERN ARIZONA

There is only one place in the United States where four states come together at the same point. Arizona, New Mexico, Colorado, and Utah all meet at a spot called the Four Corners, which also includes the huge surrounding area and a large piece of northeastern Arizona. Most of the land within the Four Corners region of Arizona is Navajo and Hopi reservation land, and it is also some of the most spectacular countryside in the state, with majestic mesas, rainbow-hued deserts, gravity-defying buttes, cliffs, and canyons. Among the most spectacular of these are the 1,000-foot buttes of Monument Valley. For years these evocative and colorful monoliths have symbolized the Wild West of cowboys and John Wayne movies.

Native American cultures consider the region the center of the universe. The Navajo and Hopi peoples who have lived on this land for hundreds of years have adapted different means of surviving in the arid Four Corners region. The Navajo have become herders of sheep, goats, and cattle. Their homes are scattered across the countryside, and many are still the traditional log-walled hogan. The Hopi, on the other hand, have congregated in villages atop mesas and built houses of stone. They farm the floors of narrow valleys at the feet of their mesas in much the same way Native Americans of the Southwest have done for centuries.

The Hopi and the Navajo are, however, only the most recent Native Americans to inhabit what many consider to be a desolate, barren wilderness. The ancient Anasazi and, not far to the southwest, the Sinagua have left their mark throughout the canyons of the Four Corners region with cliff dwellings dating back 700 years and more, the most spectacular being those at Canyon de Chelly National Monument and Navajo National Monument. No one is sure why the Anasazi moved up into the cliff walls, but there is speculation that unfavorable growing conditions brought on by drought may have forced them to use every possible inch of arable land. The cliff dwellings were mysteriously abandoned in the 13th century, and with no written record, the disappearance of the Anasazi may forever remain a mystery.

Northern Arizona is bisected by I-40, which runs from east to west. The Four Corners region lies to the north of the Interstate, while to the south the landscape changes dramatically; Eastern Arizona is a land of mountains and forests, where towns with such names as Alpine and Pinetop have become summer retreats for the people who live in the state's low-lying, sun-baked deserts. In only a few hours you can drive up from the cacti and creosote bushes of Phoenix to the meadows and pine forests of the White Mountains. Along the Mogollon Rim (pronounced Mug-*gee*-un

WHAT'S SPECIAL ABOUT THE FOUR CORNERS REGION & EASTERN ARIZONA

Native American Ruins
- ☐ Canyon de Chelly, full of ancient Anasazi cliff dwellings.
- ☐ Keet Seel and Betatakin, at Navajo National Monument, two of the largest and best-preserved Anasazi ruins in Arizona.

Natural Spectacles
- ☐ Canyon de Chelly, a narrow canyon that has been home to Native American cultures for 2,000 years.
- ☐ Monument Valley, a breathtaking landscape of eroded buttes, mesas, and pinnacles.
- ☐ The Petrified Forest, where trees have turned to stone.
- ☐ The Mogollon Rim, a 2,000-foot escarpment that stretches from central Arizona into New Mexico.
- ☐ Rainbow Bridge, the largest natural bridge in the world.

Events/Festivals
- ☐ Hopi ceremonial dances, held throughout the year at various Hopi villages
- ☐ Navajo tribal fairs, held throughout the year at different Navajo communities

Activities
- ☐ Hiking to the ruins at Betatakin and Keet Seel.
- ☐ Exploring Canyon de Chelly by Jeep, on foot, or on horseback.
- ☐ Skiing at Sunrise ski area.

Great Towns/Villages
- ☐ The Hopi villages, some of which have been occupied for hundreds of years and are built atop mesas.

TV and Film Locations
- ☐ Monument Valley, which has served as a backdrop for dozens of movies, television programs, and commercials.

by the locals), the climatic and vegetative change is dramatic. This 2,000-foot-high escarpment divides the arid lowlands from the cool mountain forests. Western author Zane Grey made his home near the Mogollon Rim and many of his novels capture the scenic beauty of this often-overlooked part of Arizona.

Trout fishing, hiking, horseback riding, and hunting are the main warm-weather pastimes of eastern Arizona. However, snow skiing at the Sunrise ski area makes this a winter destination as well. Sunrise is operated by the Apache, whose reservations cover a large part of eastern Arizona. There isn't as much to see or do in this region as there is in the Four Corners area, but if you've been down in the heat of the desert for a while and desperately need a respite from the sun, the White Mountains and Mogollon Rim offer quick relief.

1. THE HOPI RESERVATION

250 miles NE of Phoenix, 67 miles N of Winslow,
100 miles SW of Canyon de Chelly, 125 miles NE of Flagstaff,
140 miles SE of Page/Lake Powell.

GETTING THERE   By Plane   The nearest airports with regularly scheduled service are in Flagstaff and Page. See the respective sections of Chapter 6 for details.

By Train   Amtrak (tel. toll free 800/872-7245) passenger trains stop in Winslow, 67 miles south of Second Mesa. The train station is on East Second Street.

By Bus   Buses of **Greyhound/Trailways Lines** stop in Winslow and Holbrook, but there is no regularly scheduled bus service north to the Hopi pueblos. **Navajo**

Transit System (tel. 602/729-5457, 729-5458, or 729-5449) operates a bus service Monday through Friday throughout the Navajo and Hopi reservations with service between the following cities: Farmington, Gallup, and Crown Point (all in New Mexico) and Window Rock, Kayenta, Chinle, and Tuba City. The route between Window Rock and Tuba City stops at several of the Hopi villages, including Second Mesa.

By Car   This section of Arizona is one of the state's most remote regions. Distances are great but highways are generally in good condition. Ariz. 87 leads from Winslow to Second Mesa, while Ariz. 264 runs from Tuba City in the west to the New Mexico state line in the east. If you're coming from Flagstaff, you might want to take Indian Route 15 east to Indian Route 2, which leads northeast to the village of Kykotsmovi near Second Mesa.

ESSENTIALS   For more information before you leave home, contact the **Hopi Tribal Council,** P.O. Box 123, Kykotsmovi, AZ 86039 (tel. 602/734-2441). Because each of the Hopi villages is relatively independent, you might want to contact the Community Development Office of a particular village for specific information on ceremonies and dances taking place in that village: Bacavi (tel. 602/734-2404), First Mesa (tel. 602/737-2670), Hotevilla (tel. 602/734-2420), Kykotsmovi (tel. 602/734-2474), Mishongnovi (tel. 602/737-2520), Moenkopi (tel. 602/283-6684), Shungopavi (tel. 602/734-2262), and Shipaulovi (tel. 602/734-2570). These offices are open Monday through Friday from 8am to 5pm. The telephone **area code** is 602.

Completely surrounded by the Navajo Reservation, the Hopi Reservation has at its center the grouping of mesas that are home to the Hopi pueblos. This remote region of Arizona, with its flat-topped mesas and rugged, barren landscape, is the center of the universe for the Hopi peoples. The handful of villages that together make up the Hopi pueblos are ancient and independent communities that have today been brought together under the guidance of the Hopi Tribal Council. This land has been inhabited by the Hopis and their ancestors for nearly a thousand years and many aspects of the ancient pueblo culture remain intact. However, much of the Hopi culture is hidden from the view of non-Hopis. Though the Hopis perform elaborate religious ceremonies throughout the year, these ceremonies are not scheduled for a specific date until a few weeks before they occur. This makes it difficult to plan to attend a ceremony even though non-Hopis are usually welcome.

Please remember when visiting the Hopi pueblos that you are a guest of the Hopis and your privileges can be revoked at any time. Respect all posted signs at village entrances, and remember that *photographing, sketching, and recording are all prohibited in the villages and at ceremonies.* Also keep in mind that kivas (ceremonial rooms) and ruins are off-limits.

WHAT TO SEE & DO

The place to start your visit to the Hopi pueblos is at the **Hopi Cultural Center** on Ariz. 264 (tel. 734-2401) in Second Mesa. This museum, motel, and restaurant is the tourism headquarters for the area. Here you can visit the museum and learn about the Hopi culture and its history. Be sure to take notice of signs indicating when villages are open to visitors. The museum is open Monday through Friday from 8am to 5pm. Admission is $3 for adults and $1 for children.

VILLAGES

The Hopis have for centuries built their villages on the tops of mesas in northeastern Arizona, and claim that Oraibi, on Third Mesa, is the oldest continuously inhabited town in the United States. Whether or not this claim is true, several of the Hopi villages are quite old and for this reason they have become tourist attractions. Most of the villages are built on three mesas, known simply as First, Second, and Third Mesa, which are numbered from east to west. These villages have always maintained a great deal of autonomy, which over the years has led to fighting between villages. The appearance of missionaries and the policies of the Bureau of Indian Affairs have also created conflicts between and within villages. One such conflict led to the division of Oraibi and the formation of Hotevilla.

At the foot of First Mesa is **Polacca,** a village founded in the late 1800s by Walpi villagers who wanted to be closer to the trading post and school. At the top of First Mesa is the village of **Walpi,** which was located lower on the slopes of the mesa until the Pueblo Rebellion of 1680 brought on fear of reprisal by the Spanish. The villagers moved Walpi to the very top of the mesa so that they could better defend themselves in the event of a Spanish attack. Walpi looks much like the Anasazi villages of the Arizona canyons, with small stone houses that seem to grow directly from the rock of the mesa top, and ladders jutting from the roofs of kivas. The view stretches for hundreds of miles around. **Sichomovi,** lower down on the mesa, was founded in 1750 as a colony of Walpi, whereas **Hano** was founded by Tewa peoples either seeking refuge from the Spanish or offering aid to the people of Walpi.

Second Mesa is today the center of tourism in Hopiland, as the Hopi country is called, and where you'll find the Hopi Cultural Center. Villages on Second Mesa include **Shungopavi,** which was moved to its present site after Old Shungopavi was abandoned in 1680 after the Pueblo Revolt against the Spanish. Below Shungopavi is Gray Spring. The Snake Dance is performed here in even-numbered years. **Mishongnovi,** which means "place of the back man," is named for the leader of a clan that came here from the San Francisco Peaks around A.D. 1200. This village was also abandoned in 1680 and moved to its present location. The Snake Dance is held here in odd-numbered years. **Shipaulovi** may also have been founded after the Pueblo Revolt of 1680.

Oraibi, which the Hopi claim is the oldest continuously occupied town in the United States, is located on Third Mesa. The village dates from 1150 and, according to legend, was founded by people from Old Shungopavi. A Spanish mission was established in Oraibi in 1629 and the ruins are still visible north of the village. For centuries Oraibi was the largest of the Hopi villages, but in 1906 a schism occurred over Bureau of Indian Affairs policies and many of the villagers left to form **Hotevilla.** This latter village is considered the most conservative of the Hopi villages and has had frequent confrontations with the federal government. **Kykotsmovi,** also known as Lower Oraibi or New Oraibi, was founded in 1890 by villagers from Oraibi who wanted to be closer to the school and trading post. **Bacavi** was founded in 1907 by villagers who had helped found Hotevilla but who later decided that they wanted to return to Oraibi. The people of Oraibi would not let them return, and rather than go back to Hotevilla, they founded a new village.

One last Hopi village, **Moenkopi,** is located 40 miles to the west. Founded in 1870 by people from Oraibi, Moenkopi sits in the center of a wide green valley where plentiful water makes farming more reliable. Moenkopi is only a few miles from Tuba City off U.S. 160.

DANCES & CEREMONIES

The Hopi, who long ago adopted a farming life-style, have developed the most complex religious ceremonies of any of the Southwest tribes. Masked kachina dances, for which the Hopis are most famous, are held from January to July, while the equally well-known Snake Dances are held from August through December.

Kachinas, whether in the form of dolls or as masked dancers, are representative of the spirits of everything from plants and animals to ancestors and sacred places. There are more than 300 kachinas that appear on a regular basis in Hopi ceremonies, and another 200 that appear occasionally. The kachina spirits are said to live in the San Francisco Peaks to the south and at Spring of the Shadows in the east. According to legend, the kachinas lived with the Hopis long ago, but the Hopi people made the kachinas angry, causing them to leave. Before leaving, though, the kachinas taught the Hopis how to perform their ceremonies. Today the kachina ceremonies serve several purposes. Most important, they bring clouds and rain to water the all-important corn crop, but they also ensure health, happiness, long life, and harmony in the universe. The kachina season lasts from the winter solstice until shortly after the summer solstice. These months are marked by various **kachina dances** and ceremonies, with men wearing the elaborate costumes and masks of whichever kachinas have been chosen to appear. Clowns known as *koyemsi, koshares,* and *tsukus* entertain spectators between the more serious dances, with ludicrous and sometimes lewd mimicry, bringing a lighthearted counterpoint to the very serious nature of the kachina dances. Preparations for the dances take place in the kivas (circular ceremonial rooms) that are entered from the roof by means of a ladder. The kachina dancers often bring carved wooden kachina dolls to village children to introduce them to the various kachina spirits.

Despite the importance of the kachina dances, it is the **Snake Dance** that has captured the attention of non-Hopis. The Snake Dance is held only every other year in any given village and involves the handling of both poisonous and nonpoisonous snakes. The ceremony takes place over 16 days with the first 4 days dedicated to collecting all the snakes from the four cardinal directions. Later, foot races are held from the bottom of the mesa to the top. On the last day of the ceremony, the actual Snake Dance is performed. Men of the Snake Society form pairs of dancers—one to carry the snake in his mouth and the other to distract the snake with an eagle feather. When all the snakes have been danced around the plaza, they are rushed down to their homes at the bottom of the mesa to carry the Hopi prayers for rain to the spirits of the underworld.

The following is a general **calendar of Hopi ceremonies:** January, Buffalo Dances; February, Bean Dances; March, Night Dances (kachinas); April, Day Dances (kachinas); May, Day Dances (kachinas); June, Day Dances (kachinas); July, Home Dances, Social Dances; August, Snake Dance, Flute Dance, Social Dances; September, Social Dances; October, Ladies' Society Dances; November, Men's Society Dances; December, Men's Prayer Feather Ceremony. Keep in mind that the exact dates for these dances and ceremonies are not known until a few weeks before they are held.

The best way to find out about attending dances or ceremonies is to call the Hopi Tribal Council (tel. 602/734-2441).

SHOPPING

Shopping for Hopi crafts is the main pursuit of visitors to the Hopi Reservation. There are literally dozens of small shops selling crafts and jewelry of different quality. These shops often sell the work of only a few individuals, so you should stop at several to get some idea of the variety of work available. Perhaps the single best place to stop is the **Hopi Arts & Crafts–Silvercraft Cooperative Guild,** beside the Hopi Cultural Center on Second Mesa. This arts and crafts cooperative was founded in 1962 and has as its goal the perpetuation of excellence and authenticity in Hopi arts and crafts. The guild's membership of more than 300 people includes potters, weavers, basketmakers, kachina carvers, painters, and silversmiths.

Other reliable sources of Hopi arts and crafts are **Keams Canyon Arts & Crafts,** at Keams Canyon east of First Mesa (tel. 738-2295), and **Honani Crafts Gallery,** on Second Mesa (tel. 737-2238).

KACHINAS These elaborately decorated wooden dolls are representations of spirits of plants, animals, ancestors, and sacred places. Traditionally they have been given to children to initiate them into the pantheon of kachina spirits, who play important roles in ensuring rain and harmony in the universe. In recent years kachinas have become popular with non-Hopis and Hopi kachina carvers have changed their style to cater to the new market. Older kachinas were carved from a single piece of cottonwood, sometimes with arms simply painted on. This older style of kachina is much simpler and stiffer than the currently popular style that emphasizes action poses and realistic proportions. A great deal of carving and painting goes into each kachina and prices today are in the hundreds of dollars for even a simple kachina. Currently gaining popularity with tourists and collectors are the *tsuku,* or clown, kachinas, which are usually painted with bold horizontal black and white stripes. The tsukus are often depicted in humorous situations or carrying slices of watermelon.

OVERLAY SILVERWORK Overlay silverwork has come to be considered the characteristic Hopi style of silverwork, but only since World War II have the Hopis been almost exclusively making this sort of jewelry. After the war, the G.I. bill provided for Hopi soldiers to study silversmithing at a school founded by famous Hopi artist Fred Kabotie. The overlay process basically uses two sheets of silver, one with a design cut out of it. The two sheets are fused together with heat to form a raised image. Designs used in overlay jewelry are often borrowed from other Hopi crafts such as baskets and pottery, as well as from ancient Anasazi pottery designs. Belt buckles, bola ties, and bracelets are all popular.

BASKETS Though the Tohono O'odham of the deserts of central and southern Arizona are better known for their basketry, the Hopis also produced beautiful work. Wicker plaques and baskets are made on Third Mesa from rabbit brush and sumac and are colored with bright aniline dyes. Coiled plaques and baskets are made on Second Mesa from dyed yucca fibers. Yucca-fiber sifters are made by plaiting over a willow ring. This style of basket is made throughout the reservation.

POTTERY With the exception of undecorated utilitarian pottery that is made in Hotevilla on Third Mesa, most Hopi pottery is produced on First Mesa. Contemporary Hopi pottery comes in a variety of styles including a yellow-orange ware that is decorated with black and white designs. This style is said to have been introduced by the potter Nampeyo, a Tewa from the village of Hano who stimulated the revival of Hopi pottery in 1890. A white pottery with red and black designs is also popular. Hopi pottery designs tend toward geometric patterns.

WHERE TO STAY & DINE
SECOND MESA

HOPI CULTURAL CENTER RESTAURANT AND MOTEL, P.O. Box 67,
  Second Mesa, AZ 86043. Tel. 602/734-2401. 33 rms (all with bath). TV
  TEL
$ Rates: $52 single; $58 double. Children 12 and under stay free in parents' room.
  DC, MC, V.
This is the only lodging for miles around so be sure you have a reservation before heading up here for an overnight visit. The Hopi Cultural Center is the locus of visitor activities in the Hopi pueblos and its modern pueblo architecture fits in with its surroundings. Rooms are comfortable and were all recently renovated; some are wheelchair accessible. The restaurant serves American and traditional Hopi meals. There is also a museum.

WINSLOW

Though it's nearly 70 miles south of Second Mesa, this is the next closest place to stay if you're planning to tour the Hopi pueblos.

BEST WESTERN ADOBE INN, 1701 N. Park Dr., Winslow, AZ 86047.
  Tel. 602/289-4638. 72 rms (all with bath). A/C TV TEL
$ Rates: $36–$54 single; $40–$62 double. AE, DC, DISC, MC, V.
You'll find this modern motel at Exit 253 off I-40 is your best choice in Winslow. The contemporary pueblo exterior design is complemented by spacious guest rooms done in soothing pastels and featuring contemporary furnishings. The guest rooms all have balconies or patios opening onto the indoor pool area, and potted plants both in the rooms and by the pool give the whole motel a very homey feel. There are also a whirlpool bath, no-smoking rooms, and facilities for the disabled. The restaurant and lounge at the motel provide economical continental meals and a quiet place to have a drink and relax at the end of the day. Room service and in-room movies are also available.

BEST WESTERN TOWNHOUSE LODGE, 1914 W. Third St., Winslow, AZ
  86047. Tel. 602/289-4611. 67 rms (all with bath). A/C TV TEL
$ Rates: $30–$48 single; $34–$54 double. AE, CB, DC, DISC, MC, V.
Located near downtown Winslow at Exit 252 from I-40, the Townhouse Lodge is an older one-story motel. Guest rooms are large and have all been recently renovated,

with new carpeting and modern furniture. The hotel also offers in-room movies, a swimming pool, playground, and coin laundry.

There is a large coffee shop/dining room and lounge in a separate building in front of the hotel.

SUPER 8 MOTEL, 1916 W. Third St., Winslow, AZ 86047. Tel. 602/289-4606. 46 rms (all with bath). A/C TV TEL
$ Rates: $37–$43 single; $43–$49 double. AE, CB, DC, DISC, MC, V.

Take Exit 252 into Winslow to find this economical choice. Rooms are pretty standard but do include clock radios, free local calls, and in-room movies. Facilities for the disabled and no-smoking rooms are also available. The motel doesn't have a restaurant, but there are a couple within walking distance.

---

2. THE NAVAJO RESERVATION

To Navajo National Monument: 140 miles NE of Flagstaff,
90 miles E of Page, 60 miles SW of Monument Valley,
110 miles NW of Canyon de Chelly
To Monument Valley Navajo Tribal Park:
200 miles NE of Flagstaff, 60 miles NE of Navajo National Monument,
110 miles NW of Canyon de Chelly, 150 miles E of Page

GETTING THERE By Plane The nearest airports with regularly scheduled service are in Flagstaff and Page. See the respective sections of Chapter 6 for details.

By Train There is **Amtrak** (tel. toll free 800/872-7245) passenger service to Winslow, south of the reservation.

By Bus The **Navajo Transit System** (tel. 602/729-5457, 729-5458, or 729-5449) operates bus service Monday through Friday throughout the Navajo nation with service between the following cities: Farmington, Gallup, and Crown Point (all in New Mexico) and Window Rock, Kayenta, Chinle, and Tuba City. The route between Window Rock and Tuba City also stops at several of the Hopi villages. **Greyhound/Trailways Lines** stops in Winslow, Holbrook, and Houck. Check your local telephone directory for the phone number of your nearest Greyhound/Trailways station.

By Car The Navajo Indian Reservation is a vast area the size of West Virginia and is laced with a network of excellent paved roads as well as many unpaved roads that are not always passable to cars without four-wheel drive. From Flagstaff, Navajo National Monument can be reached by taking U.S. 89 north to U.S. 160; Monument Valley Navajo Tribal Park is a bit farther on U.S. 163. The most direct route to Canyon de Chelly National Monument from Flagstaff is by way of I-40 to U.S. 191 north. Window Rock is east of the north end of U.S. 191 on Ariz. 264.

ESSENTIALS The Navajo Reservation observes daylight saving time, unlike the rest of Arizona, so remember to set your watch forward an hour if visiting in the summer. Also keep in mind that *alcohol is not allowed on the reservation.*

Before taking a photograph of a Navajo, always ask permission. If permission is granted, a tip of 50¢ to $1 is expected.

For more information before visiting, contact the **Cultural Resources Department Visitors Services,** P.O. Box 308, Window Rock, AZ 86515 (tel. 602/871-4941), or **Navajoland Tourism Office,** P.O. Box 663, Window Rock, AZ 86515 (tel. 602/871-6659). The telephone **area code** is 602.

Roughly the size of West Virginia, the Navajo Reservation covers an area of 25,000 square miles of northeastern Arizona, as well as parts of New Mexico, Colorado, and Utah. It's the largest Native American reservation in the United States and is home to nearly 200,000 Navajos. Though there are now modern towns with supermarkets, shopping malls, and hotels on the reservation, most Navajos still follow a pastoral life-style—they are herders. As you travel the roads of the Navajo Reservation, you will frequently encounter flocks of sheep and goats, as well as herds of cattle and horses. These animals have free range of the reservation and often graze beside the highways, so take care when driving, especially at night.

Unlike the pueblo tribes such as the Hopis and Zuñis, the Navajos are relative newcomers to the Southwest. Their Athabascan language is most closely related to the languages spoken by Native Americans in the Pacific Northwest, Canada, and Alaska. It is believed that the Navajos migrated southward from northern Canada beginning around A.D. 1000, arriving in the Southwest sometime after 1400. At this time the Navajo were still hunters and gatherers, but contact with the pueblo tribes, who had long before adopted an agricultural life-style, began to change the Navajo into farmers. When the Spanish arrived in the Southwest in the early 17th century, the Navajo acquired horses, sheep, and goats through raids and adopted a pastoral way of life, grazing their herds in the high plains and canyon bottoms.

The continued use of raids, made even more successful with the acquisition of horses, put the Navajo in conflict with the Spanish settlers who were beginning to encroach on Navajo land. In 1805 the Spanish sent a military expedition into the Navajo's chief stronghold, Canyon de Chelly, and killed 115 people, who by some accounts are claimed to have been all women, children, and old men. This massacre didn't stop the conflicts between Navajo and Spanish settlers. In 1846, when this region became part of the United States, American settlers encountered the same problems that the Spanish had. Military outposts were established to protect the new settlers, and numerous unsuccessful attempts were made to establish peace. In 1863, after continued Navajo attacks, a military expedition led by Col. Kit Carson burned crops and homes late in the summer, effectively obliterating the Navajos' winter supplies. Thus defeated, the Navajo were rounded up and herded 400 miles to an inhospitable region of New Mexico near Fort Sumner. This march became known as the Long Walk, and had a profound influence on the Navajo. Living conditions at Fort Sumner were deplorable and the land was unsuitable for farming. In 1868 the Navajo were allowed to return to their homeland.

Upon returning home, and after continued clashes with white settlers, the Navajo eventually settled into a life-style of herding. In recent years, the Navajo have had to turn to different livelihoods. Though weaving and silverwork have become a lucrative business, the amounts of money it garners for the tribe as a whole is not significant. Many Navajo now take jobs as migrant workers; gas and oil leases on the reservation provide more income.

Though the reservation covers an immense area, much of it is of no value other than as scenery. Fortunately, the Navajo are recognizing the income potential of their spectacular land. Monument Valley is operated as a tribal park and there is also a Navajo-owned marina on Lake Powell in Utah.

As you travel the reservation you may notice small hexagonal buildings with rounded roofs. These are hogans, the traditional homes of the Navajo, and are usually made of wood and earth. The doorway of the hogan always faces east to greet the new day. At the Canyon de Chelly and Navajo National Monument visitor centers, you can look inside hogans that are part of the parks' exhibits. If you take a tour at Canyon de Chelly or Monument Valley, you may have an opportunity to visit a hogan that is still someone's home. Most Navajo now live in modest houses or mobile homes, but a family will usually also have a hogan for religious ceremonies.

WHAT TO SEE & DO
PARKS & MONUMENTS

MONUMENT VALLEY NAVAJO TRIBAL PARK, P.O. Box 93, Monument Valley, UT 84536. Tel. 801/727-3287.

You may not know it, but you have almost certainly seen Monument Valley before. Nature, in its role as sculptor, has created a garden of monoliths and spires in the north-central part of the Navajo Reservation at Monument Valley. This otherworldly landscape has been an object of fascination for years, and has served as backdrop for many western movies, including *Stagecoach* (1938) by John Ford, as well as for television shows and commercials.

Located 30 miles north of Kayenta just across the Utah state line, Monument Valley is a vast flat plain punctuated by natural cathedrals of sandstone. These huge monoliths rise up from the sagebrush with sheer walls that capture the light of the rising and setting sun and transform it into fiery hues. Evocative names reflect the shapes the sandstone has taken on as the forces of nature have eroded it: the Mittens, Three Sisters, Camel Butte, Elephant Butte, The Thumb, and Totem Pole being some of the most awe-inspiring natural monuments. A 17-mile unpaved loop road winds among these 1,000-foot-tall buttes and mesas.

Human inhabitation has also left its mark. Within the park there are more than 100 ancient Anasazi archeological sites, ruins, and petroglyphs dating to before A.D. 1300. The Navajo have been living in the valley for generations, long after the Anasazi departed, herding their sheep through the sagebrush scrublands, and some families continue to live here today.

At the valley overlook parking area you'll find a small museum, gift shop, snack bar, and campground ($10 per night per site), and numerous local Navajo guides who offer tours of Monument Valley, including **Bennet Tours,** P.O. Box 360285, Monument Valley, UT 84536 (tel. 801/727-3283 or 727-3287), which offers tours of various durations and prices. Another option is to book a tour with **Goulding's Tours,** P.O. Box 1, Monument Valley, UT 84536 (tel. 602/697-3231 or 801/727-3231). This company has its office on the edge of the valley at Goulding's Lodge, just a few miles from the park entrance. Half-day tours are $25 for adults and $13.50 for children under 12; full-day tours are $47.50 for adults and $23.75 for children under 12.

Admission: $3 per car.
Open: May–Sept, daily 8am–7pm; Oct–Apr, daily 8am–5pm.

NAVAJO NATIONAL MONUMENT, HC 71, Box 3, Tonalea, AZ 86044-9704. Tel. 602/672-2366.

Located 30 miles west of Kayenta and 60 miles northeast of Tuba City, Navajo National Monument encompasses Tsegi Canyon and three of the best-preserved Anasazi cliff dwellings in the region—Betatakin, Keet Seel, and the Inscription House. It's possible to visit both Betatakin and Keet Seel, but fragile Inscription House has been closed to the public since 1968. The name Navajo National Monument is a bit misleading. Although the Navajo people do inhabit the area now, it was the ancient Anasazi who built the cliff dwellings. The Navajo arrived centuries after the Anasazi had abandoned the area.

The inhabitants of Tsegi Canyon were known as the Kayenta Anasazi. The Chaco Anasazi and the Mesa Verde Anasazi built the spectacular pueblos in New Mexico. All the Anasazi began abandoning their well-constructed homes around the middle of the 13th century for reasons unknown and disappeared without a trace. Tree rings suggest that a drought in the latter part of the 13th century prevented the Anasazi from growing sufficient crops. However, in Tsegi Canyon, there is another theory for the abandonment. The canyon floors were usually flooded each year by spring and summer snow melt, which made farming quite productive, but in the mid-1200s weather patterns changed and streams running through the canyons began cutting deep into the soil, forming deep narrow canyons called arroyos, which lowered the water table and made farming much more difficult.

Betatakin, which means "ledge house" in Navajo, is the only one of the three ruins that can be easily seen. Built in a huge amphitheaterlike alcove in the canyon wall, Betatakin was occupied only from 1250 to 1300, and its height of occupation may have housed 125 people.

Two short trails from the visitor center lead to overlooks of Betatakin. The shorter of the two trails is paved, while the slightly longer trail is not. The strenuous five-mile round-trip hike to Betatakin itself takes about 5 hours and involves descending more than 700 feet to the floor of Tsegi Canyon and later returning to the rim. This ranger-led hike is conducted from May to September or October and leaves from the visitor center. All hikers are required to carry 2 quarts of water. This hike is very popular and the number of people allowed on each hike is limited; many people line up at the visitor center an hour or more before the center opens. During the summer months there are two hikes a day, while in spring and fall there is only one hike a day.

Keet Seel, which means "broken pieces of pottery" in Navajo, has a much longer history than Betatakin, with occupation beginning as early as A.D. 950 and continuing until 1300. At one point Keet Seel may have housed 150 people.

The 16-mile round-trip hike to Keet Seel is even more strenuous and requires an overnight stay at a primitive campground near the ruins. You must carry enough water for your trip since none is available along the trail. Only 20 people a day are given permits to visit Keet Seel, and in 1991 the trail was only open Friday through Monday from Memorial Day to Labor Day. If Keet Seel is your goal, be sure to call ahead and find out when the trail is open.

The **visitor center** has informative displays on the Anasazi culture, including numerous artifacts from Tsegi Canyon. You can also watch a 25-minute film or a short slide show. There is no lodge at the national monument, but there is a campground that's open from mid-April through mid-October. There are only 30 campsites here and in summer they are usually full by dark. There is no fee for camping.

Admission: Free.

Open: National monument, daily 24 hours; visitor center, spring through fall, daily 8am–5pm (longer hours in summer).

HUBBELL TRADING POST NATIONAL HISTORIC SITE, P.O. Box 150, Ganado, AZ 86505. Tel. 602/755-3475.

Located just outside the town of Ganado in the southeastern part of the reservation, the Hubbell Trading Post is the oldest continuously operating trading post on the Navajo Reservation. The trading post was established in 1876 by Lorenzo Hubbell, who did more to popularize the arts and crafts of the Navajo people than any other person. The trading post includes a small museum where you can watch Navajo weavers in the slow process of creating a rug. You'll soon understand why Navajo rugs cost thousands of dollars, although the women who weave the rugs usually make less than minimum wage. Silversmiths also practice their craft here at the trading post. The museum also includes exhibits on the history of the trading post with old photos and displays of old merchandise.

In the actual trading post itself, you may encounter Navajo trading jewelry or rugs for goods or cash. The squeaky old wooden floors are perpetually dusty, and an old office seems to have decades of clutter. The rug room is filled with a variety of traditional and contemporary Navajo rugs. Though it's possible to buy a small 12- by 18-inch rug for around $100, most cost in the thousands of dollars. There are also baskets, kachinas, and several cases of jewelry by Navajo, Hopi, and Zuñi in another room. Glance around the general store and you'll see basic foodstuffs (not much variety here) and bolts of cloth used by Navajo women for sewing their traditional skirts and blouses.

Trading posts have long been more than just a place to trade crafts for imported goods. They were for many years the main gathering spot for meeting people from other parts of the reservation and served as a sort of gossip fence and newsroom. You'll often see the post trader lounging around in the rug room with Navajo who have come in to trade. You can tour the grounds on your own to see how Lorenzo Hubbell and his family lived. There is a huge old barn as well as the Hubbells' living quarters. Regularly scheduled guided tours are also available.

Admission: Free.

Open: Apr–Oct, daily 8am–6pm; Oct–Apr, daily 8am–5pm.

WINDOW ROCK, ARIZONA

Window Rock, less than a mile from the New Mexico state line, is the capital of the Navajo nation. The town is named for a huge natural opening in a sandstone cliff wall just outside town, which has long been important to the Navajo. At one time there was a spring at the base of the rock, and water from the spring was used by medicine men performing the Tohee Ceremony, a water ceremony intended to bring the rains. Today Window Rock is preserved as the **Window Rock Tribal Park,** which is located 2 miles off Ariz. 264. The town of Window Rock is also home to the **Navajo Nation Museum** and **Navajo Nation Zoological and Botanical Park,** the only Native American–operated zoo in the country. The museum is located in the Navajo Arts & Crafts Enterprise next door to the Navajo Nation Inn on Ariz. 264 and contains artifacts, old photos, and contemporary crafts of the Navajo.

Open: museum, summer Mon–Sat 8am–5pm, winter Mon–Fri 8am–5pm; **zoo,** daily 8am–5pm. **Closed:** Christmas and New Year's Day.

SPECIAL EVENTS

Unlike the village ceremonies of the pueblo-dwelling Hopis, Navajo religious ceremonies tend to be held in the privacy of family hogans. However, there are numerous fairs, pow wows, and rodeos held throughout the year and the public is welcome to attend these. The biggest of these is the **Navajo Nation Fair,** held in Window Rock in early September each year. At this fair there are traditional dances, a rodeo, a pow wow, a parade, a Miss Navajo Pageant, and arts and crafts exhibits and sales.

Other important fairs include the **Central Navajo Fair** at Chinle, Arizona, in late August; the **Northern Navajo Fair** at Shiprock, New Mexico, in early October; and the **Western Navajo Fair** at Tuba City, Arizona, in mid-October.

SHOPPING

All over the Navajo Reservation you'll see stalls set up beside the road and at scenic overlooks. Though you might find quality merchandise and bargain prices, you'd do better to confine your purchases to trading posts, museum and park gift shops, and established shops where you receive some guarantee of the quality of the pieces for sale. The **Hubbell Trading Post** (see "What to See & Do," above) in Ganado has a well-deserved reputation for having an excellent selection of rugs and jewelry. Prices are not low, but neither is the quality. The **Cameron Trading Post** (tel. 679-2231), at the crossroads of Cameron where Ariz. 64 branches off U.S. 89 to Grand Canyon Village, is another historic trading post, specializing in museum-quality crafts including Navajo textiles from the period between 1860 and 1940.

NAVAJO RUGS After they acquired sheep and goats from the Spanish, the Navajo learned weaving from the pueblo tribes, and by the early 1800s their weavings were widely recognized as being the finest in the Southwest. The Navajo women primarily wove blankets, but by the end of the 19th century the craft began to die out when it became more economical to purchase a ready-made blanket or make one from purchased material. When Lorenzo Hubbell set up his trading post, he immediately recognized a potential market in the East for the woven blankets if they could be made heavy enough to be used as rugs. Having great respect for Hubbell, the Navajo adapted his ideas and soon began doing a brisk business. Although today the cost of Navajo rugs, which take hundreds of hours to make, has become almost prohibitively expensive, there are still enough women practicing the craft to keep it alive and provide plenty of rugs for shops and trading posts all over Arizona.

The best rugs are those made with homespun yarn and natural vegetal dyes. However, commercially manufactured yarns and dyes are being used more and more to keep costs down. There are more than 15 regional styles of rugs and quite a bit of overlapping and borrowing. Bigger and bolder patterns are likely to cost quite a bit less than very complex and highly detailed patterns.

NAVAJO SILVERWORK While the Hopi create overlay silverwork from sheets of silver and the Zuñi use silverwork simply as a base for their skilled lapidary or stone-cutting work, the Navajo silversmiths highlight the silver itself. Just as rug weaving did not begin until the latter part of the 19th century, silversmithing did not catch on with the Navajo until the 1880s, when Lorenzo Hubbell decided to hire Mexican silversmiths as teachers. When tourists began visiting the area after 1890, the demand for Navajo jewelry increased. The earliest pieces of Navajo jewelry were replicas of Spanish ornaments, but as the Navajo silversmiths became more proficient, they began to develop their own designs. Sandcasting, stampwork, repoussé, and file-and-chisel work create the distinctively Navajo jewelry. The squash-blossom necklace, with its horseshoe-shaped pendant, is perhaps the most distinctive Navajo jewelry design. Wide bracelets and concha belts are also popular.

SANDPAINTINGS Sandpaintings are traditionally used in healing ceremonies known as chants or chantways. The Navajo believe that when a person falls ill, that person has somehow upset the balance of the universe. Chantways are used to restore this universal balance, and include chants, prayers, herbs, and sandpaintings. Working from sunrise to sunset, a *hatathli* (medicine man) will create the appropriate sandpainting design on the floor of the ill person's hogan. After the sick person has been placed on top of the sandpainting and prayers are said, the sandpainting is destroyed.

Sandpaintings made for sale to tourists are made permanent by glueing the sand to a wood backing. Though traditional religious designs are often used, they are changed in some way to prevent duplicating the sacred designs. In recent years several Navajo sandpainters have been creating secular designs, and these are gaining popularity with tourists.

WHERE TO STAY & DINE
KAYENTA

ANASAZI INN AT TSEGI CANYON, on U.S. 60, P.O. Box 1543, Kayenta, AZ 86033. Tel. 602/697-3793. Fax 602/697-2334. 56 rms (all with bath). A/C TV TEL
$ Rates: $48 single; $53 double. Rates lower Oct–Apr. AE, CB, DC, DISC, MC, V.
Located about halfway between Kayenta and Navajo National Monument, the Anasazi Inn at Tsegi Canyon is a simple motel surrounded by wilderness, but it's the closest lodging to Navajo National Monument. If all the motels in Kayenta were full, you might be able to find something here. There is a small dining room attached to the motel.

HOLIDAY INN–KAYENTA, at the junction of U.S. 160 and U.S. 163 (P.O. Box 307), Kayenta, AZ 86033. Tel. 602/697-3221, or toll free 800/HOLIDAY. 160 rms, 8 suites (all with bath). A/C TV TEL
$ Rates: $49–$99 single; $59–$109 double; $72–$112 suite. AE, DC, DISC, MC, V.
Located in the center of Kayenta, 23 miles south of Monument Valley and 29 miles east of Navajo National Monument, this Holiday Inn is very popular with tour groups and is always crowded. Rooms are spacious and clean. The motel's restaurant is entered through a mock-up of a Navajo hogan and has a wall designed to look like part of an Anasazi ruin. The menu offers both American and traditional Navajo meals. Prices range from $6.50 to $14. The hotel also has a tour desk and gift shop.

WETHERILL INN MOTEL, P.O. Box 175, Kayenta, AZ 86033. Tel. 602/697-3231. 54 rms (all with bath). A/C TV TEL
$ Rates: $66 single; $72 double. AE, DC, DISC, MC, V.
Located 1 mile north of the junction of U.S. 160 and U.S. 163 and 20 miles south of Monument Valley, the Wetherill Inn Motel is the most convenient motel to Monument Valley. Guest rooms have recently been remodeled and all have their own coffee makers. The hotel offers airport pickup (no scheduled air service to this airport), a tour desk, and gift shop. There is a casual restaurant next door to the motel.

MONUMENT VALLEY

GOULDING'S LODGE, P.O. Box 1, Monument Valley, UT 84536. Tel. 801/727-3231. 62 rms (all with bath). A/C TV TEL
$ Rates: Apr–Oct, $84 single or double; Oct–Dec, $62 single or double; Jan–Mar, $52 single or double. AE, DC, DISC, MC, V.
This is the only lodge actually located in Monument Valley, and it offers superb views from the private balconies of the guest rooms, which are clean and modern, with southwestern decor. The Stagecoach Dining Room is located in a separate building

above the lodge. The views from here are enough to make any meal an event. Navajo and American meals are served. The hotel also features an indoor swimming pool with skylights above, a tour desk, museum, gift shop, coin laundry, and gas station.

WINDOW ROCK

NAVAJO NATION INN, 48 W. Ariz. 264 (P.O. Drawer 2340), Window Rock, AZ 86515. Tel. 602/871-4108. 54 rms, 2 suites (all with bath). A/C TV TEL
$ Rates: $55–$60 single or double; $70 suite. AE, MC, V.
Located in Window Rock, the administrative center of the Navajo Indian Reservation, the Navajo Nation Inn is a modern lodging featuring rustic southwestern furniture in the guest rooms. The restaurant and coffee shop are open daily from 6:30am to 9pm serving American and traditional Navajo dishes. The hotel also offers a tour desk and wheelchair accommodations.

---

3. CANYON DE CHELLY

222 miles NE of Flagstaff, 40 miles N of Hubbell Trading Post,
68 miles NW of Window Rock, 110 miles SE of Navajo National Monument,
110 miles SE of Monument Valley Navajo Tribal Park,
90 miles NE of Second Mesa

GETTING THERE   By Plane   The nearest airports with regularly scheduled service are in Flagstaff and Page. See the respective sections of Chapter 6 for details.

By Train   There is **Amtrak** (tel. toll free 800/872-7245) passenger service to Winslow, south of the Navajo Reservation. The train station is on East Second Street.

By Bus   Chinle, 3 miles from the entrance to Canyon de Chelly National Monument, is served by the **Navajo Transit System** (tel. 602/729-5457, 729-5458, or 729-5449). Winslow, Holbrook, and Houck are all served by **Greyhound/Trailways Lines.**

By Car   From Flagstaff, the easiest route to Canyon de Chelly is to take I-40 to U.S. 191 to Ganado. At Ganado, head west on Ariz. 264 to U.S. 191, which heads north to Chinle. If you're coming down from Monument Valley or Navajo National Monument, Indian Route 59, which connects U.S. 160 and U.S. 191, is an excellent road with plenty of beautiful scenery.

ESSENTIALS   For information before leaving home, contact **Canyon de Chelly National Monument,** P.O. Box 588, Chinle, AZ 86503 (tel. 602/674-5213). The telephone **area code** is 602.

It's hard to imagine narrow canyons less than 1,000 feet deep being more spectacular than the Grand Canyon, but in some ways the canyons of Canyon de Chelly National Monument are just that. Stand on the rim of Canyon de Chelly gazing down at an ancient Anasazi cliff dwelling as the whinnying of horses and clanging of goat bells drifts up from far below and you will be struck by the continuity of human life. For more than 2,000 years people have called these canyons home, and today there are more than 100 prehistoric dwelling sites in the area.

Canyon de Chelly National Monument consists of two major canyons—Canyon de Chelly (which is pronounced "Canyon de Shay" and is derived from the Navajo word *tségi,* meaning "rock canyon") and Canyon del Muerto (Spanish for Canyon of the Dead)—and several smaller canyons. Together the canyons extend for more than 100 miles through the rugged slick-rock landscape of northeastern Arizona, draining the seasonal runoff from the snow melt of the Chuska Mountains. These streams have for centuries carved the canyons as they bring water for farming the fertile soils of the canyon bottoms.

Canyon de Chelly's smooth vertical sandstone walls of rich reds and yellows sharply contrast with the deep greens of corn, pasture, and cottonwood on the canyon floor. Vast stone amphitheaters form the caves in which the ancient Anasazi built their homes. As you watch shadows and light paint an ever-changing canyon panorama, it's easy to see why the Navajo consider these canyons sacred ground. With mysteriously abandoned cliff dwellings and breathtaking natural beauty, Canyon de Chelly is certainly as worthy of a visit as the Grand Canyon.

WHAT TO SEE & DO

The **visitor center,** open daily from 8am to 6pm, should be everyone's first stop at Canyon de Chelly. Out front is a traditional crib-style hogan, a hexagonal construction of logs and earth that serves both as a home and as a ceremonial center. (Though most Navajo now live in modern homes or mobile homes, most also have a hogan for religious ceremonies.) Inside, a small museum acquaints visitors with the history of Canyon de Chelly, and near the front door there is usually a silversmith demonstrating Navajo jewelry-making techniques. If you want to drive your own four-wheeler into the canyon, this is where you need to get your permit. From May to the beginning of September there are daily programs, including morning coffee talks at the hogan near the visitor center, ranger-led canyon hikes (these are popular, so be sure to sign up at the visitor center), campfire programs, and natural-history programs. Saturday is Navajo day, with special programs pertaining to Navajo culture, presented in both English and Navajo.

Access to the canyons is restricted, and in order to descend into the canyon *you must be accompanied by either a park ranger or an authorized guide,* unless you are on the White House Ruins trail. The best way to see Canyon de Chelly and Canyon del Muerto is from one of the four- or six-wheel-drive trucks that operate out of **Thunderbird Lodge** (tel. 602/674-5841). These trucks are equipped with seats in the bed and stop frequently for photographs and to visit ruins, Navajo farms, and rock art. Tours cost $30 per person for a half day ($21 for children 12 and under); all-day tours are $50. Half-day tours leave at 9am and 2pm in summer, 9am and 1pm in winter; full-day trips leave at 9am and return at 5:30pm.

You can also hire a Navajo guide to lead you into the canyon on foot or in your own four-wheel-drive vehicle. The guide fee is $8 per hour. There are also two stables offering horseback tours into the canyon. **Justin Tso Horse Rental** (tel. 602/674-5678) and **Twin Trails Tours** (tel. 602/674-3466 or 674-3427) both charge around $8 per hour for a horse and $8 per hour for a guide.

THE RIM DRIVES

A very different view of the canyons is provided by the north and south rim drives. The north rim drive overlooks Canyon del Muerto, while the south rim drive overlooks Canyon de Chelly. Each of the rim drives is around 20 miles in each direction, and with stops it can easily take 3 hours to visit each rim.

THE NORTH RIM DRIVE   The first stop on the north rim is the **Ledge Ruin Overlook.** On the opposite wall, about 100 feet up from the canyon floor, you can see the Ledge Ruin. This site was occupied by the Anasazi between A.D. 1050 and 1275. Nearby, at the **Dekaa Kiva Viewpoint,** you can see a lone kiva (circular ceremonial building). This structure was reached by means of toe holds cut into the soft sandstone cliff wall.

The second stop is at **Antelope House Overlook.** The Antelope House ruin takes its name from the paintings of antelopes on a nearby cliff wall. It is believed that the paintings were done in the 1830s. Beneath the ruins of Antelope House, archeologists have found the remains of an earlier pit house dating back to A.D. 693. Though most of the Anasazi cliff dwellings were abandoned sometime after a drought began in 1276, Antelope House had already been abandoned by 1260, possibly because of damage caused by flooding. Across the wash from Antelope House, an ancient tomb, known as the **Tomb of the Weaver,** was discovered in the 1920s by archeologists. The tomb contained the well-preserved body of an old man wrapped in a blanket of golden eagle feathers and accompanied by cornmeal, shelled and husked

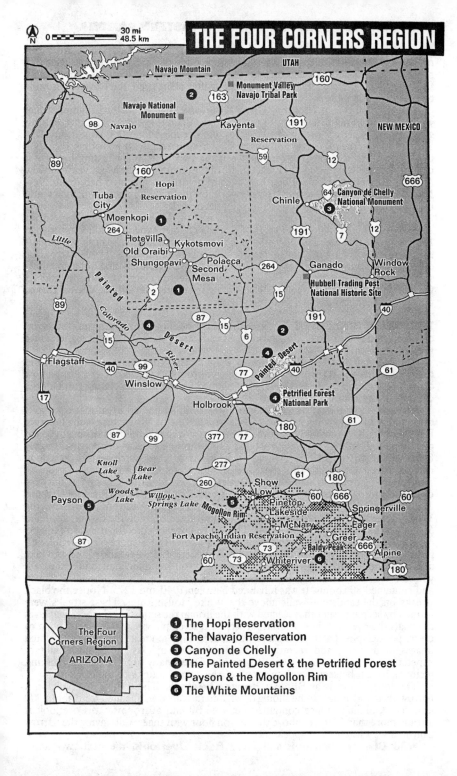

THE FOUR CORNERS REGION

30 mi
0 — 48.5 km
N

UTAH

△ Navajo Mountain

② 163 ■ Monument Valley
Navajo Tribal Park

160

Navajo National
Monument ■

98 Navajo

Kayenta

191

NEW MEXICO

Reservation

59

12

89

160

Hopi
Reservation

Tuba
City

Moenkopi

264

Chinle

64 Canyon de Chelly
③ National Monument

666

191

7

12

Hotevilla
Old Oraibi
Kykotsmovi
Shungopavi
Polacca
Second
Mesa

①

264

Ganado

Window
Rock

Little

Painted

Colorado

89

②

①

87

15

6

②

15

191

Hubbell Trading Post
National Historic Site

40

61

Desert

River

Painted Desert

④

40

Flagstaff

40

99

15

Winslow

77

40

17

Holbrook

180

④ Petrified Forest
National Park

61

87

99

377

77

180

61

Knoll
Lake

Bear
Lake

277

Show
Low

61

180

60

Woods
Lake

260

Willow
Springs Lake

Mogollon Rim

⑤

Pinetop
Lakeside

60 666

Springerville

60

Payson ⑤

McNary

Eager

87

Fort Apache Indian Reservation

73

Greer
Baldy Peak ×

666

Alpine

60

73

Whiteriver

⑥

180

The Four
Corners Region

ARIZONA

① The Hopi Reservation
② The Navajo Reservation
③ Canyon de Chelly
④ The Painted Desert & the Petrified Forest
⑤ Payson & the Mogollon Rim
⑥ The White Mountains

corn, piñon nuts, beans, salt, and thick skeins of cotton. Also visible from this overlook is **Navajo Fortress,** a red sandstone butte that the Navajo once used as a refuge from attackers. A steep trail leads to the top of Navajo Fortress, and through the use of log ladders that could be pulled up after being used, the Navajo were able to escape their attackers.

The third stop is at **Mummy Cave Overlook,** named for two mummies that were found in burial urns below the ruins. Archeological evidence indicates that this giant amphitheater consisting of two caves was occupied for 1,000 years from A.D. 300 to 1300. In the two caves and on the shelf between there are 80 rooms, including three kivas. The central structure between the two caves is interesting because it includes a three-story building characteristic of the architecture in Mesa Verde in New Mexico. Archeologists speculate that a group of Anasazi migrated here from New Mexico. Much of the original plasterwork of these buildings is still intact and indicates that the buildings were colorfully decorated.

The fourth and last stop on the north rim is at the **Massacre Cave Overlook.** The cave received its name after an 1805 Spanish military expedition killed more than 115 Navajo at this site. The Navajo at the time had been raiding Spanish settlements that were encroaching on Navajo territory. Accounts of the battle at Massacre Cave differ. One account claims that there were only women, children, and old men taking shelter in the cave, though the official Spanish records claim 90 warriors and 25 women and children were killed. Also visible from this overlook is **Yucca Cave,** which was occupied about 1,000 years ago.

THE SOUTH RIM DRIVE The south rim drive follows the south rim of Canyon de Chelly and climbs slowly but steadily. At each stop you are a little bit higher above the canyon floor.

The first stop is at **Tségi Overlook.** *Tségi* means "rock canyon" in Navajo, and that's just what you'll see when you gaze down from this viewpoint. A short narrow canyon feeds into Chinle Wash, which is formed by the streams cutting through the canyons of the national monument.

The second stop is at the **Junction Overlook,** so named because it overlooks the junction of Canyon del Muerto and Canyon de Chelly. Visible here is the Junction Ruin, with its 10 rooms and one kiva. The Anasazi occupied this ruin during the great pueblo period, which lasted from around 1100 until the Anasazi disappeared shortly before 1300. Also visible is First Ruin, which is perched precipitously on a long narrow ledge. Within this ruin there are 22 rooms and two kivas.

The third stop, at **White House Overlook,** provides the only opportunity for descending into Canyon de Chelly without a guide or ranger. The White House Ruins Trail descends 600 feet to the canyon floor, crosses Chinle Wash, and approaches the White House Ruins. These buildings were constructed both on the canyon floor and 50 feet up the cliff wall in a small cave. Though you cannot enter the ruins, you can get close enough to get a good look. You are not allowed to wander off this trail, and please respect the privacy of those Navajo living here. It's a 2½-mile round-trip hike and takes about 2 hours. Be sure to carry water. If you aren't inclined to hike the trail, you can view the ruins from the overlook. This is one of the largest ruins in the canyon and contained 80 rooms. It was inhabited between 1040 and 1275. Notice the black streaks on the sandstone walls above the White House Ruins. These streaks were formed by seeping water that reacted with the iron in the sandstone. Iron is what gives the walls their reddish hue. Anasazi artists used to chip away at this black patina to create petroglyphs. Later the Navajo would use paints to create pictographs, painted images of animals, and records of historic events such as the Spanish military expedition that killed 115 Navajo at Massacre Cave. Many of these petroglyphs and pictographs can be seen if you take one of the guided tours into the canyon.

The fourth stop is at **Sliding House Overlook.** These ruins are built on a narrow shelf and appear to be sliding down into the canyon. Inhabited from about 900 until 1200, Sliding House contained between 30 and 50 rooms. This overlook is already more than 700 feet above the canyon floor with sheer walls giving the narrow canyon a very foreboding appearance.

Wild Cherry Overlook and **Face Rock Overlook,** the next two stops, provide further glimpses of the ever-deepening canyon. Here you are gazing down 1,000 feet to the bottom of the canyon. The last stop on the south rim is one of the most spectacular—**Spider Rock Overlook.** This viewpoint overlooks the junction of Canyon de Chelly and Monument Canyon, and at this wide spot in the canyon stands the monolithic pinnacle called Spider Rock. Rising 800 feet from the canyon floor, the free-standing twin-towers of Spider Rock are a natural monument, a geologic wonder. Across the canyon from Spider Rock stands the almost-as-striking **Speaking Rock,** which is connected to the far canyon wall.

WHERE TO STAY & DINE

In addition to the two motels listed below, there is a year-round free campground near Thunderbird Lodge that does not take reservations. In the summer the campground has water and rest rooms, but in the winter you must bring your own water and only portable toilets are available.

CANYON DE CHELLY MOTEL, P.O. Box 295, Chinle, AZ 86503. Tel. 602/674-5875. 68 rms (all with bath). A/C TV TEL
$ Rates: $52–$70 single; $56–$74 double. AE, DC, MC, V.
Located in the center of Chinle, the Canyon de Chelly Motel is a modern lodging with medium to large rooms that feature modern furnishings. There are beamed ceilings and coffee makers in all the rooms, and tribal-motif bedspreads. The new restaurant is large and the menu features American and Navajo meals, with dinner prices ranging from $7 to $15. There are also an indoor swimming pool and no-smoking rooms.

THUNDERBIRD LODGE, P.O. Box 548, Chinle, AZ 86503. Tel. 602/674-5841 or 674-5842. 72 rms, 1 suite (all with bath). A/C TV TEL
$ Rates: $67–$72 single; $73–$77 double; $130–$142 suite. Rates lower Oct–Apr. AE, DC, DISC, MC, V.
★ Built on the site of an early trading post at the mouth of Canyon de Chelly, the Thunderbird Lodge is the most appealing of the lodges in this region. The pink adobe construction is reminiscent of ancient pueblos, and guest rooms have rustic furniture and Navajo sandpaintings on the walls. Rooms come in two different sizes, with either two double beds or two queen-size beds. Ceiling fans and air conditioners keep the rooms cool in the hot summer months. Carpets and bathrooms are new. The original trading post building now serves as the lodge dining room. Open daily, the dining room serves both American and Navajo meals. The lodge also has a tour desk, gift shop, and rug room.

---

4. THE PAINTED DESERT & THE PETRIFIED FOREST

25 miles E of Holbrook, 58 miles E of Winslow, 90 miles E of Flagstaff, 118 miles S of Canyon de Chelly, 55 miles N of Pinetop-Lakeside, 180 miles N of Phoenix, 230 miles W of Albuquerque

GETTING THERE   By Plane   The nearest airport with regularly scheduled service is in Flagstaff. See "Flagstaff" in Chapter 6 for details.

By Train   There is **Amtrak** (tel. toll free 800/872-7245) passenger service to Winslow, 33 miles west.

By Bus   Holbrook is served by **Greyhound/Trailways Lines.** Check your local telephone directory for the phone number of the nearest bus station.

By Car   The north entrance to Petrified Forest National Park is 25 miles east of Holbrook on I-40. The south entrance is 20 miles east of Holbrook on U.S. 180.

ESSENTIALS   For more information on the Painted Desert or the Petrified Forest, contact the **Petrified Forest National Park,** Petrified National Forest, AZ 86028 (tel. 602/524-6228). For information on Holbrook and the surrounding region, contact the **Holbrook Chamber of Commerce,** 100 East Arizona Street, Holbrook, AZ 86025 (tel. 602/524-6558). The **telephone area code** is 602.

While environmentalists in the Northwest fight to preserve the last remaining ancient forests, 20 miles east of Holbrook, at the Petrified Forest National Park, visitors can see truly ancient forests that have been preserved as petrified wood. Though petrified wood can be found in almost every state, the "forests" of downed logs here in northeastern Arizona are by far the most spectacular. A 27-mile scenic drive winds through the petrified forest and a small corner of the Painted Desert, providing a fascinating desert experience.

Petrified wood has intrigued people for years and when, in the 1850s, it was discovered scattered like kindling across this section of Arizona, enterprising people began exporting it wholesale to the East. By 1900 so much had been removed that in 1906 several areas were set aside as the Petrified Forest National Monument.

It's hard to believe when you drive across this arid landscape, but at one time this area was a vast humid swamp. That was 225 million years ago, when dinosaurs and huge amphibians ruled the earth and giant now-extinct trees grew on the high ground around the swamp. Fallen trees were washed downstream and gathered in piles in still backwaters of the swamp. There they were eventually covered over with silt, mud, and volcanic ash. Preserved from decay by this burial, the logs lay as they were when they fell until water, bearing dissolved silica that had leached from the volcanic ash, seeped into the logs. The dissolved silica filled the cells of the wood and eventually recrystallized into stone to form petrified wood.

This region was later inundated with water and thick deposits of sediment buried the logs ever deeper. Eventually the land was transformed yet again as a geologic upheaval thrust the lake bottom up above sea level. This upthrust of the land cracked the logs into the segments we see today. Eventually wind and water eroded the landscape to create the many colorful and spectacular features of northern Arizona, including the Painted Desert, and the petrified logs were once again exposed on the surface of the land.

Throughout the region you'll see petrified wood in all sizes and colors, natural and polished, being sold in gift stores. Though this petrified wood comes from the same period as that found in the park, it all comes from private land. No petrified wood, no matter how small, may be removed from Petrified Forest National Park.

WHAT TO SEE & DO

PETRIFIED FOREST NATIONAL PARK (including the Painted Desert), 25 miles east of Holbrook on I-40 or 20 miles east on U.S. 180. Tel. 602/524-6228.

The park has two visitor centers. Both have maps and books about the region, and also give out the free permits necessary to backpack and camp in the park's wilderness areas. The **Painted Desert Visitor Center** is at the north end of the park and is open daily from 8am to 5pm. A 17-minute film here explains the process by which wood becomes fossilized. The **Rainbow Forest Museum,** at the south end of the park, is open daily from 8am to 5pm. Exhibits, including letters written by people who had taken pieces of petrified wood and who later felt guilty and returned the stones, chronicle the area's geologic and human history. Connecting the two visitor centers is a 27-mile scenic road with more than 20 overlooks. The petrified logs are concentrated in the southern part of the park, while the northern section overlooks the Painted Desert.

Starting at the southern end of the park, there is the **Giant Logs self-guided trail.** This trail starts behind the Rainbow Forest Museum and a booklet explaining the numbered stops is available at the front desk. The trail lives up to its name, with huge logs strewn about the hilly area. Almost directly across the parking lot from the Rainbow Forest Museum is the entrance to the Long Logs and Agate House areas. On the **Long Logs trail** you can see more big trees, while at **Agate House** you will see the ruins of a pueblo built from wood that was turned into colorful agate. Minerals such as iron, manganese, and carbon are what give petrified wood its distinctive colors.

Heading north, you pass by the unusual formations known as the **Flattops.** These structures are caused by the erosion of softer soil deposits from beneath a harder and more erosion-resistant layer of sandstone. The Flattops area is one of the park's wilderness areas. **Crystal Forest** is the next stop to the north and is named for the beautiful amethyst and quartz crystals that were once found in the cracks of petrified logs. Concern over the removal of these crystals was what led to the protection of the petrified forest.

At the **Jasper Forest Overlook,** you can see logs that include petrified roots, while at **Blue Mesa** pieces of petrified wood form capstones over easily eroded clay soils. As wind and water wear away at the clay beneath a piece of stone, the balance of the stone becomes more and more precarious until it eventually comes toppling down. At the **Agate Bridge** stop, the soil has been washed away under a petrified log creating a natural agate bridge.

Erosion has played a major role in the formation of the Painted Desert and to the north of Blue Mesa you'll see some of the most interesting erosional features of the area. It is quite evident why these hills of sandstone and clay are known as the **Teepees.** The layers of different color are due to different types of soils and stone and to minerals dissolved in the soil.

Human habitation of the area dates back more than 2,000 years, and at **Newspaper Rock** you can see petroglyphs (rock carvings) left by generations of Native Americans. At **Puerco Indian Ruins** you can see the homes of the people who made the carvings prior to the abandonment of the area around 1400.

North of Puerco Ruins, the road crosses the Santa Fe Railroad and then I-40. From here to the Painted Desert Visitor Center there are eight overlooks onto the southernmost edge of the **Painted Desert.** Named for the vivid colors of the soil and stone that cover the land here, the Painted Desert is a Technicolor dreamscape of pastel colors washed across a barren expanse of eroded hills. The colors are created by minerals dissolved in the sandstone and clay soils that were deposited during different geologic periods. There is a picnic area at **Chinde Point** overlook, and at **Kachina Point,** where the Painted Desert Inn Museum is undergoing renovation. From here, there is access to the park's other wilderness area.

At the north end, the **Painted Desert Oasis** provides a full-service cafeteria. It's open September through May, daily from 8am to 5pm; June through August, daily from 6am to 7pm. At the south end of the park there's a snack bar serving sandwiches and ice cream. It's open September through May, daily from 8am to 5pm; June through August, daily from 7am to 7pm.

Admission: $5 per car.
Open: Daily 8am–5pm.

WHERE TO STAY
HOLBROOK

The best place to look for lodgings in Holbrook is along East Navajo Boulevard (Exit 289 from I-40), where there are half a dozen modern motels, including the first two of the following:

COMFORT INN, 2602 E. Navajo Blvd., Holbrook, AZ 86025. Tel. 602/ 524-6131, or toll free 800/228-5150. 84 rms (all with bath). A/C TV TEL
$ Rates: $42–$62 single; $44–$66 double. AE, DC, DISC, MC, V.
This is the first lodging you'll come to after you get off I-40 at Exit 289. Rooms are what you'd expect from an Interstate off-ramp motel—not too big, but clean and with good beds.

Jerry's Restaurant is open 24 hours a day and serves economical meals. The hotel also offers free coffee, in-room movies, a swimming pool, wheelchair accommodations, and no-smoking rooms.

DAYS INN, 2601 E. Navajo Blvd., Holbrook, AZ 86025. Tel. 602/524-6949, or toll free 800/325-2525. 54 rms, 3 suites (all with bath). A/C TV TEL
$ Rates: $36–$56 single; $46–$62 double; $50–$85 suite. AE, CB, DC, DISC, MC, V.

This is one of the newest motels in Holbrook. Rooms are modern, clean, and comfortable. The suites have in-room whirlpool bathtubs. The hotel also offers free coffee and doughnuts, free local phone calls, an indoor swimming pool, whirlpool bath, coin laundry, no-smoking rooms, and wheelchair accommodations. You'll find it at Exit 289 from I-40.

WIGWAM MOTEL, 811 W. Hopi Dr., Holbrook, AZ 86025. Tel. 602/524-3048. 15 rms. A/C TV TEL
$ Rates: $25 single; $30 double. MC, V.

Here in Holbrook you can have your chance to sleep in a very modern concrete wigwam. This unusual motel was built in the 1940s when unusual architecture was springing up all over the country. Owned by the same family since it was built, the Wigwam was renovated a few years ago. You'll still find the original rustic furniture and colorful bedspreads in the small wigwam-shaped buildings. There is also a gift shop and small museum here at the motel. You'll find the Wigwam on old Route 66 (U.S. 66), the main drag through downtown Holbrook.

WHERE TO DINE

BUTTERFIELD STAGE CO., 609 W. Hopi Dr. Tel. 524-3447.
Cuisine: CONTINENTAL. **Reservations:** Not necessary.
$ Prices: Appetizers $3.50–$4.50; main courses $9–$17. AE, MC, V.
Open: Dinner only, daily 4–10pm.

It's natural to assume that finding a decent meal in an out-of-the-way town might be near impossible, so the Butterfield Stage Co. is a pleasant surprise. The owners are from Yugoslavia, and I'm not sure how they got to Holbrook, but I do know that meals here are excellent. The soup and salad bar is always fresh and there isn't a better espresso or cappuccino for miles around. The restaurant is named for the famous overland stagecoach line that carried the mail from St. Louis to San Francisco in the mid-19th century.

5. PAYSON & THE MOGOLLON RIM

94 miles NE of Phoenix, 90 miles SW of Winslow,
90 miles SE of Flagstaff, 100 miles W of Pinetop-Lakeside

GETTING THERE By Plane The nearest airports with regularly scheduled service are in Phoenix and Flagstaff. See Chapters 4 and 6 for details.

By Train The nearest **Amtrak** (tel. toll free 800/872-7245) stations are in Winslow, Flagstaff, and Phoenix, all of which are about 90 miles from Payson. From there you'll have to drive or take a bus.

By Bus The **Payson Express** (tel. 602/256-6464 in Phoenix or 602/474-5254 in Payson) operates one bus a day between Phoenix and Payson and offers door-to-door service.

By Car Payson is 94 miles from Phoenix on Ariz. 87, the Beeline Highway. Ariz. 87 also connects Payson to Winslow, which is 90 miles away. Ariz. 260 runs east from Payson, climbing the Mogollon Rim and continuing into the White Mountains.

ESSENTIALS For more information on Payson, contact the **Payson Chamber of Commerce,** P.O. Box 1380, Payson, AZ 85547 (tel. 602/474-4515). The **telephone area code** is 602.

Ninety miles from Phoenix and at 5,000 feet above sea level, Payson is one of the closest places for Phoenicians to find relief from the summer heat. Summer temperatures are 20° cooler than in the Valley of the Sun, and the surrounding Tonto

National Forest provides opportunities for hiking, swimming, fishing, and hunting. It isn't quite high enough to be the mountains, but it certainly isn't the desert. The Mogollon Rim, a 2,000-foot escarpment that runs from central Arizona into New Mexico, is only 22 miles north of town. The Mogollon Rim country was featured in many of the western novels of Zane Grey, who made his home in a cabin near Payson. In recent years, retirees have discovered the nearly perfect climate of Payson. Summer highs are usually in the 80s while winter highs are usually in the 50° to 60° range.

WHAT TO SEE & DO

The first thing you should know about Payson is that Zane Grey's cabin is no more. It was destroyed by a forest fire in 1990 and there are no plans to reconstruct it. So all of you Zane Grey fans will have to content yourself with simply seeing the country Grey wrote about.

Tonto Natural Bridge State Park (tel. 602/476-4202), located 15 miles north of Payson on Ariz. 87, is the largest natural travertine bridge in the world. Discovered in 1877 by a gold prospector named David Gowan, who was being chased by Apaches, the bridge is 183 feet high and at its widest point, is 150 feet across. This state park preserves not only the bridge, but a historic lodge built by Gowan's nephew and the nephew's sons. Today the lodge has been restored to the way it looked in 1927 and is a bed-and-breakfast inn. For more information, contact **Tonto Natural Bridge and Historic Lodge,** P.O. Box 1600, Pine, AZ 85544 (tel. 602/476-3440). Admission to the park is $3 per car or $1 per pedestrian. The park is open April through May, daily from 8am to 6pm; June through September, daily from 8am to 7pm; and October through March, Monday through Friday from 9am to 5pm and Saturday and Sunday from 9am to 6pm.

Other attractions in the Payson area include the small **Payson Zoo,** which is located less than 7 miles east of town on Ariz. 260 (tel. 474-5435). Most of the animals in this zoo have appeared in movies, television shows, and commercials. There are bears, tigers, a lion, a wolf, a leopard, a cougar, and many other animals from around the world. Admission is $3 for adults and $1 for children.

The **Highline Trail** is a 51-mile-long hiking trail along the lower slope of the Mogollon Rim. You can find out more about the trail at the Payson Ranger Station on Ariz. 260 at the east end of town. Up on the top of the Mogollon Rim are seven lakes well known for their excellent fishing. The lakes are reached from a forest road that leaves Ariz. 260 just past the top of the Mogollon Rim.

SPECIAL EVENTS

Payson calls itself the "Festival Capital of the World" and though this claim may be a bit overstated, there certainly are plenty of festivals here. The **world's oldest rodeo** (a claim also made by Prescott's rodeo) takes place each year in August, while an **Old Timers Rodeo** is held in May. In June there's the annual **Country Music Festival,** and in July, the **Loggers Sawdust Festival.** In September there's the **State Fiddler's Contest & Bluegrass Festival,** and in October, the **October Art Festival.**

WHERE TO STAY

MODERATE

BEST WESTERN PAYSONGLO LODGE, 1005 S. Beeline Hwy., Payson, AZ 85541. Tel. 602/474-2382, or toll free 800/772-9766, 800/872-9766 in Arizona. Fax 602/474-1937. 26 rms, 18 suites (all with bath). A/C TV TEL

$ Rates (including continental breakfast): $48–$80 single or double; $76–$180 suites. Rates lower Nov–Apr. AE, DC, DISC, MC, V.

Located on the south side of town, the Paysonglo is Payson's best motel. As soon as you walk into the lobby, you'll sense that this is not your average motel. A comfortable seating area looks more like a living room than a lobby, and in winter there is always a fire in the marble fireplace. Guest rooms feature contemporary furnishings and several have their own fireplaces. The hotel also offers free coffee and cookies, a swimming pool, whirlpool bath, and no-smoking rooms.

KOHL'S RANCH RESORT, E. Ariz. 260, Payson, AZ 85541. Tel. 602/478-4211, or toll free 800/331-KOHL. 41 rms, 8 cabins (all with bath). A/C TV TEL

$ Rates: $30–$41 single; $38–$84 double; $84–$147 cabin. AE, DISC, MC, V.

Kohl's Ranch is 17 miles east of Payson on Ariz. 260 and is surrounded by quiet forests. Situated on the banks of Tonto Creek, this casual family resort is an excellent base for exploring the Mogollon Rim region. The lodge's lobby is a towering glass-fronted A-frame with a large stone fireplace and many exposed beams. Guest rooms vary from modern lodge rooms with hardwood-look carpets and log cabin look-alike walls to rustic wood paneled two-bedroom cabins. Some of the smaller rooms have fireplaces, as do the cabins. Rates here are highest on summer weekends and lowest on midwinter weekdays. The Zane Grey Dining Room gives you the impression that you're eating in the streets of an old Wild West cow town. The Saloon and Dance Hall features live western music on weekends, and across the parking lot by the stables is a real cowboy bar and pool hall. The hotel also offers horseback riding ($15 per hour), hayrides, a swimming pool, sauna, and video arcade.

SWISS VILLAGE LODGE, 801 N. Beeline Hwy. (P.O. Box 399), Payson, AZ 85541. Tel. 602/474-3241, or toll free 800/24-SWISS in Arizona. 99 rms, 1 suite (all with bath). A/C TV TEL

$ Rates: $39–$89 single or double; $109 suite. AE, MC, V.

The Swiss Village is across the street from Payson's Swiss-style shopping center. All the guest rooms here have small refrigerators and some have kitchenettes. In addition, some rooms have wet bars and fireplaces. Furnishings in the rooms are a bit old but are clean, and bathrooms are large. The Swiss Village Restaurant serves American and continental dishes at reasonable prices. There's live dance music in the Matterhorn lounge on weekends. A swimming pool is available for guests use.

BUDGET

CHRISTOPHER CREEK LODGE, Ariz. 260 (Star Rte., Box 119), Payson, AZ 85541. Tel. 602/478-4300. 6 rms, 15 cabins (all with bath).

$ Rates: $40–$65 single or double. MC, V.

Located 23 miles east of Payson on Ariz. 260, the Christopher Creek Lodge is a family-oriented rustic mountain retreat. You can choose between motel-style rooms with sleeping lofts; large spartan creekside cabins complete with full kitchen, woodstove, and sleeping loft; or tandem cabins with woodstoves, sliding glass doors, and picnic tables in the dining areas. All the accommodations are under the trees with Christopher Creek running along the edge of the property.

PAYSON PUEBLO INN, 809 E. Ariz. 260, Payson, AZ 85541. Tel. 602/474-5241. 31 rms, 1 suite (all with bath). A/C TV TEL

$ Rates: $35–$60 single; $40–$60 double; $69–$90 suite. AE, DC, MC, V.

You can't miss this eye-catching pale-blue pueblo-style building with its red trim. It's on the right as you're heading out of town on Ariz. 260. Rooms here are modern and clean, and all have small refrigerators. Tile accents on the bathroom counters are a nice touch. The motel's biggest drawback is its lack of a pool, but there is free morning coffee, and no-smoking rooms are available.

WHERE TO DINE

HERITAGE HOUSE GARDEN TEA ROOM, 202 W. Main St. Tel. 474-5501.

Cuisine: SALADS/SANDWICHES. **Reservations:** Not necessary.

$ Prices: $4.50–$6. MC, V.

Open: Lunch only, Mon–Sat 11am–3pm.

Tucked away in the back of this crafts store is a popular lunch spot and tearoom. The short menu features delicious sandwiches and crisp salads, but for many people the real draw here is the dessert tray. There's always a great selection of tempting cakes, cheesecakes, and mousses, as well as respectable cappuccinos and espressos. You'll find Heritage House only steps away from the Oaks.

THE OAKS RESTAURANT, 302 W. Main St. Tel. 474-1929.
   Cuisine: AMERICAN. **Reservations:** Suggested.
$ Prices: Appetizers $4–$6.50; main courses $8.50–$13. MC, V.
   Open: Lunch Tues–Sat 11am–2pm; dinner Tues–Sat 5–9pm, Sun 5–8pm; brunch Sun 11am–2pm.

Taking its name from the grove of oak trees spreading over it, the Oaks Restaurant is a quiet place for a meal in Payson. The large patio dining area beside the grassy front lawn is a great spot for lunch or dinner on a warm night. The dinner menu, which changes monthly, is short and to the point: Steaks and seafood, simply prepared, are the mainstays. The Caesar salad is good, as are the various cakes. The lunch menu features a variety of hot and cold sandwiches as well as several salads.

---

6. THE WHITE MOUNTAINS

To Pinetop-Lakeside: 185 miles NE of Phoenix, 140 miles SE of Flagstaff, 50 miles S of Holbrook, 90 miles NE of Payson

GETTING THERE   By Car   There is no regularly scheduled bus or air service, so the only way to reach this area is by car. Pinetop and Lakeside are both located on Ariz. 260. McNary and Greer are just a few miles south of this highway. Alpine is 27 miles south of the end of Ariz. 260 on U.S. 666 (the Coronado Trail).

ESSENTIALS   For more information on Alpine, Pinetop-Lakeside, or Greer, contact the **Alpine Chamber of Commerce,** P.O. Box 410, Alpine, AZ 85920 (tel. 602/339-4330); the **Pinetop-Lakeside Chamber of Commerce,** P.O. Box 266, Pinetop, AZ 85935 (tel. 602/367-4290); or the **Greer Chamber of Commerce,** P.O. Box 54, Greer, AZ 85927 (tel. 602/735-7230). For more information on the White Mountain Apache Reservation, contact the **White Mountain Apache Tribe,** P.O. Box 700, Whiteriver, AZ 85941 (tel. 602/338-4346). The **telephone area code** is 602.

When most people think of Arizona, they think of deserts and saguaro cacti. However, Arizona has more mountainous country than Switzerland and more forest than Minnesota. Folks from Phoenix and its surrounding cities long ago discovered how close the desert was to the cool mountain pine forests. And when weather reports from up north have Phoenicians dreaming about snow (it's true, they really do), they head for the White Mountains of eastern Arizona for a bit of skiing. This sparsely populated region of trout streams, ponderosa pine forests, lakes, meadows, and small towns caters primarily to family vacationers, though fishermen and hunters also know the White Mountains well. All four seasons can be experienced here, and while summer fishing and hiking and winter skiing may be the main attractions, wildflowers in spring and golden aspen groves in autumn attract vacationers who are simply searching for mountain beauty and tranquility.

WHAT TO SEE & DO
SKIING

Though there are cross-country skiing opportunities throughout the White Mountains, the only downhill ski area is **Sunrise,** P.O. Box 217, McNary AZ 85930 (tel. 602/735-7669; for snow conditions, toll free 800/882-SNOW, 800/772-SNOW in Arizona). Located just off Ariz. 260 on Ariz. 273, this ski area is on the White Mountain Apache Reservation and is operated by the Apache people. The ski area usually opens in November and receives more than 20 feet of snow per year. There is also snow-making equipment to enhance natural snowfall, and lights for night skiing on the weekends. Sunrise is one of the largest ski areas in the Southwest and is the most popular in Arizona. Plenty of winter sun makes skiing here almost as pleasant as lounging by the pool down in Phoenix. There are 11 lifts and more than 60 ski trails on Apache and Sunrise peaks. At the top of 11,000-foot Apache Peak is a day lodge offering meals and a view that goes on forever. There's also a ski school that offers classes for beginners as well as advanced skiers.

TOWNS & VILLAGES

The farther into the White Mountains you journey, the more peaceful and picturesque become the towns.

PINETOP-LAKESIDE Pinetop-Lakeside, two towns that have grown together over the years, is the busiest town in the White Mountains. There are dozens of motels and cabin resorts strung out along Ariz. 260 as it passes through the area. Pinetop-Lakeside is also a sort of ski resort in the winter. Sunrise ski area is only 30 miles away, and on weekends the town is packed with skiers. With **Apache Sitgreaves National Forest** on one side of town and the **Fort Apache Indian Reservation** on the other, Pinetop-Lakeside is well situated for exploring the miles of forests.

The **Pinetop Lakes Riding Stable,** off Buck Springs Road (tel. 369-0505), offers 1-hour ($13), 2-hour ($20), half-day ($35), and full-day ($50) horseback rides. For evening entertainment, there is **Theatre Mountain,** 1304-K Rainbow Lake Drive (tel. 368-8888), which stages melodramas and vaudeville shows.

GREER Greer is a tiny village of only 125 permanent residents 8,525 feet up in the White Mountains. It is located 5 miles south of Ariz. 260 in a green valley surrounded by forested mountains. The Little Colorado River flows through the middle of Greer on its way to the Grand Canyon, and though little more than a babbling brook up here, it's well known for its trout fishing. Several lakes and ponds in the area also provided good fishing. In winter there are more than 12 miles of cross-country ski trails around Greer; ice skating, ice fishing, and sleigh rides are also popular activities. Greer happens to be the closest town to Sunrise ski area, and there are several rustic mountain lodges and a number of rental-cabin operations.

ALPINE Alpine is another small community located not far from the New Mexico state line on U.S. 666 and U.S. 180. This area is known as the Alps of Arizona, and Alpine's picturesque setting in the middle of a wide grassy valley at 8,030 feet certainly lives up to this image. There isn't much to do in Alpine other than enjoy the natural beauty of the area. However, hunting for elk, deer, mountain lion, bobcat, and bear and fishing the 200 miles of nearby trout streams and lakes are very popular. Alpine is surrounded by Apache Sitgreaves National Forest, which has miles of hiking trails and several campgrounds. In spring wildflowers abound and the trout fishing is excellent. In summer there are forest trails to be hiked. In autumn the aspens in the Golden Bowl above Alpine turn a brilliant yellow. In winter, there is cross-country skiing and ice fishing. The Coronado Trail (U.S. 666), a serpentine scenic highway running down the eastern edge of Arizona, passes through Alpine. This road twists and turns its way through miles of forest just waiting to be explored.

WHERE TO STAY

PINETOP

BEST WESTERN INN OF PINETOP, Ariz. 260 at Billy Creek Rd. (P.O. Box 1006), Pinetop, AZ 85935. Tel. 602/367-6667, or toll free 800/528-1234. Fax 602/367-6672. 41 rms (all with bath). A/C TV TEL

$ Rates: $49–$65 single; $59–$75 double. AE, DC, DISC, MC, V.

Though it's right on busy Ariz. 260, the Best Western Inn of Pinetop is set back a little from the road so rooms are as quiet as you would hope. A modern two-story motel, the inn has a spacious lobby with cathedral ceiling and fireplace. Rooms feature extra-long beds, coffee makers, and radios. The hotel offers free cider, tea, and coffee in lobby; no-smoking rooms; and a whirlpool bath.

PINETOP ECONO LODGE, Ariz. 260 and Billy Creek Rd., Pinetop, AZ

85935. **Tel. 602/367-3636,** or toll free 800/55-ECONO. 42 rms (all with bath). A/C TV TEL
$ Rates: $49–$79 single or double. AE, CB, DC, DISC, MC, V.
Adjacent to the Best Western Inn of Pinetop, the Econo Lodge is a Tudor-style motel with basic rooms. The highest rates are weekends in ski season. The Econo Lodge offers free coffee and doughnuts in the morning, free local phone calls, in-room movies, a whirlpool bath, and no-smoking rooms.

WHISPERING PINES RESORT, P.O. Box 1043, Pinetop, AZ 85935. Tel. 602/367-4386, or 258-3437 in Phoenix. 29 cabins (all with bath). TV
$ Rates: $49–$84 single or double. MC, V.
Situated on 12½ wooded acres beside Ariz. 260 in Pinetop, the Whispering Pines Resort is a rustic family retreat. The cabins have one or two bedrooms and some are newer and nicer than others. All have fireplaces so you'll stay cozy and warm even in winter. One of the older cabins is a genuine log cabin with stone fireplace, and though this is not one of the better cabins, it does have a rustic appeal that may be suitable for the less finicky traveler. Other more luxurious cabins have their own saunas. The hotel also offers a whirlpool bath, volleyball, horseshoes, and coin laundry.

LAKESIDE

LAKE OF THE WOODS, P.O. Box 777, Lakeside, AZ 85929. Tel. 602/368-5353. 23 cabins (all with bath). TV
$ Rates: $56–$120 single or double. Rates lower in spring and fall. MC, V.
Located on its own private lake just off Ariz. 260, Lake of the Woods is a rustic mountain resort that appeals to families. The kids can fish in the lake, play in the snow, or row a boat. The resort also offers a whirlpool bath, sauna, exercise equipment, tennis court, table tennis, pool table, shuffleboard, horseshoes, a playground, and coin laundry. The resort's cabins range from tiny to huge, with rustic and deluxe side by side. The smallest sleep two or three while the largest sleep 10 or more. Some are on the edge of the lake while others are tucked away under the pines. The Lakewood Inn is just across the lake and features steaks, prime rib, and other American dishes. Early-bird dinners have smaller portions and prices. Drinks are available in the restaurant lounge.

THE PLACE RESORT, Ariz. 260 at Larson Rd. (Rte. 3, Box 2675), Lakeside, AZ 85929. Tel. 602/368-6777. 20 rms (all with bath). TV
$ Rates: $51–$78 single or double. MC, V.
Started as a trailer park nearly 20 years ago, the Place now has only cabins and is popular with families who come back year after year. The modern wood-paneled cabins of this mountain resort vary in size from cozy to spacious. Stone fireplaces and beamed high ceilings capture the flavor of the mountains, while fully equipped kitchens make the cabins as convenient as home. Recreational facilities include a playground, basketball court, horseshoes, badminton, volleyball.

LAKESIDE INN, 1637 Ariz. 260 (P.O. Box 1130-D), Pinetop, AZ 85935. Tel. 602/368-6600, or toll free 800/843-4792. 54 rms, 1 suite (all with bath). A/C TV TEL
$ Rates (including continental breakfast): Apr–May and Sept–Nov, $45–$75 single or double; May–Sept and Nov–Dec, $55–$85 single or double; Jan–Mar, $55–$79 single or double; suites $95 year round. Hol rates slightly higher. AE, DC, DISC, MC, V.
This is one of the newest hotels in the Pinetop-Lakeside area, and though its address is Pinetop, it's actually closer to Lakeside and is located on Ariz. 260. Rooms here are quite large and all have small refrigerators and clock radios. Many rooms also have fireplaces. The hotel also offers VCR, movie, and Nintendo rentals; free coffee; playing cards; a Whirlpool bath, games room, and guest library.

MCNARY

SUNRISE PARK HOTEL, P.O. Box 217, McNary, AZ 85930. Tel. 602/

735-7676, or toll free 800/55-HOTEL. Fax 602/735-7474. 98 rms, 2 suites (all with bath). TV TEL
$ Rates: $54–$94 single or double; $175–$275 suite. AE, CB, DC, DISC, MC, V.
Closed: Mar–Nov.

This is the closest lodge to Sunrise ski area and is only open during ski season. Most of the rooms are very comfortable, and there is also a deluxe suite with its own private whirlpool tub. About half the rooms overlook Sunrise Lake. The dining room and lounge are a cozy place to gather after a day of skiing. On weekends there is live popular dance music in the lounge. The hotel also offers a ski area shuttle bus, indoor swimming pool, tennis courts, indoor/outdoor whirlpool baths, sauna, volleyball, video arcade, and adult video room.

GREER

GREER LODGE, P.O. Box 244, Greer, AZ 85927. Tel. 602/735-7515. 9 rms, 6 cabins (all with bath).
$ Rates: $55 single, $110 double (full breakfast included); $65–$85 double (cabins). MC, V.

The Little Colorado River, which truly lives up to its name here in Greer, runs right past the deck of the largest log lodge in the White Mountains. There are a variety of accommodations here including spacious rooms in the main lodge. These rooms all have views of the mountains or river and come with a filling breakfast. Though most of the cabins are quite modern, there is one rustic log cabin that sleeps six and has a sleeping loft and fireplace. Only 15 minutes from Sunrise ski area, and with its own trout ponds and section of river, the lodge is popular with skiers and anglers both. The hotel also offers ski rentals, ice fishing, croquet, volleyball, horseshoes, a barbecue area, fishing ponds, and cross-country ski trails.

ALPINE

TAL-WI-WI LODGE, U.S. 666 (P.O. Box 169), Alpine, AZ 85920. Tel. 602/339-4319. 20 rms (all with bath).
$ Rates (including continental breakfast): $27–$29 single; $35–$89 double. MC, V.

Located 4 miles north of Alpine on U.S. 666, the Tal-Wi-Wi Lodge is the best lodging in Alpine. Some of the rooms here come with their own hot tub and fireplace, both of which are appreciated on cold winter nights. (Alpine is usually the coldest town in Arizona.) Furnishings in the guest rooms are old but clean. Wood-paneled walls and large front porches give the lodge its country appeal. The lodge's rustic dining room serves steaks and seafood. Guests also gather by the lounge's woodstove.

WHERE TO DINE
PINETOP/LAKESIDE

CHARLIE CLARK'S STEAK HOUSE, Ariz. 260 on the east side of town. Tel. 367-4900.
Cuisine: STEAK/SEAFOOD. **Reservations:** Accepted.
$ Prices: Appetizers $4–$9; main courses $10–$18. AE, MC, V.
Open: Dinner only, Sun–Thurs 5–9pm, Fri–Sat 5–10pm.

Charlie Clark's has been the uncontested best restaurant in Pinetop since it opened in 1938. The rustic building is equally divided between a dark bar with a big-screen TV tuned to sports events and a dining room with a bison head on the wall and a barber chair in the waiting area. Though steaks, prime rib, and traditional seafood dishes are the staples of the menu, there are also a few more exotic dishes such as escargots bourguignons, deep-fried frogs' legs, roast pheasant, and broiled quail.

FARMER DUNN'S VITTLES, four blocks behind Lauth's Country Store. Tel. 367-3866.
Cuisine: AMERICAN. **Reservations:** Not necessary.
$ Prices: Appetizers $2.50–$3.50; main courses $4–$11. MC, V.
Open: Mon–Thurs 11am–9pm, Fri–Sun 7am–9pm.

Turn down the road beside the more expensive Charlie Clark's and in a few blocks you'll come to a small lake. Sitting on the shore of the lake is this family restaurant that became popular as soon as it opened. There are daily lunch and dinner specials such as the Friday all-you-can-eat fish fry and the Saturday all-you-can-eat barbecued ribs and chicken. Farmer Dunn's will even cook any fish your kids catch in the adjacent trout pond.

ALPINE

SUNDOWNER RESTAURANT, 100 Main St. Tel. 339-4451.
    Cuisine: AMERICAN. **Reservations:** Not necessary.
$ Prices: Meals $3.50–$9. MC, V.
    Open: Daily 7:30am–8pm.
With shingle sides and a big dance hall-saloon, the Sundowner is everything you'd expect from a restaurant in this remote mountain setting. A huge elk head, guarding the pastry table, greets you as you enter the restaurant. The menu sticks to good, old-fashioned meat-and-potatoes meals. Take a seat in the front sun room for a view of the surrounding mountains.

CHAPTER 9

WESTERN ARIZONA

1. KINGMAN
- **WHAT'S SPECIAL ABOUT WESTERN ARIZONA**
2. LAKE MEAD
3. BULLHEAD CITY & LAUGHLIN, NEVADA
4. LAKE HAVASU & THE LONDON BRIDGE

They call it Arizona's West Coast, and for all intents and purposes that's exactly what it is—a 340-mile-long coast bordering the Colorado River and the string of lakes formed by damming the river—Lake Havasu, Lake Mohave, and Lake Mead—which in themselves offer thousands more miles of shoreline. In some ways Arizona's West Coast is better than the Pacific Coast of California. Though there aren't any waves, the weather and the water are warmer, the fishing is some of the best in the country, and sailboarding, jet skiing, and waterskiing are popular on all the lakes.

Despite the lakefront resorts, hotels, and campgrounds on all three lakes, the most popular accommodations are houseboats, which are perfect for family or group vacations. When you find a remote cove, the best fishing, or the most spectacular views, you can just anchor for a few days. You can even houseboat to the London Bridge on Lake Havasu.

If you aren't a water person, how about a bit of gambling? In Laughlin, Nevada—just across the Colorado River from Bullhead City, Arizona—you just might hit the jackpot. A hundred or so years ago, prospectors ventured into this barren landscape hoping to strike it rich with gold, silver, or any other valuable ore. They did occasionally find pay dirt, but it never lasted long and now western Arizona has its share of ghost towns. Oatman, near Kingman, is one of the best known and most visited, though it can hardly be called a ghost town now that a handful of real flesh-and-blood people call it home.

---

1. KINGMAN

90 miles SE of Las Vegas, 180 miles SW of Grand Canyon Village, 150 miles W of Flagstaff, 30 miles E of Laughlin

GETTING THERE   By Plane   Mesa airlines (tel. 602/225-5150, or toll free 800/637-2247) flies between Phoenix and Kingman Airport, 7000 Flightline Drive (tel. 602/757-2134).

By Train   There is **Amtrak** (tel. toll free 800/872-7245) passenger service to Kingman from Chicago and Los Angeles. The train stops along Andy Devine Avenue downtown.

By Bus   **Greyhound/Trailways Lines** provides service to Kingman Station, 305 Metcalfe Road (tel. 602/753-2522).

By Car   Kingman is on I-40 at the junction with U.S. 93 from Las Vegas. One of the last sections of old Route 66 (U.S. 66) connects Kingman with Seligman, Arizona.

ESSENTIALS   For more information about Kingman, contact the **Kingman Area Chamber of Commerce,** 333 West Andy Devine Avenue (P.O. Box 1150), Kingman, AZ 86402 (tel. 602/753-6106). The center is open daily from 8am to 5pm. The telephone **area code** is 602.

WHAT'S SPECIAL ABOUT WESTERN ARIZONA

Beaches
- [ ] Lakes Mead, Mohave, and Havasu, all with numerous beaches along their shores.

Activities
- [ ] Fishing for striped bass in Lake Mohave.
- [ ] Houseboating on Lake Mead, Mohave, or Havasu.
- [ ] Gambling in Laughlin, Nevada, across the Colorado River from Bullhead City, Arizona.

Ace Attractions
- [ ] The London Bridge, which was moved to Lake Havasu City before falling down.
- [ ] Hoover Dam, one of the tallest in the world.

Great Towns/Villages
- [ ] Oatman, an old mining town where wild burros roam the streets.
- [ ] Chloride, another old mining town, home to a growing number of artists and craftspeople.

Though Lt. Edward Fitzgerald Beale, leading a special corps of camel-mounted soldiers, passed through this area in 1857, Kingman was not founded until 1882, by which time the railroad had come to this region. Gold and silver were discovered in the nearby mountains in the 1870s and mining successfully continued well into the 1920s, until the mines eventually became unprofitable and were abandoned. These boom-towns-turned-ghost-towns are today tourist attractions.

During the 1930s Kingman was a stop on the road to the promised land of California as tens of thousands of unemployed people followed U.S. 66 from the Midwest to Los Angeles. The old "Route 66" has since been replaced by I-40, but the longest remaining stretch of the old highway runs between Kingman and Seligman. Over the years old "Route 66" has taken on legendary qualities. People come from all over the country searching for pieces of this highway's historic past.

Remember Andy Devine? No? Well, Kingman is here to tell you all about its squeaky-voiced native-son actor. Devine starred in hundreds of short films and features in the silent-screen era, but he is perhaps best known as cowboy sidekick Jingles on the 1950s television western *Wild Bill Hickok*. In the 1960s he played Captain Hap on the popular program *Flipper*. Devine died in 1977, but here in Kingman his memory lives on in a room in the local museum, on an avenue named after him, and during every October, when the town celebrates Andy Devine Days.

WHAT TO SEE & DO
MUSEUMS & PARKS

BONELLI HOUSE, 430 E. Spring St. Tel. 753-3195.
Characteristically territorial in design, this two-story mansion was built in 1915 after an earlier Bonelli home was destroyed by fire. To avoid the possibility of another fire, the Bonellis had this house constructed of locally quarried tufa stone. Rooms are furnished much as they would have been in the early part of this century, and many of the pieces are the Bonellis' original furnishings.

If you're interested in the historic buildings of Kingman, pick up a copy of the "Survey Our Past in Kingman" brochure at the chamber of commerce information center.
Admission: By donation.
Open: Thurs–Mon 1–5pm. **Closed:** Major hols.

HUALAPAI MOUNTAIN PARK, Hualapai Mountain Rd. Tel. 757-0915.
Located southeast of town, Hualapai Mountain Park is a cool mountain refuge 7,000 feet up in the Hualapai Mountains, excellent for picnicking, hiking, and camping. There are also a few rustic rental cabins available within the park.

Developed in the 1930s by the Civilian Conservation Corps, the park offers a pine-shaded escape from the desert.

Admission: Free.

Open: Daily 24 hours.

MOHAVE MUSEUM OF HISTORY AND ARTS, 400 W. Beale St. Tel. 753-3195.

If you're curious about the history of the Kingman area, stop in at this little museum. One room is dedicated to Andy Devine and contains photos, portraits, and memorabilia of the local actor. Kingman is also well known for its turquoise mines, and one museum exhibit features animals carved from Kingman turquoise. Dioramas and murals depict the history of the region, while an outdoor display contains wagons, railroad cars, and other large vehicles and machines that helped shape Kingman history. In the back room is a gallery of portraits of U.S. presidents and first ladies.

Admission: $1.

Open: Mon–Fri 10am–5pm, Sat–Sun 1–5pm.

GHOST TOWNS

OATMAN   Located 30 miles southwest of Kingman on what was once "Route 66," Oatman is a busy little ghost town. Founded in 1906 when gold was discovered here, Oatman quickly grew into a lively little town of 12,000 people and was an important stop on Route 66—even Clark Gable and Carole Lombard once stayed here. However, when the U.S. government closed down many of Arizona's gold-mining operations in 1942 because gold was not essential to the war effort, Oatman's population plummeted. Today there are fewer than 250 inhabitants, and the once-abandoned old buildings have been preserved as a ghost town. The historic look of Oatman has attracted filmmakers for years, and among the movies filmed here was *How the West Was Won.*

One of the biggest attractions of Oatman is its population of almost-wild burros. These animals, which roam the streets of town begging for handouts, are descendants of burros used by gold miners.

On weekends there are staged shootouts in the streets and dancing to western music in the evening. Three saloons, three restaurants, and a couple of very basic hotels provide food and lodging if you decide you'd like to stay in Oatman for a while.

CHLORIDE   Not exactly a ghost town, Chloride is located about 20 miles northwest of Kingman. The town was founded in 1862 when silver was discovered in the nearby Cerbat Mountains and is named for a type of silver ore that was mined here. By the 1920s there were 75 mines and 2,000 people in Chloride. When the mines shut down in 1944 the town lost most of its population. Today, there are about 300 residents.

Much of the downtown area has been preserved as a historic district and includes the oldest continuously operating post office in Arizona, the old jail, the Silverbelle Playhouse, and the Jim Fritz Museum. Many of the downtown buildings now serve as studios and shops for artists, and craftspeople. Melodramas are performed at the Silverbelle Playhouse on the first and third Saturday of every month, and on the last Saturday of June the town celebrates Old Miners Day with a parade, shootouts, melodramas, music, and dancing.

For more information about Chloride, contact the **Chloride Chamber of Commerce,** P.O. Box 268, Chloride, AZ 86431 (tel. 602/565-2204).

WHERE TO STAY

ALLSTAR INN, 3351 E. Andy Devine Ave., Kingman, AZ 86402. Tel. 602/757-7151. 118 rms (all with bath). A/C TV TEL

$ Rates: $18 single or double. MC, V.

You aren't likely to find anything cheaper than this anywhere in the country. For this low rate you get a modest but clean carpeted room. You'll find the Allstar just off I-40.

DAYS INN—KINGMAN, 3023 E. Andy Devine Ave., Kingman, AZ 86401. Tel. 602/753-7500, or toll free 800/325-2525. Fax 602/753-4686. 60 rms (all with bath). A/C TV TEL

$ Rates: $30–$52 single; $40–$62 double. AE, CB, DC, DISC, MC, V.
Just south of I-40, the Days Inn is one of Kingman's newest motels. You can't miss this Spanish colonial-style building with its tile roof and stucco walls. Rooms are fairly standard for off-ramp motels, but some of the rooms have whirlpool tubs that feel great after a long day of driving. The hotel also has a swimming pool and offers free coffee.

HOLIDAY INN–KINGMAN, 3100 E. Andy Devine Ave., Kingman, AZ 86401. Tel. 602/753-6262, or toll free 800/HOLIDAY. Fax 602/753-7137. 120 rms (all with bath). A/C TV TEL
$ Rates: $45–$69 single; $52–$75 double. AE, CB, DC, DISC, MC, V.
This courtyard motel south of I-40 on Andy Devine Avenue caters primarily to travelers coming in off the Interstate. Rooms are arranged around the central garden and swimming-pool area. All rooms have been recently redone with new carpets, drapes, wallpaper, and furniture. C. W. Dandy's restaurant and lounge serves inexpensive American food. The hotel also offers passes to Kingman Fitness and Racquet Club, in-room movies, a swimming pool, no-smoking rooms, and a coin-operated laundry.

QUALITY INN–KINGMAN, 1400 E. Andy Devine Ave., Kingman, AZ 86401. Tel. 602/753-5531, or toll free 800/228-5151. 98 rms (all with bath). A/C TV TEL
$ Rates (including continental breakfast): $40–$54 single; $45–$59 double. AE, CB, DC, DISC, MC, V.

Andy Devine Avenue used to be the famous "Route 66," and this motel, located 2 miles south of I-40, cashes in on the fame of the former highway. There are antique gas pumps and other "Route 66" memorabilia in the motel lobby. Rooms here are a bit cramped, but are clean and have newer carpets. There are two sinks in the bathrooms and a coffee maker in every room. The hotel also offers in-room movies, a swimming pool, whirlpool bath, sauna, fitness room, gift shop, and a beauty salon.

WHERE TO DINE

DAM BAR & STEAK HOUSE, 1960 E. Andy Devine Ave. Tel. 753-3523.
   Cuisine: STEAK. **Reservations:** Not necessary.
$ Prices: Dinner $8–$20. AE, CB, DC, MC, V.
   Open: Dinner only, Mon–Sat 4–10pm.
It's hard to miss the Dam Bar—just watch for the steer on the roof of a rustic wooden building as you drive along Andy Devine Avenue. Inside, the atmosphere is very casual, with sawdust on the floor and wooden booths. Mesquite-broiled steaks are the name of the game here. Locals claim they're the best in town.

HOUSE OF CHAN, 960 W. Beale St. Tel. 753-3232.
   Cuisine: CHINESE. **Reservations:** Not necessary.
$ Prices: Lunch $5–$7; dinner $8–$20. AE, MC, V.
   Open: Mon–Sat 11am–10pm.
For six generations the Chan family has lived in Kingman and today their Chinese and American restaurant just off I-40 on U.S. 93 (the road to Las Vegas) is the most popular Chinese restaurant in Kingman. The menu offers plenty of choices of both Chinese and American meals, but one of the house favorites, prime rib, isn't on the menu. The house special dinner is a feast of Chinese specialties, a good choice if you have a large family with you.

---

2. LAKE MEAD

30 miles SE of Las Vegas, 70 miles NW
of Kingman, 256 miles NW of Phoenix

GETTING THERE   By Plane   The closest airport to Lake Mead is in Las Vegas, Nevada, which is served by numerous airlines. You'll have to drive from there.

By Train   There is **Amtrak** (tel. toll free 800/872-7245) passenger service to Las Vegas from Chicago and Los Angeles. You'll have to drive from Las Vegas.

By Bus   **Greyhound/Trailways Lines** offers service to Las Vegas. Check your local telephone directory for the phone number of the station nearest you.

By Car   U.S. 93, which runs between Las Vegas and Kingman, crosses over the Hoover Dam, which forms Lake Mead. Several small secondary roads lead to various marinas on the lake.

ESSENTIALS   For more information, contact the **Lake Mead National Recreation Area,** 601 Nevada Highway, Boulder City, NV 89005 (tel. 702/293-8906). The telephone **area code** for Arizona addresses is 602; in Nevada it's 702.

Formed by the damming of the Colorado River by the Hoover Dam, Lake Mead is one of Arizona's favorite recreation areas. Annually more than eight million people visit the lake to boat, ski, fish, swim, and camp. There are a number of marinas on both the Arizona and Nevada sides of the lake, offering boat rentals, resorts, and campgrounds. Temple Bar is the easiest marina to reach on the Arizona side, while on the Nevada side, Boulder Beach and Echo Bay are the most easily accessible. On nearby Lake Mohave, Katherine Landing, just outside Bullhead City, Arizona, provides all amenities. Though the Lake Mead National Recreation Area is best known for its two lakes, it also covers quite a bit of mountainous desert land that is home to bighorn sheep and roadrunners, among other wild animals. This land was also once home to several Native American tribes who left reminders of their presence in petroglyphs.

WHAT TO SEE & DO

HOOVER DAM, U.S. 93. Tel. 702/293-8367.

The Hoover Dam is a colossal structure that's able to make a number of superlative claims. Constructed between 1931 and 1935 and now a National Historic Landmark, it was the first major dam on the Colorado River, and by providing huge amounts of electricity and water to Arizona and California, it set the stage for the phenomenal growth that this region has experienced this century. At 726 feet from bedrock to roadway, it is the highest concrete dam in the western hemisphere. The 110-mile-long Lake Mead, which was created by damming the Colorado River, is the largest human-made reservoir in the United States. The base of the dam is 660 feet thick, but the top is only 45 feet thick.

Admission: Free.

Open: Memorial Day–Labor Day, daily 8am–6:45pm; Labor Day–Memorial Day, daily 9am–4:15pm. **Closed:** Dec 25.

LAKE MEAD NATIONAL RECREATION AREA, 601 Nevada Hwy., Boulder City, NV 89005. Tel. 702/293-8906.

Containing both Lake Mead and Lake Mohave, this national recreation area offers all manner of aquatic activities as well as camping and hiking opportunities. The largest human-made reservoir in the United States, Lake Mead is 110 miles long and has more than 800 miles of shoreline. Fishing for monster striped bass is one of the most popular activities on the lakes, but waterskiing, boardsailing, and jet skiing are also popular. There are campgrounds and marinas at Boulder Beach, Callville Bay, Overton Beach, Temple Bar, Cottonwood Cove, Katherine Landing, and Willow Beach. Evening programs are held at Boulder Beach, Katherine Landing, and Cottonwood Cove.

Black Canyon, between Hoover Dam and Lake Mohave, is one of the last undammed stretches of the Colorado River and is part of the recreation area. It's possible to canoe or raft down this section of river, and along the way you will encounter rapids and several small side canyons worth exploring. Several of these canyons have hot springs.

Admission: Free.

Open: Daily 24 hours.

WHERE TO STAY & DINE

A RESORT

TEMPLE BAR RESORT, Temple Bar, AZ 86443-0545. Tel. 602/767-3400, or toll free 800/752-9669. 22 rms (all with bath). A/C TV TEL
$ Rates: $39–$89. MC, V.

Though basically just a motel, the Temple Bar Resort has a wonderfully remote setting with a beach that makes it an excellent getaway, especially if you enjoy waterskiing or fishing. Waterskiers in particular like Temple Bar because it offers 20 miles of unobstructed skiing in either direction. Directly across from Temple Bar is a huge monolith called the Temple. A restaurant and lounge overlook the lake and provide economical meals. The resort offers ski rentals, powerboat rentals, shuffleboard, boccie ball, horseshoes, and a convenience store.

The same company that operates this resort also operates two others on the Nevada side of the lake. Contact the above toll-free number for more information.

HOUSEBOATS

SEVEN CROWNS RESORTS, P.O. Box 16247, Irvine, CA 92713. Tel. toll free 800/752-9669. A/C
$ Rates: $250–$400 per day, $970–$1,975 per week. MC, V.

Why pay extra for a lake-view room when you can rent a houseboat that always has a 360° water view? There is no better way to explore Lake Mead than on a houseboat. You can cruise for miles, drop anchor at some remote beach, and have a wilderness adventure with all the comforts of home. Houseboats come complete with full kitchens (microwaves, refrigerator/freezer, gas range/oven, coffeepots, toasters, blenders), air conditioning, and room to sleep up to 12 people. There are even sun roofs, stereos, and barbecue grills.

---

3. BULLHEAD CITY & LAUGHLIN, NEVADA

30 miles W of Kingman, 216 miles NW
of Phoenix, 60 miles N of Lake Havasu City

GETTING THERE By Plane There are daily flights between Bullhead City and Phoenix on USAir Express (tel. 602/258-7355, or toll free 800/428-4322) and Mesa Airlines (tel. 602/225-5150, or toll free 800/637-2247). The round-trip fare is around $70.

By Train The nearest **Amtrak** (tel. toll free 800/872-7245) passenger service is in Kingman. You'll have to drive from Kingman.

By Bus **Greyhound/Trailways Lines** provides service to Bullhead City. The station is at 1010 Ariz. 95 (tel. 602/754-4655).

By Car From Phoenix, take U.S. 60, which becomes U.S. 93, northwest to I-40. From Kingman, take Ariz. 68 west to Bullhead City.

ESSENTIALS For more information on Bullhead City and Laughlin, Nevada, contact the **Bullhead City / Laughlin / Mohave Valley Chamber of Commerce,** 625 Ariz. 95 (P.O. Box 66), Bullhead City, AZ 86430 (tel. 602/754-4121). The telephone **area code** for Bullhead City is 602; for Laughlin, Nevada, it's 702.

You may find it difficult at first to understand why anyone would ever want to live in Bullhead City. According to the U.S. Weather Service, this is the hottest town in the country, with temperatures regularly topping 120° Fahrenheit during the summer.

However, to understand Bullhead City, you need only gaze across the Colorado River at the Emerald City—the promised land of Laughlin, Nevada, where the slot machines are always in action and the gaming tables are always as hot as the air outside (well, sometimes). Laughlin, Nevada, is the southernmost town in Nevada, and is therefore the closest place to Phoenix to go gambling. This makes Bullhead City one of the busiest little towns in Arizona.

Laughlin is a perfect miniature of Las Vegas. High-rise hotels loom above the desert like so many glass mesas. Miles of neon lights turn night into day. Acres of asphalt are always covered with cars and RVs as hordes of hopeful gamblers go searching for Lady Luck. Cheap rooms and cheap meals lure people into spending on the slot machines what they save on food and a bed. It's a formula that works well. Why else would anyone endure the heat of this remote desert?

WHAT TO SEE & DO

There are only a couple of reasons to venture into this rugged and remote corner of Arizona. You are either headed for Lake Mohave to do some fishing or houseboating, or you're here to do some gambling. I'll bet money that you're here to gamble.

Laughlin is a very popular weekend destination for Phoenicians and other Arizonans who can't gamble in their own state. The **casinos** of Laughlin are known for having liberal slots—that is, the slot machines pay off frequently. There is also keno, blackjack, poker, craps, off-track betting, and sports betting. If you want to learn how to play a game that requires a bit more thinking than slot machines, you can take a lesson in poker, blackjack, or craps at most of the casinos. To help you spread your wealth around, there's a free casino shuttle, and free ferries also shuttle gamblers across the Colorado River.

If you'd like to see a bit more of the Colorado, there are daily cruises on the paddlewheelers *Little Belle* (tel. 298-2453, ext. 2118), which leaves from the Edgewater Casino, and *Fiesta Queen* (tel. 298-1047), which leaves from Harrah's Del Rio Casino.

If you'd rather take the helm yourself, you can rent ski boats, fishing boats, bass boats, and pontoon boats at **Lake Mohave Resort** (tel. 754-3245). Rates range from $60 to $200 per day. Fishermen will be interested to know that Lake Mohave is home to awesome striped bass that really put up a fight. If you'd like to find out more about why Lake Mohave is there for you to play in, stop by the **Davis Dam** for a free self-guided tour. The dam is open to the public daily from 7:30am to 3:30pm.

EVENING ENTERTAINMENT

All the hotels in Laughlin offer live entertainment of some sort, but gambling is still the main event as far as evening entertainment is concerned.

WHERE TO STAY & DINE
BULLHEAD CITY

LAKE MOHAVE RESORT, Katherine Landing, Bullhead City, AZ 86430-4016. Tel. 602/754-3245, or toll free 800/752-9669. 41 rms, 10 suites (all with bath). A/C TV TEL

$ Rates: $60–$73 double; $83 suite. AE, MC, V.

Just up the lake from Davis Dam and only a few minutes outside Bullhead City, the Lake Mohave Resort is an older motel, but the huge rooms are ideal for families on vacation. All rooms face the lake and have chairs on their patios. Down at the marina, you can feed the giant carp that congregate waiting for handouts. Tail O' the Whale, the resort's nautical-theme restaurant and lounge, overlooks the marina. The resort also offers baby-sitting, boat rentals, a convenience store, and a tackle and bait store.

LAUGHLIN, NEVADA

COLORADO BELLE HOTEL & CASINO, 2100 Casino Dr. (P.O. Box 2304), Laughlin, NV 89029. Tel. 702/298-4000, or toll free 800/458-9500. 1,225 rms, 13 suites (all with bath). A/C TV TEL

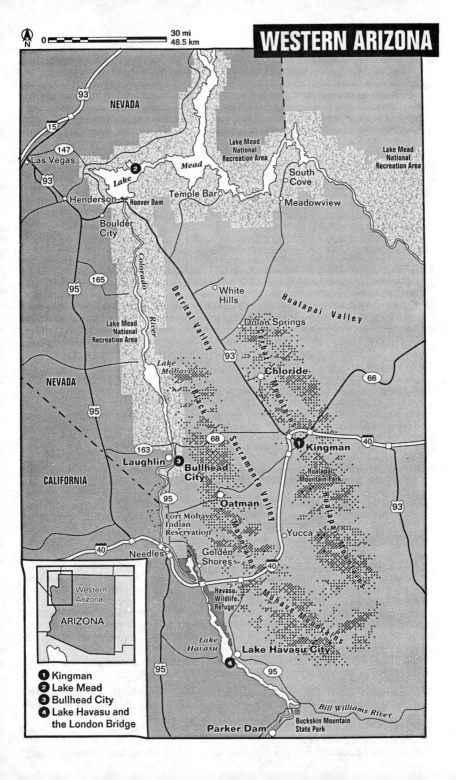

$ Rates: $19–$29 single or double Sun–Thurs, $49–$59 single or double Fri–Sat; $75–$85 deluxe rooms; $120 suite. AE, CB, DC, MC, V.

Nevada gambling casinos and hotels have always been given over to Disneyesque flights of fancy when it comes to architectural themes, and Laughlin is no exception. The Colorado Belle is built to resemble an unbelievably huge paddlewheel riverboat, complete with smokestacks and eight-story paddlewheels. Of course the guest rooms are all done in nautical themes as well.

Mark Twain's Chicken & Ribs restaurant features waitresses dressed in farm clothes and serves barbecue and steaks. The Mississippi Lounge & Seafood Bar serves clams, oysters, and shrimp in a dance-hall atmosphere. The Orleans Room is the resort's most elegant dining room and serves full-course dinners. The Captain's Food Fare offers walk-through dining where you can pick the meal the most appeals to you. For light meals and snacks, there is Huckleberry's Snack Bar and Bakery. Last, there is the 24-hour Paddlewheel Restaurant. The Riverboat Lounge offers nightly Dixieland jazz or contemporary pop music.

The hotel and casino offers free ferry service to Bullhead City, swimming pools, whirlpool baths, three gift shops, and a video arcade.

EDGEWATER HOTEL & CASINO, 2020 S. Casino Dr. (P.O. Box 642), Laughlin, NV 89029. Tel. 702/298-2453, or toll free 800/257-0300. 1,468 rms, 4 suites (all with bath). A/C TV TEL
$ Rates: $22–$49 single or double; $120 suite. AE, DISC, MC, V.
Located right on the riverbank next door to the Colorado Belle, the Edgewater offers the lowest room rates of the Laughlin casinos. Riverfront rooms are slightly more expensive than other rooms, but there really isn't an expensive room in the house. Though you'll have to stand in line to check in and deal with the racket in the casino, the rooms are cool, quiet, and comfortable.

Three restaurants provide a variety of dining options at the Edgewater. The best deals in the hotel are the bountiful buffets. For under $4 you can eat dinner and get something other than a burger and fries. Truly amazing! The hotel's main lounge is a sports bar, but another lounge offers dancing to live bands performing pop music.

The hotel also offers room service, a free ferry to Bullhead City, car-rental desk, airport transportation, complimentary gaming lessons, a swimming pool, whirlpool bath, video arcade, gift shop, jewelry store, and no-smoking rooms.

FLAMINGO HILTON, 1900 S. Casino Dr., Laughlin, NV 89029. Tel. 702/298-5111, or toll free 800/HILTONS or 800/FLAMINGO. 1,970 rms, 30 suites (all with bath). A/C TV TEL
$ Rates: Sun–Thurs, $21–$55 single or double; Fri–Sat $36–$85 single or double; single or double; suite $200–$275. holidays, $75. AE, CB, DC, DISC, MC, V.
Two shimmering glass towers reflect all the neon in Laughlin at night, and make the Flamingo impossible to miss. Guest rooms are attractively decorated and feature modern furnishings. Rooms up on the higher floors offer good views.

Alta Villa serves Italian food amid a Laughlin-style Old World atmosphere. The Beef Baron is a western-theme dining room featuring mesquite-broiled steaks and seafood. The Flagship Buffet offers filling meals at economical prices with a view of the river. Lindy's is a 24-hour New York–style deli. There's even a Burger King and a snack bar offering pizza, snacks, and ice cream. The Club Flamingo features a Broadway revue Sunday through Thursday nights at 5, 7, and 9pm; on Friday and Saturday there is live pop dance music. The Outdoor Amphitheater brings in nationally known performers for frequent concerts.

The hotel and casino also offers room service, valet parking, a tour desk, swimming pool, tennis courts, gift shop, and a video arcade.

RIVERSIDE RESORT HOTEL & CASINO, P.O. Box 500, Laughlin, NV 89029. Tel. 702/298-2525, or toll free 800/227-3849. 633 rms, 27 suites (all with bath). A/C TV TEL
$ Rates: $39–$58 single or double; $51–$71 suite (available Sun–Thurs only) AE, CB, DC, DISC, MC, V.
This is Don Laughlin's original Laughlin casino and hotel, and offers as many

entertainment and dining options as you'll find under any one roof in Laughlin. Guest rooms are spacious and modern.

The Riverview Room restaurant is open 24 hours a day. The East Buffet serves three buffet meals daily. The West Buffet serves lunch and dinner, with chicken and seafood the specialties. The Prime Rib Room specializes in build-your-own stuffed potatoes and prime rib. The Gourmet Room is open for dinner only and is the hotel's best restaurant. The Losers' Lounge features Top-40 dance music. Well-known performers appear regularly at Don's Celebrity Theatre. The Starview Showroom is the stage for Broadway plays and other specialty shows.

The hotel and casino also offers a casino shuttle, room service, two swimming pools, three movie theaters, a post office, gift shop, beauty salon, and dance studio.

4. LAKE HAVASU & THE LONDON BRIDGE

200 miles NW of Phoenix, 60 miles S of Bullhead City, 61 miles S of Kingman, 150 miles S of Las Vegas

GETTING THERE **By Plane** Mesa airlines (tel. 602/225-5150, or toll free 800/637-2247) and USAir Express (tel. 602/258-7355, or toll free 800/428-4322) both provide service between Phoenix and Lake Havasu City.

By Train The nearest **Amtrak** (tel. toll free 800/872-7245) passenger service is in Kingman, from which you'll have to drive.

By Bus **KT Services** (tel. 702/644-2233) stops in Lake Havasu City at the Easy Stop Texaco Station, 54 North Lake Havasu Drive, on its route between Las Vegas and Phoenix.

By Car From Phoenix, take I-10 west to Ariz. 95 north. From Las Vegas, take U.S. 93 south to Kingman, then I-40 west to Ariz. 95 south.

ESSENTIALS For more information on Lake Havasu and Lake Havasu City, contact the **Lake Havasu City Area Chamber of Commerce,** 1930 Mesquite Avenue, Suite 3, Lake Havasu City, AZ 86403 (tel. 602/855-4115). The telephone **area code** is 602.

"London Bridge is falling down, falling down, falling down. . . ." Once upon a time this children's rhyme was true, but that was before Robert McCulloch, founder of Lake Havasu City, hit upon the brilliant idea of buying the bridge and having it shipped to his undertouristed little town in the middle of the Arizona desert. Today the London Bridge sits like a mirage on the banks of Lake Havasu in this hot and dusty desert town. An unlikely place for a bit of British heritage it's true, but Lake Havasu City and the London Bridge have become the second-most-popular tourist destination in Arizona. Only the Grand Canyon attracts more visitors.

Lake Havasu was formed in 1938 by the building of the Parker Dam, but it wasn't until 1963 that the town of Lake Havasu City was founded by McCulloch. Not too many people were keen on spending time out in this remote corner of the desert where summer temperatures are often over 110° Fahrenheit. Despite its name, Lake Havasu City was little more than an expanse of desert with a few mobile homes on it. It was then that McCulloch began looking for ways to attract more people to his little city on the lake. His solution proved to be a stroke of genius.

WHAT TO SEE & DO

LONDON BRIDGE In the mid-1960s the British government decided to sell the London Bridge, which was indeed falling down—or more correctly, sinking—into the Thames River because of too much heavy car and truck traffic. McCulloch and his partner paid $2,460,000 for the famous bridge and had it shipped 10,000 miles to

Long Beach, California, and then trucked to Lake Havasu City. Reconstruction of the bridge was begun in 1968 and the grand reopening was held in 1971. Oddly enough, the 900-foot-long bridge was not built over water. It connected only desert to more desert on a peninsula jutting into Lake Havasu. It wasn't until after the bridge was rebuilt that a 1-mile-long channel was dredged through the base of the peninsula, thus creating an island offshore from Lake Havasu City.

The London Bridge has a long history, though the bridge that now stands in Arizona is not very old by British standards. The first bridge over the Thames River in London was probably a pontoon bridge built by the Romans in A.D. 43. However, the first written record of a London Bridge comes from the mention of a suspected witch being drowned at the bridge in 984. In 1176 the first stone bridge over the Thames was built. They just don't build 'em like that bridge anymore—it lasted for more than 600 years, but was eventually replaced in 1824 by the bridge that now stands in Lake Havasu City.

BOAT TOURS   There are several companies offering different types of boat tours on Lake Havasu. **Blue Water Charters** (tel. 855-7171) offers jet-boat tours that leave from the London Bridge and spend 2 hours cruising up the Colorado River to the Topock Gorge, a scenic area 25 miles from Lake Havasu City. The tours cost $15 for adults, $10 for children 6 to 12, and are free for children under 6. **Lake Havasu Boat Tours** (tel. 855-7979) provides a more leisurely narrated pontoon-boat tour of the island that was formed when the London Bridge was built.

WATER SPORTS   After the London Bridge, water sports on 45-mile-long Lake Havasu are the most popular local attraction. If you didn't bring your own boat, you can rent one at **Resort Boat Rentals,** in the English Village beside the the bridge (tel. 453-9613). They offer half-day and full-day rentals of ski, pontoon, and fishing boats. Rental rates start at $40 an hour for a pontoon boat and $45 for a ski boat. They also rent water-skiing equipment for $25 a day.

Jet skis and Waverunners are available from **Jet Ski Plus Rentals** (tel. 855-5019), which is located on the island at the state beach. Rates range from $40 to $55 an hour.

If you prefer a cheaper mode of transportation and don't mind using a little muscle power, stop by the **Fun Center** (tel. 453-RFUN) in the English Village. They have paddle boats, canoes, and aqua cycles for $10 an hour, as well as jet skis, Waverunners, and mini-powerboats for $40 to $55 an hour. They also offer parasailing for $30 to $40.

If you prefer to sail, you can rent a sailboat, go for a cruise, or take sailing lessons at **Adler's London Bridge Sailing Center,** on the island side of the bridge (tel. 855-1555).

HORSEBACK RIDING   This is still the west and before there were lakes, there were cowboys and, of course, horses. **Havasu Horse Rentals** (tel. 680-2939) offers daily guided rides, sunset and moonlight rides, and riding lessons. They're located 10 miles north of the bridge on Ariz. 95 between milepost markers 194 and 195.

GOLF   And what would an Arizona desert community be without its golf course. Lake Havasu City has four, all of which are open to the public. They are **Queens Bay Golf Course,** 1480 Queen's Bay (tel. 855-4777), at the Ramada London Bridge Resort; **London Bridge Golf Club,** 2400 Clubhouse Drive (tel. 855-2719); **Nautical Inn Resort,** 1000 McCulloch Boulevard (tel. 855-2131); and **Stonebridge Golf Course,** 2400 Clubhouse Drive (tel. 855-2719). Greens fees are around $20 for 18 holes.

WHERE TO STAY

HOTELS & MOTELS

HOLIDAY INN LAKE HAVASU CITY, 245 London Bridge Rd., Lake Havasu City, AZ 86403. Tel. 602/855-4071, or toll free 800/HOLIDAY. Fax 602/855-2379. 157 rms, 5 suites (all with bath). A/C TV TEL

$ Rates: Rooms $39–$79 single or double; Suites $97 single, $105 double. Special packages available. AE, CB, DC, DISC, MC, V.

Located half a mile north of the London Bridge, the Holiday Inn is a more economical choice than the previous listings. Yet despite the lower prices, you still get an attractive, newly renovated room with modern furnishings.

The Bridge Room Restaurant serves basic American food in a casual atmosphere. On weekends there's a 50-item buffet in the evening. The Reflections Lounge has dancing nightly to recorded Top-40 music and a free appetizer bar during happy hour Monday through Friday. A big-screen TV caters to the sports crowd.

The hotel also offers in-room movies, free transportation to and from the airport, free transportation to and from Laughlin, Nevada, a swimming pool, whirlpool bath, and a games room.

NAUTICAL INN RESORT & CONFERENCE CENTER, 1000 McCulloch Blvd., Lake Havasu City, AZ 86403. Tel. 602/855-2141, or toll free 800/892-2141. 120 rms, 4 suites (all with bath). A/C TV TEL

$ Rates (for one to four people): $80–$109 room Sun–Thurs, $110–$139 Fri–Sat; $140–$170 suite Sun–Thurs, $170–$200 Fri–Sat. Rates slightly higher on holiday weekends. AE, CB, DC, DISC, MC, V.

It's hot and there's plenty of sand, a beach, blue water—therefore it must be the beach. Wrong, this is the desert. The Nautical Inn is a beach resort in the middle of the desert. Though the landscape around the resort is quite barren and resort landscaping is minimal, this should still be your first choice in the area. Where else can you fish from your guest room patio? Guest rooms are huge, with new contemporary furnishings. Large windows look out on the lake and there are comfortable chairs both inside and out on the patio. The guests here are generally an active crowd, with powerboating and waterskiing the most popular activities.

The Captain's Table, open for breakfast, lunch, and dinner, is a multilevel restaurant overlooking Lake Havasu and the mountains beyond. Though Lake Havasu is a long way from the nearest ocean, seafood is the specialty. Before or after dinner you can have a drink in the lounge. The Captain's Cove is a lively disco by night and a grill where you can get a quick bite by day. And what would a beach resort be without an open-air cocktail lounge, here known as the Tiki Terrace.

The resort offers Waverunner, jet ski, and bicycle rentals; valet service; a swimming pool, whirlpool bath, 18-hole golf course, two tennis courts, water-sports center, parasailing, pro shop, gift shop, sportswear boutique, and a general store.

RAMADA LONDON BRIDGE RESORT, 1477 Queens Bay, Lake Havasu City, AZ 86403. Tel. 602/855-0888, or toll free 800/624-7939 or 800/2-RAMADA. Fax 602/855-9209. 183 rms, 15 suites (all with bath). A/C TV TEL

$ Rates: $75–$85 single or double Sun–Thurs, $125–$140 Fri–Sat; $125–$250 suite. Higher rates on hols. Special discounted rates and golf packages available. AE, DC, DISC, MC, V.

It doesn't take much to figure out that this resort was built after the London Bridge made its historic move to the Arizona desert. Merrie Olde England is the theme here, with Tudor half-timbers jumbled up with turrets, towers, ramparts, and crennelations. Just inside the main entrance is a replica of the gold State Coach that's used by the British royal family for coronations and the opening of Parliament. The coach is covered with gold leaf and looks quite authentic. Behind the check-in desk is an intricately carved wooden panel that took 4,000 hours to carve. You'll notice that it bears the name Queen's Bay Hotel, which was the name of this hotel before it was taken over by the Ramada chain.

Rooms are large, but even the view rooms have only small windows. There are prints and photographs of London Bridge (even in rooms that actually have a view of the real bridge). The hotel's main dining room serves primarily continental cuisine, with British favorites such as Yorkshire pudding also making appearances. There's live music in the evenings in the more casual café.

The hotel offers a nightly complimentary cocktail hour; complimentary bus to Laughlin, Nevada; complimentary airport shuttle; two swimming pools, whirlpool baths, nine-hole golf course, tennis courts, a beach, beauty salon, and a gift shop.

HOUSEBOATS

HAVASU SPRINGS RESORTS, Rte. 2, Box 624, Parker, AZ 85344. Tel. 602/667-3361.

$ Rates: Mar 15–Sept, $1,150–$1,975 per week; Oct–Mar 14, $695–$1,350 per week. No credit cards.

One of the most popular ways to enjoy Lake Havasu is on a rented houseboat. You can spend your days motoring from one good fishing or swimming spot to the next. There are beaches and secluded coves where you can drop anchor and stay for days. If you feel like doing a bit of sightseeing or shopping, you can cruise right up to the London Bridge. Houseboats come in four sizes, with the large boats providing much more luxury (such as air conditioning). Boats sleep 10 to 12 people and are very popular with families.

WHERE TO DINE

SHUGRUE'S, 1425 McCulloch Blvd. Tel. 453-1400.
   Cuisine: CONTINENTAL. **Reservations:** Suggested.
$ Prices: Appetizers $3–$7.50; main courses $7–$28. AE, MC, V.
   Open: Lunch daily 11am–3pm; dinner Sun–Thurs 5–10pm, Fri–Sat 5–11pm.

Located just across the London Bridge from the English Village shopping complex, Shugrue's offers flavorful food at very reasonable prices. The large restaurant has been built with many windows, so most diners get a view of the London Bridge. In addition to the seafood, steaks, and prime rib, there's a short list of Cajun favorites. Dieters, and those who like to save room for dessert, may want to choose from the menu of lighter fare.

CAPTAIN'S TABLE, in the Nautical Inn, 1000 McCulloch Blvd. Tel. 855-2141.
   Cuisine: AMERICAN. **Reservations:** Suggested.
$ Prices: Lunch $6–$8; dinner $12–$17; sunset dinners (Sun–Thurs 5–6pm) $7. AE, CB, DC, DISC, MC, V.
   Open: Breakfast Mon–Sat 7–11am; lunch Mon–Sat 11am–2:30pm; dinner Sun–Thurs 5–9pm, Fri–Sat 5–10pm; brunch Sun 10:30am–2pm.

While Shugrue's offers a view of the London Bridge, this casual multilevel restaurant provides a panorama of Lake Havasu, the city, and the desert mountains beyond. The decor is a mixture of tropical and British gentry, which seems only fitting in a lakefront beach town that has made its fortune off the London Bridge and all things British. Seafood is the specialty here—whatever types of fish are available that day can be grilled, char-broiled, baked with herb butter, blackened, served provençal, or mesquite broiled.

CHAPTER 10

SOUTHERN ARIZONA

Southern Arizona, which is roughly the strip of land between the Mexican border and Interstate 8 and 10, is an often-overlooked region. Aside from Tucson, which can be considered part of southern Arizona but is so large that is was given its own chapter (see Chapter 5), this region is without any major cities. Native American reservations, a national monument, a national forest, national wildlife refuges, and an air force bombing range take up most of the land here, leaving most of southern Arizona to its natural beauty.

Giant saguaro cactus cover the slopes of the Sonoran Desert which covers much of southern Arizona. However, numerous mountain ranges also rise up in the desert. Cacti gives way to pines in the cool mountains, where passing clouds give off snow and rain. Narrow canyons and broad valleys, fed by the rain and snow melting on the high peaks, provide habitats for birds and other wildlife unique to the region. No fewer than 14 species of hummingbirds call southern Arizona home.

Many of the high valleys between the mountain ranges receive enough rain to support some of the best grasslands in the country. This is prime grazing land, and huge ranches have sprawled across the landscape for more than a century.

Perhaps because of this prime ranch land, it was here much of America's now-famous western history took place. Wyatt Earp and the Clantons shot it out at Tombstone's O.K. Corral, and Doc Holiday played his cards. Cochise and Geronimo staged the last Native American rebellions from strongholds in the rugged mountains of this region, cavalries charged against the Apaches, and prospectors scoured the wastelands in search of mineral wealth, leaving behind them a string of ghost towns.

The very first Spanish expedition into the American Southwest, led by Francisco Vásquez de Coronado in 1540, marched up the San Pedro River valley past present-day Sierra Vista, where a national memorial commemorates his unfruitful search for the Seven Cities of Cíbola. These cities were rumored to be filled with gold and precious jewels, but all Coronado found were poor Native American pueblos. Nearly 150 years later Fr. Eusebio Francisco Kino would found a string of Jesuit missions across the Pimeria Alta, a region that would later become northern Mexico and southern Arizona. Converting the Native Americans and building mission churches, Father Kino left a long-lasting mark on this region. Today two of the missions founded by Father Kino—San Xavier del Bac and San José de Tumacacori—still stand (see "Attractions" in the Tucson chapter, Chapter 5).

Native Americans still make their homes here in southern Arizona, and the Papago Indian Reservation covers a vast expanse south of Casa Grande and west of Tucson. This reservation belongs to the Tohono O'odham tribe, who were formerly known as the Papagos. Well known for their basketry, the Tohono O'odham also sponsor one of the largest annual Native American festivals in the country. The O'odham Tash is held each February in Casa Grande and attracts dozens of tribes, who participate in rodeos, parades, arts and crafts exhibits, and dance performances. Near Willcox, the Amerind Foundation, one of the state's finest museums dedicated to the cultures of Southwest peoples, provides insightful exhibits on Native American culture.

WHAT'S SPECIAL ABOUT SOUTHERN ARIZONA

Natural Spectacles
- ☐ The rocks of Chiracahua National Monument.
- ☐ Organ Pipe Cactus National Monument, where huge cactus grow.

Birdwatching
- ☐ Ramsey Canyon Preserve, home to 14 species of hummingbirds.
- ☐ Patagonia-Sonoita Creek Sanctuary, home to more than 200 species of birds.

Monuments
- ☐ The Coronado National Memorial, commemorating the early Spanish explorer Francisco Vásquez de Coronado.
- ☐ Cochise Stronghold, the rugged mountains where this Apache chief and his men hid from U.S. troops.

Buildings
- ☐ The Gadsden Hotel in Douglas, featuring a classic grand lobby.

Museums
- ☐ Yuma Territorial Prison State Historic Park, a 19th-century prison.
- ☐ The Amerind Foundation, in Texas Canyon near Willcox, with an outstanding collection of art and artifacts from Native American cultures.

Great Towns/Villages
- ☐ Bisbee, a former copper-mining town that's becoming an artists' community.
- ☐ Tombstone, "the town too tough to die," home of the O.K. Corral.

Shopping
- ☐ Nogales, Mexico, where Mexican crafts are available at low prices.

1. YUMA

180 miles SW of Phoenix, 180 miles E of San Diego, 240 miles W of Tucson

GETTING THERE By Plane The **Yuma Airport,** Pacific Avenue and 32nd Street (tel. 602/726-5882), is served by Skywest (tel. toll free 800/453-9417) and America West (tel. toll free 800/247-5692).

By Train There is **Amtrak** (tel. toll free 800/872-7245) passenger service to Yuma from Los Angeles and New Orleans. The station is at 281 Gila Street (tel. 602/344-0300 for ticket information).

By Bus Buses of **Greyhound/Trailways** stop in Yuma on their way between San Diego and Phoenix. The station is at 170 East 17th Place (tel. 602/783-4403).

By Car Yuma is on I-8, which runs from San Diego, California, to Casa Grande, Arizona.

ESSENTIALS For more information about Yuma, contact the **Yuma Convention and Visitors Bureau,** 377 Main Street, Suite 203 (P.O. Box 230), Yuma, AZ 85364 (tel. 602/782-2567). The telephone **area code** is 602.

Though you may never have heard of Yuma, Arizona, it was once one of the most important towns in the Southwest. Founded on a shallow spot along the Colorado River, Yuma was once the Rome of the Southwest, for all roads led to the river crossing, and through it passed Quechan peoples, Spanish missionaries and explorers, Kit Carson and his mountain men, 49-ers heading for the gold fields of California, pioneers, and soldiers. Despite its location in the middle of the desert, Yuma was a busy port town when shallow-draft steamboats began traveling up the Colorado River from the Gulf of California in the 1850s. From here military supplies were transported overland to the many forts and camps throughout the Southwest during the Apache wars of the 1870s and 1880s. When the railroad pushed westward into California in the 1870s, it also passed through Yuma. Even today I-8, which connects San Diego with Tucson and Phoenix, crosses the Colorado at Yuma.

Hotter than Phoenix, Yuma's summer temperatures regularly top 120° Fahrenheit, and the U.S. Weather Service says that Yuma is the sunniest city in the United States. However, Yuma is gloriously warm and sunny in the winter and has become the winter home of tens of thousands of "snowbirds" (winter visitors from up north), who drive their RVs down from as far away as Canada.

WHAT TO SEE & DO

MUSEUMS & HISTORICAL BUILDINGS

ARIZONA HISTORICAL SOCIETY CENTURY HOUSE MUSEUM, 240 S. Madison St. Tel. 782-1841.

Located downtown not far from the river, the Century House was once the home of a prosperous Yuma merchant. Today the old home is surrounded by palm trees and lush gardens. In back is a garden restaurant where diners are surrounded by aviaries (see "Where to Dine," below, for details). Inside the museum are historic photographs and artifacts from Arizona's territorial period.

Admission: Free.
Open: Tues–Sat 10am–4pm. **Closed:** Dec 25.

QUARTERMASTER DEPOT STATE HISTORIC PARK, Second Ave. and the Colorado River. Tel. 343-2500.

Yuma was a busy river port during the mid-19th century and a depot for military supplies shipped from California. After unloading in Yuma, supplies were shipped to military posts throughout the region. In 1877 the railroad arrived in Yuma and the Quartermaster Depot began losing its importance in the regional supply network. By 1883 the depot had been closed. Today the large wooden buildings are set back a bit from the new channel of the Colorado River, but it's easy to imagine being stationed at this hot and dusty outpost in the days before air conditioning. Exhibits tell the story of the people who lived and worked at Yuma Crossing. Costumed guides happily answer questions about the depot and its role in Arizona history. A short video documentary tells the story of Yuma Crossing, when it acted as a stopover point for travelers heading for southern California.

Admission: $2 adults, $1.50 senior citizens, $1 children 6–15, free for children 5 and under.
Open: Thurs–Mon 10am–5pm. **Closed:** Dec 25.

QUECHAN INDIAN MUSEUM, Indian Hill Rd. Tel. 619/572-0661.

Across the Colorado River from Yuma Territorial Prison is California and the buildings of Fort Yuma, which were built in 1850 and played an important role in territorial Arizona. Today the old fort is the headquarters of the Quechan tribe and site of the Quechan Indian Museum. The museum is housed in the former fort kitchen, which once also served as a school for Quechan children. Having learned the importance of Yuma Crossing, the Quechan were one of eight tribes living and farming along the Colorado River when the Spanish first arrived in this region in 1540. The tribe's reservation now covers 44,000 acres on the California side of the Colorado River. Displays of tribal arts and crafts and historic photos and artifacts cover both past and present Quechan culture. Each year in the first week of March there's a Southwest Native American Pow-Wow featuring traditional dances and dress.

Admission: 50¢.
Open: Mon–Fri 8am–noon and 1–5pm. **Closed:** Major hols.

YUMA TERRITORIAL PRISON STATE HISTORIC PARK, Prison Hill Rd. Tel. 783-4771.

Yuma is one of the hottest places in the world, so it comes as no surprise that the Arizona Territory chose this bleak spot for a prison (although there is a view of the confluence of the Gila and Colorado rivers from Prison Hill). The prison first closed its doors on convicts in 1876 and operated for only 33 years before being replaced by a larger prison. Despite the stone walls (albeit thick ones) and iron bars, this prison was considered a model penal institution in its day. It even had its own generating plant for electricity and a ventilation system. The prison museum has some interesting displays, including photos of many of the 3,069 prisoners who were incarcerated at Yuma over the years; 29 were women. After the prison was shut down, the building served as a high school and as housing for the homeless during the Depression.

Admission: $2 adults, free for children 17 and under.
Open: Daily 8am–5pm. **Closed:** Dec 25.

ORGANIZED TOURS

The Colorado River has been the life blood of the southwestern desert, and today there is a wealth of history along its banks. **Yuma River Tours,** 1920 Arizona Ave (tel. 783-4400), operates narrated jet-boat tours of varying lengths between Yuma and the Imperial Wildlife Refuge to the north. Along the way, you'll learn about the homesteaders, boatmen, Native Americans, and miners who relied on the Colorado River. Tours cost $17.50 to $49.

SPORTS & RECREATION

The **Mesa del Sol Golf Resort,** 10602 Camino del Sol (tel. 342-1283), off I-8 at the Fortuna Road exit, is the most challenging course open to the public. Others include **Arroyo Dunes Golf Course,** 32nd Street and Avenue A (tel. 726-8350); **Desert Hills Municipal Course,** 1245 Desert Hills Drive (tel. 344-4653); and **Cocopah Bend RV Resort,** 6800 Strand Avenue (tel. 343-1663).

At the **Yuma Greyhound Park,** 4000 South Fourth Avenue (tel. 726-4655), you can wager on the hounds Wednesday through Sunday nights from 6pm on. There are also matinees on Saturday and Sunday starting at 2pm. General admission is free, with seating in the air-conditioned clubhouse going for $2.

WHERE TO STAY
MODERATE

BEST WESTERN INN SUITES, 1450 S. Castle Dome Ave., Yuma, AZ 85365. Tel. 602/783-8341, or toll free 800/842-4242. Fax 602/783-1349. 166 suites (all with bath). A/C TV TEL
$ Rates (including full breakfast): $52–$80 single studio; $59–$94 double studio; $64–$89 one-room suite; $69–$94 two-room suite. AE, DC, DISC, MC, V.
If you've come to Yuma to escape the cold weather up north and want to enjoy some active sports, the Best Western Inn Suites hotel should be just what you're looking for. They've got a swimming pool, whirlpool bath, an exercise room, tennis courts, and there is a golf course nearby. For quiet moments, there is a library. Rooms are spacious and attractive and feature in-room movies, an alarm clock, microwave oven, coffee maker, a small refrigerator, and a hairdryer in the bathroom. Decor is in blue green and shades of pink. All this comfort and value is located just off the Interstate at 16th Street.

P.J.'s Poolside Café serves breakfast, sandwiches, snacks, and cocktails. Wednesday nights there's a free barbecue for guests. The hotel also offers a complimentary afternoon cocktail and morning newspaper and coffee.

LA FUENTE TRAVELODGE, 1513 E. 16th St., Yuma, AZ 85364. Tel. 602/329-1814. 96 rms, 46 suites (all with bath). A/C TV TEL
$ Rates (including continental breakfast): $60–$70 single; $63–$75 double; $70–$86 suite. AE, DC, DISC, MC, V.
Conveniently located just off the Interstate on 16th Street, this appealing hotel is done in Spanish colonial style with red-tile roof, pink-stucco walls, and a fountain out front. Inside the lobby the theme is continued with rustic furnishings, tile floor, and a kiva ladder leaning against the wall. French doors open onto the swimming pool terrace and a large courtyard, around which the guest rooms are arranged. These

rooms feature contemporary furnishings in shades of pink and pale gray. The hotel also offers a complimentary newspaper, evening happy hour, whirlpool bath, fitness room, coin laundry, no-smoking rooms, and poolside gas barbecue grills.

PARK INN, 2600 S. Fourth Ave., Yuma, AZ 85364. Tel. 602/726-4830, or toll free 800/473-PARK. 164 suites (all with bath). A/C MINIBAR TV TEL

$ Rates (including continental breakfast): $60 single; $70 double. AE, DC, MC, V.
Located on Yuma's main thoroughfare, the modern Park Inn is a Spanish colonial-inspired hotel with a vaulted ceiling, exposed beams, tile floors, and reproduction colonial furniture in the large lobby. Should you be visiting between January and April, you might share the hotel with the San Diego Padres, who have their spring training camp in Yuma. During these months the hotel does not accept reservations, so reserve in advance. Guest rooms are two-room suites, and have two TVs, a microwave oven, scales, a hairdryer, a desk, a table, and a sofa. Some have whirlpool tubs and sofabeds as well. The pool area includes a large quiet patio that's ideal for soaking up the desert sun.

There is no restaurant on the premises, but the poolside Cabaña Club serves the hotel's complimentary breakfast and cocktails. There are several restaurants nearby.

The hotel offers use of nearby health club (fee), airport shuttle, complimentary cocktails, a swimming pool, whirlpool bath, no-smoking rooms, wheelchair accommodations, and a coin laundry.

SHILO INN HOTEL, 1530 S. Castle Dome Ave., Yuma, AZ 85365. Tel. **602/782-9518,** or toll free 800/222-2244. 133 rms, 1 suite (all with bath). A/C MINIBAR TV TEL

$ Rates: $77–$110 single or double, $197 suite. AE, DC, DISC, MC, V.

Located on the edge of town overlooking farmland and desert, the Shilo Inn is Yuma's most luxurious hotel. The elegant lobby has a three-story-high ceiling, marble floors and mirrored columns, unusual artichoke-pattern chandeliers, and wall-sconce lighting. The gardens are neatly manicured and provide an oasis of greenery in this dry landscape. The bright guest rooms are done in pastel greens and pinks, with comfortable chairs, a couch, and a patio. In the tile bathroom you'll find plenty of counter space. The hotel's more expensive rooms are those with a view of the desert. For long-term stays, there are also suites with kitchenettes.

The hotel's spacious dining room offers both indoor and terrace dining. The international menu features Cajun, Mexican, and Caribbean specialties, as well as steaks and prime rib. To one side of the dining room is a lounge with a dance floor. In the evenings there is recorded Top-40 music and occasionally a comedy show.

The hotel also offers complimentary newspaper and coffee, room service, a large swimming pool, whirlpool bath, exercise room, sauna, and a steam room.

BUDGET

YUMA CABANA, 2151 Fourth Ave., Yuma, AZ 85364. Tel. 602/783- **8311.** 63 rms, 4 suites (all with bath). A/C TV TEL

$ Rates: $25–$62 single or double; $38–$75 suite. AE, CB, DC, DISC, MC, V.
Fourth Avenue is Yuma's main drag and is lined with numerous aging motels that offer rooms at very reasonable rates if you aren't too fussy. The renovated Yuma Cabana is probably the best of them. Rooms are large and have balconies, new green carpeting, modern furniture, and coffee makers, and in-room movies. There are also kitchenette rooms and suites. Facilities include a swimming pool and shuffleboard court.

WHERE TO DINE

HUNGRY HUNTER, 2355 S. Fourth Ave. Tel. 782-3637.
Cuisine: STEAK/SEAFOOD. **Reservations:** Suggested.
$ Prices: Appetizers $4.25–$8; main courses $13–$18; sunset dinner (served 5–6pm) $10; lunch $5–$8. AE, DC, MC, V.
Open: Lunch Mon–Fri 11am–2:30pm; dinner Sun–Thurs 5–9:30pm, Fri–Sat 5–10pm.
Yuma's poshest restaurant sports an Eddie Bauer hunt-club decor with duck images everywhere. Frosted-glass dividers, liberal use of brass and oak, and a rich forest-green

color scheme may have you expecting a cool forest when you step outside. All meals are served with a cup of soup, fresh bread, a potato or rice pilaf, and a lazy-susan salad bar that's brought to your table. If this isn't enough to satisfy your hunger, you may want to precede your meal with an appetizer of spicy scallops, baked Brie, or crab-stuffed mushrooms, or top off your meal with mountain-high mudd pie made with two ice creams, Grand Marnier, hot fudge, and whipped cream. In between, save room for one of the well-prepared steaks or seafood dishes. Most of the same dishes are available in smaller portions and at lower prices at lunch.

GARDEN CAFE, 250 Madison Ave. Tel. 783-1491.
   Cuisine: SANDWICHES/SALADS. **Reservations:** Accepted.
$ Prices: $4–$6. AE, MC, V.
   Open: Breakfast/lunch Tues–Fri 9am–2:30pm, Sat–Sun 8am–2:30pm.

★ In back of the Century House Museum, you'll find Yuma's favorite breakfast and lunch café. Set amid quiet terraced gardens and large aviaries full of singing birds, the Garden Café is a cool retreat from Yuma's heat. On the hottest days, misters spray the air with a gentle fog that keeps the gardens cool. There is also an indoor dining area. The menu consists of various well-constructed sandwiches, daily-special quiches, salads, and rich desserts. On Sunday there's a brunch buffet.

LUTES CASINO, 221 Main St. Tel. 782-2192.
   Cuisine: BURGERS. **Reservations:** Not accepted.
$ Prices: $2.50–$3.50. No credit cards.
   Open: Mon–Thurs and Sat 10am–7pm, Fri 10am–8pm, Sun 10am–6pm.

⑤ You won't find any slot machines or poker tables at Lutes Casino anymore, but back in the 1920s when this place opened, gambling was legal in Arizona. Today it's a dark and cavernous pool hall and the state's only domino parlor, but it's better known as a family restaurant serving the best hamburgers in town. You don't need to see a menu—just walk in and ask for a Special, or Especial (this is a bilingual joint). What you'll get is a combination of a cheeseburger and a hot dog. Then cover your Special with Lutes's own secret-recipe hot sauce to make it truly special.

EN ROUTE TO NOGALES

ORGAN PIPE NATIONAL MONUMENT, Ariz. 5, Ajo. Tel. 602/387-6849.
   Located 70 miles south of Gila Bend on Ariz. 5, Organ Pipe National Monument is a preserve for the rare organ pipe cactus. This massive cactus resembles the saguaro in many ways, but instead of forming a single main trunk, it forms many trunks, some 20-feet-tall, that resemble organ pipes. This is a rugged region with few towns or services. Be sure to gas up your car before leaving Ajo. Inside the park there is only one campground, and the only roads other than Ariz. 85 are gravel. In the western section of the national monument, 15 miles down a gravel road, is Quitobaquito Spring, which was relied on by Native Americans and pioneers as the only reliable source of water for miles around.
   Admission: $3 per car; $8 per night for camping.
   Open: Visitor center, daily 8am–5pm.

---

2. NOGALES

175 miles S of Phoenix, 63 miles S of Tucson, 65 miles W of Sierra Vista

GETTING THERE   By Plane   The nearest airport with regular service is Tucson International Airport. Take a bus or drive from there.

By Train   The nearest **Amtrak** (tel. toll free 800/872-7245) passenger service is in Tucson. Take a bus or drive from there.

By Bus   Citizens Auto Stage has service between Nogales and Tucson. There is also bus service from Mexico. The bus station is at 126 Terrace Avenue (tel. 602/287-5628).

By Car   Nogales is the last town on I-19 before reaching the Mexican border. Ariz. 82 leads northeast from town toward Sonoita and Sierra Vista.

ESSENTIALS   For further information on Nogales, contact the **Nogales–Santa Cruz County Chamber of Commerce,** Kino Park, Nogales, AZ 85621 (tel. 602/287-3685). The telephone **area code** is 602.

Situated on the Mexican border 63 miles south of Tucson, the twin towns of Nogales, Arizona, and Nogales, Sonora, Mexico, (known jointly as Ambos Nogales) together form a bustling border town. All day long U.S. citizens cross into Mexico to shop for bargains on handcrafted items and duty-free imports from around the world, while Mexican citizens cross into the United States to buy products not available in their own country. Nogales is also the busiest produce port in the world. During the harvest season more than 700 truckloads of produce daily cross into the United States from Mexico.

WHAT TO SEE & DO

Most people who visit Nogales, Arizona, are here to cross the border to Nogales, Mexico. The favorable exchange rate makes shopping in Mexico very popular with Americans. If you'd like to learn more about the history of this area, stop by the **Pimeria Alta Historical Society,** at the corner of Grand Avenue and Crawford Street (tel. 287-5402), near the border crossing in downtown Nogales. The historical society maintains a small museum, library, and archives on this region of northern Mexico and southern Arizona, which was once known as Pimeria Alta.

Just a couple of miles outside Nogales on the road to Patagonia, you'll see signs for the **Arizona Vinyard Winery** (tel. 287-7972). You may not think of Arizona as wine country, but the Spanish began growing grapes and making wine as soon as they arrived in the area several centuries ago. You can taste free samples of white burgundy, blanc de blanc, chablis, vin rosé, tino tinto, haut sauterne, mountain Rhine, and worker's red.

SHOPPING

As you can probably guess, **Nogales, Mexico,** is a typical border town filled with tiny shops selling Mexican crafts and souvenirs and dozens of restaurants serving simple Mexican food. (There is however, quite a bit of poverty in Nogales, Mexico, so anyone crossing the border should be prepared to encounter numerous beggars.) Some of the better deals are on wool rugs, which cost a small fraction of what a Navajo rug will cost but also are not nearly as well made. Pottery is another popular buy, though my personal favorite items are the hand-blown blue drinking glasses and pitchers.

All the shops and restaurants in Nogales, Mexico, are within walking distance of the border, so unless you're planning to continue farther into Mexico, it's not a good idea to take your car across the border. There are numerous pay parking lots and garages on the U.S. side of the border where your car will be secure for the day. If you should take your car into Mexico, be sure to get Mexican auto insurance before crossing the border—your U.S. auto insurance is not valid. There are plenty of insurance companies set up along the road leading to the border.

Most shops and restaurants in Nogales, Mexico, accept U.S. dollars, but you should be sure to carry small bills, as change will be given in Mexican pesos. You may bring back $400 worth of merchandise duty free. This allowance includes 1 quart of liquor (if you are 21 or older).

WHERE TO STAY

BEST WESTERN TIME MOTEL, 1200 Grand Ave., Nogales, AZ 85621.
   Tel. 602/287-4627, or toll free 800/528-1234. 43 rms (all with bath). A/C TV TEL

$ Rates: $30–$40 single; $32–$45 double. AE, CB, DC, DISC, MC, V.

Located only a mile from the border on the road leading to the border crossing, the Time Motel has recently been renovated inside and out and is an eye-catching pink and blue outside. Guest rooms are rather cramped with two beds in them, but the furnishings are all new and done in tasteful pastels. Bathrooms are also rather small. There are, however, VCRs and free in-room movies in all the rooms.

The motel also offers free coffee and doughnuts, free local phone calls, a swimming pool, whirlpool bath, and no-smoking rooms.

RIO RICO RESORT & COUNTRY CLUB, 1550 Camino a la Posada, Rio Rico, AZ 85621. Tel. 602/281-1901, or toll free 800/288-4746. Fax 602/281-7132. 175 rms, 10 suites, 5 apts (all with bath). A/C TV TEL

$ Rates: $70–$88 single; $80–$98 double; $130 suite; $195 apt. Special packages available. AE, CB, DC, DISC, MC, V.

A few miles north of Nogales, Rio Rico is the site of a secluded and little-known golf resort. The hotel is built atop a low hill, and all the guest rooms have excellent views over the golf course and desert. Guest rooms are rather spartan and bathrooms are fairly basic, but there are new carpets. Rooms have in-room movies and sliding glass doors that open onto patios or balconies.

La Cima, the resort's dining room, sports southwestern decor and features a mixture of American and Mexican dishes on the menu. The Cantina Lounge features live dance bands on the weekend. Margaritas are the house specialty.

The resort also offers horseback riding, Mexico shopping shuttle, an 18-hole golf course, swimming pool, whirlpool bath, sauna, exercise room, four tennis courts, pro shop, shuffleboard, and volleyball.

SUPER 8 MOTEL, 700 W. Mariposa Rd., Nogales, AZ 85621. Tel. 602/281-2242, or toll free 800/843-1991. Fax 602/281-2242, ext. 400. 101 rms (all with bath). A/C TV TEL

$ Rates: $39–$41 single; $43–$47 double. AE, DC, DISC, MC, V.

This is the largest and newest motel in town and is located just off I-19 at the Mariposa Road exit. Though it's located next to a shopping center, the motel has a very attractive pool and garden area, and from some of the rooms there are views across the desert. Rooms are of average size, though those with only a single queen-size bed seem quite spacious. There are clock radios in all the rooms, and some have in-room whirlpool tubs.

Barrow's Bar & Restaurant serves three meals daily.

The hotel also offers free local phone calls, a swimming pool, tennis court, coin laundry, and no-smoking rooms.

WHERE TO DINE

LAS VIGAS, 180 W. Loma St. Tel. 287-6641.
   Cuisine: STEAK/MEXICAN. **Reservations:** Not necessary.
$ Prices: $4.50–$10. MC, V.
   Open: Daily 9am–10pm.

To reach Las Vigas, head down Grand Avenue toward the border. Before you get to downtown Nogales, watch for Arroyo Boulevard, which forks to the right; Las Vigas is just past the fork. It's a western-style building with a covered sidewalk in front and old photos of Mexican men and women inside. Animal heads and skins on the walls give Las Vigas a very rustic feel. Meals are inexpensive and filling, and there are daily specials.

MR. C'S SUPPER CLUB, 282 W. View Point Dr. Tel. 281-9000.
   Cuisine: CONTINENTAL. **Reservations:** Suggested.
$ Prices: Appetizers $3–$9; main courses $11–$20. MC, V.
   Open: Mon–Sat 11:30am–midnight. **Closed:** Hols.

Located atop a hill on the north side of town just off Mariposa Road, Mr. C's is Nogales's best restaurant. The menu leans heavily toward fresh fish dishes, with the day's menu written over the salad bar. Start your dinner with an order of botanas, an

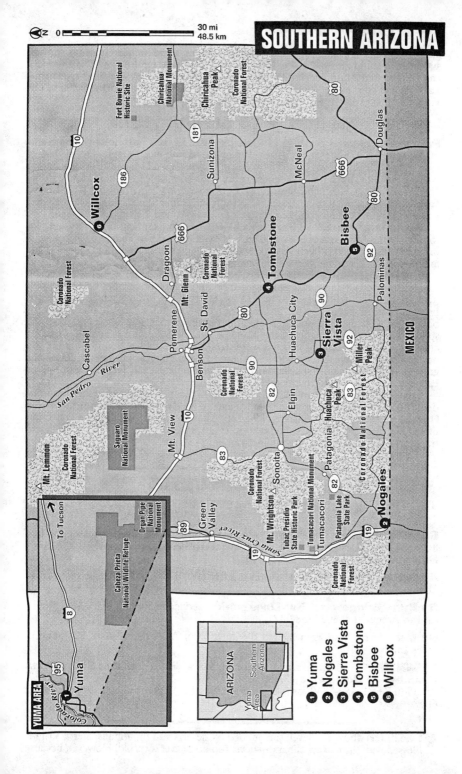

assortment of Mexican appetizers. For main dishes, there are fat Guaymas shrimp, succulent quail in mustard sauce, Norwegian salmon, and tender steaks. Most dishes can be prepared a number of different ways, which makes for a very extensive menu. Early diners can take advantage of the early-bird specials for $8.50 to $10.50. On Friday and Saturday nights, there's live music in the lounge.

EN ROUTE TO SIERRA VISTA

Patagonia, 18 miles north of Nogales on Ariz. 82, is a historic old mining and ranching town 4,000 feet up in the Patagonia Mountains. Surrounded by higher mountains, the little town has for years been popular with film and television crews. Among the films that have been shot here are *Oklahoma, Red River, A Star Is Born, David and Bathsheba,* and most recently, *Arrowtooth Waltz* starring Jerry Lewis, Faye Dunaway, and Johnny Depp. Television programs filmed here have included *Little House on the Prairie, Red Badge of Courage,* and *The Young Riders.*

Patagonia Lake State Park (tel. 287-6965), a popular boating and fishing lake formed by the damming of Sonoita Creek, is 11 miles south of Patagonia. The lake is 2.5 miles long and has been stocked with bass, crappie, bluegill, and catfish. Park facilities include a picnic ground, a campground, and a swimming beach.

The **Patagonia–Sonoita Creek Sanctuary** is a nature preserve owned by the Nature Conservancy and protects a mile and a half of Sonoita Creek riparian (riverside) habitat, which is important to migratory birds. More than 250 species of birds have been spotted on the preserve, which makes this a very popular spot with birders from all over the world. Among the rare birds that may be seen here are 22 species of flycatchers, kingbirds, and phoebes, and the Montezuma quail. A forest of cottonwood trees, some of which are 100 feet tall, lines the creek and is one of the best examples of such a forest left in southern Arizona. At one time forests such as this grew along all the rivers in southern Arizona. The sanctuary is located 3 miles south of Patagonia on a dirt road that parallels Ariz. 82.

Patagonia is horse country and is home to the only museum in the country dedicated to horses and horse-drawn vehicles. The **Straddling Museum of the Horse,** on McKeown Avenue (tel. 394-2264), has an amazingly thorough collection of saddles, harnesses, bridles, horseshoes, straps, chariots, wagons, and other horse trappings. The museum is open daily from 9am to 5pm.

---

3. SIERRA VISTA

189 miles SE of Phoenix, 70 miles SE of Tucson,
33 miles SW of Tombstone, 33 miles W of Bisbee

GETTING THERE By Plane   Mesa airlines (tel. 602/225-5150, or toll free 800/637-2247) has regular flights from Phoenix to Sierra Vista Airport, 2100 Airport Drive (tel. 602/459-8575).

By Train   The nearest **Amtrak** (tel. toll free 800/872-7245) passenger service is in Tucson.

By Bus   Bridgewater Bus Lines provides service to Sierra Vista. The station is on Fab Avenue (tel. 602/458-3471).

By Car   Sierra Vista is located at the junction of Ariz. 90 and Ariz. 92 about 35 miles south of I-10.

ESSENTIALS   For further information on Sierra Vista, contact the **Sierra Vista Chamber of Commerce,** 77 South Calle Portal, Suite A-140, Sierra Vista, AZ 85635 (tel. 602/458-6940, or toll free 800/288-3861). The telephone **area code** is 602.

At 4,620 feet above sea level, surrounded by deserts and mountains, Sierra Vista is blessed with the perfect climate—never too hot, never too cold. However, because it's a long way from any population centers and is not on an Interstate highway, few people know about Sierra Vista. If it were not for the U.S. Army's Fort Huachuca, it's likely that no one would have ever settled here, but when Camp Huachuca (later to become Fort Huachuca) was founded in 1877, the seeds of Sierra Vista were sown. Today, however, retirees, free from the necessity of living where there are jobs available, have discovered the climate and settled down here.

Though the town itself is modern and has very little character, the surrounding countryside has much to offer. Within a few miles' drive of town are a national conservation area, a national memorial, and a Nature Conservancy preserve. No other area of the United States attracts more attention from birders, who come for the 300 bird species in southeastern Arizona. With its many inexpensive motels, Sierra Vista makes a good base for exploring all of this region.

WHAT TO SEE & DO

FORT HUACHUCA MUSEUM, Grierson Rd. inside Fort Huachuca U.S. Army base. Tel. 533-5736.

Fort Huachuca, an army base located at the mouth of Huachuca Canyon northeast of Sierra Vista, was established in 1877 and, though it has been closed a couple of times, is still active today. The buildings of the old post have been declared a National Historic Landmark and one is now a museum dedicated to the many forts that dotted the Southwest in the latter part of the 19th century. Near the museum stands a row of Victorian officers' quarters.

Though not exactly a part of the museum, the **B Troop, 4th Regiment, U.S. Cavalry (Memorial)** is one of Sierra Vista's most famous attractions. The original B Troop was formed in 1855 and saw action at Little Big Horn. To celebrate the horseback days of the cavalry, the new B Troop memorial was formed. The troop of about 30 members dress in the blue-and-gold uniforms of the 1880s, have made appearances across the country, including at the Tournament of Roses Parade, and can often be seen right here in Sierra Vista. Phone 533-2714 or 533-2622 to find out if they will be riding while you're in town.

Admission: Free.
Open: Mon–Fri 9am–4pm, Sat–Sun 1–4pm.

RAMSEY CANYON PRESERVE, Ariz. 92. Tel. 378-2785.

A buzzing fills the air in Ramsey Canyon, but it's not the buzzing of mosquitoes. Instead it's the buzzing of curious hummingbirds. Wear bright-red clothing when you visit this preserve and you're certain to attract the curious little avian dive bombers, which will mistake you for the world's largest flower. Located 5 miles south of Sierra Vista on Ariz. 92, this wildlife preserve is owned by the Nature Conservancy and is internationally known as a home to 14 species of hummingbirds—more than anywhere else in the United States.

Covering only 280 acres, the preserve is situated in a wooded gorge in the Huachuca Mountains. A short nature trail leads through the canyon, with an explanatory guidebook that points out the reasons for and difficulties in preserving Ramsey Canyon. A second trail leads higher up the canyon. Ramsey Creek is a year-round stream, a rarity in this region, and attracts a wide variety of wildlife, including bears, bobcats, and nearly 200 species of birds.

Because the preserve has become very popular and has only a few parking spaces, a parking reservation is an absolute must on weekends and is suggested during the week. April and May are the busiest time of year here and August is the best time to see hummingbirds. To avoid parking problems, you can stay in a cabin at the preserve (see "Where to Stay," below, for details).

Admission: $3 (free for Nature Conservancy members).
Open: Daily 8am–5pm.

CORONADO NATIONAL MEMORIAL, Montezuma Canyon Rd. Tel. 458-9333 or 366-5515.

About 20 miles south of Sierra Vista is a 5,000-acre memorial dedicated to Francisco Vásquez de Coronado, the first European to explore this region. Coronado, leading more than 700 people, left Compostela, Mexico, on February 23, 1540, in search of the fabled Seven Cities of Cíbola. These cities were said to be rich in gold and jewels, and Coronado had dreams of becoming wealthy from his expedition. Coronado led his band of weary men and women up the valley of the San Pedro River sometime between 1540 and 1542. The forested Montezuma Pass, in the center of the memorial, is situated at 6,575 feet and provides far-reaching views of Sonora, Mexico, to the south, the San Pedro River to the east, and several mountain ranges and valleys to the west. A visitor center tells the story of Coronado's fruitless quest for riches and features a bird observation area where you might see some of the memorial's 140 or more species of birds.

Admission: Free.
Open: Daily 8am–5pm.

SAN PEDRO RIPARIAN NATIONAL CONSERVATION AREA, Ariz. 90. Tel. 457-2265.

Located 8 miles east of Sierra Vista, the San Pedro Riparian National Conservation Area is a rare example of a natural riparian (riverside) habitat. Over the past 100 years the southwestern landscape has been considerably altered by the human hand. Most deleterious of these changes has been the loss of 90% of the region's free-flowing year-round rivers and streams that once provided water and protection to myriad plants and animals, including humans. Fossil findings from this area indicate that people were living along this river 11,000 years ago. At that time this area was not a desert but a swamp, and the San Pedro River is all that remains of this ancient wetland (today then there isn't much water on the surface because most of the river water has flowed underground since an earthquake a century ago). The conservation area is particularly popular with birders who have a chance of spotting more than 300 species of birds here. Also living along the river are 80 species of mammals, 14 species of fish, and 40 species of amphibians and reptiles.

There are three main parking areas for the conservation area, at the bridges over the San Pedro River on Ariz. 92, Ariz. 90, and Ariz. 82. This latter parking area is at the ghost town of Fairbank, which now is the site of the conservation area's headquarters. The headquarters building, open Monday through Friday from 8am to 5pm, has handouts and maps of the area. At the Ariz. 90 parking area, the San Pedro House, a 1930s ranch, operates as a visitor center and bookstore. It's open on Saturday from 10am to 4pm and on Sunday from noon to 3pm.

Admission: Free.
Open: Daily 24 hours.

WHERE TO STAY
MODERATE

RAMADA INN–SIERRA VISTA, 2047 S. Ariz. 92, Sierra Vista, AZ 85635. Tel. 602/459-5900, or toll free 800/825-4656. Fax 602/458-1347. 152 rms, 3 suites (all with bath). A/C TV TEL

$ Rates: $69 single; $73 double; $95–$110 suite. AE, CB, DC, DISC, MC, V.

This modern three-story motel is one of Sierra Vista's best lodgings. There's a piano in the lobby and you're welcome to play. In the courtyard pool area there are plenty of tables where you can have a drink or two between swims. There is also a whirlpool bath. Guest rooms feature contemporary furnishings, coffee makers, large closets, and plenty of counter space in the bathrooms. Colorful landscape prints and big windows brighten the rooms. No-smoking rooms are available.

Nickels Restaurant is a family restaurant with a contemporary feel. It's open for three meals a day and has very reasonable prices. The Oyster Club lounge features an old-fashioned jukebox and DJ dancing on weekends. The hotel also offers room service and free coffee.

RAMSEY CANYON INN, 31 Ramsey Canyon Rd. (P.O. Box 85), Hereford, AZ 85615. Tel. 602/378-3010. 6 rms (4 with bath), 3 cottages.

$ Rates: $65 single or double without bath, $75 single or double with bath (including full breakfast); $85 cottage single or double. No credit cards.

★ Just outside the gates of the Nature Conservancy's Mile Hi/Ramsey Canyon Preserve, the Ramsey Canyon Inn is a pleasant bed-and-breakfast inn with a country flavor. Located on both sides of Ramsey Creek, the inn has rooms in the main building and small cabins that are reached by a footbridge over the creek. Hummingbird feeders set up on the inn's front porch attract 14 species of hummers throughout the year, with different species appearing at different times of year. A large country breakfast is served in the morning, and in the afternoon you're likely to find a fresh pie made with fruit from the inn's orchard. Breakfast is not included in the cottage rates because they have their own kitchens.

BUDGET

MILE HI, Ramsey Canyon Preserve, 27 Ramsey Canyon Rd., Hereford, AZ 85615. Tel. 602/378-2785. 6 cabins (all with bath).
$ Rates: $60–$70 single or double. No credit cards.
Located inside the Ramsey Canyon Preserve and operated by the Nature Conservancy, Mile Hi is a collection of very basic cabins beside Ramsey Creek. Each cabin is different, but all have kitchens where you can fix your own meals. There are also patio chairs and barbecue grills. If you're used to roughing it, these cabins should be fine for you—and there's no better location. You can be out birding at dawn and dusk when most birds are busily feeding. If you're planning to visit during the summer, you should make a reservation at least a year in advance. People come from all over the world to stay in these cabins. Unless you want to drive all the way back into Sierra Vista, bring all your own food.

SIERRA SUITES, 391 E. Fry Blvd., Sierra Vista, AZ 85635. Tel. 602/459-4221. Fax 602/459-8449. 96 rms, 4 suites (all with bath). A/C TV TEL
$ Rates (including continental breakfast): $39–$52 single; $44–$58 double; $70–$76 suite. AE, DC, DISC, MC, V.
Located only a few blocks from the front gate of Fort Huachuca, Sierra Suites offers comfortable accommodations with several extras. Though the most of the rooms are not true suites, they are slightly larger than most motel rooms and many have refrigerators and microwave ovens. The lobby is attractively done in southwestern style, with red-tile floor, brick walls, a fireplace, and wicker furniture. There is no restaurant, but just off the lobby is the sunny lounge where breakfast and free afternoon cocktails are served.

The hotel offers free local phone calls, health club membership, a swimming pool, whirlpool bath, and no-smoking rooms.

WHERE TO DINE

BUNBUKU, 297 W. Fry Blvd. Tel. 459-6993.
Cuisine: JAPANESE. **Reservations:** Accepted.
$ Prices: Appetizers $2.50–$7.50; main courses $6–$14. MC, V.
Open: Lunch daily 11am–2:30pm; dinner daily 4:30–9pm.
Because Sierra Vista is home to a military base and many of the servicemen have Asian wives, the town supports quite a number of excellent Asian restaurants. Serving good Japanese meals, this place is packed at lunch when everyone from the base heads into town to eat, but at dinner there's usually no problem getting a seat. Donburi (pork cutlets), yakitori (chicken on a skewer), tempura, sushi, and sashimi are all available.

KAREN'S, 4907 S. Ariz. 92. Tel. 378-2355.
Cuisine: CONTINENTAL. **Reservations:** Required.
$ Prices: Fixed-price dinner $25.40. MC, V.
Open: Dinner only, Thurs–Sat 5:30–8:30pm.
★ Located south of town near the turnoff for Ramsey Canyon, Karen's is a culinary oasis in southern Arizona. The restaurant is an unpretentious place with a tile roof and green awning. The menu changes weekly and all meals are a fixed price. A recent menu offered a choice of grilled top sirloin with sweet- and

hot-pepper purée; grilled chicken breast stuffed with mozzarella and herbs, and served with a sauce of sun-dried tomatoes; and orange roughy baked in parchment with a garlic-basil butter. Meals are served with perfectly prepared vegetables such as roast baby potatoes with lemon and mint or marinated green beans with roasted walnuts. Desserts, such as poached pear with bittersweet-chocolate sauce and raspberry coulis, are delicious.

---

4. TOMBSTONE

181 miles SE of Phoenix, 70 miles SE of Tucson, 24 miles N of Bisbee

GETTING THERE   By Plane   The nearest airport with regular service is in Sierra Vista, which is served by Mesa airlines (tel. 602/225-5150, or toll free 800/637-2247) from Phoenix. You'll have to drive from Sierra Vista.

By Train   The nearest **Amtrak** (tel. toll free 800/872-7245) passenger service is to Benson, 25 miles north. You'll have to drive from Benson.

By Bus   The nearest bus service is to Benson, on **Greyhound/Trailways Lines.** You'll have to drive from Benson.

By Car   From Tucson, take I-10 east to Benson, from which U.S. 80 heads south to Tombstone. From Sierra Vista, take Ariz. 90 north to Ariz. 82 heading east.

ESSENTIALS   For more information on Tombstone, contact the **Tombstone Tourism Association,** P.O. Box 917, Tombstone, AZ 85638 (tel. 602/457-2211). The telephone **area code** is 602.

"The town too tough to die" is today one of Arizona's most popular tourist attractions, though I'll leave it up to you to decide whether the town deserves its reputation (either as a tough town or as a tourist attraction). Although the name Tombstone alone would be enough to interest most visitors, this old mining town's claim to fame is that of the Wild West—"cowboys and Indians," and the cavalry. It was here in Tombstone that once stood a livery stable known as the O.K. Corral, and when Wyatt Earp, his brothers Virgil and Morgan, and Doc Holiday took on the outlaws Ike Clanton and Frank and Tom McLaury on October 26, 1881, the ensuing gun battle sealed the fate of this town.

Tombstone was named by Ed Schieffelin, a silver prospector who had been warned against venturing into this region, which at the time was home to Apache tribes who were fighting to preserve their homeland. Schieffelin was warned that the land would be his tombstone, so when he discovered a mountain of silver here, he named it Tombstone. Within a few years, Tombstone was larger than San Francisco. Between 1880 and 1887 an estimated $37 million worth of silver was mined here. Such wealth created a sturdy little town, and as the Cochise County seat of the time, Tombstone boasted a number of imposing buildings, including the county courthouse, which is now an Arizona State Park. In 1887 the silver mines were flooded by an underground river. Despite attempts to pump the water out, the mines were never reopened, and the population rapidly dwindled. Today the historic district consists of both original buildings built after the town's second fire and newer buildings built in keeping with the architectural styles of the time. Most of the buildings are souvenir shops and restaurants, which should give you some indication that this is a classic tourist trap, but kids (and adults raised on Louis L'Amour and John Wayne) love it, especially when the famous shootout is reenacted on Sunday at 2pm.

WHAT TO SEE & DO

The shootout has come to epitomize the Wild West in western novels, movies, and television shows of the 1950s and 1960s. All over Arizona there are regular reenactments of gunfights, with the sheriff in his white hat always triumphing over the bad guys in their black hats. But nowhere is this great American phenomenon more glorified than here in Tombstone, where the star attraction is the famous **O.K. Corral,** site of a brief gun battle that has taken on mythic proportions. Six days a week you'll have to be content to view the lifelike figures posed in the corral in the position they were in when the fighting started, but each Sunday at 2pm there is a live reenactment of the famous shootout.

When the shooting was over, three men lay dead. They were later carted off to the **Boot Hill Graveyard** on the edge of town. The cemetery is open to the public and is entered through a gift shop on U.S. 80 just north of town. The graves of Clanton and the McLaury brothers, as well as those of others who died in gunfights or by hanging, are well marked.

When the residents of Tombstone weren't shooting each other in the streets, they were likely to be found in the saloons and bawdy houses that lined Allen Street. The most famous of these is the **Bird Cage Theatre,** so named for the large cagelike cribs that hang from the ceiling. These velvet-draped cages were used by prostitutes to ply their trade. The town's other famous drinking and gambling emporium is the **Crystal Palace,** at the corner of Allen Street and Fifth Street. The high-ceilinged saloon, built in 1879, has been completely restored and is a hangout for costumed members of the Wild Bunch, the local group that stages the Sunday shootout at the O.K. Corral.

On a much lighter note is the **Rose Tree Inn Museum** at Fourth Street and Toughnut Street. The museum claims to have the world's largest rose bush growing on its grounds. The shrub is indeed impressive as it sprawls across an arbor and covers 7,000 square feet. Inside the museum you'll see antique furnishings from Tombstone's heyday in the 1880s.

The most imposing building in town is the **Tombstone Courthouse State Park,** at the corner of Third Street and Toughnut Street. Built in 1882, the courthouse is now a state historic park and museum, containing artifacts, photographs, and newspaper clippings chronicling Tombstone's lively past. In the courtyard, the gallows that once ended the lives of outlaws and bandits still stand.

SPECIAL EVENTS

Tombstone's biggest annual celebrations are **Territorial Days,** held the first weekend of March, and **Helldorado Days,** held the third weekend of October. The latter celebrates the famous gunfight at the O.K. Corral and includes countless shootouts in the streets, mock hangings, a parade, and contests.

EVENING ENTERTAINMENT

Tombstone was once well known for its saloons, and a couple of historic drinking establishments are still in business. Try the **Crystal Palace,** at the corner of Allen Street and Fifth Street. Built in 1879, this saloon has been fully restored to the way it might have looked on the day of the famous shootout.

WHERE TO STAY

ADOBE LODGE MOTEL, 505 Fremont St., Tombstone, AZ 85638. Tel. 602/457-2241. 15 rms (all with bath). A/C TV TEL
$ Rates: $25–$30 single; $35–$45 double. MC, V.
Located in the heart of Tombstone only a block off historic Allen Street, the Adobe is a small motel with clean, no-frills rooms. If you prefer being close to the historic district, where you can walk back to your room after dinner or a nightcap, this is the best choice.

BEST WESTERN LOOKOUT LODGE, U.S. 80 (P.O. Box 787), Tombstone, AZ 85638. Tel. 602/457-2223, or toll free 800/528-1234. 40 rms (all with bath). A/C TV TEL
$ Rates (including continental breakfast): $35–$50 single; $45–$60 double. Senior-citizen discounts available. AE, CB, DC, DISC, MC, V.
The biggest and best lodging in Tombstone is located 1 mile north of town. Stone walls give the spacious rooms an Old West feel, and all overlook the Dragoon

Mountains. Rooms come with king- or queen-size beds, and some are no-smoking. In the summer, the pool is very welcome after a long hot day. The hotel also offers complimentary coffee.

WHERE TO DINE

THE LUCKY CUSS RESTAURANT, 412 Allen St. Tel. 457-3561.
   Cuisine: AMERICAN. **Reservations:** Not necessary.
$ Prices: Complete dinner $11–$14. MC, V.
   Open: Daily 11am–8:30pm. **Closed:** Thanksgiving, Dec 25.
Named for the second mine that Tombstone founder Ed Schieffelin opened, the restaurant was opened in the early 1960s and is a condensed replica of old Tombstone. Paintings and props depict the Bird Cage Theatre, the Wells Fargo office, railroad depot, and the Lucky Cuss Mine, which houses the restaurant's barbecue pit. Barbecued ribs and smoked chicken are the house specialties and have been for 30 years. If she's still as spry as when I last visited, 96-year-old Nettie will entertain you with old, old favorites on the piano.

5. BISBEE

205 miles SE of Phoenix, 94 miles SE of Tucson, 24 miles NW of Douglas

GETTING THERE   By Plane   The nearest airport with regular service is in Sierra Vista, which is served by Mesa airlines (tel. 602/225-5150, or toll free 800/637-2247) from Phoenix. You'll have to drive from Sierra Vista.

By Train   The nearest **Amtrak** (tel. toll free 800/872-7245) passenger service is in Benson, from which you'll have to drive.

By Bus   The nearest bus service is on **Greyhound/Trailways Lines** to Douglas or Sierra Vista, from which you'll have to drive.

By Car   Bisbee is on U.S. 80, which begins at I-10 in the town of Benson, 45 miles east of Tucson.

ESSENTIALS   For further information on Bisbee, contact the **Bisbee Chamber of Commerce,** Naco Road (P.O. Box BA), Bisbee, AZ 85603-0560 (tel. 602/432-2141). The telephone **area code** is 602. In an **emergency,** phone 432-2261 for the police, fire department, or an ambulance.

Arizona abounds in ghost towns that boomed on mining profits but then quickly went bust when the mines played out. When the Phelps Dodge company shut down its copper mines here, Bisbee nearly went the way of those other abandoned mining towns. However, because Bisbee is the county seat of Cochise County, it was not fated to disappear into the dust of the Southwest desert. The town did stop growing in the early part of this century, so today it's one of the best-preserved turn-of-the-century towns anywhere in the Southwest. Old brick buildings line the narrow winding streets of the old section of town. Television and movie producers have discovered these well-preserved streets and in recent years Bisbee has doubled as New York City, Spain, Greece, Italy, and, of course, the Old West.

The rumor of silver in "them thar hills" is what first attracted prospectors to the area in 1877, and within a few years the diggings attracted the interest of some San Francisco investors, among them a Judge DeWitt Bisbee. However, it was copper and other less-than-precious metals that would make Bisbee's fortune. With the help of outside financing, large-scale mining operations were begun in 1881 by the Phelps Dodge Company. By 1910 the population had climbed to 25,000 and Bisbee was the largest city between New Orleans and San Francisco. The town boasted that it was the liveliest spot between El Paso and San Francisco—and the presence of nearly 50 saloons and houses of prostitution along Brewery Gulch backed up the boast.

Tucked into a narrow valley surrounded by red hills a mile high in the Mule

Mountains, Bisbee is best approached from the north on U.S. 80. From this direction, you pass through a tunnel known as the Time Tunnel just before reaching town. Many of the town's old buildings have been restored in recent years, and there are now quite a few bed-and-breakfast inns offering accommodations in all price ranges. There are also a couple of excellent restaurants and a few galleries and antiques stores. Though the copper mines are shut down, they are now the main tourist attraction. For such a small and remote town, Bisbee today has a very cosmopolitan air about it. Several artists now call the town their home and urban refugees have been dropping out of the rat race to open small inns and restaurants. Between the rough edges left over from its mining days and this new cosmopolitan atmosphere, Bisbee is rapidly becoming one of Arizona's most interesting towns.

WHAT TO SEE & DO

At the Bisbee Chamber of Commerce visitor center, located at the south end of town near the traffic circle, you can pick up three walking-tour brochures that will lead you past the most important buildings and sites in town. Climb the hills above town for an excellent panorama of the jumble of old buildings. After you've seen the **old town,** you might want to drive out to the **Warren district,** where the wealthier citizens of old Bisbee built their homes.

MUSEUMS & TOURS

BISBEE MINING AND HISTORICAL MUSEUM, 5 Copper Queen Plaza. Tel. 432-7071.

Housed in the 1897 Copper Queen Consolidated Mining Company office building, this small museum features several rooms of old mining equipment. In the mine tunnel room you'll learn how underground mines were blasted and "mucked" out. There's also an exhibit of minerals that are found in the ground beneath Bisbee. In addition there are exhibits pertaining to the history of the town itself. In the founder's room of the museum you can see the luxury that surrounded the mine's executives.

Admission: $2 adults, free for anyone under 18.
Open: Daily 10am–4pm. **Closed:** Dec 25.

MUHEIM HERITAGE HOUSE, 207B Youngblood Hill. Tel. 432-4461.

Built between 1902 and 1915 by Swiss immigrant Joseph Muheim, the Muheim House has an unusual semicircular porch that overlooks the rest of town. Inside there is period furniture and old wine-making equipment used by Muheim, who owned several saloons in town. You'll find the historic home up Brewery Gulch from Main Street.

Admission: $1.
Open: Fri–Mon 1–4pm.

QUEEN MINE TOURS, 118 Arizona St. Tel. 432-2071.

Copper built Bisbee, and the closing of the mines nearly made it a ghost town. Between 1880 and 1975 the mines here produced $6.1 *billion* worth of metals, and though the Queen Mine hasn't produced any ore for years, people still head into the tunnels daily on the Queen Mine Tours. You'll find the ticket office and mine just south of the old Bisbee business district at the U.S. 80 interchange. You can tour either the underground Queen Mine or the Lavender Pit open mine.

Admission: Queen Mine tour, $7 ($6 May–Nov) adults, $3 children 7–11, $1.50 children 3–6, free for children under 3; Lavender Pit tour, $4 per person.
Open: Daily 10:30am–3:30pm.

SPECIAL EVENTS

Bisbee's population of artists, writers, and other creative souls demand an active cultural life, so throughout the year you can enjoy classical music performances, gallery exhibits, comedy nights, theater performances, and that old western standby, the melodrama. More athletic events include the **Vuelta de Bisbee** bicycle race in

April, the **Mule Mountain Marathon** in May, a **Poetry and Jazz Festival** in late August, and **Brewery Gulch Days, La Fiesta de Vinos** wine festival, the **Bisbee Art Festival,** and the **Fall Festival of Arts and Crafts,** all in September.

SHOPPING

Shopping is one of Bisbee's main attractions. There are several art galleries selling both traditional western art and very avant-garde contemporary works by artists from Bisbee and around the state. There are also a number of antiques stores, the largest of which is **Main St. Antiques,** 67 Main Street (tel. 432-4103). Several jewelry-makers in town work with turquoise and malachite mined in Bisbee. Visit **Gloria's Jewelry & Gemstones,** 86 Main Street (tel. 432-2179), for a look at some of the best local jewelry.

Bisbee's most famous shop has to be the **One Book Bookstore,** 38 Main Street, operated by Walter Swan. The store now sells two books, both of which were written by Swan. *Me 'n Henry* and *Adventure Stories* both contain recollections and tales of Swan's life in the Bisbee area. The down-home flavor and the fascinating tidbits of historical information have made these books very popular. In fact, after Swan published his first book and opened his bookstore to sell it, he found himself garnering national attention and making television talk-show appearances.

EVENING ENTERTAINMENT

Once home to more than 50 saloons, Bisbee now has only a handful of authentic Old West saloons. The **Bisbee Grand Saloon,** at 61 Main Street (tel. 432-5900), boasts a back bar from Tombstone and has both a saloon and a ladies' lounge. There are occasional comedy nights and melodramas here. The **Stock Exchange,** 15 Brewery Gulch (tel. 432-2775), was once the Bisbee stock exchange. You can catch live bands (country-and-western and rock) on the weekends.

WHERE TO STAY

MODERATE

COPPER QUEEN HOTEL, 11 Howell Ave. (P.O. Drawer CQ), Bisbee, AZ 85603. Tel. 602/432-2216, or toll free 800/247-5829. 41 rms (all with bath). TV TEL
$ Rates: $57–$72 single; $57–$80 double; from $77 suite. AE, MC, V.

⭐ Located in the center of Bisbee, the Copper Queen Hotel was built just after the turn of the century by the Copper Queen Mining Company. At that time Bisbee was a booming mining town and the "Queen" played hostess to such notables as Teddy Roosevelt and Gen. "Black Jack" Pershing. Having recently undergone a renovation and restoration and the addition of a swimming pool, the hotel is once again the center of activity in Bisbee. The atmosphere is casual and authentic. The old safe behind the check-in desk has been there for years, as has the oak roll-top desk. There are even swinging screen doors to usher you into the lobby. Spacious halls with their own lounges lead to guest rooms furnished with antiques and decorated in turn-of-the-century colors.

The hotel's dining room, through the swinging screen doors off the lobby, has a very casual feel. The menu is primarily steaks and Italian favorites, with prices from $13 to $16. There is a terrace out front for al fresco dining. For drinks, there's the Old Saloon.

THE WHITE HOUSE OF WARREN, 800 Congdon Ave., Bisbee, AZ 85603. Tel. 602/432-7215. 2 suites (both with bath). A/C
$ Rates (including full breakfast): $75–$100. No credit cards.

⭐ Warren is Bisbee's old wealthy neighborhood, and several of its old mansions are today operating as bed-and-breakfast inns. You'll find Warren by driving past the Lavender Pit Mine, which is downhill from Bisbee, and taking Bisbee Road at the traffic circle

Once the local schoolhouse, the White House of Warren is today a fascinating bed-and-breakfast inn run by a former student of the school and his wife. The guest rooms, lounge, and breakfast room are set up around a large central hall that features an upright piano. The two suites are both very distinctive. The Honeymoon Suite is elegant and has a huge bathroom with whirlpool bath for two, ceiling fans, and a view toward Mexico. The Library Suite has floor-to-ceiling shelves filled with books both old and new. A traditional kiva ladder provides access to books on the higher shelves. Be sure to notice the towels here; they bear the seal of the White House in Washington, D.C. Massage service is available.

BUDGET

BISBEE GRAND HOTEL, 61 Main St. (P.O. Box 825), Bisbee, AZ 85603. Tel. 602/432-5900. 9 rms (2 with bath), 2 suites (both with bath).
$ Rates (including full breakfast): $45–$65 single or double; $90 suite. AE, MC, V.
The Bisbee Grand Hotel is the sort of hotel you'd expect Wyatt Earp and his wife to patronize. At street level there is a historic saloon with a high pressed-tin ceiling and a 109-year-old back bar from Tombstone. Adjacent to the saloon is the ladies' lounge, where there's live piano music on Wednesday nights. There is even a small theater that hosts comedy nights and the occasional melodrama. Upstairs are beautifully decorated turn-of-the-century guest rooms. The Oriental Suite has a ceiling fan, brass bed, clawfoot tub, and skylight, and the Victorian Suite has a red-velvet canopy bed. All the other rooms are equally attractive and sport their own themes, such as the cherub room. Though only a couple of rooms have private bathrooms, they all have sinks. Skylights keep most of the hotel much brighter than it was in its early days.

BISBEE INN, 45 OK St. (P.O. Box 1855), Bisbee, AZ 85603. Tel. 602/432-5131. 18 rms (none with bath).
$ Rates (including full breakfast): $29 single; $34–$39 double. MC, V (5% is added to your bill).
Originally built as the LeMore Hotel and opened in 1917, the Bisbee Inn overlooks the infamous Brewery Gulch. Though still maintaining much of the original interior style, the building has been modified a bit for the convenience of guests. There is now a tiled and enclosed courtyard dining area. There are, however, no private bathrooms because of the difficulty of putting plumbing in all the rooms. Showers and toilets are separate from one another and are kept quite clean. Rooms are furnished with antique oak furniture and iron bed frames. Because this is one of Bisbee's historic buildings, you can take a tour without staying at the hotel. There is no smoking permitted in the rooms.

WHERE TO DINE

MUDDY'S SOUTH, 18 Main St. Tel. 432-7687.
   Cuisine: DELI. **Reservations:** Not necessary.
$ Prices: Sandwiches $1.75–$6.50; salads $3.50–$4.75. No credit cards.
   Open: Mon–Thurs 7am–midnight, Fri–Sat 7am–2am, Sun 8:30am–10pm.
If you're wondering where the literati, artists, and street-corner philosophers hang out in Bisbee, take a peek in the door at Muddy's late on a Friday night. You may find yourself quite surprised at the urban sophistication of the clientele. The unusual local artworks in the window should tip you off before you even walk past the sign proclaiming: ON THIS SITE IN 1897 NOTHING HAPPENED. However, by day the place is likely to be full of tourists passing through town. The Caesar salad is good and vegetarians will be warmed by the miso soup and brown rice. Soups are all homemade and there are daily pasta specials.

THE WINE GALLERY BISTRO, 41 Main St. Tel. 432-3447.
   Cuisine: NOUVELLE. **Reservations:** Accepted only for large parties.
$ Prices: Lunch $4.50–$5; dinner $9–$14. No credit cards.
   Open: Lunch Tues–Fri 11am–2:30pm; dinner Tues–Thurs 5:30–8:30pm, Fri 6–9pm, Sat 5:30–9pm.

⭐
Ⓢ
The quality and creativity of the meals served at this tiny restaurant are a testament to the type of people who are repopulating Bisbee, and the low cost of a meal is reason enough to dine in Bisbee. During the recent filming of a movie nearby, star Jerry Lewis ate here as often as he had time off. The menu is short (seven items in the evening), but there are also daily specials. Pastas are the main events here, with such succulent combinations as roast duck with spinach, pecans, and black currants. The chicken pasta with cilantro pesto was delicious, as was the sun-dried tomato polenta with Gorgonzola and roasted vegetables. As the name suggests, wines are not overlooked here. They're in a rack against the back wall. Don't be discouraged if the four tables are full—they have additional seating in the basement.

EN ROUTE TO WILLCOX: A STOP IN DOUGLAS

This town's one and only true tourist attraction is the elegant lobby of the Gadsden Hotel (see "Where to Stay & Dine," below, for details), which is on the National Register of Historic Places.

About 20 miles east of Douglas on a gravel road is the verdant San Bernardino Valley. In 1884, former Texas Ranger John Slaughter bought the valley and turned it into a **cattle ranch,** one of the finest in the West. Slaughter later went on to become the sheriff of Cochise County and helped rid the region of the unsavory characters who had flocked to the many mining towns of this remote part of the state. Today the ranch is a National Historic Landmark and has been restored to its turn-of-the-century look. Long shady porches, whitewashed walls, and dark-green trim give the ranch a well-manicured look, while inside antique furnishings present a picture of a very comfortable life. But it also plays an important role as a gateway to Mexico. Just across the border is **Agua Prieta,** Sonora, where Pancho Villa lost his first battle. Whitewashed adobe buildings, old churches, and sunny plazas provide a contrast to Douglas. Curio shops and Mexican restaurants abound, as they do in almost all border towns.

WHAT TO SEE & DO

COCHISE STRONGHOLD, Coronado National Forest. Tel. 826-3593.

The Apache peoples first moved into this region of southern Arizona sometime in the early 16th century. They pursued a hunting and gathering life-style that was supplemented by raiding neighboring tribes for food and other booty. When the Spanish arrived in this area, the Apaches acquired horses and became even more efficient raiders. They continued to attack Spanish, Mexican, and eventually American settlers, and despite repeated attempts to convince them to give up their hostile way of life, the Apaches refused to change. Not long after the Gadsden Purchase of 1848 made Arizona U.S. soil, more people than ever before began settling in the region. The new settlers immediately became the subject of Apache raids, and eventually the U.S. Army was called in to put an end to the attacks.

By the mid-1880s only Cochise and Geronimo and their Chiracahua Apaches were continuing to attack settlers and fight the U.S. Army. Cochise used this rugged section of the Dragoon Mountains as his hideout, and managed to elude capture for years because the granite boulders and pine forests made it impossible for the army to track Cochise and followers. Cochise eventually died and was buried at an unknown spot somewhere within the area now called Cochise Stronghold. Today there are hiking trails, a campground, and a picnic area. A hike among the spectacular rock formations will give you an idea of how impregnable was Cochise's last stronghold.

Admission: Free.
Open: Daily 24 hours.

AMERIND FOUNDATION MUSEUM, off I-10 in Texas Canyon, between Benson and Willcox. Tel. 586-3666.

It may be out of the way and difficult to find, but this museum is well worth seeking out. Established in 1937, the Amerind Foundation is dedicated to the study, preservation, and interpretation of prehistoric and historic Native American cultures. To that end the foundation has compiled the nation's finest private collection of Native American archeological artifacts and contemporary items. The museum comprises two buildings, one containing the anthropology museum and the other containing the art gallery. The first exhibit of the anthropology museum is devoted to the dances and religious ceremonies of the major southwestern tribes, including the Navajo, Hopi, and Apache. The next two exhibits on the first floor of the museum contain archeological artifacts amassed from the numerous Amerind Foundation excavations over the years. Many of the pieces came from right here in Texas Canyon.

The museum's second-floor exhibits contain fascinating ethnology displays, including amazingly intricate beadwork from the Plains tribes, a large collection of Northwest Coast tribe wood carvings including masks, a case full of old Zuñi fetishes, Pima willow baskets, 18 old kachinas, 100 years of southwestern tribal pottery, Navajo weavings, and a *santos* and *retablos* from the Southwest's Hispanic culture.

The art gallery contains works by 19th- and 20th-century American artists, such as Frederic Remington, whose works focused on the West. There is also a room full of paintings on paper by Hopi artists. (Because of a staff shortage, the art gallery is only open occasionally.) The museum store is small but has a surprising selection of books and Native American crafts and jewelry.

The Amerind Foundation is located 64 miles east of Tucson in the heart of Texas Canyon, a small but rugged canyon strewn with huge rounded boulders. To reach the museum take the Triangle T–Dragoon exit (Exit 318) from I-10 between Benson and Willcox. There is no museum sign on the highway so you must pay attention. The museum entrance is 1 mile east.

Admission: $3 adults, $2 seniors and children 12–18, free for children under 12. **Open:** Daily 10am–4pm. **Closed:** Major hols.

WHERE TO STAY & DINE

GADSDEN HOTEL, 1046 G Ave., Douglas, AZ 85607. Tel. 602/362-4481. 145 rms, 4 suites (all with bath). A/C TV TEL
$ Rates: $27–$47 single; $30–$49 double; $50 suite. AE, CB, DC, MC, V.

Unless you're on your way to or from Mexico, there aren't many reasons to stay in Douglas, but this hotel is one of them. Built in 1907, the Gadsden bills itself as "the last of the grand hotels," and its listing on the National Register of Historic Places backs up that claim. The marble lobby, though dark, is a classic. Vaulted stained-glass skylights run the length of the large lobby, and above the landing of the wide Italian marble stairway is a genuine Tiffany stained-glass window. Though the carpets in the halls are old and well worn, many of the rooms have been renovated and refurnished in various styles. The bathrooms are also a bit worse for the wear, but at these prices, who expects everything to be brand new?

The Saddle & Spur Lounge is a popular local hangout, with more than 200 cattle brands painted on the walls. In the El Conquistador Dining Room there's a large tile wall mural. Meals reflect the Mexican and American heritage of the area. The Cattleman's Coffee Shop is popular for breakfast and lunch. The hotel also offers a dress shop and a beauty shop.

6. WILLCOX

192 miles SE of Phoenix, 81 miles E of Tucson,
74 miles N of Douglas, 62 miles NE of Tombstone

GETTING THERE By Plane The nearest regularly scheduled service is to Sierra Vista on Mesa Airlines (tel. toll free 800/637-2247). You'll have to drive from Sierra Vista.

By Train The nearest **Amtrak** (tel. toll free 800/872-7245) passenger service is in Benson, from which you'll have to drive.

By Bus Willcox is served by **Greyhound/Trailways Lines.** The station is at 144 South Haskell Avenue (tel. 602/384-2183).

By Car Willcox is located on I-10, with Ariz. 186 heading southeast toward Chiracahua National Monument.

ESSENTIALS For more information on Willcox and the surrounding area, contact the **Willcox Chamber of Commerce & Agriculture,** 1500 North Circle I Road, Willcox, AZ 85643 (tel. 602/384-2272). The telephone **area code** is 602.

There isn't much to do in Willcox itself, but this quiet cattle town does make a good base of operations for exploring southeastern Arizona. Once known as the "Cattle Capital of America," Willcox still relies heavily on ranching for its livelihood, and holds Arizona's largest livestock auction.

WHAT TO SEE & DO

CHIRACAHUA NATIONAL MONUMENT. Tel. 824-3560.
Sea Captain, China Boy, Duck on a Rock, Punch and Judy—these may not seem like appropriate names for landscape features, but Chiracahua National Monument is no ordinary landscape. These gravity-defying rock formations sculpted by nature—called "the land of the standing-up rocks" by the Apaches and the "wonderland of rocks" by pioneers—are the equal of any of Arizona's many amazing rocky landmarks. Rank upon rank of monolithic giants seem to have been turned to stone as they marched across the forested Chiracahua Mountains. Big Balanced Rock and Pinnacle Balanced Rock threaten to come crashing down at any moment. Formed about 25 million years ago by a massive volcanic eruption, these rhyolite badlands were once the stronghold of renegade Apaches. If you look closely at Cochise Head peak, you can even see the famous chief's profile.
The Chiracahuas are still an important refuge, but now it's for animals and plants. Many species of birds, mammals, and plants that are normally found only far to the south in Mexico have found just the right climate to survive here in the Chiracahuas. Keep your eyes open and you might see a trogon or a sulphur-bellied flycatcher.
Within the monument are a campground, picnic area, visitor center, many miles of hiking trails, and a scenic drive that provides views of many of the most unusual rock formations.
Admission: $3 per car.
Open: Visitor center, daily 8am–5pm. **Directions:** To reach Chiracahua National Monument, take Ariz. 186 southwest from Willcox for about 30 miles and watch for signs.

FORT BOWIE NATIONAL HISTORIC SITE, off Ariz. 186. Tel. 847-2500.
The Butterfield Stage, which carried mail, passengers, and freight across the Southwest in the mid-1800s, followed a route that passed through the heart of Apache territory in the Chiracahua Mountains. Fort Bowie was established in 1862 near the mile-high Apache Pass to protect the slow-moving stage as it traversed this difficult region. It was from Fort Bowie that federal troops battled Geronimo until the Apache chief finally surrendered in 1886. Today there's little left of Fort Bowie but some crumbling adobe walls. To reach the historic site, drive southeast from Willcox on Ariz. 186; after about 20 miles, watch for signs. It's another 6 miles up a dirt road and then a 1.5-mile hike to the ruins of the fort.
Admission: Free.
Open: Ranger station, daily 8am–4:30pm; grounds, daily dawn–dusk.

REX ALLEN MUSEUM, Rail Road Ave. Tel. 384-4583.
Rex Allen, for those of you too young to remember, was a singing cowboy back in the days when singing cowboys were the latest rage. It was Allen who made famous the song "Streets of Laredo." Allen starred in a few western movies in the early 1950s, moved on to do the television program *Frontier Doctor* in the mid-1950s, and then went on to narrate several Walt Disney movies. This memorable career has led Rex

Allen to be lionized in his hometown of Willcox. He has his own museum downtown, a life-size bronze statue in the park across from his museum; his horse, Koko, is buried beneath his statue. Last, but certainly not least, he has his own annual festival every year in October. The museum houses Rex Allen memorabilia, of course.

Admission: $3 per person or $5 per family.
Open: Daily 10am–4pm.

MUSEUM OF THE SOUTHWEST, Willcox Chamber of Commerce Visitor Center, 1500 N. Circle I Rd. Tel. 384-2272.

Located just off the Interstate at the Rex Allen Drive exit (Exit 340), the Museum of the Southwest is a good place to find out more about southeastern Arizona. There are exhibits on the geology of the region, the Apaches, and settlement by pioneers and the conflicts that arose with Native Americans. Cattle ranching has played an important role in the history of Willcox and a large display in the museum is dedicated to this mainstay of the West. The museum also includes a cowboy hall of fame and an information center where you can find out more about Willcox and the surrounding region.

Admission: Free.
Open: Mon–Sat 8am–5pm, Sun 1–5pm.

WHERE TO STAY & DINE

BEST WESTERN PLAZA INN, 1100 W. Rex Allen Dr., Willcox, AZ 85643. Tel. 602/384-3556, or toll free 800/262-2645 outside Arizona. 92 rms, 3 suites (all with bath). A/C TV TEL

$ Rates (including full breakfast): $45–$55 single or double; $80 suite. Weekend rates available. AE, CB, DC, DISC, MC, V.

Located just off I-10, this motel offers clean, comfortable rooms and a quiet place for drinks and a meal. Rooms vary in size, and all have coffee makers; many also have small refrigerators. Suites have whirlpool tubs and in-room movies. The hotel also offers a complimentary daily newspaper, free local phone calls, a swimming pool, coin laundry, beauty salon, no-smoking rooms, and wheelchair accommodations.

The Solarium dining room specializes in mesquite-broiled steaks. The Hopi Lounge serves cocktails in a quiet setting.

COMFORT INN, 724 N. Bisbee Ave., Willcox, AZ 85643. Tel. 602/384-4222. Fax 602/384-3785. 73 rms (all with bath). A/C TV TEL

$ Rates (including continental breakfast): $38–$44 single; $44–$50 double. AE, CB, DC, DISC, MC, V.

Another convenient choice in Willcox, the Comfort Inn features a swimming pool and free local fax service. All rooms have modern furnishings, queen-size beds, and in-room movies.

The adjacent restaurant serves economical American food.

INDEX

GENERAL INFORMATION